AMERICAN WEST CHRONICLE

CONSULTANTS
Walter Nugent, Ph.D.
William Deverell, Ph.D.

WRITERS
Barton H. Barbour, Ph.D.
Wim Coleman
William Deverell, Ph.D.
Anthony O. Edmonds, Ph.D.
Christy Nadalin
Walter Nugent, Ph.D.
Bill O'Neal
Pat Perrin
B. Byron Price
Bradley Shreve, M.A.

FOREWORD
U.S. Senator Ben Nighthorse Campbell,
Council of 44 Chiefs of the Northern Cheyenne Nation

Publications International, Ltd.

Louis Weber, CEO
Publications International, Ltd.
8140 Lehigh Avenue
Morton Grove, IL 60053

Permission is never granted for commercial purposes.

ISBN: 978-1-68022-833-5

Manufactured in China.

8 7 6 5 4 3 2 1

Contributors

Foreword Author:

Ben Nighthorse Campbell is the only citizen of Native American heritage to serve in both the United States Senate (1993–2005) and the U.S. House of Representatives (1987–93). He is also a former Olympian, a noted artist, a rancher, and one of 44 chiefs of the Northern Cheyenne Nation. In 1997 Senator Campbell made history when he became the first Native American to chair the Indian Affairs Committee. In this role, he collaborated with tribes to gain input on legislation that served Indian health, education, economic needs, sovereignty, self-governance expansion, and arts and crafts protections. During his two decades in Washington, he was a key figure in the conception and founding of the National Museum of the American Indian. He led the effort to change the name of Custer Battlefield National Monument to Little Bighorn Battlefield National Monument, and he sponsored bills that created the Sand Creek Massacre National Historic Site, the Great Sand Dunes National Park, and the Black Canyon of the Gunnison National Park.

Consultants and Essayists:

Walter Nugent, Ph.D., (consultant, essayist) is Tackes Professor of History, Emeritus, at the University of Notre Dame. He has written more than 150 essays, articles, and reviews on American and comparative history, and is the author of 11 books, including *Into the West: The Story of Its People,* which won the Caughey Book Prize of the Western History Association. He served as president of the Western History Association in 2005-06.

William Deverell, Ph.D., (consultant, essayist) earned his doctorate in history from Princeton University. A professor at the University of Southern California and a noted historian of the 19th and 20th century American West, he is the director of the Huntington-USC Institute on California and the West. Professor Deverell is the author or editor of nine books, including *Whitewashed Adobe.*

Contributing Writers:

Barton H. Barbour, Ph.D., (sidebars and captions writer) teaches Early North American history and U.S. Indian Policy at Boise State University. He is the author of five books, including *Fort Union and the Upper Missouri Fur Trade,* which was a finalist for the Western Writers of America SPUR Award in nonfiction.

Wim Coleman (sidebars and captions writer) has written books, plays, and articles about U.S. history for READ, Appleseeds, Greenhaven, Perfection Learning, Discovery Enterprises, Portable Press, and Enslow—including four titles in the Enslow series *The Wild History of the American West,* in collaboration with Pat Perrin.

Anthony O. Edmonds, Ph.D., (captions writer) is the George and Frances Ball Distinguished Professor of History at Ball State University. He is the author of several books about American history, and wrote for *The Sixties Chronicle* and *The Fifties Chronicle.*

Christy Nadalin (timeline writer and fact-checker) is a freelance writer, editorial researcher, and documentary television producer whose work has appeared in publications and productions by the National Geographic Society, the Discovery Channel, A&E Television Networks, and Time Life Books. She also contributed to *Civil Rights Chronicle, The Sixties Chronicle,* and *The Fifties Chronicle.*

Bill O'Neal (captions writer) has written more than 30 books, including *Best of the West, Ghost Towns of the American West, The Sons of the Pioneers,* and *The Johnson County War,* which was named 2005 Book of the Year by the National Association for Outlaw and Lawman History.

Pat Perrin (sidebars and captions writer) has authored, with Wim Coleman, U.S. history books, plays, articles, and stories for Greenhaven, Perfection Learning, Discovery Enterprises, Portable Press, ETS, Appleseeds, and Enslow.

B. Byron Price (sidebars writer) is director of the Charles M. Russell Center for the Study of Art of the American West at the University of Oklahoma. Formerly, he was director of the National Cowboy and Western Heritage Museum and the Buffalo Bill Historical Center. He has written or edited more than three dozen articles and 10 books and monographs on western American history and art.

Bradley Shreve, M.A., (sidebars writer) is a doctoral candidate and teaching assistant at the University of New Mexico. He has published several articles and is currently working on his dissertation, *Red Power Rising: The Origins of Pan-Indian Activism in the United States.* He also wrote for *The Sixties Chronicle* and *The Fifties Chronicle.*

Additional writing by **David Devendorf**

Factual Verification and Research:

Joseph Bator, Ph.D., (fact-checker) earned his doctorate in history from Northwestern University. He has taught university-level courses on the history of the American West, and is currently a freelance researcher.

Marci McGrath, M.A., (fact-checker) holds a master's degree in history from the University of New Orleans. She has taught history at the secondary school level.

Richard A. Sauers, Ph.D., (researcher) is the author of more than two dozen books, including *America's Battlegrounds: Walk in the Footsteps of America's Bravest* and *Gettysburg: The Meade-Sickles Controversy.* He is director of the Packwood House Museum in Lewisburg, Pennsylvania.

Chris Smith (fact-checker) is a New Orleans-based writer and researcher.

Index by **Ina Gravitz**

Acknowledgments can be found on page 447.

Contents

The "American West" dates only to about 1800. However, humans lived on the continent as long ago as 28,000 B.C. Hunter-gatherers established themselves by 4000 B.C. Europeans, though daring and ambitious, were late arrivals indeed.

1800–1815 With the May 1803 purchase from France of the enormous North American province of Louisiana, President Thomas Jefferson doubled the size of the United States. The president envisioned the American West as a settlement for countless farmers, as well as a major boost to America's political standing in the world. Next, Jefferson wanted to discover what lay west of St. Louis. Enter two bold men, Meriwether Lewis and William Clark. Let the exploration begin.

1816–1829 Although the leader of an 1820 U.S. Army expedition to present-day Colorado pronounced the vast West worthless, other hardy trailblazers, notably mountain men and traders, knew better. Fur-bearing animals were abundant, and the men who trapped them set the tone for America's western experience: curious, tough, enterprising, a little brazen. Speculators realized that money could be made in a variety of enterprises. The West was waiting.

1830–1848 By 1830 the American sense of self was motivating the nation's leaders to action. By now quite separate from the Old World, Americans regarded themselves as people of providence, whose religious faith and other ways of life qualified them to settle and control the West and Southwest. Never mind that Mexico and native Indians had legitimate claims to these regions. America was motivated by a new notion, purportedly sanctioned by God: Manifest Destiny.

1849–1860 It was a yellow metal that stirred the imaginations of men and touched the desires of women. It was "goald," discovered in California's Sacramento Valley in 1848. A year later, gold fever spread through the East, and even to Europe. Suddenly, the American vision of the West was more than just farming and timber. Speculators both naive and devious insisted that vast wealth awaited those who had the backbone to claim it. The Gold Rush was on.

Foreword

THE VAST AMERICAN WEST. It evokes images of cowboys and Indians, gunfighters and outlaws, buffalo hunts and cattle drives, adventurous settlers in covered wagons, and trappers and prospectors seeking their fortune. It stirs feelings of independence and spirited toughness, a determination to overcome the odds as well as the elements. The West was all of these things. Even today, in many ways, much of the West still embodies an aura of toughness and independence. However, when my thoughts turn to the American West, they first acknowledge a time predating America and our definition of the "West."

I am always quick to remind folks that at one time the "West" was a continent, inhabited by tens of millions of people from a variety of indigenous cultures, many now long gone, who lived in communities with established governmental structures, many using a unique system of self-governance we now call "democracy." These communities were home to farmers and doctors, teachers and craftsmen, housewives and soldiers, priests and astronomers. They were here while many European cities were in their infancy. They were here before the birth of a boy king in Egypt named Tutankhamen. They were here before the Greek poet Homer wrote *The Iliad*, before Caesar watched the chariots race at Circus Maximus, and before Christ walked the hills near the Sea of Galilee.

They knew not of alcohol or drug abuse, tuberculosis or cholera, smallpox or AIDS, or even the common cold. They had many different languages, but in every language they referred to themselves, in the collective,

Senator Ben Nighthorse Campbell

as simply "The People." They were not known as "Indians" until Christopher Columbus traveled off course and believed he had landed in India. Whether Columbus or Leif Ericson arrived first is up for debate, but it was inevitable that Europeans would locate this land of plenty. I find it interesting, though, that every famed explorer who traveled farther west to a place where their kind had not been before seemed not to notice that the land was already inhabited, and took it upon themselves to claim their "discovery" and declare ownership for their sponsoring governments.

The boundary of this great land called the West was adjusted over time as the eastern land of this continent was colonized by Europeans, eventually giving birth to a new nation. The West represented the "frontier," where civilization ended and the unknown vastness began. At one time, the western frontier was Appalachia. But as the young country quickly grew in population, and in land mass through purchases of large tracts of wilderness, the frontier pushed farther west until it reached a mighty river, unlike any seen before. Even today, most folks agree, the Mississippi River is the natural boundary that delineates the West from the East.

Famed explorers Lewis and Clark were dispatched to this new land, west of the Mississippi, in search of the Northwest Passage. Their travels and those of many intrepid explorers that followed paved the way for expansion of a nation—a nation in need of more land and more resources to fuel its fast-paced growth. Their citizenry were encouraged to tame the wilderness, to settle the land. It was cloaked in heroic terms, such as "Manifest Destiny" and "westward expansion," but it meant only one thing for the native people of the West: loss. It was a loss of land and hunting grounds, loss of access to sacred sites, and ultimately loss of their way of life.

Many of the early trappers and mountain men built alliances and trading relationships with Indians, often marrying into their tribes. But as more and more settlers and fortune-seekers went west, fewer and fewer bothered to befriend those upon whose land they encroached…eventually at their own peril. The nation's military might was then called upon to protect the settlers and drive the native people from their lands. We know how much was gained; sometimes we must remember how much was lost.

I was speaking at a conference in Great Falls, Montana, recently, when a reporter approached me and asked, "What was the greatest benefit to Native Americans that arose from Lewis and Clark's expedition?"

I must say, that one threw me for a loop. I stood in stunned silence to see if he was joking; he was not. I finally, politely replied, "I can't think of any."

In the initial 400 years that passed after the Europeans began settlement of North America, tens of millions of indigenous people died due to sickness, slavery, starvation, and war. By 1900 their numbers had dwindled to just over 200,000 souls scattered on postage stamp-sized reservations throughout the United States. Their loss was great indeed.

As a student of the West, I have many heroes. In fact, the West provided fertile ground for the growth of many legends in American history. Such names as Buffalo Bill Cody, Wyatt Earp, Doc Holliday, Jim Bridger, Chief Joseph, Sitting Bull, Geronimo, and Ten Bears are but a few of the legendary figures, white and Indian alike, who made their mark in the American West.

Among those who interested me is the Bent family. Brothers William and Charles were trappers who built a thriving business trading with the Indians in the West. William identified so much with the Indian culture that he married into the Cheyenne tribe. He and his wife, Owl Woman, had a son, George Bent. George lived his life in both cultures, receiving his schooling among the whites in St. Louis and then returning to live among the Cheyenne in the West. Many are not aware that he was with the Cheyenne and neighboring Arapaho on November 29, 1864, a day when most of the young men—hunters and warriors—were away on a hunting expedition to feed their starving tribe.

Their chief, Black Kettle, flew the American flag, for he had been told by the Great White Father that under it his people had protection. But not on this day. Colonel John Chivington led the Colorado Militia in an attack on the women, children, and elderly at Sand Creek and massacred them in one of the most shameful acts in American history. George Bent survived that day, but his mother, Owl Woman, did not. George turned his back on his white side and lived as an Indian until his death.

I study the West because I am proud of my western roots. I have three places that I call home. My boyhood home was in the mountains of Northern California, in the town of Weimar, not far from the placer mines of gold country, in an area long inhabited by the Miwok and Maidu Indians. My ancestral home is on the Northern Cheyenne Reservation in Lame Deer, Montana. It is among the poorest communities in this country, in economic terms, but among the richest in spirit. For nearly 30 years, my wife Linda and I have lived on a ranch in southwestern Colorado, among the Southern Ute Indian tribe. This is not far from the cliff dwellings of Mesa Verde, where long ago lived one of those great cultures that I wrote of earlier, the Anasazi, the forefathers of the many Pueblo Indian tribes of New Mexico.

As an artist, the West inspires me, with its broad vistas, towering mountains, deep canyons, painted mesas, and the sense of space and freedom. The Indian people understood that the most beautiful cathedral made by man cannot exceed the beauty of our Earth Mother and all she provides us. It is in this vein that I understand the stirrings of the early settlers and their desire to live among this beauty and stake their claim to the American dream. I also understand the very different desire of those running from something in their life and seeing the vastness of the West as a place to lose themselves, or make a new start. I understand the stirring of an adventurer's heart whose happiness is in the quest for what lies over the next horizon. In America, those adventures have often taken us west.

THE HONORABLE BEN NIGHTHORSE CAMPBELL
U.S. SENATOR—RETIRED
COUNCIL OF 44 CHIEFS OF THE NORTHERN CHEYENNE NATION

Introduction

WHAT IS THE American West? In the physical world, the American West is a reasonably well-defined geographical region with an enormous assortment of people, wildlife, industry, and topographies. Today, it stretches from the Dakotas south to Texas, and westward to the full length of the Pacific coast.

There is another West, too, and it exists in history books, paperback novels, vintage TV shows, and in our personal confabulations. It is a place we devise from first-hand experience, myth, imagination, wishful thinking, and, sometimes, bald misinformation.

The West is a 19th century cowpoke, on the make in a lusty railhead. It's the ringing clamor of multicultural Los Angeles. It's where homesteaders put down roots and where Native Americans confronted that encroaching new culture, and battled in vain to save their own. The West is a place that Napoléon considered worthless, and sold to the young United States for a song. It's where tourists in windowless rooms push half-dollars into slot machines, and a sunny place where the elderly go to conclude their lives. Four presidents live together on a mountainside in the West. The West is Texas football and the Alamo; *Cinco de Mayo* and an Italian cowboy movie filmed in Spain.

American West Chronicle attempts what no other heavily illustrated, single-volume history has done: to cover a great and ever-expanding portion of the American landscape from 1800 to 1950—a period encompassing the Jefferson Administration, the Lewis and Clark expedition, the growth of railroads, gold and land rushes, the Civil War and two world wars, the Dust Bowl, unconscionably bad treatment of Indians and other "minorities," the endless quest for comfort, riches and power, and the beginnings of the middle class as we know it today.

As an adjunct to the main body of the book, a lively, illustrated prologue discusses the West as it existed for thousands of years prior to 1800. An insightful, picture-driven epilogue brings this enormously significant tale to the present day.

In the course of *American West Chronicle,* readers will meet a fascinating assortment of visionaries, heroes, schemers, and explorers; finaglers, military leaders, tycoons, nature lovers, and artists; Native warriors and lusty common folk; even Hawaiian royalty, for the book defines the American West as including U.S. territories, possessions, and states lying west of the Pacific coast.

American West Chronicle is very much a book of faces, captured in nearly 1,000 photographs and other compelling images. When you look at those faces, you will have a sense of what it was like to have lived and died in America's western vastness, with all the adventure, fear, joy—and even the mundane—that that entails.

For the 200 years of its modern history, the West has been a dream. But unlike other dreams, it has been most vivid when the dreamer is wide awake, eyes open to absorb the splendor and drama, eager to devour whichever experiences lie just beyond the next horizon.

Age of Discovery
⌒ Before 1800 ⌒

WHEN DID HUMANS arrive in the American West (or any other part of the Americas)? How did they get there? Since fossil remains do not go back anywhere near as far as they do in Europe, Asia, and (longest of all) Africa—and since there is no evidence either of apes and anthropoids from which modern humans might have evolved—we have to conclude that humans came to the Americas from somewhere else. We know that Europeans arrived in North and South America and adjacent islands beginning with Columbus's voyage of 1492, but we also know that Native Americans were living in the Americas long before Columbus came. How and when did the earliest people arrive?

The conventional explanation for some time has been that the first humans in the American hemisphere migrated across a land bridge that connected eastern Siberia with Alaska. The "bridge" existed during the most recent ice age, the last of several that occurred cyclically over the past 800,000 years. Vast glaciers covered much of the northern hemisphere as far south as what is now central Illinois and Indiana. They absorbed so much water from the oceans that sea levels were lower than now, perhaps by several hundred feet. As a result, dry land connected Siberia and Alaska where the Bering Strait now exists.

Daniel Boone (*center*) was the most famous frontiersman to lead settlers through the Cumberland Gap. From 1775 to 1800, more than 300,000 pioneers negotiated the Gap, the deepest pass through the Cumberland Mountains.

"I had gained the summit of a commanding ridge, and, looking round with astonishing delight, beheld the ample plains, the beauteous tracts below...."
—Daniel Boone, describing Kentucky, c. 1770

BEFORE 1800

28000 B.C.: Early man begins to populate the North American continent, arriving from Asia via the Bering Land Bridge.

6400 B.C.: "Kennewick Man" lives in what is now Washington State. His remains will be discovered in 1996, and shed new light on what we know about early human migration to North America.

4000 B.C.: Humans on the North American plains begin to adapt to a hunter-gatherer culture, as the large mammals prevalent during the Ice Age die off.

700 A.D.: The Mogollon Indians begin to populate what is now the Southwest United States.

750–1150 A.D.: The Anasazi, an early Pueblo Indian culture, flourish in the Southwest. The hallmark of the Anasazi farming communities is their above-ground adobe buildings, examples of which still exist at Chaco Canyon and Mesa Verde.

1100: Cahokia Mounds (in present-day Illinois), the site of the largest prehistoric Indian community outside of Mexico, boasts a population of between 8,000 and 20,000.

Late 1200s: A long drought and threats by other Native American groups lead the Anasazi to abandon their adobe cliff-side communities.

1492: Christopher Columbus brings Europeans to the shores of the New World.

1500: At this time, there are some 240 tribes (speaking several hundred languages) living in the American West.

1540: Francisco Vásquez de Coronado sets out on an expedition to discover the "seven cities of Cibola," in what is now New Mexico. He is disappointed to find that Cibola is a simple Zuni pueblo, and there is no gold for the taking.

Prehistoric Native American hunters had only bows and arrows and spears to battle mammoths and other massive animals.

But while the glaciers covered the interior of North America rather completely, they made an exception of enough of Alaska and Siberia to permit humans to live there, cold though it must have been. An ice-free zone along the east face of the Rocky Mountains may have provided a corridor for migration southward, as did the coastline of the North Pacific. When the glaciers finally melted, world sea levels rose, inundating the land bridge and converting it into the Bering Strait.

This bridge may have been a hundred or more miles wide and not visibly different from the Asian and Alaskan lands that it connected. It may have been a hilly meadowland, home to animals large (mammoths, mastodons, elk) and small (many species) that provided the food supply for the roving humans. In physical characteristics, those humans were much like other East Asians, as recent comparisons of DNA and teeth shapes confirm. Once across the bridge into North America, the theory goes, these humans increased and multiplied, migrating ever southward and eastward. They ultimately reached the tip of South America and could have done so within a few thousand years. Some of them, of course, moved on to populate the present United States, the Caribbean islands, Brazil, and the rest of North and South America.

The popularity of the Bering land bridge hypothesis rests in part on timing. In 1926, in Folsom, New Mexico, human-fashioned spear points dating from 10,000 to 11,000 BP (Before the Present) were discovered in conjunction with the bones of bison. And in 1932 in Clovis, New Mexico, slightly older (about 12,000 BP) and more numerous spear points turned up. Tools and weapons similar to those found in Clovis have since surfaced in a number of places. Because the last ice age ended at about the same time, archaeologists conjectured that the Clovis people arrived by way of the land bridge.

Alternative Theories

The Bering land bridge hypothesis of migration continues to be the most popular one among most archaeologists. However, little hard evidence (in the form of settlements, charred artifacts, bones, or even more spear points) has been discovered along the routes the migrants must have taken. That may be because rising seas would have covered it, and the harsh and moist North Pacific climate would have decayed anything organic.

Archaeologists have offered other hypotheses about how humans migrated to the Americas. In southern Chile, about 500 miles south of Santiago, American archaeologist Tom Dillehay and his team uncovered a settlement called Monte Verde in the early 1990s. Carbon-dated to about 13,000 BP, a thousand years earlier than Clovis, Monte Verde's treasures included stone tools, house foundations, edible plants, and other items. To have arrived and settled that far south of the Bering Strait suggests that the migration from Asia probably happened significantly earlier than previously thought.

How? One plausible suggestion is that people inched along the coast of the North Pacific in boats. Certain Native Americans both in the western United States and as depicted in old Peruvian pottery resemble the Ainu people of northern Japan. Some of them may have followed coastlines all the way around to the Americas. Another possibility is boat travel across the Pacific from Polynesia. We know that Pacific islanders reached Hawaii, Tahiti, and Easter Island, and some are still able to navigate by dead reckoning, without compasses, across a thousand miles of open Pacific. Might not a few, at least, have made it all the way to the west coast of South America, at some point in the past? Not terribly likely, perhaps, and certainly not easily, but nonetheless possible.

Another site, older even than Monte Verde, has been partially excavated at Meadowcroft in western Pennsylvania. It may go back as far as 19,000 BP. Another at Pedra Furada in Brazil is possibly 40,000 years old. However, these and several other pre-Clovis sites have yet to gain full acceptance from archaeologists.

Various cultures, called Paleo-Indian (from Clovis to about 10,000 BP) and Archaic (to around 4,500 BP), sprinkled themselves across what is now

Early seafarers who stopped at Easter Island, west of Chile, gazed in wonder at more than 600 gigantic stone statues. The mystery of their origin remains unsolved.

1581: The first Spanish expedition crosses El Paso del Norte (The Northern Pass), a desert chasm between two mountain ranges that will evolve into the border cities of Ciudad Juárez, Mexico, and El Paso, Texas.

1658: While hunting furs west of Lake Superior, French traders Médard Chouart des Grosseilliers and Pierre-Esprit Radisson become the first Europeans to contact Indians of the Northern Plains tribes.

June 17, 1673: A team of explorers led by Jacques Marquette and Louis Jolliet reaches the Mississippi River and begins to paddle south toward the Gulf of Mexico.

1675: Juan Francisco de Treviño, governor of New Mexico, publicly hangs three Pueblo Indians and whips 43 others on the grounds that their religion constitutes practice of witchcraft.

August 10, 1680: A Pueblo uprising involving more than 20 far-flung settlements results in widespread destruction and the deaths of some 400 Spanish settlers and missionaries in New Mexico.

April 9, 1682: French explorers René-Robert Cavelier (his title is Sieur de La Salle) and Henri de Tonti arrive at the mouth of the Mississippi and claim the entire valley for France, naming the region Louisiana.

1684: La Salle returns to Louisiana with the intent to establish a permanent French settlement, but he misses the mouth of the Mississippi River and lands on the coast of Texas.

1687: On his third desperate attempt to reach Louisiana by traveling overland from Texas, La Salle is murdered when his own men mutiny.

the United States. Some of these peoples gradually adopted agriculture and grew domesticated crops. Archaic Indians in Mexico were the first to develop edible corn, and the process spread northward into the present southwestern and central United States.

On the Great Plains and in the Pacific Northwest, however, hunting remained a way of life. In 1996, a skeleton turned up in Kennewick, Washington, on the banks of the Columbia River. A middle-aged male, he had been wounded by a spear but had recovered. He carried his own spear-throwing device and showed other signs of leading the life of a hunter. While not as old as the Clovis people, Kennewick Man—as he was quickly named—has been dated at 8,400 BP.

Pictured is a facial reconstruction of the "Kennewick Man," the remains of a prehistoric male found near Kennewick, Washington, and dated at 8,400 years old.

Indian Cultures Flourish

The astonishing thing about Kennewick Man was his close resemblance to Europeans, or to the Ainu people of northern Japan, rather than modern American Indians. Indians in the Northwest claimed the skeleton as an ancestor, but it has been held under court order at the University of Washington Museum in Seattle, and examined by forensic experts in the meantime. Whoever Kennewick Man finally proves to be, his morphology—indeed his existence—only deepens the mystery of human origins in the Americas.

More certain are some of the ancestral Native American civilizations of the present United States. (We pass over the splendid civilizations of Central and South America, such as the Toltecs, Olmecs, Mayans, Aztecs, and the many successive cultures of Peru, not because they are unimportant but because they flourished outside of the *American* West.) In the Southwest, three cultures flourished from around 2,000 BP until about the year 1200 or 1300. These include the Hohokam in southern Arizona (possibly ancestors of today's Tohono O'odham), the Mogollon in southwest New Mexico and adjacent Chihuahua and Sonora, and the Anasazi. The latter were cliff-dwellers who built Mesa Verde in Colorado, the Chaco Canyon city in northern New Mexico, and other sites around the Four Corners. The Anasazi are probably ancestors of the Pueblos, Hopi, and Zuñi. Each of the Anasazi, Mogollon, and Hohokam cultures dwindled or disappeared before the Spanish arrived, for unclear reasons—possibly drought, intertribal warfare, or some other unknown reason.

Two thousand miles to the east, a collection of peoples shared the Mississippian culture. They lived, farmed, created artistic masterpieces, and built extensive cities—from Arkansas and Louisiana to Georgia and Alabama, and northward to Illinois and Indiana. Cahokia (Illinois), which existed as a village or city from about 800 to 1400 (again, it became deserted well before Europeans arrived), may have

The Anasazi were gifted agriculturalists and builders. Their cliff dwellings in the current Southwest, erected with mud and clay mortar, faced south for maximum sun exposure during winter.

been home to 20,000 people at its peak. Its remnants include the extensive Cahokia Mounds about 10 miles across the Mississippi from St. Louis. Mississippians also bequeathed some remarkably elegant art works, fully comparable to what was being done at that time in Western Europe. But the disappearance of Cahokia's people, and other Mississippians, is as shrouded in darkness as the end of the Anasazi and their neighbors.

On the eve of Europeans' first arrival in the Americas around 1500, more than a million people were living in what is now the United States west of the Mississippi River, the majority of them in California and the Southwest. Europeans arrived in the West gradually. They appeared among the pueblos of the upper Rio Grande in 1598, but they would not meet the roving tribes of the Great Plains and Rocky Mountains until much later. Whenever contact did occur, Indian population plummeted. Armed conflict was one reason, but a more deadly one was the diseases brought by the Europeans, for which the Natives had no immunity.

In the meantime, however, life went on as it had for centuries, and the West was no garden of Eden. Indian nations pushed each other back and forth across the Plains and the Southwest. Some, like the Crow and Lakota, were traditionally at odds. Some tribes outnumbered or out-generalled other tribes, pushing them aside. Mandans and then Hidatsas and Arikaras forced Apacheans (the ancestors of Apaches and Navajos) from the Central Plains into the Southwest. Ojibwas pushed the Sioux westward out of the Upper Mississippi. And Kiowas and Comanches chased Wichitas and Caddos eastward out of the Southern Plains. Other examples abounded.

"SAVAGE AND WILD"

THESE ARE PEOPLE dwelling to the west of this place, toward the great river named Messipi.... They do not use muskets but only bows and arrows, with which they shoot very skillfully. Their cabins are not covered with bark, but with deerskins, carefully dressed, and sewed together with such skill that the cold does not enter. These people are, above all the rest, savage and wild, appearing abashed and as motionless as statues in our presence. Yet they are warlike, and have conducted hostilities against all their neighbors, by whom they are held in extreme fear.

—FATHER CLAUDE ALLOUEZ OF FRANCE, DESCRIBING NATIVE AMERICANS, LATE 1600s

1690: Alonso de León establishes the first Spanish settlement in what is now east Texas, a mission at San Francisco de los Tejas. The settlement will be abandoned in 1693 under pressure from Indians disinclined to conversion.

1692: Twelve years after being routed by the Pueblo Indians, Don Diego de Vargas—supported by 200 soldiers—successfully reclaims New Mexico for Spain.

1714: Etienne Veniard de Bourgmont of France explores and documents the Missouri Valley when he travels with the Missouri Indians back to their lands. He produces two documents on his return, translated as *Route to Be Followed for Ascending the Missouri River* and *Exact Description of Louisiana*.

1716: Spain establishes permanent settlements in east Texas as a bulwark against the increasing French presence in adjacent Louisiana.

1718: The French establish the city of New Orleans in their Louisiana territory.

May 5, 1718: San Antonio is established at the junction of the San Antonio River and San Pedro Springs by Martín de Alarcón, the Spanish governor of Texas.

1736: German Socialist missionary Christian Gottleib Priber settles among the Cherokee of western Carolina and begins to preach his notions of a communal Indian republic.

1741: Russian-backed explorers Vitus Bering and Alexei Chirikov launch a voyage of discovery along the Alaskan coast.

1741: French fur traders Pierre and Paul Mallet are the first Europeans to tell of the existence of the uncharted Rocky Mountain range, when they return from a 2,000-mile exploration of the North American interior.

As indicated by this Charles Russell painting of Blackfoot and Sioux warriors, Native Americans fought not just with Europeans but with other Indian tribes as well.

The Mississippi Valley and Great Plains, in particular, were the scene of moving, jostling peoples for several centuries before and during the arrival of the Spanish and (later) the Americans. Tribal alliances and enmities turned much of the West into an almost constant battleground, with mortality among Indian males chronically high. Nonetheless, native peoples survived, and often thrived, whether as farmers and irrigationists, pueblo builders, or hunters of the millions of buffalo and other animals living on the Plains and in the mountains.

Spaniards Populate the Southwest

Such was the scene that Europeans came upon when they entered the West. Wherever and whenever contact took place, Indian population fell. Epidemics of smallpox, measles, and other previously unknown contagions decimated tribe after tribe. By 1900 the Indian population in the West had dwindled to around a quarter-million, a small fraction of their pre-contact peak. The impact of the new diseases was felt for more than 200 years. Tribes that suffered early, such as the eastern Sioux, actually increased in numbers in the 19th century because they had acquired a level of immunity. They were at a military advantage over their neighbors who had not yet done so.

Europeans came to the trans-Mississippi West in a sequence: Spanish first, then French, and finally English and Americans. Africans (some free, most of them slaves) often accompanied the Spanish and English. Intermarriage among Spaniards, Indians, Africans, and French was common in many areas, producing mestizos in the Southwest and métis farther north. Scots

Spain's Reign in North America

SPAIN STUMBLED UPON a fabulous New World bonanza when it conquered the Aztec Empire in 1521 and the Inca Empire by the 1530s. Enormously wealthy and powerful, Spain held sway over Europe throughout the century. Decline began after the Great Armada met defeat by England in 1588, but two centuries would elapse before the curtain fell on Spain's New World empire.

From the heartland of New Spain—later the Republic of Mexico—explorers, missionaries, and colonists fanned out over a vast extent of land from Florida to Texas and on to California. When France surrendered Canada to Britain at the end of the Seven Years' War (1756–63), King Louis XV of France ceded Louisiana (a vast amount of land stretching from the Gulf of Mexico to present-day Canada) to his Spanish Bourbon cousin. Spain's acquisition of Louisiana expanded its North American colonies, but it necessitated costly administrative restructuring. The era of the "Bourbon reforms" (c. 1760–1800) brought French influence to Spanish administration and helped maintain peace on the frontiers.

Teodoro de Croix and Juan Bautista de Anza were among the able administrators who injected new vitality into Spain's Indian policies and efforts to govern the land from Florida to California. After American independence, Spain grew fearful of the aggressive and acquisitive *yanquis* east of the Mississippi River. From 1783 to 1800, Spain retained its feeble grip on the North American borderlands, but its power rapidly evaporated. No longer was it possible to maintain this extensive, weakly defended "buffer zone" against meddling American interlopers.

In 1800 Napoléon forced Spain to retrocede Louisiana to France, and in 1803 dumped the white elephant of Louisiana on the United States for a pittance. New Spain soon rebelled, and other Latin American rebellions erupted after 1810. Squandering its resources in futile campaigns to stifle independence movements, Spain devoted little attention to the borderlands. By 1820 the United States seized East and West Florida, and began casting covetous eyes toward Texas, New Mexico, and California.

and Irish, after they arrived in the present South in the 1700s, also intermarried with Indians (Cherokee and Creek leaders with names like Ridge and McGillivray resulted), but English newcomers did so rarely.

Hernán Cortés's rapid and lucrative conquest of Aztec Mexico (1519–21) provoked dreams of gold and glory much farther north. This resulted in two exploratory expeditions around 1540 into the future South and Southwest—by Hernando de Soto and Francisco Vásquez de Coronado, respectively. Both failed to find riches and ran into serious Indian resistance, and de Soto died. Coronado managed to slouch back to Mexico City with about a hundred survivors of the 1,400-man force he set out with, but his trip was also regarded as a failure.

It was almost 60 years before another expedition sallied north from central Mexico. Juan de Oñate, sometimes called "the last conquistador," led at least 400 soldiers and their families, and a dozen or so Franciscan missionaries, up to the Rio Grande. They crossed it at El Paso del Norte and followed the river into the land of 40,000 Pueblo Indians. Unlike Coronado, Oñate and his band survived and stayed. In 1609–10, the Spanish founded Santa Fe

Hernando de Soto, a noted captain under Pizarro, led an exploratory party into Florida in 1539. De Soto probed much of the lower South and Southwest before dying of fever.

1743: François and Louis-Joseph de La Vérendrye, the first Europeans to explore what is now the state of South Dakota, leave a marker claiming the region for France.

1744: The Treaty of Lancaster allies the Six Nations (Indians of the western territories of Pennsylvania, Maryland, and Virginia) with the British, against the French.

1752: The poem *Destiny of America*, which concludes with the stanza "Westward the course of empire takes its way," is published. It was penned by Britain's George Berkeley, Bishop of Cloyne.

May 28, 1754: The Battle of Jumonville Glen begins the French and Indian War, a conflict over land and fur. The war will spread to Europe and become known as the Seven Years' War. This battle soon will be followed by the Battle of Fort Necessity, notable as the only battle in which George Washington ever surrendered.

1759: In an effort to reduce the growing number of Indian raids against Spanish settlers in Texas, several hundred Spanish soldiers (with Indian allies) battle thousands of Comanche and members of other Plains tribes. The Spaniards are forced to retreat.

February 10, 1763: The Seven Years' War ends with the Treaty of Paris. The settlement forces France to relinquish its claim on most of its North American possessions. The British gain Canada while Louisiana comes under Spanish control.

May 9–October 30, 1763: Ottawa Indians led by Pontiac lay siege to Fort Detroit.

1764: Russian Tsarina Catherine II repeals the fur tax and calls for increased exploration of Alaska, encouraging the establishment of a Russian settlement in North America.

as the capital of the province of Nuevo México. In 1680 most of the Pueblos revolted against harsh Spanish rule, killing about 400 and chasing the other 2,000 or so back down the river past El Paso. It took 12 years before the Spanish returned, but the reconquest of 1692 became permanent. New Mexico has had a continuous multiculture—combining Spanish, Pueblo, Navajo, and (after 1846) Anglo-Americans—ever since.

In the 1680s and 1690s, Spanish Jesuit missionaries, supported by the military, began crossing the Sonoran Desert into present Arizona south of the Gila River. They called the region Pimería Alta, or (roughly) "upper Pima land," after the most prominent Indians there. The area could scarcely be called a colony, for it never attracted settlers. It remained the smallest and least accessible of Spain's four principal entries into what is now the Southwest.

The third effort, following New Mexico and Arizona, was in Texas, where Spaniards tried with little success from 1690 to 1693 to establish missions among the Caddo Indians of eastern Texas. Their other objective was to head off any French colonization along the Gulf coast and the lower Mississippi River. Spain hardly colonized Texas, but it was determined not to let France do so after La Salle's visit of 1682. Spain returned in 1716 to create a presidio (a military base) at Nacogdoches in east Texas and another in 1718 at San Antonio de Valero in south Texas. Efforts to expand farther north, notably in the late 1750s, were thoroughly smashed by the Comanches, rightly called the "Lords of the Plains." By 1760 the Spanish population of Texas was no more than 1,200 or so—larger than their presence in Arizona but smaller than in New Mexico.

In 1769 Spain began its fourth missionizing and colonizing effort in the future American West. This time the target was California. Fray Junípero Serra and several other Franciscans accompanied a small military detachment to the gorgeous bay of San Diego de Alcalá. They created the first of nearly two dozen missions that by 1823 would dot the *camino real*, or royal road,

Swashbuckling English seaman Sir Francis Drake led several looting expeditions against New Spain. During a circumnavigation of the world (1577–80), he explored the Pacific coast of the future United States.

northward beyond San Francisco Bay. Presidios, missions, and settlements—notably the *villa* of Los Angeles (1781)—sprouted along that several hundred miles of California coast. The people were by no means purely Spanish but a mixture of European, African, and Indian origins. However, the missionaries never managed to convert more than a minority of the Indians. Diseases wiped out a great many. Moreover, the Central Valley lay beyond the Spaniards' reach. The number of soldiers, settler families, and clergy settled there never passed 3,300 as of 1821. During that year, Mexico, and with it the Southwest, became independent from Spain. Numbers stayed small during the ensuing 25 years of Mexican governance as well.

French Explore Northern Regions

France was the second European power to secure a foothold in the future American West. Beginning in 1608 with the founding of Quebec City, the French established themselves in the St. Lawrence Valley and far into the interior around the Great Lakes. The French began exploring the Gulf coast with La Salle's expedition of 1682. They opened Louisiana in the early 1700s, and they founded New Orleans in 1718. The French encroachment disturbed the Spanish, but the two powers never came to blows in the future United States.

Other than Quebec, Montreal, and some widely scattered fur-trading posts in what is now the Upper Midwest, the French created few towns or farm settlements. Frenchmen did explore the North American interior. They traded with many Indian nations, intermarried, and established a "middle ground," in the words of historian Richard White, between Europe and Indian country. They rarely fought with Indians and did not force colonial domination on them as the Spanish did. Nor did they disrupt, destroy, and drive them away as the English and (later) Americans so often did. In truth, the French were too few in number to do so had they wanted to.

By 1760 it appeared on maps that the French controlled a vast arc from the mouth of the St. Lawrence westward and southward to the mouth of the Missis-

In 1673 and '74, Father Jacques Marquette and trader Louis Jolliet led a small party of fellow Frenchmen in an epic exploration of the Mississippi River.

sippi. But real control was an illusion. Only along the St. Lawrence River in Quebec were French men and women truly settled and in the majority. Elsewhere they were a scattered few among tens of thousands of Indians. Only 70,000 French and French-speaking métis lived in all of New France. By 1760

February 15, 1764: French workers begin to build the city of St. Louis.

May 1, 1769: Daniel Boone, John Finley, and four others set out on an expedition to explore the West beyond the Cumberland Gap, which cuts through the Cumberland Mountains region of the Appalachian Mountains.

1769: Franciscan priest Junípero Serra establishes San Diego de Alcalá, the first of his series of missions in Alta California, near what is now the city of San Diego. Serra will found nine of the 21 California missions.

1769: Scottish inventor James Watt receives a patent for an improved steam engine that will help fuel the Industrial Revolution.

1774: Explorer Juan Bautista de Anza conducts a successful expedition northwest from Arizona to the Pacific coast, establishing overland communication between Alta California and Sonora.

1775: An Indian rebellion rocks the San Diego mission. Every building is burned and most of the missionaries, including the head priest, are murdered.

April 1775: The American Revolutionary War begins.

1776: Following an arduous journey of more than 2,000 miles from Mexico, a group of some 240 Spanish settlers establish Monterey on San Francisco Bay.

July 4, 1776: The Declaration of Independence is signed at Philadelphia's Independence Hall.

September 22, 1777: John Bartram dies. He was the "Father of American Botany" and had explored the area around Lake Ontario.

they were completely outnumbered by upwards of two million British colonists to their south and east along the Atlantic seaboard.

Britain Flexes Its Muscles

The story of British colonization is much better known than those of the Spanish and French, for the obvious reason that the United States developed out of that colonization. The stories of Jamestown, the Pilgrims, the Massachusetts Bay Colony, William Penn, and other familiar names from colonial history have long been the narrative taught in American schools. By 1760 a series of firmly established settlements and colonial societies had displaced and driven out virtually all Indians from the coastal strip from Maine to Georgia. Rarely did English-speaking settlement penetrate very far inland. Kentucky and Tennessee would soon open up as extensions of Virginia and North Carolina, but as of 1760 the English-speakers thinned out rapidly as they approached the Appalachian chain of mountains, and were only beginning to consider going farther west.

From 1756 to 1763, the colonies were caught up in the struggle between France and England known as the Seven Years' War. In America, the war was virtually over in late 1759, when British forces defeated a French army on the Plains of Abraham above Quebec City. Though further engagements occurred in 1760, the win at Quebec was decisive. The Treaty of Paris of 1763, which formally ended the war, turned over to Britain whatever France had claimed title to east of the Mississippi and north of the Ohio: in other words, the Great Lakes and much of Trans-Appalachia. (France had already, in 1762, transferred its claims west of the Mississippi, including New Orleans, to Spain.) The French Empire on the mainland of North America went out of existence. French culture and language lingered for two or three generations in parts of the Midwest,

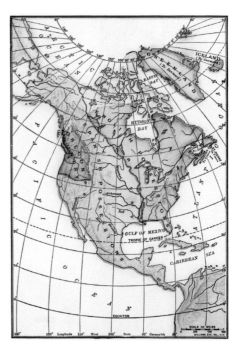

At the close of the Seven Years' War in 1763, France had lost its vast North American empire. Great Britain took possession of Canada, and Spain gained control of Louisiana.

but eventually nothing was left but some mispronounced place names such as Vincennes, Prairie du Chien, Bourbonnais, and—more importantly—Detroit, St. Louis, and New Orleans.

Britain appeared in 1763 to be the dominant power, certainly east of the Mississippi, facing only distant Spain. The actual residents of the lands west of the Appalachians continued to be a few hundred thousand Indians. The future looked good for the British Empire in North America. However, the 18th century's long list of surprising changes on the map of North America was not yet complete.

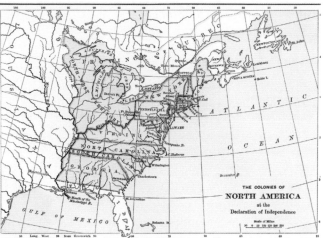

After the Seven Years' War, the boundary of the English colonies was extended to the Mississippi River, and American pioneers thronged into the Northwest Territory.

America Pushes Westward

Britain's acquisition of much of New France did not come without problems. Indeed, "the problem of the West"—how to govern not only Trans-Appalachia but the established colonies themselves—proved within a dozen years to be too difficult for Britain. Many conflicts developed and accelerated between the coastal colonies and the mother country between 1763 and 1775. Not the least of them was the attempt by the British Crown to decree in 1763 that all land west of a "Proclamation Line" along the crest of the Appalachians was off-limits to settlers.

Britain feared being drawn into clashes between settlers and Indians, which had chronically occurred and threatened to get worse. Moreover, settlements west of the mountains would be even less easy to govern than those on the seaboard, which were becoming difficult enough. By 1775, just when battles erupted between colonists and British troops at Lexington and Concord in Massachusetts, groups of settlers led by Daniel Boone and others were edging into Kentucky through the Cumberland Gap—where Virginia, Tennessee, and Kentucky meet—and were paddling down westward-flowing streams into Tennessee. The departure of the French enticed settlers into western Pennsylvania around Fort Pitt. In New York, the westward push was thwarted by the Iroquois nations from moving very far up the Mohawk River, but American victories in that area early in the Revolutionary War ended that resistance. In northern New England, particularly along the Connecticut River in Vermont and New Hampshire, the settlement frontier boomed from 1760 on.

By 1782 the 13 American colonies had won their struggle for independence. The edge of new settlement, the frontier zone, had moved west of the Appalachians. Kentucky and Tennessee held thousands of white, British-

The Five Nations of the Iroquois confederacy—Mohawk, Seneca, Cayuga, Oneida, and Onondaga—fiercely battled New York settlers for a century and a half until their final defeat in the late 1700s.

stock settlers, while similar people poured into western Pennsylvania, central New York, and Vermont. Those places were the "American West" of the post-Revolutionary years. South of Virginia, white settlement had been less dense. The true and numerous occupants of much of Georgia, and the future states of Alabama and Mississippi west of it, were the tens of thousands of members of the Indian nations known as the "Civilized Tribes"—Cherokee, Choctaw, Chickasaw, Creek, and Seminole. They would stay until they were forced out by military defeat (notably by Andrew Jackson against the Creeks in 1814), imposed treaties, deprivation of legal rights by the State of Georgia, and physical removal in the 1820s and 1830s.

The King's Proclamation Line of 1763 had been intended to create a semipermanent Indian reserve in much of the Trans-Appalachian region that Britain had taken from France. It would have cooped up the 13 colonies between the sea and the mountains. But the peace treaties of 1782–83 gave the newborn United States a huge bonus. The treaties not only ended royal authority and the Proclamation Line, but they set the western boundary of the new country at the Mississippi River.

Trans-Appalachia became the United States' first major land acquisition. This was a stunning development, because neither in actual population on the ground nor by military victories had the United States come close to occupying or conquering that huge region. The American negotiating team at the Paris peace conference in 1782—Benjamin Franklin, John Adams, and John Jay—fought stubbornly to push the boundary all the way to the Mississippi. Franklin, in fact, kept after the British to give up Canada, though American invaders had failed twice to take it or to persuade its people to join their cause. The peace negotiations came very close to giving the United States what became southern Ontario as well as Trans-Appalachia.

France and Spain provided the Americans with essential financial aid during the Revolu-

For two years after the British surrender at Yorktown, peace negotiations were conducted by Ben Franklin, John Adams, and John Jay. The resulting 1783 Treaty of Paris guaranteed Americans a frontier extending to the Mississippi River.

Treaty of Paris

As the American War of Independence wound down, negotiators produced a preliminary treaty in November 1782. In early 1784, Congress ratified a final draft of the Treaty of Paris that John Adams, Benjamin Franklin, and John Jay had hammered out with conciliatory British diplomats. Ignoring French allies whose motives they mistrusted, the Americans won remarkable concessions from Great Britain, considering the new nation's state of disarray.

Most importantly, the former colonies became free sovereign and independent states. Britain yielded its land east of the Mississippi River, from Canada to Florida, and the negotiators drew a boundary between the U.S. and British Canada. The U.S. secured valuable fishing rights in the Grand Banks off New England. In addition, the U.S. agreed to pay prewar debts to British merchants, offer amnesty to Loyalists, and indemnify them for land and other confiscated property. In exchange, Britain agreed to evacuate its western fur trade and military forts.

Neither party fulfilled its treaty obligations. The U.S. failed to honor its debts to Britain and did not compensate Loyalists, who suffered discrimination in the United States. In response, Britain refused to evacuate its western posts. It also continued to profit from the fur trade while encouraging Native allies to harass frontier settlements. Failure to deal with these nagging issues over the next 25 years, or to grapple with emerging problems, would bring the two nations to blows again in 1812.

---

tionary War. The French also sent troops and ships, which were decisively helpful at the Battle of Yorktown in October 1781—an American triumph that ended serious British resistance. Yet both France and Spain, though eagerly pitching in to defeat Britain, did not mean to replace it with a powerful United States. They much preferred to keep the Americans east of central Kentucky.

British diplomats at the peace negotiations hoped to retain the land west of the Appalachians and north of the Ohio River. But Franklin, Jay, and Adams negotiated a deal with Britain, breaking their promise to their French benefactors not to conclude a separate peace. France had no choice but to accede, not wanting to throw the Americans into the arms of the British, and even lent Franklin more money when he had the nerve to ask for it. Thus, in 1783 the western boundary of the United States became the Mississippi all the way south to Spanish Florida.

A Free-for-all Out West

While the United States was being legally born in Paris as a generously outsized infant, land and sea explorations that would ultimately benefit it continued to take place in and around North America. France was no longer a colonial power, but French speakers continued to play many roles in the fur trade of the Great Lakes and beyond. Russia had sent Danish sailor

In 1741 Vitus Bering, a Danish explorer sailing under a Russian flag, shipwrecked on what would be named Bering Island, where he died of scurvy. His expedition proved that Asia and America were separated by water.

23

November 3, 1791: While camped near the upper Wabash River, an ill-trained militia commanded by Northwest Territory Governor Arthur St. Clair is routed by Indians. More than 600 whites are killed. It is one of the most successful campaigns ever by Indians against whites.

1792: British Captain George Vancouver explores the Pacific coast from present-day Oregon up to British Columbia.

1792: Robert Gray explores the Pacific Northwest, naming the Columbia River after his well-traveled ship.

1793: North West Company fur trader Alexander Mackenzie embarks on a journey from Lake Athabasca to the Pacific, becoming the first European man to cross the continent.

October 27, 1795: The Treaty of San Lorenzo establishes the Mississippi River as the western boundary and the 31st parallel as the southern boundary between the United States and Spanish territory.

1796: At a meeting of the American Philosophical Society in Philadelphia, Thomas Jefferson expresses disappointment that no reliable cartography of the continent's western lands exists.

1797: The trading post at Pembina, in what is now North Dakota, is established by a North West Company fur trader named Charles Chaboillez.

1799: Kentuckian Daniel Boone resettles west of the Mississippi, in Spanish territory. He will ultimately make his home near St. Charles on the Missouri River.

1799: The Russian-American Company, created to settle Alaska and oversee trade in the region, makes Sitka, Alaska, the site of its headquarters.

Vitus Bering to explore the most remote coasts of the North Pacific in 1741. He not only located the strait that is named after him, but he laid the basis for the Russian-American Company's forts and trading posts in Alaska. Russian seal-hunters proceeded all the way south to Bodega Bay, about 50 miles north of San Francisco (officially Spanish territory), and remained there into the early 1800s.

Britain retained Newfoundland, Nova Scotia, and the other coastal provinces of Canada, as well as Lower Canada (i.e., Quebec) and Upper Canada (later Ontario). The North West Company and the Hudson's Bay Company, both British, oversaw the enormous interior of western Canada by means of crown-granted fur-trading and other monopoly rights. A Scottish associate of the Northwest Company, Alexander Mackenzie, became the first European to cross the continent, which he did in 1793, reaching the Pacific coast 12 years ahead of the famous Lewis and

Ambitious explorer Sir Alexander Mackenzie blazed a trail across northwestern Canada to the Arctic Ocean in 1789. Four years later, he led an expedition over the Canadian Rockies to the Pacific.

Clark expedition. Britain also occupied several forts along the Great Lakes, including Mackinac and Detroit until 1796. The British presence to the north was not a comfortable one for the United States, particularly when allied with Indians unhappy about American expansion into their lands.

The Americans' more problematic neighbor, however, was Spain, though not because of any demographic pressure. The Spanish colonies in Florida and Texas remained lightly populated. Despite lingering land claims on the east side of the Mississippi, Spain posed no aggressive threat to the western United States, even when disreputable Americans such as General James Wilkinson and Vice President Aaron Burr intrigued with Spanish authorities to possibly detach the West from the United States and make it independent. These cloudy plots never went anywhere, fortunately, because if they had, the central government had few ways of preventing them. Spain, however, was not belligerent or aggressive. Indeed, it gave up Natchez and its other claims north of Florida in 1795. The real problem for the United States was Spain's possession of New Orleans.

As American settlers and their exports multiplied in Trans-Appalachia, the Mississippi River route to the sea steadily grew to critical importance. As Thomas Jefferson would write in 1802, New Orleans was the sole spot on the globe whose possessor was the United States' mortal enemy—unless the United States possessed it itself. There were also, to be sure, cultural and religious antipathies separating Anglo-Americans from Spain, despite its help in the Revolutionary War. But New Orleans, by the end of the 1790s, was becoming the urgent sore spot.

The infant United States struggled through the 1780s and 1790s to govern its great land mass. Much of it was still unsettled by Americans but was seductively inviting (if the Indians would only get out of the way). The Congress of the Articles of Confederation (1781–89) managed to pass two key laws before it gave up the ghost after the Constitution of 1787 became the law of the land. In 1785 Congress passed an ordinance that established how public land was to be surveyed and sold to private owners. Essentially without any money, the Confederation government in the early 1780s took over the land claims of several states. Thus, the United States Public Domain came into being.

George Washington supervised slaves at his Mount Vernon plantation during his presidency. Prior to the 19th century, slavery was prohibited in Massachusetts as well as in the Northwest Territory.

From the start, the central government—Confederation and then Constitutional—passed measures to turn the domain over to individuals, and also, if possible, to turn a profit from it. The profit motive waned over the years, but the transfer would continue in the form of cash sales, auctions, preemptions, homesteading, and other laws well into the 20th century. Speculators, developers, railroad companies, and other buyers and sellers came along. Abuses and inequities inevitably occurred, but the federal government as a landlord and seller provided generations of American settlers of middling and poorer classes with ways to own land that were unheard of in Europe. The Land Ordinance of 1785 paved the way.

The other key law of the Confederation Congress was the Northwest Ordinance of 1787. While the 1785 law had concerned transfer of ownership, the 1787 law set forth how the West would be governed. It created a three-step territorial system based on increases in settlement that would culminate in statehood once an area was sufficiently peopled. And, most remarkable of all, each new state would become a state fully equal to Massachusetts or Virginia or any of the original 13. The West would never be a colonial empire of the East—not in constitutional or legal terms, at any rate.

For decades after the first U.S. census in 1790, the population of the West roughly doubled every 10 years. Many pioneer children attended one-room schools, although they spent more time working on family farms.

In 1790 Miami Indians, led by Chief Little Turtle, ambushed General Josiah Harmar, killing 183 men. The next year, Little Turtle led a dawn attack against General Arthur St. Clair, leaving more than 600 dead.

The 1787 Ordinance created the Northwest Territory, a region that was west of the Appalachians, north of the Ohio River, and east of the Mississippi River. Five states ultimately were carved from it by means of the territorial process the ordinance set forth, Ohio being the first in 1803. The ordinance also forbade slavery north of the Ohio River. A subsequent law creating the Southwest Territory was similar except in that crucial respect; slavery would be legal in Alabama, Mississippi, and other southern territories.

Baby Boom

The Ordinances of 1785 and 1787 laid down the essential legal framework for western settlement. The ordinances thereby promoted it. But by themselves, they were only the framework and not the settlement itself. That resulted from the urgent propensity for Americans to reproduce themselves. The American birth rate in 1800 was explosive. In a country of young people—the median age in 1790, when the first census was taken, was about 16 years—marriage took place early and children came soon and frequently. As they reached adulthood, and the parents' homestead could not hold them all, they looked for new land to settle farther west. Fortunately for them (though not for the Indians who lived on it), the land was out there. Those lands lay, after 1783, within the sovereign limits of the United States. The combination of available land and high fertility was synergistic. There was no penalty of poverty for having large families, because children helped as farmhands and land would be available for following generations. Land availability, plus high fertility, powered westward expansion.

One problem remained to bedevil this idyllic mechanism. The Indians, who were the true, traditional, and numerous inhabitants of Trans-Appalachia (and areas west of that region), did not feel obliged to turn over their land to the invading whites. Conflict had been chronic in colonial times; Anglo-Americans had never seemed able to live in peace with the Indians whose lands they pressed into. American independence did nothing to end such conflict. In the late 1780s, war was chronic in the Ohio Valley and Old Northwest, with no certain outcome. Miami leader Little Turtle led his forces in 1790 and 1791 in the worst defeats ever inflicted by Indians on the U.S. Army.

Only in 1794, at Fallen Timbers near Toledo, did American troops, under Anthony Wayne, defeat the northwestern Indians. The subsequent Treaty of Greenville "extinguished Indian title," in the euphemism of the time, to much of northwest Ohio and nearby lands. Jay's Treaty with Britain in 1794 and the Treaty of San Lorenzo in 1795 with Spain further opened Trans-Appalachia to American settlement. By then, the West was producing the first new states after the original 13: Vermont in 1791, Kentucky in 1792, and Tennessee in 1796, with a combined 1790 population of nearly 200,000, almost none of whom had lived there 30 years earlier.

By 1800 the second census counted about five million Americans, white and black (Indians were not enumerated). From one million around 1750, this meant a fivefold increase in 50 years. Most of the increase came from the high birth rate rather than from migration. Amazingly, the extremely rapid growth continued. Fifty years later, the 1850 census revealed growth that was again fivefold, to nearly 25 million. Throughout the half-century ending in 1800 and the full century up to 1850, nearly all of that population growth took place among a predominantly rural population. It grew fastest of all near the frontiers of settlement, as they moved westward from the Atlantic seaboard over the mountains to Trans-Appalachia and then beyond the Mississippi.

Mrs. John Merrill defends her wilderness home in Kentucky in 1791. All the while, the native warriors were defending their homelands against the invasion of white settlers.

As of 1800, the American West—the region of fresh settlement and white occupation—was a vast banana-shaped region running from Vermont at its northeastern tip through western New York and Pennsylvania, down the Ohio Valley to include the southern edges of Ohio and Indiana, through western Kentucky and Tennessee, to the Spanish-controlled lower Mississippi. In Georgia, Cherokee and Creek stood in the way—momentarily—of white movement west. In the Old Northwest, Indians not only lived virtually unimpeded by white inroads, but they resented their recent forced retreats in Ohio and Indiana. Moreover, they awaited leaders who would keep their lands and even recover (possibly with British help) some losses.

West of the Mississippi, centered in St. Louis and New Orleans, the Spanish Empire still governed. It, too, contended with powerful Indian nations, such as the Osages in Missouri, the Caddos in Louisiana and east Texas, and the Comanches on the Texas Plains. The region that we now call the American West, stretching from the Great Plains through the Rocky Mountains and from the Great Basin to the Pacific, was virtually unchallenged Indian territory. The Spanish posts at Nacogdoches, San Antonio, Albuquerque, Santa Fe, and the California coast were tiny white (or, really, mestizo) atolls amid a sea of Indians. This situation was to change radically within a very short time.

From Sea to Shining Sea
∞ 1800–1815 ∞

O N MAY 2, 1803, the United States bought the vast North American province of Louisiana from France for the bargain price of $15 million. The extraordinary purchase actually doubled the size of the United States. During that particularly hopeful spring, President Thomas Jefferson's grandiose dreams for the West, and for America, were beginning to come true.

The Louisiana Purchase coincided with Jefferson's vision for his country. Convinced that farmers (whom he called "the chosen people of God") were key to the infant republic's experiment in democracy, Jefferson believed that the new territory would provide enough land for American farmers to flourish forever. And with their prosperity literally rooted in good and presumably inexhaustible soil, the republic would undoubtedly thrive. The Louisiana Purchase, Jefferson told the United States Congress, would provide "an ample provision for our posterity" and "a widespread field for the blessings of freedom and equal laws." Through optimism and naïveté, Jefferson believed that the Louisiana Territory provided enough land for white Americans and Native Americans to live in peace.

The President's fertile imagination did not stop there. For centuries, explorers had speculated that a Northwest Passage—a waterway shortcut to

Sacagawea, a Shoshone Indian, points the way for the Corps of Discovery. In reality, Sacagawea merely pointed out a couple landmarks to the explorers. She did, however, facilitate negotiations between the Corps and the Shoshone, who traded horses to the Pacific-bound explorers.

"[I]t is impossible not to look forward to distant times, when our rapid multiplication will expand itself beyond those limits, and cover the whole northern, if not the southern continent...."

—PRESIDENT THOMAS JEFFERSON, LETTER TO JAMES MONROE, NOVEMBER 24, 1801

President Jefferson was not satisfied with the newly acquired Louisiana Territory. He wanted to extend America's holdings all the way to the Pacific Ocean.

President Jefferson was legitimately concerned that Lewis and Clark would be captured by the Spanish or British. Thus, he developed this code matrix in case his explorers needed to pass information secretly to Washington.

Asia—existed somewhere on the North American continent. Jefferson believed this, too. He thought eastern, Mississippi, or Missouri Valley rivers might flow west all the way to the Pacific Ocean. Finding the passage, and using it, would only enhance America's economic and political position. Meanwhile, Easterners wondered what else loomed in the far, far West. Maybe, some thought, the region was home to a lost tribe of Welsh-speaking Native Americans. Perhaps it brimmed with active volcanoes, giant prehistoric creatures, or monsters.

Jefferson resolved to find out and, in doing so, stake the young nation's claim to the North American West. Writing to his personal secretary, Meriwether Lewis, in June 1803, President Jefferson outlined the objectives of the expedition that Lewis, along with his friend William Clark, was to organize and supervise. "The object of your mission," Jefferson wrote, "is to explore the Missouri River" in order to determine how one might travel on it or its branches all the way to the Pacific Ocean.

Instructed to examine and document the interior of North America and to interact with the Native American populations as peaceably as possible, Lewis and Clark set off on a two-year journey as captains of the Corps of Discovery. They took with them boats, food, and medical supplies, including thousands of pills to induce sweat (a favored cure-all of the era). They also packed a large number of gifts and trinkets for the Native Americans they would encounter along the way, including sewing needles, beads, scissors, ribbons, and combs.

From 1804 to 1806, Lewis and Clark traversed the continent with a party of several dozen people. Included were York (Clark's African slave) and Sacagawea (the teenaged Shoshone Indian wife of one of the party's interpreters). The Corps of Discovery made it all the way to the Pacific Ocean at the mouth of the Columbia River before heading back to St. Louis. Lewis and Clark did not find the Northwest Passage; it didn't exist. But they did find the American West, and through their writings and drawings, they shared their discoveries with the rest of the nation.

Thomas Jefferson imagined America would become an "empire for liberty" and that the American West would play the critical role in sustaining that empire. His notions of liberty, while undoubtedly enthusiastic, were nonetheless slightly peculiar. Though beguiled by and fascinated with Native

Americans, Jefferson did not pay much attention to whether or not Native peoples *wanted* to share the interior reaches of North America with westward-moving Americans. Such uncertainty inevitably would harden into outright, protracted hostility between Native Americans and white Americans in the decades following the Lewis and Clark expedition. As Jefferson grew older, his own thoughts about Indians became more antagonistic, even as he held on to the belief that the West was so big as to be almost infinite in size. If Native Americans would not adopt the ways of white America, Jefferson wrote to John Adams in 1812, "we shall be obliged to drive them, with the beasts of the forest into the Stony mountains."

Jefferson's vision for his "empire for liberty" allowed for the freedom of African Americans as the nation expanded westward. But while initially opposed to the exportation of slavery into the West, Jefferson revised his ideas as time went on. Even William Clark's slave, York, who believed he should have been set free due to his service to the nation, would not be freed by his owner for another 10 years after the completion of the expedition.

Clearly, many obstacles lay ahead for Jefferson and future American leaders. Even Jefferson's own vice president, Aaron Burr, conspired against him and his hopes for the sustainability of the young nation. In 1806 Burr, along with Louisiana Territory Governor James Wilkinson, hatched a scheme to foment rebellion near New Orleans and perhaps establish their own nation in the West. Burr's precise objective remains unclear, but his shenanigans were anything but an endorsement of Jefferson's ideas or dreams. On a much bigger scale of enmity, unresolved antagonism between Great Britain and the United States erupted into the War of 1812, a clash that threatened the very existence of the American republic.

Despite the turbulence, one thing is certain: Because of the remarkable Lewis and Clark journey, and subsequent expeditions launched by Jefferson and other leaders, the far West became someplace real for Americans in the early 19th century. And having read about it, looked at pictures of it, and imagined it, many wanted to see it for themselves.

The United States proved victorious in the Battle of Lake Erie (*pictured*) in 1813, a key triumph on its road to a stalemate with Great Britain in the War of 1812.

1800: The Harrison Land Act goes into effect. Under the new law, the federal government will sell land in the Northwest Territory to individuals in order to encourage settlement of that region.

October 1, 1800: France and Spain sign the secretly negotiated Treaty of San Ildefonso, which returns possession of the Louisiana Territory to France.

1801: Army Captain Meriwether Lewis accepts the invitation of President-elect Thomas Jefferson to serve as his private secretary. Jefferson likely envisions Lewis as the leader of the transcontinental expedition he has been planning for a decade.

October 1802: Concerned with the expansionist goals of the United States, Spain closes the port of New Orleans to U.S. cargo.

January 18, 1803: President Jefferson asks Congress to allocate funds for an expedition in search of a water route across the North American continent.

March 1, 1803: Ohio becomes the 17th state to join the Union.

October 1803: Congress approves the acquisition of the Louisiana Territory, after French Emperor Napoléon Bonaparte agrees to sell the territory to the U.S. for $15 million.

1804: In the wake of the Louisiana Purchase, trading posts are opened across the West along existing trade routes.

May 14, 1804: Meriwether Lewis and William Clark lead their expedition team, the Corps of Discovery, out of St. Louis, Missouri, in their quest for a Northwest Passage to the Pacific Ocean.

October 1804: Lewis and Clark establish Fort Mandan as their winter headquarters, in what is now North Dakota. It is here that they will meet Sacagawea and her husband, Toussaint Charbonneau.

Napoléon gives up on America French leader Napoléon Bonaparte (*right*) negotiates the sale of Louisiana to the United States. Why was a man who was enchanted by dreams of conquest willing to give up so vast a territory? For one thing, he needed cash to bankroll his intended invasion of England. Also, he had grown heartily sick of the Americas. He recently had tried, unsuccessfully, to put down a slave rebellion in the West Indies. Moreover, it would be difficult for him to establish a strong military presence in Louisiana. "Damn sugar, damn coffee, damn colonies!" Napoléon reportedly exclaimed.

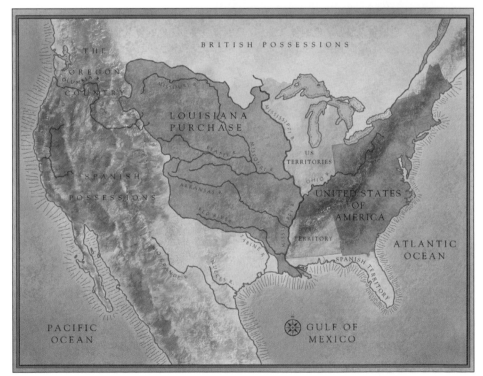

Scope of the Louisiana Purchase Although the Louisiana Purchase did not extend U.S. territory to the Pacific Ocean, President Thomas Jefferson hoped that the United States would eventually reach there. Musing in a letter to James Monroe even before the purchase, Jefferson dreamed of the U.S. covering "the whole northern, if not the southern continent, with a people speaking the same language, governed in similar forms, & by similar laws." Such an empire would have to be easily traversable. Jefferson hoped that exploration of newly acquired Louisiana and the British-controlled Oregon Territory would reveal a convenient water route across the continent—the fabled Northwest Passage. It was never found.

The Louisiana Purchase

In A Letter Dated May 26, 1801, President Thomas Jefferson remarked to his friend and political colleague, James Monroe, "There is considerable reason to apprehend that Spain cedes Louisiana...to France. It is a policy...very ominous to us."

Jefferson had good reason to worry about Louisiana, which was then much more vast than the boot-shaped southern state that bears the name today. Louisiana was bounded on the east by the Mississippi River and on the west by the Rocky Mountains. The territory included the port of New Orleans on the Gulf of Mexico, and it reached as far north as British Canada.

France exerted control over the territory during the 17th and 18th centuries, but turned it over to Spain in 1762. In 1795 the Spanish gave Americans unlimited access to the Mississippi River and allowed them to ship goods out of New Orleans duty-free. These advantages were essential to the survival of Americans settling west of the Appalachian Mountains.

Jefferson's suspicion was soon confirmed: Spain had secretly ceded Louisiana to France's consul for life, Napoléon Bonaparte. Although sentimentally attached to France, Jefferson did not trust its leader. It was no secret that Napoléon harbored ambitions to conquer all of Europe. Did his dreams include conquering America as well?

Jefferson quickly ordered the U.S. minister in Paris, Robert Livingston, to learn if Louisiana had already passed into French hands. If so, Livingston was to try to purchase New Orleans. Jefferson then sent James Monroe to France to assist Livingston. By the time Monroe arrived in Paris in April 1803, French officials had already made Livingston an astounding offer—to sell all of Louisiana to the U.S. Napoléon was no longer interested in the Americas; the far-off land was too difficult and too costly to control.

Haggling with Napoléon's representatives, Monroe and Livingston managed to get the price of Louisiana down to $15 million. It was an unbelievable real estate bargain, more than doubling the size of the United States

Monroe and Livingston with Charles Maurice de Talleyrand

at less than three cents per acre. Out of this 828,000-square-mile wilderness would come all or parts of 13 states. A treaty ceding Louisiana to the U.S. was signed on May 2 and backdated to April 30.

Jefferson received news of the agreement with as much alarm as delight. Because America's Constitution made no provision for adding territory or for nationalizing its inhabitants, Jefferson felt that two constitutional amendments were needed to make the purchase truly legal. But severely pressed for time, Jefferson swallowed his scruples and proceeded toward ratification.

Considerable controversy ensued. Jefferson's political enemies, the Federalists, were furious that a president avowedly devoted to small government would use big-government tactics to achieve his political ends. Moreover, northeastern Americans worried that they might fade into helpless obscurity if the U.S. expanded so far westward. There was even talk of northeastern states seceding from the Union.

Even so, the U.S. Senate ratified the Louisiana Purchase by a vote of 24 to 7 on October 20, 1803. The largely unexplored region of Louisiana with its barely defined boundaries was now officially part of the United States. The time was ripe for an expedition to find out just what America had gained.

April 1805: Tenskwatawa, brother of Shawnee leader Tecumseh, awakens from a trance with a message from the Great Spirit, who tells him that Indians must cut all ties with whites and their culture. *See* November 7, 1811.

Mid-August 1805: Lewis and Clark (with interpreter Sacagawea) reach the end of the navigable Missouri River and continue their journey on foot. They encounter a band of Shoshone Indians while crossing the Continental Divide, and in a remarkable coincidence, Sacagawea recognizes their chief as her brother.

Late fall, 1805: Lewis and Clark set up their winter camp in view of the Pacific Ocean. They will name their camp Fort Clatsop, after a band of local Indians.

1806: U.S. merchant ships are regularly seized by British and French as the two countries set blockades and a flurry of naval decrees against each other. The British Navy begins the practice of impressing American sailors into service.

March 23, 1806: Lewis and Clark leave Fort Clatsop to begin their long trek back to St. Louis. They will soon separate to explore different regions on the return trip.

April 1806: Frontiersman Thomas Freeman and botanist Peter Custis set out to map the Red River, along the Texas-U.S. border. This is the southern counterpart to the Lewis and Clark journey; both expeditions are organized by President Jefferson.

July 1806: Zebulon Pike departs for an exploration of the Arkansas River from Nebraska to Colorado.

September 23, 1806: Lewis and Clark arrive in St. Louis, having led separate divisions of their expedition to the Great Falls of the Missouri and the Yellowstone River, respectively.

New Orleans changes hands On December 20, 1803, the French flag was lowered over New Orleans, and the United States flag was raised in its place. During this ceremonial transfer of Louisiana from French to American hands, there was much cheering—all of it by U.S. citizens. In contrast to the jubilation shown in this illustration, the city's French and Spanish citizens watched in uneasy silence. Although by treaty they were guaranteed U.S. citizenship and religious freedom, the primarily Catholic inhabitants felt apprehensive about falling under the rule of an essentially Protestant power. Watching from his balcony, the French colonial prefect of Louisiana, Pierre Clément de Laussat, burst into tears.

Indians on the hunt An Indian hunts pronghorn antelope on the Great Plains. Although Native Americans killed animals for subsistence, hunting also had a ritualistic, religious element. Indians took care to respect the slain animals' spirits, and a shaman (medicine man) often played a role in the hunt. The introduction of horses by early Spanish explorers transformed Indian hunting techniques. So did the advent of the repeating rifle in the late 1860s, which led many Indians to abandon spears, darts, and even bows and arrows.

Lewis and Clark

William Clark

Meriwether Lewis

ON JUNE 20, 1803, President Thomas Jefferson sent his faithful secretary, Meriwether Lewis, instructions for an expedition Lewis and William Clark would make into the newly acquired Louisiana Territory. "The object of your mission," the President related, "is to explore the Missouri river, & such principal stream of it, as, by it's [sic] course & communication with the waters of the Pacific Ocean, may offer the most direct & practicable water communication across this continent, for the purposes of commerce." A naturalist and a product of the Enlightenment, Jefferson also requested that the two explorers take detailed notes of their journey. They were to record data on the region's flora, fauna, soil, climate, and indigenous peoples.

Lewis and Clark began their storied journey in May 1804, when the Corps of Discovery—a company of some 33 men—set out from Camp Dubois, heading up the Missouri River on a 55-foot-long keelboat. They brought with them basic provisions, such as flour, cornmeal, salt pork, and coffee, as well as 120 gallons of whiskey. Clark, the more experienced boatman, guided the raft and meticulously surveyed the land and the river. Meanwhile, Lewis followed his companion along the riverbank. He hunted to supplement the company's rations, and took notes on the animals and vegetation they encountered.

In October, the Corps of Discovery set up camp with the Mandan Indians in what is now North Dakota. After a brutally cold winter, the expedition resumed. The corps survived a grueling trek through the Rocky Mountains and eventually made its way to the headwaters of the Columbia River. When the company reached the mouth of the Columbia, Clark was elated: "Great joy in camp we are in *view* of the *Ocian,* this great Pacific Octean which we been so long anxious to See."

Their elation, however, was short-lived. They wintered at Fort Clatsop in Oregon Country, where constant rain and an unvarying diet of salmon dampened their spirits. The explorers were so anxious to leave that they hastily started their return trip in March. When they reached the Bitterroot Mountains (which create the border of present-day Idaho and Montana), the company was forced to set up camp for more than a month due to heavy snow in the high mountain passes. Finally, with the help of the hospitable Nez Percé Indians, they found a clear trail by late June.

Lewis and Clark parted ways for a portion of the return trip, but they reunited near the Little Knife River (in present-day North Dakota) on August 12. Their return trip down the Missouri went quickly, as they flowed with the river. Seven months after leaving Fort Clatsop, the Corps of Discovery arrived in St. Louis to great fanfare on September 23, 1806.

The mission was a huge success. In two years, Lewis and Clark had made it to the Pacific Ocean and back, losing only one man (who died from illness). Despite confrontations with Blackfeet and Sioux, their trip was mostly peaceful, and friendships were made with many of the land's Native peoples. Moreover, Clark's exceptional maps of the region and Lewis's descriptive commentary about the landscape and its inhabitants—and observations of flora and fauna—became invaluable resources. Perhaps most significantly, the expedition opened Americans' eyes to their future in the West.

October 1806: General James Wilkinson sends a letter to President Jefferson outlining a treasonous conspiracy to separate the West from the United States. Wilkinson fingers Jefferson's former vice president, Aaron Burr, but neglects to mention his own role in the plot. Jefferson will send Wilkinson to arrest Burr.

1807: The geysers of what is now Yellowstone National Park are discovered by fur trader John Colter, a veteran of the Lewis and Clark Expedition.

1807: Fur trader and New Orleans native Manuel Lisa builds the first trading post in what is now the state of Montana, at the mouth of the Bighorn River.

March 1807: The Monroe-Pinkney Treaty does not make it past President Jefferson's desk because the language contains no assurances from the British that they will stop their practice of forcing Americans into service with the British Navy.

June 22, 1807: The British ship *Leopard* fires on the American frigate *Chesapeake,* killing several sailors. British sailors then press four of the Americans into their service, an incident that will become a rallying cry during the War of 1812.

August 1807: The steamboat *Clermont,* Robert Fulton's creation, embarks on a 150-mile maiden voyage from New York City to Albany. The trip will take about 32 hours.

December 22, 1807: Congress passes the Embargo Act, restricting trade with Europe during the Napoleonic Wars, in an effort to project neutrality. The act will have the unintended effect of bringing American commerce to a virtual standstill.

The expedition begins The Corps of Discovery leaves Camp Dubois, about 11 miles upstream from St. Louis, on May 14, 1804. The team of about three dozen men left in three boats—a 55-foot-long keelboat and two 40-foot pirogues (large canoes). The expedition members had wintered at Camp Dubois, rigorously training for all aspects of the journey, and were relieved to get under way at last. Using sails, oars, poles, and tow ropes from the shore, the expedition began a slow, upstream navigation of the Missouri River.

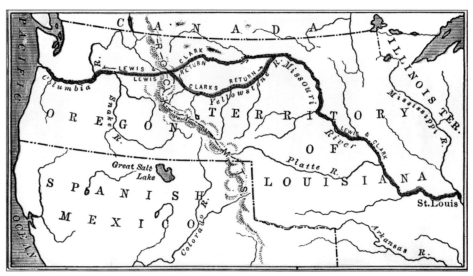

Up the Missouri President Jefferson ordered Lewis and Clark's Corps of Discovery to follow the Missouri River and find "the most direct and practicable water communication across this continent." Although the corps members were not the first white men to cross North America, they were the first to follow the Missouri River to its source. Some parts of the river proved unnavigable, forcing men to carry boats overland. Moreover, the Missouri ended with no sign of a cross-continental water route. Instead, the corps faced its toughest obstacle—the Bitterroot Range of the Rocky Mountains.

Wintering with the Indians In October 1804, in what is now North Dakota, the Corps of Discovery sighted a Mandan earth lodge village like the one pictured here. Rather than continue their Missouri River exploration into the winter, Lewis and Clark decided to camp among the friendly Mandans and Hidatsas. The corps built Fort Mandan across the river from the Indians' main village. During their winter stopover, Lewis and Clark hired Toussaint Charbonneau, a French-Canadian fur trader, and his Indian wife, Sacagawea, to continue on with them as interpreters. The corps resumed its westward journey the following April.

The mysterious Sacagewea
Although she was not an expert guide, as has often been claimed, Sacagawea's wilderness knowledge and bravery proved invaluable to Lewis and Clark. Especially crucial were her services as an interpreter when the Corps of Discovery arrived among her native Shoshones in what is now Montana. A mysterious figure whose life remains clouded by legend, Sacagawea is believed to have been born around 1787. In 1805 she gave birth to a boy, Jean Baptiste. Although historians generally agree that she died in 1812, Shoshone tradition holds that she lived among her people until 1884.

A fork in the river On June 3, 1805, the Corps of Discovery arrived at a fork in the Missouri River. The expedition's mission was to follow the Missouri to its source—but which fork was the true Missouri? Lewis and Clark both believed it to be the south fork, while their men believed it to be the north fork. The men loyally followed their commanders, with fortunate results. They had been told by Indians that they would find waterfalls on the Missouri River; on June 13, they arrived at those falls.

1808: John Jacob Astor founds the American Fur Company in an effort to break up the fur-trading monopoly held by Canada's Hudson's Bay Company.

1808: U.S. government officials detain a band of Cherokee that has been launching raids against settlers in Tennessee. The officials forcibly relocate the Indians to Arkansas.

1809: Russia's expansionist plans for North America are well under way. By year's end, about 25 Russian colonies will exist in the Pacific Northwest.

October 11, 1809: Meriwether Lewis dies of a gunshot wound in a Tennessee tavern. He was traveling to Washington to address concerns about his performance as governor of Louisiana.

1810: Zebulon Pike publishes an account of his adventures during his Red River exploration and his subsequent detention by Spanish forces.

September 16, 1810: Mexican priest Father Miguel Hidalgo y Costilla incites a revolt against Spanish rule in Mexico.

1811: Fort Astoria, the first permanent American settlement on the Pacific coast, is established in northwest Oregon by John Jacob Astor's Pacific Fur Company.

November 7, 1811: Tenskwatawa, Shawnee prophet and brother of Tecumseh, leads an attack on William Henry Harrison and his 1,200-man army at the Battle of Tippecanoe.

November 11, 1811: The 12th Congress convenes. U.S. representatives known as the War Hawks, from the South and West, push for war against the British. Southerners desire to acquire Florida, and Westerners blame the British for their troubles with the Indians in their region.

Discovering plant life Meriwether Lewis began his scientific training under Thomas Jefferson, himself no middling naturalist. On their westward journey, Lewis and his team discovered or described more than 178 forms of plant life, including blue flax, fringed sagebrush, Indian tobacco, lanceleaf sage, and wild alfalfa. They brought back many such plants as specimens. Upon learning that Shoshone Indians boiled the bitterroot (*pictured*) for food, Lewis attempted the experiment himself, only to find the taste "naucious to my pallate." He gave the root to the Indians, who ate it "heartily."

Sketches of wildlife William Clark drew this sketch of a "cock of the plain," or sage grouse. The keenly observant Meriwether Lewis wrote of the bird: "the beak is large short curved and convex. the upper exceeding the lower chap. the nostrils are large and the beak black." Lewis and Clark discovered or described 122 types of mammals, birds, reptiles, and fish, contributing vastly to America's knowledge of its western animal life. A man of boundless scientific curiosity, President Jefferson was not disappointed by the expedition's findings.

BRAVING THE ELEMENTS

A TREMENDIOUS WIND from the S. W. about 3 oClock this morning with Lightineng and hard claps of Thunder, and Hail which Continued untill 6oClock a. m. when it became light for a Short time, then the heavens became sudenly darkened by a black cloud from the S. W. and rained with great violence untill 12 oClock, the waves tremendious brakeing with great fury against the rocks and trees on which we were encamped.... It would be distressing to See our Situation, all wet and colde our bedding also wet, (and the robes of the party which compose half the bedding is rotten and we are not in a Situation to supply their places) in a wet bottom scercely large enough to contain us our baggage half a mile from us, and Canoes at the mercy of the waves, altho Secured as well as possible, Sunk with emence parcels of Stone to wate them down to prevent their dashing to pecies against the rocks.

—JOURNAL ENTRY OF WILLIAM CLARK, NOVEMBER 12, 1805, WHILE ENCAMPED NEAR THE PACIFIC OCEAN

Salt Makers by John F. Clymer courtesy of Mrs. John F. Clymer and the Clymer Museum of Art

Reaching the Pacific Three members of the Corps of Discovery make salt from seawater as Indians look on. The explorers reached the Pacific Ocean in November 1805, and their joy at completing their mission wasn't dampened even by the constant rainfall. Lewis and Clark's men built their winter camp, Fort Clatsop, on the south bank of the Columbia River. The campsite was decided by a vote that famously included Sacagawea, an Indian woman, and York, an African American slave. After a dreary winter, the Corps of Discovery set out on its long voyage back to St. Louis on March 23, 1806.

Burr's Ugly Schemes

As U.S. PRESIDENT, George Washington distrusted a U.S. senator from New York named Aaron Burr. Yet not even Washington could have imagined how low Burr would go in his quest for power.

The trouble started in 1800 when Burr ran as Thomas Jefferson's vice presidential nominee. During the campaign, Burr secretly connived to gain the presidency. Alexander Hamilton, one of America's Founding Fathers, did his best to derail Burr's scheme. "[T]his man has no principle, public nor private," stated Hamilton. "[H]is sole spring of action is an inordinate ambition."

Burr lost the presidency and settled for the VP position. Then, in 1804, Burr ran for governor of New York. Again Hamilton orchestrated his defeat, angering Burr to the point where he challenged Hamilton to a duel. The combatants faced each other in New Jersey on July 11, 1804. Hamilton held his fire but Burr shot, mortally wounding Hamilton. Burr was indicted for murder in New Jersey, but never tried.

In 1805 Burr began hatching a scheme with the early republic's greatest scoundrel, Major General James

Aaron Burr

Wilkinson. A Revolutionary War veteran, U.S. Army commander, and governor of Louisiana Territory, Wilkinson also was a spy. For years, he peddled secret information to Spain. In 1793 he informed Spanish officials of American plans to attack New Orleans. During the tumultuous 1790s, Wilkinson considered plans to lead wavering western territories into alliance with Spain, or establish a new nation under his dictatorship. By 1806 the two conspirators evidently decided that Burr would lead a small army down the Ohio River, join Wilkinson near New Orleans, and foment rebellion.

Newspaper reports and informants kept President Jefferson apprised of Burr's progress, and by January 1807 arrest warrants were issued. Burr fled but was soon captured. Charged with treason—a capital crime—Burr stood trial before Federalist Chief Justice John Marshall. In a characteristic betrayal, Wilkinson offered damning testimony against Burr. The trial created a public sensation, but Wilkinson escaped charges and Marshall acquitted Burr due to lack of evidence. Disgraced in the U.S, Burr spent several years in Europe before returning to practice law in New York. He died in obscurity in 1836.

1812: With the steamboat *New Orleans,* Robert Fulton and Edward Livingston initiate a regularly scheduled steamboat and freight route along the Mississippi River between New Orleans and Natchez.

1812: The United States, hoping to annex Canada while the British are busy fighting Napoléon, attempt three invasions across the northern border by the end of the year. All end in failure.

March 1812: Russia establishes Fort Ross near Bodega Bay, California, as a trading post and a base for sea otter hunters.

March 17, 1812: U.S. troops attack East Florida in an effort to wrest control of the region from Spain.

April 30, 1812: Louisiana is officially named the 18th state of the United States of America.

June 19, 1812: After years of preparation that focused on building the strength of the U.S. Navy, America declares war against the British, launching the War of 1812.

August 15, 1812: Dozens of settlers are massacred by Potawatomi Indians while attempting to evacuate Fort Dearborn in Illinois.

August 16, 1812: General William Hull surrenders Detroit to the British.

August 19, 1812: The USS *Constitution* battles Britain's HMS *Guerriere* off the coast of Nova Scotia. Within an hour, the *Guerriere* loses all her masts and surrenders.

December 1812: Fort Daer, a Hudson's Bay Company fort and the first permanent settlement in what would become North Dakota, is established by Irish and Scottish immigrants from Winnipeg, Canada.

Pike the spy Zebulon Pike grew up on frontier military posts and became a zealous soldier. In 1805 and '06, he was sent on several explorations by Major General James Wilkinson, but Pike's real assignment was to spy on the Spanish along the southwestern border of the Louisiana Purchase. When Wilkinson tipped off the Spanish that Pike would be in their territory, Pike was captured— although later released. It is not known whether Pike's capture was planned as an opportunity for espionage—just as it is not known whether Pike ever climbed, or even saw, the Colorado peak named after him.

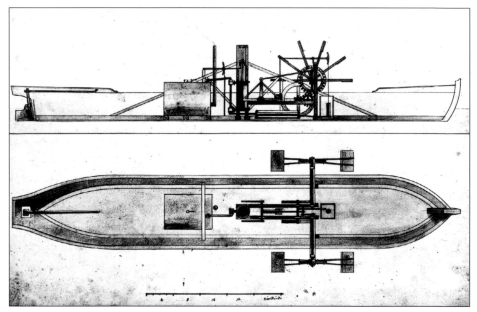

Fulton's steamboat While exhibiting his landscape paintings in England and France, Robert Fulton became fascinated with technology. He took advantage of opportunities to work on canals, mines, torpedoes, a submarine, and a steam-powered boat. In 1806 Fulton returned to the United States and built his own steamboat— not the country's first, but the first that was commercially successful. Fulton piloted his *Clermont* up the Hudson River in 1807. Spectators and boatmen were astonished. A contemporary described how they sought protection from "the approach of the horrible monster which was marching on the tides, and lighting its path by the fires which it vomited."

Lisa expands the frontier

Manuel Lisa, who helped Lewis and Clark prepare for their western explorations, headed the first large fur company on the upper Missouri River. In 1807 he established Fort Raymond as a trading post, and in 1809 he joined with Pierre Chouteau and others to found the St. Louis Missouri Fur Company. Lisa got along well with Native Americans, while his trading companions and

competitors characterized him as bold and daring. Lisa also was the first U.S. settler of Nebraska, establishing Fort Lisa in the territory in 1812.

Astor and the American Fur Company

Soon after the American Revolution, German immigrant John Jacob Astor arrived penniless in New York City. By 1800 Astor was one of the leading American merchants in the fur trade. In 1808 Astor set up the American Fur Company to organize trading around the Great Lakes, which helped to open that "Northwest Territory" to commerce and settlement. Under subsidiaries, Astor's company expanded control over the fur trade into the Rockies and the Pacific Northwest. His Fort Astoria on the Columbia River became important in establishing the U.S. title to the Oregon territory. At his death, Astor was by far the richest man in America, having amassed a fur-bearing estate worth an estimated $20 million.

Republic of West Florida

After the Louisiana Purchase from France in 1803, West Florida fell under dispute. The United States claimed to possess the region as part of the purchase, while Spain claimed to have controlled it since 1783. In 1810 U.S. and British settlers in West Florida rebelled against Spanish rule. On September 26, they founded the Free and Independent Republic of West Florida (all of which actually lay within today's states of Louisiana, Mississippi, and Alabama). The republic lasted a mere 74 days, after which the U.S. took possession of the area. In 1819 Spain ceded all of Florida to the U.S.

Stuart discovers the South Pass

For all its successes, the Lewis and Clark expedition of 1804–06 failed to find a passable route through the Rocky Mountains. In November 1812, Robert Stuart (*pictured*), leading six other explorers employed by fur magnate John Jacob Astor, succeeded where Lewis and Clark had failed. Stuart discovered the South Pass, a 20-mile-wide valley that cut through the Rockies in what is today southwestern Wyoming. For some years afterward, the pass was neglected by travelers except for trappers, missionaries, and soldiers. However, it eventually became part of the Oregon Trail, one of the key pioneering routes across North America.

January 1813: The U.S. attempt to retake Detroit ends in defeat when British and Indian forces kill close to 400 U.S. troops on the battlefield.

August 30, 1813: Hostile "Red Stick" Creek Indians attack Fort Mims, Alabama, killing peace-seeking "White Stick" Creeks, white setters, and slaves. It will become known as the Fort Mims Massacre of the Creek War.

September 10, 1813: Commodore Oliver Hazard Perry leads the U.S. to victory over the British in the Battle of Lake Erie, securing the Northwest Territory for the Americans.

October 5, 1813: Shawnee chief Tecumseh dies at the Battle of the Thames in Ontario, Canada. The U.S. wins the battle.

March 27, 1814: William Weatherford (Red Eagle), who led the Red Sticks in the Creek War, suffers a final defeat at the hands of Andrew Jackson in the Battle of Horseshoe Bend in the Mississippi Territory.

August 9, 1814: Andrew Jackson signs the Treaty of Fort Jackson, which relieves the Creek Indians of 23 million acres of their ancestral lands in present-day Alabama and Georgia.

August 24–25, 1814: The White House and the U.S. Capitol burn at the hands of the British.

September 11, 1814: The U.S. defeats the British in the Battle of Lake Champlain—a key victory.

December 24, 1814: British and American diplomats agree to the terms of the Treaty of Ghent, which calls for a return to the prewar status quo.

January 8, 1815: Andrew Jackson and his troops enjoy a decisive victory at the Battle of New Orleans.

February 17, 1815: The U.S and Britain ratify the Treaty of Ghent, marking the end to the War of 1812.

War of 1812

THOUGH HISTORIANS HAVE generally attributed the War of 1812 to the British seizure of American ships and impressment of American sailors, the most ardent supporters of the war were Westerners. Those living on the frontier believed that their Canadian neighbors to the north were encouraging Indian attacks on American settlements in hopes of gaining a foothold in the fur-rich Mississippi Valley. Westerners and Southerners hoped that war would lead to the annexation of Canada and Florida, the latter being under the control of Britain's ally, Spain.

Battle of the Thames

War with Britain had many detractors, most notably those in the Northeast who relied on trade with Canada and Britain. But it was the War Hawks in the South and West who had President James Madison's ear. When hostilities finally commenced, the United States recognized that it was futile to engage the mighty British navy and instead focused the bulk of its military brunt on attacking forts along the Canadian border. Success was limited. Despite victories at Thames River, Put-in-Bay, and York, American troops could hope for little more than a stalemate.

The U.S. achieved just that when peace negotiators met in Ghent, Belgium. British envoys insisted on navigation rights on the Mississippi and hoped for a Missouri River border between Canada and the United States. The Americans, however, stood firm, rejecting the British demands outright. In the end, the two countries merely agreed to stop fighting, with neither ceding or acquiring territory.

"Tecumseh's War"...and "Curse"
Shawnee leader Tecumseh fought against the American occupation of Indian lands. Insisting that all Native American land was owned communally, he warned William Henry Harrison, then governor of the Indian Territories, not to occupy areas acquired by treaties with individual tribes. "Tecumseh's War" against the American intruders continued into the War of 1812, in which he fought on the side of the British. Tecumseh was killed in an 1813 battle in Ontario, Canada. Harrison, elected U.S. president in 1840, died in office, as did the next six presidents elected in a year ending in zero—due, some say, to "Tecumseh's Curse."

Battle of Tippecanoe On November 7, 1811, Major General William Henry Harrison (*far left, on horse*) defeated Shawnee forces in the Battle of Tippecanoe. The conflict took place in the Indian capital of Prophetstown (present-day Battle Ground, Indiana). Harrison cunningly advanced when the brilliant Shawnee leader, Tecumseh, was away. The defeat shattered Tecumseh's dream of an Indian confederacy and made Harrison a hero. In 1840 Harrison ran successfully for president with running mate John Tyler. Their slogan was "Tippecanoe and Tyler, too!"

Fort Dearborn Massacre When the War of 1812 began, Fort Dearborn stood in a wilderness that is now Chicago, harboring 54 soldiers, 12 militiamen, nine women, and 18 children. The region's Indians allied themselves with the British against the Americans. In August 1812, the fort's commander, Captain Nathan Heald, was ordered to evacuate. When he did so, his party was attacked by a force of about 500 Potawatomi Indians. Eighty-six of the fort's men, women, and children were killed in the ensuing slaughter. The Fort Dearborn Massacre strengthened Tecumseh's Indian Confederacy.

Tenskwatawa's visions Tenskwatawa, the "Shawnee Prophet" (*center*), declared a religious vision to the Shawnees in 1805 and accurately predicted a solar eclipse in 1806. According to Tenskwatawa, Indians were made by the Creator, while white men were made by the evil Great Serpent. He commanded his people to abandon white men's ways, including textile clothing, manufactured goods, and alcohol. Tenskwatawa was not a military leader like his brother, Tecumseh, and his defeat at the Battle of Tippecanoe in 1811 destroyed his credibility completely. He died in what is now Kansas City in 1836.

Battle of Lake Erie Commodore Oliver Hazard Perry leaves his disabled flagship, *Lawrence,* during the hotly contested Battle of Lake Erie on September 10, 1813. Commodore Perry had overcome great obstacles to build a fleet of nine vessels that could contest a British flotilla on Lake Erie. The *Lawrence,* a 20-gun brig, was named after Perry's friend, Captain James Lawrence, who recently had died in action after uttering, "Don't give up the

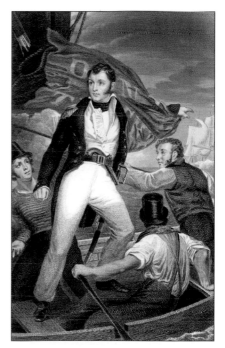

ship"—words that were emblazoned on Perry's battle flag. After transferring to the *Niagara,* Perry directed a victory that placed Lake Erie in American control. He proudly relayed the message, "We have met the enemy and they are ours."

Battle of New Orleans On January 8, 1815, an army commanded by Andrew Jackson defeated General Edward Pakenham's British forces in the Battle of New Orleans. British troops suffered hundreds of deaths, including that of Pakenham, while only a few Americans were killed. News that a peace treaty between Britain and the U.S. had been signed in Belgium had not yet reached America. However, the treaty would not go into effect until its ratification and proclamation on February 17–18, so the U.S. victory may have prevented further concessions to the British.

War Against the Creeks

WHEN THE UNITED STATES declared war on Britain in 1812, Native nations—including the Creeks—found themselves embroiled in the conflict. Maintaining neutrality became impossible. Americans aimed to acquire Indian lands by force or coercive negotiations. American frontiersmen, many of whom were "Indian haters," feared that British or Spanish agents had incited Indians to attack vulnerable communities. Among Native nations, tribal politics began to fracture as debates raged over which side to support.

Tecumseh, a charismatic Shawnee politician and warrior, traveled south to enlist Creeks and other tribes against the Americans. Through trade and military affiliations with the British, Tecumseh helped develop a pan-Indian alliance. Many "Red Sticks" (Upper Creeks) sympathized with Tecumseh. When a leader named Little Warrior devastated a white settlement on the Raisin River in 1813, "White Sticks"—Creek peacekeepers desperate to avoid war—arrested and executed him.

After some Creeks procured arms and ammunition at Pensacola, Florida, Americans deemed them enemies. In August 1813, Creek warriors attacked Fort Mims near the Alabama River, killing almost 400 American settlers. When news of the shocking massacre reached Nashville, the Tennessee legislature ordered state militia commander Andrew Jackson to punish them.

From November 1813 until March 1814, Jackson hunted the Creeks, culminating in a bloody battle at

Andrew Jackson's Tennessee militia defeats the Creeks

Horseshoe Bend on the Tallapoosa River. Among the soldiers were David Crockett and Sam Houston. Jackson's militia and regular soldiers surrounded a Creek town, set it ablaze, and killed nearly a thousand Indians. Many roasted inside their burning homes. Said Crockett, "We shot them like dogs and then set the house on fire."

The slaughter at Horseshoe Bend transformed Jackson into a national hero, and boosted his political career. The surviving Creeks signed a treaty at gunpoint later that summer, surrendering 23 million acres of land to the U.S. as war "reparations." Ironically, much of the land belonged to the White Sticks, who had been at peace with the U.S. and had even aided Jackson's military campaign.

Fort Mims Massacre On August 30, 1813, Creek Indians of the antiwhite "Red Stick" faction attacked Fort Mims, Alabama, near the Alabama River. In addition to the white settlers and slaves who lived in the fort, Creeks and mixed-bloods who opposed the Red Sticks had gathered there for safety. As many as 500 militiamen, settlers, and friendly Creeks were killed in the attack. The Fort Mims Massacre transformed the Creek War from a civil war among the Creeks into a conflict between Red Stick warriors and the U.S.

The Red Sticks surrender William Weatherford (Red Eagle) surrenders to Colonel Andrew Jackson. Weatherford had led the Red Sticks against U.S. forces throughout the Creek War. His final defeat came on March 27, 1814, in the Battle of Horseshoe Bend, which occurred on the Tallapoosa River in present-day Alabama. After escaping the battle, Weatherford turned himself over to Jackson, who was impressed both by his bravery and eloquence. Weatherford helped the U.S. negotiate peace with the Red Sticks and was pardoned by Jackson.

Building prisons After American colonists achieved independence, they began to reform draconian penal systems imposed on them by England. Such reforms spilled over into the West. When Kentucky became a state in 1792, it inherited laws that had made the death penalty all too frequent. In 1798 politician John Breckenridge spearheaded the state's reformed penal code, requiring capital punishment only for first-degree murder. A prison became a necessity, so the State Penitentiary of Kentucky (seen here in 1813) was built in 1799. The prison often held those convicted of antislavery activities. Distinctions were seldom made between slave stealers and genuine abolitionists.

To the Rockies ...And Beyond
∞ 1816–1829 ∞

A

FTER RETURNING from an expedition to the Rocky Mountains in present-day Colorado in 1820, U.S. Major Stephen H. Long reported bad news. The vast sweep of prairie that lay like a grassy carpet at the eastern flank of the Rockies was, according to Long, worthless, "almost wholly unfit for cultivation" and "uninhabitable by a people depending upon agriculture for their subsistence." This part of the West, which Long called the "Great American Desert," was good only for defensive purposes. It would help prevent hasty migration of American settlers westward because, after all, who would want to rush west into such an inhospitable place? And it would provide a barrier that few enemies of the nation would dare cross.

Major Long was sketchy about the details of just who this eastward-moving enemy might be (he could have been thinking of the Russians, Spanish, or British). But his dour description of the Plains stretching from modern-day Nebraska to Oklahoma created an image of a harsh West and gave credence to those who thought the Louisiana Purchase had been pure folly.

But if the West, or large sections of it, appeared to be a risky bet for farmers, it seemed like something else entirely to others. In the three-plus decades following the triumphant return of Lewis and Clark, mountain men and traders began their wide-ranging travels across the expanse of the North American

Fur trappers toiled in the great outdoors, explored new territories, and were basically their own boss. Yet the hazards were many: exposure to the elements, lack of medical treatment, and intense lonliness. Bears, snakes, Indians, and fellow trappers were all potential enemies.

"There is, perhaps, no class of men on the face of the earth . . . who lead a life of more continued exertion, peril, and excitement, and who are enamored of their occupations, than the free trappers of the West."

—Writer Washington Irving

continent. Motivated by various objectives, from curiosity to a yearning for adventure to greed, several thousand men fanned out across the West.

What they were after were furs (mostly beaver, but otter and buffalo also were high on the list), and they found them in abundance in the rivers and streams of the far West. For more than a generation in the early 1800s, until their aggressive fur-trapping decimated the animal populations of the interior West, these celebrated mountain men were the lifeblood of a niche industry in North America. Never likely to get rich, the mountain men lived dangerously in the West. Those unprepared risked death from starvation, dehydration, or excessive cold or heat. Potential enemies included grizzly bears, Indians, and even rival trappers and traders from British companies.

Though they seemingly lived the ultimate life of freedom, trappers were basically independent contractors working for fur-trading

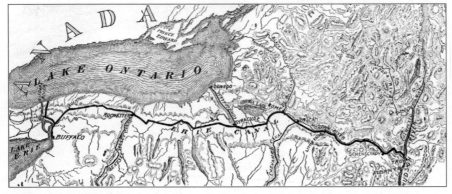

Opened in 1825, the Erie Canal became the gateway to the Upper Midwest. Goods could now be transported easily into and out of the region. Many eastern and immigrant farmers moved west, and population subsequently boomed in western New York and Michigan.

companies. Even the annual trapper celebration, the famed "Rendezvous," reveals the ties that mountain men inevitably forged with the world that they had never fully left behind. These summertime gatherings in the Rocky Mountains not only offered mountain men a week or two of fun and frivolity, but they were opportunities for trappers to bargain and sell pelts to traders who had journeyed from St. Louis. They also exchanged news and employment information.

The western fur trade was an economic bonanza in the early 19th century. Worldwide fashion trends, driven in part by European excitement over beaver-felt hats, created a frenzy of economic opportunism. Even William Clark got involved in the excitement, helping to form the Missouri Fur Company in 1808 not long after returning from his western adventures as co-leader of the Corps of Discovery.

John Jacob Astor was the most successful fur trader of all. An immigrant to New York from Germany, by way of London, Astor already was among the nation's most prominent fur traders by the time President Thomas Jefferson dispatched Lewis and Clark to explore the Louisiana Purchase. When he formed the Pacific Fur Company in 1810, Astor aimed to dominate the fur trade of the newly explored region. Within a year, Astor's company established a trading post (Astoria) at the mouth of the Columbia River in the Pacific Northwest. There, in competition with the British-owned Hudson's Bay Company, the Pacific Fur Company trapped and traded beaver and other pelts until the War of 1812 forced Astor out of the region.

The fur trade, and the exploratory wanderings of the men involved in it, helped hasten the opening of the West. A year before his 1820 Rocky Mountain expedition, Stephen Long had been part of a journey up the Missouri River into the Rockies, where Lewis and Clark had traveled earlier. But while Lewis and Clark had used pirogues (small riverboats) to make their way, the famed "Yellowstone Expedition" of 1819 traveled upriver from St. Louis on a steamboat called the *Western Engineer*.

Numerous transportation advancements were made in the 1820s and '30s. The way to the West was carved out by trails and canals, and boats found their way upriver to faraway places. When the Erie Canal opened in 1825, the Great Lakes region became connected by waterway to the Atlantic Ocean. It created a conduit for commerce and settlers (Michigan's population soared from 9,000 in 1820 to more than 200,000 in 1840), and it set off a flurry of canal building throughout the nation.

Westward-bound pioneers found flatboats useful for transporting cargo, including cows and horses, as seen here. Flatboats could only travel downstream. Once they reached their destinations, they were sold as lumber.

By the 1820s, the signals were clear, if subtle. An acre, a county, or a state at a time, Americans extended the western frontier. The far West remained generally unknown and seemed endlessly vast, but the country was changing.

In 1826 fur trapper and explorer Jedediah Smith, a man who knew the West perhaps better than any other American of his time, astonished Spanish officials and priests when he showed up on horseback in Southern California not far from Los Angeles. Asked where he had come from, Smith informed the Spanish that he had traveled overland, from the east. Releasing Smith from captivity, angry officials ordered him to go back the way he had come, perhaps thinking that such incursions would not happen again.

They could not have been more wrong. The genie was out of the bottle— and he was headed west.

November 5, 1816: James Monroe is elected as the fifth president of the United States.

December 11, 1816: Indiana becomes the 19th state to join the Union.

Spring 1817: The grand steamboat *Washington,* built by Henry Miller Shreve, travels upstream from New Orleans to Louisville, Kentucky.

September 29, 1817: The Treaty of Fort Meigs is signed. It cedes all remaining lands belonging to the Ohio Valley Indian tribes to the U.S. government.

December 10, 1817: Mississippi becomes the 20th state.

December 26, 1817: Major General Andrew Jackson leads an attack against the Seminole Indians in Spanish Florida.

1818: The Treaty of Peace is signed by the United States and Britain. It establishes a northern boundary for the future states of Montana and North Dakota at the 49th parallel.

March 1818: Major General Andrew Jackson defeats the Seminoles in Spanish Florida.

December 3, 1818: Illinois enters the Union as the 21st state.

Late 1818: By the end of the year, construction on the National Road reaches the Ohio River in Wheeling, Virginia. The westward progress of this highway will open the Midwest to settlement and trade.

February 22, 1819: The U.S. and Spain sign the Adams-Onís Treaty. The U.S. renounces its claims to Texas, Spain relinquishes Florida, and the U.S.-Mexican border (stretching all the way to the Pacific) is defined.

May 28, 1819: The *Independence* becomes the first steamboat to travel up the Missouri River, from St. Louis to Franklin, Missouri.

Spain's missions in California In the mid-1700s, Spain's King Charles III decided to use religion to conquer the territory that would become California. He put Father Junípero Serra in charge of what was called the "Sacred Expedition" to convert and civilize the Native American population of the region. Father Serra and his followers began building their first mission in San Diego in 1769. Eventually, 21 missions, including San Gabriel Arcángel near present-day Los Angeles (*pictured*), ranged along a 650-mile-long road from San Diego in the south to Sonoma in the north.

Missions miserable for Indians The purpose of the Spanish missions in California was to convert Native Americans to Catholicism; to teach them Spanish; to instruct them in such useful practices as agriculture, weaving, and blacksmithing; and ultimately to make them full citizens of the Spanish empire. However, as this illustration suggests, Indian life in the missions was little better than slavery. Moreover, between the missions' founding in 1769 and their secularization in 1834, European diseases, changes of diet, and poor living conditions wiped out about 75 percent of the coastal Indian population.

Expansion After the War of 1812

To MANY EARLY AMERICANS, the Appalachian Mountains seemed to be the natural western boundary of their nation. Although explorers reported a huge expanse of land on the other side of that barrier, the territory was hard to reach.

In 1775 Daniel Boone and his team of men started clearing a road through the Cumberland Gap in the Appalachians, and in 1792 the Wilderness Road was widened for settlers' wagons. A flurry of road building culminated in the federal construction of the National Road, which stretched from Maryland through the Cumberland Gap into what would become West Virginia.

Even so, the land beyond the mountains was already occupied by Native Americans, who often resented incursions from the east. The British in Canada supported the idea of an independent Native American state that would limit U.S. expansion, so when the War of 1812 broke out between Britain and the United States, most western tribes sided with the British.

When the war ended in 1815, Secretary of the Treasury Albert Gallatin commented that the conflict had made Americans "feel and act more as a nation." The surge of nationalism was accompanied by a sense of entitlement to the lands across the mountains. The U.S. government, eager to make the West safer for settlers, sanctioned the defeat and removal of Native American tribes.

Mail stagecoach and freight wagons on the National Road

Pioneers poured across the Appalachians and into the lands beyond. Wagons, people on foot, and an occasional family with a wheelbarrow moved westward. Indiana became a state in 1816, as did Mississippi and Illinois in 1818. On midwestern rivers, barges, keelboats, and great paddle wheel steamboats carried settlers farther into the West.

During the War of 1812, the difficulties of moving troops and supplies in the Great Lakes area drew attention to transportation problems in that region. Work on the Erie Canal began in 1817 and ended in 1825. Thus, the wilderness trading post of Buffalo, New York, soon became another major gateway to the West.

Steamboats spur westward migration In 1818 *Walk-in-the-Water* became the first steamboat on Lake Erie. With their large steam-powered paddle wheels, steamboats could manage strong currents in the open water. They also could go upstream on rivers much more easily than boats powered by poles, oars, tow ropes, or sails. Steamboats dramatically increased migration, creating new towns and new industries. By the 1830s, huge paddle wheelers made regular runs on midwestern rivers, cutting earlier water travel and delivery times by half and more.

December 14, 1819: Alabama becomes the 22nd state to join the Union.

1820: A contingent from the Army Corps of Engineers, under the command of Major Stephen Long, travels across Kansas to the Rocky Mountains on a scouting and mapping expedition. Team member Dr. Edwin James succeeds in climbing Pikes Peak.

March 1820: The Missouri Compromise brings two states into the Union—Missouri as a slave state and Maine as a free state. The compromise officially prohibits slavery in areas west of Missouri above latitude 36 degrees, 30 minutes.

March 15, 1820: Maine becomes the 23rd state.

Late 1820: By the end of this year, the California missions hold 20,000 American Indians.

February 24, 1821: Mexican liberals and conservatives declare independence from Spain.

August 10, 1821: With the Missouri Compromise settled, Missouri finally becomes the 24th state in the Union.

September 1821: Missouri trader William Becknell discovers a market for his goods in Santa Fe, part of the newly independent Mexican Republic. Becknell will repeat the journey from Missouri to Santa Fe several times over the next few years and become known as the "Father of the Santa Fe Trail."

1822: William Henry Ashley advertises in a St. Louis newspaper for trappers willing to go into the Rocky Mountains, marking the beginnings of the Rocky Mountain Fur Company.

1822: Frontiersman James Bridger makes the first trapping expedition into the Rocky Mountains.

Maroons settle among the Seminoles A well-armed maroon soldier prepares to fight for his freedom. The name *maroons* was given to black slaves who escaped within a generation of their arrival from Africa. Maroon communities formed throughout the Americas, frequently preserving aspects of African culture. Maroons who lived among the Seminoles in Florida joined the Indians to fight the U.S. in the three Seminole Wars. Today, many descendents of Florida maroons live in Oklahoma. The word *maroon* may have come from the Spanish word *cimarrón,* which means wild or untamed—interestingly, the same word from which *Seminole* is derived.

The First Seminole War Near the Florida border, Seminole Indians prepare to ambush U.S. troops as they approach Fort Scott in Georgia. Such hostilities between Indians and whites in Georgia arose largely over escaped black slaves who had settled among the Seminole in Spanish-controlled Florida. General Andrew Jackson led U.S. troops into the region in December 1817, marking the beginning of the First Seminole War. In Florida, Jackson's men destroyed Seminole and maroon villages. After the war ended in 1818, the Spanish ceded control of Florida to the U.S. Two more Seminole Wars would force most of the Florida Indians to move west of the Mississippi River.

The Missouri Compromise

JUST BEFORE 1820, the United States government became involved in frantic gerrymandering on a continental scale. That term had come into use in 1812, when Massachusetts Governor Elbridge Gerry's Antifederalist Party redistricted his state to maintain its own majority. One district came out looking like a salamander, and a newspaper editor called it a "Gerrymander." The reasons behind national gerrymandering included political power, slavery, and disputes over the rights of the federal government.

Trouble began in 1819, when the slaveholding territories of Alabama and Missouri both applied for statehood. Alabama was admitted, giving the Union an equal number of slaveholding states and nonslaveholding states—although the North still held a majority in the House of Representatives. If Missouri was admitted as a slave state, the balance of power would swing to the South.

Northerners found slavery repugnant and did not want it to spread; Southerners were economically dependent on slavery and did not want it limited. Each side was eager to prevent the other from controlling the nation's economy and future development.

To calm the congressional uproar, Illinois Senator Jesse Thomas suggested drawing a line across the Louisiana Purchase. Except in Missouri, slavery would never be allowed north of that line. To maintain the balance of political power, Missouri would enter the Union as a slave state and Maine would enter as a free state.

That sounded like a workable solution, but was it legal? Representative John Randolph of Virginia insisted that the federal government could not limit slavery, which was, after all, allowed by the U.S. Constitution. Before Randolph had the opportunity to bring his objections on the floor, House Speaker Henry Clay moved quickly. Clay signed the Missouri statehood bill and slipped it secretly to the Senate, where it passed without further debate.

President James Monroe also believed that the bill violated the Constitution, but fearing civil war without the Missouri Compromise, Monroe signed it. Secretary of State John Quincy Adams astutely observed that the raging arguments were only "a title page to a great tragic volume" yet to be written.

The Missouri Compromise 1820

Free state or territory

Slave state or territory

Territory closed to slavery

Slave state, free state A map of 1820 shows how the westward movement played a significant role in the sectional problems between North and South. The Louisiana Purchase doubled the size of the U.S. and produced the first state west of the Mississippi River (Louisiana, 1812). Louisiana was a slave state, so the next western state admitted to the Union was a free state (Indiana, 1816). Maintaining the balance, a slave state was admitted the next year (Mississippi, 1817), followed by a free state (Illinois, 1818) and then a slave state (Alabama, 1819). When Missouri then sought admission as a second consecutive slave state, Congress erupted in conflict. The resulting Missouri Compromise of 1820 allowed statehood for Maine (free state) and then for Missouri (slave state).

1822: Jedediah Smith and Mike Fink embark on a fur trading expedition to the upper Missouri, sponsored by William Ashley and Andrew Henry. The team establishes Fort Henry near the mouth of the Yellowstone River.

1822: President James Monroe warns Russia not to encroach further on U.S. territory in the Pacific Northwest.

1822: Congress abolishes the 28 government-operated fur trading posts in the West, including Fort Osage, Missouri.

Spring 1822: The Western Department of John Jacob Astor's American Fur Company is established in St. Louis, Missouri. Within five years, it will absorb the competition.

1823: The first American settlement in Texas, consisting of 300 families, is established by Stephen Austin along the San Antonio River. Mexico granted permission for the settlement on the condition that the settlers become Mexican citizens and Roman Catholics.

1823: A Red River expedition led by Army Corps Major Stephen Long marks a point along the 49th parallel, north of Pembina, North Dakota, as the U.S.-Canadian border.

1823: Stephen Long publishes a map of his 1820 Rocky Mountain expedition in which he labels the plains east of the mountains the "Great American Desert." This pronouncement will ward off potential settlers for a generation.

1823: The first trading post in the territory of Nebraska is established in Bellevue.

September 1823: Joseph Smith, the 18-year-old son of a New York State farmer, claims to have been visited by the angel Moroni, who gave him a set of golden plates, which he translated as the Book of Mormon.

Log cabins in Indiana Many fur traders, explorers, and emigrants heading west passed through Indiana Territory, and many others settled there. When Indiana gained statehood in 1816, it boasted about 60,000 citizens. This 1820 log cabin allegedly was the first one built in Indianapolis, Indiana. Introduced to the American colonies by Scandinavian immigrants, this style of home was used in most forested areas. The rough-hewn logs, notched to fit together at the corners, did not require nails. Spaces between the logs generally were filled with clay and rags, and the sturdy structures often were covered with clapboard siding.

The "Father of Texas" In 1821 Stephen Fuller Austin (*center*) moved to Texas to develop the first Anglo-American colony in the Mexican province. As an *empresario* (land agent), Austin was the political, judicial, and military leader of his colony, which included hundreds of families. Worn out after 15 years of cease-less labors on behalf of his colonists, Austin died in 1836 at age 43, shortly after accepting appointment as the first secretary of state of the new Texas Republic. The state's capital would be named after Austin, who is known as the "Father of Texas."

Long discovers "Great Desert" In 1820 Major Stephen Long led an expedition across the Midwest. Long discovered and named the Rocky Mountains and Long's Peak, and made useful reports on Native Americans. However, Long did not consider the Great Plains useful for anything more than a buffer between American civilization and lands held by other nations. On his map, Long labeled the middle of the country the "Great American Desert." He reported that the area was "unfit for cultivation and of course uninhabitable by a people depending upon agriculture." It was a notion that had to be overcome before settlers would move westward.

Adams's Treaty and Monroe's Doctrine

WHILE THE LOUISIANA PURCHASE of 1803 greatly enlarged the United States, the new territory's boundaries were ill-defined. In subsequent years, the U.S. and Spain squabbled about borders—with Spanish leaders feeling vulnerable. As U.S. population and power grew, Spain lost much of its influence in the West. Spanish leaders also feared American threats against Texas and other possessions. In 1819 Spain had no option but to sign the Adams-Onís Treaty. John Quincy Adams, the secretary of state under James Monroe, drafted the treaty with Luís de Onís, the Spanish minister to the U.S.

The treaty stipulated the Louisiana Purchase's western and southern boundaries, and it extended the 42nd parallel to the Pacific. This became the first U.S. assertion of a "legal" claim to the Pacific coast south of the Columbia River. In addition, Spain relinquished claims to "Oregon Country" (Russia would follow suit in 1824). Adams secured east and west Florida in exchange for a highly questionable claim to Texas.

Four years later, in a December 1823 speech to Congress, President Monroe outlined a new hemispheric policy. The Monroe Doctrine asserted that the Americas were closed to further European colonization, and that the U.S. would tolerate no European meddling in the hemisphere. If intervention became necessary, the United States would assume police power. The U.S. promised not to intervene in European affairs, nor would it interfere with existing European colonies.

Many Americans believed that only a U.S.-British naval alliance would make the doctrine enforceable. But the canny Adams realized that Great Britain had to support U.S. policy. At the time, an array of European autocratic monarchies threatened Britain's constitutional monarchy, and Britain would not alienate its greatest potential ally—the United States. Besides, Adams insisted, "It would be more candid, as well as more dignified, to avow our principles explicitly to Russia and France, than to come in as a cockboat in the wake of the British man-of-war." Adams was correct, and the U.S. felt confident in enforcing the Monroe Doctrine. In the 1840s, the U.S. aggressively pursued Spanish-held land in the West, including Texas and California.

"America, North and South, has a set of interests distinct from those of Europe, and peculiarly her own. She should therefore have a system of her own, separate and apart from that of Europe.... [O]ur endeavor should surely be, to make our hemisphere that of freedom."

—THOMAS JEFFERSON, TO PRESIDENT JAMES MONROE, OCTOBER 24, 1823

The Monroe Doctrine As U.S. president in 1823, James Monroe issued the Monroe Doctrine, which asserted the United States' commitment to keep European powers from restoring their waning control over North and South America. Monroe's other diplomatic accomplishments contributed greatly to U.S. westward expansion. Assisted by his able secretary of state, John Quincy Adams, Monroe forged treaties that defined U.S. borders with Canada and Mexico, limited Russian expansion down the Pacific coast, and placed Oregon under joint British and American control. At last, U.S. citizens were free to settle across the continent.

December 2, 1823: In an address to Congress, President James Monroe states that the Americas should hereafter be free of European colonization, a concept that will become known as the Monroe Doctrine.

1824: William Ashley and Andrew Henry revive the fur trade when they send small brigades of mounted trappers into the Rocky Mountains.

1824: Frontiersman James Bridger, deep into Utah on an expedition for Ashley and Henry, is thought to be the first white man to see the Great Salt Lake. He mistakenly exclaims, "Hell, we are on the shores of the Pacific!"

Spring 1824: In preparation for the mass migration of Cherokee and Choctaw Indians to the new Indian Territory, the U.S. Army opens Fort Towson and Fort Gibson in what is now Oklahoma.

March 11, 1824: War Secretary John Calhoun creates the Bureau of Indian Affairs. He puts former Supervisor of Indian Trade Thomas McKenney in charge of the new bureaucracy.

April 1824: Russia and the United States agree to set Russia's southern border in the western hemisphere at 54 degrees, 40 minutes, and to allow American ships inside its 100-mile security radius.

October 4, 1824: A new Mexican constitution proclaims the United Mexican States a republic with equality for all Mexicans, freedom of the press, and one religion: Catholicism.

November 2, 1824: In the presidential election, Andrew Jackson wins the popular vote over John Quincy Adams, but fails to win an electoral majority. That leaves the election in the hands of the House of Representatives, which elects Adams.

Cooper romanticizes the frontier James Fenimore Cooper, a prolific American novelist, exerted an enormous influence on later western literature through The Leatherstocking Tales. Working from Cooperstown, the New York community founded by his father, the author created the stalwart frontier character Natty Bumppo, who was based partly on Daniel Boone. Cooper carried Bumppo through adventures from his youth to old age in a series of five novels: *The Pioneers* (1823), *The Last of the Mohicans* (1826), *The Prairie* (1827), *The Deerslayer* (1841), and *The Pathfinder* (1840). The popular Leatherstocking Tales established a precedent for frontier romance and heroes that subsequent generations of writers would try to recreate.

The trail to Santa Fe In 1821 Missouri trader William Becknell found a route to the Mexican town of Santa Fe, New Mexico. Newly independent from Spain, Mexico was now receptive to trade with Americans. Becknell returned eastward with news of a good market on a trail wide enough to accommodate wagons. As seen in this illustration, Missouri traders began flowing into Santa Fe. By 1825 the Santa Fe Trail had become the West's first major trade route. Consequently, America soon became interested in acquiring the territory.

The Erie Canal The first canal boat carries dignitaries, including ardent canal supporter and New York governor DeWitt Clinton, to celebrate the 1825 opening of the Erie Canal. New York's 363-mile-long, 40-foot-wide Erie Canal connected the upper Hudson River with Lake Erie. A system of locks compensated for the 568-foot difference in height between the two bodies of water. The Erie Canal drastically reduced travel time and shipping costs between New York City and the country's interior. Thousands of farm families traveled westward via the canal, populating the Midwest with people from northern states—a fact that became significant when the Civil War approached.

The strategic Fort Snelling After the War of 1812, the U.S. decided to dominate the Upper Mississippi Valley in earnest, building forts and other outposts between Lake Michigan and the Missouri River. The most crucial of these was Fort Snelling, built from 1819 to 1825 at the confluence of the Minnesota and Mississippi rivers, where it helped end British control of the fur trade in the region. A lonely outpost of civilization in a vast wilderness, Fort Snelling became a meeting place for Indians, traders, immigrants, and even tourists.

Ogden explores Northwest

Peter Skene Ogden was a Canadian fur trader and an explorer of the American West. In 1825 he led a Hudson's Bay Company brigade of more than 100 French Canadians, British, and Native Americans—including women and children—into Utah. He encountered other trappers, and squabbled with one American group over territorial rights (even though they were all in Mexican territory at the time). About 30 of Ogden's men switched sides, solely because the Americans paid better prices for furs. Ogden's daily journals of his travels in Utah, Idaho, Oregon, northern California, and Nevada proved especially valuable to mapmakers.

Adams helps expand the U.S.

As a diplomat abroad, John Quincy Adams (son of the United States' second president, John Adams) became convinced that America's destiny lay not with foreign alliances but in westward expansion. While serving as secretary of state to President James Monroe from 1817 to 1825, Adams negotiated treaties that brought much of the West under U.S. control. After an undistinguished term as president (1825–29), Adams served in the House of Representatives, where he promoted the annexation of Oregon to the U.S. However, as an abolitionist, he opposed the annexation of Texas because it would have meant the westward expansion of slavery.

1825: When the first seasonal meeting of Ashley and Henry's trapping brigades becomes an open rendezvous, attracting Indians and free-trappers as well, it replaces the trading post and the trading company as the point of purchase in the fur trade.

1825: New U.S. government policy mandates the exchange of Indian lands in the East for public land in the West, ostensibly allowing the tribes to live with some self-determination.

June 3, 1825: The U.S. government appropriates the Kansa Indian ancestral lands. The government will move the Indians to a reservation and open the state of Kansas for resettlement.

October 26, 1825: The opening of the Erie Canal links the Hudson River and Lake Erie, creating new opportunities for commerce with the West.

November 7, 1825: Missouri's Shawnee Indians sign a treaty with the U.S. government. They consent to give up their lands in exchange for a 2,500-square-mile reservation in Kansas and some provisions.

1826: James Fenimore Cooper releases his novel *The Last of the Mohicans,* which tells of the massacre at Fort William Henry during the French and Indian War.

1826–27: Trapper Jedediah Smith leads the first overland expedition to California, from the Great Salt Lake in Utah to Mission San Gabriel near present-day Los Angeles.

1827: The Hudson's Bay Company builds a lumber mill at Fort Vancouver, the first in the Pacific Northwest.

May 8, 1827: Colonel Henry Leavenworth establishes Fort Leavenworth on the Missouri River to guard the western frontier and the Santa Fe Trail.

Russians in California The Russian-American Company, chartered by Czar Paul I in 1799, established colonies in Alaska for sea otter hunters and fur traders. In 1812 the company set up an outpost, called Fort Ross, in northern California. The chapel seen in the center of this illustration was constructed around 1825 and dedicated to Saint Nicholas. When sea otters became scarce in 1841, the Russians sold their fort to Johann Sutter and withdrew from California. The new owner would become famous a few years later when gold was discovered at Sutter's Mill.

CONSTITUTION

OF THE

CHEROKEE NATION,

MADE AND ESTABLISHED

AT A

GENERAL CONVENTION OF DELEGATES,

DULY AUTHORISED FOR THAT PURPOSE.

AT

NEW ECHOTA,

JULY 26, 1827.

PRINTED FOR THE CHEROKEE NATION,
AT THE OFFICE OF THE STATESMAN AND PATRIOT,
GEORGIA.

Cherokee Constitution
In 1827 the Cherokee Nation adopted a legal constitution. Strongly influenced by the U.S. Constitution, it was a politically sophisticated document that divided governmental power into executive, legislative, and judicial branches. Largely the creation of John Ross, who became the Cherokee's principal chief, the Cherokee Constitution's main purpose was to preserve the nation's territory and autonomy. However, gold was soon discovered on tribal land in Georgia, and the forced western relocation of the Cherokee by the U.S. government became all but inevitable.

Indian Women

REPRESENTATIONS OF INDIAN WOMEN of the Old West have been, for the most part, erroneous and misleading. Sometimes depicted as the fair princess frolicking and carefree, and at other times as the toiling, stooped-over wife living a life of drudgery, they were in reality neither. Rather, women played diverse roles in Native American society, serving as homemaker, farmer, mother, doctor, and even architect.

The majority of Indian women got married once they reached puberty. Such marriages typically were prearranged and in some cases occurred without courtship. Once wedded, women took up their ascribed roles. In most Indian cultures, men did the hunting while women maintained the home. This frequently meant that women were responsible for constructing the family's shelter, whether that be a tipi, a hogan, a wikiup, or a more permanent adobe dwelling.

In many tribes, it was women who tended to and cultivated crops and other plants used in daily living. Being experienced horticulturalists, they were familiar with the medicinal properties of certain plants, which in some societies made them the primary health care providers. But perhaps the Indian woman's greatest duty was as mother. It was she who raised the children, instilling in them the folkways and mores of the tribe or band.

Of course, women's roles varied as much as the myriad cultures of the American West. Life for Indian women in the Pacific Northwest, for example, was very different than in the Great Plains or the Southwest. In some matriarchal societies, family life, lineage, and leadership were female-centered, while in others women's roles were more akin to their non-Indian pioneer counterparts. Regardless of the culture, Indian women fulfilled roles often ignored in the discourse on Native America and the West.

Gifts for the Indians Fur company agents met with Native Americans to trade for bear, deer, moose, muskrat, beaver, lynx, otter, and marten hides and pelts. Before the bargaining began, the agent generally presented the Indians with gifts, such as the necklace the trader in this illustration is presenting to a young warrior. Among many Native American tribes, the giving and accepting of gifts was part of sealing a contract. Native Americans especially liked to receive glass beads, blankets, clothes, guns, horses, and steel items, such as knives, sewing needles, and ax heads.

Slavery expands westward Slaves work on a plantation in the Old Southwest. The growth in the demand for cotton around the beginning of the 19th century caused the plantation system to expand westward from the Atlantic seaboard into Kentucky, Tennessee, western Georgia, Alabama, and Mississippi. To meet the cotton demand, slavery also grew; from 1790 to 1860, the number of slaves in the U.S. increased from about 700,000 to 4.5 million. The need for slave labor introduced a market for "surplus" eastern slaves to be sold to southwestern plantation owners.

1828: The Shawnee, under the leadership of prophet Tenskwatawa, arrive at the Shawnee Reserve in Kansas after an arduous journey.

1828: The U.S. Senate ratifies a treaty that establishes the Sabine River as the official U.S.-Mexico border. (The river separates modern-day Texas and Louisiana.)

1828: Jedediah Smith leads an expedition from California into Oregon, where his party is attacked by a band of Indians on the Umpqua River. Smith and three others survive and make it to the safety of Fort Vancouver.

1828: The Arkansas Cherokee reach a resettlement agreement with the U.S. government. They will cede their lands and relocate west of the Mississippi River.

February 21, 1828: The Georgia Cherokee publish the first issue of their weekly newspaper, *Cherokee Phoenix*. It will run until 1834 when the Georgia Guard will destroy the printing press, four years before the Cherokee's forced relocation west.

Spring 1828: Joseph Smith and Martin Harris, his scribe, complete the translation of the Book of Mormon. Harris shows the manuscript to his family, who destroys it. *See* Summer 1829.

November 4, 1828: Andrew Jackson, a proponent of the Indian relocation policy, is elected as the seventh president of the United States.

1829: President Andrew Jackson offers to take Texas off Mexico's hands for $5 million, but Mexico rejects the offer.

Summer 1829: Joseph Smith retranslates the Book of Mormon, with Oliver Cowdery serving as his new scribe.

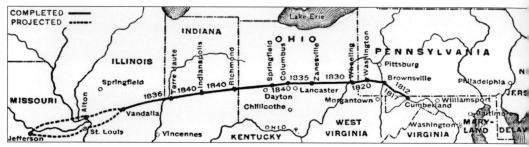

The National Road In 1811 construction began on the National Road, which was designed to open land west of the Allegheny Mountains to settlement. Also called the Cumberland Road and the National Pike, it reached what is now Wheeling, West Virginia, in 1818 and Vandalia, Illinois, in 1841. The 20-foot-wide, crushed-gravel road was centered in a cleared, 60-foot right-of-way. Traffic included wagons, faster coaches drawn by teams of horses, individuals on horseback, and herds of animals. In 1879 an old-timer recalled that the "traffic was so heavy that generally it was safe from highway robbery."

The beaver hat business Tall beaver hats were considered essential to gentlemen in eastern U.S. cities, England, and other European countries. Beaver fur clipped from the hide could be matted into a natural waterproof felt, which was in demand for women's hats as well as men's. In the early 1800s, the European beaver population drastically declined and American beaver pelts brought excellent prices. By 1840, when the mountain men held their last Rendezvous, few beavers remained in the American West. In any case, European styles soon changed, and silk hats became more popular.

> "I have held my hands in an ant-hill until they were covered with ants, then greedily licked them off. I have taken the soles of my moccasins, crisped them in the fire, then eaten them."
> —Mountain man Joe Meek

Smith blazes new trails

Jedediah Smith combed his hair to cover the terrible scars inflicted by a grizzly bear on his scalp, left ear, and eyebrow. A tireless fur trapper, Smith collected 668 beaver pelts in 1824–25 to set a single-season record. As leader of trapping expeditions, Smith roamed the entire West in classic journeys of adventure and exploration. He covered at least 16,000 miles across trackless wilderness, making significant contributions to American geographical knowledge. Smith retired from the fur trade and settled in St. Louis, but at age 32 he went West again—and was killed by Comanche warriors.

DYING OF HEAT

IN THOSE MOMENTS how trifling were all those things that hold such an absolute sway over the busy and the prosperous world. My dreams were not of Gold or ambitious honors, but of my distant, quiet home, of murmuring brooks, of Cooling Cascades. After a short rest we continued our march and traveled all night. The [sound] murmur of falling waters still sounding in our ears and the apprehension that we might never live to hear that sound in reality weighed heavily upon us....

When morning came it saw us in the same unhappy situation, pursuing our journey over the desolate waste, now gleming in the sun and more insuportably tormenting than it had been during the night. [About] at 10 O Clock Robert Evans laid down in the plain under the shade of a small cedar, being able to proceed no further. [We could do no good by remaining to die with him and we were not able to help him along, but we left him with feelings only known to those who have been in the same situation and with the hope that we might get relief and return in time to save his life.]

—Diary of explorer Jedediah Smith, June 24–25, 1827, while crossing the Great Salt Lake Desert

The annual Rendezvous

Trapping was a lonely occupation, but the mountain men at least could look forward to the annual Rendezvous. The first Rendezvous was held in 1825 at Wyoming's Green River, and for the next decade and a half it was the most important business and social event of the fur trade. Rendezvous sites, which usually changed from year to year, brought together trade caravans, trappers, and Native Americans each summer, when no trapping was done. After selling the pelts, the trapper purchased what he needed for another year in the mountains, then spent a few weeks in riotous debauchery. Along with drinking, gambling, and womanizing, men competed in wrestling, horse racing, and shooting contests.

The Hudson's Bay Company Fur traders in boats and wagons arrive at a Hudson's Bay Company trading post. The mission of the company, chartered in 1670 by King Charles II, was to claim resources of the New World for England. The British claimed control over all of the waterways that drained into Hudson Bay—as did the French. After decades of raids and skirmishes, the territory was finally recognized as British. In 1821 the HBC absorbed the North West Company of Montreal, thus monopolizing the fur trade in Canada and the Oregon Territory.

Manifest Destiny
⁃ 1830–1848 ⁃

THE AMERICANS CAME prepared for a fight. Sailing up the California coast from the south, sailors and marines sharpened cutlasses and cleaned pistols. They took target practice with their 80 cannons, aiming at objects as far away as two miles. Commodore Thomas ap Catesby Jones, in charge of the United States Pacific fleet (all of six ships in 1842), drilled his men incessantly, preparing them for war.

Commodore Jones knew there might be trouble once he sailed to Monterey, the capital of Mexican California. Who knew if the Mexican authorities wished to attack the American ships? England and France might cause trouble, too. Rumors circulated about English warships in the waters off the California coast, and a French fleet had recently sailed from South America on a mysterious assignment. Jones knew he commanded a formidable force. If England or France or Mexico wanted to fight the United States, they would have to take on Jones and his men.

On October 19, 1842, the commodore made his decision. He notified the Mexican authorities of Monterey, as well as the 29 Mexican soldiers there, that they must surrender to the United States. They did. The next day, Jones marched his men six abreast into the small village from the coastline while his band played "Yankee Doodle" and "The Star-Spangled Banner." But the

American Progress, an 1870s painting by John Gast, represents Manifest Destiny. The angelic figure (interpreted by some as "Columbia," the personification of the United States), leads white settlers westward while stringing telegraph wire as she goes. Native Americans (*left*) clear out of her path.

"Unless this country is soon occupied by some of our own people, there is every reason to believe that some other nation will avail itself of the advantages which it offers."

—HALL J. KELLY, FOUNDER OF THE AMERICAN SOCIETY FOR THE SETTLEMENT OF THE OREGON TERRITORY, SEPTEMBER 21, 1832

When Commodore Thomas ap Catesby Jones seized Monterey, California, in October 1842, he thought that the U.S. and Mexico were at war. He was wrong; the war would not begin for another three and a half years. A gunner aboard one of Jones's ships drew this sketch of the misadventure, complete with a song lampooning Jones's orders.

A highly influential political writer, John O'Sullivan helped James Polk—a great advocate for U.S. expansion—win the presidency in 1844. According to O'Sullivan, it was God's will for Americans to occupy and spread democracy across the continent.

United States was not at war with Mexico—or England or France, for that matter. On the 21st of October, Commodore Jones returned Monterey to Mexico, shook hands, apologized, and lowered the American flag from the briefly christened Fort Catesby, then sailed away.

Why did Commodore Jones seize Monterey? Understanding this one-day war, or understanding America in the half century before the Civil War, requires that we wrestle with a phrase rarely heard anymore: "Manifest Destiny." What is, or what was, Manifest Destiny, and why did it grab hold of the American imagination in the 1840s?

Part of the answer lies in what Americans of European descent thought about their special place in history and in the New World. Many Americans saw themselves as an especially chosen people, sure to gain favor in God's eyes. They also saw great significance in their separation from the Old World and what they believed to be Europe's moral and political decay. In the New World, they believed, God had bestowed upon Americans a divine gift, an entire continent upon which to act out a special future. From their communities in the East, Americans looked west and saw endless emptiness, as if the diverse and numerous Native American societies hardly existed at all. Surely, Americans thought, God had made the West because he had special plans for the young nation.

By the 1840s, this view—equal parts expansionist fervor, religious doctrine, and patriotism—had become attached to the single phrase "Manifest Destiny," a belief that the future of the nation lay in expanding ever westward across the continent. Yet, this faith could not disguise deep divisions in American society, most notably the conflict over slavery. Expansion during the 1840s would make those divisions even more prominent and troubling.

A newspaperman named John O'Sullivan, writing about American expansion into the West and Southwest in the 1840s, declared that territorial additions to the young nation were "the fulfillment of our manifest destiny...to overspread the continent allotted by Providence for the free development of our yearly multiplying millions." To those who believed it, this expansion was obvious and inevitable. The nation grew, he wrote, "by the right of our manifest destiny."

True believers in Manifest Destiny expected, as O'Sullivan put it, that the United States would soon "possess the whole of the continent which Providence has given us for the development of the great experiment of liberty and…self government entrusted to us. It is right such as that of the tree to the space of air and the earth suitable for the full expansion of its principle and destiny of growth." In other words, America had both a right and an obligation to spread out from the Atlantic to the Pacific, maybe even across all of North America. Overriding belief in this duty set into motion cycles of westward migration and conquest.

Of course, European Americans had been moving into the West, and into Native territory, for hundreds of years prior to the 1830s and 1840s. But unlike earlier periods, in which the federal government was often a reluctant partner of settler and other movements into the West, the 1830s and 1840s saw the federal government leading the way west. The government paid for western explorations, supplied the Army, declared war, and pushed the idea of Manifest Destiny to the very ends of the continent. Individuals still played critical and important roles in moving to and claiming parts of the West, but they had a much more powerful partner than in earlier years.

This illustration appeared during Lewis Cass's run for the presidency in 1848. The artist implies that Cass was willing to wage bloody war solely for the purpose of "Manifest Destiny." Earlier in the decade, America's zealous quest to expand its territory was a major reason why the U.S. went to war against Mexico.

John O'Sullivan invented a catchy phrase, but he did not invent the idea or ideas behind that phrase. Americans had been thinking about their supposedly special place in the world and in North America long before O'Sullivan put "manifest" and "destiny" side by side in his newspaper column. As John Quincy Adams wrote to his father, former President John Adams, in 1811, "The whole continent of North America appears to be destined by Divine Providence to be peopled by one nation, speaking one language, professing one general system of religious and political principles."

Through the first several decades of the 19th century, Americans moved in greater and greater numbers to the West. At first, that West encompassed mostly the rich farmlands near the Ohio and Mississippi river systems. But as knowledge of the Louisiana Purchase territory gradually filtered throughout American society, people began to think about a West much bigger and farther away.

By the 1830s, more and more American farm families began to imagine new lives in such places as far-off Oregon Territory. A trickle of settlers began to make the arduous journey to the far western reaches of the continent. As they and their horses, mules, oxen, and wagons made the slow and often dangerous trips, they imagined new lives built on hope: hope that they would live through the journey (many did not), hope that the Indians they would encounter would be friendly (they usually were), and hope that Manifest Destiny really did mean that the territory to which they were emigrating would soon become part of America.

It was as if God himself had thrown open the West to the young nation. The era exploded with American expansionist aggression. Manifest Destiny signaled a change in American thinking and behavior. In earlier years, a belief in God's plans for America could provoke a kind of passive faith in the minds of Americans: *God will take care of the details.* But by the 1840s, Americans felt compelled to take a more active role: *Working with God, we will produce our Manifest Destiny.* This change in thinking might appear slight, but it meant that American expansion from the 1840s forward would be energetic, ambitious, and bloody.

Caught up in "Oregon Fever" during the 1840s, thousands of Americans braved the elements and migrated to Oregon Country, where fertile soil awaited them. British and Americans debated over claims to the region until 1846, when the two sides agreed on a border at the 49th parellel.

Manifest Destiny became the blueprint for conquest. Native American claims upon western land did not concern the expansionists. The nation's response to Native America was encompassed in the simple phrase "the Indian Problem." This problem can be expressed in deceptively simple terms of citizenship and geography. One, Indians were not Americans, and Americans were not about to let them become members of that exclusive national category. And two, Indians most definitely *were* in the way of the journey that Manifest Destiny insisted America take. Americans and their national leaders spent much of the 19th century pushing Indians out of the way.

Those convinced of the righteousness of Manifest Destiny figured that Native Americans were obstacles to everything God had in mind for the young nation. This left Indians with few choices. They could try to avoid westward-pushing Americans by staying a step ahead of the settler juggernaut. Or they could adopt American mores, embrace Christianity, and learn to farm. As a last resort, Natives could fight their American enemies.

The first option could work only if there was an inexhaustible supply of land (which there was not), and if those Indians migrating west could exist relatively peacefully with the Native groups they encountered. The second option could work only if the dominant American society respected those Native peoples who chose to adopt, or assimilate to, American ways. The last choice, violent resistance, could last only if the various Native societies could maintain hostilities in the face of an overwhelming foe. As understood by whites, Manifest Destiny insisted that the end result, regardless of the choices Native Americans made, would be the same: The entire continent would inevitably belong to the white race.

Faith in Manifest Destiny encouraged Americans to think big. Instead of scaling back desires to meet the challenges of geography, Americans simply added size to their dreams. That much of North America already was claimed by other foreign powers—including Great Britain, Russia, and Mexico—did little to shake American confidence in the future.

By the 1830s, the West looked like a checkerboard of international interests, with several countries drawing the maps differently. Mexico, Great Britain, and the United States all laid claim to lands in the West, Southwest, and Northwest. But the boundary lines that separated, for instance, the Louisiana Purchase from the Oregon Territory were not at all clear. At several junctures in the 1840s, this confusion, coupled with American aggression, nearly led to war. By 1846, with the Mexican-American War, it did.

The Mexican-American War was triggered in 1846 by disputes and skirmishes regarding the Texas-Mexico border. Upon defeat in 1848, Mexico ceded enormous territory to the United States: Texas, New Mexico, and California.

In an 1844 speech, Ralph Waldo Emerson wondered about Manifest Destiny and the nation's headlong territorial expansion across North America. By gobbling up land, America might become great, he believed. But the true judge of that greatness would be how well the nation, and the nation's leaders, grappled with the social and moral problems of the era. Emerson understood as well as anyone that Manifest Destiny was like a runaway train across America. It had to be controlled; otherwise, expansionism would lead to inevitable conflict within American society, especially regarding the conflict between those advocating the expansion of slavery and those pushing for its abolition.

"The United States will conquer Mexico," Emerson wrote. He was correct, but the result would spell trouble. The conquest of Mexican territory raised unanswerable questions about the ways in which American society would move forward. Would the land gained in victory be slave or free? Emerson predicted that the ingestion of territory gained as the spoils of war "will be as the man swallows the arsenic, which brings him down in turn. Mexico will poison us."

1830-1848

1830: A wagon train led by Jedediah Smith and William Sublette crosses the Rocky Mountains at South Pass. They journey through Indian and Mexican territory to the Pacific coast.

1830: Mexico imposes strict limits on American immigration to Texas.

1830: Congress moves to protect squatters from land speculators with the passage of the Preemption Act. This act will enable settlers to buy public lands that they have cultivated for a year or more.

1830: Regular steamboat service is established on the Missouri River.

April 6, 1830: Joseph Smith organizes the Church of Christ in upstate New York. Eventually, Smith and his followers will change the name to The Church of Jesus Christ of Latter-day Saints. Followers will be commonly known as Mormons.

May 28, 1830: President Jackson signs the Indian Removal Act, paving the way for the destruction of southeastern American Indian culture and their mass relocation to western reservations.

December 1830: A group of Mormon missionaries from New York and Ohio arrives in Independence, Missouri. They believe that they have reached the Center Place of Mormon lore and their future City of Zion.

1831: The Northwest missionary movement begins in earnest when a Nez Percé delegation travels to St. Louis seeking white teachers for its tribe.

January 1831: Looking to grow his church in the West, Mormon leader Joseph Smith arrives in Kirtland, Ohio, with some of his followers.

January 1831: James Black designs a knife for James Bowie. The bowie knife will become the weapon of choice among many Westerners.

Cherokee newspaper

In 1828 Elias Boudinot, a Cherokee, became the first editor of the *Cherokee Phoenix*, a newspaper published weekly in English and Cherokee. It was the first newspaper ever published by American Indians. Boudinot strongly opposed government policies to distribute Cherokee lands in Georgia among white settlers. He advocated tribal migration to Indian Territory as the only hope of keeping the Cherokee Nation intact. However, a leadership faction regarded Boudinot as a traitor. He resigned from the *Cherokee Phoenix* in 1832, and after migrating to Indian Territory was assassinated.

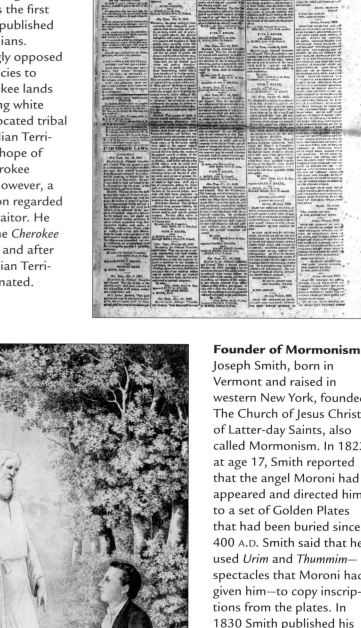

Founder of Mormonism

Joseph Smith, born in Vermont and raised in western New York, founded The Church of Jesus Christ of Latter-day Saints, also called Mormonism. In 1823, at age 17, Smith reported that the angel Moroni had appeared and directed him to a set of Golden Plates that had been buried since 400 A.D. Smith said that he used *Urim* and *Thummim*—spectacles that Moroni had given him—to copy inscriptions from the plates. In 1830 Smith published his translations of those inscriptions as the *Book of Mormon*. His followers considered him a prophet and attested to appearances by angels, Jesus, and several Old Testament figures. They followed him to Ohio, Missouri, and finally Illinois, where he was assassinated in 1844.

Journeys of the Latter-day Saints

DURING THE 1820s AND 1830s, the Second Great Awakening ignited waves of religious revivalism in western New York. Numerous denominations emerged from the area but the most important was The Church of Jesus Christ of Latter-day Saints, whose followers were known as Mormons.

Founded by Joseph Smith, Jr., in 1830, the church grew rapidly, recruiting converts from the U.S. and Europe. Relations between Mormons and "Gentiles" (non-Mormons) in New York, Ohio, Illinois, and Missouri often seethed with tension, forcing Mormons to relocate several times. Missourians especially mistrusted Mormons' political behavior, economic power, "northern" attitudes regarding slavery, and the practice of polygamy. In 1838 the Missouri governor's "extermination order" forced the Mormons across the Mississippi to Illinois. After an Illinois mob murdered Joseph Smith and his brother, Hyrum, in 1844, leadership passed to Brigham Young.

Gathering information from explorers and trappers, Young led the "Saints" westward in 1846. The Mormon exodus coincided with the onset of the Mexican-American War. Some Mormons joined the Army for two rea-

Joseph Smith, Jr.

sons: to get to the West and to prove their much-questioned loyalty. Other Mormons journeyed west in "handcart companies," some of whom suffered terribly during the trek to present-day Utah's Great Salt Lake Valley, which they named Deseret. In 1848 the Treaty of Guadalupe-Hidalgo made Deseret part of the U.S.

Brigham Young ruled Utah for decades, serving concurrently as governor, Indian agent, military strategist, and church prophet. Communitarian Mormons built towns, cleared fields, developed irrigation systems, and made the desert bloom. Continuing enmity with Gentiles resulted in the Utah Mormon War of 1857–58, a virtually bloodless conflict during which the U.S. Army reestablished federal authority in Utah Territory.

The infamous Mountain Meadows Massacre also occurred in 1857. Possibly with Young's approval, Mormon militiamen and a few Natives murdered more than 120 men, women, and children from an Arkansas wagon train with alleged connections to Joseph Smith's killers. The sensational murders spurred changes in Utah's territorial government. After church leaders repudiated polygamy, Utah achieved statehood in 1896.

Choctaw perish on march German artist Karl Bodmer painted Choctaw Indians along the Mississippi River, which ran through their original homelands. In the early 1830s, the Choctaw were relocated to Indian Territory. More than half of the 20,000-plus Choctaw Indians who walked to Oklahoma died on the journey, many of starvation. In 1847, after hearing of the Irish potato famine, a group of Choctaw collected $710 and sent it to help the starving Irish. The Choctaw were known as one of the Five Civilized Tribes because they adopted an American-style government and public school system.

March 18, 1831: The U.S. Supreme Court refuses to grant the Cherokee Nation an injunction preventing the state of Georgia from passing laws hostile to the Cherokee. The court claims a lack of jurisdiction over such "domestic dependent nations." However, the ruling leaves the door open to subsequent decisions more favorable to the Cherokee. *See* March 3, 1862.

April 1831: Pierre Chouteau, Jr.'s steamboat, *Yellowstone,* makes its maiden voyage up the Missouri River.

Summer 1831: Smallpox breaks out among the Shawnee Indian tribe of the Ohio River Valley.

1831-33: The Choctaw of Tennessee reluctantly relocate to present-day Oklahoma with the assistance of Army escorts.

1832: Famed Shawnee Indian Tenskwatawa poses for portrait artist and Indian chronicler George Catlin.

1832: George Catlin, who travels some 2,000 miles up the Missouri River with American Fur Company trappers, paints Indian portraits and pictures of Indian life.

February 8, 1832: The War Department orders that Cantonment Leavenworth (in present-day Kansas) be renamed Fort Leavenworth.

March 3, 1832: The Supreme Court's landmark decision in *Worcester v. State of Georgia* determines that jurisdiction over Indian territories belongs to the federal government.

March 24, 1832: Foreshadowing years of anti-Mormon persecution, Joseph Smith and Sidney Rigdon are tarred and feathered in Hiram, Ohio. Both survive.

June 6, 1832: While Sauk chief Black Hawk tries to lead his band back to Illinois, panicky militia shoot his emissary. This begins the Black Hawk War.

Cherokee v. Georgia In 1828 Georgia enacted laws calculated to seize Cherokee tribal lands and force Indians to leave them. After appealing in vain to the U.S. Congress and President Andrew Jackson, a Cherokee delegation led by Chief John Ross took the dispute to the U.S. Supreme Court. In the 1831 case *Cherokee Nation v. State of Georgia,* the court stated that the Cherokee Nation was neither a state nor a foreign entity, but rather a "domestic dependent nation." In the 1832 case *Worcester v. State of Georgia,* the Supreme Court ruled that Georgia had no authority over the Cherokee Nation. The state of Georgia, with President Jackson's approval, ignored this ruling.

THE CASE

OF

THE CHEROKEE NATION

against

THE STATE OF GEORGIA:

ARGUED AND DETERMINED AT

THE SUPREME COURT OF THE UNITED STATES,

JANUARY TERM 1831.

WITH

AN APPENDIX,

Containing the Opinion of Chancellor Kent on the Case; the Treaties between the United States and the Cherokee Indians; the Act of Congress of 1802, entitled 'An Act to regulate intercourse with the Indian tribes, &c.'; and the Laws of Georgia relative to the country occupied by the Cherokee Indians, within the boundary of that State.

America's bird man In the 1820s, John James Audubon sailed down the Mississippi on a quest to record America's birds. When Audubon found a bird he wanted to paint, he shot it, wired it into a position that would show important details, and painted it in a natural habitat—as seen in this image of the great blue heron. Unable to find an American publisher for his work, Audubon traveled to London in 1826, where he gained admiration and success. His images and descriptions in *Birds of America* and other publications intensified American interest in the western wilderness.

The bowie knife James Bowie was a frontier adventurer who smuggled slaves, gambled, and drank. Wounded in an altercation, he began carrying a large hunting knife given to him by his brother, Rezin. The blade was more than nine inches long with a cutting edge on both sides and a crosspiece between blade and handle. During a melee near Natchez, Mississippi, Bowie, despite terrible wounds, used his knife to kill Major Norris Wright. Bowie moved to Texas, engaged in an epic battle with Indians, and was slain at the Battle of the Alamo. For years afterward, versions of the bowie knife were made for frontiersmen for close-quarter fighting.

Fort Leavenworth In Kansas, Fort Leavenworth stands today as the oldest active Army post west of the Mississippi River. In 1827 Colonel Henry Leavenworth established an encampment on the west bank of the Missouri River near the mouth of the Little Platte River. The location proved unhealthy for the garrison, and in the late 1830s Fort Leavenworth was moved 12 miles to the south. The new site proved to be a portal into the western frontier. One of the most notable expeditions launched from Fort Leavenworth was Colonel Stephen Kearny's Santa Fe column during the Mexican-American War.

The Natives of California Hundreds of years ago, many different Native American groups lived in California's forests, mountains, valleys, deserts, and coastal areas as well as on offshore islands. Independent villages were home to hundreds of people. Most tribes enjoyed plentiful food supplies and animal furs, and practiced such crafts as basket making. Families like the one pictured here either produced what they needed or traded with others. But soon after the Spanish arrived, new diseases began to devastate Indian tribes. Spanish missions, grazing grants, and later Mexican land grants all disrupted traditional Indian lifestyles—even before the Gold Rush drew prospectors and settlers to California.

The Black Hawk War Many Sauk and Fox Indians, including Chief Black Hawk (*pictured*), were outraged by early-1800s treaties that ceded their lands to the U.S. government. In 1830 Black Hawk's village was occupied by white settlers, but two years later Black Hawk and about 1,000 followers attempted to take back their Illinois homeland. Federal troops pursued the Indians, killed many of them, and captured Black Hawk and his followers. The end of the Black Hawk War concluded a major conflict between settlers and Indians in Illinois, Iowa, and Wisconsin, and opened the Upper Mississippi Valley to settlement.

July 9, 1832: An act of Congress creates the office of Commissioner of Indian Affairs.

Fall 1832: President Andrew Jackson, a strong supporter of the Indian relocation program, is reelected.

October 1, 1832: Texas colonists gather at the Convention of 1832 to seek reforms from Mexico.

1833: Inventor Samuel Colt unveils his revolver.

1833: Following in the footsteps of George Catlin, Prince Maximilian of Germany and Swiss painter Karl Bodmer travel the Missouri River, observing Indian life.

June 30, 1833: Indian Country is the official name give to the territories to the west of Missouri.

July 1833: Mobs converge on the Mormon colony near Independence, Missouri. • Zion's Camp is disbanded, having been laid low by a cholera outbreak. Joseph Smith leaves Missouri to return to Kirtland, Ohio.

October 31, 1833: A mob attacks and burns a Mormon colony in Jackson County, Missouri.

1834: The Bureau of Indian Affairs reorganizes as the Department of Indian Affairs. It assumes responsibility for the new Indian Territory.

1834: Fort Laramie is established on Wyoming's North Platte River. It becomes the first permanent trading post in the area.

1834: Bent's Fort, also known as Fort William, is established as a trading post on the upper Arkansas River. This will spur the development of the Bent's Fort branch of the Santa Fe Trail.

Spring 1834: The houses of roughly 200 Mormon families in Jackson County, Missouri, are burned.

Osceola's defiance According to legend, Seminole leader Osceola defiantly thrust a dagger into the 1832 Treaty of Payne's Landing, which ceded the Indians' Florida lands to the United States. Beginning in 1835, Osceola led a guerrilla war against U.S. efforts to relocate the Seminole. Fighting from the Everglades, Osceola's small army was highly successful against vastly superior U.S. forces. In 1837 General Thomas Sidney Jesup used deceit to capture Osceola, whose 1838 death in captivity from malaria led to a weakening of Seminole resistance.

The Crow and their horses The Crow were a nomadic Plains Indian tribe who lived in the Yellowstone River area. In their matriarchal society, women could hold high positions, and family relationships were recorded through the female line. The Crow first encountered horses in the 1730s, and they soon acquired large herds. As seen here, horses allowed Crow hunters to ride alongside buffalo and bring them down easily. Crow men, women, and children all rode, and they used packhorses to carry their belongings.

Walker forges new paths

Joseph Reddeford Walker was one of five brothers who found the lure of the frontier irresistible (brother John died at the Alamo). A man of impressive physique and commanding presence, Joe Walker led trapping parties into the Rocky Mountains and successfully battled hostile warriors. He led probably the first party into Yosemite (1833), opened Walker's Pass in the southern Sierra Nevada Mountains (1834), and guided the first wagon train overland from Salt Lake to California (1843). Walker served explorer John Frémont as scout during two expeditions, and pursued other western adventures until he was nearly 70.

McCormick's reaper

Cyrus Hall McCormick's wheat-reaping machine, patented in 1834, spurred a revolution in agriculture. The horse-drawn machine could do the work of a dozen or so men, and after McCormick expanded his reaper for two horses, then for four, the labor-saving results were astounding. McCormick established his plant in Chicago and became a millionaire by age 40. Wheat production across the land skyrocketed from 30 million bushels in 1850 to 100 million in 1860. Sales of reapers for the 1862 harvest season totaled $33,000, increased to $40,000 the next year, and rose to $85,000 one year later.

The importance of Bent's Fort

In 1833 brothers William and Charles Bent and their business partner, Ceran St. Vrain, built an adobe trading post, Bent's Old Fort (*pictured*), on the Arkansas River in present-day Colorado. The fort became the most important white settlement along the Santa Fe Trail, serving explorers, traders, mountain men, Indians, Mexicans, and U.S. soldiers. In 1846, during the Mexican-American War, Colonel Stephen Kearny's Army of the West stopped there on its way to conquer New Mexico. In 1849 Bent blew up the fort after he failed to sell it to the U.S. government.

The formidable Creeks

Pictured is Me-Na-Wa, a Creek warrior. The Creek confederacy of nearly 50 towns was located in present-day Alabama and Georgia. During the 1700s, the Creeks were prosperous farmers, and they fielded a large force of warriors. During the War of 1812, a Creek band called Red Sticks went on the warpath against American frontiersmen but was defeated by General Andrew Jackson at the Battle of Horseshoe Bend. The Creeks suffered great loss of life during the winter of 1834–35 when they were forced to move west to Indian Territory, where they became one of the Five Civilized Tribes.

Varieties of tomahawks

For close combat, Native American warriors used tomahawks and war clubs. The heads of these weapons were fashioned from stone, while the wooden handles were covered with buckskin. White traders introduced metal heads for tomahawks, which held a sharp edge better than stone hatchets. Metal tomahawks were greatly prized, and sometimes their handles were wrapped with cloth instead of buckskin. Well-balanced tomahawks could be thrown, and mountain men often added these hatchets to their arsenals.

1830-1848

May 5, 1834: Mormon leader Joseph Smith leads "Zion's Camp" (200 armed men) from Kirtland, Ohio, toward Independence, Missouri.

1835: In response to Mexican President Antonio López de Santa Anna's efforts to centralize authority and reduce the freedom of action of the states, American settlers in Texas proclaim independence with their "Declaration of the People of Texas."

April 22, 1835: The Florida Seminole Indians, led by Chief Osceola, refuse to recognize the relocation treaty they agreed to in 1832.

October 2, 1835: The Texas War of Independence begins when Mexican troops attempt to repossess a cannon from U.S. settlers in Texas, sparking a skirmish near the town of Gonzales.

October 28, 1835: A Tejano force soundly defeats the Mexican troops who were sent by Santa Anna to quell the Texas rebellion.

December 10, 1835: Santa Anna loses San Antonio to the Texas insurgents.

December 29, 1835: Some Cherokee Indians agree to the Treaty of New Echota, ceding their ancestral territory in the East for land in what is now Oklahoma. Other Cherokees object. *See* May 23, 1836.

Late 1835: Chief Osceola leads the Florida Seminole Indians in the War of Resistance against forced removal to the West.

1836: War Secretary Lewis Cass unveils a plan for a military road from Minnesota to the Texas border. This will unite the forts of Indian Territory.

1836: Dr. Marcus Whitman and his wife, Narcissa—along with Reverend H. H. Spalding and his wife, Eliza—respond to the Nez Percé request for teachers by establishing a mission at the junction of the Columbia and Snake rivers.

Bonneville's adventures In 1832 American author Washington Irving traveled to the American frontier, a trip that inspired three books, including *The Adventures of Captain Bonneville* (1837). This book was based on a colorful and adventurous frontiersman named Benjamin Louis Eulalie de Bonneville (*pictured*). In May 1832, Bonneville ventured from the East to the West Coast. No one heard from him for three years, but he returned with a journal that detailed his adventures on the frontier. Bonneville sold his journal to Irving for $1,000. The book is often cited as the most literate description of the fur-trapping era.

Ridges sign fateful treaty As tensions between whites and Indians mounted, Cherokee leader John Ridge (*pictured*) and his father, Major Ridge, became convinced that the Indians' survival depended on cooperating with the U.S. government. The Ridges were among the signers (later known as the Ridge Party) of the 1835 Treaty of New Echota, which exchanged Cherokee lands for territory west of the Mississippi. An illegitimate document that was not supported by most Cherokees, the treaty nevertheless doomed them to a forced western migration. In retaliation for their role in the treaty, Major and John Ridge were assassinated by Cherokee Indians in 1839.

The Second Seminole War The warriors of Seminole leader Osceola attack Fort King, Florida, in 1835—an episode that triggered the second of three Seminole wars. During the First Seminole War of 1817–18, General Andrew Jackson had invaded Florida, primarily to drive out escaped black slaves living among the Indians. An estimated 1,500 U.S. soldiers died in the Second Seminole War of 1835–42, which forced most of the Seminoles to leave Florida and settle west of the Mississippi. By the end of the Third Seminole War of 1855–58, as few as 200 Seminoles still lived in Florida.

JOHN RIDGE.
A CHEROKEE.

Removing the Eastern Indians

IN THE 19TH CENTURY, American politicians wrestled with "the Indian question." Should Natives be exterminated to guarantee whites' safety? Could "untutored children of the forest" be assimilated, or would they be ostracized by white society? One thing was certain: Generations of dwellers on the frontiers of "Indian Country" developed deep suspicions—even hatred—of Indians.

As early as 1636, the Massachusetts Bay Puritans attempted to exterminate the Pequots, and New England's Native resistance continued until King Philip's War of 1676. Indian-white wars in the "Old Northwest" accelerated U.S. Indian policy developments in the 1790s. Defeated Indian nations were forced to sign treaties ceding vast amounts of territory.

An Indian-removal policy emerged after Andrew Jackson's election in 1828. Jackson's inaugural address promised Indians a "just and humane policy." But in 1830 Congress passed a removal act requiring relocation of eastern Indians, by force if necessary, to "Indian Territory" west of the Mississippi River. The first targets were the Southeast's Five Civilized Tribes: Choctaw, Chickasaw, Creek, Seminole, and Cherokee. The Cherokee Indians challenged the new policy's legality.

Cherokees had adjusted to life within the United States while maintaining tribal traditions. They wrote a constitution resembling that of the U.S. A scholar named Sequoia invented a written language and published a bilingual newspaper, the *Cherokee Phoenix*. Cherokee military power had declined by 1820, but many mixed-blood Scots-Natives had gained tribal leadership positions and understood white men's ways. Wealthy planters, some owning slaves, dominated Cherokee politics, though "traditional" leaders remained influential. Cherokees possessed immense livestock herds. They dwelled in houses and built handsome towns. Cherokee society was obviously "civilized."

In the late 1820s, Georgia passed laws designed to destroy the Cherokee Nation. Tribal lands became counties, Cherokee government was declared illegal, and Cherokees were denied recourse to courts. But Cherokees had signed treaties with Great Britain and later the U.S., whose constitution forbade states to make Indian policy. Jackson faced a dilemma. Would he honor his presiden-

The Trail of Tears by Robert Lindneux

tial oath to uphold treaties, or would he support Georgia's laws?

In crucial Supreme Court cases, Chief Justice John Marshall deemed Georgia's laws unconstitutional, but declared that Indians were "wards" of the federal government, deserving protection as "domestic dependent nations." Jackson detested Justice Marshall and refused to enforce his decisions.

Vainly seeking justice, the Cherokees resisted removal as neighboring nations were forced westward. In 1835 a small faction of Cherokees signed the Treaty of New Echota, agreeing to sell its land and move west, but this was opposed by the majority of Cherokees. In 1838 Georgia and the U.S. Army forcibly removed the remaining Cherokees. One fourth of roughly 16,000 emigrants died from exhaustion and disease on the bitter 800-mile winter trek from Georgia to Oklahoma. The Cherokees' "Trail of Tears" was the most horrific of dozens of removals that continued to the 1860s.

After rebuilding their lives in Indian Territory, Indians encountered further destruction during the Civil War, when many sided with the Confederacy. In the aftermath of rich oil discoveries in Oklahoma around 1900, corrupt politicians and oil prospectors targeted Native Americans. Indians were kidnapped, murdered, and hoodwinked into selling land as greedy whites fleeced them of valuable resources. The Indian removals left an ugly blot on U.S. history, surpassed in their day only by the stain of slavery.

The Texas Revolution

SOON AFTER ASSUMING the Mexican presidency in 1833, Antonio López de Santa Anna attempted to form a more centralized federal government—throwing out Mexico's 1824 Constitution in the process. Mexican Federalists in Zacatecas revolted, but were easily crushed by Santa Anna's forces. The news of their slaughter traveled north, where the American settlers colonizing Texas had their own issues with Santa Anna.

In fact, these Anglo settlers outnumbered Mexicans in Texas, an imbalance that Santa Anna could not let stand, as he believed that the United States would use that leverage to foment rebellion and annex Texas. In response, he tried to enforce Mexico's antislavery laws in Texas for the first time, as well as collect customs duties. Predictably, the proslavery American settlers (most of whom came from southern states) revolted, beginning with the October 1835 Battle of Gonzales.

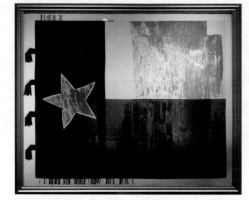

Texas's Lone Star Flag, adopted 1839

Meanwhile, elected representatives from many Texas settlements attended a "consultation" held at San Felipe to determine the future course of the revolt. On November 13, delegates organized a temporary government, headed by the General Council and Provisional Governor Henry Smith. They also established an army under the command of Sam Houston.

Enraged by this turn of events, Santa Anna led 6,000 troops into Texas in January 1836 to put down the rebellion. In February and March, the invaders vanquished the Texas garrison at the Alamo, a mission fortress at San Antonio, and forced Colonel James Fannin's command to surrender at the Battle of Coleto. On March 27, Mexican troops brutally executed nearly 350 Texan prisoners of war near Goliad.

Panic swept Texas settlements in the wake of these events, and thousands of refugees fled to the United States. By this time, however, the insurgents had signed a Declaration of Independence and formed the Republic of Texas, electing David Burnet as president.

With his retreating army clamoring for a fight, Sam Houston finally engaged Mexican forces at the Battle of San Jacinto on April 21, 1836. Houston's stunning 18-minute victory over Santa Anna ended the Texas Revolution and helped secure international recognition for the new republic. However, due to concerns over the balance of slave and nonslaveholding states, Texas would not become a state until 1845.

The hated dictator General Antonio López de Santa Anna was the self-proclaimed "Napoléon of the West." A political chameleon, Santa Anna unscrupulously changed sides throughout his long career. He became president of Mexico 11 times, on each occasion assuming dictatorial powers, and eventually was overthrown. When he first seized power, during the mid-1830s, the despotic Santa

Anna was deeply resented by Anglo settlers in Texas. He foolishly incarcerated Stephen Austin, who had used his great influence to restrain Texas hotheads. In 1835 Austin returned to Texas to fight for independence from Mexico. Revolution erupted immediately, and Santa Anna marched north—toward the Alamo and San Jacinto.

The Alamo When General Santa Anna led a large army into San Antonio in 1836, defiant Anglos and Tejanos forted up inside the walls of the Alamo, an old mission just outside of town. Former Tennessee Congressman Davy Crockett and legendary knife fighter James Bowie were the best-known men among nearly 200 defenders, but William Travis ably commanded the garrison. During a 13-day siege, Mexican artillery pounded away at the walls, and before dawn on March 6, Santa Anna commenced a frontal assault. Faced with overwhelming numbers, all (or nearly all) of the defenders were slain. But the Mexican army suffered heavy casualties. Santa Anna's men needed to regroup for more than two weeks in San Antonio before resuming their campaign in Texas.

"Freemen of Texas" In the fall of 1835, relations were tense between the Anglo settlers of Mexican Texas and the dictatorial Mexican government of Santa Anna. When a company of Mexican soldiers marched from San Antonio to Gonzales to seize a cannon that settlers had used against Indian raiders, Anglo rebels gathered to offer resistance. Following a skirmish on October 2, the Mexicans retreated and the rebels issued a call to arms, as this publication indicates. Texans volunteered in large numbers, while Santa Anna organized an army to stamp out the revolution.

Crockett fights for Texas A legendary bear hunter on the Tennessee frontier, Davy Crockett parlayed his notoriety into a congressional career, sometimes wearing buckskins and a coonskin cap in the U.S. Capitol halls. After rejection by the voters, Crockett announced that they could go to hell. He was going to Texas. Crockett journeyed to San Antonio hoping to acquire land grants, but soon found himself fighting as "a high private" against the Mexican army. During the Battle of the Alamo, he either went down while swinging his rifle butt (as pictured here) or, as later evidence indicated, surrendered and was executed.

December 8, 1836: General Thomas S. Jesup takes command of the Seminole War, ordering 8,000 troops to march against 1,500 Indians in Florida.

1837: Some 75 percent of all Plains Indians have died, largely as a result of the presence of whites, who carry smallpox and other European diseases.

1837: Following a congressional refusal to annex slaveholding Texas, President Andrew Jackson recognizes the Republic of Texas on his last day in office.

January 1837: Released by Sam Houston, Santa Anna returns to Mexico. He is denounced for agreeing to recognize Texas's independence. Mexicans and Texans will continue to engage in border skirmishes for the next decade.

January 26, 1837: Michigan is admitted to the Union.

March 6, 1837: Although General Jesup reaches an accord with some Seminole chiefs, he continues to wage war against the great Chief Osceola.

Summer 1837: A smallpox epidemic sweeps the High Plains. The Mandan are nearly wiped out, and the Arikara and Hidatsa suffer enormously.

July 1837: A thousand western Indians are pressed into service for General Jesup against the Seminole Indians. • In New Mexico, Pueblo Indians upset over the existing tax structure revolt, driving out Governor Albino Pérez.

October 21, 1837: General Jesup captures Chief Osceola under a flag of truce.

November 7, 1837: Abolitionist newspaper editor Elijah Lovejoy is murdered while defending his press from a proslavery mob in Alton, Illinois.

The hero of Texas At 6'3" and 240 pounds, Sam Houston was a larger-than-life force in Texas during the revolution and early statehood. Before arriving in Texas, he was a wounded hero at the Battle of Horseshoe Bend, governor of Tennessee, and a major general of militia. After defeating the Mexican army at San Jacinto, Houston became president of the Texas Republic, one of two charter senators of the state of Texas, and Texas governor. It was Houston who magnanimously named Stephen Austin the "Father of Texas"—a title he could have claimed for himself.

Travis writes for help at the Alamo WilliamTravis, a young lawyer from Alabama, journeyed to Texas in 1831 under a cloud of scandal. During the political tensions of the next few years, Travis was twice jailed by Mexican authorities, and he became a leading agitator for Texas independence. Upon the outbreak of the war, Travis obtained a commission as a lieutenant colonel of cavalry, and he was in San Antonio when the Mexican army approached. With James Bowie bedridden, Travis took command of a small garrison in the Alamo, where he staged a stubborn defense and penned appeals for help. During the final assault, he died at his post on the north wall.

TRAVIS'S DESPERATE PLEA

Fellow-Citizens and Compatriots: I am besieged by a thousand or more of the Mexicans under Santa Anna. I have sustained a continued bombardment for twenty-four hours, and have not lost a man. The enemy have demanded a surrender at discretion; otherwise the garrison is to be put to the sword, if the place is taken. I have answered the summons with cannon shot, and our flag still waves proudly from the walls. I shall never surrender nor retreat! Then I call on you, in the name of liberty, of patriotism, and of everything dear to American character, to come to our aid with all dispatch. The enemy are receiving re-inforcements daily, and will no doubt increase to three or four thousand in four or five days. Though this call may be neglected, I am determined to sustain myself as long as possible, and die like a soldier who never forgets what is due to his own honor or that of his country. Victory or death!

—WILLIAM TRAVIS, TEXAS COMMANDER AT THE BATTLE OF THE ALAMO, IN A LETTER ADDRESSED TO "THE PEOPLE OF TEXAS AND ALL AMERICANS IN THE WORLD," FEBRUARY 24, 1836

The Goliad Massacre At the Battle of San Jacinto, the Texan soldiers of General Sam Houston (*left*) tore into the Mexican army with the vengeful shout, "Remember the Alamo! Remember Goliad!" Several weeks earlier, fewer than 200 Texans had died courageously defending the Alamo. Another mission-fortress at Goliad housed more than 400 Texans under the command of Colonel James Fannin. Trying to retreat, Fannin allowed himself to become surrounded, then surrendered his force unconditionally. General Santa Anna ordered the execution of Fannin and 341 of his men, all of whom were killed on March 27, 1836. Little wonder that Texans wanted revenge from Santa Anna (*center*) and his brother-in-law, General Cos (*right*).

The Texas border dispute The boundary line enclosing the word "TEXAS" indicates the generally accepted perimeter of Texas prior to the 1836 Battle of San Jacinto. But Santa Anna, the captured general and president of Mexico, feared for his life. On May 14, 1836, he signed the Treaties of Velasco, which recognized Texas independence and designated the Rio Grande (the line separating the pink and yellow areas) as the border. Although the Mexican government refuted Santa Anna's treaty, the Republic of Texas happily claimed a vast area (yellow) that extended into modern Wyoming. A decade later, Mexicans were further angered when Texas was admitted to the Union. President Polk sent General Zachary Taylor to the north bank of the disputed Rio Grande. Taylor's army was attacked, provoking a declaration of war against Mexico.

"As battles go, San Jacinto was but a skirmish; but with what mighty consequences! The lives and the liberty of a few hundred pioneers at stake and an empire won!"

—KATE SCURRY TERRELL, A 19TH CENTURY JOURNALIST

Revenge at San Jacinto On the afternoon of April 21, 1836, the Mexican army of General Santa Anna relaxed at its camp near the San Jacinto River, close to present-day Houston. But the nearby Texan army, despite weeks of retreat and even though considerably outnumbered, launched an unexpected assault led by General Sam Houston. The 900 Texans, advancing in a single rank 1,000 yards wide, fired a deadly rifle volley as the Mexican officers tried to form their men. Vengefully shouting "Remember the Alamo," the Texans barreled into the confused encampment. Within 18 minutes, the Mexican army was routed. More than 600 Mexicans died in the slaughter and another 730 were captured—including Santa Anna.

December 25, 1837: Zachary Taylor's brigade retreats after routing Seminole warriors in the Battle of Okeechobee.

1838: The Cherokee Indians march from Georgia to Oklahoma along the "Trail of Tears" under the oversight of General Winfield Scott.

1838: Johnny Appleseed, whose real name is John Chapman, moves his horticultural mission from Ohio to northern Indiana.

January 12, 1838: With the Mormon colony in Kirtland, Ohio, failing, leader Joseph Smith flees to the new Mormon center in Missouri.

January 26, 1838: While the war in Florida still rages, indomitable Seminole Chief Osceola dies in the Army's Fort Moultrie prison.

October 1838: Gallatin, Missouri, is plundered by a secret Mormon militia known as the Danites, led by Apostle David Patten.

October 27, 1838: Lilburn Boggs, governor of Missouri, orders that Mormons be "exterminated or driven from the state."

October 30, 1838: The massacre at Haun's Mill in Missouri, perpetrated by Missouri militiamen, leaves 17 Mormons dead.

October 31, 1838: Joseph Smith surrenders to Missouri officials and only narrowly escapes execution. He and his followers agree to disarm and leave the state empty-handed.

November 30, 1838: Joseph Smith and other Mormon leaders are jailed in Liberty, Missouri.

February 1839: The last of the Mormons to be driven from Missouri depart for Illinois, leaving their community abandoned.

Detroit grows up Founded by the French in 1701, Detroit remained essentially a fur-trading center for more than a hundred years. It passed from British to U.S. hands in 1796, then became the capital of the Michigan Territory in 1805. Detroit's transition from trading to manufacturing was hastened by a steamboat connection to the Great Lakes in 1818. By 1836, the date of this picture, Detroit was a thriving port where agricultural goods were brought, processed, and shipped. The city became especially important as a flour-producing center.

Farmers, loggers head to Michigan With the completion of the Erie Canal in 1825, it became easy for settlers to migrate to the Michigan Territory. Consequently, families and businesses took advantage of the region's rich farmlands and vast forests of white pine. From 1830 to its achievement of statehood in 1837, Michigan's population increased from 31,639 to 174,543. America's growing construction needs turned lumber into the state's greatest industry. Clear-cutting soon replaced selective cutting, and logging crews replaced lone lumberjacks.

Arkansas emerges In 1803, when present-day Arkansas was part of the Louisiana Purchase, the area was home to only a few hundred white people. Settlement there increased when it became an official territory in 1819. By 1836 the Arkansas Territory boasted 60,000 residents, enough for it to achieve statehood that year. The removal of Indians from 1832 through 1839 opened the state to more settlers, most of whom became farmers. By the beginning of the Civil War, Arkansas's population exceeded 435,000, about 25 percent of whom were black slaves.

Schoolcraft's many gifts Born in 1793, Henry Rowe Schoolcraft became deeply accomplished in the fields of geology, geography, topography, and ethnology. His explorations took him to the Lake Superior region, where he discovered the source of the Mississippi River. Serving the territory as a federal Indian agent and in other posts, he made peace among warring tribes, inoculated Indians against smallpox, and negotiated treaties that added vast lands to the U.S. His marriage to a half-Ojibwa woman added to his knowledge of Native American culture.

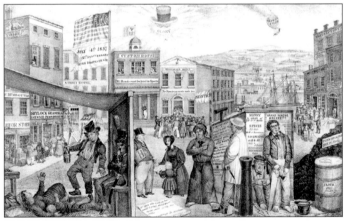

The Panic of 1837 This political cartoon shows the chaos caused by the Panic of 1837, including a run on the bank, shoeless workmen, and begging mothers. The financial crisis could be blamed on rampant speculation in western states and President Andrew Jackson's banking policies. Investors frantically bought western land from the federal government, anticipating that canals and railroads would increase the land's value. When the financial bubble burst, Jackson's chosen successor, President Martin Van Buren, took no effective action, and the entire nation was plunged into an economic depression that lasted until 1843. Thousands of land speculators were ruined.

The hospitable Mandan The Mandan lived along the Missouri River in present-day North and South Dakota, practicing agriculture and living in villages like the one shown here. After their first contact with Europeans in 1738, they formed an important link between French traders and neighboring Plains Indians. The Lewis and Clark Corps of Discovery stayed among the Mandan during the winter of 1805–06, and benefited from their hospitality. After they were almost wiped out by smallpox in 1837 and 1838, the Mandan were forced to band together with other tribes.

March 1839: The final contingent of Cherokee refugees arrives in Indian Country. In total, the forced removal of the Eastern Cherokee has cost 4,000 lives out of a total population of 15,000.

April 1839: Joseph Smith and his followers escape prison in Missouri and flee to Illinois.

1840: The era of the mountain trapper comes to an end with the final annual rendezvous on the Green River in present-day Wyoming.

1840: Aligning itself with Mexican antigovernment rebels, Texas sends a small flotilla to the Mexican coast.

1840: Thomas Cole, founder of the Hudson River School style of painting, creates his masterpiece, *The Voyage of Life*. With its focus on majestic American landscapes, the Hudson River School popularizes the concept of Manifest Destiny.

November 3, 1840: William Henry Harrison is elected as the ninth president of the United States.

1841: Russia's tenure in California ends when European immigrant Johann Sutter buys Fort Ross, north of San Francisco. Sutter dismantles Fort Ross and transports sections of it to his Fort Sutter at the junction of the Sacramento and American rivers.

April 4, 1841: President Harrison dies of pneumonia at age 68. Vice President John Tyler becomes president.

May 1, 1841: The Western Emigration Society takes its first wagon train (led by John Bidwell) across the Rockies. The Bidwell-Bartleson party leaves Independence, Missouri, bound for California.

November 4, 1841: The wagon train that originated in Independence, Missouri, becomes the first to make it all the way to California.

Potawatomi evicted from Midwest The Potawatomi belonged to Tecumseh's Native American Confederacy and took part in Tecumseh's War in 1811. In the early 1800s, the U.S. government annexed much of the Potawatomi land. Here, Indians, government officials, Army troops, and onlookers gather at Fort Dearborn in 1833 to witness the Treaty of Chicago, in which the Potawatomi exchanged their Illinois, Wisconsin, and Michigan lands for territory in southwestern Iowa. That year, the town of Chicago was incorporated on the Fort Dearborn site. In the late 1830s and the 1840s, the Potawatomi people were forcibly moved farther west to Kansas.

A SOMBER FAREWELL

THEY FELT THAT they were bidding farewell to the hills, valleys and streams of their infancy; the more exciting hunting grounds of their advanced youth; as well as the stern and bloody battle fields, where they had contended in riper manhood, on which they had received wounds, and where many of their friends and loved relatives had fallen, covered with gore and with glory. All these they were leaving behind them to be desecrated by the plowshare of the white man. As they cast mournful glances back toward these loved scenes that were rapidly fading in the distance, tears fell from the cheek of the downcast warrior, old men trembled, matrons wept, the swarthy maiden's cheek turned pale, and sighs and half-suppressed sobs escaped from the motley groups as they passed along, some on foot, some on horseback, and others in wagons—sad as a funeral procession.

—SANFORD C. COX, A SETTLER, COMMENTING ON THE
REMOVAL OF THE POTAWATOMI INDIANS OF INDIANA, 1838

A Glimpse of California

MORE THAN A DECADE before the California Gold Rush of 1849, a young Harvard law student with a literary flair penned the first important American account of life in that far-flung territory. Born in Cambridge, Massachusetts, in 1815, Richard Henry Dana went to sea in 1834 to regain his health after a bout with measles. He joined the crew of a vessel headed for the Pacific Coast to exchange a cargo of manufactured goods for cattle hides (popularly known as "California bank notes").

Richard Henry Dana

After a grueling five-month-long voyage around Cape Horn (the southern tip of South America), Dana's ship reached California. For more than a year, it called at ports from San Diego to San Francisco. Dana spent his liberty ashore visiting towns and missions. He mingled with the local population, observed their customs, partook in fandangos, and recorded his observations and impressions in a journal.

After returning home in 1836, Dana expanded his diary into a book-length narrative that he hoped would expose the dismal working conditions and other injustices endured by merchant seamen. Published in 1840, *Two Years Before the Mast* enjoyed widespread critical acclaim and sales that exceeded 100,000 copies.

The book not only led to reforms in maritime law but also was devoured by readers hungry to learn more about the intriguing lands that lay west of the Mississippi River. Often romantic in tone, Dana's travelogue portrayed Mexican California as an exotic garden blessed with abundant natural resources but cursed with an ignorant, indolent population and a capricious government.

The author also took note of a growing class of American and British merchants who had married Mexican women and had risen to positions of prominence in California society. "In the hands of an enterprising people," he mused, "what a country this might be!" Although some subsequent writers took issue with Dana's harsh characterization of the "Californios," his influential prose quickened the pulse of a nation just beginning to embrace the doctrine of Manifest Destiny.

Wilkes surveys the Pacific coast Lieutenant Charles Wilkes was given command of the United States Exploring Expedition in 1838. Over the next four years, the expedition circumnavigated the world, traveling about 87,000 miles and exploring regions as remote as the Antarctic continent. Along the way, Wilkes carefully surveyed the west coast of North America, charting San Francisco Bay, the Columbia River, and Puget Sound. Wilkes wrote about this phase of his journey in *Western America, including California and Oregon,* which was published in 1849. The timely book featured a detailed map of Sacramento Valley, where gold recently had been discovered.

Redwoods soar to the heavens Two members of Charles Wilkes's United States Exploring Expedition measure a California redwood in 1841. For centuries, Native Americans had been familiar with these trees, which are the most massive organisms on earth. In 1769 Spanish priest Juan Crespi became the first European to record seeing them; he called them *palo colorado*—"red wood." There are actually two species of giant redwoods in America: the giant sequoia, which grows in the Sierra Nevadas in eastern California, and the coast redwood, which grows from southern Oregon to central California. Redwoods of both species can grow more than 300 feet tall.

1830-1848

1842: Kit Carson guides John Frémont's scientific and mapping expedition into the Rocky Mountains. Frémont's maps and journals from the expedition will be published by Congress upon his return.

1842: With the discovery of gold dust in the roots of a freshly dug onion, Francisco Lopez sets off a local gold rush to Southern California's San Feliciano Canyon.

1842: The Military Road through Indian Territory from Missouri to Texas is completed.

May 16, 1842: The first organized wagon train along the Oregon Trail leaves Elm Grove, Missouri, en route to the Oregon Territory.

May 30, 1842: Fort Scott is established along the Military Road through Indian Territory.

August 9, 1842: The Webster-Ashburton Treaty is signed, ending the U.S.-British disputes over the boundaries of Maine, Nova Scotia, and Quebec.

August 14, 1842: The Second Seminole War ends without the benefit of a peace treaty.

September 18, 1842: Mexican troops attack San Antonio in what will come to be known as "Dawson's Massacre."

October 19, 1842: Incorrectly believing that the U.S. is at war with Mexico, Commodore Thomas ap Catesby Jones, commander of the U.S. Pacific fleet, sails to Monterey, California, and proclaims California's annexation by the United States. Two days later, Jones will realize his mistake and return Monterey to Mexico's control.

1843: Dr. Marcus Whitman leads the Great Migration, an exodus of about 1,000 pioneers, along the Oregon Trail. The mass migration to Oregon will become an annual event.

Scott oversees Cherokee removal In May 1838, General Winfield Scott was assigned the grim task of rounding up Cherokee Indians and marching them to the region west of the Mississippi. After many Indians set out on the Trail of Tears, Scott heeded a petition to delay further marches. He then made the controversial decision to allow Chief John Ross to oversee the removal of the remaining Cherokees. Scott, who had served heroically in the War of 1812, would later lead U.S. forces to victory in the Mexican-American War in 1846–48.

Haun's Mill Massacre During the 1830s, Joseph Smith centered his Morman activities in Missouri. Missourians, however, strongly disliked the Mormons' religious beliefs and Smith's prophecies that his people would inherit the Earth. Anti-Mormon mobs formed in Missouri during the summer of 1838, and violence began in the fall. Smith appealed to Governor Lilburn Boggs for protection. Boggs's response: "The Mormons must be treated as enemies, and must be exterminated or driven from the State...." At Haun's Mill (*pictured*) on October 30, 17 Mormons were killed and 15 were wounded, including several children. Pragmatically, Smith led his people to Illinois.

The First Railroads

O N JULY 4, 1828, MORE THAN 50,000 people turned out in Baltimore to watch Charles Carroll lay the cornerstone for the Baltimore and Ohio Railroad. Nearly two years later, in May 1830, a horse-drawn railcar made its way down the B&O's 13 miles of track. In December of that same year, the first steam-powered locomotive sped along the world's longest railroad—a 136-mile stretch from Charleston to Hamburg, South Carolina. Soon, railway lines opened in Pennsylvania, New York, and Massachusetts. America had embraced the most modern form of transportation and embarked on a course that, in subsequent decades, would radically transform the nation.

For most Americans, the railways of the 1830s were more of a novelty than a practical way to transport goods and people. It was still much cheaper to use canals or roads than to pay the relatively steep rates that the railroads charged. Also, some people were hostile toward the new technology, distrusting the safety of locomotives and the changes they would bring to American society.

Nevertheless, nationalist political leaders, such as Henry Clay and former president John Quincy Adams, encouraged rail development. They maintained that railroads would bind the nation together, bring internal unity, and curb the rising tensions between the North and the South. Though top government officials supported rail construction, most development was privately

B&O Railroad, 1830

financed by forward-thinking entrepreneurs who recognized that railroads were the future of transportation in the United States.

Most of the early railroads were concentrated along the eastern seaboard, where the nation's great centers of trade and commerce were located. Gradually, however, lines were extended into the interior and beyond the Appalachian Mountains. Just 10 years after the B&O began service, all but four states had laid a combined 3,000 miles of track. By midcentury, that figure tripled to nearly 9,000 miles, making railroads the dominant form of transportation in the United States.

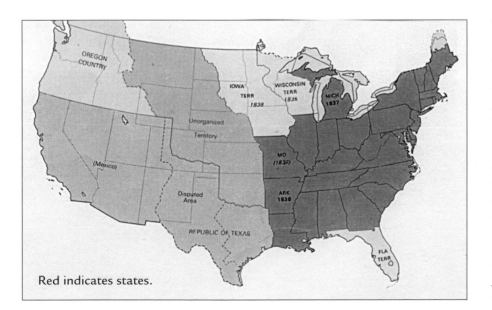

Red indicates states.

The West in 1840 This 1840 map of the West gives little indication that American pioneers were on the verge of a sweeping westward movement. At the time, the Republic of Texas, populated by American settlers, was seeking annexation by the United States. American traders were probing northern Mexico along the Santa Fe Trail. Oregon Country was jointly claimed by Great Britain and the U.S., but a steady stream of Americans was about to enter the territory via the Oregon Trail. American whalers and trading vessels were utilizing the excellent harbors of Mexican California. The 1844 election of an expansionist president, James K. Polk, would lead to the aggressive acquisition of these regions.

1843: Mexican President Santa Anna comes back to power and warns that Mexico will consider American annexation of Texas an act of war.

1843: Frontiersmen James Bridger and Louis Vasquez establish Fort Bridger as a supply post for travelers on the Oregon Trail.

1844: Abolitionists block Senate ratification of an annexation treaty between Texas and the United States.

May 24, 1844: Samuel Morse sends the first words via telegraph, from Washington, D.C., to Baltimore: "What hath God wrought?"

June 27, 1844: A mob storms the jail in Carthage, Illinois, and kills Joseph Smith and his brother, Hyrum, who were being held on charges of treason.

August 1844: Explorer and cartographer John Frémont returns to St. Louis at the end of a lengthy journey through the West.

August 8, 1844: Following the murder of Joseph Smith, Brigham Young takes over as head of The Church of Jesus Christ of Latter-day Saints.

November 5, 1844: James K. Polk is elected as the 11th U.S. president on a popular expansionist platform.

February 19–20, 1845: Troops led by Manuel Micheltorena, the unpopular Mexican governor of California, clash with Juan Bautista Alvarado's army of Californios at the Battle of Cahuenga.

March 1845: Mexico severs diplomatic relations with the United States after outgoing President Tyler signs a resolution to annex Texas. Texas will accept annexation on July 4.

March 3, 1845: The state of Florida is admitted to the Union.

Gateway to the West St. Louis was founded in 1764 by French fur traders and named for King Louis IX, who had been canonized as a saint. The exploratory expeditions of Lewis and Clark and Zebulon Pike set out from the St. Louis area. By the 1820s, trappers and traders left St. Louis in keelboats, returning with fortunes in furs. The "Gateway to the West" boasted a population of nearly 5,000 by 1830 and was the largest community in the new state of Missouri. As the principal port for Mississippi River steamboats north of New Orleans, St. Louis's population rose to 16,000 by 1840. It then grew tenfold over the next 20 years.

"Broken Hand" Fitzpatrick Born in Ireland in 1799, Thomas Fitzpatrick arrived in America in 1816 and went west to become a fur trapper. Known as "Broken Hand" Fitzpatrick after losing two fingers to an exploding gun, he eventually became a valued scout. In 1841 he led John Bidwell's party of California-bound emigrants and also guided missionary priest Pierre-Jean DeSmet to the Oregon Territory. In 1843 Fitzgerald joined John Frémont's Oregon expedition. During the 1846–48 Mexican-American War, he guided Colonel Stephen Kearny's army across the Southwest. As an Indian agent, he negotiated several important peace agreements, including the Fort Laramie Treaty of 1851.

The Telegraph

Samuel Morse

WELL KNOWN AS A portrait artist, Samuel Morse also was fascinated with the properties of electricity. Traveling from France to New York in 1832, he enjoyed shipboard conversations about European and American experiments with electricity and magnets. The notion of telegraphing messages was already in the air, and Morse started working out how it could be done. He also made notes for a dot-and-dash code system.

While still a professor of fine arts at New York University, Morse worked on his telegraph machine. In 1837 he gave up painting entirely, and in 1843 he was granted a patent for his invention. The following year he telegraphed the first message: "What hath God wrought?"

Workers soon erected telegraph lines, connecting major eastern cities. During the American Civil War, both sides put up thousands of miles of new lines—and also went to great lengths to destroy lines belonging to the opposition. At times, telegraph lines dangling from Union Signal Corps observation balloons relayed messages back to President Lincoln's War Department in Washington.

The Pacific Railroad Act of 1862 called for constructing a transcontinental railroad across America, and for building a telegraph line alongside the tracks. On May 10, 1869, the Union Pacific and Central Pacific tracks met at Promontory Summit, Utah. A telegraph line attached to the railroad's last spike (which was steel), and another attached to the hammer, sent the sound of the final blow west to San Francisco and east to New York City.

Throughout the West, stations were built so that settlers and travelers could send and receive telegraph messages. Women soon realized that they could learn the Morse code as well as men could. In fact, in an early venture into a technical profession, women operated some of the most remote telegraph stations on the western plains.

Drawing the black beans Texas prisoners draw beans from a pot, with life or death riding on the draw. Following a Mexican invasion of the Republic of Texas in September 1842, a retaliatory force marched to the Rio Grande. About 300 Texans aggressively invaded the Mexican town of Mier before losing a battle to Mexican troops. Survivors of the Mier Expedition killed five guards in an escape attempt, and Mexican dictator Santa Anna ordered the decimation of the 176 prisoners. On March 25, 1843, a pot was filled with 159 white beans and 17 black ones; blindfolded captives took their luck. The 17 unlucky ones were shot, while the others were imprisoned.

Summer 1845: *Democratic Review* editor John O'Sullivan coins a famous phrase about American expansionist zeal when he argues that it is "our manifest destiny . . . to overspread the continent allotted by Providence for the free development of our yearly multiplying millions."

October 1845: Voters in Texas approve the soon-to-be state's constitution.

December 1845: John Frémont reaches Sutter's Fort, near the confluence of California's Sacramento and American rivers.

December 29, 1845: Texas, annexed by mutual agreement, officially joins the Union as the 28th state.

1846: Mexican authorities order explorer and cartographer John Frémont out of California.

1846: The 500-strong Mormon Battalion follows a division of the Army of the West to California. Along the way, they discover a good location for a Pacific railroad route.

1846: The first permanent Mormon settlement in Idaho is established in the Upper Bear River Valley.

1846: The Santa Fe Trail becomes a major trade route. Four hundred wagons carrying $1.7 million in goods make the journey.

January 13, 1846: On President Polk's orders, General Zachary Taylor reports to the Texas border on the north bank of the Rio Grande. However, Mexico asserts that the boundary is actually 100 miles to the north at the Nueces River.

January 14, 1846: Reaching an agreement with the U.S. government, the Kansa Indians relinquish another two million acres.

The martyrdom of Joseph Smith Joseph Smith was commander of the Mormon militia and wielded great political power among his followers. Many Christian communities considered his religious doctrines blasphemous, his practice of polygamy immoral or illegal, and his power threatening. In 1844 he and his older brother, Hyrum (one of the witnesses who had originally testified to the reality of the Golden Plates), were arrested in Carthage, Illinois, on charges of treason. As depicted here, a mob of about 200 armed men attacked the jail on June 27, 1844, killing both Joseph and Hyrum.

The Mormons' "Moses"
Brigham Young joined The Church of Jesus Christ of Latter-day Saints in 1830, after reading the Book of Mormon. When Joseph Smith was killed in 1844, Young became the second Mormon leader and prophet. He is sometimes called "The American Moses" because he led his followers through the desert to their "promised land" at Utah's Great Salt Lake. When Utah became part of the United States, Young attempted to create a new state called Deseret. Instead, he was made governor of the new Utah Territory.

> "[G]et up into the mountains, where the devil himself cannot dig us out, and live in a healthy climate where we can live as old as we have mind to."
>
> —JOSEPH SMITH, FEBRUARY 20, 1844

Mormons grow strong in Nauvoo In 1839 the Mormons founded a new city in Illinois. Nauvoo ("beautiful place") soon became the 10th largest U.S. city. By 1844 the community militia—the Nauvoo Legion—boasted 3,000 troops (more than a third as many as the U.S. Army of that time). This Mormon show of strength raised alarm in nearby communities and led to violence, including the assassination of the Smith brothers. In 1846 the Mormons were forced to leave Illinois. The Nauvoo Legion re-emerged in Deseret the following year, and in 1852 it became Utah's territorial militia.

THE MORMONS' FRANTIC FLIGHT

THIS SCENE OF confusion, fright and distress was continued throughout the forenoon. In every part of the city scenes of destitution, misery and woe met the eye. Families were hurrying away from their homes, without a shelter,—without means of conveyance,—without tents, money, or a day's provision, with as much of their household stuff as they could carry in their hands. Sick men and women were carried upon their beds—weary mothers, with helpless babes dying in the arms, hurried away—all fleeing, they scarcely knew or cared wither, so it was from their enemies, whom they feared more than the waves of the Mississippi, or the heat, and hunger and lingering life and dreaded death of the prairies on which they were about to be cast. The ferry boats were crowded, and the river bank was lined with anxious fugitives, sadly awaiting their turn to pass over and take up their solitary march to the wilderness.

—M. BRAYMAN, LEGAL COUNCIL TO GOVERNOR THOMAS FORD OF ILLINOIS, ON THE EXPULSION OF MORMONS FROM NAUVOO, ILLINOIS, 1846

The Mormon Trail
Because many non-Mormon communities felt threatened, Mormons frequently were forced to relocate. In 1847 Brigham Young led a group of his followers to the Great Salt Lake; over the next 20 years, about 30,000 additional Mormons would follow. Groups such as the one seen here, called "handcart companies," pushed and pulled their belongings in carts because they could not afford pack animals. Their route from Illinois and Iowa to their settlement in Utah is known as the Mormon Trail.

February 1846: The first Mormon refugees to leave their colony at Nauvoo, Illinois, cross the Mississippi into Iowa. • Directed to "flee Babylon," members of The Church of Jesus Christ of Latter-day Saints board the ship *Brooklyn* in New York, bound for San Francisco.

March 1846: Sam Houston of Texas begins his first term as a U.S. senator.

March 13, 1846: Colonel Jose Castro, the Mexican military governor at Monterey, denounces John Frémont and his fellow officers, claiming they are nothing more than a band of highwaymen.

April 18, 1846: Pio Pico is sworn in as (the last) governor of the Mexican state of Alta (northern) California.

April 24, 1846: Mexican troops encounter an American scouting party on the north bank of the Rio Grande, part of General Zachary Taylor's army that had proceeded south of Nueces into Mexican territory. On the basis of this skirmish, President Polk will announce that "American blood has been shed on the American soil," and ask Congress to declare war.

May 8, 1846: Troops led by General Zachary Taylor defeat Mexican forces in the Battle of Palo Alto.

May 9, 1846: Mexican forces retreat back across the Rio Grande after being soundly defeated in the Battle of Resaca de la Palma.

June 14, 1846: John Frémont helps launch the Bear Flag Rebellion in California, raising the bear flag over Sonoma and establishing the California Republic.

June 15, 1846: The Oregon Treaty between the United States and Great Britain is ratified. The agreement ends joint occupation of the territory and sets the Oregon border at the 49th parallel.

Horseback warriors The arrival of the horse in the Americas served both the nomadic and warlike inclinations of the Native American Comanche. After Comanche Indians acquired horses, they separated from the Shoshone and emerged as a distinct group. During the 1700s, while armed with native weapons adapted for mounted battle and guns acquired in trade with the French, the Comanche ruled the Great Plains. They fiercely attacked wagon trains (as seen in this illustration) and fought U.S. Cavalry units, holding back white settlement for more than 100 years. The Comanche were broken in the mid-1800s, largely by epidemics of smallpox and cholera.

Polk expands U.S. territory In 1845 James K. Polk assumed the U.S. presidency with an ambitious agenda, which included westward expansion. President Polk threatened war against Great Britain to end joint occupancy of Oregon Country. Britain agreed to a boundary at the 49th parellel, assuring U.S. possession of Washington, Oregon, and Idaho. In 1845 Polk achieved the long-delayed annexation of Texas, adding a vast western state. Desirous of California and the rest of the Southwest, Polk offered to buy the northern half of Mexico; when his offer was declined, he incited hostilities. Through the ensuing Mexican-American War, the U.S. gained the entire Southwest, completing the enormous expansion dreams of President Polk.

Frémont at the forefront Nicknamed "The Pathfinder," topographer, explorer, soldier, and politician John Frémont became a legend in his own lifetime. During his third expedition to the far West, begun in 1845, he joined California's Bear Flag Rebellion as well as the U.S. military campaign to wrest California from Mexico. Frémont negotiated the Treaty of Cahuenga, which ended hostilities in California, and became one of the first two senators from California. He later became the first presidential candidate of the Republican Party, and briefly served as a Union major general during the Civil War.

Bear Flaggers seize Mexican commander When an uncouth band of the Bear Flag Republic raided Sonoma on June 14, 1846, the wealthy and educated Mariano Guadalupe Vallejo was the Mexican military commander there. Vallejo treated the rebel leaders courteously and even served them breakfast, assuring them that he supported U.S. rule of California. He was promptly imprisoned by the Bear Flaggers under such poor conditions that he contracted malaria, and his estate was nearly destroyed. Nevertheless, Vallejo accepted U.S. rule of the territory. He served in California's constitutional convention and in its first state senate.

The fight for California By 1845 Mexican-ruled California was home to more than 800 U.S. settlers. In June 1846, some of them revolted, founding the California Bear Flag Republic. Their republic, which never really governed California at all, lasted a mere 25 days before U.S. military forces arrived, bringing the region into the already-raging Mexican-American War. Californios (Mexican natives of California), such as the lancers portrayed on the left, fought bravely but unsuccessfully against rebel settlers and U.S. troops. The Treaty of Cahuenga, signed in January 1847, ended the fighting in California.

The Bear Flag Republic On June 14, 1846, 33 unruly, English-speaking settlers who called themselves *Osos* (Bears) marched into Sonoma, a Mexican military outpost in northern California. They seized the town without a fight, striking the first blow in a struggle that eventually would lead to California's U.S. statehood. The Osos promptly proclaimed the founding of the California Bear Flag Republic and raised a makeshift flag (*pictured*) above Sonoma's plaza. The flag amused the town's Spanish-speaking residents, who thought that its crudely painted beast looked more like a pig than a bear.

July 2, 1846: U.S. Commodore John Sloat anchors the *Savannah* at Monterey, California.

July 7, 1846: The U.S. claims to have annexed California with Commodore John Sloat's capture of Monterey.

July 9, 1846: A contingent of marines and sailors marches into San Francisco's Plaza and replaces the Mexican flag with the Stars and Stripes.

July 11, 1846: The California Republic's bear flag makes way for the American flag at Sutter's Fort.

July 23, 1846: Commander Robert Stockton replaces an ailing Commodore Sloat at Monterey.

July 31, 1846: The ship *Brooklyn* arrives in San Francisco with approximately 230 Mormon emigrants on board.

August 1846: Mexican President Santa Anna is recalled to Mexico. President Polk makes a misguided decision in allowing Santa Anna to pass through the U.S. naval blockade.

August 2, 1846: Mexican General Vallejo is released from his imprisonment at Fort Sutter.

August 10, 1846: The frigate *Congress*, under the command of Commodore Stockton, arrives in San Francisco Bay.

August 13, 1846: John Frémont and Commodore Robert Stockton take possession of Los Angeles.

August 18, 1846: Colonel Stephen Kearny and his troops enter Santa Fe and take possession of New Mexico.

September 17, 1846: Santa Anna is restored to the command of the Mexican army. • After a three-day battle with a prejudiced mob, the last Mormons are run out of Nauvoo, Illinois.

Bridger's explorations Jim Bridger, who became a fur trapper while still a teenager, traversed the Rocky Mountains with the instincts of a born explorer. The Bridger Mountains, Bridger Creek, Bridger Crossing, Bridger's Ferry, Bridger Flat, Bridger Pass, Bridger Peak, and the Bridger Trail testify to his expertise as an explorer. The husband of three Native American women, he was a master of Plains sign language and spoke about six Indian tongues—as well as English, Spanish, and French. From 1843 to 1853, he operated Fort Bridger, a Wyoming trading post, and into his 60s he worked as a guide and army scout.

Benton promotes Manifest Destiny
During his 30 years as a U.S. senator from Missouri (1821–51), Thomas Hart Benton vigorously promoted westward expansion. He was initially angry when, in 1841, young army topographer John Frémont eloped with his teenaged daughter, Jessie. But after Benton realized that Frémont was, like him, a believer in Manifest Destiny, the two men became partners in conquering the West. Benton was not above exaggerating for propaganda purposes. For example, he described the bloodless, almost comical 1846 seizure of undefended Sonoma, California, by rebellious Bear Flaggers as a courageous assault on "a fortified, well-garrisoned presidio."

Sloat takes Monterey, Yerba Buena
Commodore John Sloat of the U.S. Navy's Pacific Squadron was ordered in 1845 to seize Alta (northern) California if war broke out with Mexico. On June 7, 1846, he received word that General Zachary Taylor had engaged and defeated Mexican forces at Palo Alto and Resaca de la Palma. After waiting indecisively for three weeks, Sloat and his men sailed for Monterey Bay. After delaying a few more days, Sloat sent Captain John Montgomery and 70 troops to take possession of tiny Yerba Buena (soon to become San Francisco) and Monterey. His troops faced almost no resistance, and the American flag was raised over the small communities.

The Oregon Treaty

IN THE MID-1840S, the United States and Great Britain nearly went to war over the hotly contested Oregon Country. The territory in question was bounded by the Rocky Mountains and the Pacific Ocean and stretched from the 54°40′ parallel (now the border between Alaska and British Columbia) south to California. In all, it covered a half million square miles.

Inhabited by native peoples for millennia, European powers vied for the region through much of the 18th and 19th centuries. Great Britain and the United States boasted the strongest claims to Oregon Country. In 1793 British explorer Alexander Mackenzie staked out the territory, and the British-owned Hudson's Bay Company established Fort Vancouver on the northern bank of the Columbia River in 1825. Americans Lewis and Clark reached the mouth of the Columbia in 1805, and Spain ceded to the United States its prior claim to much of the region with the signing of the Adams-Onís Treaty in 1819. The U.S. and Great Britain initially settled this ambiguity by agreeing to joint occupation.

But as word of the Oregon Country's fertile soil and open lands reached Americans back east, "Oregon fever" led to a swell of migration. In just four years (1841–45), the number of Americans in the territory jumped from less than 500 to 5,000. The British population, on the other hand, stagnated at roughly 700.

The new migrants believed that it was their "Manifest Destiny" to occupy the region, and began clamoring for complete American control. They found a champion in the newly elected President Polk, who talked tough to Great Britain and took up the war cry "54-40 or fight!" Fortunately for both countries, level heads prevailed. In 1846 negotiators agreed to avoid a potentially destructive and costly war by setting the border at the 49th parallel.

The Oregon Trail During the Great Migration of the mid-1800s, thousands of settlers made a four- to six-month trip to claim good farmland in the Northwest. They traveled the Oregon Trail, which was at first just a 2,000-mile string of natural landmarks that a knowledgeable traveler could follow. The way soon became clearer as more and more wagons followed it. The Oregon Trail (romanticized in this painting by Albert Bierstadt) generally is thought of as beginning in Independence, Missouri, and ending in Oregon City, Oregon. However, many travelers started at different "jumping-off towns" and took branches leading into other areas, including northern California.

Stockton captures Los Angeles Commodore Robert Stockton arrived at Monterey Bay in the frigate *Congress* in July 1846, shortly after Commodore John Sloat had taken possession of Monterey. Aggressive and ambitious, Stockton took command of naval forces from the prudent Sloat, who sailed for home. Stockton and his men moved southward, seized Los Angeles on August 13, 1846, and proclaimed the annexation of California to the United States on August 17. Californios soon launched a counter-rebellion, but Stockton resolutely battled the rebels. Reinforced by an army column led by Colonel Stephen Kearny, Stockton reestablished American authority over California by January 1847.

September 24, 1846: Zachary Taylor leads his troops into Monterey after a four-day siege.

September 25, 1846: Needed on two fronts, the Army of the West splits. Some troops will march on Chihuahua, Mexico, while others will secure California.

October 8, 1846: The Battle of the Old Woman's Gun ends with a defeat of the U.S. Marines by Californio rebels, who will keep Los Angeles in their hands for several more months.

November 2, 1846: The Donner Party is trapped by a snowstorm while trying to cross the Sierra Nevada. When their supplies run out, some members of the party will resort to cannibalism.

December 1846: Santa Anna resumes both his position as president of Mexico as well as his dictatorial ways.

December 28, 1846: Iowa joins the Union as the 29th state.

1847: Lawmakers in Missouri pass legislation outlawing the education of black people, regardless of their status as slaves or freedmen.

1847: Dr. Marcus Whitman and his wife, Narcissa, are among a group of 14 massacred by Cayuse warriors in reprisal for an earlier measles epidemic. *See* 1850.

January 1847: Commodore Stockton appoints John Frémont governor of California, but Frémont is detained and charged with mutiny. *See* November 2, 1847.

January 8, 1847: U.S. troops defeat rebelling Californios in the Battle of San Gabriel.

January 16, 1847: The Russian brig *Constantine,* from Sitka, Alaska, arrives in a harbor in northern California. The U.S. remains concerned about the presence of Russian interests in the Pacific Northwest.

The Donner Party The ill-fated Donner Party was organized in 1846 in Springfield, Illinois, by the Donner brothers, Jacob and George. Bound for California, the 87 emigrants reached Fort Bridger that summer and decided to follow a trail toward San Francisco called the "Hastings Cutoff." A series of fateful delays and difficulties brought the Donner Party atop the Sierra Mountains in late October, when the first snowstorm of the season blocked the pass to the western slope. By mid-December, 15 members of the snowbound party set out for help. As starvation took its toll, both groups resorted to cannibalism. When rescue parties finally arrived in February 1847, only 46 survivors remained.

The travails of westward travelers Settlers went westward full of hope for good land, new opportunities, and better lives. Most walked all the way in order to save their animal teams and because their brakeless wagons were subject to catastrophes, such as tumbles into ravines. Many succumbed to cholera and other diseases; others died from accidental gunshots, animal stampedes, violence among fellow travelers, gunpowder explosions, suicide, Indian attacks, and being run over by wagon wheels. Children were especially vulnerable. The Oregon–California Trails Association estimates that graves along the Oregon Trail averaged 10 per mile.

The San Patricio Battalion The San Patricio Battalion was a turncoat artillery unit during the Mexican-American War. These Irish Americans switched sides after being persecuted by southern troops. In April 1846, a month before hostilities began, Sergeant John Riley left General Zachary Taylor's army and accepted a commission in the Mexican army. Later deserters would serve under him in the San Patricio "Battalion" (never more than two companies), which fought against the U.S. Army at Buena Vista and Churubusco. Captured after Churubusco, about 50 San Patricios were sentenced to death and hanged.

U.S. invades Mexico City On the morning of September 14, 1847, General John Quitman and his brigade of Mississippi volunteers took possession of the Grand Plaza, the heart of Mexico City. The day before, the Mexican stronghold at Chapultepec Castle had fallen, with fierce fighting in the streets. The exhausted Mississippians were in need of reinforcements. Other troops soon arrived, and then—as depicted here—General Winfield Scott arrived in a triumphant march. Sporadic fighting in the countryside continued for a month, and in February 1848 the war was formally ended by the Treaty of Guadalupe-Hidalgo.

U.S. takes New Mexico Colonel Stephen Kearny proclaims U.S. possession of New Mexico in August 1846. President Polk had offered Mexico $25 million for California, $5 million to recognize the Rio Grande boundary for Texas, and another $5 million for "New Mexico," a vast area that also included what would become Arizona, Utah, Nevada, and parts of Colorado and Wyoming. Rebuffed, Polk incited war. Kearny, a cavalryman, was ordered to raise an "Army of the West" and seize New Mexico and California. After a long march across the Santa Fe Trail, the Army of the West took Santa Fe without bloodshed. Kearny established a provisional government before moving toward California.

The Whitman murder Dr. Marcus Whitman is about to be murdered by a Cayuse Indian at his mission in Oregon's Walla Walla Valley. Dr. Whitman had arrived in the Pacific Northwest in 1835 as a missionary to Native Americans. The next year his bride, Narcissa, and another missionary wife became the first white women to cross the Rocky Mountains. The Whitman Mission became a way station for overland travelers, and many sick immigrants sought treatment from the doctor. But nearby, Cayuse Indians were dying from white men's diseases, and on November 29, 1847, angry warriors killed Dr. Whitman, Narcissa (*shown at right*), and 12 others. They then burned down the mission.

January 19, 1847: During the Taos Rebellion in New Mexcico, Charles Bent—the American-appointed governor of New Mexico—is assassinated.

January 30, 1847: The northern California town of Yerba Buena is renamed San Francisco.

February 23, 1847: U.S. General Zachary Taylor's 5,000 troops defeat Santa Anna's 20,000 men in the Battle of Buena Vista.

February 25, 1847: U.S. troops defeat a Mexican army in the Battle of the Sacramento.

March 27, 1847: Some 12,000 American troops, under the command of General Winfield Scott, overwhelm the Mexican defenders at the fortress of San Juan de Ulua in Vera Cruz, Mexico.

July 1847: Brigham Young and a party of emigrants arrive in the Valley of the Great Salt Lake, where the persecuted Mormons will finally establish a permanent community.

August 19, 1847: Captain Johann Sutter and James Marshall agree to build a lumber mill on the American River, near present-day Sacramento.

September 14, 1847: U.S. troops under General Winfield Scott capture Mexico City, while Santa Anna flees. This virtually guarantees that the Americans will win the war.

November 2, 1847: John Frémont's court-martial begins in Washington, D.C. *See* January 31, 1848.

January 24, 1848: James Marshall discovers gold at California's Sutter's Mill.

January 31, 1848: John Frémont's court-martial ends with a guilty verdict. He turns down the pardon offered by President Polk, believing it would imply guilt.

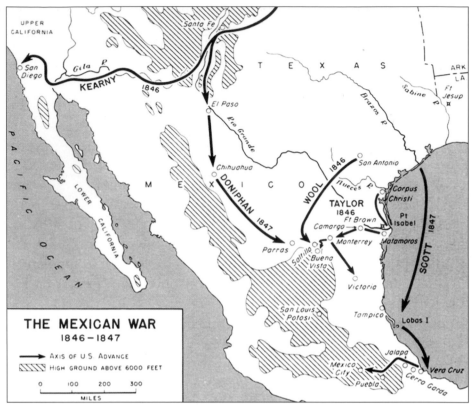

THE MEXICAN WAR
1846–1847

→ AXIS OF U.S. ADVANCE
▨ HIGH GROUND ABOVE 6000 FEET

0   100   200   300
MILES

Mexican-American War campaigns In May 1846, General Zachary Taylor launched an invasion of northern Mexico with his small army. Even after being reinforced by General John Wool's 2,400-man force of volunteers, Taylor was outnumbered. Nevertheless, he scored a series of victories that would vault him to the presidency in 1848. Meanwhile, Colonel Stephen Kearny marched west, seized Santa Fe, then continued on to California. In 1847 General Winfield Scott sailed to Vera Cruz, then marched across mountains and jungle toward Mexico City with 11,000 men. Despite the opposition by General Santa Anna's 30,000 men, Scott executed a brilliant campaign and captured the Mexican capital.

AN AVAILABLE CANDIDATE.

"Old Rough and Ready" elected president This political cartoon from the 1848 presidential campaign vilifies the Whig candidate, General Zachary Taylor. Although he was criticized as a killer by political opponents, the public regarded the general as a war hero, and they elected him president. Taylor had spent 40 years in the Army after enlisting as a militia private. Cool under fire and a casual (even sloppy) dresser, he was affectionately called "Old Rough and Ready" by his men. Stationed on the Rio Grande when war with Mexico broke out, Taylor aggressively advanced across the border. He won battle after battle—then prevailed in the presidential race.

Treaty of Guadalupe-Hidalgo

IN 1846 THE U.S. CONGRESS declared war against a "sister republic," Mexico. Some Americans—including Henry Thoreau and Abraham Lincoln—considered the war unjust and immoral, but most celebrated the nation's first invasion of foreign soil. Within one year, the United States' largely volunteer Army captured Mexico City.

On behalf of the U.S., Nicholas Trist negotiated the Treaty of Guadalupe-Hidalgo, which was agreed to by Mexican President Manuel de la Peña y Peña and the Mexican Congress. The treaty was signed on February 2, 1848, and Americans rejoiced at the news. For $15 million, Mexico had ceded Texas, New Mexico, and California to the United States. The treaty conferred U.S. citizenship on Hispanic residents of the acquired territories. It promised protection of Catholicism and the Spanish language. And it legitimized earlier Spanish and Mexican land grants to Hispanos and the Pueblo Indians, who had inhabited the land before the Spanish arrived.

Not surprisingly, American racism undermined the treaty. Many U.S. citizens viewed Mexicans as a "mongrel race" and Indians as mere "savages." From Texas to California, Hispanos were barred from voting, denounced for speaking Spanish, and relegated to an inferior status in U.S. society. Anglo lawyers and politicians systematically defrauded legitimate Hispano and Native American landowners. Much of the best land rapidly passed into the hands of newcomers. Land thefts and repression continued until about 1920, when the situation began to improve.

Nicholas Trist

The unfulfilled treaty left a bitter legacy. Chicano political activism erupted shortly after World War II, and spread throughout the West. In the mid-1960s, the fiery Reyes López Tijerina sparked an angry Chicano rebellion to reclaim community land grants in northern New Mexico. Pueblo Indians and non-Native sympathizers also strove to regain lost land in the 1920s, and they later won important courtroom battles over the future of Pueblo land. As with treaties made with Native Americans, the Treaty of Guadalupe-Hidalgo is another example of U.S. failure to keep its promises.

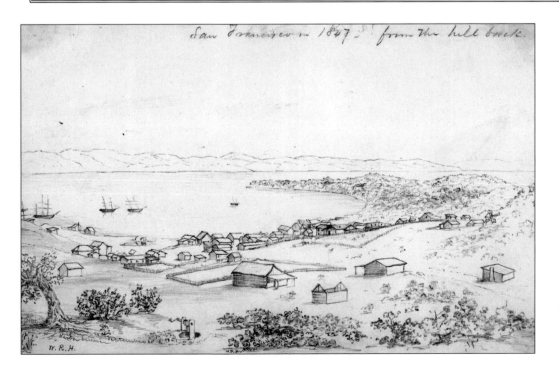

Yerba Buena renamed San Francisco Yerba Buena was founded in the early 1800s on the southern peninsula of San Francisco Bay. The town is seen here in 1847, shortly after it had been claimed by the United States and renamed San Francisco. Even though the bay was one of the finest natural harbors in the world, the town itself seemed unpromising, lacking especially in drinking water and firewood. Early in 1848, only about 800 people lived there. But the discovery of gold that year on the nearby American River began San Francisco's sudden transformation into a thriving city.

February 2, 1848: The Treaty of Guadalupe-Hidalgo is signed, ending the Mexican-American War. • The first Chinese workers in America arrive in San Francisco aboard the brig *Eagle*.

March 11, 1848: Mormons discover gold on the south fork of the American River.

March 15, 1848: *The Californian* reports that gold was discovered along the American River at a sawmill owned by Johann Sutter, but the news is met with more disbelief than excitement.

April 3, 1848: In San Francisco, Thomas Douglas becomes the first teacher at the first public school in California.

May 12, 1848: The California Gold Rush is on when Sam Brannan runs through San Francisco waving a bottle of gold dust and shouting, "Gold! Gold! Gold from the American River!"

May 29, 1848: Wisconsin becomes the 30th state admitted to the Union.

August 14, 1848: Oregon is officially established as a territory by Congress after it is determined that slaveholding will not be permitted.

October 6, 1848: The Pacific Mail Steamship Co. sends a ship from New York to California.

November 1848: The first ship full of East Coast gold seekers sets sail for California.

November 1, 1848: Johann Sutter announces his plan to build Sacramento City on the Sacramento River.

November 7, 1848: General Zachary Taylor is elected the 12th president of the United States, fending off a challenge from General Lewis Cass.

Inns sprout up across the land Public inns, offering food, drink, and lodging, had always been popular among affluent travelers in the eastern states. But in the mid-1800s, inns sprang up along the trails that settlers followed into the Northwest, especially in towns along the Oregon Trail and its branches. An inn offered travelers the chance to relax and enjoy a little festivity. Frontier dances, such as the one seen here, usually were variations of traditional Virginia reels and Irish jigs. When the Southwest and California became part of the United States, inns for American travelers soon opened along southern routes.

The publishing boom Frontier newspapermen were among the most important pioneers. Journalists brought hand-operated printing presses in covered wagons to fledgling western communities, where they reported on local events while airing their political views. Publishing boomed in the 1800s thanks to improvements in technology. In 1847 Richard M. Hoe introduced rotary presses that printed 18,000 sheets on both sides per hour. In 1884 the Linotype revolutionized typesetting. Those developments made large circulation newspapers feasible. Book publishing also prospered, leading to countless books that glorified the West.

Sutter and His Fort

A NATIVE OF KANDERN, Germany, Johann August Sutter became a pivotal figure in the shaping of California. Back in Europe, he had accrued substantial debt after several ill-fated business ventures. In 1834 he left his wife and children and started off for the United States in hopes of striking it rich in the American West. He eventually arrived in California in 1839.

That summer, he set up camp near the confluence of the Sacramento and American rivers. Sutter traveled to Monterey, where he met with Juan Bautista Alvarado, the governor of Mexican California. Alvarado told the émigré that he could have title to 11 square leagues in the Sacramento Valley, provided that he become a Mexican citizen. Sutter agreed.

After bringing the local Indians into line through a combination of diplomacy and intimidation, Sutter used

Johann August Sutter

their labor to build a fort. Sutter's Fort soon became a popular trading post for trappers and a resting point for travelers making their way to the West Coast. As business boomed, Sutter expanded his outpost. The fort had its own blacksmith shop, tannery, bakery, cobbler, distillery, and prison. A farm on the Feather River supplied the settlement with grain and other crops.

By the mid-1840s, Sutter presided over a prosperous agricultural empire. His luck, however, soon changed when James Marshall discovered gold on his property in 1848. Sutter's employees quit, his land was overrun, and his own attempts at digging gold proved futile. "It was high time to quit this kind of business," he wrote. "The whole expedition proved to be a heavy loss to me." Broken and defeated, Sutter moved to Lititz, Pennsylvania. He died in 1880.

> "I reached my hand down and picked it up; it made my heart thump, for I was certain that it was gold. The piece was about half the size and of the shape of a pea. Then I saw another piece in the water."
>
> —JAMES MARSHALL, RECALLING HIS DISCOVERY OF GOLD IN THE AMERICAN RIVER ON JANUARY 24, 1848

Marshall cursed by gold Finding gold was the unluckiest thing that ever happened to James Marshall. In 1847, before his gold discovery, he signed a contract with Johann Sutter to build a sawmill in Coloma, California, about 40 miles from Sutter's Fort. On January 24, 1848, Marshall discovered gold in the mill trace. His workmen immediately abandoned his sawmill to search for gold, and before long he lost his land to rampant prospectors. In the years that followed, Marshall vainly tried his hand at raising vineyards and even prospecting for gold. He died in 1885 as a penniless subsistence farmer.

Brannan's get-rich-quick scheme By the time gold was discovered in 1848, a Mormon named Samuel Brannan had started San Francisco's first newspaper and owned a store outside Sutter's Fort. Brannan cunningly took advantage of the imminent Gold Rush. He collected bogus tithes from Mormons and used the money to buy all the prospecting gear in the region, which he sold to gold hunters at outrageous prices. He also ran through the streets of San Francisco, shouting about the gold discovery. Half of San Francisco's population fled to the gold fields, and Brannan became California's first millionaire. Bad luck and alcoholism eventually caught up with him; he lost his fortune and died broke.

The Rush to California

⌒◦1849-1860◦⌒

IN 1847 A EUROPEAN ÉMIGRÉ to the far West named Johann Sutter built a sawmill on the American River at his ranch in California's Sacramento Valley. It was the first large-scale attempt to use the power of rushing water for industrial purposes in California. A few months later, in early 1848, a Sutter employee named Henry Bigler wrote an entry in his diary. "This day," he scribbled on January 24, "some kind of mettle was found...that looks like goald."

It *was* "goald." A man named James Marshall had spotted a pea-sized nugget of gold in the tail of the millrace and plucked it out. His discovery, he admitted, caused him to "think right hard." Nothing like the California Gold Rush had ever taken place in the history of the world. The Gold Rush changed California, changed the West, changed America, and changed the world. It allowed thousands of people to lift their heads from their ordinary lives (agricultural drudgery for most of them) and imagine something—and someplace—very different.

For hundreds of years, immigrants' dreams had been limited to farms and land. Europeans sailed to North America in search of that dream, and eventually—as the soil of the East began to play out—they worked their way west in search of better land. Farmers in the East and Midwest wished to

After hearing spectacular stories of treasure-laden rivers in California, tens of thousands of gold seekers poured into the state during the spring and summer of 1849. By the end of that summer, miners had excavated a combined $10 million worth of gold.

"The whole country, from San Francisco to Los Angeles and from the seashore to the Sierra Nevada, resounds with the sordid cry of 'gold! Gold!! GOLD!!!' while the field is left half planted, the house half built, and everything neglected but the manufacture of shovels and pickaxes."

—San Francisco *Californian*

accumulate, by the end of their lives, enough land to pass on to the next generation.

However, the new discovery in California inspired people to dream bigger. The nugget that caused Marshall to think right hard caused people in the United States—and all over the world—to do just the same. Tens of thousands of them journeyed to California, hoping to find exactly what Marshall had found, and more of it. And whether they were North Americans, South Americans, Mexicans, Chinese, or French, their mere presence in the far West changed the place forever.

Sailing from the East Coast to California appeared to be the least hazardous route, yet it was incredibly long. Because ships could not "cut through" the Americas, they had to sail south of South America before going north to California. The 17,000-mile journey took three to eight months.

The Gold Rush, and other rushes that followed, were remarkably successful in remaking the West. The rushes led to the construction of cities, and settlers brought with them law and legal traditions. The settlers inaugurated a powerful labor movement in the West, and they invented modern practices of mining and the modern mining corporation.

But the Gold Rush and its spin-offs would have been more remarkable if they had not been so transitory and wasteful. Gold seekers were like so many whirlwinds in the West, eating up resources and the landscape at one spot before setting off in another direction in search of another discovery of precious gold, silver, or some other valuable mineral. Atop all the excitement and wonder of the Gold Rush, we must consider the costs of such events. People, trees, water, and the soil itself were put to work and used up by miners who paid no heed to the future.

Oh, but it was a tremendously alluring adventure. Not all who went thought they would get rich, but most of the Gold Rush migrants figured they might do better out in far-off California than by staying home. And if *we* worked a small farm in the mid-19th century, sunrise to sunset, we might think about going west, too.

Agricultural laborers in the mid-1800s were lucky if they made a dollar a day. Gold miners splashing about in a freezing Sierra Nevada stream could pull out $20 worth of gold a day, especially if they had arrived in California early, in 1848 or '49. If our hardy miner combined skill with luck, he might make $100 a day. Even if a miner did not know what he was doing (and most did not, at least at first), he might see more money in a month than the average American family saw in a year. By the summer of 1849, after word had spread that there was gold (GOLD!) in California, $10 million already had been pulled out of the Sierra streams. Within five years, that figure would skyrocket to $200 million.

Once news of Marshall's discovery became known (and, given communication and transportation challenges, it took a while), the result was foreordained. People came in droves, more than a quarter-million in just a few years. Most gold seekers were not well prepared for the journey. No railroads to California existed. Would-be miners walked or rode across the middle of the continent. Or they took a ship, either all the way around South America and then north to San Francisco, or to the eastern edge of Central America, where they ventured through the jungles of Panama (the Panama Canal was still more

This painting romanticizes the overland journey to California. In reality, many died on the hellacious, months-long trek, be it from disease, starvation, accidents, Indian attacks, or exposure to extreme heat or cold.

than 60 years in the future) and hoped to catch a ship on the far side.

However they chose to go, the trips were hard and full of danger. As Alonza Delano, a journalist of the era, wrote, "Any man who makes a trip by land to California deserves to find a fortune." Bad weather, bad food, accidents, and disease killed many a '49er long before he had a chance to try to get rich in California. One group of gold seekers happened into Death Valley, got lost, and wandered around for months trying to get out.

The early days of the California Gold Rush were symbolized by the spectacle of men working alone or in small partnerships, panning for gold in a stream. The process was not especially difficult. The gold was not locked away in deep, below-ground veins—at least not at first. It was in the "placers," gold-bearing creeks and streambeds, dry or wet. It had started out in veins, but the geology of the Sierra Nevada Mountains had exposed those veins to erosion. The gold eroded and was washed down the mountain. The hard work had already been done; the gold was free from the rock. The gold miner only had to find it and separate it from the gravel surrounding it. This was a task perfectly suited to people with little money or skill but the will to work hard.

Most men who arrived during the early days of the Gold Rush did not expect to stay long—five years at the most. Then, they hoped, they would return home rich. In the meantime, they had to withstand the difficulties of camp life. Fresh food was scarce, and miners frequently became malnourished on their diet of biscuits, coffee, beans, dried beef, and molasses. Their world was nearly all male, at least in the earliest years of the Gold Rush. Miners grew lonesome quickly; many never had been away from home. They missed their parents, their friends, their wives, and their children.

But most stuck it out. And others came. Almost overnight, San Francisco became the supreme city of the far West. In 1850 the City by the Bay boasted 25,000 residents. Inland, gold miners created the new city of Sacramento at the confluence of the American and Sacramento rivers. Sacramento was an all-important depot for mining supplies, and in 1854 it became the state capital. The non-Indian population of California mushroomed during the Gold Rush, growing from just 14,000 people in 1848 to more than 200,000 in just four years.

California grew so much and so quickly that it was ready for statehood by 1850. But discussions of its admittance to the Union erupted into heated debates. Prior to California statehood, 15 states prohibited slavery and 15 allowed it. Northerners wanted California admitted as a free state, but that would be considered "unfair" to the South.

Thus, legislators hammered out the Compromise of 1850: California would join as a free state while proslavery forces would gain certain concessions. Most notable was the Fugitive Slave Law, which criminalized those who aided runaway slaves. The "compromise" infuriated both Northerners and Southerners, and in the end accomplished hardly more than a decade's postponement of the Civil War.

Gold Rush-era tensions and antagonisms roiled life in California. The mining camps and the mining world were notoriously discriminatory and brutal. Chinese miners not only faced hostility by racist whites, but they were forced to pay an expensive Foreign Miners' Tax. Violence, generally aimed at nonwhites by whites, was hardly uncommon in the gold camps. Moreover, the Gold Rush period marked a particularly grim chapter in the lives of California's Native American population. In the first decade of the Gold Rush, tens of thousands of California Indians died due to violence, disease, or starvation. Indian women were raped; children were captured and sold into slavery. Some Indians were even hunted for sport.

As compensation for California entering the Union as a free state in 1850, the South reaped the benefits of the Fugitive Slave Law. The law not only allowed southern whites to recapture fugitive slaves, but it opened the door for the kidnapping of free blacks in the North.

After '49ers scooped out most of the gold in the creeks and streams, people devised new mining techniques to go after gold locked in the earth. Mining companies were formed to penetrate deep into hillsides and mountainsides. Beginning in 1852, gold seekers aimed high-pressure water hoses at hillsides (with force enough to kill a man), blasting away dirt and rock to expose the gold. A man with a hose could do in a day what several men could not do in a week.

Hydraulic mining, brutally efficient and environmentally catastrophic, was California's chief technological innovation of the Gold Rush era. It allowed miners, in the words of one observer, to "make a sad mess of the country in their search for the precious metal." It proved extremely destructive, especially to the farmers in downriver valleys whose land became choked with silt and debris in the runoff from hydraulic operations. Such mining eventually was banned in the state in the 1880s.

Others responded to the challenges of finding ever more elusive treasure by moving. The Gold Rush encouraged Americans and others simply to look

California's population swelled so much that it created an urgent need to connect the East to the West. In the 1850s, stagecoach companies created comfortable vehicles (notably Concord stagecoaches) for cross-country travel. Transcontinental telegraph and railroad lines would be completed in the 1860s.

over the next rise, to search in the next river or the next mountain in their quest for mineral wealth. California and its Gold Rush, the heyday of which lasted from 1848 to 1855, was the first and most important chapter of western mining. But from there, miners leapfrogged all over the West, looking for the "big strike" in Nevada, Colorado, Idaho, Montana, and Arizona.

The Gold Rush also hastened transportation and communication from the East to the West. In 1857 Congress passed a bill to fund an overland mail service from the East Coast to California. In 1861 the transcontinental telegraph line was completed. And in 1862 Congress passed the Pacific Railroad bill, which allocated funds to companies to build a transcontinental railroad. Each of these dramatic breakthroughs had once been only a pipe dream, but the California Gold Rush spurred men into action to make all of these dreams come true.

1849–1860

1849: Nearly 80,000 '49ers from around the globe converge on California, hoping to strike it rich in the gold fields.

1849: An estimated one in every five "Argonauts" (gold seekers) who journey to California in 1849 die within six months.

1849: "Pretty Juanita," convicted of murder for killing a man who allegedly tried to rape her, is hanged at a mining camp in Downieville, California.

1849: Brigham Young organizes the Perpetual Emigrating Company to help Mormons overseas make their way to Utah. He does so in response to what he sees as the alarming number of non-Mormons moving west.

1849: The American Fur Company sells Fort Laramie to the U.S. government, which immediately moves to fully staff and arm the facility.

February 28, 1849: The Pacific Mail steamer *California* arrives on the West Coast, establishing regular steamboat service to California.

April 1849: The first wagon train of gold seekers departs from Missouri and Iowa.

May 18, 1849: The ship *Grey Eagle* arrives in California with 34 passengers following a record-setting 113-day journey from the East.

June 4, 1849: The USS *Ohio* loses 18 sailors to dreams of fortune when they desert their posts and head for the gold fields.

July 4, 1849: The first steam printing press in the West, belonging to the Robert Semple daily *Alta California,* is put into service.

July 29, 1849: Stakeholders in the gold fields gather to pass a resolution forbidding African Americans, either slaves or freedmen, from owning claims or working in the gold mines.

Panning for flakes
This grizzled '49er uses a tin pan to wash gold from streambed gravel, where millions of dollars' worth of the precious metal lurked. The first miners in California utilized this simple process. The miner gently shook the pan to spill out sand and gravel, leaving the heavier flakes of gold in the pan. Placer deposits, containing loose gold washed out of rocky hillsides, were relatively easy to work. With gold around $16 an ounce in 1948–49, a lucky miner could produce $15 to $80 per day in gold dust.

Dreaming of riches Easterners read news about gold in California. Exaggerated reports of the gold discoveries near Sutter's Fort swept across the United States and ignited a "rush" to California. Newspaper stories, letters, and dazzling offers of inexpensive transportation inspired the first waves of "Argonauts," who dropped everything to join the surge of gold seekers. For every man who found wealth, hundreds went bust and returned home, sadder but wiser. A handful of entrepreneurs, such as Leland Stanford and Levi Strauss, made fortunes by supplying miners with tools, gear, and clothing.

Life in the Gold Fields

IN MAY 1849, a man named Shufelt boarded the steamer *Panama* with a heavy heart and dollar signs in his eyes. His journey took him from the docks of New York City to California's gold fields. Shufelt left behind his wife and young child, gambling that the fortune he stood to make would be worth the temporary hardship. Months later, while lying ill on a filthy mat in a cabin he shared with six other miners, Shufelt might have gained some perspective about his situation—had his illness not left him deranged and near death.

Nothing about life in the gold fields was easy. It was backbreaking work, performed at all hours of daylight and under whatever conditions nature delivered. Searing summer heat, bitter winter cold, freezing mountain streams, filthy drinking water, and inadequate housing, food, and medicine took their toll. Scurvy, cholera, typhus, accidents, and snakebites were widespread in the mining camps. Historians claim that one out of every five miners who journeyed to California in 1849 died within six months. This was not lost on Shufelt, who observed:

"Many, very many, that come here meet with bad success & thousands will leave their bones here. . . . Some will have to beg their way home, & probably one half that come here will never make enough to carry them back."

The men who rushed to California's gold fields also suffered emotionally. They were achingly lonely, as most had left their families behind. Rumors of great mother lodes caused excitement that turned to crushing disappointment when the rumors were found to be false. While some '49ers got rich, most barely made enough to survive. Moreover, gold country inflation resulted in $6 frying pans, $8 jars of pickles, and $3 eggs.

For some miners, the only thing worse than working the gold fields was the thought of stumbling home as a penniless failure. Many couldn't afford return passage. Others went to nearby towns to beg for jobs, while perhaps a thousand a year chose to end their own lives. Not surprisingly, it was often the speculators and the men who capitalized on gold country inflation who truly struck it rich.

Word spreads to Europe
Satirical depictions of the Gold Rush, such as this one by the French cartoonist Cham, reflected Europeans' enthusiasm for the gold discovery. Reports of enormous nuggets, including one found in 1854 that weighed 195 pounds, lent credence to the wildest stories. Europeans, though skeptical of the exaggerated hoopla, came to the diggings by the thousands. Among them were French engineers who helped develop large-scale flume operations. Many Cornish men with mining experience also joined the exodus to gold country.

October 1849: The first European gold seekers head for California.

October 13, 1849: The California constitution is approved by a convention in Monterey. The constitution states that Indians have no political or legal rights. Voters elect Peter Burnett governor of the soon-to-be-official state.

November 18, 1849: John and Amanda Pelton open a public school in California, in an old Baptist church in San Francisco. It initially is free to poor children only, but it will be made free for all children in 1850.

December 9, 1849: The Martin Van Buren engine, so named because it once was used on the President's estate in New York, arrives in San Francisco. This first city fire engine will be used to pump water out of the mines.

December 10, 1849: Chinese laborers working in California hold their first organizational meeting to discuss working conditions and other issues.

December 24, 1849: Most of San Francisco is destroyed as the First Great Fire ravages the city • F. P. Wierzbicki publishes his *California as it is and as it May be, or a Guide to the Gold Region,* the first English-language book printed in California.

December 28, 1849: Edward Otis organizes the Independent Unpaid Axe Volunteer Fire Company to help guard against another major fire in San Francisco. The town council allocates $800 toward the purchase of fire-fighting equipment for the new company.

1850: Congress establishes New Mexico and Utah as U.S. territories.

1850: For gold miners, Levi Strauss markets twilled cotton trousers made of a heavyweight cloth that is known as "genes" in France.

"We ketch a piece of meat in the fingers & crowd like a lot of Swine. The ship perhaps so careened that you will have to hold on or stagger and pitch like a Drunken man. Many behave so swineish that I prefer to stay a way unless driven to it by hunger."

—HIRAM PIERCE, A BLACKSMITH FROM TROY, NEW YORK, DESCRIBING HIS SEA VOYAGE TO CALIFORNIA IN 1849

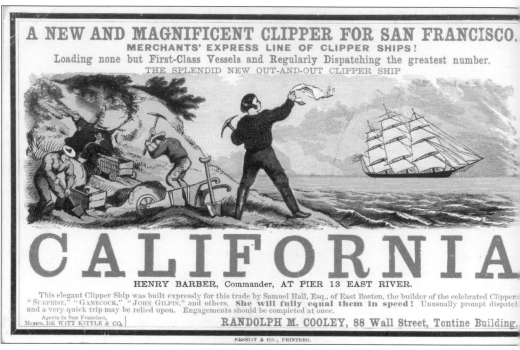

Sailing to California During the Gold Rush, tens of thousands of gold seekers arrived in California by ship. Many came from East Coast ports, sailing around Cape Horn (the southern tip of South America). Crowded quarters, spoiled food, seasickness, and deadly diseases such as cholera all threatened to make the ocean voyage a horrific experience. The famed Clipper Ships were the fastest vessels afloat, and could shorten the trip considerably. Still, the ocean route to California could consume up to eight months, and fares ranged from $100 to $1,000.

BURY 'EM AND MOVE ON

THE POOR WOMEN arrive, looking as haggard as so many Endorean witches; burnt to the color of a hazel-nut, with their hair cut short, and its gloss entirely destroyed by the alkali, whole plains of which they are compelled to cross on the way. You will hardly find a family that has not left some beloved one buried upon the plains. And they are fearful funerals, those. A person dies; and they stop just long enough to dig his grave and lay him in it, as decently as circumstances will permit, and the long train hurries onward, leaving its healthy companions of yesterday, perhaps, in this boundless city of the dead. On this hazardous journey, they dare not linger.

—19TH CENTURY WRITER LOUISA AMELIA KNAPP SMITH CLAPPE

Perils of the Overland Trails

OVERLAND TRAVEL to California and Oregon prior to the transcontinental railroad was daunting, dangerous, and, for many, deadly. Luzena Wilson described the hardships in a memoir of her 1849 trek to the West Coast: "Many an unmarked grave lies by the old emigrant road.... [B]rave souls gave up the battle and lie there forgotten, with not even a stone to note the spot where they sleep the unbroken, dreamless sleep of death."

Of the estimated half million people who attempted the 2,000-mile trip, between four and six percent perished along the way. Disease claimed most. During the early 1850s, outbreaks of Asiatic cholera killed hundreds, perhaps thousands, of emigrants as they crossed the Great Plains. Scarlet fever, influenza, diphtheria, measles, smallpox, and scurvy took many others, as did dysentery due to bad water and poor sanitation.

Because doctors and medicine were scarce on the overland trails, midwives delivered most of the babies and dispensed home remedies to treat illness and injuries. Scores of emigrants were run over by wagons, kicked by draft animals, and shot by accident or on purpose. Indian attacks, however, claimed only a few hundred lives, most of them on the Oregon Trail west of South Pass. The Mountain Meadows Massacre, the most notorious incident of violence and bloodshed on the overland trails, occurred in 1857, when a party of Mormons and Paiutes murdered about 120 California-bound emigrants traveling through Utah.

Exposure, hunger, and exhaustion killed far more victims than did firearms. Such conditions took their greatest toll on young children, the elderly, and adult males. In 1856, for example, more than 200 members of two Mormon handcart companies bound for Salt Lake City succumbed to the vicissitudes of winter weather.

The "gambler's route" Travelers might cut 8,000 miles and several months from the trip to California if they crossed the Isthmus of Panama instead of sailing all the way around South America, but the choice was risky and often deadly. The "gambler's route" might pay off if travelers did not fall ill from cholera, dysentery, or malaria, and avoided conflicts with Natives. Indian canoes carried thousands of men along the short Chagres River, and prices charged for this service skyrocketed as demand increased. Men who completed the crossing often found themselves stranded for weeks or months in Panama City while they waited for ships bound for California.

1850: Chief Tiloukaikt and four other Cayuse Indians turn themselves in to U.S. authorities, claiming responsibility for the Whitman Massacre in Oregon Territory. They are subsequently hanged.

1850: The California legislature passes the Indenture Act, which permits white settlers to declare Indians vagrant and enslave them for up to four months. The law extends to Indian children, leading to an epidemic of kidnappings.

January 14, 1850: A group of western businessmen petitions the U.S. Senate Committee on Roads and Canals, requesting the construction of a St. Louis–San Francisco railroad and telegraph line.

April 13, 1850: In response to the many foreigners working in the gold fields, California's legislature enacts the Foreign Miners' Tax, which requires all foreign miners to pay $20 a month for a license. *See* March 14, 1851.

September 9, 1850: As part of the Compromise of 1850, California is admitted to the Union as a free state. Designed to balance the desires of slaveholders and abolitionists, the compromise will include four other legislative measures: New Mexico and Utah will join the Union and decide the slavery question through their legislatures; Texas will be compensated for giving up its claim to lands east of the Rio Grande; Washington, D.C., will outlaw the slave trade; and the passage of the Fugitive Slave Act will be ensured.

October 29, 1850: A grand ball in San Francisco celebrating the admission of California into the Union turns tragic when the steamer *Sagamore* explodes at Central Wharf, killing some 40 people.

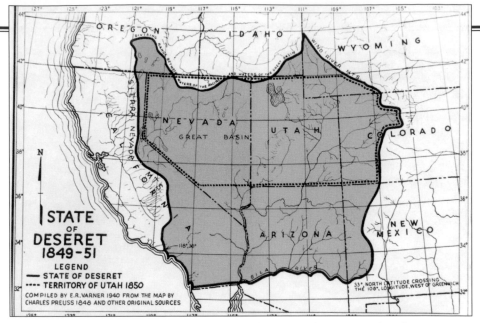

Brief life of Deseret In 1849 Mormon settlers near the Great Salt Lake organized Deseret ("honeybee," from the *Book of Mormon*) as a provisional U.S. state. The area included large parts of present-day Utah, Nevada, California, and Arizona as well as smaller sections of Colorado, New Mexico, Wyoming, Idaho, and Oregon. The provisional state established a legislature, a court system, and laws that served as the only government in the Great Basin for about two years. Deseret was never recognized by the United States government. After the establishment of Utah Territory, with Brigham Young as its first governor, Deseret was dissolved.

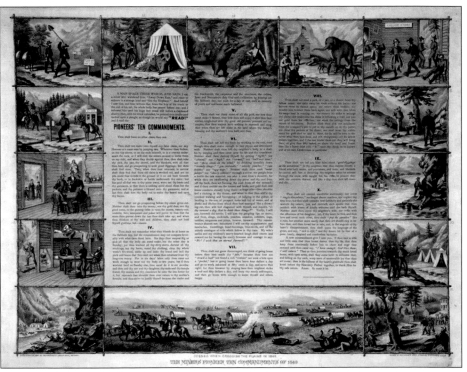

The proverbial elephant Pictured is a romanticized representation of life in the gold fields. Elephants (*top row, second from right*) did not march through the fields, but the phrase "seeing the elephant" was popular. For gold seekers, it meant a man had made it to the gold fields and lived to tell the tale. In the absence of law, miners created their own "Ten Commandments," such as, "Thou shalt not steal a pick, or a shovel, or a pan from thy fellow-miner."

Thousands flock to San Francisco
The sleepy port of Yerba Buena, boasting about 1,000 residents in 1848, was transformed into San Francisco when the Gold Rush began. The forest of masts on abandoned ships visible in this image indicates that many vessels sailed to San Francisco but few left when their crews deserted. By August 1849, the city claimed 6,000 residents, and by December the population reached 25,000. Not only was the city a main entry point for people and goods, but it became the center of financial operations.

Sacramento grows up Near the site of the original gold discovery, Sacramento grew like a mushroom. Sam Brannan established the settlement on the Sacramento River, which offered access to the San Francisco Bay. It soon became the leading supply center for the northern diggings (while Stockton served that purpose for more southerly regions). During the Gold Rush years, men in Sacramento hastily constructed gambling parlors, hotels, banks, and stores, where prices were exorbitantly high. Floods ravaged Sacramento in 1850 and 1852. Construction of a levee system soon commenced, but the town was washed out again in 1862.

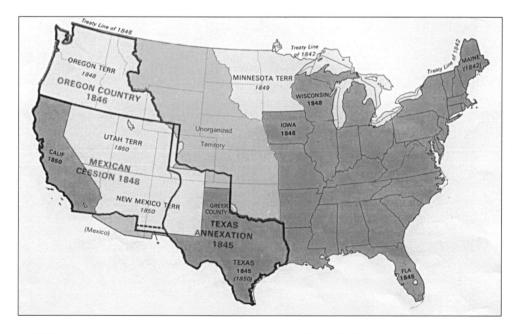

The West's new look From 1840 to 1850, maps of the West changed dramatically. By 1850, the Republic of Texas had become the 28th state, and the U.S. had acquired an enormous amount of land in the Southwest from Mexico by war and treaty. The discovery of gold in California attracted tens of thousands of people to the West Coast. The Compromise of 1850, a major attempt to settle the growing political difficulties between North and South, awarded statehood to California and created the territories of New Mexico and Utah. In addition, the U.S. persuaded Great Britain to relinquish its claims to Oregon Country.

November 6, 1850: President Millard Fillmore decrees that he will reserve the right to possess properties in the San Francisco area for military purposes, including the Presidio, Goat Island, Angel Island, Black Point, and Point San Jose.

1851: As more whites cross the nation, attacks on wagon trains by Plains Indians escalate. In an effort to quell the violence, the U.S. signs the Fort Laramie Treaty of 1851 with Plains tribes, including the Lakota, Crow, Arapaho, Cheyenne, Mandan, and others.

1851: While pursuing a band of Indians suspected of raiding trading posts, frontiersman James Savage becomes the first white man to travel to the Yosemite Valley.

1851: In an effort to put an end to the cruel treatment of Indians in California, U.S. agents negotiate 18 treaties with California tribes, promising 8.5 million acres of reservation lands. *See* 1852.

1851: *Terre Haute Express* editor John Soule pens the famous line: "Go West, young man, and grow up with the country," but the line is somehow credited to *New York Tribune* editor Horace Greeley.

March 14, 1851: The Foreign Miners' Tax is repealed after its passage leads to violence and unrest in mining camps across California. *See* 1852.

May 4, 1851: San Francisco's business district is destroyed in another great conflagration. Eighteen blocks, including 2,000 buildings, go up in flames.

June 22, 1851: The California legislature decides to move the state capital to Vallejo.

November 15, 1851: San Franciscan Sam Brannan lands in the Kingdom of Hawaii but fails to convince King Kamehameha III to give him and his party land for a colony.

Creative engineering Rerouting river channels constituted California's first large-scale civil engineering projects. Carpenters and innovative designers built wooden flumes to redirect watercourses to expose the gravelly streambeds, which boasted immense quantities of placer gold. Once the streambeds were laid bare, pick-and-shovel men dug down six to 10 feet to bedrock to remove the gold-bearing gravels, which then were processed in sluice boxes. This whole process required collective organization, signaling the end of the brief heyday of the individual miner.

Chinese do the dirty work Chinese laborers played a crucial role in the gold mines. They were hard workers who sometimes made substantial sums by reworking gravel beds and providing needed services to miners. Nevertheless, the Chinese struggled to make gains since they often were the victims of legal and informal discrimination. From 1850 to 1882, California passed numerous laws designed to oust the "coolies." Ironically, Chinese workers thrived because they took on work that most white Americans refused to do, such as laundry operations, gardening, and laying rail track.

Boomtowns In the late 1840s, Gold Rush towns grew phenomenally in central California. By 1849 some 40,000 miners swarmed the diggings. Inflation was rampant: Boots fetched up to $40 a pair, and one prostitute claimed she earned $50,000 in 1849. As miner William Swain observed, "it is no unusual sight to see hundreds of dollars staked on the upturning of a certain card." Some boomtowns, like Placerville (*pictured*), became commercial centers and thus survived beyond the initial boom years. Many towns were victims of raging fires, which readily consumed the closely packed wooden structures.

Slaves and freedmen go west Many southern whites brought slaves with them to California. As many as 2,000 African Americans joined the Gold Rush. Some were freedmen—former slaves who had become free—while others remained slaves. The nation at the time was growing nervous over the slavery issue, and slave owners in California were a small minority. One Alabaman lamented, "With twenty good Negroes and the power of managing them as at home, I could make from ten to fifteen thousand dollars per month. But here a fellow has to knock it out with his own fist or not at all." California became a free state in 1850.

December 1851: By the end of the year, California has exported $34,492,000 worth of gold since the rush began.

1852: California politicians successfully lobby Congress to reject a series of treaties signed the previous year, which agreed to provide 8.5 million acres of land to California's Indians.

1852: The Foreign Miners' Tax is reinstated at a rate of $4 per month.

1852: Harriet Beecher Stowe's watershed novel, *Uncle Tom's Cabin*, further polarizes the two sides of the slavery issue.

1852: By the end of the year, U.S. immigration records show that more than 20,000 Chinese have come to San Francisco to make their fortunes in the gold fields.

June 8, 1852: Chinese laborers constructing the Parrott granite building demand more money, kicking off the first known labor strike in San Francisco's history.

November 12, 1852: The infrastructure for the first magnetic telegraph—which eventually will connect San Francisco with San Jose, Stockton, Sacramento, and Marysville—is installed at Montgomery and Merchant streets in San Francisco. *See* October 1, 1853.

December 10, 1852: San Francisco holds its first legal public hanging. José Forner is executed on a gallows on Russian Hill in front of an audience of 10,000 people.

1853: Oregon's Willamette University opens, becoming the first university west of the Rockies.

1853: The first Buddhist temple in the United States, the Kong Chow Temple, opens in San Francisco.

Compromise of 1850 U.S. Senator Henry Clay of Kentucky presents the Compromise of 1850 to Congress. According to the approved deal, California entered the Union as a free state. The U.S. territory of New Mexico, which included Utah and Arizona, was to apply "popular sovereignty" to decide the issue. To appease the South, the compromise provided that federal fugitive slave laws would be firmly enforced in the North, where they often had been ignored. To please Northerners, no more slave auctions were to take place in Washington, D.C., although slavery in the nation's capital would not be interfered with. In addition, Texas received money for relinquishing its claim to land east of the Rio Grande. Not surprisingly, the cobbled-together compromise satisfied few.

Statehood for California In 1849 Californians proudly designed a seal in confident anticipation of statehood, which was granted the next year to the wealthy, booming providence. The grizzly bear in the foreground represented determination and recalled the Bear Flag Revolt of 1846. Seated behind the bear is Minerva, Roman goddess of wisdom. Above Minerva is "EUREKA," Greek for "I have found it!" In the background, a miner works with pick and shovel to uncover gold. The mountains suggest the magnificent Sierra Nevada, source of the spectacular gold strike. The ships indicate the commercial greatness that emerged when San Francisco became a major seaport almost overnight.

New West Coast States

WITH THE TREATY of Cahuenga, signed on January 13, 1847, Mexican authorities in California ceded their territory to the United States. With the Treaty of Guadalupe-Hidalgo, which ended the Mexican War on February 2, 1848, the Mexican government ceded a vast region, which included California, to the U.S.

But what was to become of California? Growing tensions between northern and southern states stirred a seemingly irresolvable debate as to whether to admit California as a slave or free territory. When President James K. Polk, a champion of western expansionism, left office in 1849, he sadly wondered if the U.S. would lose California altogether.

The 1849 Gold Rush drastically changed California's fate. In need of a strong civil government because of a huge influx of settlers, Californians in October 1849 adopted their own state constitution, which prohibited slavery. Congress admitted California as a free state on September 9, 1850.

Questions about the region north of California were resolved during the same period. Back in 1818, the United States and Great Britain had agreed to jointly occupy the huge territory known as Oregon. But in June 1846, shortly after the beginning of the Mexican War, Britain acknowledged U.S. claims to all of Oregon south of the 49th parallel. From this area, the coastal state of Oregon was admitted to the U.S. in 1859. The Oregon Territory also included land that eventually became the states of Washington and Idaho and parts of Montana and Wyoming.

The "Sydney Ducks" Many Australians sought wealth in California, including escaped convicts nicknamed "Sydney Ducks." These criminals populated Sydney Town in San Francisco's Barbary Coast district. Local vigilante mobs (*pictured*) captured, "tried," and hanged several Ducks in 1851. Widely seen as outcasts from a convict colony, the rowdy Aussies were markedly different from Englishmen. Ironically, gold strikes in New South Wales and Victoria in 1851 persuaded many Ducks to return to Australia. Several hundred thousand people from Britain and elsewhere joined them.

Cards, booze, and sex Gambling parlors, saloons, and bordellos abounded in the gold regions and San Francisco. Miners congregated to make or break partnerships, trade stories, spend money, and seek a break from their dirty, backbreaking work. Faro, monte, poker, and other card games offered entertainment as well as a chance to make big money. Hotels rented space to professional gamblers, and wherever gambling took place, liquor was sure to flow in large quantities. Lucius Fairchild, later Wisconsin's governor, wrote: "Gambling, drinking, and *houses of ill fame* are the chief amusements of this country."

1853: Chocolatier Domingo Ghirardelli opens the first retail outlet of his San Francisco-based landmark confectionery.

1853: Mexico and the U.S. reach agreement on the Gadsden Purchase. The U.S. pays $10 million for land along Mexico's northern border.

1853: Congress organizes Washington as a U.S. territory.

October 1, 1853: The California State Telegraph Company line from San Francisco to San Jose is operational, with the line to Marysville slated for completion within the month.

1854: Congress establishes both Nebraska and Kansas as U.S. territories.

1854: Sir George Gore of England leaves Fort Leavenworth on a three-year, 6,000-mile buffalo hunting expedition on the Great Plains. This expedition represents the beginning of the end of the American buffalo herd.

1854: Congress approves the Kansas-Nebraska Act, which allows the two territories to choose whether to allow slaveholding within their borders.

1854: The fledgling Republican Party, which emerged from the fallout of the Kansas-Nebraska Act, declares itself firmly in the abolitionist camp.

February 25, 1854: The California state legislature moves the capital to Sacramento, where it will remain.

June 2, 1854: A lighthouse on Bird Island in the San Francisco Bay is illuminated for the first time.

August 19, 1854: Lakota chief Conquering Bear is killed in Wyoming when U.S. troops meet resistance in the Lakota encampment. They had come to arrest a warrior who shot a calf belonging to a Mormon settler. *See* September 3, 1855.

Chicago begins its boom Potawatomi Indians called the swampy area on which Chicago took shape *Checagou,* which means wild onion or garlic. An 1833 census of Chicago listed about 400 dwellings, five churches, 26 liquor dispensaries, 19 groceries, 17 law offices, and three drugstores. But Chicago grew from its humble origins as a fur trading post into one of the greatest American cities. The city and its hinterlands blossomed during the 1840s, when the Illinois and Michigan Canal made transportation to and from the Great Lakes both cheap and rapid. Here, ships lug cargo along the Chicago River.

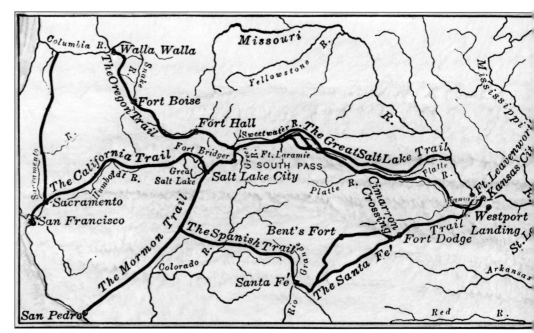

Western trails This map displays several well-known western trails. Most famous is the California–Oregon Trail, which followed the south bank of the Platte River. The Mormon Trail ran generally along the north side of the Platte. The Santa Fe Trail—longest lived of them all—was primarily a military and commercial route from Missouri to New Mexico. Several thousand "Argonauts" took that trail for much of their journey to California. Also visible are portions of the Old Spanish Trail, which ran from New Mexico to California. Some cutoffs are not shown, such as the so-called "Donner Trail" that the unfortunate Donner Party followed to its sad fate in 1846.

White Man's Diseases

As Europeans colonized the New World, they brought with them diseases that ended up killing millions of indigenous people. In some regions, more than 90 percent of the population was wiped out. These "white man's diseases" included measles, mumps, chicken pox, typhoid fever, influenza, dysentery, scarlet fever, diphtheria, hepatitis, cholera, smallpox, and venereal diseases. Although many such infections were seldom fatal for European explorers, Native Americans had no immunity to even a child's disease, such as chicken pox. In the 1840s, white hunters, traders, and emigrants carried these diseases westward across North America.

The deadliest of all was the very contagious smallpox, and its spread among Native Americans might not have been entirely accidental. During the Seven Years' War (1756–1763), many Indians sided with the French against the British. According to several letters, British officers probably attempted to deliberately infect Native Americans with smallpox. In a 1763 letter, the commander-in-chief of British forces in North America, Lord Jeffrey Amherst, inquired whether smallpox could be used to effectively reduce the Native population. In response to Amherst's letter, Colonel Henry Bouquet wrote, "I will try to inoculate the Indians by means of Blankets that may fall in their hands, taking care however not to get the disease myself."

It has been suggested that a similar plan was carried out by the U.S. Army. However, most historians agree that no evidence exists that indicates that smallpox infection was anything more than a tragic accident.

Fort Laramie Treaty The 1851 Fort Laramie Treaty was the first major treaty the United States negotiated with Plains Indians. (The fort, and a nearby camp of Plains Indians, is pictured.) Guaranteeing permanent reservations for the Lakota, Cheyenne, Arapaho, Assiniboine, Arikara, and several other nations, it promised trade goods, annual cash gifts, and government assistance. U.S. negotiators incorrectly assumed they could order tribes to change their ways, stop fighting one another, and avoid harassing westbound emigrants. Never fully ratified, the treaty quickly became a dead letter. Within a decade, the U.S. commenced a series of bloody wars to subjugate Plains Indians.

Trophy scalps "Taking scalps" was part of war craft for many, but not all, North American Natives. Scalps constituted war "trophies" for Native Americans, just as heads or other body parts had throughout European war history. To take a scalp, a knife-wielding warrior kneeled on a downed adversary, snatched a handful of hair in one hand, and slashed off a portion of the scalp with the other hand. In rare instances, victims of scalping survived to tell the tale.

1855: Northern abolitionists form Emigrant Aid Societies to send activists into Kansas to vote the abolitionist side of the ballot. Similar societies with the opposite agenda form in southern states.

1855: Kansans elect a proslavery legislature following an election marred by intimidation and ballot box stuffing on the part of "border ruffians" from neighboring Missouri.

September 3, 1855: In a final act of retribution for the incident that began when an Indian killed a cow, U.S. Army General William Harney directs hundreds of troops in a massacre of an entire Indian village in Ash Hollow, Nebraska.

January 4, 1856: A law is passed requiring postage stamps on all letters handled by the postal service.

May 24, 1856: Abolitionist John Brown leads a night raid on proslavery settlers at Potawatomi Creek, Kansas, killing five men. Proslavery settlers retaliate by rioting in Lawrence, Kansas, killing one.

June 17, 1856: Explorer and military officer John Frémont declares himself the first Republican candidate for the presidency. He promises to end polygamy and slavery.

1857: President James Buchanan sends U.S. troops to Utah to enforce the federal law prohibiting polygamy. Buchanan also fears a Mormon theocracy and Mormon rebellion against the U.S.

1857: The Lecompton Constitution is drafted, making Kansas a slave state. Abolitionists boycott this election, and convince the acting governor of Kansas to convene a special session of the legislature. In this session, a second vote decisively rejects the Lecompton Constitution.

Fires ravage San Francisco The Great Fire of 1851 was the fifth big blaze that devastated San Francisco in its early years. Hastily erected wood and canvas buildings were reduced to ashes by untended flames, and many brick and iron structures were destroyed as well. The May 4 fire engulfed at least 1,500 houses. In the wake of the fires, rents skyrocketed, as did the costs of building materials. After several disastrous conflagrations, city leaders chose a phoenix—the mythic Greek bird of rebirth—to adorn the city's official seal.

Women bring stability to camps Women and children were a rarity among the initial wave of Gold Rushers bound for California. In the following years, however, their presence grew, and they were considered a "civilizing" influence on the rowdy, male-dominated mining camps. Some women worked as "soiled doves" (prostitutes), but many others helped to build communities that resembled those the miners had left behind. By the mid-1850s, family life began to stabilize. Towns matured, and the wild days of the Gold Rush became a memory.

Digging deep for gold

Hard-rock mining rapidly supplanted placer mining at the California gold diggings. While individuals had found bits of gold in stream gravel, the veins of gold that lay in quartz deposits called for a different method. Beginning in the early 1850s, companies employed miners to work underground. Large numbers of men dug shafts deep in the earth. Immense amounts of ore were excavated, crushed, and refined with vast quantities of mercury used to separate the gold. Though lucrative, underground mining was difficult and dangerous. Lanterns near a gas leak could cause an explosion, and hill collapses could bury miners alive.

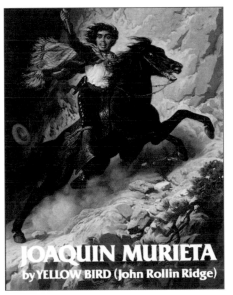

The legend of Joaquin Murieta

Anglo-Americans in California vehemently disdained Mexicans and abused Hispanos, whose lands they invaded and overran. To Hispanos, a bandit named Joaquin Murieta was a heroic avenger, and a mythology sprang up around him that resembled that of Billy the Kid. California Governor John Bigler assembled a team of California Rangers to track down Murieta in 1853. The Rangers killed a man said to be Murieta, but many Hispanos claimed that the "real" Joaquin Murieta escaped. To Hispanos, the story perpetuated a spirit of resistance in the face of overwhelming numbers of white men in California.

Blasting the hillsides

Hydraulic mining represented a major shift in mining tactics. Engineers designed flumes and water-containment structures that generated great pressure. Water was fed through heavy hoses to teams of men, who blasted rock and dirt out of hillsides and into processing structures, where gold was recovered. Vast amounts of waste flowed down the rivers. This highly productive form of mining had its drawbacks. Thousands of miners lost their jobs, and hydraulic operations fell under the control of a few San Francisco capitalists. Hydraulic mining continued unabated from 1852 until 1883, when public outcry over the destruction of downstream farmlands led to laws prohibiting the practice.

1849-1860

March 1857: In *Dred Scott v. Sandford*, the U.S. Supreme Court declares that the U.S. territories cannot prohibit slavery and that blacks—even free blacks—do not have constitutional rights.

April 29, 1857: The U.S. Army's Division of the Pacific establishes its permanent headquarters at San Francisco's Presidio.

August 1857: The Fancher Party, emigrants from Arkansas and Missouri en route to California, arrives in Salt Lake City.

September 7, 1857: The Fancher Party is attacked by Paiute Indians working in concert with Mormon militiamen. The Fancher Party gains a defensive position, and spends the next five days under siege.

September 11, 1857: The Mormons negotiate a surrender with the Fancher Party, offering safe passage. The emigrants agree and lay down their weapons, only to be slaughtered by the Mormons in what is called the Mountain Meadows Massacre. *See* 1871.

1858: The first nonstop stagecoach arrives in Los Angeles, California, from St. Louis, Missouri.

1858: The "Mormon War" ends with a federal pardon for the Mormons' violation of federal polygamy law.

May 11, 1858: Minnesota is admitted as the 32nd state in the Union.

1859: The Pikes Peak gold rush is sparked when gold is discovered in Boulder Canyon, Colorado. Some 100,000 fortune seekers will converge on the Rocky Mountain canyon.

1859: A Wyandotte, Kansas, convention results in consensus and a new constitution, which makes Kansas a free state. Although voters overwhelmingly approve the new constitution, it is delayed in Congress by proslavery southern legislators.

Rigged elections in Kansas Missouri "border ruffians" cast their votes—in Kansas Territory—before receiving a free drink of whiskey. In November 1854, Kansans held an election for a congressional delegate. In response, thousands of armed proslavery men from Missouri poured over the border and voted for a candidate who shared their views. Half of the ballots were cast by nonresidents, and the proslavery candidate won. On March 30, 1855, votes by out-of-staters helped elect proslavery members to the Kansas territorial legislature. Abolitionists responded by establishing the Free State legislature in Topeka. The opposing factions clashed until 1861, when southern states seceded and Kansas joined the Union as a free state.

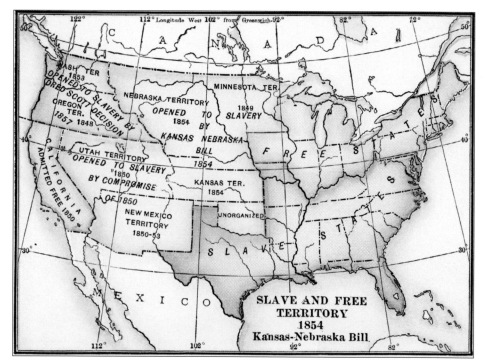

A nation divided This map illustrates free and slave territories within the United States. The date "1854" at the bottom of the map is misleading. The Oregon Territory bears the legend "Opened To Slavery By Dred Scott Decision," which the Supreme Court handed down in 1857. That case, decided by a court dominated by Southerners, had the effect of "nationalizing" slavery. Negating the Missouri Compromise of 1820, it guaranteed all citizens the right to take their "property" (i.e., slaves) wherever they wished. The court's decision horrified the North, greatly inflaming militant abolitionists.

The Camel Corps Beginning in 1856, 74 imported camels were led to a special stable at Camp Verde, Texas. The innovative secretary of war, Jefferson Davis, was convinced that these desert beasts could provide superior service as Army pack animals along the vast distances of the arid Southwest. But even though the camels proved useful, the Army abandoned the experiment before the Civil War. The animals proved to be too aggressive, and their soft feet couldn't handle rocky terrain. Most of the camels were auctioned off, while others lived wild in the Texas desert until century's end.

Kidnapped by Indians Olive Oatman (born in 1838) was one of two sisters captured by Yavapai Indians in 1851 while their Mormon family was crossing the desert near modern-day Yuma, Arizona. The Yavapai hunted and farmed in the Arizona-California desert region, and were not a particularly warlike people. The Yavapai traded Olive and her sister, Mary Ann, to the Mohave Nation. At that time, the sisters were given tattoos on their chins marking them as slaves. Mary Ann died of starvation, but Olive was redeemed from captivity in 1856. She eventually married. Whites often characterized Natives' captives as "slaves" who endured horrible suffering or were raped, but Oatman said the Indians "never offered the least unchaste abuse to me."

Mountain Meadows Massacre In September 1857, the Fancher Party from Arkansas passed through Utah en route to California. Mormon fears of a U.S. Army invasion were at a high pitch that summer, and many Mormons believed that the Fancher Party included men who recently had murdered a prominent Mormon in Arkansas. Possibly encouraged by Mormon leader Brigham Young, 70 or 80 militiamen and a few Paiute Natives besieged the wagon train. A few days later, the overlanders surrendered. The Mormon militiamen then murdered about 120 men, women, and children in Mountain Meadows. They spared 17 children deemed too young to be killed. The Mountain Meadows Massacre remains the most troubling event in Mormon history.

1859: Prospectors at the Comstock Lode in Nevada discover silver, spurring rapid development in nearby Virginia City.

1859: U.S. immigration rates have surged this past decade; 2.5 million foreign nationals (including 66,000 Chinese) have entered the U.S.

1859: Hudson River School painter Albert Bierstadt travels through the American West for the first time.

February 14, 1859: Oregon enters the union as the 33rd state—and a free state.

October 16, 1859: Attempting to incite an antislavery revolution in the South, abolitionist John Brown and several followers seize the U.S. arsenal at Harper's Ferry, Virginia, but are unable to hold it. Brown will hang for treason.

1860: President Buchanan vetoes a homestead bill designed to provide grants to settlers in the West. Buchanan's veto divides his Democratic Party.

1860: Republican upstart Abraham Lincoln is elected president on a pro-homestead legislation/antislavery platform.

1860: Some 30,000 settlers leave Kansas in the wake of a killer drought.

1860: According to the U.S. census, about half of the nation's 31 million people live west of the Appalachian Mountains.

April 14, 1860: The first Pony Express delivery completes its 1,966-mile journey from St. Joseph to Sacramento in 11 days.

October 8, 1860: A telegraph line is opened from Los Angeles to San Francisco.

December 20, 1860: South Carolina becomes the first state to secede from the Union.

Miller paints the West In 1837 Alfred Jacob Miller left his New Orleans studio to journey with an American Fur Company trade caravan—a group that traveled along the Oregon Trail to the 1837 Rendezvous in Green River, Wyoming. Miller became the first American artist to see and paint such landmarks as Fort Laramie, Chimney Rock, Scott's Bluff, and Independence Rock. At the weeks-long Rendezvous, he sketched trappers at work, Native Americans, wrestling, horse racing, and other scenes from the colorful pageantry of the Rendezvous. Ultimately, Miller finished more than 400 works that depicted a rapidly vanishing way of life.

Indians journey to Washington Pawnee, Ponca, Potawatomi, and Chippewa Indians pose in front of the White House in 1857 or '58. Native diplomats often paid visits to the "Great Father" in Washington, D.C. Sometimes such visits took place when tribal leaders sought confirmation of treaty rights. Other times Indian agents persuaded selected Indians to tour the nation in hopes they would be awed by the power and numbers of whites, and would then more willingly accept policies dictated from afar. Too often, the parties to such meetings worked at cross-purposes, and only rarely did these conferences significantly affect policy.

Douglas's Master Plan

Two-term U.S. Senator Stephen Douglas of Illinois badly wanted to be president. In 1854, hoping to secure his candidacy, Douglas found an opportunity to benefit Illinois and Chicago, where he owned considerable property, and enhance his bid for the White House. His master plan relied on the success of his proposed Kansas-Nebraska bill.

At the time, Kansas and Nebraska were not U.S. territories, and Congress refrained from making them such since to do so would invite the slavery question for each territory—a hot-button topic that congressmen were afraid to touch. Douglas, however, argued that "popular sovereignty" (the "people's will"), and not Congress, should determine slavery's future in Kansas and Nebraska.

Ignoring the 1820 Missouri Compromise, which prohibited slavery north of the 36°-30′ border of the Arkansas Territory (excluding Missouri), the 1854 Kansas-Nebraska Act allowed men in Nebraska and Kansas to allow or eliminate slavery before petitioning for statehood. Douglas hoped they would not vote for slavery, but his main objective was to help Kansas and Nebraska become U.S. territories and then states regard-

Stephen Douglas

less of how they voted. This would lead to railroads through Nebraska and Kansas, which could greatly benefit Chicago economically. Thus, by letting "the people" decide, Douglas thought he could win over American citizens with his support of popular sovereignty, claim an economic victory for Illinois, improve his personal financial situation due to a railroad hub in Chicago, and—perhaps— win the 1856 presidential election.

However, anarchy, murder, and voting irregularities in "Bleeding Kansas" quickly exposed Douglas's faulty reasoning. Proslavery and antislavery factions established competing territorial governments, and a shooting war began in 1856. Nebraska, meanwhile, fell under the control of Free Soilers, who had little affection for black people but who strongly opposed slavery.

As Kansas bled, Douglas's dreams withered. Despised in the North and South alike for his popular sovereignty plan, Douglas watched angry crowds burn him in effigy from his train window while he traveled from Washington, D.C., to Illinois. Though he ran in the North as a Democratic nominee in 1860, Republican Abraham Lincoln won the presidency, garnering 180 electoral votes to Douglas's 12.

FORCING SLAVERY DOWN THE THROAT OF A FREESOILER

Power of the press This inflammatory newspaper cartoon from 1856 depicts several famous politicians: Senator Stephen Douglas, former President Franklin Pierce, future President James Buchanan, and Lewis Cass, Michigan's territorial governor. They are portrayed as proslavery politicians bent on forcing slavery on the entire nation. Newspapers and magazines kept important issues before the American voters, and satirical editorial cartoons helped shape public opinion. Many newspaper editors were unabashedly partisan and closely allied with particular political parties.

Massacre in Kansas The Marais des Cygnes Massacre in May 1858 occurred in Kansas two years after John Brown's 1856 Potawatomi Massacre. Like the other violence in "Bleeding Kansas," this event involved proslavery and antislavery men willing to kill to attain political goals. In this somewhat exaggerated image, proslavery men murder five Free Soilers. Though the number of killings did not rise above a hundred or so, the violence in Kansas produced grave fears in every state north and south. It also presaged the far greater slaughter and devastation to come in the Civil War.

Nevada Gold Rush Ten years after the '49er Gold Rush, another bonanza, the Comstock Lode, was discovered on the eastern side of the Sierra Nevada Mountains. The incredible wealth of gold and silver produced by the Comstock mines was the principal factor in awarding territorial status to Nevada in 1861, and statehood three years later. Virginia City (*pictured*), the boomtown at the center of the mining district, experienced spectacular growth. The city's population exceeded 25,000, and the hotels, restaurants, saloons, opera houses—and brothels—rivaled those of San Francisco.

Gold in Colorado A group of '59ers works gold diggings in Colorado. Paydirt was found at the foot of the Rocky Mountains in 1858, and the next year thousands of prospectors swarmed to the region. Central City, Black Hawk, Denver City, and other ramshackle towns boomed. "Pikes Peak or Bust" was a popular slogan, and for years other strikes were made, most spectacularly at Cripple Creek in 1890. Denver experienced impressive growth as a supply center, becoming one of the premier cities of the West. Colorado achieved statehood in 1876, and Denver became the state capital.

> "Old John Brown drew his revolver and shot the old man Doyle in the forehead, and Brown's two youngest sons immediately fell upon the younger Doyles with their short two-edged swords."
>
> —JAMES TOWNSLEY, DESCRIBING THE BEGINNING OF THE POTAWATOMI CREEK MASSACRE IN MAY 1856

John Brown and "Bleeding Kansas"

John Brown

JOHN BROWN WAS probably slightly deranged, but no American worked more zealously to end the "peculiar institution" of slavery. Brown's father was a New England abolitionist, and his mother died when John was a boy. Deeply religious, Brown became a drifter who left a trail of failed business ventures. As an impassioned abolitionist, however, he helped slaves flee from bondage on the Underground Railroad, and established a short-lived experimental colony for free blacks in New York's Adirondack Mountains.

By the time Congress passed the Kansas-Nebraska Act in 1854, Brown believed that God had chosen him to end slavery. Free Soilers rapidly dominated Nebraska, preserving it from slavery. But Kansas lay next to Missouri, a slave state, and it seemed that slavery would spread to Kansas. Many Northerners grew angry when what they perceived as a spineless Congress and president, the "dough-faced" James Buchanan, took no preventive action.

Brown and several of his sons traveled to Kansas, where they brutally murdered five proslavery men in the "Potawatomi Massacre." Numerous abolitionists shared Brown's belief that Kansas must not be sacrificed to fuel slavery's expansion. If some Americans balked at outright murder, others did not, and heavily armed proslavery and antislavery men swarmed into Kansas. In a dress rehearsal for the coming Civil War, Kansas started "bleeding" in 1856.

Even ministers supported the guerrilla warfare led by John Brown. Reverend Henry Ward Beecher, an East Coast abolitionist, shipped dozens of Sharps rifles to Kansas, where they were dubbed "Beecher's Bibles." Federal troops quelled most of the violence in "Bleeding Kansas" by 1857, but they were powerless to defuse the nation's looming "irrepressible conflict."

Departing Kansas in 1858, Brown laid plans to capture a federal arsenal and foment a slave rebellion at Harper's Ferry in western Virginia. Though it failed and Brown died on the gallows, many Northerners celebrated him as a martyr. Brown's hanging galvanized thousands to oppose slavery at all costs. In January 1861, Kansas joined the Union as a free state. Three months later, the Civil War began.

Brown's raid on Harper's Ferry Fanatical abolitionist John Brown, who was responsible for the 1856 murders of five proslavery settlers in "Bleeding Kansas," developed a wild scheme to arm and liberate southern slaves. To initiate his slave uprising, Brown led 17 followers into unsuspecting Harper's Ferry, Virginia, on October 16, 1859. They seized the federal arsenal and a nearby rifle manufactory. Although Brown held 11 hostages, the arsenal was assaulted by federal troops led by Lieutenant J.E.B. Stuart. Brown was wounded and 10 of his followers, including two of his sons, were killed. Rapidly tried and hanged for treason, Brown became a martyr throughout the North.

Other Gold Rushes

THOUGH THE DISCOVERY of gold in California drew the largest number of people and ultimately proved to be the most prosperous strike, it was just one of many gold rushes in the West during the mid-19th century. In 1858, for example, 30,000 fortune seekers made their way to British Columbia.

The following year, rumors of bountiful gold deposits near Pikes Peak drew thousands to Colorado, while Henry Comstock's discovery in the Sierra Nevada Mountains created a near frenzy, sending a wave of migrants scrambling back toward the California border. In the early 1860s, strikes in the future states of Idaho and Montana enticed an estimated 25,000 to the Boise basin. Another 10,000 to 15,000 headed to the Montana towns of Bannack and Virginia City, east of the Bitterroot Mountains.

The various discoveries did not all pan out. People who crossed the Canadian border to look for gold along the Fraser River had to purchase a permit from the local authorities and then forge their way up the steep forested canyons. Most turned back, broken and discouraged. In Colorado, the rumors of gold proved more prevalent than the metal itself. On the other hand, the Comstock Lode and the discoveries in Idaho and Montana were bountiful enough, but the sheer competition for a claim practically extinguished one's chances of striking it rich.

Pine Creek in Colorado

Besides failure and ruin, the gold rushes also gave rise to "boomtowns" that festered with vice and crime. Boredom, greed, frustration, and/or heavy drinking drove many disgruntled miners to violence. Outside the towns of Bannack and Virginia City, organized gangs patrolled the roads, ambushing unsuspecting prospectors. The lawlessness, along with the influx of people that came with the western gold rushes, forced federal lawmakers to create new territorial governments in Colorado, Nevada, Idaho, and Montana.

Wells, Fargo wagons Henry Wells and William Fargo, along with other experienced expressmen, organized Wells, Fargo & Co. in 1852 to capitalize on express and banking opportunities in California. The first Wells, Fargo office opened in San Francisco, and the efficient company soon began buying smaller express operations. By 1860 the company boasted 147 offices and a network of stagecoach lines, as well as express riders who delivered packages wherever needed. The company realized great profits in handling gold dust.

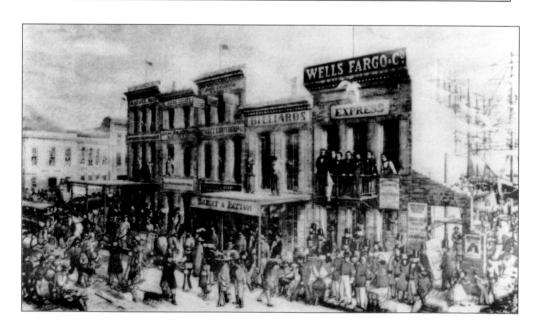

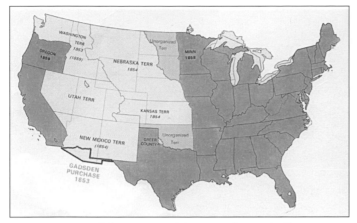

Prewar map of the West This map of 1860 indicates important developments in the West related to the Civil War. To facilitate a southerly railroad route to California, southern politicians engineered the Gadsden Purchase, acquiring the land from Mexico in 1853. But northern politicians lobbied for a northerly route, and the resulting stalemate delayed the transcontinental railroad until the Civil War, when Northerners had Congress to themselves. Meanwhile, in creating Kansas and Nebraska territories, the Kansas-Nebraska Act of 1854 violated the Missouri Compromise of 1820. This enraged the North and led to the creation of the Republican Party.

The "Queen City" Cincinnati, located on the Ohio River, was one of the most important inland ports of 19th century mid-America. Hundreds of flatboats, barges, and (later) steamers cruised up and down the Ohio and Mississippi rivers loaded with farm produce, livestock, hemp, and other commodities. Cincinnati's population grew from 4,000 in 1813 to 115,000 in 1850, making it the sixth largest city in America. Land speculation, urban development, manufacturing, and banking all flourished in a "wildcat" atmosphere that sometimes resulted in fiscal crashes and heavy losses. Meanwhile, the "Queen City" boasted such cultural resources as colleges and theaters.

Surveyors' risky work In 1853 Congress appropriated $150,000 to find a railway route between the Mississippi River and the Pacific. No maps existed for most of that area, so surveyors often doubled as explorers. David Dodge and Peter Dey laid out the Union Pacific route; Theodore Judah headed up the western team. In the Sierra Nevadas, surveyors found themselves working above drops as terrifying as 1,500 feet. On cliffs such as this, they tied themselves to long ropes that looped around trees above and were anchored by other men. Everywhere, surveying was dangerous work. Surveyors died from falls, natural hardships, and Indian attacks.

The 1860 presidential election The Republican Party, a northern-based, antislavery coalition, was organized in 1854 to challenge the Democratic Party, which was dominated by southern politicians. The 1860 Republican convention was held in Chicago, where Illinois lawyer and politician Abraham Lincoln was named the party's presidential candidate. The Democrats convened in Charleston, South Carolina, a hotbed of secessionist sentiment. But the leading Democratic candidate was a Northerner, Illinois Senator Stephen Douglas, and the convention disintegrated. The Republicans, as the only united party, commanded a large electoral majority. Six weeks after Lincoln's election, South Carolina voted to secede from the Union.

Civil Wars and the Railroads
∽1861-1876∾

I N THE FALL OF 1864, a different kind of civil war came to the Cheyenne Indians of eastern Colorado. On November 29, violence between Native Americans and white soldiers exploded in ways every bit as bloody, brutal, and tragic as any fight between Confederate and Union troops. Alongside the banks of Sand Creek, Cheyenne Chief Black Kettle camped with his followers as well as Arapaho Indians. Most of the men of the camp were away on a hunting expedition that day. Women and children stayed behind, and Black Kettle flew the American flag over his people. It did not do them any good.

A colonel in the Colorado militia, a former Methodist minister and anti-slavery activist named John Milton Chivington, wanted to enhance his reputation as an Indian fighter. Tensions in Colorado between the Cheyenne and settlers were at an all-time high, with many indiscriminate killings of both whites and Natives. Chivington arrived at the banks of Sand Creek that day with a distinguished military record. At the 1862 Battle of Glorieta Pass in New Mexico—the Civil War's most important western battle—Chivington defeated Confederate forces who had come west from Texas. This victory held the Santa Fe Trail and the Southwest for the Union. At Sand Creek more than two years later, Chivington envisioned more glory. With the 700 men

The federal government, the railroads, and individuals all worked in consort to populate the American West. The government granted western land to companies in exchange for laying the tracks, and the railroads sold the land cheaply to settlers who were eager for a fresh start.

"There are 10 spikes to a rail, 400 rails to a mile, 1,800 miles to San Francisco—21,000,000 times those sledges to be swung: 21,000,000 times are they to come down with their sharp punctuation before the great work of modern America is complete."

—DR. WILLIAM A. BELL, IN AN 1866 NEWSPAPER ARTICLE ABOUT THE TRANSCONTINENTAL RAILROAD

under his command, he marched the Third Colorado Regiment to Sand Creek from Fort Lyon, about 40 miles away, and prepared to wage war on a cold autumn day.

At dawn, and within sight of Black Kettle's American flag waving over the Indian camp, Chivington ordered his men to attack. The Cheyenne and their Arapaho friends never had a chance. Chivington's men killed more than 130 men, women, and children, many of whom they mutilated after death. Indian body parts were displayed in public in Denver. Despite the horrors of the massacre, many people in Colorado sided with Chivington. A newspaper editorial in Denver insisted that the men under Chivington's command "all acquitted themselves well, and Colorado soldiers have again covered themselves with glory."

But word of exactly what happened at Sand Creek leaked out. The U.S. Army ordered an investigation. "It is difficult to believe," the investigative panel later reported, "that beings in the form of men could commit or countenance the commission of such acts of cruelty and barbarity." Chivington blamed a subordinate for insisting that the Indians were hostile. The slaughter ruined Chivington's military career, although he did not go to prison for it.

After the Sand Creek Massacre (*pictured*), perpetrators brought scalps and body parts of the dead Indians to Denver's Apollo Theater for display. Vengeful Cheyenne "Dog Soldiers" responded by killing scores of white settlers in the region.

The Chivington massacre reminds us that the battle of North and South wasn't the only "civil war" that plagued America in the 19th century.

Robert E. Lee's 1865 surrender and the close of the Civil War had an ironic impact in the American West, as the end of one war coincided with the acceleration of another. Despite the misplaced optimism of some whites that a peace might be hammered out between the United States and those Native Americans who violently resisted encroachment by settlers, miners, and others, the end of the sectional conflict ushered in a period of renewed warfare in the West. Once Ulysses S. Grant accepted Lee's surrender, the United States was generally more free to send soldiers out to western forts, where they engaged in battles with the last bands of Native Americans not yet forced onto reservations.

Yet the end of the Civil War also ushered in a period of remarkable progress and growth in the West, at least in some parts and for some people. Not since the days of the California Gold Rush had the West seen such rapid and deep changes. In the years following the Civil War, thousands of miles of new railroad lines crisscrossed western spaces. Cities grew up almost overnight, and millions of people journeyed as tourists and settlers to this vast region of the nation. The American West came of age in the decades following the Civil War, but it did so at a high price.

When the war ended, the nation looked to the West as a place to heal the national wounds of warfare. And once the nation looked west, it went west: by rail, by ship, on horseback, and on foot. In the process, new Westerners, and those who were already there, began the complicated processes of remaking the nation.

Even though the Civil War had shattered the country and left hundreds of thousands of Americans dead and wounded, Americans still believed in the promise of the nation. For many, this meant continued faith in the land and farming. With the war over, and with railroad expansion increasing with each passing year, Americans again looked to the West as the place where national destiny could work itself out on territory much less bloodied by the war. The Civil War did not kill Thomas Jefferson's vision of a nation of small farmers tending the soil and living lives of virtuous citizenship, but it did push that vision westward.

In the late 1860s, both the Central Pacific Railroad Company (heading eastward from California) and the Union Pacific Railroad Company worked at a furious pace to complete the transcontinental railroad. On April 28, 1869, Central Pacific workers set a still-standing record by laying 10 miles and 56 feet of track in one day.

The federal government shared in this vision. In 1862 Congress passed the Homestead Act, a major revision to the Land Ordinance of 1785. The new legislation enticed Americans to move to the Great Plains. The Homestead Act allowed settlers to claim western (or other) lands, up to 160 acres. After five years, the land would become theirs. All settlers had to do was to make the requisite improvements to the land, build structures, and pay a total of $18 in fees.

Never before had the United States government flatly given away land for only a filing fee, as it began doing on January 1, 1863. The act is in many ways the perfect symbol of the 19th century American faith in farming, land ownership, and the American West. American men and women answered the challenge put to them by the Homestead Act. New migrants to the West filed their claims under the act. Claimants had to be heads of families or at least 21 years old, citizens or naturalized citizens, and those who had not served in the Confederate military or who had ever "borne arms against the United States Government or given aid and comfort to its enemies."

Hand in hand with reforms in landholding came new railroad legislation. With the Civil War over, the nation not only looked west, it built west. The Pacific Railroad Act of 1862 jump-started the engine of rail development by bringing the United States directly into the railroad business. The act authorized Congress to help pay for a transcontinental railroad "from the Missouri River to the Pacific Ocean." Federal assistance came in the shape of federal loans and generous grants of land to the rail companies building the railroad. As the war dragged on, and northern and southern soldiers killed one another by the thousands, the nation began to invest more and more hope in railroad technology, almost as if the railroad being built across the belly of the nation could be a giant suture tying the wounded country back together.

The transcontinental railroad project started off fairly modestly in the far West. Four Gold Rush migrants to California, together with a visionary civil engineer, figured that they could start a railroad company that would build the western leg of a transcontinental railroad. These four men eventually would be called the Big Four. But in 1863, the year they began construction in Sacramento, California, they were known for other things.

Leland Stanford had journeyed to California to find a treasure of gold, but instead struck it rich in merchandising. Riding the wave of Republican Party politics that swept Abraham Lincoln into the presidency, Stanford became governor of California. Partnering with him in the Central Pacific Railroad venture were Mark Hopkins and Collis Huntington, two men who had become rich in the hardware business in Sacramento, and Charles Crocker, another New Yorker. Theodore Judah, a brilliant engineer, offered the technical know-how. It was Judah who believed that a railroad could be built across the rugged Sierra Nevada Mountains, that same range that had spelled disaster for the Donner Party back in 1847.

For six years, the Central Pacific, employing thousands of Chinese laborers, built tracks eastward from California, while the Union Pacific laid its own track westward from Omaha. No one knew quite where the two lines would meet (at several points, it even looked as if they might miss one another). The two companies laid track as fast as possible, since each additional mile meant more in federal loans and grants of land.

The Central Pacific's Chinese workers proved extremely valuable to the project. Railroad executives put them into the most dangerous situations in

This Union Pacific Railroad advertisement announces the completion of the transcontinental railroad—and all the advantages that will come with it. It promises a trip from Omaha to San Francisco in fewer than four days, connections to other destinations (including gold mines), and luxurious accommodations along the way.

the Sierra Nevada Mountains (although all railroad construction was dangerous), and Chinese workers handled much of the explosive work needed to blast a rail route through rock. And though rail officials admired the work the Chinese performed, they essentially considered these workers expendable. They paid them less than other workers, and they insisted that the numbers of Chinese workers grow with each year of construction.

In the spring of 1869, at a lonely spot in northwestern Utah, the tracks of the Union Pacific and Central Pacific met. Officials from both railroad corporations, as well as assorted dignitaries and politicians, gathered to celebrate the event. The transcontinental rail project, an engineering marvel of the 19th century, was finished! "This railroad unites the two great oceans of the world," declared one of the speakers that day.

Tied to the celebration by telegraph wires, the nation joined in the excitement. In fact, the completion of the transcontinental railroad was the first simultaneously experienced event in American history. Photographers recorded the scene for posterity, twice. One set of photographs included the Chinese workers who had been so instrumental in laying track through inhospitable western terrain; the "official" photographs of the event show only white workers and railroad executives.

Only several feet wide, the railroad nonetheless changed forever the western landscape and the lives of the people living on it. Once the transcontinental project provided the key link, other railroad lines began to push into western territory. With that growth came fat governmental grants of land to western railroad companies—an outlay that eventually would amount to well over 100 million acres of land. The post-Civil War Congress provided to railroads nearly as much land as it gave to actual settlers. The railroads subsequently sold much of the land to developers and aspiring settlers.

After the Civil War, huge numbers of Americans moved west thanks largely to the Homestead Act. By the end of the 19th century, those taking advantage of the act filed roughly 600,000 claims for more than 80 million acres of western land.

Thanks largely to the Homestead Act and the transcontinental railroad, state populations boomed in the West. From 1860 to 1880, South Dakota's population soared from 4,837 to 98,268, Nebraska's shot from 28,841 to 452,402, and that of Kansas jumped from 107,206 to 996,096—a figure greater than the populations of 11 East Coast states. This phenomenal growth would alter the face of America forever.

1861: As Congress seeks to exert more control over the West, hoping to bring the new states into the Union fold, Colorado and Nevada are organized as territories—as is Dakota Territory.

1861: Texas Governor Sam Houston, a Unionist, is forced from his office when his beloved state sides with the Confederacy.

January 1861: South Carolina calls a state convention, and delegates vote to secede from the Union. Mississippi, Florida, Alabama, Georgia, Louisiana, Texas, Virginia, Arkansas, Tennessee, and North Carolina will soon follow.

January 29, 1861: After years of bitter divisiveness over the slavery issue, Kansas is admitted to the Union as a free state.

February 1861: The South creates the Confederate Constitution and names Jefferson Davis provisional president of the Confederacy.

March 4, 1861: Abraham Lincoln is inaugurated as U.S. president. He claims that while he has no plans to end slavery in existing slave states, he will not permit those states to secede from the Union.

April 12, 1861: The Civil War begins with the Confederate assault on Fort Sumter, South Carolina.

May 1861: More than a month after the attack on Fort Sumter, the news of the Civil War reaches California, which promptly sides with the Union.

June 1861: West Virginia is born when it splits off from Virginia in disagreement over Virginia's decision to join the Confederacy.

June 1861: Missouri, Kentucky, Maryland, and Delaware decide not to secede, despite the fact that all are slave states.

The Pony Express A Pony Express rider waves his hat at telegraph construction workers. In 1860 business mail began to be carried back and forth from California by courageous relay riders of the colorful Pony Express, founded by Kansas-based business partners William Russell, Alexander Majors, and William Waddell. The company placed 157 relay stations at intervals of 20 miles or less along the 1,840-mile route. The 80 youthful riders were each assigned a 75-mile route to ride back and forth, east and west. But when the coast-to-coast telegraph line was completed in October 1861, the Pony Express was rendered obsolete.

The "promised land" *Westward the Course of Empire Takes Its Way* (1861), by painter Emanuel Leutze, boldly proclaims some of the most important themes in the much-celebrated westward movement. Visible are suggestions of an Old Testament Moses leading people to the "promised land." Meanwhile, sublime nature—beautiful but perilous—is a barrier surmounted by hardy Americans surging into the "Great West" to civilize it and wrest it from the grip of unworthy Indians. Gazing into California, a mystical land that promises a rich, providentially ordained future, the haggard but persevering overlanders believe their trials will soon be over. Congress commissioned this painting for a mural in the U.S. Capitol.

"Crazy Judah"

Theodore Judah, who was dubbed "Crazy Judah" because he kept insisting that a transcontinental railroad could be built, proved his point by finding a route across the Sierra Nevadas. In 1861 Judah presented California financiers with surveys and maps. He became a partner in the Central Pacific, but was shut out when he objected to some of the Big Four's decisions and their financial manipulations. On his way back east to find backers who would help him buy out the Central Pacific, Judah fell ill, probably from yellow fever or typhoid contracted in Panama. He died in 1863, a few days after reaching New York.

Baylor and the Texas Mounted Rifles

When Texas became a Confederate State in February 1861, a lawyer, farmer, and Indian fighter named John Baylor (*pictured*) worried about Union troops still stationed there. To meet any threat from them, Baylor secretly formed a militia that became known as the Texas Mounted Rifles. When Texan Union troops proved to be of no threat to the Confederacy, Baylor turned his attention elsewhere. The Texas Mounted Rifles, after being accepted for Confederate service, easily invaded southern New Mexico, which in August 1861 became the Confederate Territory of Arizona. Colonel Baylor served as that territory's first and only governor.

Denver emerges Destined to become the largest city between St. Louis and the Pacific coast, Denver began in 1858 as a prospector's camp along the eastern slope of the Rocky Mountains. Word of a gold strike brought a rush of "'59ers" to the growing encampment. In the 1860s, miners brought gold dust into Denver banks, and the town became a trade center. Although the first transcontinental railroad missed Denver by more than 100 miles, a board of trade aggressively obtained other rail connections to secure the city's future.

Cochise's rampage Cochise, a legendary war chief of the Chiricahua Apache, concentrated his warfare against Mexicans south of the border—until 1861. That year, American authorities falsely accused him of kidnapping and attempted to arrest him while under a flag of truce. Cochise escaped, and after further provocations he killed several hostages. Six Apache captives were hanged in retaliation. Cochise launched a vicious hit-and-run warfare campaign against Anglos, which lasted for a decade. When the great chief died, apparently of cancer, his body was interred in a secret place in his beloved Chiricahua Mountains.

October 24, 1861: The transcontinental telegraph line is completed at Fort Bridger in the Utah Territory, heralding the end of the Pony Express. The first transcontinental telegram carries a message from Utah's chief justice to President Lincoln.

December 1861: The pro-Union Kansas Jayhawkers attack Independence, Missouri, burning many buildings and killing several civilians.

1862: The Pacific Railroad Act passes Congress. It provides public lands to the Union Pacific Railroad and Central Pacific Railroad so that they can construct a transcontinental rail line along the 42nd parallel.

1862: The so-called Five Civilized Tribes—the Creek, Cherokee, Seminole, Chickasaw, and Choctaw—are divided by the Civil War. Most join with the Confederacy, but the Creeks split into two factions and will fight among themselves for the duration of the conflict.

1862: The Morrill Anti-Bigamy Act, designed to prohibit polygamy among Utah's Mormon community, is passed by Congress.

1862: Montana's gold rush begins in earnest with a strike in Bannack. Gold was first found in Montana a decade earlier in Deer Lodge Valley.

January 10, 1862: In his inaugural address, California Governor Leland Stanford suggests curbs to Asian immigration, claiming that "Asia, with her numberless millions, sends to our shores the dregs of her population."

March 28, 1862: In the Civil War, General Henry Sibley's Confederates are defeated at Glorieta Pass, New Mexico, by Union forces, including a Colorado volunteer unit. Glorieta Pass becomes known as "the Gettysburg of the West."

Watkins showcases Yosemite Carleton Watkins was one of the West's most talented landscape photographers. At age 21, he left New York for California during the Gold Rush years, soon finding work as a daguerreotype operator in San Jose. Lugging photographic equipment into Yosemite, Watkins developed 30 plate pictures and 100 stereograph views. These images of Yosemite were among the first seen in the East. In 1865 Watkins was appointed official photographer for the California Geological Survey. In 1871, he opened the Yosemite Art Gallery in San Francisco, which was destroyed by the San Francisco earthquake and fire in 1906.

Battle of Pea Ridge By early 1862, Confederate forces had been pushed entirely out of Missouri into Arkansas, leaving Missouri in Union hands. On March 7–8 of that year, Confederate troops, led by generals Earl Van Dorn, Ben McCulloch, and Sterling Price (*seen here, center, with his arm in a sling*), stormed back into Missouri at the Battle of Pea Ridge in northwestern Arkansas. Outnumbered Union forces led by General Samuel Curtis eventually prevailed, winning Missouri for the Union for the rest of the Civil War.

The Homestead Act

IN THE MID-19TH CENTURY, many U.S. leaders were eager to increase the westward migration of settlers in order to expand and strengthen the nation. They came up with the revolutionary idea of giving free land to settlers who would live there and improve the property. The politicians, however, faced opposition from northern businessmen who did not approve of the idea of free land, and who were afraid they would lose their supply of cheap laborers. In an odd alliance, Southerners who did not want to see an increase in slave-free states joined that opposition.

The argument went on for 20 years, until southern opposition disappeared when the southern states withdrew from the Union. Finally, Congress passed the Homestead Act, and President Abraham Lincoln signed it into law on May 20, 1862.

According to the act's rules, a settler would receive 160 acres of surveyed public land if he or she paid $18 in fees and lived on the land for five continuous years. The homesteader had to be the head of a household or at least 21 years old. Any who had served in the Confederate military were ineligible. He or she also had to agree to make improvements on the land, such as building a house and farming the property. Farm families who could not afford land in the East—as well as single women, former slaves, and new immigrants—were among those who filed.

When all requirements had been completed and the homesteader was ready to take legal possession, two of the homesteader's neighbors or friends had to accompany him or her to the local Land Office, where they had to vouch for the truth of statements about the improvements that the owner had made. The successful homesteader then paid the final fee and received the deed for the property.

Although most homesteaders settled in the western Plains, they inhabited 30 states in all. By 1900 homesteaders had filed 600,000 claims for a total of 80 million acres.

Homesteaders' cabins This Nebraska family, with its log cabin situated near a stream, was better off than most homesteaders. Only those who staked early claims had access to wood and water. Latecomers built sod homes on the open plains, and even though they dug wells, they often had to haul water from miles away. The typical homestead cabin was a single 10′×20′ room that served for living, dining, working, cooking, and sleeping. Some also had sleeping lofts or lean-to additions. It was not unusual for an entire family of six to 10 people to live in one cabin.

April 16, 1862: The Confederate Congress calls for a draft of able-bodied men between the ages of 18 and 35, although the order will be relaxed for those owning more than 20 slaves.

April 25, 1862: Flag Officer David Farragut captures New Orleans for the Union.

May 5, 1862: Mexican forces defeat the French at the Battle of Puebla, but Napoleon III will continue to press his imperialist agenda in Mexico.

May 20, 1862: The Homestead Act, which allows citizens to "improve to own" up to 160 acres of unclaimed public land, passes Congress.

June 1862: Confederate soldiers drive pro-Union Wyandot Indians from the Seneca Reserve in Indian Territory back to Kansas—and confiscate their property.

June 19, 1862: The federal government abolishes slavery in all U.S. territories.

Summer 1862: The New Haven Arms Company sells the first Henry repeating rifles. Though not the first repeating rifles on the market, they are clearly the best, and will soon become the gold standard for Union soldiers.

July 1, 1862: President Lincoln signs off on the Pacific Railroad Bill, authorizing construction of a transcontinental railroad.

July 17, 1862: The Second Confiscation Act is passed by Congress. The act states that Confederates who do not surrender by September are to be punished by having their slaves freed. The act also guarantees freedom for all slaves taking refuge behind Union lines.

Battle of Glorieta Pass Texas Confederates engaged Union soldiers on March 26–28, 1862, at the narrow defile in New Mexico known as Glorieta Pass. Earlier in the Civil War, Lieutenant Colonel John Baylor had led the Second Texas Mounted Rifles into lower New Mexico and created the Confederate Territory of Arizona. In San Antonio, General H. H. Sibley formed an "Army of New Mexico" and marched west to expand Baylor's conquest. Sibley captured Albuquerque and Santa Fe, then advanced with 1,100 men on Fort Union. However, the Texans were intercepted by 1,300 Union troops in Glorieta Pass. When about 60 wagons of the Confederate baggage train were destroyed, Sibley ordered a withdrawal to Texas. The Battle of Glorieta Pass became known as the "Gettysburg of the West."

The "Comstock Lode" In 1859 gold was discovered at what would soon become the lively town of Virginia City, Nevada. The "Comstock Lode" was named after a miner who insisted that it was on his claim, although neither he nor the initial discoverers would profit much from the find. Digging for Comstock gold was complicated by an annoying gray mud that turned out to be nearly pure silver. When the ore near the surface gave out, new technologies were developed for deeper mining. Here, in one of the first flash-lit photographs ever taken, miners are about to descend into the Comstock tunnels.

The Sioux Uprising According to an 1852 treaty with the U.S. government, the Santee (or Dakota) Sioux were forced to live along the upper Minnesota River on a strip of land 150 miles long and 10 miles wide. The treaty assured the Santee of compensation in money and goods, much of which was stolen by white traders. In August 1862, the desperate and starving Santee began a six-week revolt known as the Sioux Uprising. The Santee took the lives of hundreds of whites in Minnesota, many of them settlers. Some teachers and missionaries (*pictured*) escaped after being warned by friendly Indians of impending violence.

Mass executions After the Sioux Uprising was put down by U.S. troops, 303 Indian prisoners were convicted and sentenced to death for murder and rape. Because such a huge number of pending executions was shocking even to many whites, President Abraham Lincoln commuted most of the convictions. This illustration portrays the execution of 38 Indians on December 26, 1862, in Mankato, Minnesota. Because all the traps were sprung by a single rope, the hangings were simultaneous. The following spring, some 1,700 Santee were forced to move out of Minnesota to Nebraska and South Dakota.

Emancipation Proclamation President Lincoln drafted the Emancipation Proclamation in 1862, declaring slavery ended in the 11 states that had joined the Confederacy. Texas was the only western state in the Confederacy. More than 200,000 slaves lived in Texas, but even as they heard rumors of their freedom, it seemed impossible to run away because no Union armies were within reach. At the end of the war, a significant number of freedmen became cowboys, and many African American families penetrated the West as homesteaders.

1861-1876

August 17, 1862: The Sioux Uprising begins when four Dakota Indians kill five settlers in Minnesota and decide to wage war against the U.S. government.

August 18, 1862: In the first organized attack of the Sioux Uprising, Dakota warriors storm the Redwood Agency in Minnesota. The warriors kill 44 whites and capture 10.

August 19, 1862: Governor Alexander Ramsey of Minnesota gives Colonel Henry Sibley the command of the American forces mustered to fight the Dakota. Meanwhile, 16 more Americans are killed by the Dakota near New Ulm, Minnesota.

August 23, 1862: Thirty-four settlers are killed and much of New Ulm is destroyed when approximately 650 Dakota attack. However, the town is ultimately defended.

August 25, 1862: A wagon train that includes some 2,000 displaced settlers from the sacked town of New Ulm heads toward Mankato, Minnesota.

August 28–30, 1862: The Second Battle of Bull Run ends in disaster for federal troops.

September 2, 1862: Some 200 Dakota attack American troops in the 31-hour Battle of Birch Coulee. Thirteen U.S. troops (and nearly 90 horses) are killed, and many more are mortally wounded.

September 6, 1862: After losing to the Confederates at the Battle of Bull Run, Union Major General John Pope is given command of U.S. troops in the Northwest—and the action against the Dakota.

Railroad heavyweights
Congressman Oakes Ames (*center*) of Massachusetts and his brother Oliver (*top*) helped finance the Union Pacific Railroad (Oakes got stuck with most of the blame for the UP's financial scandals). Continuing clockwise, Charles Crocker, the Central Pacific partner in charge of building the railroad, hired Chinese laborers and actually spent time working on the line. Sidney Dillon was president of the Union Pacific in the 1870s and '80s. Colorado financier David Moffat (*bottom*) built railroads that were bought by the UP. Central Pacific partner Leland Stanford was elected governor of California in 1861. Collis Huntington also was one of the CP "Big Four" partners.

Carson's Indian battles From the 1830s to 1850s, famed mountain man and scout Kit Carson battled Indians on more than two dozen occasions. Despite aggression toward Natives, Kit married an Arapaho maiden and served for a decade as an Indian agent in New Mexico. In 1861 he resigned to join the Union Army. As colonel of the First New Mexico Cavalry, Carson rounded up 500 renegade Apaches. In 1863 he led a successful campaign against hostile Navajos, and the next year General Carson skillfully fought off 3,000 Comanche and Kiowa warriors at the First Battle of Adobe Walls. Only George Custer ever faced as large a force of Native Americans.

How to Get a Farm in the West

"I HOPE IT WILL be a good home for us," Rosa Ise said when she saw the Kansas acres that her husband had claimed. "It surely looks like good land." The Ises—like many other Americans during the 19th century—had headed west to homestead. Settlers could get western farmland by moving onto it, legally claiming it, buying it, or some combination of all three.

When Texas became independent, Texas farmers simply claimed the cattle and land abandoned by Mexicans who had left. Often, the U.S. government looked the other way when white settlers moved onto lands that belonged to Native Americans. After the eventual massive Indian relocations, territorial or state governments encouraged and organized the incoming tide of white settlers. Those who moved before the U.S. government declared an area open to settlement were protected by "graduation" and "pre-emption" policies that allowed settlers to buy the property later.

In Oregon, the 1850 Donation Land Act granted 320 acres of free land to each unmarried male settler—and 640 to married couples. ("American half-breed Indians" also were "granted" land if they already lived there.) The U.S. Homestead Act of 1862 gave federal land to farmers who would live on the land and make improvements. Railroad companies had been granted millions of acres of federal land along their routes. They provided free or very inexpensive train trips into the West and offered long-term loans to those who bought railroad land.

In general, western land was plentiful and either free or cheap. But wherever they settled, successful homesteaders such as Rosa Ise and her family generally faced a lifetime of hard work to turn their homestead into a comfortable home.

Homesteaders rely on windmills Prairie winds, especially the remorselessly hot winds of summer, were a curse to settlers—except when those winds could be harnessed to pump water. Homesteaders often had to settle far from streams and rivers. Windmills were a godsend, as they allowed homesteaders to pump water from 100 to 200 feet underground. The demand for windmills led to their manufacture in prairie states. From 1880 to the 1950s, as many as 50 companies manufactured windmills in Kansas alone.

September 17, 1862: More than 23,000 casualties at the Battle of Antietam in Maryland make this the bloodiest single day in American history to date.

September 23, 1862: American forces defeat the Dakota at the Battle of Wood Lake. This same day, antiwar Dakota "friendlies" take control of 269 American hostages from the prowar Dakota faction.

September 26, 1862: Dakota "friendlies" release American captives, while the Americans respond by detaining 1,200 Dakota. Eventually, another 800 Dakota will surrender to Americans.

September 28–November 3, 1862: Nearly 400 Dakota are summarily tried for murder and other wartime atrocities. In the final accounting, 323 Dakota are found guilty; 303 are sentenced to die. Most of the untried and acquitted are not released. *See* November 9, 1862.

October 17, 1862: Quantrill's Raiders, a Confederate guerrilla band, attack Shawneetown, Kansas. They kill two and loot the town.

November 9, 1862: The 303 Dakota who have been sentenced to die are moved to Camp Lincoln, near Mankato, Minnesota. Their route takes them through New Ulm, where they are attacked by a mob.

December 4, 1862: Soldiers guarding the condemned Dakota thwart an attack by a mob of several hundred armed settlers.

December 6, 1862: President Lincoln orders that 39 of the planned 303 executions go forward. One more Dakota eventually will be pardoned.

December 26, 1862: At 10 A.M., the 38 condemned Dakota are publicly hanged on gallows in the town of Mankato. They will be buried in a mass grave.

West Coast star In 1863 a young actress, painter, dancer, and poet named Adah Isaacs Menken decided that New York City was not sufficiently sophisticated to appreciate her talent. Thus, she went to San Francisco, where she appeared in the title role of the play *Mazeppa,* adapted from a poem by Lord Byron. Menken became an instant star, in no small part because, at the play's climax, she appeared on horseback in tights—which made her appear nude. During her short, tempestuous life, she had many famous friends, including Mark Twain, Charles Dickens, and Walt Whitman.

Drum Barracks In 1862, when General James Carleton began organizing the "Column from California" to march against Confederate forces in New Mexico, a base was established at the post of New San Pedro, near Los Angeles. Camp San Pedro soon was designated Camp Drum, in honor of a departmental adjutant, and later was renamed Drum Barracks. An elaborate set of buildings was enclosed by a picket fence, 1,480′×1,638′. The final stage of the Army's camel experiment, begun in the 1850s, saw 36 camels stationed at Drum Barracks as pack animals. Drum's use as a military facility ended in 1871.

Confederate guerrilla fighter Before the Civil War, William Clarke Quantrill taught school for several years in Missouri and Kansas. He also tried making his living as a gambler, and in 1860 he fled Kansas as a wanted horse thief. Quantrill enthusiastically joined the Confederate Army at the outbreak of the Civil War, but early in the war he formed his own guerrilla band to harass Union troops and to destabilize their supporters. The Union declared Quantrill an outlaw, while the Confederacy officially promoted him to the rank of captain. He was killed in a Kentucky raid in 1865.

Quantrill's Raiders Quantrill's Raiders began as a dozen men harrying Union soldiers and sympathizers along the Kansas-Missouri border. By the time of their 1863 strike on Lawrence, Kansas (*pictured*), the group expanded to about 450 riders. In Lawrence, Quantrill's Raiders burned homes and murdered 183 men and boys in front of their families. Soon, Union retaliation forced the Raiders to break into smaller groups. In Missouri, they were folk heroes; to the Union, they were vicious renegades.

The murderous Maddox George Maddox rode as a scout for the Confederate guerrilla force led by the notorious William Clarke Quantrill. Maddox cut a dashing figure with cavalry boots and a brace of Remington New Model Army revolvers. But like most of Quantrill's men, he was more of a murderous brigand than a soldier. Maddox killed and looted alongside "Bloody Bill" Anderson, Quantrill's vicious lieutenant. Fellow guerrillas included Frank and Jesse James and Cole and Jim Younger, who formed the infamous James-Younger Gang after the Civil War.

1863: Arizona and Idaho are organized as United States territories.

1863: The Bozeman Trail opens. It is the route of choice from Colorado to the Montana gold fields, but it cuts through the hunting territory of the Northern Plains Indians.

1863: Quantrill's Raiders, a Missouri-based band of Confederate guerrillas that includes future outlaw James and Younger brothers, set Lawrence, Kansas, afire and murder 150 of its townspeople.

January 1, 1863: President Lincoln frees the Confederacy's slaves with his public issuance of the Emancipation Proclamation.

January 8, 1863: Leland Stanford, California governor and key investor, breaks ground for the construction of the Central Pacific Railroad, which begins in Sacramento.

April 1863: Congress passes a law that authorizes the removal of the Dakota from Minnesota (most of the tribe will go to South Dakota). The Sioux Wars will continue until Wounded Knee in 1890.

April 1863: The Shawnee Friends Mission school reopens as a school for Indian orphans.

May 2, 1863: Legendary Confederate General Stonewall Jackson is felled by friendly fire at the Battle of Chancellorsville.

May 22, 1863: Failing to succeed with frontal assaults on Vicksburg, Mississippi, Union General Ulysses S. Grant begins to lay siege to the city.

June 20, 1863: West Virginia is admitted to the Union after splintering off from Confederate Virginia.

July 1–3, 1863: Union forces are victorious at the Battle of Gettysburg in Pennsylvania. Fighting results in 51,000 total casualties.

The Navajos' "Long Walk" Many Navajo Indians in the Southwest refused to accept confinement on a government reservation. But Colonel "Kit" Carson (as directed by Union Army Brigadier General James Carleton) waged an economic war against the Navajo to force them to move. Beginning in 1863, Carson marched his troops through Navajo territory, destroying crops, orchards, livestock, and homes. Other Native Americans who were longtime enemies of the Navajo joined Carson's campaign. In 1864 approximately 8,000 Navajos, such as those pictured here, were forced on a 300-mile "Long Walk" through the Arizona desert to Bosque Redondo in New Mexico.

Working on the railroad Track-layer gangs such as this one laid ties and rails in place and hammered in spikes—three blows to each spike, 10 spikes to a rail, and 400 rails to a mile. Stable bosses managed the horses, mules, and supply wagons, and other bosses watched everybody. Workers were paid from $2.50 to $4 a day, and they were charged $5 weekly for food (prepared by cooks) and sleeping space in a railroad car. Surveyors worked well ahead of these crews, as did graders, who hauled dirt in wheelbarrows to make a raised bed for the tracks.

> **"Damn any man who sympathizes with Indians. I have come to kill Indians and I believe it is right to use any means. I long to be wading in gore."**
>
> —Colonel John Chivington, who orchestrated the massacre at Sand Creek

Sand Creek Massacre

Colonel John Chivington

In 1864 festering tensions between Indians and whites in Colorado Territory exploded. Raids and counter-raids bloodied the summer and autumn, and white settlers howled for vengeance. Colonel John Chivington, a Civil War hero, was ordered to punish the Cheyennes.

Black Kettle, a Cheyenne chieftain, never made war against the United States. His mixed band of Cheyennes and Arapahos pitched winter lodges along Sand Creek in eastern Colorado. The commander at nearby Fort Lyon guaranteed their safety. In front of Black Kettle's tipi fluttered an American flag, signifying peace.

Nevertheless, on a bitterly cold late November dawn, Chivington's raiders surged into Black Kettle's camp. Militiamen slaughtered and savagely mutilated more than 130 Indians, mostly old men, women, and children.

After torching the village and killing or scattering hundreds of ponies, the troopers rode to Denver, where cheering crowds gawked at scalps and body parts displayed as "trophies."

Most Westerners applauded Chivington, but mass murder of Indian noncombatants outraged other Americans. Indian agent Kit Carson denounced "that dog Chivington and his dirty hounds," and offered damning evidence to an 1865 congressional investigation of the "Sand Creek Massacre." No congressional charges ensued, but Chivington's reputation was destroyed.

In the wake of the Sand Creek slaughter and similar events, the government reexamined its failed "kill or conquer" Indian policy. During Ulysses Grant's administration, Congress revised its Indian Policy and opened the reservation era.

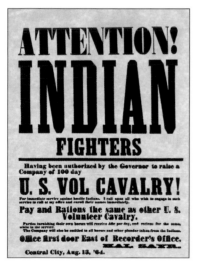

Chivington's recruits Most men who answered this advertisement for volunteer Indian fighters, issued on August 13, 1864, were poorly disciplined Colorado frontiersmen bent on vengeance against Comanche raiders. Colonel John Chivington's eagerness to harness their rage before their 100 days of service ended was perhaps one reason for his notorious attack on Sand Creek on November 29 of that year. It has been alleged that many of the volunteers were drunk on the morning of the massacre.

Mutilation at Sand Creek On the morning of November 29, 1864, Colonel John Chivington's troops surrounded a camp of Cheyennes and Arapahos at Sand Creek, Colorado, then suddenly attacked with rifles and howitzers. Most of the warriors were away hunting, leaving only a small number of able-bodied men to defend fleeing villagers from charging troops. Before a U.S. Congressional hearing in 1865, one witness testified that he saw bodies "worse mutilated than any I ever saw before; the women cut all to pieces." Victims, he said, included "children two or three months old; all ages lying there, from sucking infants up to warriors."

"Father of Arizona"

Charles Poston, known as the "Father of Arizona," formed a mining company there in 1854. Five years later, he published Arizona's first newspaper. After successfully lobbying Congress in 1863 for a territorial government, Poston became Arizona's first superintendent of Indian affairs and one of its first delegates to Congress. Poston is buried at "Poston's Butte" near a pyramid-like monument, which some claim was built in his honor while others insist it was built by him as a sun temple.

"Buffalo soldiers" Following impressive performances during the Civil War, African American soldiers were retained by the U.S. Army in four regiments. Stationed almost constantly on the frontier, these segregated regiments were officered by white men, who often were ostracized by officers of white units. Off-duty black soldiers frequently were unwelcome in the frontier communities they protected. But they were steady, dependable troops who earned the respect of Cheyenne Indians, who nicknamed them "buffalo soldiers" due to their dark skin and thick hair.

A Cherokee Confederate leader Stand Watie was among the signers of the 1835 Treaty of New Echota, which forced the Cherokee Nation to move from southeastern states to Indian Territory west of the Mississippi. Unlike the treaty's other three principal signers, Watie escaped assassination by angry Cherokees. A slave owner, he built a thriving plantation in present-day Oklahoma before joining the Confederate cause during the Civil War. Leading a volunteer Cherokee regiment, Watie rose to the rank of brigadier general and fought successfully in a number of battles. In June 1865, he became the last Confederate general to surrender to the Union.

European railroad workers Railroad work crews such as this one in Wyoming included many Irish and other European immigrants. From 1847 to 1854, more than one and a half million Irish had immigrated to the United States. Irish comprised the largest number of railroad workers, especially on eastern lines. Germans, Swedes, and some other immigrants generally headed for cities or established family farms, but they also were actively recruited by railroad companies that desperately needed laborers.

The Cattle Industry

IN THE LAST QUARTER of the 19th century, a booming market for beef fueled the rapid expansion of the range cattle industry in the American West. The removal of bison and Indians from much of the Great Plains left cattlemen free to graze their herds on a veritable sea of grass. For a few years, ranchers operated unfettered on the public domain. They conducted annual roundups to mark or brand new calves and to thin out the number of mature steers, which were driven overland and sold to midwestern feeders and meat packers. From 1865 to 1890, drovers trailed as many as 10 million head of Texas cattle northward to Kansas railheads and to finishing pastures on the Northern Plains.

Due to rising cattle prices in the late 1870s, the livestock industry began to attract huge amounts of eastern and foreign capital, particularly from Great Britain. Cattle corporations bought up western land and livestock with abandon, absorbing many small-scale ranches in the process. The newcomers erected permanent shelters, barbed-wire fences, and other improvements. Moreover, they introduced expensive breeding stock to produce larger animals with better-tasting meat. They also established cooperative associations to help protect themselves from rustlers and to lobby federal and state lawmakers for favorable legislation.

For a brief period in the early 1880s, investors in some cattle companies enjoyed dividends that exceeded 30 percent. Such conditions encouraged speculation, overgrazing, and other slipshod business practices that soon proved disastrous. By the mid-1880s, cattle prices began to weaken and herds were decimated by summer droughts and hard winters. The hardships forced many ranchers to dump their remaining stock onto already glutted markets.

Many cattle companies could not satisfy their creditors and went bankrupt. Investors on both sides of the Atlantic lost millions of dollars. Chastened by the experience, most of the ranchers who survived the disaster began to reduce the size of their operations and pay more attention to range conservation. The American cattle industry would thrive ever after, eventually generating $79 billion a year.

Goodnight blazes trails

As a young man, Charles Goodnight was a pioneer cattleman and a Texas Ranger who battled Comanches. On cattle drives, Goodnight took great precautions, armed each of his drovers with a rifle and four pistols, and rarely suffered damage from raids. He opened a number of trails, including the famous Goodnight-Loving Trail in 1866. He invented the chuck wagon (for his trail crews) as well as the first safe sidesaddle (for his wife, Molly). The greatest of the ranches he established was the JA, which ranged 100,000 cattle on 1.3 million acres in the Texas Panhandle.

CATTLE DRIVE DRUDGERY

2ond Hard rain & wind Storm Beeves ran & had to be on Horse back all night Awful night. wet all night clear bright morning. Men still lost quit the Beeves & go to Hunting Men is the word—4 P.M. Found our men with Indian guide & 195 beeves 14 Miles from camp. allmost starved not having had a bite to eat for 60 hours got to camp about 12 M *Tired....*

5th Oh! what a night—Thunder Lightning & rain—we followed our Beeves *all* night as they wandered about—put them on the road at day break found 90 Beeves of an other mans Herd travelled 18 miles over the worst road I ever saw & come to Boggy Depot & crossed 4 Rivers It is well Known by that name We Hauled cattle out of the Mud with oxen half the day

—DIARY OF GEORGE C. DUFFIELD, JUNE 2 AND 5, 1866

July 4, 1863: General Grant succeeds in Vicksburg, Mississippi, effectively splitting the Confederacy in half.

July 9, 1863: Port Hudson, Louisiana, surrenders to federal forces, giving the Union control of the Mississippi River.

July 26, 1863: Sam Houston dies at age 70 on his Huntsville, Texas, farm.

August 25, 1863: General Thomas Ewing, Jr., issues "Order No. 11," requiring Missouri residents living on the border with Kansas to establish their loyalty to the Union, and to move to within one mile of a federal post.

October 6, 1863: Quantrill's Raiders defeat a small contingent of federal cavalry and execute 17 bystanders in an attack on Baxter Springs, Kansas.

October 17, 1863: President Lincoln names General Ulysses S. Grant supreme commander of the federal forces in the West.

November 19, 1863: Lincoln delivers his Gettysburg Address.

1864: Colonel Kit Carson spearheads a campaign against the Navajo of northwest New Mexico, forcing 8,000 Indians to surrender. Carson leads his captives on a "Long Walk" across the territory to a reservation on the Pecos River, where they will spend four years in detention.

1864: Congress passes a second Pacific Railroad Act, which improves per-mile track land grants and subsidies in an effort to stimulate investment in the railroad.

1864: Montana becomes the newest United States territory.

February 1864: Kansas's state legislature calls for the removal of all American Indians from the state.

March 12, 1864: Ulysses S. Grant is promoted to the rank of lieutenant general and named general-in-chief of the Armies of the United States.

Railroad leads to Omaha boom Pictured here is the Omaha, Nebraska, state capitol as it appeared in the 1860s. The Homestead Act of 1862 brought a wave of settlers to the Nebraska Territory. In 1863 President Lincoln declared that the Union Pacific Railroad would start at Omaha, and the first rails were laid there in 1865. When the transcontinental railroad was completed in 1869, Omaha became the gateway to the West for settlers and the shipment of goods. The demand for Nebraska land—free and for sale—boomed. The population rose from 28,841 in 1860 to 122,993 in 1870.

The wagons of choice John Studebaker and his four brothers began their careers as blacksmiths, but in 1852 two of the brothers started building wagons in South Bend, Indiana. John traveled on to California, where he repaired miners' tools and made wheelbarrows. He returned in 1858 with enough money to expand the family business. During the peak years of westward migration, about half of the wagons on the trails were Studebakers. Seen here is the Studebaker Victoria carriage that Abraham and Mary Todd Lincoln used to ride around Washington, D.C., on the day of Lincoln's assassination. From 1902 to 1966, Studebaker manufactured automobiles.

All about tipis Tipis were developed by nomadic Plains Indians as portable housing. The cover was fashioned from buffalo hides and was waterproof. A dozen poles provided a frame for the cover. The interior was about 15 feet high and, at ground level, about 15 feet in diameter. A smoke flap at the top provided ventilation, and a door flap covered the entrance. In warm weather, the bottom of the cover was raised so that air could circulate. A tipi could be erected within a couple hours. The tipi was so efficient and comfortable that the U.S. Army designed a canvas version.

Proud Kiowas In 1866 Lone Wolf was chosen as principal chief of the Kiowa, a Plains tribe about 2,000 strong. At the time, the tribe was in conflict with white settlers who were encroaching upon traditional Kiowa hunting grounds. Although a large contingent of Kiowa wanted peace and agreed to the Medicine Lodge Treaty of 1867, life on the Kiowa Reservation in western Indian Territory proved difficult for Lone Wolf and other proud warriors. Kiowa war parties often slipped away from the reservation for raids, and Comanche warriors also raided actively. In 1874 the U.S. Army launched a major campaign, and in February 1875 Lone Wolf was captured. He was incarcerated in Florida, while his followers were returned to the reservation.

Hell on Wheels Pictured is a "Hell on Wheels" town. Late in 1866, the Union Pacific Railroad halted construction for the winter at the village of North Platte in Nebraska Territory. Saloonkeepers, gamblers, prostitutes, pickpockets, and other riffraff flocked to the site. Tents and ramshackle frame structures served as restaurants, while railroad workers slept in bunkhouse cars. With a temporary population of 5,000, North Platte was a Hell on Wheels town for just a few months. The next Hell on Wheels was Julesburg, Colorado, a railroad division point that boomed until Cheyenne, Wyoming, became Hell on Wheels for the winter of 1867–68.

April 12, 1864: Confederate General Nathan Bedford Forrest commands the attack at Fort Pillow, Tennessee, resulting in the deaths of 574 U.S. troops, including some 200 black Union soldiers.

September 2, 1864: Quantrill's Raiders slay and scalp 150 Union soldiers—many of whom are unarmed—in Centralia, Missouri.

Fall 1864: Union General William Tecumseh Sherman marches through Georgia, capturing Atlanta and Savannah from the Confederate Army.

October 23, 1864: The Battle of Westport in Missouri, the largest Civil War battle west of the Mississippi, ends with a Confederate retreat.

October 31, 1864: Nevada joins the Union, in part to ensure additional electoral votes for President Lincoln's reelection.

November 8, 1864: President Lincoln is reelected, with Andrew Johnson as his vice president.

November 14, 1864: *Camanche,* the U.S. Navy's first ironclad warship on the Pacific Coast, is launched from San Francisco's Union Iron Works.

November 29, 1864: Army Colonel John Chivington leads his troops against a band of peaceful Indians in Sand Creek, Colorado. They murder and mutilate more than 130 Indians, mostly women and children who were gathered under an American flag.

1865: Many East Coast Americans get their first glimpse of the Wild West when writer Mark Twain publishes "The Celebrated Jumping Frog of Calaveras County," which is set in a California mining camp.

March 3, 1865: Congress establishes the Freedmen's Bureau to aid former slaves.

Winchester's rifles Oliver Winchester began as a shirt manufacturer in New Haven, Connecticut. During the 1850s, Winchester invested $40,000 in the Volcanic Repeating Arms Company in New Haven. When the firm declared bankruptcy, Winchester took control, adopting the name New Haven Arms Company. By 1860 gunsmith B. Tyler Henry developed a lever-action rifle that Winchester christened the "Henry." A magazine beneath the barrel held 15 rounds, but it had to be loaded from the front. An 1866 model with a loading chamber on the side was named the "Winchester," and the company was renamed the Winchester Repeating Arms Company.

"Soiled doves" In the gold fields, mining towns, cow towns—in boomtowns of every kind—prostitutes went to work and men lined up to visit them. Wells, Fargo coaches even transported prostitutes and dance-hall girls to such locales as Virginia City, Nevada. After lonely months on the trail, many cowboys were eager for female company. Sometimes romanticized as "soiled doves," prostitutes often faced miserable living conditions and the constant risk of physical violence. Many fell into drug addiction or alcoholism. It was not uncommon for prostitutes to take their own lives.

> "Questionable women stayed in their shoddy rooms by day, but came boldly out at night when fiddles began to play, flitting about the saloons, dance halls, and gambling dens like bright fireflies."
>
> —AUTHOR FRANK COLLINSON, DESCRIBING THE COW TOWN OF FORT GRIFFIN, TEXAS, IN THE MID-1870s

Cattle Towns

IN THE TWO DECADES that followed the Civil War, a succession of small communities flourished on the Kansas prairie. These areas were railroad shipping points for several million head of cattle driven north from Texas on the Chisholm, Great Western, and associated trails. Although the economic significance of these "cattle towns" was short-lived, the places earned colorful and lasting reputations for lawlessness and violence.

By the mid-1860s, the increasing density of agricultural settlement in Missouri and eastern Kansas—and quarantine laws barring Texas cattle carrying the fatal disease splenic fever—had denied drovers overland access to midwestern livestock markets. In 1867, however, Joseph G. McCoy, a visionary Illinois entrepreneur, overcame these difficulties by building stockyards along the Kansas Pacific Railroad at the sparsely settled town of Abilene. A host of merchants, saloon keepers, gamblers, and prostitutes was not far behind.

Cowboys delivered more than a million cattle to Abilene during the town's four-year tenure as the principal cattle shipping point in the West. By 1871, however, arriving farmers and stricter enforcement of the quarantine law had forced shippers to establish a new trailhead at Newton, Kansas, 60 miles to the southwest. The following year, drovers pointed their herds to the towns of Ellsworth and Wichita—and in 1875 to Dodge City, which began a decade-long reign as the "Queen of the Cow Towns." After 1880, Dodge shared the droving trade with Caldwell, the state's last important cattle transportation center.

During shipping season, violence often flared in the towns as cowboys—after months on the trail—overindulged in liquor, gambling, and prostitutes. The resulting mayhem and bloodshed gained national attention and caused towns to prohibit the carrying of firearms and segregate districts devoted to vice from the rest of the community. Towns also hired tough lawmen, such as "Wild Bill" Hickok and Wyatt Earp, to maintain order.

In 1885 Kansas lawmakers extended the quarantine on Texas cattle to the entire state, bringing the colorful era of the Kansas cow towns to an end. Few Kansans mourned its passing. "The cattle traffic made money for its citizens," declared one Dodge City reformer, "but it did not make a town."

The first cattle town "At this writing, Hell is now in session in Abilene." This pronouncement by the *Topeka Commonwealth* fittingly described the raucous cattle town. In 1864 Abilene, Kansas, boasted only a handful of shabby log structures near the tracks of the Kansas Pacific Railroad. Cattle buyer Joseph McCoy built shipping pens, barns, a bank, and a three-story hotel called the Drover's Cottage. Abilene became the rollicking terminus of the Chisholm Trail. On Texas Street, cowboys swaggered into such saloons as the Alamo and the Bull's Head, establishing a Wild West atmosphere that other cattle towns would try to emulate.

March 4, 1865: President Lincoln is inaugurated for his second term.

March 13, 1865: The Confederate Congress authorizes enlistment of slaves for military service with no change in their relations to their owners.

April 9, 1865: The Civil War ends with the surrender of Confederate General Robert E. Lee to Union General Ulysses S. Grant in Appomattox Court House, Virginia.

April 14, 1865: President Lincoln is shot by actor and Confederate sympathizer John Wilkes Booth during a performance of *Our American Cousin* at Ford's Theatre in Washington, D.C. Lincoln will die the following day, and Andrew Johnson will become president.

April 26, 1865: John Wilkes Booth is cornered and killed by U.S. soldiers in a barn outside of Bowling Green, Virginia.

May 10, 1865: Confederate guerrilla William Quantrill is mortally wounded by Union soldiers in Kentucky. • Confederate President Jefferson Davis, wearing his wife's cloak, is captured by Union soldiers near Irwinville, Georgia.

July 1865: General Patrick Connor invades South Dakota's Powder River Basin with three columns of soldiers. Their orders: "Attack and kill every male Indian over 12 years of age."

July 7, 1865: Four of John Wilkes Booth's accomplices are executed in Washington, D.C.

July 10, 1865: Dennis N. Cooley replaces outgoing Indian Affairs Commissioner William P. Dole.

July 26, 1865: In the Battle of Platte Bridge in Wyoming, Lakota, Cheyenne, and Arapaho ambush a small detachment escorting an Army supply wagon train.

Useful mules Two soldiers load a pack mule for western travel. A hybrid of horse and donkey, the mule is more surefooted and enduring than the former, and larger and stronger than the latter. These characteristics made it a favorite beast of burden for the rugged and varied country of the Old West. Some town streets were widened to make room for mule teams. The 20-mule teams of Death Valley became legendary.

Dodge and the railroads General Grenville Dodge left his work as a railroad surveyor and engineer to join the Union Army during the Civil War. A superb combat officer, Dodge rose to major general of volunteers. General Dodge also rebuilt southern railroads for Army use, and at war's end he became chief engineer of the Union Pacific Railroad. Following his key role in building the nation's first transcontinental line, he worked on other western railroads. During his career, he surveyed 60,000 miles of railroad line, making an enormous contribution to the settlement of the West.

Building bridges Spindly looking wooden railroad bridges managed to support a locomotive, tender, and string of cars, even in the high winds of western plains and mountains. Lumber for Central Pacific bridge trestles was cut in northwest forests, shipped down the coast by schooners, and sent to the site on flatcars. Trestles for Union Pacific bridges were prefabricated in Chicago and brought by train to the end of the line. The Union Pacific Dale Creek Bridge seen here, a triumph of 19th-century engineering, was 700 feet long and stood 126 feet above a tiny creek in Wyoming's Black Hills.

Pseudo-slavery in California During the California Gold Rush, prospectors violently evicted Native Americans from the gold fields. Even though California entered the Union as a free state in 1850, new state laws legalized the forcible indenture of Indians, including children. Indian communities were moved to areas lacking in game, farmable land, or water. By the time such harsh laws were repealed in 1863, California's once plentiful and independent Indian population had been reduced to scattered groups, such as the one seen in this photograph. By then, they were completely dependent on whites for their survival.

The stagecoach kings In 1852 Henry Wells and William Fargo started providing banking and mail services to mining camps. They soon formed the Wells, Fargo company to make deliveries by wagon and stagecoach. By 1863 the company boasted 180 stagecoach depots throughout the West. By 1866 Wells Fargo had bought out major competitors. Their Concord stagecoaches, such as the one seen here, came in several sizes, seating six, nine, or 12 passengers and up to a dozen more on the roof. They were pulled by four- or six-horse teams.

August 1865: In the Battle of Tongue River in Wyoming, Brigadier General Patrick Connor and his troops destroy an Arapaho village and kill more than 50 Indians. The attack is in retaliation for raids on the Bozeman Trail and overland mail routes.

September 1865: Cheyenne warrior Roman Nose, avenging the Sand Creek Massacre, leads hundreds of Cheyenne warriors in a siege of U.S. soldiers who are attempting to return to Fort Laramie in Wyoming.

September 19, 1865: The Missouri Pacific Railroad between St. Louis and Kansas City is completed.

October 14, 1865: Intimidated in the wake of the Sand Creek Massacre, southern Cheyenne chiefs sign a treaty handing over most of Colorado Territory to the U.S. government.

December 18, 1865: Secretary of State William H. Seward declares that the 13th Amendment to the Constitution has been ratified. The amendment officially outlaws slavery everywhere in the United States.

December 24, 1865: The Ku Klux Klan is organized in Pulaski, Tennessee, by a group of Confederate veterans looking to resist Reconstruction.

1866: A trader named Jesse Chisholm transports a large load of buffalo hides from Texas to Kansas, cutting what comes to be known as the Chisholm Trail.

1866: U.S. forces in the West come under the command of General Philip Sheridan, who expressed his plan to bring peace to the Great Plains by suggesting, "Kill the buffalo and you kill the Indians."

1866: A nationwide cholera epidemic sweeps through many American cities on both coasts.

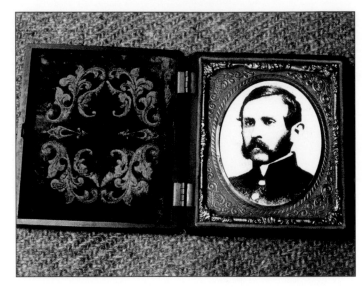

Fetterman gets restless The son of a career Army officer, William Fetterman compiled a brilliant combat record during the Civil War and was promoted to lieutenant colonel. When the Civil War ended, he accepted a regular commission as a captain in the 18th Infantry. By late 1866, Captain Fetterman was stationed at Fort Phil Kearny (in Wyoming) on the Bozeman Trail, which was commanded by Colonel Henry Carrington, who had been a desk officer during the Civil War. Fetterman became contemptuous of Carrington's timidity against Sioux raiders, and he lobbied for an offensive campaign. He succeeded in converting most of the younger officers to his aggressive policy.

The Fetterman Massacre "With 80 men, I could ride through the Sioux nation," boasted Captain William Fetterman at Fort Phil Kearny. On December 21, 1866, he was given his opportunity following a morning attack on a woodcutting detail. Fetterman led an 80-man pursuit party of infantry and cavalry. Defying orders, he aggressively marched out of sight of the fort, lured by a decoy party commanded by the great Sioux warrior Crazy Horse. When the cavalrymen moved ahead of the foot soldiers, the trap was sprung by 2,000 Sioux, Cheyenne, and Arapaho warriors. Launching 40,000 arrows, the warriors annihilated Fetterman and his soldiers, then stripped and mutilated the bodies. The Fetterman Massacre stood as the worst military fiasco in the West until Custer's failure at the Little Bighorn 10 years later.

"As a class [the Chinese] are quiet, peaceable, patient, industrious and economical. Ready and apt to learn all the different kinds of work required in railroad building, they soon become as efficient as white laborers. More prudent and economical, they are contented with less wages."

—A REPORT BY CALIFORNIA GOVERNOR LELAND STANFORD TO PRESIDENT ANDREW JOHNSON, OCTOBER 10, 1865

The industrious Chinese Famine in China drove immigrants such as this one to California, where they met harsh discrimination. The Central Pacific, facing a severe labor shortage, tried out a few Chinese workers. At first, the railroad paid them less than the $30 monthly wage of white workers, but the Chinese were so industrious that the CP soon raised their wages and actively recruited more workers in China. The Chinese cooked their own healthy food, lived in tents or cabins, and organized themselves into efficient work teams. To conquer the daunting Sierra Nevadas, the Chinese used techniques they had learned on cliffs above the Yangtze River.

Conquering the Sierras If tracks could not be laid through the Sierras—mostly double-summit ranges, with the highest point being 14,000 feet—a transcontinental railroad could not be built. Even at the single-summit Donner Pass, workers had to blast and build to achieve a usable grade. Seen here, Chinese workers construct a trestle and cut through the mountain in the background. When working on very steep cliffs, they lowered themselves in baskets from the top. A man in the basket hand-drilled a hole in the cliff face, tamped in powder, lit it, and scrambled back up the rope. No records were kept of the lives lost.

Blasting through mountains Central Pacific work crews blasted their way through the Sierra Nevada Mountains. At first, they crept along slowly—seven inches per day in tunnels such as this one—using black powder. Then English chemist James Howden manufactured powerful (though unstable) nitroglycerin at work sites, and progress increased to two feet per day. In Utah, Union Pacific crews also used the dangerous substance. No one knows how many workers died in unplanned explosions, but the CP stopped using nitroglycerine after they punched through the Sierra Nevada summit. Mountain rainstorms and snowstorms added to the dangers of tunneling. Avalanches covered tunnels and buried workers in their sleeping quarters.

The Alaska Purchase Concerned about the expense of maintaining Alaska as part of the Russian empire, and fearing the possible loss of the vast province to Great Britain, Russia indicated its willingness to sell the territory to the United States early in 1867. Secretary of State William H. Seward, shown here at the treaty signing (*second from left*), quickly negotiated a price of $7.2 million. Envisioning a barren land of glaciers and Eskimos, Americans jeered "Seward's Folly" and "Seward's Icebox." But in 1897, gold was discovered in the Yukon, triggering a memorable rush and producing enough wealth to more than cover the purchase price.

Mormons head to Ogden The Mormon exodus to Salt Lake Valley, Utah, began in 1846. Soon, some 12,000 "Saints" fanned out and established communities. About 35 miles northwest of Salt Lake City was Ogden, the territory's second largest town. Established at the confluence of the Weber and Ogden rivers, just west of the rugged Wasatch Range, the town was built on the site of a briefly occupied trading post, Fort Buenaventura. For many years, the community focused on farming. But when the Union Pacific Railroad reached Ogden in 1868, the town was rapidly transformed into a major western freight hub.

Union Pacific's photographer In 1867 in Junction, Kansas, a group of travelers on the partially completed Union Pacific Railroad poses for the official photographer of the UP, Alexander Gardner. A native of Scotland, Gardner migrated to the United States in 1856. Gardner was fascinated by the scientific aspects of photography, and he was a key assistant to famed photographer Matthew Brady throughout the Civil War. Immediately after the war, Gardner began photographing the westward progress of the UP Railroad while also recording images of nearby Native Americans. He issued a photographic volume, *Across the Continent on the Union Pacific Railway*, as a companion to his Civil War book.

Cowboy boots During the trail drive era, manufacturers began to make boots with high heels, narrow toes, and thin soles. High heels allowed a cowboy to brace his feet in the stirrups or, while roping on foot, to dig his heels into the dirt. The narrow cut permitted a cowboy to catch the stirrup of a wheeling horse or, if thrown from the saddle, to slip his boot free and escape being dragged to death. Thin soles gave the rider a feel for the stirrup. Intricate stitching added decoration while stiffening the tops to better withstand the constant wear of the saddle fenders. Boots also symbolized the proud superiority felt by cowboys over men who made their livings on foot.

Chisholm's trail Jesse Chisholm was the son of a Cherokee mother and a Scottish father. An enterprising trader, Chisholm constantly moved among the tribes in Indian Territory (later Oklahoma), and established several trading posts. Conversant in more than a dozen Native American dialects, he frequently found employment as an interpreter, helping to negotiate treaties and ransom for captives. The north-south trader's route that he blazed became the legendary Chisholm Trail, the most famous of all western cattle trails.

Buffalo Bill William Cody earned the nickname "Buffalo Bill" while working as a contract hunter for railroads. Buffalo Bill claimed that he killed 4,280 buffalo in 1867 and '68, providing a tremendous amount of meat for hungry construction crews. As a teenager, the adventurous Cody had worked in the West as a teamster, prospector, and trapper, and reputedly rode for the Pony Express. During the Civil War, he enlisted in the Seventh Volunteer Kansas Cavalry, and after the war he served the Army as an Indian scout. In 1883 Buffalo Bill began to capitalize on his fame through a spectacular show business career.

Railroads threaten Indians Native Americans had been alarmed by settlers and soldiers on the Plains and by the reduction of buffalo herds. The railroad was clearly going to be more permanent than passing wagons, and Indians saw it as a greater threat. The bodies of Union Pacific surveyors, train crews, and telegraph workers were occasionally found riddled with arrows and sometimes scalped. As seen here, Cheyenne warriors tore up tracks near Plum Creek, Nebraska, in August 1867, and set up a barricade. They attacked telegraph workers and then derailed and looted a freight train, killing members of both crews.

1866: The first cattle trail is blazed when Charles Goodnight and Oliver Loving drive a herd of 2,000 longhorns from Texas to New Mexico.

February 12, 1866: Secretary of State William H. Seward formally demands that France withdraw its forces from Mexico.

February 13, 1866: Former Quantrill Raiders Frank and Jesse James rob a Liberty, Missouri, bank.

April 9, 1866: Congress passes the Civil Rights Act, which grants equal rights to all native-born Americans (with the glaring exception of untaxed American Indians).

June 1866: The Tauromee and other Indians on the Seneca Reserve in what is now Oklahoma risk starvation when a flood destroys their crops.

June 13, 1866: Several hundred U.S. soldiers begin building forts along the Bozeman Trail, from present-day Colorado to Montana, even while Indian chiefs are at Fort Laramie negotiating a treaty governing access to the Powder River Basin. Given this incontrovertible evidence of bad faith on the part of the U.S. government, Red Cloud's War begins. • The 14th Amendment to the Constitution, which grants rights of citizenship to blacks, goes to the states for ratification.

July 1866: Congress authorizes the creation of the first peacetime African American army units. Of these, it will be the mounted Ninth and 10th Cavalry regiments that will attract the attention of the Cheyenne and Comanche, who will call them "buffalo soldiers."

July 4, 1866: The U.S. government signs a treaty with the Delaware. The agreement allows the U.S. to acquire the tribe's remaining land in Kansas and sell it to the Missouri River Railroad Company for $2.50 per acre.

Exploiting Yosemite Today, Yosemite National Park covers 1,189 square miles of the Sierra Nevada Mountains. Among its attributes are rich meadows, granite cliffs, clear streams, thousands of lakes and ponds, groves of giant sequoias, mountain peaks exceeding 10,000 feet, and some of the highest waterfalls in the world. Unlike Yellowstone, the Yosemite Valley and its surrounding wonders came in danger of commercial exploitation soon after their discovery by whites in the 1850s—especially groves with valuable timber and meadows suitable for grazing. The area did not became a national park until 1890, and wasn't brought fully under governmental protection until 1906.

The Bozeman Trail The shortest route to the Montana gold fields around Virginia City was the Bozeman Trail. Mapped out by John Bozeman in 1863, the trail angled from Fort Laramie in Wyoming to Montana, then westward through 6,000-foot Bozeman Pass to Virginia City. Although the Army built three forts along the route, Chief Red Cloud of the Sioux conducted attacks that halted virtually all traffic. The Army pulled out in 1868, and the Bozeman Trail was abandoned. Nine years later, with the Sioux confined to reservations, the old route reopened as an important cattle trail.

Red Cloud's War Red Cloud, of the Oglala Sioux, claimed his first scalp at 16 while riding against Pawnee warriors. During another raid he killed a Crow chief, then earned even more glory by killing four Pawnee braves. Red Cloud began fighting U.S. soldiers in 1854. Widely acknowledged as the best war leader of the Oglala, Red Cloud enjoyed his greatest triumphs from 1866 to '68, when the Bozeman Trail was laid out through some of the richest hunting grounds of the Northern Plains Indians. Red Cloud's War was marked by an incessant series of attacks against soldiers and travelers.

The Fort Laramie Treaty Following two years of relentless assaults on travelers and Army units by Chief Red Cloud and 2,000 Sioux warriors, the U.S. government decided to work for peace in 1868. Red Cloud insisted that war would continue unless the Army agreed to leave the three forts that guarded the Bozeman Trail. Forts Reno, Phil Kearny, and C. F. Smith were abandoned, and warriors set them ablaze. In April 1868, Sioux chiefs (*pictured*) signed the treaty at Fort Laramie in Wyoming, and Red Cloud triumphantly visited the fort in November. The government agreed to stay out of the Black Hills—a promise it would renege on in 1874, when whites discovered gold in that region.

Laying track in the desert By summer 1868, Central Pacific workers headed eastward across the hot, treeless Nevada desert. They had to haul thousands of gallons of water and all their building materials to the work sites by train. Nevertheless, their speed picked up on this flatter land; Central Pacific crews were soon laying four to six miles of rail a day. Meanwhile, Union Pacific workers on Wyoming's alkali desert faced 100-degree heat, freezing nights, and Indian attacks on people and animals. The bodies of dozens of mules were left to rot alongside the Union Pacific track.

BRAVE HEARTS AND BRAWNY MUSCLES

IT WAS WORTH THE DUST, the heat, the cinders, the hurrying ride, day and night, the fatigue and the exposure, to see with one's own eyes this second grand "March to the Sea." Sherman, with his victorious legions, sweeping from Atlanta to Savannah, was a spectacle less glorious than this army of men, marching on foot from Omaha to Sacramento, subduing unknown wildernesses, scaling unknown mountains, surmounting untried obstacles, and binding across the broad breast of America the iron emblem of modern progress and civilization. All honor, not only to the brains that have conceived, but to the indomitable wills, the brave hearts and the brawny muscles that are actually achieving the great work!

—*PHILADELPHIA BULLETIN*, 1868

1861-1876

July 13, 1866: Colonel Henry B. Carrington and his men break ground on the construction of Fort Phil Kearny in Wyoming, in desirable Plains Indians hunting territory. Workers draw constant harassment from neighboring Lakota, Cheyenne, and Arapaho groups.

August 20, 1866: President Andrew Johnson declares the Civil War officially over, although at this point this is simply a formality.

December 21, 1866: Lakota Sioux, Northern Cheyenne, and Arapaho warriors in Wyoming annihilate Captain William J. Fetterman and 80 of his troops near Fort Phil Kearny.

1867: In an effort to remove Indians from areas desirable to white settlers, the U.S. government presses the Comanche, Kiowa, Cheyenne, Arapaho, and other southern Plains Indian tribes to sign the Medicine Lodge Treaty.

1867: The first cattle drive up the Chisholm Trail arrives in Abilene, Kansas, after a long journey from Texas.

March 1, 1867: Nebraska becomes the 37th state to join the Union.

March 30, 1867: Secretary of State William H. Seward reaches an agreement with Russia to purchase Alaska for $7.2 million (equivalent to two cents per acre).

Summer 1867: Great Indian chiefs Crazy Horse, Red Cloud, and Sitting Bull attend the 6,000-tribe Grand Council at Bear Butte, South Dakota, and agree to put a stop to white encroachment.

August 12, 1867: President Johnson suspends Secretary of War Edwin Stanton from office while Congress is not in session. *See* February 24, 1868.

Western frontier This Currier & Ives lithograph, created in 1868, glorifies the western frontier at the time. Ahead are snowcapped mountains, winding rivers, fertile land, and endless possibilities. Settlers have built homes and a school, and now they chop wood for further construction. Wagons head out on a dusty trail, while a train rumbles westward—perhaps all the way to the Pacific Ocean. Two Indians on horseback look on, undoubtedly impressed.

Battle of Beecher Island
In 1868 Major General George Forsyth and 50 frontiersmen pursued Cheyenne Indians who had been launching raids in Kansas and Colorado Territory. On September 17, Forsyth and his men were trapped by Cheyenne warriors on a sandbar in the Republican River in Colorado. During the nine-day siege that followed, Forsyth's men fought off about 750 Indians led by Chief Roman Nose, who was killed. On the 25th, cavalry troops arrived and rescued the surviving frontiersmen. This episode became known as the Battle of Beecher Island after Forsyth's slain second in command, Lieutenant Frederick Beecher.

Incident at Washita Almost four years after escaping the massacre of Sand Creek, Chief Black Kettle was still seeking peace with the U.S. in 1868. At the time, he was living at a Cheyenne camp on the Washita River in present-day Oklahoma. One late November dawn, Lieutenant Colonel George Custer's Seventh Cavalry surprised the camp, attacking it from four sides and killing more than 100 Indians, including Black Kettle and his wife. Because most Indian casualties were women, children, and old men, it remains a matter of controversy whether Custer's attack at Washita River should be called a battle or a massacre.

Sherman turns wrath toward Indians During the Civil War, General William Tecumseh Sherman achieved notoriety for his savagely destructive march through Georgia. As a commander after the war, Sherman fought against Indian uprisings throughout the West. His methods, which included the wholesale slaughter of bison in order to deprive Indians of their food supply, reflected his earlier "total war" tactics against the Confederacy. He didn't mince words about his goals, famously commenting that "the more I see of these Indians, the more convinced I am that they will all have to be killed or be maintained as a species of paupers."

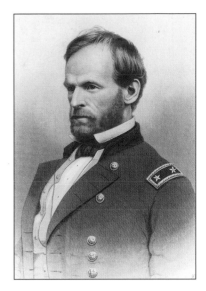

Harte captures California "color"
The picturesque prospectors and gamblers of the California gold fields were brought to life for Easterners through a series of delightful short stories by Bret Harte. A native of Albany, New York, Harte published his first poem at age 11, and he was still in his teens when he journeyed to California in 1854. Impressionable and talented, he picked up the "local color" of the gold fields, and incorporated this fresh, captivating material in such stories as "The Luck of Roaring Camp," "Tennessee's Partners," and "The Outcasts of Poker Flat." Although his work became imitative and his popularity declined, Bret Harte earned a permanent niche in western fiction.

Bierstadt opens eyes to the West Beginning in 1859, Albert Bierstadt made a number of journeys into the West, returning with sketches, photographs, and Indian artifacts. In his New York City studio, he painted huge canvases of western scenes, wildlife, and Indians. His work fueled American fascination with lesser-known parts of their country and helped to draw settlers westward. During the 1860s and 1870s, Bierstadt was considered America's foremost painter. In 1867 he toured Europe and England and had an audience with Queen Victoria. *Among the Sierra Mountains, California* (*pictured*) was exhibited at London's Royal Academy.

December 1867: The Delaware Indians begin their relocation from Kansas to Indian Territory, with each family required to make the 200-mile journey at its own expense and risk.

1868: The Kiowa Indians are relocated to a reservation in Oklahoma, and the Crow are moved to a reservation in Montana.

1868: The U.S. signs the Fort Laramie Treaty of 1868 with the Sioux, agreeing to abandon the forts on the Bozeman Trail. The Sioux retain their hunting grounds in the Montana, Wyoming, and Dakota territories, but agree to become "civilized."

1868: The Senate agrees to permit open immigration from China.

1868: Congress organizes Wyoming as a U.S. territory.

1868: The Chinese workers building the Central Pacific rail line succeed in making their way through the High Sierras.

1868: George Armstrong Custer and his troops attack a Cheyenne community on the Washita River in present-day Oklahoma, the same people who were decimated at Sand Creek four years earlier. This time, Chief Black Kettle is killed along with about 100 of his people.

1868: Former Confederate states Florida, Alabama, Louisiana, North Carolina, and South Carolina are readmitted to the Union following their ratification of the 14th Amendment. The amendment asserts that no state can make any law that would deny any U.S. citizen equal protection under the law, in part addressing the passage of Black Codes in southern States.

1868: The size of Utah Territory is reduced to that of the present state of Utah.

The golden spike Union Pacific and Central Pacific tracks met at Promontory Point, Utah, on May 10, 1869, triggering a nationwide celebration over the completion of the first transcontinental railroad. When a golden spike was driven into a pre-drilled hole, a waiting telegrapher tapped out the news. The Liberty Bell pealed in Philadelphia, and fireworks exploded across the nation. A hundred cannons were fired in the nation's capital, and 220 boomed in San Francisco. The golden spike, engraved with official signatures, was quickly removed. Today the spike is on display at Stanford University, which was founded by Leland Stanford of the Central Pacific, who swung the sledgehammer at Promontory Point.

Traveling in style Following the completion of America's first transcontinental railroad in 1867, world travelers sought to make the adventurous coast-to-coast journey. In 1870 first-class passengers were charged $100 to travel from Omaha to Sacramento. George Pullman's new sleeping cars were staffed by courteous porters, and boasted fresh linen and steam heating. The Palace Hotel Express offered excellent meal service in a dining car (*pictured*) for the four-day trip.

The Transcontinental Railroad

WHEN THE 1800s BEGAN, Americans still traveled on foot, in animal-drawn vehicles, and on the backs of such tractable creatures as horses, mules, and donkeys. In the 1840s, trains carried people and goods between major U.S. cities. By 1869 it became possible to cross the entire country in seven days on the transcontinental railroad.

When he took office, President Abraham Lincoln saw the need for a railroad to connect the east and west coasts. In 1862 Congress authorized two companies to build a cross-country track—one from each side of the country.

In 1863 Central Pacific workers started laying tracks from Sacramento, California, building eastward through the daunting Sierra Nevada Mountains. Most of their workers would be Chinese immigrants. That same year, the Union Pacific broke ground at Omaha, Nebraska, and its laborers began laying tracks into the West beginning in 1865. Many of their workers, recently released from service, still wore their blue or gray Civil War uniforms. Large numbers of Union Pacific employees were Irish immigrants.

On May 10, 1869, the two lines were joined with much ceremony at Promontory Point, Utah. However, the work was not over. Since the companies had been paid by the mile, both had focused on quantity of line rather than quality, and many repairs had to be made even after cross-country passenger service began on May 15.

Soon, other problems drew public scrutiny, especially in the East. The railroad had been financed largely by the federal government, but private companies had been in charge of the work. Although the Union Pacific Railroad wound up broke, investors in those private companies had become very rich. The financial manipulations have been attributed to Union Pacific Vice President Thomas Durant. He distributed cash and railroad shares to influential politicians and friends, then stuck a luckless congressman with most of the blame. Similar shenanigans likely took place among the "Big Four" officials of the Central Pacific. They grew wealthy from the railroad, but

A Cumbres and Toltec steam locomotive

it was discovered that all of that company's records were lost or burned.

The transcontinental railroad helped change the distribution of the nation's population. Granted property along the tracks by the government, railroad companies were eager to sell that land. To gain passengers and land buyers, railroads advertised cheap fares in the East and in Europe. They set up immigrant passenger cars, where travelers rode on simple benches, slept on straw mattresses, and cooked their own meals. The railroads also offered special boxcar rates for household goods, farm equipment, animals, and hired hands. These newcomers cleaned up some of the wildest railroad towns and other frontier towns and settled down to family life in the West.

Frontier life was no longer as isolated as it had been. Residents of the West could now import goods easily, visit back East, and read new books and magazines. Since the railroads had to publish schedules, the country was divided into four regularized time zones, and each locale could no longer decide for itself what time it was there. The telegraph line that ran alongside the transcontinental tracks flashed messages across the country—a country that was beginning to feel like a single nation.

1861-1876

February 24, 1868: The House of Representatives impeaches President Andrew Johnson for his attempt to strip Secretary of War Stanton of his office.

May 26, 1868: President Johnson is acquitted when the Senate—by a single vote—fails to reach the two-thirds majority needed for conviction.

July 28, 1868: The secretary of state declares that 28 of the 37 states have ratified the 14th Amendment to the Constitution.

1869: John Wesley Powell leads an expedition through the Grand Canyon, paving the way for a government-funded geologic study of the West.

1869: Women are granted suffrage in Wyoming, making it the first U.S. state or territory in which women may vote.

1869: Wild Bill Hickok becomes marshal of Hays City, Kansas.

May 10, 1869: The transcontinental railroad is completed by the Central Pacific and Union Pacific railroad companies. A ceremonial golden spike joins the two railways together in Promontory Point, Utah.

1870: Virginia, Texas, and Georgia are readmitted to the Union.

1870: The U.S. government relocates the Osage Indian tribe to a northeastern Oklahoma reservation.

1870: Motivated by a growing demand for buffalo meat and hides, and transported by the new transcontinental railroad, buffalo hunters head to the Plains in droves. Within a decade, America's buffalo will be almost completely wiped out.

1870: Mormons gain a political edge when the Utah legislature gives women the right to vote, at the behest of Mormon leader Brigham Young.

Emperor Norton Was he crazy, eccentric, or extremely clever? On September 17, 1859, a bankrupt San Francisco resident named Joshua Norton declared himself Norton I, "Emperor of These United States and Protector of Mexico." The numerous decrees of Emperor Norton's 21-year "reign" included the abolition of the U.S. Congress and the Democratic and Republican parties. Although penniless and powerless, Norton was treated with deference and honor by his fellow San Franciscans. Moreover, a few of his decrees—including the construction of a bridge and a tunnel across San Francisco Bay—were eventually realized.

Norton der Erſte,

Grant's shifting Indian policy Ulysses S. Grant commanded the U.S. Army after the Civil War until he became president early in 1869. Although General Grant was preoccupied with the turbulent Reconstruction of the South, he generally supported a forceful military policy toward Native Americans of the West. But as president, he was influenced by humanitarian reformers. President Grant's "Peace Policy" featured civilian control of reservations and appointment of Indian agents by church groups. The Army's role was to drive the tribes onto the reservations. But civilian, rather than military, control of the reservations led to corruption and mistreatment, which triggered hostile outbreaks that belied the term "Peace Policy."

Grant's "Peace Policy"

WHEN CIVIL WAR HERO Ulysses S. Grant became president in 1869, the nation's Indian policy was in terrible shape. Many citizens feared that a military solution to the "Indian problem" would lead to genocide. The humanitarian organization "Friends of the Indian"—mostly wealthy Easterners who lived where Indians were practically nonexistent—implored Grant to do something. The result was the Quaker Policy, aka the Peace Policy. Congress, admitting it had utterly failed to fulfill its constitutional duty, handed control of Indian policy to religious groups, notably Quakers, who enjoyed a reputation for fair dealings with Indians.

Though motivated by high-minded intentions, the religious men's ethnocentrism, ignorance, and inexperience doomed the policy. Recruiting reliable and honest men to serve as Indian agents at remote reservations proved difficult. Various denominations fell into bitter squabbling over the distribution of agencies; Protestants received the majority. Making matters worse, Grant's administration was deeply tainted by corruption. Powerful lobbyists routinely bribed congressmen, and Grant's own Cabinet members hatched criminal schemes, including the sale of Indian agencies and annuity contracts to scoundrels who defrauded both Indians and the U.S. government.

Far from bringing peace, the closing decades of the 19th century saw more bloodshed than ever in the West. Custer's fights at the Washita River and Little Big Horn,

Red Cloud speaks with President Grant

the Nez Percé War, the Apache Wars, the slaughter at Wounded Knee, and other conflicts occurred during the Peace Policy years (circa 1868–90). Indians suffered military defeat and then underwent forced relocation, losing much land in the process. Meanwhile, as railroads pushed into the West, thousands of bigoted whites stormed—legally and illegally—into the Plains Indians' homelands.

Ultimately deemed a near total failure, the Peace Policy was jettisoned by 1882. It served the greed and illusory fantasies of whites, but failed to improve Indians' already grim situation. The results for Indians included substantial land losses and further demoralization.

Great Salt Lake City Jim Bridger and other fur trappers visited the Great Salt Lake in the 1820s, but no Americans settled the area until 1847. That year, 148 Mormon pioneers led by Brigham Young laid out Great Salt Lake City with streets 132 feet wide. The "Temple Block" was intended as the future site of a grand temple. Great Salt Lake City prospered from the traffic of the California Gold Rush, and in 1856 it was designated the capital of Utah Territory. "Great" was dropped from the city name in 1868. The next year, the nation's first transcontinental railroad was completed at nearby Promontory Point, assuring further growth and prosperity.

1870: The Paiute tribe becomes noted for its newfound devotion to the Ghost Dance movement, the tenets of which include the imminent disappearance of the white man. The movement will spread to parts of Nevada, California, and Oregon.

1870: Bret Harte establishes a set of stereotypes about eccentric and coarse frontier characters with the publication of his book *The Luck of Roaring Camp and Other Sketches.*

1870: California has perpetrated the worst treatment of American Indians in U.S. history, based on outright genocide on the missions. From 1845 to 1870, California's Indian population has declined by 80 percent.

January 23, 1870: In retaliation for an attack on a white settler and his son, some 173 Blackfoot Indians are murdered by U.S. soldiers on Montana's Marias River.

February 23, 1870: The state of Mississippi is readmitted to the Union.

March 30, 1870: The secretary of state proclaims that 29 of the 37 states have ratified the 15th Amendment to the Constitution. The amendment states that the right to vote cannot be denied based on a man's race or status as a former slave.

1871: Congress passes the Indian Appropriations Act, which calls for all Indians to be treated as individuals. The act effectively ends the practice of treating Indian tribes as sovereign nations.

1871: A contingent of Papago Indians, along with members of the Tucson Committee of Public Safety, murders more than 100 Apaches, their historic enemies, outside Camp Grant, Arizona.

Wheeler aims to map the West In 1869 Lieutenant George Montague Wheeler of the Army Corps of Engineers was placed in charge of a geographical expedition of central Nevada. As its purpose grew, the expedition assumed the formidable title of the Geographical Survey of the Territory of the United States West of the 100th Meridian. Wheeler's mission was to make maps, locate Indian tribes, and undertake geological and zoological studies. The impressive achievements of this expedition, which continued until 1879, included photographs of the Grand Canyon. Declining health kept Wheeler from fulfilling his goal of mapping the entire western United States.

Texas Longhorns It is believed that Longhorn cattle descended from Mexican herds that were driven northward to stock Texas missions. As these herds crossed the Rio Grande, strays wandered into a harsh, virtually uninhabited land of cactus, brush, and mesquite trees. To deal with predators and wilderness conditions, these cattle boasted horns six feet or more in width, along with aggressive temperaments and remarkable agility. Lanky and multicolored, these wild beasts—up to 10 million of them—roamed southern Texas by the end of the Civil War. The tough and ornery longhorn would become an icon of the state of Texas.

California vineyards The California wine industry began modestly in the 1700s when Franciscan padres began growing the "Mission" variety of grape to provide sacramental wine for their services. Beginning in 1824, American pioneer Joseph Chapman cultivated Mission grapevines for commercial purposes near Los Angeles. Hungarian immigrant Agoston Haraszthy transplanted cuttings from his family's vineyards in the hills of Sonoma County in 1857. In 1861 the state of California sent Haraszthy to Europe, and he returned with 100,000 vines from the finest vineyards. Cuttings were distributed to growers throughout the state, and by 1870 California vintners were producing three million gallons of wine a year.

Pinkerton Detective Agency In 1850 a Chicago deputy sheriff organized a detective agency with the motto "We never sleep." Alan Pinkerton's National Detective Agency succeeded in driving many outlaws

out of the train-robbing business. His agents included Kate Warne, the first American female detective, and Charles Angelo Siringo, who chased down the James Gang. Pinkerton agents caught stagecoach robber Black Bart and hounded the Wild Bunch until Butch and Sundance left the country. The Federal Bureau of Investigation, founded in 1908, was modeled after Pinkerton's agency.

Born to kill John Wesley Hardin was named by his father, a Texas preacher, after the founder of Methodism. But from a young age, Hardin revealed the instincts of a killer. As a boy, he stabbed a youngster in the chest, and at 15 he shot a former slave to death. Pursued by Reconstruction troops, the young killer defended himself with deadly aggressiveness. Hardin drank and gambled, and from 1868 through 1874

he was embroiled in one gunfight after another. He escaped to Florida only to be captured there and sentenced to a long prison term. Released in 1894, Hardin reverted to his reckless ways. He was killed by adversary John Selman during a dice game the following year.

Deadly shoot-outs In the frontier West, the population was overwhelmingly male, almost everyone carried firearms, and drinking and gambling were popular recreational activities. When armed men, fortified with whiskey, quarreled over a card game or a dance hall girl, gunplay often erupted. A study of 590 gunfights proved that seven out of every 10 gunfights produced one or more fatalities. In this tableau, two soldiers from Fort Hays, Kansas, lie dead outside a Hays City dive.

The Hayden Survey During the 1850s, Ferdinand Hayden (*seated at far end of table*) accompanied scientific expeditions into the West. After the Civil War, he conducted far-ranging geological surveys, persuading botanists, zoologists, anthropologists, painters, and photographers to accompany him. In 1870 Congress appropriated $25,000 to fund the Hayden Survey of the Western Territories for the Department of the Interior. Hayden launched expeditions into Yellowstone country in 1870 and 1871, which were instrumental in the creation of Yellowstone National Park.

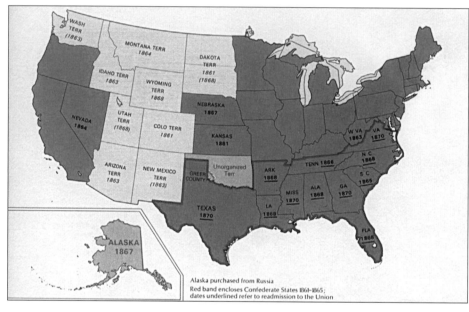

Alaska purchased from Russia
Red band encloses Confederate States 1861-1865;
dates underlined refer to readmission to the Union

New states and territories Throughout the 1860s, the West experienced constant development. Mining activity led to the creation of the state of Nevada and the territories of Colorado, Idaho, Washington, Montana, and Arizona. Kansas and Nebraska achieved statehood, and Dakota, Utah, and New Mexico Territories were organized. Wyoming Territory was created because of the appearance of the railroad. Construction of the first transcontinental railroad, which began during the Civil War, was completed in 1869.

Powell's expeditions Major John Wesley Powell overcame the loss of an arm during the Civil War to lead a series of exploratory expeditions through the West from 1867 through 1875. Undaunted by dangers and hardships, Powell brought his small parties to one spectacular site after another. Powell's photographer, John Hillers, provided views of Arizona's Canyon de Chelly (*pictured*) during the 1871 expedition. Such photographs supplemented surveys and maps compiled by Powell and his men.

Shooting buffalo On the Plains, buffalo herds once extended as far as the eye could see. However, they were dramatically reduced by Indians hunting from horseback, white hunters in search of buffalo meat for railroad workers and hides for leather, and soldiers shooting the animals for sport. Even passengers on railway lines shot buffalo for the fun of it, especially when they blocked the track (*as pictured here*). According to historian Donald Fixico, by the late 1800s only about 1,200 buffalo were left in the West.

O'Sullivan photographs the West Frontier photographer Timothy O'Sullivan captured this view of Black Canyon on the Colorado River. O'Sullivan trained under famed photographer Matthew Brady during the Civil War, then headed to the West for new challenges. O'Sullivan loaded about 300 pounds of photographic equipment into a roofed wagon with sides that provided a traveling darkroom. The wagon was drawn by four mules. In mountainous country, the camera, tripod, chemicals, and heavy glass negatives had to be packed tightly. Until his death at 42, O'Sullivan provided accurate visual documentation of America's West.

Sheridan's hatred of Indians An 1853 graduate of West Point, General Philip Sheridan performed superbly as a cavalry leader during the Civil War. After the war, he intended to subdue the Indians of the West by aggressively confining them to reservations. General Sheridan encouraged buffalo hunters to violate treaties and kill off the herds that made possible the lifestyle of Plains Indians. He also insisted upon winter campaigns into the Indian heartlands, and was quoted as saying, "The only good Indians I ever saw were dead." Sheridan's harsh strategy succeeded, and in 1884 he was named commanding general of the U.S. Army.

1871: Federal Judge James McKean orders Mormon leader Brigham Young arrested on polygamy charges. Federal prosecutors also bring John Lee and other Mormons up on murder charges for the 1857 Mountain Meadows Massacre. *See 1875.*

1871: Anti-Chinese riots rock Los Angeles. By the time the dust settles, about 25 of the city's 200 Chinese are dead.

1871: Apache Chief Cochise surrenders to Army General George Crook, but flees when it becomes clear that Crook intends to send the Apaches to a New Mexico reservation. *See 1872.*

1871: Wild Bill Hickok becomes the marshal of Abilene, Kansas.

October 8, 1871: The Great Chicago Fire begins. Almost simultaneously, the Great Peshtigo Fire, one of the worst forest fires in recorded North American history, starts in Wisconsin. It will spread to Michigan.

1872: A year after fleeing from General Crook, Apache Chief Cochise surrenders to General Oliver Otis Howard. He is sent to an Arizona reservation.

1872: Cheyenne, Wyoming, hosts the first rodeo.

1872: Mark Twain publishes *Roughing It,* his account of his travels and writings in the West.

1872: "Buffalo Bill" Cody receives the Congressional Medal of Honor in recognition of his military service in the campaign against the Cheyenne.

1872: Canada passes the Dominion Lands Act, similar to the U.S. Homestead Act of 1862.

1872: Yellowstone National Park is established by an act of Congress. The act sets aside more than two million acres in northwest Wyoming for Yellowstone.

Corruption of Indian agents Indian agents were employees of the Bureau of Indian Affairs. Their thankless, difficult, and sometimes dangerous job was to distribute government annuities and supplies on reservations. All the while, they were to protect Indians from unscrupulous traders and make sure treaties were upheld by both Indians and whites. Because agents were underpaid, it is not surprising that many of them were corrupt. As this cartoon shows, some agents made small fortunes by pocketing federal annuities and selling goods intended for the Indians, who were forced further into poverty and starvation.

Making use of buffalo hides From 1870 to 1883, white hide hunters followed buffalo herds across the Great Plains, establishing camps wherever there were large kills. A good hunter employed two to four skinners, and traveled with one or two wagons. Freshly skinned hides were stretched and pegged to the ground, flesh side up for drying. A special poison was applied to kill insects that would infest the hides. Two out of three hides were ruined by bugs, by careless skinners, or by improper drying. Usable hides were brought by wagon to railheads, where buyers paid $1 to $3.50 for each. The hides then were shipped in bales to tanners in the East.

Chinese Exclusion

In the decades following the California Gold Rush, hundreds of thousands of Chinese made their way to American shores, with more than 90 percent settling in the West. Most came from the economically depressed Taishan district, north of Hong Kong, and nearly all were men. In many ways, those who journeyed to America were like all immigrants—they came to prosper in a land where opportunity abounded. But the Chinese experience was very different from that of their European counterparts. They endured appalling levels of racism, discrimination, and extralegal violence. The Chinese were so reviled that they eventually were barred entry into the nation with the passage of the Exclusion Act of 1882.

Organized labor especially detested "coolies" (Chinese laborers). White miners and railroad workers contended that the new immigrants depressed wages and heightened competition for jobs. Whites formed vigilance committees to intimidate Chinese laborers. When the economy faltered in the 1870s, the amount of oppression increased. In Los Angeles, white mobs swept through a Chinese neighborhood, killing 19. One particularly gruesome episode in Chico, California, saw whites open fire on a group of orchard workers and then set their bodies ablaze.

Besides violence, workingmen's organizations zealously lobbied for restrictions on Chinese immigration and civil rights. The Foreign Miners License Law forced immigrants to pay special taxes, while the Naturalization Act of 1870 limited citizenship to whites and blacks only. Asian children were prohibited from attending public schools, and California enacted legislation that curbed legal protection by forbidding Chinese testimony against whites.

Anti-Chinese legislation culminated in the Exclusion Act, but the racism and violence continued for decades. On September 2, 1885, in Rock Springs, Wyoming, a seemingly minor argument escalated into a massacre, leaving 28 Chinese laborers dead. That same year in Tacoma, Washington, whites burned down Chinese homes and businesses and drove them out of town. In 1892 labor successfully lobbied for the passage of the Geary Bill, which renewed the Exclusion Act and required the Chinese still in the country to carry residency papers. The Exclusion Act remained in effect until 1943.

Chinese Massacre Virulent anti-Chinese sentiment in California triggered the infamous Chinese Massacre in Los Angeles on October 24, 1871. In Chinatown, two Asian men quarreled over a Chinese woman. When gunplay erupted, a white man was killed in the crossfire. A mob of 500 white men, representing a 10th of the population of 5,000, went on a rampage. Nineteen Chinese men and boys were slain. Few Chinese left Los Angeles, however, and despite other racist acts their presence in the community steadily grew.

THE HANGING PLACE

Men were dragged forth, many of them mortally wounded, and hurled headlong from a raised sidewalk to the ground. To the neck of some of the most helpless the mob fastened ropes and, with a whoop and a hurrah, rushed down Los Angeles Street to the hanging place, dragging some writhing wretch prone upon the ground. More doomed and bleeding miserables were jerked along by as many eager hands as could lay hold of clothing and queue, cuffed and cursed in the meantime by the infuriated multitude. A boy was thus led to the place of slaughter. The little fellow was not above twelve years of age. He had been a month in the country and knew not a word of English. He seemed paralyzed by fear—his eyes were fixed and staring, his face blue-blanched and idiotic. He was hanged.

—Journalist P. S. Dorney, describing the anti-Chinese riot in Los Angeles in October 1871

Buffalo hunting The buffalo was the staff of life of Plains Indians, who utilized many parts of the animal. White men had their own reasons for killing the great beasts. Professional hunters killed bison to provide eastern gourmets with buffalo humps and tongues. Also, hunters were contracted to provide railroad crews with meat. In 1870 tanners developed a process for turning the thick, tough buffalo hides into commercial leather. Hide hunters began killing bison in vast numbers, skinning the carcasses and leaving the rest to rot. The enormous herds were nearly exterminated by 1883, and Plains tribes found their traditional way of life impossible.

A frustrated Kiowa Satanta was a bold, fearless Kiowa warrior who eventually became a chief. A gifted orator, he had a booming laugh and reveled in his role of Plains Indian leader. Disgusted when Kiowas moved onto a reservation, Satanta often slipped away for raids. Arrested and sentenced to be executed in 1871, he was pardoned back to his reservation. Satanta promptly went back on the warpath, but in 1874 he was seized again and sent to prison. In 1878 the old war chief committed suicide by jumping headfirst from a second-story window.

King's survey In 1867, 25-year-old mountaineer and mining engineer Clarence King (*pictured*) headed a U.S. government-sponsored geological survey along the route of the Union Pacific Railroad in Colorado. The survey's primary goal was to locate mineral sources, but by its completion in 1878 its far-ranging achievements included the earliest discovery of a glacier in the United States (Mount Shasta in California). Based on the survey, King wrote *Systematic Geology*, considered one of the great scientific works of its time. He also used his expertise to expose a fraudulent diamond field in Colorado.

Yosemite and Yellowstone

SOON AFTER WHITE PEOPLE learned of its existence in 1851, California's magnificent Yosemite Valley was threatened by commercial interests. During the decade, homesteader Galen Clark publicized the need to protect the giant sequoias in Yosemite's neighboring Mariposa Grove from the timber industry.

A coalition of environmentalists, who were devoted to wilderness preservation, and capitalists, who were tantalized by the possibilities of tourism, took their concerns to the federal government. In 1864, while the Civil War still raged, the U.S. Congress passed a bill ceding Yosemite Valley and the Mariposa Grove to the state of California, "upon the express conditions that the premises shall be held for public use, resort, and recreation." Once President Abraham Lincoln signed the bill, a remarkable precedent was set. The U.S. government was in the business of protecting public lands.

In 1871 another great wilderness area was explored—the Yellowstone Valley. With its canyons, waterfalls, mountain peaks, geysers, and other natural wonders, Yellowstone dazzled the public imagination and seemed in urgent need of protection from private interests. But unlike Yosemite, Yellowstone could not be ceded to a state; it lay in both the Montana and Wyoming territories. And so, in 1872, the federal government took the remarkable step of bringing the 3,300-square-mile area directly under its control, making Yellowstone not only America's, but the world's, first national park.

Meanwhile, the Yosemite Valley had been poorly managed by the state of California. The sequoias were in renewed danger from logging, and high country meadows were threatened by the overgrazing of sheep—described by environmentalist John Muir as "hooved locusts." Largely through Muir's efforts, Yosemite became a national park in 1890. In 1906 the environmentally conscious President Theodore Roosevelt signed a bill that brought Yosemite completely under federal control.

In 1916 an act of Congress created the National Park Service. Today, the service oversees 57 national parks and many other sites of historical or natural significance.

The wonders of Yellowstone In 1870-71, when the first reports of Yellowstone were published in the East, the public was entranced by the area's plentiful wonders. In addition to the Mammoth Hot Springs (shown here in an 1872 photograph by William Henry Jackson), Yellowstone featured fossil forests, lakes and rivers, a mountain of volcanic glass, and a colorful 19-mile-long gorge with two stunning waterfalls. Yellowstone was devoid of gold, silver, and other commercially valuable metals and minerals, and it was not suitable for timber or grazing interests. Therefore, Congress found it fairly easy to declare Yellowstone the nation's and the world's first national park in 1872.

April 10, 1872: The tree-poor state of Nebraska is host to the nation's first Arbor Day celebration.

May 1872: The passage of the Mining Act of 1872 ensures a streamlined system for staking a claim on public land.

1873: General George Custer begins to wage war against the Sioux. Crazy Horse and Sitting Bull, though clever opponents, are worn down by Custer's tenacity.

1873: San Francisco's first cable car carries passengers up and down the city's steep streets.

1873: President Ulysses S. Grant vetoes a law protecting the North American buffalo herd, despite overwhelming evidence that the animals are in dire jeopardy.

1873: The first railroad line in South Dakota connects Yankton with Sioux City, Iowa. The arrival of the railroad will encourage white settlement in the territory.

1873: Northern California's Modoc Indian War ends with the capture of their leader, Kintpuash, also known as Captain Jack.

1873: George Custer and his Seventh Cavalry encounter Sitting Bull while on assignment guarding Northern Pacific Railroad surveyors.

1873: The American economy collapses following the panic of 1873.

1874: The legal precedent for school segregation is set in a California court (*Ward v. Flood*).

1874: Joseph Glidden receives a patent for barbed wire.

1874: The "Great American Desert" begins its transition to America's breadbasket when Russian Mennonites reach Kansas and plant drought-resistant "Turkey Red" wheat.

The Modoc War When Oregon settlers demanded that the Army remove warlike Modocs from their traditional homeland, the Native Americans resisted, then retreated to the Lava Beds, a natural fortress. During the ensuing Modoc War of 1872–73, the Army instituted a lengthy siege, but assaults against the outnumbered warriors were repeatedly repulsed. The Spencer repeating rifle that's pictured was Army issue, and probably was one of the spoils of war seized by Modoc braves. Not until Modocs were betrayed by deserters was the Army able to flush their skillful enemies.

Captain Jack Young Modoc leader Kintpuash, known to whites as Captain Jack, was reluctant to go to war, but he resisted confinement to a reservation. During the Modoc War, he proved to be a fierce and able war chief. On April 11, 1873, while Brigadier General E.R.S. Canby led peace discussions, Kintpuash produced a pistol and shot the Civil War veteran in the face. In the ensuing melee, other members of the white delegation became casualties, but Canby would be the only general killed during the Indian Wars. Within months, Kintpuash was betrayed and then surrendered. He was hanged on October 3, 1873.

The General Mining Act

FROM CALIFORNIA to Nevada to Colorado, Americans in the mid-1800s discovered precious metals imbedded in the earth, including gold and silver. But who had a right to the land in which these treasures were buried? This situation was addressed by a federal mining law in 1866, which eventually was revised into the General Mining Act of 1872. Much like the Homesteading Act of the same period, the Mining Act made public land readily and cheaply available to U.S. citizens.

Individuals, however, did not benefit from this law. Once lone prospectors exhausted surface soil and streambeds of gold, their work was through. The ongoing quest for gold, silver, and other metals (such as copper and zinc) required mine shafts, crushing mills, and other technologies of large-scale mining. These in turn required large-scale capital. And so corporations, not individuals, reaped the greatest advantage from public land made available at outrageously low prices.

While corporations profited from the government's generosity, miners suffered from declining wages and increasingly dangerous work—a development that made the West ripe for strikes, labor violence, and radicalism during the 1890s and the early years of the 20th century. Thus, the General Mining Act of 1872 stirred up problems that still trouble American society today.

Indeed, the law itself remains very much in force. Numerous attempts have been made to reform it, raising issues of environmental concerns and the possibility of royalty payments to the federal government. Despite these issues, the law remains much as it was in 1872. Moreover, public lands continue to be sold at the original 1872 prices of $2.50 or $5.00 an acre.

Silver boomtown Silver City, New Mexico, was founded in 1870 by Captain John Bullard, who laid out streets on his farm after discovering silver on a nearby hill. Prospectors swarmed into the valley, and a tent city sprang up where Apaches recently had camped. Early in 1871, Captain Bullard was killed in a fight with Apaches, but Silver City continued to boom. Frame and brick buildings replaced the tents, and the streets teemed with ox trains and other traffic. In 1873 a 13-year-old boy moved into town along with his brother, mother, and stepdad. The young teen was Henry McCarty, aka Billy the Kid.

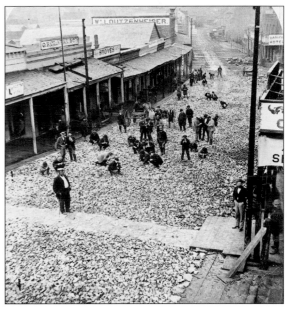

Streets paved with gold Grass Valley, California, was truly the sort of town from which legends were made. According to one story, gold was found in the area when a miner stubbed his toe against a rock that was rich with the precious metal. During the 1850s and afterward, Grass Valley became the center for three of California's richest mines—the Empire, the Idaho-Maryland, and the North Star. In this 1873 photograph, prospectors try to confirm the rumors that Grass Valley's streets were literally paved with gold.

1874: A gold rush grips the Lakota's sacred Black Hills. U.S. authorities assist the miners' interests at the expense of the Lakota and in violation of the 1868 Fort Laramie Treaty.

1874: The ancient Anasazi cliff dwellings at Colorado's Mesa Verde are captured on film by notable photographer William H. Jackson.

1875: John Lee is tried for the 1857 Mountain Meadows Massacre. The non-Mormon jurors vote to convict while the Mormons vote to acquit, forcing a mistrial. The nation is outraged, and Mormon leaders turn their backs on Lee. *See* September 1876.

1875: Pinkerton agents try and fail to assassinate the outlaw James brothers by firebombing their Missouri farm. Archie Samuel, Jesse and Frank's half brother, dies in the attack.

1875: A Senate commission offers Red Cloud and other Lakota chiefs $6 million for their sacred Black Hills. The Lakota decline and vow to defend their lands from intruders.

1875: Judge Isaac Parker arrives in Fort Smith, Arkansas. In 21 years as a frontier judge, he will sentence 168 people to death, 88 of whom will hang. Parker will earn the moniker "Hanging Judge."

1875: In Oklahoma, Bass Reeves becomes probably the first black deputy U.S. marshal west of the Mississippi.

1875: Legendary western lawman Wyatt Earp takes a law enforcement position in Wichita, Kansas.

1875: Deadwood, South Dakota, is born when miners in the Black Hills find gold in Deadwood Creek. The town soon will gain a reputation as one of the West's wildest outposts.

1876: Jack McCall shoots Wild Bill Hickok in the back of the head in Deadwood, South Dakota.

Colt's revolvers Samuel Colt of Hartford, Connecticut, invented and manufactured revolvers—handguns that could shoot six bullets without reloading. Colt earned a U.S. patent for a revolver in 1836 and then improved the design in 1846 (with the help of Army Ranger Captain Samuel H. Walker). When the Army ordered 1,000 revolvers, Colt set up a factory to produce the first gun with truly interchangeable parts. Colt's .45-caliber "six-shooter" became known as "The Peacemaker," and was called "the gun that won the West." The model shown here, adopted by the U.S. Cavalry in 1873, was the most widely used in the Wild West.

Trigger-happy Hickok The cast of *The Scouts of the Plains,* a popular stage drama of the 1870s, included "Wild Bill" Hickok (*second from left*). James Butler Hickok never took comfortably to the stage; during one performance of *Scouts,* he shot out an annoying spotlight. Hickok, a Pony Express station attendant, wagon driver, Army scout, trail guide, gambler, and gunfighter, is said to have killed 100 men. In 1876, as marshal in Deadwood, South Dakota, he was shot from behind and killed while playing poker. He was holding two black aces and two black eights, which became known as "the dead man's hand."

Shipping pens In 1874 Wichita, Kansas, like every other cattle town, boasted shipping pens alongside railroad tracks. Following delivery to the pens, the cattle were delivered by train to stockyards or "livestock hotels," with adjacent slaughter facilities (or meat-packing plants) that processed the animals for shipment to customers. Chicago, where the Union Stockyards were incorporated in 1865, was the first dominant shipping point. Other major stockyards soon were established in Kansas City, St. Louis, Omaha, Fort Worth, and, in 1887, Wichita.

Moran's view of the Grand Canyon In 1871 Thomas Moran accompanied government surveyor Ferdinand Hayden to Yellowstone. Moran's watercolor sketches, and the large oil paintings he made from them, caught the public's imagination and influenced the campaign to make Yellowstone a national park. In 1873 Moran went westward again—this time with John Wesley Powell—and saw the Grand Canyon. Moran would return there many times and paint hundreds of images of the area. Congress bought a large Moran oil painting of Yellowstone in 1872, and two years later bought *The Chasm of the Colorado* (*pictured*), which featured the Grand Canyon. Both paintings were hung in the nation's Capitol.

Mackenzie's triumphs Ranald Slidell Mackenzie already had distinguished himself as a Union officer during the Civil War before going west to join the Indian Wars as a colonel. Commanding primarily out of Texas, he became an exceptionally able Indian fighter. His most notable victory was the September 1874 Battle of Palo Duro Canyon in Texas, which ended the Red River War against combined forces of Kiowa, Apache, Comanche, Arapaho, and Sioux. After routing the Indians at Palo Duro, Mackenzie crippled further resistance by ordering more than a thousand of their horses slain.

Sharps rifles Patented by Christian Sharps in 1848, the Sharps breechloading rifle achieved immediate popularity because it was powerful and quick to load. In 1854 Reverend Henry Ward Beecher shipped Sharps carbines to fellow abolitionists in Bleeding Kansas. The crates were marked "Bibles," and the carbines became known as "Beecher's Bibles." More than 100,000 were purchased for the Union Army during the Civil War. In 1874 Sharps hunting rifles (*pictured*) began to be manufactured. The Sharps rifles were utilized by hide hunters to slaughter the enormous herds of buffalo in the West.

Showdown at Adobe Walls On June 27, 1874, hundreds of Comanche, Cheyenne, Arapaho, and Kiowa warriors launched a dawn attack on Adobe Walls, a lonely cluster of structures that serviced buffalo hunters in the Texas Panhandle. Only 28 men were available to defend Adobe Walls. Three of the hunters were killed, but the professional hunters, armed with powerful buffalo guns, drove off their attackers. The young chief, Quanah Parker, was wounded, and Billy Dixon shot another war leader off his horse at seven-eighths of a mile. The Army responded with a major campaign. In the resulting Red River War of 1874–75, more than a dozed engagements occurred between the Army and Plains Indians in the Texas Panhandle region. Victorious, the Army drove the Comanche and Kiowa onto reservations.

Remington revolvers Remington percussion cap revolvers began to be produced in 1857. The Remington New Model Army in .44 caliber was especially popular, with 122,000 manufactured. The United States Army purchased more than 125,000 Remingtons during the Civil War, when the Remington was the principal competitor of Colt revolvers. After the war, the Colt Peacemaker became the most popular cartridge revolver. Remington's first cartridge pistol was the 1875 Single Action Army Model in .45 caliber (*pictured*). This excellent revolver was similar in appearance to the Civil War percussion weapon.

Railroads recruit Mennonites As the Atchison, Topeka and Santa Fe Railway laid its tracks across Kansas, the company was anxious for capable farmers to settle along the route. Members of the Mennonite religious sect were famous worldwide for their farming skills. So during 1873–74, the railroad encouraged Mennonites who were persecuted in Russia to immigrate to Kansas, offering them land on extremely generous terms. Before they could establish permanent dwellings, Mennonite settlers lived in harsh conditions—some in tar paper shacks provided by the railroads, others in communal longhouses like the one shown here.

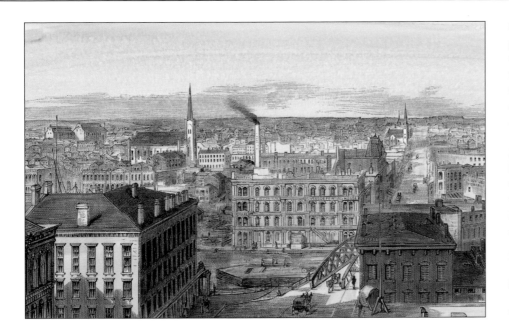

Germans influence Milwaukee's growth By the 1830s, Milwaukee expanded from its beginnings as a fur trading center and became a growing metropolis. Incorporated by the Wisconsin territorial legislature in 1836, Milwaukee grew to 20,000 residents by 1850. By 1890 its population exceeded 200,000, making it one of the 20 largest U.S. cities. A mixed populace of German, Irish, and "Yankee" residents transformed the city into a thriving industrial center by the late 19th century. The substantial German population helped promote socialism in the city, and some early "reform" governors were Socialists. German influence also boosted Milwaukee's fame as a major beer-producing region.

America's largest ranch King Ranch cowboys ready cattle for a drive to market. Founded in 1853 in south Texas by Captain Richard King and Gideon Lewis, the ranch grew and was consolidated between 1861 and 1875. It was frequented by Confederate General Robert E. Lee, who supposedly chose the site for the main house. King's success driving cattle, especially longhorns, came in part from his practice of allowing trail bosses to own an interest in the herds. The contemporary King Ranch is the largest in the United States. It sprawls across six counties and covers an area larger than Rhode Island.

Black Hills War On June 17, 1876, at Rosebud Creek in the Montana Territory, General George Crook's troops repulsed an attack by Lakota and Cheyenne warriors led by the Oglala Sioux leader Crazy Horse. The battle (*pictured*) was soon followed by Custer's disastrous defeat at Little Bighorn. Both battles took place during the Black Hills War, which was triggered by an illegal rush of gold prospectors into land that had been ceded to the Sioux according to the 1868 Fort Laramie Treaty. The Sioux refused to give up the Black Hills not because of its precious gold, but because they considered the land itself to be the sacred center of their universe.

Battle of the Little Bighorn

IN THE SPRING OF 1876, three columns of U.S. troops converged on Indian hunting grounds along Powder River in present-day Montana and Wyoming. Their intent: to force defiant bands of Lakota, Cheyenne, and Arapaho to abandon their nomadic ways for permanent reservations. On June 22, near the confluence of the Yellowstone River and Rosebud Creek, U.S. Army Brigadier General Alfred Terry dispatched Lieutenant Colonel George Custer and some 600 men of the Seventh Cavalry to search the upper Little Bighorn Valley for hostiles.

On June 24, Custer's scouts located a large village inhabited by as many as 7,000 Natives under the leadership of Sitting Bull, Gall, Two Moons, Crazy Horse, and others. Fearing that his presence had been discovered by Indian hunting parties and that his adversaries would soon scatter, Custer decided to attack immediately. Dividing his command, he left 135 men to escort the regiment's slow-moving pack train and sent Captain Frederick Benteen with three companies (115 men) to reconnoiter to the southwest. Custer then ordered Major Marcus Reno with 175 men across the Little Bighorn River to attack the village. Custer and the rest of his command rode northward along the high ground east of the river hoping to cut off a possible Indian retreat.

Although surprised by the sudden attack, determined warriors soon routed Reno's force. Moreover, they slaughtered Custer and his outnumbered men, some of them in vicious hand-to-hand fighting. Benteen's battalion and the laggard pack train arrived on the battlefield as the fighting waned. Joining with the remaining Reno troopers, Benteen's men held their ground until the Indians finally retired on the evening of June 26.

In all, 263 Cavalry troopers and an unknown number of Indians died in the fighting. In the years that followed, the Battle of the Little Bighorn, sometimes called Custer's Last Stand, became a powerful symbol of Native American resistance and a tribute to the heroism of combatants on both sides.

Custer's last stand

George Armstrong Custer graduated from West Point the same year the Civil War erupted, 1861, and vaulted in rank from lieutenant to major general of volunteers. The "Boy General" was a bold and fearless officer, leading slashing cavalry charges that would influence his tactics during the Indian Wars. In 1868 he led the Seventh Cavalry in a headlong charge that shattered a large Cheyenne village at the Washita. Eight years later, Custer and his troops approached a vast Sioux and Cheyenne encampment along the Little Bighorn. He divided his regiment and demanded hard-striking attacks from different directions to overcome superior numbers. But the warriors withstood the onslaught and killed more than 260 white men, including Custer.

The glorification of Custer Just three weeks after Custer and his troops were slain to a man at the Little Bighorn, a New York City newspaper featured a woodcut of the soldiers heroically battling their "savage" attackers. Depictions of Custer's Last Stand became immensely popular throughout the nation. The 1895 lithograph *Custer's Last Fight* was placed in 150,000 saloons by the Anheuser-Busch brewery, and Buffalo Bill Cody re-created Custer's Last Stand in his Wild West show. In this painting, artist John Mulvaney incorrectly armed Custer with a saber. A host of novelists and, later, moviemakers added their own inaccurate touches while glorifying the Last Stand.

"My heart was bad that day."

—GALL, A LAKOTA CHIEF WHO HELPED COORDINATE RESISTANCE AT THE LITTLE BIGHORN AFTER THE U.S. ARMY HAD KILLED HIS TWO WIVES AND THREE OF HIS CHILDREN

The legend of Crazy Horse This drawing is a rare image of Crazy Horse, who spent only the last few months of his life on a reservation. For more than two decades, Crazy Horse rode as a warrior of the Oglala Sioux, launching daring attacks against Crows, Shoshones, and the U.S. Army. He was a key leader in the Red Cloud War (1866–68), engineering the Fetterman Massacre and the Wagon Box Fight. In 1876 he masterfully led his warriors against General George Crook at Montana's Rosebud River and against Custer at the Little Bighorn. Reluctantly submitting to reservation life in 1877, he was bayoneted by a guard within a few months.

Chief Sitting Bull By his mid-20s, daring Sioux warrior Sitting Bull rose to the leadership of the elite military society Strong Hearts. A few years later, he became chief of the Hunkpapa Sioux, who revered him for his exceptional spiritual powers as well as his courage in battle. Chief Sitting Bull conducted numerous engagements against the U.S. Army, although he was not in tactical command when the vast force of Plains warriors he assembled triumphed over George Custer in 1876. Five years later, he reluctantly submitted to reservation life. The legendary chief was shot to death during the Ghost Dance disturbance of 1890.

Public reacts to "Custer Massacre" Although the "Custer Massacre" took place on June 25, 1876, news of the debacle did not reach Seventh Cavalry headquarters at Fort Abraham Lincoln until July 6, the same date as this newspaper account by the Bismarck (North Dakota) *Tribune*. The startling news was telegraphed around the nation. Day after day, for the rest of July and into August, every possible element regarding Custer and the battle was related to a public hungry for information. Recruits known as "Custer's Avengers" enlisted in the Army, which launched determined campaigns to avenge the defeat and crush Indian resistance.

1876: Bat Masterson and his friend Wyatt Earp become officers of the law in Dodge City, Kansas.

January 1876: The U.S. government announces that all Sioux Indians who do not report to the reservation by January 31 will be considered hostile. However, some Sioux will not hear of the ultimatum.

March 17, 1876: General George Crook's men attack an Indian camp on the Powder River in southeastern Montana. Many of the Sioux and Cheyenne in the camp are murdered, and the camp is destroyed.

Spring 1876: Sitting Bull coordinates the largest Plains Indians gathering in history. It is estimated that 11,000 Indians converge on the area in Montana, just in time for Sitting Bull's stand against General George Custer.

June 25, 1876: Sitting Bull's forces kill General George Armstrong Custer and more than 260 white men under his command at the Battle of the Little Bighorn in Montana.

August 1, 1876: Colorado enters the Union as the 38th state.

September 1876: John Lee is easily convicted in his second trial for the 1857 Mountain Meadows Massacre.

September 1876: The James-Younger Gang's botched robbery attempt of the First National Bank in Northfield, Minnesota, ends with the deaths of two members. Cole Younger takes 11 bullets but survives.

October 1876: Red Cloud, Spotted Tail, and the other Sioux reservation chiefs sign their sacred Black Hills territory over to the U.S. government when given the choice of giving up the land or starving.

Black cowboys It has been estimated that about 15 percent of cowboys were African Americans. Many were former slaves who had been freed, had bought their own freedom, or had escaped. Some had been "buffalo soldiers" in the U.S. Army's first all-black regiments during the Civil War. Black cowboys faced racism on western ranges, but some gained acceptance through their exceptional courage and abilities. Perhaps the most famous black cowboy was Nat Love, also known as Deadwood Dick. In 1876 Love won the Deadwood City (Dakota Territory) competitions in revolver and rifle marksmanship, roping, saddling, and wild-mustang riding.

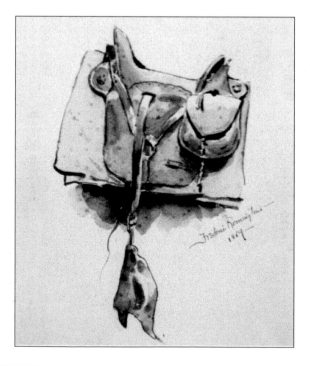

The cowboy's saddle The western stock saddle was the cowboy's workbench. Cowboys often spent 14 or more hours a day on horse-back, and light eastern saddles were inadequate for such work. *Vaqueros* developed large saddles from Spanish war saddles. Wide leather fenders extended from seat to stirrup, protecting the rider's legs from horse sweat. The cowboy could "dally" the loose end of his lariat to the saddle horn in front. Although most cowboys earned only $30 per month, they willingly spent at least $40 for a well-crafted saddle.

War honors The Indian Wars Medal (or Indian Campaign Medal) honored soldiers who showed gallantry in fighting against Native Americans from 1865 to 1891. During the 19th century, Indian fighters were widely regarded as heroes for their role in realizing Manifest Destiny and opening the West to settlement and industry. In those times, many white Americans agreed with the now notorious proverb, "The only good Indian is a dead Indian."

The James-Younger Gang Jesse James (*left*) and his brother Frank (*right*) fought as Confederate guerrillas during the Civil War, then formed the most notorious outlaw band of the 19th century. Chief among the accomplices were Cole, Jim, and Bob Younger. The James-Younger Gang, usually led by the charismatic and ruthless Jesse, committed robberies for a decade after the Civil War. But in 1876 the citizens of Northfield, Minnesota, resisted and pursued the bank robbers. They killed three outlaws, then captured the wounded Younger brothers. The James brothers escaped, but Jesse later was murdered for a reward while Frank turned himself in and was exonerated. Frank and Jesse's mother, Zerelda (*pictured*), would sell pebbles from Jesse's gravesite for a quarter each.

Stinky fuel Nowhere was the adaptability and inventiveness of American frontier folk more needed than on the Great Plains, where homesteaders struggled to adjust to arid, treeless, windy prairies. For water, settlers dug deep wells and built windmills that harnessed underground aquifers. Lacking logs for home construction, they built houses out of sod. For heating and cooking fuel, families gathered "chips," meaning dried buffalo or cow dung. "On the plains," a saying went, "the wind draws the water and cows chop the firewood."

Breeds of cattle As the range cattle industry spread throughout the West, ranchers began improving the beef qualities of lean Texas longhorns. Favorite "American breeds" included Herefords (*pictured*), shorthorns, and angus. Herefords were developed in the county of Hereford in England. These cattle are stocky with red bodies, white faces, and white patches. Herefords also were called "white faces," and when wealthy ranchers dressed in formal attire, they referred to their white shirt fronts as "Herefords."

Boom Time
◈ 1877-1893 ◈

AMERICA REINVENTED ITSELF in the decades following the Civil War, and nowhere was this more obvious than in the American West. Railroads made iron webs across the western landscape, forever changing cities, towns, and villages. Innovations in technology followed, enhancing American industrial growth. Western cities grew prodigiously during the last three decades of the 19th century, and western industrialization—whether represented by railroads, factories, mines, or other examples—remade places, lives, and futures.

During the post-Civil War era, most Americans had been born into rural lives on small farms. The U.S., including the West, was still overwhelmingly rural in 1870 and 1880, but it was also a nation of great cities, some of which seemed to sprout and grow in a matter of a few years. Out west in the Rocky Mountains, cities such as Denver and Salt Lake City began to flex economic and industrial muscle in the post-Civil War period. Out on the edge of the Pacific, San Francisco added to its clout as the West's most important urban center. Already by 1870, San Francisco was America's 10th largest city.

Many envision the American West of the latter 19th century as a region of long vistas and wide-open spaces. But that view represents only one aspect of the West of that era. Just as in the East, where industrialization and immi-

Major cities emerged in the West in the late 1800s, including San Francisco, which boasted a population of 300,000 when it was photographed here in 1890. Streetcars, street lamps, telegraph wires, towering buildings, and a diverse range of businesses all signify the city's entry into the modern age.

> "The greatest and most interesting land boom was that of the 1880's.... Exuberant auction sales, accompanied by brass bands and free lunches, helped sell $100,000,000 of southern-California real estate during the boom's peak year."
>
> —AUTHOR GLENN S. DUMKE, *THE BOOM OF THE EIGHTIES IN SOUTHERN CALIFORNIA*

gration led to urban growth on a grand scale, western cities grew as a result of the period's massive social changes.

We cannot overstate the power of the railroad in all this change. To Americans of the 1870s and '80s, the railroad seemed to be everywhere. A railroad chugging through a small town might mean that the town would soon become a city. But if the railroad bypassed that town, the community might wither. Without a railroad, how would visitors and settlers find their way there? Without a railroad, and without the railroad's ability to spread news, how could the town's attractions and promise be advertised? How could goods and products get taken to and from market?

Guthrie, Oklahoma, was one of the many towns that survived and thrived due to its close proximity to a railroad. Towns without railroad access simply withered away.

With the railroad and expanding cities came boosters: breathless individuals or eager companies who championed the delights of a particular place. They papered the nation with pictures, maps, and pamphlets that extolled their city or town as the next best thing in America. Every western city, or smaller towns that dreamed of being cities, had its share of tireless promoters. And boosters, of course, had a stake in all this, with land to sell or businesses to promote. Part hucksterism, part good business sense, boosterism undoubtedly helped make the West better known far and wide. The railroads, especially such giant corporations as the Southern Pacific and the Atchison, Topeka and Santa Fe, were among the most important boosters of all.

People from all over heeded booster calls and went west. Some came from the East, South, and Midwest; others from much farther away. New immigrants, from Southern and Eastern Europe, came to America by the millions. Many found their way to the American West, especially to the West's cities. Denver, nestled at the foot of the Rocky Mountains, grew by nearly 70,000 people in 10 years near the end of the century. Denver, the capital of the new state of Colorado was, one British tourist remarked, "altogether an astounding place, with a future quite dazzling."

More remarkable yet was Los Angeles. From a village of only a few thousand people in the middle of the century, Los Angeles grew with amazing speed once the railroad (1876) and a real estate boom (1880s) arrived. Already by the 1880s, a visitor could see Los Angeles getting crowded before her very eyes. "It has business thoroughfares, blocks of fine stone buildings, hotels, shops, banks, and is growing daily," wrote Helen Hunt Jackson. "Its outlying regions are a great circuit of gardens, orchards, vineyards, and corn-fields, and its suburbs are fast filling up."

In their enthusiasm, boosters looked the other way when it came to the problems of the West. And there were problems. Poorer neighborhoods grew increasingly crowded in western cities, and living conditions deteriorated with equal speed. Epidemic diseases—smallpox and others—struck over and over again. Legions of Westerners battled tuberculosis. Some caught the contagion in their neighborhoods or at their jobs; others already afflicted went west in vain hopes of finding a cure in dry western air. Water became a problem in western cities: too little of it, or too little of it that was clean. Sewage and other infrastructural problems vexed city councils and bureaucrats.

Labor troubles polarized workers and employers—in the cities, in the mines, and on the railroads. Anti-immigrant behavior, directed particularly at Chinese, became a grim part of everyday life. Places as different as booming Los Angeles and little Rock Springs, Wyoming, proved that they had something awful in common. In L.A. (1871) and Rock Springs (1885), murderous rampages took the lives of dozens of Chinese.

Racial discrimination ran rampant in the West. Mexican Americans continued to bear the brunt of racial enmity in the far West and Southwest in the latter decades of the 19th century. African Americans, many of whom migrated from the South in search of better lives out west, often found greater opportunities and freedom. At the same time, however, many of those new Westerners discovered that racial isolation—in one of the handful of all-black western towns that arose late in the century—was their only hope of a better life. The American West of the 1870s, '80s, and '90s was not nearly so racially egalitarian or "free" as either rumor or hope suggested it might be.

From all regions of the United States, trains carried aspiring settlers to western states and territories. Some would start their own homesteads, while others would toil in factories or mines. Nearly all would face some form of hardship.

Indians continued to face hardship in the decades following the Civil War. Having crushed Native America through its tried and true policy of warfare, the U.S. government changed tactics regarding Indian affairs in the last decades of the century. The government increasingly approached the so-called "Indian Problem" of the era through assimilation aims. Arguments that Native Americans could and should be brought into the mainstream of American society offered convenient justifications for the delivery of Indian lands to the public domain.

The position of the federal government was simple: Indian tribes would no longer be allowed to occupy land in which ownership was shared among tribal members. Tribal ownership did not make sense in the U.S. system of property relations. Indians would be taught (or forced) to own property as individuals; this would teach them how to be Americans (or so the wishful theorists assumed). Indians who farmed plots of land would, as if by magic, become good, sturdy American yeomen, fashioned as if by Thomas Jefferson himself. Needless to say, Indians were not brought into the conversation, or asked if they thought this plan was a good idea.

The government pushed its aims in several ways, mixing coercion and violence with more humanitarian approaches. In the late 1860s, President Ulysses S. Grant, in his Peace Policy, boldly granted churches and missionary organizations the administration of most Indian reservations in the

Apache Indians, who had fought fiercely for their land and independence, were finally subdued by the 1880s. Here they dig an irrigation ditch in Arizona while under military supervision.

nation. This radical departure from previous policy was designed to insulate Indians from Indian agents and other federal or civilian opportunists intent upon cheating Native Americans. A recurrent theme within reform circles was that Indians needed to be brought into the embrace of American life and not isolated within tribalism, lest they become easy victims of corrupt officials or fall to depravity themselves. In the end, Grant's Peace Policy, though perhaps motivated by honorable intentions, largely failed.

Even after such setbacks, those who believed that assimilation was best for Indians figured that they had a very powerful tool with which to accomplish their goals: the congressional allotment program, which distributed Indian lands to individual Indian farmers. The idea had been around a long time, but it became prominent during this era due to a single piece of legislation. The General Allotment Act of 1887, aka the Dawes Act, was the most important piece of Indian policy in the late 19th century.

Not unlike other legislation aimed at Native Americans, the Dawes Act sprung from complex motives and goals. It was a reform measure, in that many of its supporters believed that making Indians into property-owning farmers would protect them from the Army and from speculators out to steal tribal lands. Under the act's provisions, the federal government would divide Indian land into 160-acre sections to be delivered to heads of households and made into farms. Each farmer would then become a U.S. citizen upon agreeing to take hold of a farming section. (Indians, the "first Americans," would not automatically be granted birthright American citizenship until 1924.)

Though we might see reform impulses behind the act's passage, it would be a stretch to call it a humanitarian piece of legislation. Western Americans approved of the Dawes Act not because it aimed to protect Indians but because it offered whites opportunities to get hold of Indian land. Individual parcels of 160 acres did not generally exhaust any given tribe's landholdings. What to do with all that "surplus" land? Westerners wanted it, and they got it through the Dawes Act's provisions that allowed for such land to be sold off to non-Native buyers.

Predicting the end result of the Dawes Act would have been easy. Indian lands left Indian hands, and whites took advantage of the opportunity (as they had for centuries). Tribal governance and tribal authority waned precipitously. By the end of the century, Native Americans controlled only half the land they had in the 1880s.

Indians did not necessarily accede to all this change peacefully. Attempts to force Indians to become "more American" occasionally resulted in Indians choosing instead to become "more Indian" and resist. The last violent bursts of Indian resistance to the United States can be dated to this period, when assimilationist thinking ruled the government's Indian policy.

Mistrust of (and anger at) the federal government came from many corners of the American West in the last decades of the 19th century. White western farmers expressed rising discontent with Washington by the 1880s. State and federal agrarian policies were at least partly to blame for farmer unrest, as was the harsh impact of a national depression in the early 1890s. But trouble also sprang from the speed with which the West had changed in the aftermath of the Civil War. Railroads, cities, and industrial growth had restructured the West, and farmers were not always sure that the new West (and the new America) had their best interests at heart. Nor were the farmers alone in this; the West's industrial laborers, miners, railroad workers, and others added their own anger to the swelling unrest of the period.

Grim-faced silver miners prepare for another grueling workday. While capitalists lined their pockets with the profits, miners and other hard-laborers resented doing backbreaking work in hazardous conditions for pitiful wages.

Within a few short years, this turmoil would generate a political tornado that would roar across America. For a brief moment, at the very end of the century, it looked as though a nationwide alliance of farmers and urban workers—a fleeting partnership largely forged in the American West—might threaten the established political order of the land, if not the very organization of American society. As the 20th century fast approached, it was clear that deep disagreements about the nature and meaning of America lingered, in the West and elsewhere.

1877: The Reconstruction era ends with the withdrawal of the last federal troops from the South.

1877: Mining camps and boomtowns proliferate in Wyoming's Black Hills now that the threat of Sioux raiding parties has been removed.

1877: Repealing the 1868 Fort Laramie Treaty, Congress takes the Black Hills and 40 million additional acres of land from the Lakota.

1877: "The Chinese Must Go!" becomes a rallying cry throughout California, as Irish-Catholic immigrant Denis Kearney founds the Workingmen's Party. The party sponsors several violent demonstrations, implicitly condoning aggression against Chinese laborers.

March 3, 1877: The U.S. Congress passes the Desert Land Act. This act allows an individual to buy up to 640 acres of public land (at 25 cents per acre) in exchange for a promise to irrigate the land and engage in large-scale farming.

Spring 1877: Wyatt and Morgan Earp move to Deadwood in the Dakota Territory, where Wyatt picks up various odd jobs.

March 23, 1877: A firing squad executes mass murderer John Lee in Mountain Meadows, Utah. He is perched on the edge of his own coffin when they shoot him.

May 1877: Pursued by U.S. forces, Sioux Chief Sitting Bull escapes with his followers to the Cypress Hills in Saskatchewan, Canada.

May 6, 1877: Ogala Sioux Chief Crazy Horse surrenders to U.S. authorities at Fort Robinson in Nebraska.

May 7, 1877: The Great Sioux Wars end when General Nelson Miles defeats a small band of Miniconjou Sioux.

Kearney's zealous rage In his shoddy quest to oust Chinese laborers, Denis Kearney harangued unemployed mobs, such as this one in San Francisco. An immigrant himself (from Ireland), Kearney accused Chinese immigrants of taking jobs away from white Americans by working for lower wages. He also organized the influential Workingmen's Party of California. Arrested repeatedly for inciting violence against the Chinese, Kearney played a strong role in passing the Chinese Exclusion Act of 1882, the first U.S. immigration law to target a specific ethnic group. The law severely curtailed Chinese immigration for many years.

Lee blamed for massacre In 1870, with criticism of the 1857 Mountain Meadows Massacre steadily mounting, Major John Doyle Lee was excommunicated from the Mormon Church. Four years later, Lee was tried for his leadership role in the heinous attack on the emigrant wagon train from Arkansas. Although a hung jury resulted, prosecutors and Mormon officials apparently agreed to a retrial of Lee if his superiors would be spared. At Lee's second trial, in 1877, he insisted that he had been ordered to launch the treacherous assault. He was convicted and executed by firing squad on the site of the infamous massacre. In 1961 Lee's membership in the Mormon Church was reinstated.

The Exoduster Movement

"**H**o! for the Great Solomon Valley of Western Kansas!" exclaimed an 1877 handbill directed at African Americans in the rural South. The handbill was one of many that encouraged an exodus of former slaves from Mississippi, Tennessee, Texas, and other southern states to Kansas. Into the 1880s, roughly 20,000 "Exodusters" (the word was derived from *exodus*) boarded steamboats along the Mississippi River and made their way to St. Louis. From there, they moved on to the great agricultural promised land.

"Pap" Singleton

This migration was spurred by the decline of Reconstruction in the South and the subsequent rise of white supremacist state governments. As Union troops left the war-torn South, the protection of civil rights fell by the wayside. African Americans were unable to vote, hold office, or purchase land. Many were locked into the sharecropping system, which kept them in a perpetual state of debt and servitude.

To escape this life, thousands followed the lead of Benjamin "Pap" Singleton, whose Edgefield Real Estate and Homestead Association advertised free and open land on the western prairie. But as African Americans began to leave the South, whites dependant on their cheap labor resisted. Many blacks who attempted to leave were arrested on trumped-up vagrancy charges or were threatened with violence. Others waited for weeks along the banks of the Mississippi, as steamboats heading north refused to transport them.

Still, thousands of African Americans made it to Kansas and settled throughout much of the state. All-black colonies, such as Nicodemus in Graham County, sprang up almost overnight. The exodus reached its peak in 1879, when in just a few months 6,000 migrants filtered into the region. There was not enough land, however, to absorb all of the Exodusters, leaving many stranded in St. Louis, Kansas City, and Topeka. By the 1880s, a dearth of land coupled with white resistance brought the movement to an end.

"Black freedom" in Kansas Groups of former slaves, such as those seen here, made their exodus from the South and headed to Kansas. In 1879 a Louisiana Exoduster wrote to the Kansas governor: "I am anxious to reach your state, not because of the great race now made for it but because of the sacredness of her soil washed by the blood of humanitarians for the cause of black freedom." Kansas had a long abolitionist tradition, and the state had been one of the first to ratify the 13th Amendment.

1877–1893

July 1877: Alexander Graham Bell, Gardiner Hubbard, Thomas Watson, and Thomas Sanders found the Bell Telephone Company.

August 18, 1877: In Arizona Territory, Henry McCarty, aka William Bonney and "Billy the Kid," kills Frank "Windy" Cahill, who allegedly attacked the Kid during an argument.

August 29, 1877: Mormon leader Brigham Young dies at age 76.

September 1877: Chiefs Red Cloud and Spotted Tail visit President Rutherford B. Hayes, who assures them that they can choose their own permanent settlement site within the Sioux reservation, which at the time excludes their sacred Black Hills.

September 5, 1877: Crazy Horse resists arrest at Fort Robinson in Nebraska and is fatally bayoneted by an Army soldier.

September 27, 1877: The commissioner of Indian Affairs, John Q. Smith, is fired after a bureau investigation finds "cupidity, inefficiency, and the most barefaced dishonesty."

September 28, 1877: Texas gunfighter John Wesley Hardin is sentenced to 25 years in prison for the murder of a deputy sheriff.

October 5, 1877: Nez Percé Chief Joseph surrenders after a four-month journey in which he led 700 Indians for 1,500 miles before being surrounded by U.S. troops.

November 1877: John Tunstall hires Billy the Kid, just in time to fight by his side in a feud against the Dolan Company.

1878: The Exodusters, some 40,000 African Americans seeking to escape the post-Reconstruction South, migrate to Kansas. There they will establish Nicodemus, the first all-black western town.

Sutro's tunnel In the early 1860s, businessman and miner Adolph Sutro recognized the problems of the Comstock gold and silver mines in Nevada. Deep underground, miners endured intense heat and poor ventilation and worried about floods and fires. Sutro proposed digging a horizontal ventilating tunnel. He did not get financing for the project until 1869, after a Comstock fire killed dozens of miners. He completed his tunnel in 1878. Sutro, who made a huge profit on his shares, eventually became mayor of San Francisco.

Death in Deadwood The town of Deadwood, South Dakota, developed next to a mining site during the 1874 Black Hills gold rush. In 1876 Marshal "Wild Bill" Hickok was murdered and buried in Deadwood. By that year, the town had become a settled, more prosperous community—as seen in this photograph of the town's main street. After a smallpox epidemic swept through the mining camps in 1876 and a fire destroyed much of the town in 1879, many residents moved on to other mining fields. In 1903 Martha Jane Canary ("Calamity Jane") was buried in Deadwood, next to Hickok.

Eloquent chieftain

"From where the sun now stands, I will fight no more for-ever." These oft-quoted words were pronounced by Chief Joseph, impressive leader of the Nez Percé, a peaceful tribe that inhabited magnificent territory in the Northwest. When their homeland became coveted by white men, the eloquent negotiations

of this tall, young chieftain attracted the notice of Army officers, government officials, and the nation's press. But the Nez Percé rebelled against white encroachments in 1877, then expertly dueled Army contingents during a trek that reached 1,500 miles. Although apprehended just 40 miles short of Canada, Chief Joseph became admired as the per-sonification of the Noble Red Man.

Mine dangers In 1883 a government publication described the plight of men trapped by fire in a Comstock mine in present-day Nevada: "Dead men were lying on the floor of the level as they fell in the agony of suffocation, with their mouths glued to cracks in the planks . . . turning everywhere for one last breath of fresh air." Mine workers throughout the West faced danger from fire, gas, underground water, broken mineshaft cables, and collapsing tunnels. Comstock superintendent Philip Deidesheimer designed the "square sets" of timber tunnel braces seen in this drawing, which prevented cave-ins and undoubtedly saved many lives.

Jews in California This synagogue on Mason Street in San Francisco symbolized Jewish immigration to the West. The California Gold Rush included a wave of Jews from Germany, as well as from France and other European countries. On Yom Kippur in 1849, two services were conducted, one by Germans and another by Polish immigrants. Soon, two congregations were formed, Emanu-El and Sherith Israel. Arriving with skills and/or capital, the German Jews espe-cially thrived in San Francisco. By 1877 more than 21,000 Jews had settled in western states and territories.

"Hanging Judge" Parker Missouri Congressman Isaac Parker was appointed a federal judge in 1875 and assigned to the Western District of Arkansas, which included lawless Indian Territory. Conducting court in Fort Smith, Judge Parker sent out 200 deputy U.S. marshals— far more than employed by any other jurisdic-tion—to chase down outlaws. Many lawbreakers were arrested or slain, but 65 deputies were killed during Parker's 21 years on the bench. The hard-working judge tried 13,490 cases, resulting in 9,454 convictions or guilty pleas, as well as 79 executions by hanging. Dime novelists dubbed Parker the "Hanging Judge."

1878: Samuel Colt produces the double-action revolver, which allows the shooter to fire several times in succession without pausing to cock the hammer.

February 18, 1878: John Tunstall, friend and mentor to outlaw Billy the Kid, is murdered in New Mexico. This event will spark a blood feud known as the Lincoln County War in which Billy the Kid and the Regulators will kill several men in retribution for Tunstall's death.

April 9, 1878: Bat Masterson's older brother, Marshal Ed Masterson, is killed in the line of duty in Dodge City, Kansas.

September 1878: Ruthless men called the Rustlers steal, kill, and rape their way throughout Lincoln County, New Mexico.

September 27, 1878: The last Indian battle in Kansas takes place. A band of Northern Cheyenne, attempting to flee from confinement and starvation on its Oklahoma Indian Territory reservation and return to its homelands in Yellowstone, makes its final stand against the U.S. Cavalry.

1879: An uprising on the Ute Indian Reservation in Colorado leads to the deaths of reservation administrator Nathan Meeker and some of his white assistants. Several Ute men are sent to prison, on the charge of raping white women.

1879: The United States Indian Training and Industrial School in Carlisle, Pennsylvania, welcomes its first group of Lakota children—84 of them. The boarding school, and others like it, are designed to refashion Indians as members of "civilized" society.

1879: The Supreme Court rejects the Mormon argument that polygamy is protected by the First Amendment, and upholds the constitutionality of antipolygamy laws.

O'Sullivan photographs the Southwest Lieutenant George Wheeler, leader of the U.S. Geological Survey, hoped that photographs would attract settlers to the Southwest. During the 1870s, photographer Timothy O'Sullivan worked with several goverment-sponsored surveys in that area. O'Sullivan's stark images, such as *Tufa Domes, Pyramid Lake, Nevada* (*pictured*), revealed a strange and striking landscape. (These domes of calcium carbonate rock formed in Pyramid Lake between 26,000 and 13,000 years ago.) O'Sullivan was among the first to record Native American life in the Southwest, including Navajo weavers, pueblo villages, and prehistoric ruins. In 1882 O'Sullivan died of tuberculosis at age 42.

Inside the passenger cars An 1878 magazine ran this illustration with an article that described ordinary train passengers as a "congregation of aching spines and cramped limbs." The writer commented: "It is a pathetic thing to see their nightly contrivances and poor shifts at comfort; the vain attempts to improvise out of their two or three feet of space a comfortable sleeping." Even those passengers more comfortably ensconced in Pullman cars were subject to the idiosyncrasies of fellow travelers, the heat and dust of the prairies, and the delays and dangers of spring floods and winter blizzards.

San Francisco evolves In 1878 photographer Eadweard Muybridge climbed to the roof of a Nob Hill mansion and turned his large glass-plate camera on San Francisco. His 13 exposures (three are shown here) overlapped to make a complete panorama of the city. San Francisco had grown and matured considerably since the Gold Rush days, becoming the 10th largest U.S. city by 1870. In the late 19th century, it was a cosmopolitan city of hotels, restaurants, parks, churches, synagogues, universities, and libraries—home to artists and writers, the wealthy and the poor. By 1890 a quarter of California's 1.2 million residents lived in San Francisco.

Pioneer for women's suffrage In 1862, when her husband was crippled in an accident, Abigail Duniway supported her family by writing novels, teaching, and running a hat shop. In 1871 she founded *New Northwest*, a women's newspaper in Portland, Oregon, and began lecturing on temperance and women's rights. A popular speaker in the Northwest, Duniway traveled 12,000 miles, giving more than 140 lectures. She helped women gain voting rights in Idaho in 1896 and Washington in 1910. Suffrage proved more difficult to pass in Oregon, but when the 19th Amendment was ratified in 1920, Duniway was the first Oregon woman to register to vote.

The Bannock campaign By the 1860s, the Bannocks—a fierce but small tribe—had submitted to life on the Fort Hall Reservation in Idaho. But as hunting became increasingly difficult, Bannocks, such as those photographed waiting for rations, were forced to rely on reservation handouts to avoid starvation. In 1878 Bannocks and neighboring Paiutes went on the warpath. Numbering only a few hundred, the renegade warriors raided settlers and skirmished with troopers across a rugged wilderness region. The Army's response was skillfully directed by one-armed General O. O. Howard, and the Bannock-Paiute War ended before the year was out. Casualties included 78 slain warriors, 31 dead settlers, and 24 soldiers killed or wounded.

The innovative general George Crook, a U.S. Army general, habitually rode ahead of his troops on scouting and hunting sorties, accompanied only by Native American scouts. He rode a mule, shunned uniforms, and carried a shotgun or hunting rifle. As a junior officer before the Civil War, Crook learned to fight frontier style, emulating the guerrilla tactics of warriors and living off the land while campaigning. After the war, Crook returned to the West and employed large numbers of Native American scouts. The Indian scouts settled old scores with enemy tribes. Their employment reduced the potential number of hostiles.

1879: John Wesley Powell directs the newly created Bureau of Ethnology in an ambitious program to document American Indian culture before it is destroyed by increasing white settlement.

March 3, 1879: Congress creates the United States Geological Survey at the behest of John Wesley Powell and others. The USGS will be a repository for past and future research projects and will coordinate future projects.

October 8, 1879: The James Gang robs the Chicago, Alton and St. Louis train of $40,000 in Glendale, Missouri.

November 27, 1879: Virgil Earp, Wyatt Earp's brother, is appointed deputy U.S. marshal in Tucson, Arizona.

November 29, 1879: Wyatt Earp arrives in Tombstone, Arizona, along with his brothers, Virgil and Morgan.

1880s: Carrie Nation lives in Medicine Lodge, Kansas, before embarking on her crusade against liquor.

1880: The Santa Fe Trail enters its decline with the arrival of the Atchison, Topeka and Santa Fe Railroad in Santa Fe, New Mexico.

1880: Kansas Governor John St. John and the National Women's Christian Temperance Union are the driving forces behind prohibition legislation that makes Kansas a "dry" state.

1880: The number of cattle drives up the Chisholm Trail reaches its peak this year, and will begin to decline.

1880: The Southern Pacific Railroad reaches Tucson, Arizona.

September 3, 1880: The outlaw James brothers steal $1,800 from a Mammoth Cave, Kentucky, stagecoach.

November 2, 1880: Pat Garrett is elected sheriff of Lincoln County, New Mexico.

Sam Bass and his gang
Sam Bass (*center*) was an illiterate Texas cowboy who drifted into outlawry as a horse thief. As the head of a gang of highwaymen in 1887, Bass robbed seven Black Hills stagecoaches and a train. Returning to Texas, Bass formed another gang in the spring of 1878 and pulled four train holdups in the Dallas area. A planned bank robbery in Round Rock, Texas, was betrayed by a gang member. After a wild shoot-out with lawmen, Bass was fatally wounded and died two days later, on July 21, 1878—his 27th birthday.

Stronger plows When homesteaders reached the Great Plains, they discovered that the light, inexpensive iron plows used by generations of farmers in the East could not penetrate the thick root system of prairie grass. Beginning with a plow fashioned from a saw blade in 1837, Illinois blacksmith John Deere eventually produced a heavy steel model. Deere ordered a special type of hard steel from Pittsburgh, and by 1857 he was manufacturing 10,000 plows per year. In 1868 James Oliver developed a chilled-iron plow with a smooth-surface moldboard that slipped through dense prairie soils without clogging. Equipped with superior plows, sodbusters quickly discovered the magnificent fertility of Great Plains soil.

Cowboys

In the mid-1800s, Mexican *vaqueros* withdrew from Texas, leaving most of their sturdy longhorn cattle behind. (The Spanish word *vaquero*, pronounced "ba-cah-roh" by Texans, eventually became "buckaroo.") During the next 20 years, American cowboys drove cattle to markets in St. Louis and Chicago. However, the cowboy era really began when Confederate soldiers returned from the Civil War to find Texas overrun with longhorns. What were people to do with all that beef?

Railroads provided the answer. Railroad builders bought beef for their workers, then rail lines opened access to larger markets. Cowboys led longhorns on cattle drives to railroad towns. There, the cattle were sold and shipped east to people with an appetite for steak and the money to buy it.

The men and occasional women who worked on ranches and cattle drives developed special skills. They saw themselves as different from ordinary shopkeepers and farmers. Most were young, and probably about 15 percent were African American. Many were army veterans who still wore their long blue or gray overcoats and carried military revolvers. By the 1870s, boots made especially for cowboys—with high tops, toes that could slide easily into stirrups, and high heels that would prevent the boots from sliding all the way through the stirrups—began to replace ordinary work boots.

Ranches and cowboys expanded northward, but by the late 1800s the open range was gone. Farmers fenced their fields with barbed wire, and some states passed laws barring cattle from other states from crossing their territory. The last big cattle drive was to Dodge City, Kansas, in 1881.

About that time, Buffalo Bill Cody opened his Wild West show, adding fringe, beadwork, and metal ornaments to western costumes. As other shows and rodeos competed for audiences, cowboy clothing got fancier and boots became much more colorful. The cowboy tradition continued in live performances and later in Hollywood movies.

Dodge City's swingin' saloon The Long Branch Saloon in Dodge City, Kansas, featured a five-piece band and a steer's head mounted in front to attract Texas cowboys. The best bartender in Dodge, Adam Jackson, presided over the bar as "Champion Milkpunch Mixer." Co-owner Chalkley Beeson, a talented violinist, led the band, which included another violin, a coronet, a trombone, and a piano. In 1879 the Long Branch was the scene of a fatal gunfight, when "Cockeyed Frank" Loving, a professional gambler, killed Levi Richardson. In the long-running television series *Gunsmoke*, a fictional Long Branch was owned by Miss Kitty and frequented by Marshal Dillon, Doc, and Festus.

> I've labored long and hard for bread,
> for honor and for riches.
> But on my corns too long you've tred,
> You fine-haired sons of bitches.
>
> —BLACK BART

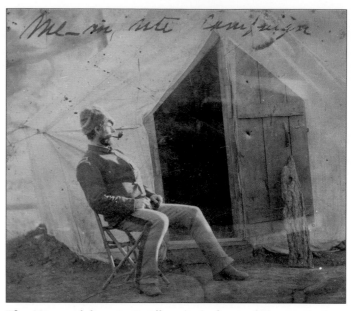

Black Bart The elusive California bandit known as Black Bart pulled off nearly 30 stagecoach robberies from 1875 to 1882. Charles Boles, a native of New York State, went west during the California Gold Rush. Eventually, he decided that the only gold he could find was inside Wells, Fargo & Co. strongboxes. After robbing an express coach at a carefully selected wilderness site, the masked highwayman would escape on foot, sometimes leaving behind scraps of poetry. Between robberies, he resided in a San Francisco hotel and dressed in Victorian finery. After stealing a total of $18,000, he was captured by a Wells, Fargo detective. He wound up serving four years in San Quentin.

The Ute uprising A. C. Allen sits in front of his tent during the Ute Campaign. The Ute uprising of 1879 was triggered by Nathan Meeker, a well-intentioned idealist who was in charge of the White River Agency in northwestern Colorado. Meeker abruptly tried to change the Ute horsemen-hunters to farmers, and when he became alarmed at their bitter reaction, a column of soldiers was summoned to the agency. In September 1879, Ute warriors attacked the approaching column, killing Major T. T. Thornburgh and inflicting heavy casualties among his men. While the soldiers were pinned down, warriors slaughtered Meeker and nine of his agency employees. The Army soon converged in force on the troubled region, establishing large encampments at three agencies while peace negotiations were conducted.

Celebrities perform in Leadville Oro City, in present-day Colorado, was a mining camp that flourished for about two years after gold was discovered near there in 1860 (*oro* is Spanish for gold). The camp was all but abandoned in 1877 when the discovery of lead containing large amounts of silver resulted in the building of the mine pictured here. In 1878 the former Oro City became the thriving town of Leadville. As its fortunes waxed and waned over the years, Leadville played host to many colorful personalities, including Harry Houdini, John Philip Sousa, and Oscar Wilde, all of whom performed at the famous Tabor Opera House.

Belle Starr Educated in a girls school in the 1850s, Myra Maybelle Shirley became a good pianist and a lover of books. She also was an accomplished horsewoman, and her brother taught her to handle firearms. As an adult, she displayed a romantic taste for desperados, including husbands Jim Reed and Sam Starr, both of whom were slain in shootouts. Known as Belle Starr, she served a prison term for horse theft, and for years she hid fugitives in her home in Indian Territory. Belle often flogged her adolescent son, and after she was blasted from her horse by a shotgun in 1889, he was suspected of killing her. The assassin of Belle Starr was never apprehended.

Quanah's commanding presence Quanah Parker was the son of Comanche chief Peta Nocona and Cynthia Ann Parker, who had been abducted in an 1836 raid on Parker's Fort. Quanah grew into a tall, strong man with bold features, and he mastered warrior skills. In 1875, after a military campaign that overwhelmed the Comanches, Quanah was the last diehard chief to bring his band onto the Fort Sill Reservation in Oklahoma. Although only 30, he proved himself a peacetime leader. He shrewdly sold reservation grazing rights, visited Washington to negotiate land settlements, and rode in President Roosevelt's 1905 inaugural parade. He installed his vast family—he married eight times and had 25 children—in the 12-room "Comanche White House" near Fort Sill.

Deringer's pocket pistols Henry Deringer was a Philadelphia gunmaker who produced a variety of pocket pistols during the first half of the 19th century. These popular little hideout guns, called derringers, included models manufactured by Colt, Remington, and other companies. Many derringers were single-shot, and calibers were as small as .22. The short barrels rendered them accurate at only a few paces. The most common derringer was the two-shot, .41 caliber "Over and Under" model seen here; Remington produced more than 150,000 of these classic backup weapons.

California soil ripe for fruit California gold production began to drop after 1852, but the decline of mineral production was offset by diversified agricultural activities. During the 1860s, wheat farming and the wine industry flourished, and in the 1870s Southern California experienced phenomenal growth in the citrus industry. The soil and climate of almost every valley proved suitable for a particular fruit, and California farmers eventually would raise more than 60 varieties. These included apples, apricots, dates, figs, grapes, lemons, and mangoes. Mexicans, Filipinos, and Chinese were hired as manual laborers.

1881: The nation is stunned by Helen Hunt Jackson's revelations about the federal government's treatment of Native Americans in the West. She publishes her findings in her book, *A Century of Dishonor*.

1881: Wyatt Earp is named the Arizona Territory's deputy U.S. marshal.

March 11, 1881: Frank and Jesse James rob a Muscle Shoals, Alabama, paymaster of $5,000.

March 15, 1881: In Arizona Territory, the driver and a passenger are killed in a failed attempt to rob the Tombstone stagecoach.

April 1881: Outlaw Billy the Kid is found guilty of first-degree murder in the death of Sheriff Brady in New Mexico.

April 13, 1881: Billy the Kid is sentenced to death. His execution is scheduled for May 13.

April 28, 1881: Billy the Kid kills both of his prison guards and escapes from death row.

Summer 1881: The last big cattle drive arrives in Dodge City, Kansas, a casualty of barbed wire and interstate commerce regulations. Texas cowboys have driven some two million longhorns to Dodge City since the drives began in 1866.

July 14, 1881: Sheriff Pat Garrett ends the brief but deadly criminal career of Billy the Kid with a single bullet, killing the notorious outlaw in Fort Sumner, New Mexico.

July 15, 1881: The James Gang holds up the Chicago, Rock Island and Pacific Railroad train. Frank James kills Frank McMillan and conductor William Westfall.

Wanted fugitive The bold gunman known during the Lincoln County War as Billy the Kid later led a band of fugitives and rustlers. Sheriff Pat Garrett launched a relentless manhunt for the Kid and his followers. In December 1880, Garrett and his posse killed Tom O'Folliard at Fort Sumner in New Mexico. Although the Kid and other gang members escaped, Garrett tracked him down a few days later, killed Charlie Bowdre, and took the Kid into custody. The Kid shot his way out of jail in Lincoln, but Garrett wouldn't give up his pursuit, trailing the fugitive to Fort Sumner.

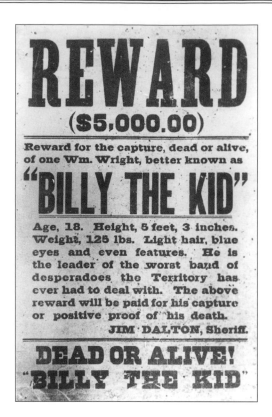

Central City's revival Central City sprang up in present-day Colorado because of the 1859 Gold Rush. During the next few years, the town declined because of a fall in gold production, the Civil War, and Indian attacks on approaching settlers. But Central City rebounded in the late 1860s due to the introduction of new methods for smelting copper, silver, and gold. By 1871 it was the most important city in the region. During the 1880s, when this photograph was taken, Central City was still solid and stable. It finally waned as a mining town in the early 20th century.

Billy the Kid During the last four years of his life, Billy the Kid (born Henry McCarty) engaged in an estimated 16 gun battles, killing four men and helping to shoot five other men to death. The Kid killed a blacksmith when he was 17, and later murdered the sheriff of Lincoln County, New Mexico. He earned murderous notoriety during the bloody Lincoln War, and he shot his way out of jail before being tracked down and killed by Sheriff Pat Garrett in 1881. Dead at 21, the personable outlaw became a western icon. Billy the Kid has been a feature character in at least 40 movies, more than any other Westerner.

The man who killed the Kid Pat Garrett had been a cowboy, buffalo hunter, bartender, and rancher when he was elected sheriff of lawless Lincoln County, New Mexico. Tall (6′5″) and resolute, Garrett killed a man in a shootout before launching a relentless manhunt for Billy the Kid and his gang of rustlers. After a series of gun battles and a bloody jail escape by the Kid, Sheriff Garrett killed Billy in a darkened bedroom. Garrett went on to raise a large family, hold other offices, engage in other gunfights, and suffer his own controversial murder. But always he was known as the man who shot the legendary Billy the Kid.

The Mythic West

THANKS LARGELY TO James Fenimore Cooper's Leatherstocking Tales, stories of the frontier West became a staple of American literature in the early 19th century. The exploits of Cooper's hero, Natty Bumppo, echoed the real-life adventures of such backwoodsmen as Daniel Boone and David Crockett. Cooper's stories captivated readers at the same time that steam-driven printing presses and an expanding railroad network were making inexpensive reading materials available to a wider audience.

In 1860 dime novels succeeded story papers as the principal mass medium for popular literature, including western tales. By the turn of the 20th century, Beadle and Adams, Street and Smith, Frank Leslie, and other enterprising publishers had sold an estimated 250 million copies of the crudely produced genre. During the post-Civil War era, dime novels embellished the already colorful deeds of such noted frontier characters as Kit Carson, "Texas Jack" Omohundro, "Wild Bill" Hickok, and "Buffalo Bill" Cody.

By some estimates, Cody alone starred in some 1,700 short novels. Most of them were penned by Edward Z. C. Judson, who wrote under the pseudonym Ned Buntline, and Colonel Prentiss Ingraham, a former Confederate veteran and soldier of fortune. Buntline's *Buffalo Bill, King of the Border Men*, a serialized tale published in Street and Smith's *New York Weekly* in 1869, was the first to romanticize the life of the handsome young buffalo hunter and army scout. Three years later, Cody appeared in Buntline's theatrical melodrama *The Scouts of the Plains*, the cast of which at various times also included Omohundro and Hickok. The play's enthusiastic reception in the East led Cody in 1883 to produce his own famous outdoor pageant, Buffalo Bill's Wild West.

By 1900 Cody's long-running show, along with the art of Frederic Remington and the prose of Theodore Roosevelt and Owen Wister, had transformed the cowboy from a common laborer and often unsavory dime novel character into an iconic American hero. Wister's influential cowboy novel, *The Virginian*, published in 1902, spawned a host of imitators in the decades that followed and reflected America's continuing romance with the Old West.

July 19, 1881: Sioux Chief Sitting Bull and 186 of his followers surrender at Fort Buford in Dakota Territory with the understanding that Sitting Bull is to be pardoned. Federal officials will break their promise, sending Sitting Bull to two years of incarceration at Fort Randall in Dakota Territory.

August 5, 1881: Spotted Tail, a Sioux leader who favors negotiation over war, is shot by his cousin and former friend Crow Dog, who thinks that Spotted Tail is too eager to appease white settlers. *See* December 1883.

September 7, 1881: The James Gang's last train robbery nets them about $3,000 in cash and jewelry.

September 8, 1881: In Arizona Territory, the stagecoach from Tombstone to Bisbee is held up. Some $2,500 is stolen from the mail and the Wells, Fargo box.

October 5, 1881: A posse is formed to chase hostile Apache Indians from the vicinity of Tombstone, Arizona.

October 26, 1881: Doc Holliday and the Earp brothers (Wyatt, Virgil, and Morgan) gun down the Clantons and the McLaurys in the legendary gunfight at the OK Corral in Tombstone.

November 30, 1881: A judge exonerates the Earps and Doc Holliday of any wrongdoing in connection with the shootout at the OK Corral.

1882: Massive copper deposits are found at Butte, Montana's Anaconda mine.

1882: Congress passes the Chinese Exclusion Act, ending Chinese immigration and naturalization for the next 10 years. Nearly 23,000 Chinese will immigrate to the United States in 1882.

"Wickedest" nightclub in America Tombstone, Arizona, founded in 1879 with 100 people, boomed to a population of more than 7,000 by late 1881. During that time, additions to the culture included a courthouse, five newspapers, saloons, dance halls, a cemetery, and the gunfight at the OK Corral. The Bird Cage Theatre (*pictured*) offered gambling, drinking, and 13 finely feathered "painted ladies" swinging from the ceiling. Deemed the "wickedest" nightclub in America by *The New York Times*, the Bird Cage never closed its doors from 1881 to 1889. Twenty-six deaths were recorded there, and 140 bullet holes remain in its walls.

Sod houses Settlers on the treeless Great Plains, unable to erect log cabins, were forced to build sod houses for free housing. They dug large sod squares out of the ground and stacked them to form walls about three feet thick. A special plow, nicknamed a "grasshopper," often was used to cut the sod strips, and a typical "soddy" required about an acre of land to be stripped. The soddy shown here was placed against a hill so that only three walls had to be built. Soddies were sturdy and snug, but when it rained the roof would drip mud for two or three days.

The adventures of Wyatt Earp

Wyatt Earp sought adventure in the West as a railroad section hand, buffalo hunter, saloonkeeper, gambler, peace officer, sportsman, and prospector. His frontier activities often included members of his clannish family, as well as such gambler/gunfighter friends as Doc Holliday, Bat Masterson, and Luke Short. He wore a badge in Wichita, Kansas; Dodge City, Kansas; and Tombstone, Arizona, where the Earp brothers and Holliday became embroiled in a bitter dispute with the Clanton and McLaury brothers. The feud, which featured a shootout at Tombstone's OK Corral and bloody retributions, vaulted Wyatt and Doc to legendary status.

Hot-tempered dentist

John Henry Holliday, a Georgia dentist who contracted tuberculosis, went west seeking a climate that might postpone his demise. Doc Holliday gravitated to numerous western boomtowns during their heydays, occasionally practicing dentistry but more frequently working as a gambler. A hot-tempered alcoholic, Doc engaged in eight gunfights, most notably alongside the Earp brothers at Tombstone's OK Corral. Grazed by a revolver bullet fired by Frank McLaury, Holliday killed Tom McLaury with a shotgun blast. Doc died at age 36 in 1887. His premature death of tuberculosis and prowess with a gun made him a captivating figure of the Old West.

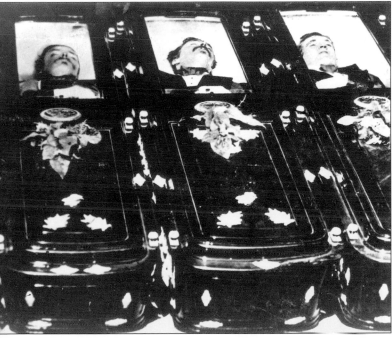

Gunfight at the OK Corral The West's most famous gunfight pitted four men against five just outside the OK Corral in Tombstone, Arizona. Wyatt, Morgan, and Virgil Earp, backed by Doc Holliday, approached Ike and Billy Clanton, Frank and Tom McLaury, and Billy Claiborne. These individuals already had clashed on several occasions, and on October 26, 1881, the Earp party forced a gun battle. A furious exchange of shots lasted less than a minute. Morgan and Virgil were wounded, while Ike and Claiborne fled. Tom and Frank McLaury and Billy Clanton (*pictured, left to right*) were killed, and so were Morgan Earp and others during the vendetta that followed.

The timber industry During the 19th century, settlers considered the West's old-growth forests to be good for nothing except clear-cutting for timber. With the Timber and Stone Act of 1878, U.S. Congress made forests and other land deemed "unfit for farming" available at $2.50 per acre, leading to rampant logging. Entrepreneurs, such as Frederick Weyerhaeuser, made vast fortunes in the burgeoning lumber industry. The floating logs pictured here are destined for a Seattle sawmill, while ships (*background*) transport the lumber internationally. By 1909 an estimated 79 million hectares (almost 200 million acres) of western old-growth forests had been cleared away.

1882: Congress passes the Edmunds Act, which makes polygamy a federal crime. The passage of the law serves its desired effect, sending many Mormon polygamists underground.

1882: Judge Roy Bean opens the Jersey Lilly saloon in Langtry, Texas, where he will dispense "the law west of the Pecos" from behind the bar until his death in 1903.

1882: Reports of an Indian uprising lead the U.S. Navy to shell the Tlingit village of Angoon, Alaska.

1882: Idaho's first electric light is turned on, near Ketchum.

1882: Congressman George Cannon, a Mormon polygamist, is forced from office. John Thomas Caine will take his seat.

1882: Swiss-born anthropologist Adolph Bandelier explores Pueblo cultures in the Southwest.

February 1882: Pat Garrett immortalizes Billy the Kid with his book *The Authentic Life of Billy the Kid*.

March 21, 1882: Authorities send Sheriff Johnny Behan a telegram ordering him to arrest Wyatt Earp for murder, but the telegraph operator warns Earp.

April 3, 1882: The James-Younger Gang's reign of terror ends with the death of Jesse James, shot in the back of the head by Robert Ford in Missouri for a $5,000 reward.

May 1, 1882: Phoebe Ann Moses makes her first public appearance at a sharpshooting show. She goes by the stage name Annie Oakley.

July 14, 1882: In West Turkey Creek Canyon in the Arizona Territory, outlaw Johnny Ringo is found propped dead against a tree. The official verdict of suicide remains questionable.

Tabor and Baby Doe Horace Austin Warner Tabor (*left*), a merchant, politician, and owner of the celebrated Matchless Mine, became the wealthiest citizen of Leadville, Colorado. In 1880 he fell in love with a divorced woman named Elizabeth Bonduel McCourt Doe, known as "Baby Doe" (*right*), and divorced his wife to marry her. Tabor's silver fortune evaporated, and he died in poverty. According to legend, on his deathbed in 1899, Tabor told Baby Doe to "hang on to the Matchless." In fact, he had already lost the mine. Ironically, Baby Doe died in a shack near the Matchless; her frozen body was found there in March 1935.

Opera houses Many western communities expressed progress and prosperity through an imposing opera house. Such facilities hosted opera performances, traveling troupes, Shakespearean plays, musical entertainment, minstrel shows, and stars such as Sarah Bernhardt, Edwin Booth, Lillie Langtry, and Oscar Wilde. Western men attended in evening attire, and women wore splendid gowns and jewelry. The Tabor Grand Opera House in Denver (*pictured*) was one of the most ornate and impressive of its kind. Financed by multimillionaire Horace Austin Warner Tabor, the entertainment palace was completed in 1881.

"Prince of Hangmen"

While George Maledon was justly called the "Prince of Hangmen" in Fort Smith, Arkansas, stories about him must be taken with a grain of salt. For example, his gallows probably could not hang 12 people at one time, as has been claimed, although he did hang as many as six simultaneously. Whether he actually hanged 60 people during his grim career is hard to determine. But he was a craftsman who took pride in the fact that his prisoners' necks snapped neatly, making their deaths quick and humane.

Shutting the door on the Chinese

In 1880, 105,000 Chinese lived in the United States. Only 5,000 were women, and 75,000 were in California. White Westerners treated Chinese as inferiors, along with Hispanics, African Americans, and Native Americans. As in other undereducated regions of the world, many whites in the West were uncomfortable with those who looked and lived differently. Published in San Francisco, *The Wasp* championed the anti-Chinese movement, and in 1882 the Chinese Exclusion Act prohibited Chinese immigration.

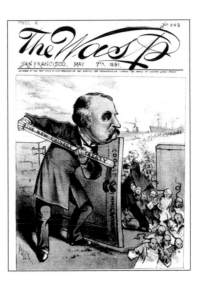

Burying children An 1880s Nebraska family visits the grave of a child, presumably their own. Nineteenth-century infant and child mortality was 20 to 30 times higher than it is today. Newly settled western areas had some of the highest rates. Children and teenagers died from infectious diseases, such as measles, scarlet fever, typhus, diphtheria, and tuberculosis. Infants also succumbed to croup, whooping cough, pneumonia, and intestinal infections, such as diarrhea. Some families lost half or more of their children to disease or accident. Also, because many women died giving birth or from later complications, a man might have a series of wives during his lifetime.

A champion for Wyoming Francis Emroy Warren was more responsible for the early development of Wyoming than anyone else. A Medal of Honor winner during the Civil War, the Massachusetts native restlessly sought opportunity in the West, settling in 1868 in the railroad boomtown of Cheyenne. Intensely ambitious and hard-working, Warren built a vast ranching enterprise (he raised sheep as well as cattle, and was called "the greatest shepherd since Father Abraham"). He exercised great political power as a mayor, governor, and, for 37 years, U.S. senator. Warren brought a stream of federal building projects and jobs to Wyoming.

> "We make our greatest mistake in feeding our civilization to the Indians instead of feeding the Indians to our civilization. . . . Kill the Indian in him, and save the man."
>
> —U.S. CAVALRY OFFICER RICHARD PRATT, FOUNDER OF THE U.S. INDIAN TRAINING AND INDUSTRIAL SCHOOL IN CARLISLE, PENNSYLVANIA

WHITEWASHED HISTORY

THEY TOLD US THAT Indian ways were bad. They said we must get civilized. I remember that word too. It means "be like the white man." I am willing to be like the white man, but I did not believe Indian ways were wrong. But they kept teaching us for seven years. And the books told how bad the Indians had been to the white men—burning their towns and killing their women and children. But I had seen white men do that to Indians. We all wore white man's clothes and ate white man's food and went to white man's churches and spoke white man's talk. And so after a while we also began to say Indians were bad. We laughed at our own people and their blankets and cooking pots and sacred societies and dances. I tried to learn the lessons—and after seven years I came home.

—SUN ELK OF NEW MEXICO, DESCRIBING HIS SEVEN YEARS (BEGINNING IN 1883) AT THE U.S. INDIAN TRAINING AND INDUSTRIAL SCHOOL IN CARLISLE, PENNSYLVANIA

"Reeducating" young Indians The United States Indian Training and Industrial School was founded in Carlisle, Pennsylvania, in 1879. Carlisle was considered a model for the "reeducation" of Native American children so they could live successfully in mainstream America. In the late 1800s, reeducation meant erasing tribal identities, languages, and traditions—as can be seen in these photos of Carlisle students in their Indian clothing and in their school uniforms. Unfortunately, the Indian schools did more to destroy Native American culture than they did to help students assimilate. As one Carlisle student wrote, "Don't look back, all that is passed away."

"Stuart Stranglers"
Granville Stuart and his brother, John, roamed into Montana during the 1850s, and their gold discoveries triggered a rush to that territory in 1862. Settling in Deer Lodge, Granville engaged in business, served in the legislature, and helped launch cattle ranching in eastern Montana. Plagued by rustlers, Stuart organized a vigilante raid in 1884 that resulted in the summary execution of 19 stock thieves. The vigilantes were dubbed "Stuart Stranglers," and Granville was elected the next president of the Montana Stockgrowers Association.

Foresight of John Wesley Powell

JOHN WESLEY POWELL understood that homesteaders were going to have a hard time trying to farm in the West. He tried to warn those who rushed to take advantage of free land. He even designed a plan that might have saved many of their lives.

As a Union soldier during the Civil War, Powell lost one arm when he was wounded at the Battle of Shiloh. That did not stop him from taking an intense interest in the American West. Powell became a geologist, and from 1867 to 1871 he headed exploring expeditions to the Rocky Mountains, the Green and Colorado rivers, and the Grand Canyon. He made accurate maps and published reports on those areas, and from 1881 to 1894 he was director of the U.S. Geological Survey.

Tau-gu (*left*) and John Wesley Powell

Other explorers had noted that the West was not as lush and green as the East. But when farmers learned that not all of the West was actually desert, it seemed to offer them a wonderful opportunity to own their own land. Their longing for independence coincided with the U.S. government's desire to populate the western reaches of the nation. Homesteaders believed that water would, somehow, be sufficient for their crops. Many suffered horribly when that turned out to be untrue.

In 1878 Powell published his *Report on the Lands of the Arid Region*, which accurately described the water problems that settlers would face. He proposed that homesteaders moving into the Great Plains and nearby mountains should make cooperative use of the water resources, much as Mormon settlements had in Utah. Powell also believed that the people of each irrigation district should pay for their own water systems and be responsible for the conservation of water resources.

Most western politicians rejected Powell's plan as involving too much regulation and restriction of development. By the beginning of the 20th century, just months before Powell died, the federal government began a program of building dams and helping some cities import water across hundreds of miles. Eventually, small farmers lost out to the water demands of corporations, mega-farms, and urban development.

Sheepherding in Montana A few cattlemen became active in Montana during the 1850s, but it was not until 1869 that the first important sheep operation was established. The livestock industry flourished on the vast ranges of Montana due to great cattle ranches and, by 1900, six million sheep. In December of that year, 11 cowboys jumped a Montana sheepherder and clubbed to death 3,000 sheep. But otherwise, only a couple of lesser incidents reflected the cattleman-sheepherder conflicts that were so violent in Wyoming, Texas, Arizona, Colorado, and Oregon. Cattlemen despised sheep because they cropped grass too close for cattle and thus "ruined" pastures for those cattle.

1877-1893

October 5, 1882: Outlaw Frank James surrenders to Missouri Governor Thomas Crittendon.

1883: Sioux Chief Sitting Bull is allowed to relocate to the Standing Rock Reservation in Dakota Territory, near his birthplace.

1883: In Texas, a drought necessitates a ban on the fencing of public lands. When ranchers' appeals to the government go unanswered, the ranchers band together and start the Fence Cutter's War.

1883: Sarah Winnemucca Hopkins pens *Life Among the Piutes*, the first autobiographical tribal history written by an Indian woman.

1883: A group of U.S. senators meets with Sitting Bull to propose opening Lakota lands to white settlement. The Sioux chief strongly resists. The U.S. government proceeds with its plan over Sitting Bull's objections.

1883: New York Assemblyman Theodore Roosevelt is among the hunters gathered on the Northern Plains for the last large buffalo kill.

1883: A group calling itself "Friends of the Indian" meets in upstate New York to develop a plan for assimilating Indians into white society.

1883: Women are granted the right to vote in the Washington Territory.

1883: After 19 years, the Northern Pacific Railroad line is finally completed. It includes a 3,850-foot tunnel in the Rocky Mountains in Montana.

1883: The Catholic Church sells the Alamo to the state of Texas, which intends to preserve the historic site.

1883: The town of Hailey receives the first commercial telephone service in Idaho.

Langtry a hit in Southwest Emilie Charlotte ("Lillie") Langtry (*right*) was a popular British beauty and actress whose male admirers included the future King Edward VII. In 1882–83, she went on a cross-continental American theatrical tour. Although she was extremely popular in the Southwest, her contribution to western legend was largely inadvertent on her part. Judge Roy Bean (*Photo, below*), the self-proclaimed "Law West of the Pecos," famously adored her from afar. Bean did not, as he claimed, name the town of Langtry, Texas, after her, but he did build the town's Jersey Lilly Saloon in her honor. The actress visited Langtry after Bean's death in 1903.

Twain pens American classics After Mississippi riverboat traffic was disrupted by the outbreak of the Civil War, a young pilot named Samuel Langhorne Clemens went west to revive his fortunes. He found a new career writing under a pseudonym, Mark Twain. He forged a distinctive voice from the idioms of the wilderness, boomtowns, and saloons, and he brought frontier humor to national popularity. Twain's novels reflected his boyhood days along the Mississippi River and became American classics.

Twain's masterpiece Huckleberry Finn and Tom Sawyer are the two most memorable characters created by Mark Twain. Both boys are featured in *The Adventures of Tom Sawyer* (1876), set in a small Missouri town before the Civil War. Twain revisited Tom and Huck and the Mississippi River frontier in his masterpiece, *The Adventures of Huckleberry Finn* (1884). Huck (*pictured*), the town outcast, helps runaway slave Jim escape, and slowly recognizes Jim's humanity. Humor is mixed with nostalgia, social criticisms, and penetrating character development.

Howe documents small-town life Edgar Watson Howe was born in Indiana and educated at rural schools in Missouri. Drawn to the West, he worked as a journeyman printer in Nebraska, Colorado, Iowa, Wyoming, and Utah. In Kansas, Howe was editor and proprietor of the *Atchison Daily Globe* from 1877 through 1911. In 1911 he established *E. W. Howe's Monthly,* which became noted for his lively editorials. The first and best of more than a dozen Howe novels was published in 1883. The highly regarded *Story of a Country Town,* which accurately depicted small-town life, was a precursor to the Realism movement in American literature.

Dodge City Peace Commission In Dodge City in 1883, a reform-minded administration arrested female "singers" in the Long Branch Saloon. Gambler and gunfighter Luke Short, a co-owner of the Long Branch, fumed over the incident, took a couple of shots at a policeman, and was run out of town. Lawyers were consulted, charges and counter-charges were made, and Short recruited a band of supporters, including Bat Masterson and Wyatt Earp, who both previously had worn badges in Dodge. The celebrated "Dodge City Peace Commission" did little aside from pose for this famous photograph (Wyatt is seated second from left, while Short and Bat stand first and second, respectively, from left). Short soon sold out and moved to Fort Worth, Texas.

1883: "Buffalo Bill" Cody's first Wild West show is held at the Omaha fairgrounds. It includes reenactments of scenes from Cody's life, including a cattle roundup and a stagecoach holdup.

November 3, 1883: Black Bart, the gentlemanly stagecoach bandit, botches his last robbery attempt and is shot. Though the wound is minor and he escapes, he leaves a clue that will ensure his capture.

November 18, 1883: U.S. railroads reset their clocks, inaugurating Standard Time.

November 21, 1883: Black Bart reports to San Quentin prison for a lenient four-year sentence. Though he had robbed Wells, Fargo stagecoaches more than 25 times, the company pressed charges only for the final robbery.

December 1883: The U.S. Supreme Court throws out Crow Dog's murder conviction for the assassination of Spotted Tail, asserting that U.S. courts have no jurisdiction over Indian affairs on Indian lands.

1884: Henry Villard, the industrialist who raised the money to build the Northern Pacific Railroad, is forced out of his own organization when cost overruns nearly destroy the project.

1884: The Kansas state legislature passes a law prohibiting the importation of Texas cattle between March 1 and December 1—an attempt to reduce the tick-borne cattle disease Texas Fever. This effectively kills the long drives.

1884: The Haskell Indian Nations University is founded in Lawrence, Kansas.

1884: With the discovery of silver this year, the mining district of Coeur d'Alene, Idaho, is on its way to becoming the nation's richest mining region.

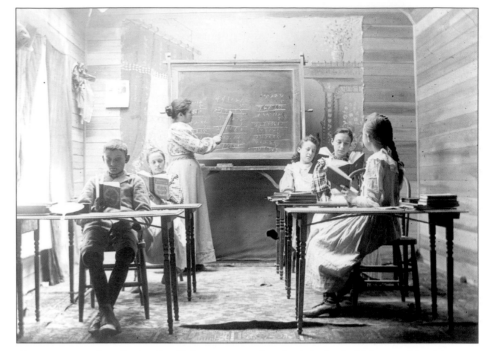

One-room schools In the Plains states, school might be held in an old cabin, a barn, or a building constructed from a community "school-raising" project. A single room and teacher, as shown here, served for first- through eighth-grade students. Teachers, nearly all of whom were women, earned up to $1 a day and lived in the building or with local families. Some taught while also working out their homestead claims. Classes were usually small, but could include as many as 50 students. When large enough, the school building also was used for meetings, community spelling bees, public debates, traveling lecturers, and/or theater groups.

Indians depend on rations Lakotas at Standing Rock Reservation gather to receive U.S. government rations. Native Americans forced onto reservations were unable to hunt or raise their customary corn, beans, and squash. Instead, they were entirely dependent on sacks of white flour and other unfamiliar foods supplied by the government. The system was highly fallible. A historical marker erected by the state of Montana reads: "The Starvation Winter of 1883–84 took the lives of about 500 Blackfeet Indians. . . . This tragic event was the result of an inadequate supply of government rations during an exceptionally hard winter."

The Failure of Reservations

TODAY, THE BUREAU OF INDIAN AFFAIRS administers roughly 300 Indian reservations, many of which resulted from mid-19th century treaties. Most late-1800s reservations were dreary, impoverished backwaters that became targets for unscrupulous parasites, both in and out of government.

Theoretically, reservations would protect Indians from whites' abuses until they were effectively assimilated into white society. Programs to achieve that elusive goal came and went, while seemingly every attempt to assimilate Indians produced greater suffering. Few whites valued Indian cultures, while Indians refused to jettison their ancestral traditions. Those who attempted to assimilate found little real success.

Indian Schools, supporters of assimilation argued, would transform Indians into "acceptable" Americans. Instructors taught the three Rs and the rudiments of Christianity while promoting a formidable cultural brainwashing program. Christian policy-makers were generally hostile to "Indian-ness."

Few Indians recalled their school experiences positively; many remembered them as a time of cultural dismemberment. Children, sometimes literally kidnapped, attended boarding schools in which abuse was common. Teachers forced boys and girls to cut their hair and wear white people's clothes. Teachers sometimes beat students who spoke Native languages. The goal was to eliminate "tribalism" and turn Indian children into "American-

Navaho youth Tom Torlino before and after "assimilation"

style" farmers, even if reservation land was utterly unfit for crop growing.

Lieutenant Richard Pratt administered the Carlisle Indian school in Pennsylvania from 1879 until 1904. Carlisle Indian students received a basic education and industrial arts training, but most eventually returned to reservations to take up Indian ways again.

The dream of "civilizing" the Indians ended badly. By the 1930s, two-thirds of reservation land had been taken away from Native Americans, plunging huge numbers of them into poverty and despair. Indian languages, crafts, and traditions also were threatened by attempts to enforce assimilation. Today, approximately a third of Native Americans live on reservations.

Imposing Christianity Nineteenth century religious revivalists encouraged Christian missionaries, such as the one pictured here with Lakotas, to spread their faith to western Indians. Like secular reformers, missionaries were confident that they were bringing superior beliefs and customs to savages desperately in need of salvation. Defeated Indians found it natural to adopt the religion of the conqueror. At first, they did not realize they were expected to discard their traditional beliefs and ceremonies rather than to integrate them into Christianity. In the 1880s, federal policies outlawed specific Indian tribal rituals and increased pressure to abandon cultural practice, sometimes resulting in Indian rebellions.

Crusader for the Indians
In 1879 author Helen Hunt Jackson heard a translated lecture by Chief Standing Bear about the deadly effects of federal Indian policies. Jackson became a crusader for Native American causes, and in 1881 she published *A Century of Dishonor*, documenting the government's broken treaties, unfulfilled promises, and corrupt mismanagement regarding Native Americans. In 1882 President Chester Arthur

designated Jackson special commissioner of Indian Affairs. Her commercially successful 1884 novel, *Ramona*—a romantic tragedy about a half-breed senorita and her Indian husband—affected eastern humanitarians and helped inspire such policies as the 1887 Dawes Severalty Act.

Charles's chuckwagons On the vast Matador Ranch in western Texas, cowboys gather around a chuckwagon for a meal. The popular chuckwagon was invented by legendary Texas cattleman Charles Goodnight. In 1866 Goodnight bought a surplus army wagon, then attached a toolbox to one side and a water barrel to the other. At the rear was a "chuck box" designed by Goodnight. It was filled with drawers and shelves and covered with a hinged lid that dropped down on a swinging leg to form a cook's worktable. The crew's bedrolls were packed into the wagon bed, as were flour sacks and other provisions.

Calamity Jane Born in the early 1850s, Martha Jane Canary earned notoriety in the West as Calamity Jane. She liked to dress like a man, curse, and chew tobacco. She also worked as a bull whacker in the Black Hills. A heavy drinker, Calamity was thrown into various frontier jails for disturbing the peace. She was married briefly and gave birth to a daughter, who was raised in a convent. Calamity claimed an intimate relationship with Wild Bill Hickok, and when she died, following years of alcoholism, she was buried near the "Prince of Pistoleers" in Deadwood, South Dakota.

Stagecoach Mary In 1832 Mary Fields was born into slavery in Tennessee, but in the post-Civil War West she earned respect as "Stagecoach Mary." The strapping woman was befriended by Mother Amadeus, an Ursuline nun who brought Mary with her to help establish St. Peter's Mission School in Montana Territory. With a cigar clenched in her teeth, Mary regularly drove a mission supply wagon to and from

nearby Cascade. Later she opened a restaurant and a laundry in Cascade, where she became the first woman permitted to drink in the town's saloons. "Stagecoach Mary" also rode shotgun and worked as a driver for a local stagecoach line.

Gamblers and their tricks Gambling was a popular pastime for many Westerners—and a serious profession for others. Professional gamblers enhanced their odds with loaded dice and marked cards. They filed their fingertips for greater sensitivity while handling marked cards. Blue tinted glasses could be worn to read the backs of cards marked with phosphorescent ink invisible to the naked eye, while other "advantage tools" could be ordered by catalog. If such equipment led to trouble, the gambler could reach for a Remington .41 caliber derringer or some other hideout gun.

Legendary saloon fighter Gambler-gunfighter Luke Short battled adversaries in saloon fights in Dodge City, Tombstone, Leadville, and Fort Worth. His friend Bat Masterson was present during Short's two most famous gun battles. At Tombstone's Oriental Saloon in 1881, Short killed Charlie Storms following a quarrel over a card game. Six years later, in a point-blank duel with the former marshal of Fort Worth, Short pumped three pistol bullets into long-haired Jim Courtright. After Short died at age 39 of dropsy (excessive fluid accumulation), he was buried within sight of Courtright's grave.

Medicine Lodge bank robbery On the rainy morning of April 30, 1884, three gunmen entered the Medicine Valley Bank of Medicine Lodge, Kansas. While a fourth outlaw held the horses, the inside men killed the bank president and teller. The bank robbers were hotly pursued and forced to surrender. Hauled back into town, the four desperados were photographed in front of Medicine Lodge's timber jail. Astoundingly, Marshal Henry Brown (*wearing light hat and neckerchief*) of neighboring Caldwell and his deputy, Ben Wheeler (*tall man at right*), were part of the gang. That night, a mob lynched all four outlaws.

Quick on the trigger Dapper Ben Thompson was the West's first great gunfighter. Beginning with adolescent shooting scrapes in Austin, Texas, Thompson engaged in gunplay from the 1850s through the 1880s. He unlimbered his guns during at least a dozen altercations, killing four men and wounding several others. Thompson served in the Confederate Army, was a gambler and saloonkeeper in the Kansas cattle towns, and wore a badge as city marshal of Austin. In 1884 Thompson and fellow gunfighter John King Fisher were assassinated in a San Antonio variety theater, whose proprietor Ben had killed the previous year.

1884: The Fort Yuma Reservation is established for the Quechan Indians of Arizona and California.

1884: By the end of this year, the Southern Plains buffalo herd is destroyed, and only small, scattered groups of the once-iconic animal remain in the American West.

1884: Theodore Roosevelt heads west to recover following the deaths of his wife and mother within hours of each other. He will develop a lifelong love for the West, which will have a great impact on his presidential policies.

April 30, 1884: Henry Brown, the future marshal of Caldwell City, Kansas, is one of a group of cowboys who attempt to rob a bank in Medicine Lodge, Kansas.

November 3, 1884: In *Elk v. Wilkins*, the U.S. Supreme Court denies citizenship to John Elk, an American Indian, because he does not give complete allegiance to the United States.

1885: Chief Sitting Bull joins Buffalo Bill's Wild West show.

1885: Charles Rushmore, for whom Mount Rushmore will be named, travels to the Black Hills to verify mining claims.

1885: President Grover Cleveland warns Oklahoma "Boomers"—white settlers who want to open Indian Territory to whites—to stay off Indian lands.

1885: The University of Arizona is founded in Tucson.

1885: More settlement in Kansas (the population quadruples from 1870 to 1890) leads to an increase in farming and a decline in ranching.

September 2, 1885: British and Swedish miners murder 28 Chinese immigrants and run the rest out of Rock Springs, Wyoming, in what will be called the Rock Springs Massacre.

Dubious cures During the late 19th century, U.S. consumers fell prey to patent medicines—especially in the West, where physicians often were scarce. Pictured is an advertisement for Dr. Edwin Wiley Grove's "Tasteless Chill Tonic," a supposed malaria cure that also made people pleasingly plump. Grove's products, which included tablets to cure cold symptoms ranging from headache to constipation, were harmless at worst and perhaps even somewhat beneficial. His chill tonic contained quinine, the only reliable treatment for malaria back then. But in those days of unregulated products, many useless and less benign medicines were laced with alcohol, morphine, opium, or cocaine.

Fires, storms, and twisters Besides insects that chewed their crops and coyotes that ate their animals, farmers on the Great Plains faced destructive weather. Hot, dry summers parched tilled soil, and without prairie grasses to anchor the soil, high winds blew up dust storms. In dry weather, prairie fires could burn for as long as six weeks. Winter blizzards buried houses beneath snow, hailstorms flattened crops, and ice storms killed livestock. Although an individual tornado, such as this 1884 Kansas funnel, did not cover a wide area, each violently rotating twister destroyed everything it touched.

Poker Alice Alice Ivers was a native of England who became famous in the West. During her long life (1851–1930), she married a mining engineer, a fellow gambler, and a sheepherder, but she was widowed all three times. Alice lived with her first husband in a mining camp, where the only recreation was watching poker games. After he died, she became an expert at faro. Her straight face at the card table earned her the nickname "Poker Alice." She ran gambling tables at numerous mining towns, and once had to kill a drunken soldier. On another occasion, she pulled a gun on a crooked gambler and made him return $1,500 she had lost.

Two-story soddy Most sod houses were low to the ground, built as part dugouts or against the side of a hill. But this impressive two-story sod house boasted a shingled roof and glass panes in the windows. The corners were reinforced by rounded buttresses. Interior walls probably were lined with paper or canvas, which controlled dust and limited the invasion of insects and snakes. Sod houses would stand as long as the roofs remained intact.

Sharpshooting Annie Oakley As a girl, Phoebe Ann Moses was a natural marksman who regularly went into the woods with a rifle to add to the family pot. At 15, she outshot Frank Butler, a traveling exhibition sharpshooter who would later marry her and form a vaudeville act. In 1885 they began touring with Buffalo Bill Cody's immensely popular Wild West show. As Annie Oakley, she was an amazing shooting machine and performer who became one of the primary assets of Cody's show for 17 years. Chief Sitting Bull nicknamed her "Little Sure Shot."

Crackdown on polygamy In 1843 Mormon founder Joseph Smith experienced a "revelation" that sanctioned plural marriage for men, popularly known as polygamy. Prior to the revelation, Smith had begun to acquire additional wives. Only about one in 10 Mormon men followed Smith's example, but the controversial practice angered other Americans, and was a primary factor in the 1844 murder of Smith. From 1849 to 1895, Utah Territory applied several times for statehood, but Congress refused as long as polygamy was practiced. Federal courts enforced laws against the practice, sending hundreds of Mormons—including these men—to prison. In 1890 the Mormon Church outlawed polygamy, and Utah became a state in 1896.

November 1885: Whites in Tacoma, Washington, force more than 700 Chinese immigrants onto open wagons, then ship them off by train to Portland, Oregon.

1886: The Division of Forestry is formally established within the U.S. Department of Agriculture.

1886: Western tourism gains momentum as The Raymond, the first luxury tourist resort in Southern California, opens in Pasadena.

January 1886: Blizzards dump heavy snow across the Plains states. High drifts and record-low temperatures kill hundreds of people, and some areas report mass livestock mortality as well.

February 1886: Whites in Seattle kill five Chinese immigrants after riot leaders vow to purge Seattle of Chinese. Some 200 victims are forced onto ships bound for San Francisco.

September 4, 1886: Apache leader Geronimo surrenders to General Nelson Miles after engaging in years of guerrilla warfare against settlers in the Southwest. Again breaking a promise to place him in his home country, authorities relocate Geronimo and his tribe to Florida.

1887: The Interstate Commerce Commission is created with the passage of the Interstate Commerce Act.

1887: Congress rejects Utah's sixth petition for statehood. The Mormons' insistence on maintaining polygamy is the deal-breaker.

1887: Settlers flock to Los Angeles, drawn by weather and prosperity. The city will grow exponentially over the next few decades.

1887: Susanna Medora Salter is elected mayor of Argonia, Kansas, becoming the first female mayor in the United States.

European homesteaders In 19th century Europe, a combination of peaceful times and better health practices led to population increases. Subsequently, economic troubles and crop failures produced widespread joblessness and starvation. Those problems, along with religious and political discontent, drove Europeans to flee their home countries. Many who immigrated to America continued westward to homesteading territory. They traveled via the Erie Canal, on paddle wheel steamboats across the Great Lakes, by wagon, on foot, and on immigrant railroad trains. European immigrants, such as the Swedish group seen here, were people of determination and conviction—characteristics that served them well in conquering the hardships of their new lives.

Cattle thieves' sneaky tricks On the vast open ranges of the West, stock thieves could steal cattle and alter their brands with minimal chance of being caught. In the designs pictured, brands were altered with running irons, which were branding irons without a face attached. The end of the running iron was slightly curved, and when heated was used to change the brand. A 7 brand, for example, could become 76. The only sure way to prove that a brand had not been altered was to skin a cow and examine the hide from the inside. Big ranches were especially vulnerable to cattle theft. The enormous ranch XIT in the Texas Panhandle designed its brand so that it was nearly impossible to alter.

Barbed Wire

IN THE LATE 1870s, barbed wire began to alter the landscape of the American West. Perfected on the Illinois prairie by farmer Joseph Glidden, barbed wire fencing changed prevailing patterns of land use and facilitated the settlement of the region west of the Mississippi. Called "devil's rope" by some, the thorny wire had its greatest impact on the vast grasslands of the Great Plains, where millions of cattle grazed the open range and traditional fencing materials were expensive and in short supply.

At first, many western farmers and ranchers greeted barbed wire fencing with skepticism and hostility. Some believed that such enclosures could not contain wild cattle. Others opined that the sharp prongs were inhumane and would injure livestock. Demonstrations to the contrary, combined with shrewd promotion, won over most of the naysayers. One enthusiastic barbed wire salesman ballyhooed his product as "light as air, stronger than whiskey, and cheap as dirt."

Many benefits derived from the investment. Herds of cattle that once mingled together on the open range and drifted unencumbered over long distances could now be confined, separated, worked, and bred more efficiently. Barbed wire facilitated range conservation, helped ranch-

ers trim their labor costs, and helped farmers protect their crops from livestock. The fencing of pastures without surface water hastened the drilling of wells and the erecting of dams and windmills.

In Texas, landless "free grass" ranchers waged a brief but violent campaign of fence cutting during the 1880s. Their rampage caused more than $20 million in damage in 1883 alone, prompting the state legislature to declare the practice a felony and send Texas Rangers to halt the destruction.

Barbed wire still fences the range today. No icon of the Old West has enjoyed a longer or more useful tenure on the land.

Battles over barbed wire As farmers moved west to stake out their 160-acre homestead claims, cattlemen began using barbed wire to fence in the public domain, where they grazed their vast herds on government grasslands. One Colorado rancher fenced off more than a million acres. In 1883 the secretary of the Interior declared that if intruders put up barbed-wire fences on settlers' legally owned land, the settlers should cut it down. About two years later, the Nebraska homesteaders pictured above donned masks and applied wire cutters to barbed wire strung by the Brighton Ranch in Custer County, which blocked them from water. On other occasions, cattlemen cut the fencing of homesteaders.

1887: Wilford Woodruff assumes leadership of The Church of Jesus Christ of Latter-day Saints following the death of John Taylor.

1887: Miners in Leadville, Colorado, discover a valuable lode of silver.

1887: Sam Blanchard discovers that Hutchinson, Kansas, is built on top of a massive salt deposit when he strikes salt at 300 feet while drilling a well.

February 8, 1887: The Dawes Severalty Act is enacted. The new law imposes private land ownership on Native American tribes, who are accustomed to communal property. The U.S. government will carve up tribal lands, reapportion them, and sell the surplus.

March 3, 1887: The Edmunds-Tucker Act is enacted. Designed to destroy the framework of Mormon society, the law will allow the federal government to disincorporate the church, confiscate the church's property, and end women's suffrage in Utah.

November 8, 1887: Fatalistic dentist-turned-gambler Doc Holliday dies of tuberculosis at age 36.

1888: Photography becomes more practical with the invention of George Eastman's Kodak camera.

1888: Sioux leader Red Cloud asks Jesuits to establish a school for Lakota children on their reservation, so as to avoid sending them off the reservation to become assimilated.

1888: A summer drought followed by an extremely harsh winter causes massive livestock mortality across the Northern Plains. Ranchers, left with fields of cattle carcasses, dub the catastrophic winter the "Great Die-Up."

January 13, 1888: The National Geographic Society is founded. It will become the largest scientific and educational nonprofit institution in the world.

The Northwest's railroad king James Jerome Hill attributed his spectacular financial success to "work, hard work, intelligent work, and then more work." Born in Canada in 1838, he moved to Minnesota as a teenager and learned the shipping business from the ground up. In 1879 Hill and business partners purchased the bankrupt St. Paul and Pacific Railroad (which would become the Great Northern Railway) and began building a vast railroad network throughout the American Northwest. By promoting farming along his 6,000 miles of track, he greatly contributed to the development of western agriculture.

Northwest railroads Crew members pose with a Northern Pacific Railroad engine. The Northern Pacific, chartered in 1864, took rail transportation westward from Minnesota into undeveloped Native American homelands, where survey and construction crews sometimes needed U.S. Army protection. In 1872 the company opened offices in Europe to entice settlers into the sparsely populated regions it served. By the 1890s, James Hill's better-run Great Northern Railway was competing for business in many of the same areas. The Great Northern eventually extended from Lake Superior to the Pacific coast and down into California.

The high life in Pasadena In 1873 Dr. Thomas Elliott and a group of 100 Indiana families who were interested in healthy living decided to move to a warmer climate. In December of that year, they bought 4,000 acres in California's San Gabriel Valley for $25,000. In 1886 they incorporated the municipality of Pasadena. That same year in Pasadena, the 200-room Raymond Hotel (*pictured*) opened with a grand ball. In 1890 the Valley Hunt Club held a parade of flower-bedecked horses and carriages, an event that would develop into the annual Tournament of Roses Parade.

Historian of the West By the 1870s, Hubert Howe Bancroft, a prosperous California bookseller and publisher, envisioned a multivolume history of western America, from Alaska to Panama. Assembling 60,000 items for his great project, Bancroft created a "History Factory" at his San Francisco headquarters. A large staff, as many as 50 at a given time, pored through his research collection and wrote vast amounts of copy. Bancroft stood behind a tall writing desk with a revolving worktable at his side. From 1874 through 1890, 39 volumes were published. Bancroft donated his enormous research library to the University of California.

Geronimo In 1886 fierce Apache leader Geronimo became the last Indian chief to surrender to the U.S. Army. Originally, he was known as Goyakla ("One Who Yawns"), but he became a ferocious foe of Mexicans after Mexican soldiers massacred his wife and children. Although Geronimo took several wives and fathered more children, he looted and killed ceaselessly throughout the 1860s and '70s. Even after submitting to reservation life, he led breakouts until finally cornered by a vast army. As an old man, Geronimo was a celebrity, appearing at numerous public events. He sold his autograph and personal clothing items while proudly showing off his many battle wounds.

NEW FACE OF THE WEST

AS NEARLY AS I CAN estimate, there were in 1865 about nine and one-half million of buffaloes on the plains between the Missouri River and the Rocky Mountains; all are now gone, killed for their meat, their skins, and their bones. This seems like desecration, cruelty, and murder, yet they have been replaced by twice as many cattle. At that date there were about 165,000 Pawnees, Sioux, Cheyennes, and Arapahoes, who depended upon these buffaloes for their yearly food. They, too, have gone, but they have been replaced by twice or thrice as many white men and women, who have made the earth to blossom as the rose, and who can be counted, taxed, and governed by the laws of Nature and civilization. This change has been salutary, and will go on to the end.

—U.S. ARMY GENERAL WILLIAM T. SHERMAN, 1886

Protectors of Texas The Texas Rangers (pictured in 1882) began as a loose-knit group in the 1820s to protect white settlers from Indians and bandits. They were formally organized during the Texas Revolution (1835–36), and participated in combat during the Mexican War (1846–48). Periodically disbanded and reorganized during the mid-19th century, the Rangers made a comeback in the 1870s. They fought Indians and bandits and settled range wars between farmers and cattlemen. Despite their success in bringing order to Texas by the turn of the 20th century, they were sometimes as capable of brutality as their most ruthless enemies.

Hearst strikes it rich George Hearst grew up in Missouri, but when he heard the news of gold at Sutter's Mill, he moved to California. According to some stories, Hearst and his wife walked all the way. Hearst eventually became a multimillionaire with shares in Nevada's Comstock Lode, South Dakota's Homestake mine, and other gold, silver, and copper mines. Although considered nearly illiterate and colorfully crude, Hearst was a U.S. senator from California from 1887 to 1891. During that time, he took little interest in the small newspaper, the *San Francisco Examiner*, that he accepted in repayment for a gambling debt.

Toxic pollution As the heyday of the lone prospector disappeared and industrialized mining arrived, so did the toxic and dangerous practice of smelting—the extraction of metal from ore. The most notorious smelting pollution of the late 19th century occurred around the mining town of Butte, Montana. Smelting plants, such as this one near Butte at Anaconda, contaminated water and created sulfur fumes so thick that one couldn't see to cross a street. Industrial residues of arsenic, cadmium, copper, lead, and zinc killed trees, vegetation, fish, livestock, pets, and people. Such problems would worsen during the 20th century.

Taking Indian Land—Legally

IN THE AFTERMATH of President Grant's scandal-ridden administration, the Navajos' "Long Walk," and the slaughters at Sand Creek and the Washita, Indians faced a grim future. Well-intentioned but ignorant Americans concluded that Indians must stop being Indians. So-called experts and government officials discussed legal and institutional means to end tribalism. Frustrated by widespread corruption in the Office of Indian Affairs, and rejecting a military solution to the "Indian Problem," reform organizations such as the Indian Rights Association and Friends of the Indian developed "humane" programs to "civilize" the Indians.

Congressman Henry Dawes

In 1871 U.S. Representative Henry Dawes of Massachusetts sponsored the bill that ended U.S. treaty-making with Native Americans. Like other "friends" of the Indian, he believed that laws could bring Indians into mainstream society. While chairing the Senate Committee on Indian Affairs in 1887, he shepherded the Dawes Severalty Act through Congress. Dawes hoped that breaking reservations into allotments for individual Indians would abolish the tribalism that perpetuated "savagery," and transform Indians into productive farmers. The large amounts of excess land sure to remain after allotment could be sold to white settlers, who would open up the West for "civilization." Before Congress passed the law, Indians still possessed about 140 million acres of land.

The Dawes Act bred disaster for Native Americans. From 1887 to 1934, when Congress repealed it, Indians lost two-thirds of their land to whites, often through chicanery. Meanwhile, Indians remained impoverished, invisible people totally outside mainstream American society. Most western reservations were unsuitable for farming, and government promises of instruction and assistance went unfulfilled. Land allotments were prematurely forced on many tribes who did not make the necessary transition to farming or ranching. Leasing land was illegal, which prevented Indians from generating income from outside sources. Scheming white politicians and businessmen frequently reserved the best parcels for themselves. Most Indians were unwilling to renounce their own traditions and culture, and resisted changes imposed from afar by doubtful "friends."

Large-scale corporate farms "Bonanza farms" appeared in the Dakota-Minnesota borderlands, and in California's Central Valley, around 1882. Funded by English, Scottish, and American investors, these were the United States' first large-scale "corporate farms." Utilizing mechanized reapers, harvesters, and the like, bonanza farms employed thousands of men who planted vast fields of wheat, much of which was sold overseas. Dry-farming tactics made the Northern Plains operations profitable in the 1880s thanks to greater than average rainfall. But after 1890, drought and the collapse of national and overseas wheat prices led to declining profits. Most of the enormous farms went bust or were divided and sold by 1900.

January 22, 1888: Stagecoach bandit Black Bart is released from San Quentin on good behavior.

1889: For the next 20 years of his life, artist Frederic Remington will paint or sketch more than 2,700 iconic western-themed pictures.

1889: In Salem, Oregon, farm and labor representatives and prohibitionists meet to form a progressive Union Party.

1889: Telluride, Colorado, is the scene of Butch Cassidy's first bank heist.

1889: Kansas adopts legislation regulating trusts, the first sign of the agrarian-based Populist movement that is about to sweep across the West.

1889: The Ghost Dance movement has a resurgence when Paiute holy man Wovoka wakes from a trance to spark a spiritual revival among Natives. The federal government interprets the movement as dangerous to U.S. interests.

February 3, 1889: "Bandit Queen" Belle Starr is gunned down near her Oklahoma Territory home. Her killer will never be brought to justice.

March 2, 1889: By passing the Sioux Act, the U.S. government breaks up the Great Sioux Reservation. The government replaces it with six smaller reservations and opens the remaining land to white settlers.

April 22, 1889: In Oklahoma, two million acres of former Indian land is made available to white settlers. On this day alone, 50,000 white settlers swarm the territory to stake their claims.

September 16, 1889: Bob Younger, outlaw member of the James-Younger Gang, dies while imprisoned at the Minnesota State Penitentiary.

Ritzy hotels In the 19th century, the wealthy enjoyed comfort and luxury at grand resort hotels. Some were built in the West during the late 1800s. The Hotel del Coronado (*pictured*) was an elegant San Diego seaside resort, a place where silver barons, politicians, and royalty rubbed elbows. Construction, mostly by Chinese laborers, began in March 1887 and was completed 11 months later at a cost of $1 million. The hotel is said to be haunted by the ghost of a 19th-century socialite.

A farmer's nightmare A Nebraska farmer uses a branch to beat grasshoppers off his crops. During insect invasions, Great Plains farmers salvaged what they could, but sometimes they lost their entire harvest. In *Sod and Stubble*, John Ise described a horrific incident on a Kansas farm in the late 1800s: "Grasshoppers—millions, billions of them—soon covered the ground in a seething, fluttering mass, their jaws constantly at work biting and testing all things, as they sought what they might devour, their wings fluttering as if with some irresistible impulse of motion, making a low crackling, rasping sound, like the approach of a prairie fire."

Killer blizzards Natural calamities on the Great Plains wrought widespread damage and hardship among settlers. But the most lethal weather hazard resulted from blizzards that struck with sudden ferocity. In January 1888, blinding snowstorms and plunging temperatures killed several hundred people in Nebraska and Dakota Territory, including schoolchildren trying to return to their homes. Relentless blizzards early in 1886 devastated the range cattle industry, wiping out ranches from Montana to Texas. In Wyoming alone that winter, hundreds of thousands of cattle were killed.

Friends of the Indian From 1883 to 1916, clergymen, social reformers, and government officials met annually at this resort in Lake Mohonk, New York. Calling themselves "Friends of the Indian"—in some cases without ever meeting an Indian—they shaped U.S. attitudes toward Native Americans. The "Friends" argued that the government could improve the lot of indigenous people by integrating them into the general American culture. The conferences at Mohonk had a powerful effect on federal Indian policy, influencing the passage of the Dawes Act and the creation of schools designed to mainstream Indian youth. Western Indians had no way of knowing who was influencing their destinies, or why.

Worshiping with peyote Native Americans have used peyote for centuries, tracing back at least to the Aztecs. A spineless cactus that grows in northern Mexico and the southwestern United States, peyote has medicinal qualities and also produces hallucinations. Comanches, Kiowas, and Apaches, when confined to reservations during the 1870s, developed religious rituals involving singing, prayer, meditation, and eating peyote as a sacrament to the supernatural spirits being worshipped. It is claimed that Quanah Parker originated peyotism rites, and the peyotist shown here is also a Comanche. Peyotism spread throughout various tribes, and was incorporated as the Native American Church in 1918.

Remington's western art A native of New York State, artist Frederic Remington drew inspiration from his travels to the West. He filled sketchbooks with drawings of cowboys, horses, cattle, roundups, prospectors, cavalrymen, warriors, and Indian camps. The popularity of his 1886 cover illustration for *Harper's Weekly* created a widespread demand for his western art. Remington wrote short stories and articles, illustrated with his drawings, and in 1895 began producing bronzes. Before his death at 48 from complications of appendicitis, Remington published illustrations in approximately 140 books and 40 magazines. He also produced more than 2,700 paintings and drawings.

Boomers pour into Oklahoma "The last barrier of savagery in the United States was broken down," wrote reporter William Willard Howard upon observing the Oklahoma land run of April 22, 1889. At a bugle call, thousands of hopeful "Boomers"—on foot, horses, wagons, trains, and even bicycles—stormed into Oklahoma to claim mile-square sections of land to settle on. Towns also sprang up with breathtaking speed, including Oklahoma's first capital, Guthrie. "Unlike Rome, the city of Guthrie was built in a day," observed Howard. "To be strictly accurate in the matter, it might be said that it was built in an afternoon."

Jackson photographs Yosemite A self-taught painter and a skilled photographer, William Henry Jackson first went west in 1866. He photographed Native Americans and the construction of the Union Pacific Railroad, and in 1870 became the official photographer of the U.S. Geological and Geographical Survey of the Territories. His spectacular photographs of Yellowstone helped persuade the U.S. Congress to declare the area America's first national park in 1872. This Jackson photo was taken at Glacier Point in Yosemite in 1888 or '89. In the latter part of his 99-year life, Jackson painted scenes depicting the changes he had seen in the West.

Oklahoma Land Rushes

AFTER THE GADSDEN PURCHASE of 1853, the United States' continental boundaries as we know them today took shape. The one area of land that remained off limits to white settlement was Indian Territory in what is now the state of Oklahoma. In 1834 Congress had created the territory to relocate eastern tribes. However, in the 1880s there was increasing talk of opening the territory's lands to whites.

The issue initially made little headway in Congress, but was kept alive by David Payne and his legion of "Boomers" who illegally "boomed" across the border into Indian Territory and set up homesteads. Despite being arrested and removed on multiple occasions, Payne and his followers continued to press for the settlement of Oklahoma. Mounting pressure finally forced Congress to acquiesce to the land-hungry Boomers. President Benjamin Harrison then declared that some two million acres of land in central Oklahoma would be opened for settlement.

Realizing that there was not enough land to accommodate the multitudes of home seekers, government officials decided that the only way to partition the territory was through a land run. When the cannon sounded at high noon on April 22, 1889, 50,000 people raced across the border and staked out 160-acre plots on a first-come, first-serve basis. The event was quite a spectacle. One witness recalled, "Looking in every direction over

Hollister, Idaho, prior to the April 22, 1889, land run

the hills and plains, the boomers are thicker than the locusts were in Egypt."

White settlers' appetite for land in Indian Territory did not stop with the great land rush of 1889. The Dawes Severalty Act broke up reservations and placed Indians on individual homesteads, leaving millions of acres of land in "surplus." In Oklahoma, land runs were organized throughout the 1890s and early 1900s to settle these surplus tracts. The result was a tapestry of Indian and non-Indian land. In 1906 the Oklahoma land rushes came to an end with the passage of the Enabling Act, which dissolved the Indian Territory and paved the way for Oklahoma statehood.

Sooners beat the Boomers Not nearly enough lots existed to accommodate the 50,000 Boomers who raced across the Unassigned Lands of Oklahoma on April 22, 1889. Like the family pictured here, people who claimed land had to guard it from latecomers. Boomers faced other problems—especially from so-called "Sooners," people who already had made claims before the land run officially started. While some Sooners were settlers who had sneaked onto the Unassigned Lands early, the most notorious Sooners were U.S. marshals and railroad employees. Although they inhabited Oklahoma legally before the run, they were prohibited from making land claims. Many did so anyway.

The Last Indian Resistance

Frozen corpse of Big Foot, a Sioux chief

FOLLOWING THE INDIAN VICTORY at the Battle of the Little Bighorn in 1876, the U.S. Army moved quickly to crush Native military resistance on the Great Plains and force recalcitrant bands onto reservations. By May 1877, starvation and unrelenting military pressure had compelled Lakota and Northern Cheyenne dissidents to capitulate. Sioux Chief Sitting Bull and his followers were notable exceptions. They fled to Canada.

As the Great Sioux War was ending, the incursions of white gold seekers and government plans to relocate the Nez Percé tribe from ancestral lands in Oregon to a reservation in Idaho provoked fresh violence. During the summer of 1877, Chief Joseph led the Nez Percé on a brilliant fighting retreat through parts of Idaho, Wyoming, and Montana in hopes of reaching Canada. After 1,500 miles of hide-and-seek, U.S. troops cornered the exhausted Nez Percé 40 miles from the international boundary. Declaring that he would "fight no more forever," Chief Joseph surrendered on October 5 after a five-day battle.

In the decade that followed, Indians' dissatisfaction with reservation life led to bloodshed on several reservations. One of the worst incidents occurred in 1879, when disgruntled Utes in Colorado killed several government employees, including Indian agent Nathan Meeker.

In Arizona, the destructive raids of a band of Chiricahua Apaches under the leadership of Geronimo bedeviled authorities on both sides of the U.S.-Mexican border until 1886, when the final holdouts laid down their arms. To prevent further trouble, the government exiled Geronimo and nearly 500 other Apaches to Florida, effectively ending Indian warfare in the Southwest.

The Ghost Dance, a spiritual movement that prophesied the return of the traditional Indian way of life, precipitated the last armed encounter between Native Americans and the U.S. Army in 1890. On December 29, fighting broke out between U.S. troops and 350 Sioux at Wounded Knee Creek on the Pine Ridge Reservation in South Dakota. Twenty-five soldiers and more than 150 Indians, many of them women and children, died in the massacre, bringing America's Indian Wars to a horrific end.

The Ghost Dance Facing cultural eradication late in the 19th century, Native Americans desperately embraced mystical religions. Notable among these messianic movements was the Ghost Dance, a nonviolent cult inspired by a Paiute named Wovoka. Ghost Dance followers prayed, chanted, and danced to bring the return of the old world, in which dead relatives and the buffalo would return. As the Ghost Dance spread among the Sioux, Cheyenne, and Arapaho, government reservation agents misinterpreted the religion, fearing it might incite rebellion—a violent situation that led indirectly to the tragic Battle of Wounded Knee.

"There I was, doing my best to teach my people to follow in the white men's road—even trying to get them to believe in their religion—and this was my reward for it all! The very people I was following... had no respect for motherhood, old age, or babyhood. Where was all their civilized training?"

—LUTHER STANDING BEAR, A SCHOOLTEACHER, REACTING TO THE SLAUGHTER AT WOUNDED KNEE

The killing of Sitting Bull As the Ghost Dance spread among the Sioux in the Standing Rock Agency in North Dakota, Indian Agent James McLaughlin feared an outbreak, and he ordered the arrest of Chief Sitting Bull. Approximately 40 Sioux policemen surrounded Sitting Bull's cabin before dawn on December 15, 1890. As a crowd of Sioux gathered, Sitting Bull defiantly declared that he would not go. Someone triggered a rifle bullet into Lieutenant Bull Head, who shot Sitting Bull as he fell. Sergeant Red Tomahawk (*center*) then fired a slug into Sitting Bull's brain. In the melee that followed, six policemen and at least seven tribesmen died. Sitting Bull was buried in the cemetery at nearby Fort Yates.

DYING AT WOUNDED KNEE

AT LAST I GAINED the dirt creek, where an Indian gave me a carbine he had taken from a dead enemy. At that moment the fast-firing cannon began to speak, and it was so close and loud that it frightened me, so I endeavored to crawl away up the ditch. I had not gone far till I met White Face, my wife. She had been shot, the ball passing through her chin and shoulder, but she mumbled: "Let me pass. Let me pass. You go on. We will all die soon, but I must get my mother. There she is." She crawled to where her mother lay, at the top of the bank, but as she lifted the body in her arms she fell dead, shot again.

—DEWEY BEARD, RECALLING THE BATTLE OF WOUNDED KNEE

Explosive violence at Wounded Knee Turmoil swept the reservation after the killing of Sitting Bull. Hundreds of soldiers were brought in. On December 29, the Seventh Cavalry moved to take charge of a large encampment on Wounded Knee Creek. Shooting broke out, with most of the firepower controlled by soldiers, who boasted four Hotchkiss guns (*pictured*). About 150 Sioux were killed, including more than 60 women and children. The Army suffered 25 killed and 39 wounded, most of them shot inadvertently by other soldiers.

Mass burial Shortly after the battle of Wounded Knee, a ferocious blizzard gripped the region for three days. A civilian burial party, which was paid $2 per day apiece and was guarded by soldiers, finally reached the site on New Year's Day, 1891. A large pit was dug, and the frozen Sioux corpses were pulled from beneath the snow and hauled by wagon to the mass grave. Four babies were found still alive, covered by the blankets of their dead mothers. Hundreds of Sioux watched from nearby hillsides as the pit was closed without ceremony. Within months, the Ghost Dance movement was over.

November 2, 1889: The Dakotas become the 39th and 40th states to join the Union.

November 8, 1889: Montana is the 41st state to be admitted to the Union.

November 11, 1889: Washington achieves statehood.

1890: Naturalist John Muir's convincing arguments in favor of the preservation of California's sequoia forests spur Congress to establish Yosemite National Park.

1890: The U. S. Supreme Court upholds the constitutionality of the 1887 Edmunds-Tucker Act. The court rejects the argument that the prohibition of polygamy denies Mormons their First Amendment rights.

1890: A census report indicates that the center of population has shifted dramatically west, and is now 20 miles east of Columbus, Indiana. The census report concludes that there is no longer an American frontier.

1890: The first major meatpacking plant in Fort Worth, Texas, opens its doors, making the city the center of meat processing in the Southwest.

1890: Congress establishes the Oklahoma Territory within the Indian Territory on land that was supposed to be preserved exclusively for Native Americans.

1890: The Cullom-Strubble Bill, designed to deny suffrage to all Mormons, is introduced in Congress. In response, Wilford Woodruff, leader of the Mormon Church, will issue the "Manifesto," a revelation that urges all members of the church to comply with federal laws regarding marriage.

January 1, 1890: Pasadena, California's Valley Hunt Club hosts the first Tournament of Roses, which features a picnic, games, and carriages covered with flowers.

Farm machinery In the 1830s, a typical farmer could cut only a few acres of wheat per day. By midcentury, with a mechanical reaper, he could increase his daily output to 20 acres or more. By the 1880s, a steam thresher (*pictured*) could process a remarkable 750 to 800 bushels of wheat per day. With planters, cutters, huskers, cream separators, potato planters, hay driers, manure spreaders, poultry incubators, automatic wire binders, and the reaper-thresher or combine, farmers moved from subsistence to commercial agriculture. Buying machinery and land not only increased farmers' yields, but also their debts. In 1900 farmers still worked longer hours than industrial workers.

Bandits target stagecoaches Stagecoach travel remained popular into the 1890s, especially in remote areas. Passengers, often crowded together, endured bumpy rides, dust, breakdowns, and runaway teams. Besides passengers and their valuables, stagecoaches transported mail, money, gold bullion, and other freight. As seen here, guards bearing double-barreled shotguns rode with the driver, and some passengers thought it only sensible to be well-armed. Indeed, stagecoaches did get held up. Notorious stagecoach bandits included the James Gang, Sam Bass and his gang, and the gentler Black Bart.

Lease preaches populism In an 1890 speech, Mary Elizabeth Lease described populism as "a religious as well as a political movement, for we seek to put into practical operation the teachings and precepts of Jesus of Nazareth." Based in Kansas, Lease was a schoolteacher, housewife, mother, temperance lecturer, author, lawyer, feminist, political activist, and divorcée. She became a major force in the Populist (or People's) Party, railing in her speeches against the power of Wall Street and mobilizing the nation's farmers and laborers. She gave more than 160 speeches in 1890 alone.

Woodruff on polygamy A leader of The Church of Jesus Christ of Latter-day Saints, Wilford Woodruff once insisted that Mormons not give up the practice of polygamy, for "then we must do away with prophets and Apostles, with revelation and the gifts and graces of the Gospel, and finally give up our religion altogether. . . ." But in 1890, after Woodruff became president of the LDS, the U.S. government seemed ready to destroy the church unless it renounced polygamy. Woodruff then declared "that my advice to the Latter-day Saints is to refrain from contracting any marriage forbidden by the law of the land." Woodruff's manifesto, signed in September 1890, officially denounced plural marriage in the LDS.

Business booms in Chicago During the 19th century, Chicago gained unparalleled access to America's waterways and became the nation's chief railroad hub. Inevitably, the city grew into a spectacular center of industry and trade. Iron ore, farm produce, and livestock all arrived there for processing and shipping. From 1860 to 1890, Chicago's population skyrocketed from 109,000 to 1.1 million. By 1910, it soared to 2.2 million. Chicago's industrial progress came with a steep price. For example, wretched working conditions at the Union Stock Yards (*pictured*) inspired Upton Sinclair's 1906 exposé novel, *The Jungle*.

Peffer speaks up for farmers William Peffer once described the financial middlemen who stood between America's farmers and the marketplace as people "who produce nothing, who add not a dollar to the nation's wealth, who fatten on the failures of other men, whose acquisitions are only what their fellows have lost." Peffer's class rhetoric was typical of the People's Party, which championed farmers and laborers against monopolies and money interests. Populism had its strongest following in the South and West. A major leader in the party, Peffer represented Kansas as a Populist in the U.S. Senate from 1891 to 1897.

July 3, 1890: Idaho is admitted to the Union as the 43rd state.

July 10, 1890: Wyoming is admitted to the Union with its women's suffrage provision intact.

December 15, 1890: Sitting Bull is murdered when Lakota policemen attempt to arrest him at the Standing Rock Reservation as part of the U.S. government's crackdown on the Ghost Dance movement.

December 20, 1890: L. Frank Baum, author of the classic children's book *The Wonderful Wizard of Oz*, states in a newspaper editorial that American Indians should be annihilated, adding, "better that they die than live the miserable wretches that they are."

December 29, 1890: Lakota Chief Big Foot and 150 of his followers are massacred by federal troops at Wounded Knee Creek on the Pine Ridge Reservation in South Dakota. The troops were determined to wipe out followers of the Ghost Dance movement.

1891: Congress passes the Forest Reserve Act, which authorizes the creation of public forests throughout the West.

1891: Fort Union, which served as a staging ground for the Union victory over the Confederates at the Battle of Glorieta Pass in New Mexico, is abandoned.

August 24, 1891: Inventor Thomas Edison files for a patent for his latest creation: the motion-picture camera.

1892: The Dawes Act opens some two million acres of Crow ancestral land to white settlers in Montana.

1892: The Sierra Club is founded in Yosemite Valley, California, by naturalist John Muir.

Queen of Hawaii In 1891 Lydia Liliuokalani became the first female monarch of Hawaii, and also the last of a dynasty of Hawaiian monarchs. By the time of her coronation, Hawaii was largely under the commercial and cultural control of the United States. Because of her resistance to American influence, Queen Liliuokalani was forced to abdicate in 1893. She never returned to the throne, despite a rebellion on her behalf in 1895. Three years later, the U.S. annexed the islands. Liliuokalani was the composer of Hawaii's most beloved song, "Aloha Oe."

Electric streetcars In 1887 the Pico Street Electric Railway, a short-lived electric streetcar service, began in Los Angeles, although its passengers often had to wait two hours for a vehicle. The next year, the first fully functional trolley cars (drawing electricity from an overhead wire) went into service in Richmond, Virginia. Trolleys rapidly swept through American cities from coast to coast. On July 1, 1891, the Belt Line Railway Company began trolley service in Los Angeles. Pictured here is Car No. 10 of the Oakland and Berkeley Rapid Transit Company, which started operating in the East San Francisco Bay Area in 1891.

The People's Party

IN HER SPEECH IN 1890, firebrand orator Mary Elizabeth Lease was said to harangue Kansas farmers to "raise less corn and more hell." She denied that she did, insisting that a newspaper made it up; nevertheless, she wryly agreed that the phrase was good advice. She also publicly declared that "Wall Street owns the country."

Known as the people's Joan of Arc, Lease was part of a huge radical movement that swept across the Midwest and West in the late 1800s. The movement began nonpolitically during the 1870s and thrived during the 1880s with the rise of the Southern Farmers' Alliance, the Colored Farmers' Alliance, and the Farmers' Alliance of the Northwest.

At first, the alliances sought to help farmers help each other through tough economic times. For example, the Southern Farmers' Alliance organized the Texas Exchange, a cooperative designed to provide farmers with cheap credit and to market their crops. Such measures proved insufficient. Commodity brokers, who bought farmers' products, defeated the alliances at every turn. Farmers responded by forming the People's (or Populist) Party.

The People's Party, in which many women were active, was opposed to the monopolies and "money power" that it claimed held ordinary Americans in a stranglehold. Populists advocated the nationalizing of the railroad industry. The party also believed in other government solutions to economic problems, especially "free silver"—a policy of expanding the currency by minting without charge all the silver coming from American mines. This would protect farmers from falling prices they received for the wheat, corn, and cotton they produced. Perhaps most significantly, the party promoted unity of all "producers"—farmers, miners, and other laborers.

Populism peaked during the elections of 1892, when the People's Party presidential candidate, James B. Weaver, carried Colorado, Kansas, Idaho, and Nevada, and won 22 electoral votes overall. Weaver's support throughout the West made the People's Party a third party to be reckoned with. By 1896 the party's causes—including free silver—had largely been adopted by the Democratic Party. Western populism quickly faded into obscurity, never to fully regain a footing in American politics.

Donnelly's visions After the panic of 1857 ruined the Minnesota utopian community he had founded, Ignatius Donnelly entered politics. He advocated education for freedmen, women's suffrage, and—in 1872—cheap paper money. In 1892 he was the Populist Party candidate for U.S. vice president. Donnelly also authored a widely read science-fiction novel, *Caesar's Column* (1890), which describes a future in which cities are brightly lit by artificial lights and documents are projected on glass screens. In Donnelly's nightmarish world of 1988, financiers control an economy in which the rich get richer and the poor get poorer. At the end, a few reformers escape to organize their own Populist state.

The Greenback Party The Panic of 1873 caused many farmers to advocate the unlimited printing of paper money—so-called "greenbacks." This interest led to the founding in 1874 of the Greenback-Labor Party, which promoted such Populist causes as a graduated income tax and women's suffrage. James B. Weaver (*pictured*), one of the party's prominent leaders, represented Iowa as a congressman for two terms. The Greenback Party declined around 1884, but Weaver went on to become a leader of the Populist Party. He was its surprisingly successful (though not victorious) third-party presidential candidate in the election of 1892, gaining most of his support in the West.

1892: Several miners are killed when a strike by silver miners in Coeur d'Alene, Idaho, turns violent.

1892: The U.S. Congress votes to extend the Chinese Exclusion Act for another 10 years. It also adds language that requires all Chinese workers to register with the federal government or be deported.

January 1, 1892: The focus of U.S. immigration policy shifts to the East with the opening of New York's Ellis Island as the U.S. immigration station.

April 1892: The Johnson County War rages in Wyoming. More than 40 "Regulators," in cahoots with the Wyoming Stock Growers Association, attempt to hunt down and kill alleged cattle rustlers. They succeed in killing two men, including Nate Champion, who held off more than 40 marksmen for 12 hours.

June 8, 1892: Bob Ford, the man who shot Jesse James, dies from a gunshot in a Creede, Colorado, saloon.

October 5, 1892: Eight die in a bloody shootout when the Dalton Gang attempts to rob two banks in Coffeyville, Kansas.

1893: The Great Northern Railway line is completed. It reaches Seattle, Washington.

1893: Women are granted the right to vote in the state of Colorado.

1893: In a dramatic career move, well-known cowboy Charles Russell becomes a full-time artist.

1893: The Western Federation of Miners in Butte, Montana, is created in the aftermath of the 1892 Coeur d'Alene strike.

Oil in L.A. One spring day in 1892, Los Angeles resident Edward Doheny learned that a brown, greasy substance that he had spotted on the wheels of a passing cart was called *brea* (Spanish for tar) and could be burned for fuel. Doheny and his partner, Charles Canfield, began digging for *brea* to sell. On April 20, 1893, they hit something even better—oil—which would make them millionaires and change the city forever. Prospectors rushed to Los Angeles, and before long 1,400 oil wells towered above the city, with more nearby. As seen in this photograph, shops, hotels, and real estate companies served the growing population.

The rowdy town of Bodie Nineteenth-century Californians crowd the main streets of Bodie during a Fourth of July celebration. Although gold was discovered in the region by Bill Bodey and other prospectors in 1859, Bodie was no more than a ramshackle mining camp until a rich vein was uncovered in 1876. The population soared to 10,000, while 65 saloons encouraged frequent gunfights. "The smoke of battle almost never clears away completely in Bodie," observed reporter Mark Twain. The area's inevitable decline in mineral production left more than 150 weathered buildings, which are preserved today in one of the West's largest ghost towns.

Johnson County Invaders Wealthy Wyoming cattlemen, plagued by rustlers, mounted an extralegal expedition in April 1892 with the goal of killing stock thieves and seizing control of Johnson County. Twenty-two hired gunmen from Texas rode alongside cattle barons, ranch foremen, and stock detectives. Although the Johnson County Invaders killed two suspected rustlers, hundreds of citizens offered unexpected resistance, and three troops of U.S. Cavalry forced their surrender. In custody at Fort D. A. Russell outside Cheyenne, 43 of the Invaders (also called Regulators) posed for this photograph. With powerful political connections and an expert legal team, the Invaders soon won their release and complete exoneration.

The Dalton Gang Bob Dalton (*left*) led an outlaw gang that included his brothers, Grat (*right*) and Emmett. In 1891 and '92, the Dalton Gang held up four trains and committed other robberies in Kansas and Oklahoma. Then the Dalton brothers boldly decided to rob two banks simultaneously, a feat never before attempted by a gang. On October 5, 1892, the three brothers along with two accomplices struck the banks in Coffeyville, Kansas. When a street fight erupted, Bob shot several citizens, three fatally, and Grat killed the city marshal. But all five outlaws were gunned down, and only Emmett survived to go to prison. The bodies of Bob and Grat were held up for the photographer of this picture.

Celebrated lynchings On February 1, 1893, a former slave named Henry Smith was tortured and burned to death in Paris, Texas, before a crowd of about 10,000 cheering citizens (*pictured*). Although lynchings of African Americans throughout the South and Southwest had been frequent in previous years, Smith's death triggered a rise in organized, public murders in which people delighted in being photographed with their victims. Some even sent out the photographs as postcards. For many years, racial lynchings received positive press and virtually no criminal reprisals. More than 3,000 black men and women were lynched from 1882 to 1968.

1893: Inspired by the view from the summit of Colorado's Pikes Peak, Wellesley College Professor Katharine Lee Bates writes her poem "America the Beautiful." Set to the music of Samuel Ward's "Materna," it will become America's alternate national anthem.

1893: The federal government offers an olive branch of sorts to Mormon polygamists, granting them presidential amnesty.

1893: Frederick Jackson Turner presents his influential essay, *The Significance of the Frontier in American History*, at an American Historical Association conference.

1893: A run on the federal gold supply causes the Panic of 1893, which leads to an economic depression.

1893: Experts estimate that of the 20 million buffalo that once roamed the Plains, fewer than 2,000 remain.

1893: Colorado becomes the second state in the Union to grant women suffrage.

1893: The Hawaiian monarchy is overthrown by government ministers, businessmen, and planters. The U.S. sends troops to maintain order and protect Americans.

January 17, 1893: American Sanford Dole heads a provisional government in Hawaii after Queen Liliuokalani is deposed.

May 1, 1893: The World's Fair opens in Chicago.

October 30, 1893: Swiss artist Karl Bodmer, who documented the expedition of Germany's Prince Maximilian through the West, dies. At the time of his death, Bodmer is unaware of the impact his work will have on the preservation of Plains Indian culture.

Cherokee Strip land run The Oklahoma land run of April 22, 1889, was neither the last nor the biggest on the American frontier. In 1893 Native Americans ceded to the U.S. a stretch of Oklahoma land called the Cherokee Strip (or Cherokee Outlet). It was 226 miles long by 58 miles wide. On September 16, 1893, a pistol shot signaled a land run onto the strip, and more than 100,000 hopeful settlers stormed across the dusty prairie to claim the 40,000 homesteads and numerous town lots in the area.

Great White City In 1893 Chicago staged the World's Columbian Exposition to celebrate the 400th anniversary of the discovery of America by Christopher Columbus. The exposition was held on a 633-acre site bisected with canals and lagoons and featuring buildings plastered in white—the Great White City. Throngs of tourists, including large numbers of Westerners, traveled to the world's fair. Afterward, communities began to devise their own fairs, such as Cheyenne's Frontier Days and Denver's Festival of the Mountain and Plain. In 1904 the St. Louis World's Fair celebrated the centennial of the Louisiana Purchase.

Turner's Frontier Thesis

IN JULY 1893, CROWDS thronged to Chicago's World Columbian Exposition, celebrating four centuries of American "civilization." Few attended the American Historical Association's annual conference, held inside one of the buildings. One speaker, a young professor named Frederick Jackson Turner, read a paper entitled "The Significance of the Frontier in American History." Initially, it caused little stir, but within a few years most historians came to believe that Turner had grasped the central theme of the American experience.

Turner rhapsodized about the frontier and its effects on American life and institutions. He believed the frontier—a "moving line between civilization and savagery"—had given rise to democracy itself. Its transformative power leveled class differences, made inventiveness more important than family bloodlines, and created the "rugged individualism" that underpins

Frederick Jackson Turner

American mythology of the West. Turner also claimed that the "free land" beyond the frontier served as a social "safety valve" to siphon off excess population and eliminate the class tensions that wracked Europe at the time. Subsequent historians have chipped away at Turner's thesis, producing some important modifications, but the core of Turner's idea remains powerful.

The frontier thesis appeared at a critical time. Although new homesteads would be granted well into the 1900s, the 1890 census proclaimed that the frontier line was no more. Consequently, a new sense of American destiny was beginning to stir. Where could the U.S. expand, citizens wondered, if the frontier was "closed"? Anxious Americans looked to the Pacific and Caribbean, where Spanish colonies still lingered. As the 20th century approached, the American frontier took on a whole new meaning.

Rise and fall of Cripple Creek The Colorado Gold Rush of 1891 created the boomtown of Cripple Creek, pictured here during its heyday in the 1890s. By 1901, the city boasted several newspapers, a stock exchange, 16 churches, 19 schools, service from three railways, and a population of about 35,000. Prosperity brought serious problems, however, including two devastating fires in 1896. In 1903–04, Cripple Creek also witnessed deadly labor violence. As gold production declined during the first couple of decades of the 20th century, Cripple Creek faded to become little more than a ghost town.

Growing Unrest
⌒ 1894–1918 ⌒

THE AMERICAN WEST of the 1890s and early 20th century was a troubled place. Political and social disorder, at times punctuated by grim violence, characterized much of the '90s. In the mining regions of the Rockies, industrial strife seemed at times to be the order of the day. Miners toiling away in the dark centers of western mountains worked not for the lure of mineral riches, but for wages. Recent immigrants found their way westward on the railroad, and mining companies hungry for immigrant brawn hired them at a furious pace. The work could be indescribably strenuous, and every bit as dangerous.

When workers organized themselves into secret or not-so-secret unions, mine owners often responded with obstinate fury. A national depression in the early 1890s made an already tense situation far worse. Mining towns from Idaho to Montana, from Colorado to Arizona, erupted in violent episodes large and small. Assassinations, shoot-outs, and bombings seemed to make life in the mining towns even more dangerous than in the mines themselves.

Mine owners hired private detectives or, in some cases, small private armies to defend their mines and their labor practices. When that failed, they courted the involvement of the federal government, which did at times send troops to quell the unrest or keep the peace. This resort to military authority

Throughout the West, miners demanded safer working conditions. Inside a Scofield, Utah, mine on May 1, 1900, blasting powder ignited coal dust, sparking an explosion and an inferno. Approximately 200 miners were killed. These men helped remove the bodies.

"I have spent my life among the American workers all over this country, slept in their homes, eaten at their tables. They are the majority of the people who have the inalienable right in our view to govern the country."

—ELIZABETH GURLEY FLYNN, ORGANIZER FOR THE WEST-BASED INDUSTRIAL WORKERS OF THE WORLD (IWW)

was viewed by many as the complete collapse of the rule of law. When the governor of Colorado declared one county to be "in a state of insurrection and rebellion," given the violence of labor troubles there, journalist Ray Stannard Baker viewed the situation as the total "breakdown of democracy" and a "reversion to military despotism."

Trouble was not limited to the mines and mining towns. Railroad turmoil vexed the West. By the late 19th century, the railroad had become the region's largest employer, and labor disputes and other conflicts erupted frequently. The Pullman strike in the summer of 1894 took railroad corporations by surprise. Officials with such rail corporations as the Southern Pacific Railroad (the largest in the West) and the Atchison, Topeka and Santa Fe were caught completely off guard when the Pullman strike paralyzed western traffic.

Railway officials draw spikes from switches in Chicago during the 1894 Pullman strike. Union sympathies were so strong during this era that rail workers all throughout the West went on strike in support of their Pullman "brethren" in Chicago.

Ostensibly tied to a dispute between workers and management at the Pullman Palace Car Company headquarters outside Chicago, the Pullman strike began as an example of local labor unrest in the Midwest. But because railroad workers throughout the nation had secretly signed up for a union called the American Railway Union, the little strike in Illinois got big very fast. Rail workers walked off the job all over the West, choosing to align with the striking employees at the Pullman works.

Out in California, striking workers occupied rail depots in Oakland, Sacramento, and Los Angeles, and shut down the state's rail traffic for weeks. The railroad company insisted that their employees continue to run trains that were pulling ornate and luxurious "Pullman palaces," private rail cars that catered to the wealthy on rail journeys around the nation. But American Railway Union members refused to hitch Pullmans to outbound trains, and the situation stalemated. Railroad workers and their families moved into the depots, set up tent communities, and waited.

Meanwhile, California farmers showed up in wagons and on horseback and supplied striking workers with food. The farmers argued that they were in dispute with the railroad, too, over the prices charged to ship fruit, vegetables, grain, or livestock to markets. What had begun as a wage conflict in an industrial setting outside Chicago had grown into what looked like broader class warfare in the far West: farmers and industrial workers siding together in mutual antipathy to corporate authority.

It took the power of the federal government to break the strike. Seizing on the clever argument that the strike prevented the transport of U.S. mail over the rails (a federal crime), authorities won the right to commit U.S. troops to the field as strikebreakers. That worked. The strike fell apart, and the trains began to run again all over the West. But the Pullman strike proved something very important about the 1890s. If farmers and industrial workers could join forces over matters of mutual interest, they could constitute a powerful challenge to the status quo.

Millions of these farmers and workers pinned their political hopes on the success of a new movement of the 1890s. This was Populism, a complex political awakening that spoke to discontented farmers and workers across the nation. Unsettled by the declining centrality of rural America within national culture, and battered by economic woes, American farmers had grown increasingly frustrated—and increasingly active politically—in the decades following the Civil War. By the early 1890s, their actions, especially in the South and the West, had attracted the support of industrial laborers and miners. These workers saw in Populism's appeal to farmers hope for redress of their own economic and other grievances. In 1892 James Weaver, the Populist candidate for president of the United States, garnered a million votes and won four states: Colorado, Kansas, Idaho, and Nevada.

Presidential candidate William Jennings Bryan, a Democrat who was nominated by the Populist Party, is caricatured here as a Populist snake swallowing the Democratic Party. He lost presidential bids in 1896, 1900, and 1908.

Four years later, Nebraskan William Jennings Bryan, the "Boy Orator of the Platte," famously carried the Populist standard to the presidential election. Bryan supported the unlimited coinage of silver money by the federal government, in opposition to reliance solely upon the gold standard. Populist farmers insisted that silver production would raise crop prices, which had fallen through the floor during the 1893 depression. Bryan's famous speech at the 1896 Democratic National Convention excoriated those who would rely solely on the gold standard. "You shall not crucify mankind upon a cross of gold," he thundered. Bryan lost the 1896 election, in part because of his remarkable abilities as an orator. His "Cross of Gold" speech so identified him with the issue of free silver that he could not rise above it as the representative of broader Populist appeals. Republican William McKinley's victory took the wind out of Populism's sails. And though Bryan would run again, the Populist moment had passed.

Political ferment and labor conflicts at the end of the 19th century hardly kept people from coming to the West. On the contrary, people came in

Alvin Langdon Coburn photographs the Grand Canyon in 1911. Thanks to innovations in photography in the late 1800s, cameras became affordable for the masses, who proceeded to take millions of photos of, and thus popularized, the West.

droves. The expanding rail networks that crisscrossed the nation fanned out to all parts west by century's end. Moreover, railroad corporations proved brilliant at advertising the West to the tourist and prospective settler. Rail companies blanketed the nation with promotional material about the region: where to live, what to plant, what to see, what to buy, what to photograph.

Innovations in technology contributed to this boom period. Lithography became cheaper and better; images of the West could be mass-marketed at low cost. By the 1890s, photography had become easier and more inexpensive. Kodak's box camera, cheap and light, helped revolutionize the picture-taking industry, and Americans went crazy for photography. The West—its parks, places, and people—became one of the favorite subjects of the "everyman" or "everywoman" photographer, and the millions of pictures that resulted helped spread the news that the West was quite a place to see.

That kind of palpable excitement, which was certainly real, masked a growing sense of national uneasiness about the West during the same period. Part of that unease was due to the nation's real concern that the West remained a coarse, often violent place, exemplified by the mining towns. All the while, America's big thinkers wondered what the West meant to the nation. The answers were not clear.

In what would become a famous address, a young historian tried to understand all of American history by explicit reference to the West, and especially to the frontier, in his thesis "The Significance of the Frontier in American History." Frederick Jackson Turner, a scholar in his early 30s in 1893, delivered his ideas to the annual meeting of the American Historical Association in Chicago. What Turner hypothesized was nothing short of a major reinterpretation of American history.

Turner argued that democracy in American history had been created and fostered by successive waves of westering Americans. By tackling the obstacles and challenges of the frontier—first in the forests of New England, then ever westward with each generation—Americans experienced and energized the national commitment to democracy over and over again. But, Turner pointed out, something had changed at the very end of the 19th century. No longer was there an unbroken line of frontier stretching north to south at any point in the United States. The West had been "tamed," and that just might mean that the nation was at a critical crossroads.

Turner's ideas, as influential as they have been, were flawed. His theory about westward-moving pioneers was too neat and abstract to accommodate history's untidy realities. For one, Turner's emphasis on "free"—or unoccupied—land revealed a blind spot in his thinking. Certainly, those generations of Native Americans who fought and died to protect their land thought of it as anything but unoccupied. Yet Turner's "frontier thesis" did hold an elemental truth within its elegant hypothesizing. Turner assumed, rightly, that something had changed, or was changing, in the American experience. He thought he saw the end of the frontier before his very eyes. That may not have been true, as parts of America in 1893 could qualify as frontier regions. But

Turner did assume that the West was changing rapidly, and he did foresee a migration to the region's cities. That aspect of the late 19th and early 20th century is critical to a greater understanding of the American West.

In the midst of all the era's cowboying, and as media and Buffalo Bill's Wild West shows glorified the old West, a new West beckoned. This was the West of cities. Western cities became magnets by the turn of the century— magnets for people from outside the West, and outside the nation, and magnets for people

At this Women of All Nations Parade in New York City on May 3, 1916, a suffragette banner announces: "Women Have Full Suffrage in Wyoming, Colorado, Utah & Idaho." The same could not be said for many other states until the 19th Amendment was passed in 1920.

who had grown up on western farms and ranches. Denver, Seattle, San Francisco, Portland, and Los Angeles were among the cities that beckoned.

Western troubles did not go away in the early 20th century. But Populism's decline and eventual disappearance did coincide with a "settling down" of the West. By the early decades of the 20th century, the West was already exhibiting new signs of political and social reform, many of which would be exported to the nation as a whole within a decade or so. On one front, the West firmed up a long-standing regional commitment to temperance and prohibition through the 1910s, as town after town, and some entire states, went "dry," prohibiting the sale of liquor.

Perhaps most impressively, the West in the 1910s made critical strides toward equal voting rights for women. The West had always led the nation in this regard; women had gained equal voting rights in parts of the West as far back as the immediate aftermath of the Civil War. Through the first decades of the 20th century, women's suffrage campaigns were active in every region of the West. American women would gain the vote in 1920, and it could be argued that western women's suffrage success paved the way.

1894: Construction is completed on the $2.5 million Colorado state capitol.

1894: William Jennings Bryan, a congressman from Nebraska known as the "Great Commoner," rises to national prominence as the West's spokesman against the gold standard and the fiscal policies of East Coast capitalists.

1894: The Wilson-Gorman Tariff, also known as the Revenue Act, imposes a two percent income tax on Americans.

1894: Conservationist and Sierra Club founder John Muir writes *The Mountains of California*.

1894: The Carey Act, which provides for large federal land grants to states that agree to irrigate the land, fails when the states realize that the necessary large-scale irrigation projects are prohibitively expensive.

1894: South Dakota homesteader Hardy Webster Campbell establishes a dry-farming experiment in Colorado. His "Campbell System" promotes both drought-resistant crops and cultivation methods that supposedly enhance the ability of soil to retain moisture. Campbell's techniques will dramatically increase cultivated acreage in some of the West's more arid regions.

May 1894: Coxey's Army, a band of about 500 unemployed men led by Jacob Coxey, marches on Washington with a petition for Congress.

May 11, 1894: Fifty thousand Pullman Palace Car Company workers go on strike. They will disrupt railroad transportation into the summer.

1895: The Supreme Court eradicates the income tax with its decision in *Pollock v. Farmers' Loan & Trust Company*.

Stanford founded in teen's honor "The children of California shall be our children." So said millionaire railroad magnate and politician Leland Stanford to his wife, Jane (*pictured*), shortly after the death of their only son, Leland Jr., at the age of 15. Working as equal partners, the couple built Stanford University in their son's honor, opening its doors in 1891. Stanford was a coeducational university when most others were all male, and it was devoted to "practical education" when higher learning was largely classical. Stanford was located far to the west of America's established academic centers, but it nevertheless grew to become one of the nation's most prestigious universities.

Lummis's sunny outlook
In 1884, while working as a journalist in Ohio, Charles Lummis was offered a job at the *Los Angeles Times*. He decided to walk to California, writing weekly articles about his journey. At the *Times*, Lummis wrote about corrupt California politicians and became a lifelong supporter of Indian rights. In late 1894, he became editor of a regional magazine, *The Land of Sunshine*, a position he held for 11 years. *The Land of Sunshine* included stories by John Muir and other well-known authors, and it envisioned California as a land of possibilities.

Free Silver at 16 to 1

At the 1896 Democratic Convention, presidential candidate William Jennings Bryan railed against America's existing gold-standard policy—the careful limitation of the amount of currency in circulation. The gold standard, he cried, oppressed the nation's workers. "You shall not press down upon the brow of labor this crown of thorns," he cried. "You shall not crucify mankind upon a cross of gold."

U.S. Currency, 1896

While demonized by Bryan, the gold standard was upheld by believers as a "sound money" policy. Those who benefited from this policy included bankers, capitalists, creditors, and the upper and middle classes in general.

By contrast, Populists and progressives promoted a "free silver" policy. According to this plan, the government would buy and mint unlimited quantities of silver at the long-held ratio of 16 ounces of silver to one ounce of gold (giving rise to the slogan "free silver at 16 to 1"). It was forthrightly reflationary, reversing the West's chronic shortage of currency. Such a drastic increase in the money supply was meant to relieve people in debt and help producers suffering from low prices for their goods.

Bryan's free silver message was extremely popular throughout the newly radicalized West, where farmers were suffering from the financial depression caused by the Panic of 1893. And, of course, it also appealed to the West's suddenly booming silver industry—both miners and owners. Bryan was, however, considered dangerously leftist by most voters in the urban Northeast. He lost the election to Republican William McKinley, who kept the U.S. on the gold standard.

Hardship on the prairie Laura Ingalls's family moved often while she was growing up, and she received an inadequate education. In 1885 she married Almanzo James Wilder, who homesteaded in Dakota Territory. The couple fell into debt as their crops died from drought. They were weakened by diphtheria, lost an infant son, and saw their cabin destroyed by an accidental fire. The Wilders finally settled with their remaining child in Missouri, where they painfully worked their way back to financial stability. In 1931, encouraged by her daughter, Rose, Laura Ingalls Wilder began writing her semiautobiographical Little House series of children's books about a pioneer family.

Leftist Bryan runs for president Although he is most remembered as a fundamentalist opponent of evolution during the Scopes Trial of 1925, William Jennings Bryan was enough of a leftist to attract the support of prominent Socialist Eugene Debs for his 1896 presidential campaign. Bryan ran for president three times—in 1896, 1900, and 1908—always campaigning on behalf of the working man against the "money power." He also advocated women's suffrage, the graduated income tax, and the popular election of senators. He resigned as President Woodrow Wilson's secretary of state in 1915 in protest against policies that tilted toward U.S. involvement in World War I.

1895: Women in Utah regain the right to vote. They had lost it in 1887 due to a congressional effort to reduce the Mormon vote and end polygamy.

1896: Women in Idaho are granted the right to vote.

1896: William Jennings Bryan's strong stand against the gold standard in his "Cross of Gold" speech makes him the presidential candidate of choice for both Democrats and Populists.

1896: A gang of well-known outlaws, operating in Wyoming under the leadership of Butch Cassidy, dub themselves the "Wild Bunch."

January 4, 1896: Utah becomes the 45th state in the Union after a protracted struggle between the federal government and the Mormon church.

March 2, 1896: The Supreme Court rules that the federal government has no claim on the estate of Leland Stanford, clearing the way for the endowment of California's Stanford University.

April 23, 1896: The first public exhibition of a "moving picture" is held in New York City, during the East's brief tenure as the capital of the film industry.

May 18, 1896: In *Plessy v. Ferguson*, the U.S. Supreme Court rules that it is constitutional for governments to maintain separate facilities for black and white citizens as long as the facilities are "equal."

August 16, 1896: Gold is discovered at Bonanza Creek off Alaska's Klondike River, though it will be some months before the news becomes widely known.

November 3, 1896: Ohio-born Republican William McKinley is elected president.

The "Sage of Emporia"
William Allen White, publisher of *The Emporia Gazette* in Kansas, railed against the Populist movement and its attacks on the rich elite. "Whoop it up for the ragged trousers," he roared in an 1896 editorial, "put the lazy, greasy fizzle, who can't pay his debts, on the altar, and bow down and worship him." White's editorial caught national attention, and is said to have helped elect William McKinley president of the United States. After 1900, White became the leading voice for progressivism, and was revered as the "Sage of Emporia." He edited the *Gazette* until 1944.

Hellacious trek in the Klondikes
After arriving at the Alaskan port of Skagway, many aspiring Klondike Gold Rush prospectors made their way up Chilkoot Pass (seen here in 1897), which rose 1,000 feet in its last half mile. A scarcely less daunting route was White Pass, where more than 3,000 pack animals died. Those who survived these trails boated more than 500 miles along the Yukon River to Dawson. Out of about 100,000 "stampeders" who set out for the gold fields near Dawson, only some 30,000 arrived—and most of them found little but hardship and disappointment.

Klondike Gold Rush

IN 1897 A YOUNG MAN named Jack London left San Francisco to join the Klondike Gold Rush. He had little luck as a prospector, but in the rowdy frontier city of Dawson, he stumbled across a new career of sorts: He told stories in barrooms in exchange for drinks. In 1898 he returned to California full of tales that would make him famous as a writer.

The Klondike Gold Rush itself is quite a story. In 1897 steamboat passengers arrived in Seattle and San Francisco carrying bags and crates of gold they had mined near the Klondike River in the Yukon. When this news got out, hordes of U.S. prospectors headed north. Their journey typically began in San Francisco or Seattle, then took them by ship to the Alaskan ports of Skagway or Dyea. From there, they usually faced steep and sometimes deadly mountain treks over the Chilkoot or White passes, at times braving fierce winds and temperatures as low as −65° F.

The prospectors' ultimate destination was the Yukon city of Dawson, near the Klondike gold fields. The town's population grew from 500 before the Gold Rush to 30,000 in 1898. Only a tiny number of the 100,000 prospectors who passed through Dawson actually struck it rich. In 1901, when readily available gold finds were exhausted, the city's population dwindled to about 9,000.

Before the Yukon stampede, gold already had been found in the neighboring U.S. possession of Alaska. Fur-

Klondike area in Yukon Territory

ther Alaskan gold discoveries at Nome in 1898 and Fairbanks in 1902 stirred U.S. interest in what often had been regarded as a useless region.

Ironically, the Klondike Gold Rush had far less impact upon Canada's economy than did discoveries of copper, lead, zinc, silver, coal, and nickel in other parts of the country. But the sheer magnitude of the Gold Rush, with its sensational successes and even more spectacular failures, continues to grip the public imagination, especially through the writings of such participants as Jack London and poet Robert Service.

Mexicans segregated in L.A.
Railroads helped create an Anglo majority in Southern California (as the Gold Rush had in the north). By the late 19th century, most California Hispanics had lost their property to new laws or debts. They found themselves segregated into poverty-stricken barrios. When Los Angeles boomed in the early 1900s, good jobs in the new economy were not open to Mexican Americans. The men were reduced to manual labor. Many families, such as the one pictured, became dependent on women working as maids, laundresses, and in other low-paying jobs.

July 1897: Two ships returning from the Klondike, carrying miners and loads of gold, arrive in Seattle and San Francisco, triggering a gold rush.

1898: South Dakota becomes the first state to adopt the progressive-era reform of initiative and referendum, which grants citizens the power to petition to add legislative measures to the state's ballot for voter approval.

1898: The Southern Pacific Co. launches *Sunset Magazine* to promote rail travel and to sell real estate.

January 1898: The de Lome letter, a private letter written by the Spanish minister in the United States, is stolen by Cuban rebels and given to newspaperman William Randolph Hearst, who publishes it. Critical of President McKinley, the letter embarrasses the U.S. government and is a contributing cause of the Spanish-American War.

February 15, 1898: An explosion sinks the USS *Maine* in Havana Harbor, leading directly to the U.S. declaration of war against Spain in April.

April 1898: The Teller Amendment is enacted. It guarantees Cuban freedom at the conclusion of the Spanish-American War.

April 25, 1898: The Spanish-American War begins when the United States declares war on Spain.

July 7, 1898: The Newlands Resolution, a congressional act that annexes the Republic of Hawaii, is signed by President William McKinley.

November 1898: The American Anti-Imperialist League is formed to oppose the acquisition of the Philippines and additional territories by the United States.

Brigham Young University The massive Academic Building of Brigham Young Academy sits nestled among the Utah mountains. Founded by Mormon leader Brigham Young in 1875, the academy was incorporated as a subsidiary of The Church of Jesus Christ of Latter-day Saints in 1896. Its board transformed the academy into Brigham Young University in 1903 when it added a College Department to the secondary school. Most faculty members and students have been LDS members, and enrollment has skyrocketed in recent years with the worldwide growth of church membership. BYU remains a religiously oriented institution with strict rules of behavior for its students.

The last stagecoach robbery Barely 10 years after she had left a Canadian boarding school, a young woman named Pearl Hart took part in America's last stagecoach robbery. On May 30, 1899, Hart (dressed as a boy) and her partner, Joe Boot, held up an Arizona stagecoach bound from Benson to Globe. After politely returning a dollar apiece to the travelers, Hart and Boot made away with more than $400, but quickly got caught. Hart wound up in Yuma Territorial Prison, where she became a much-visited celebrity. She posed for photographs such as this one—with unloaded weapons, of course.

An American Empire?

IN A LETTER TO Theodore Roosevelt, Secretary of State John Hay called the Spanish-American War of 1898 "a splendid little war." Many Americans agreed.

In the years between the Civil War and the Spanish-American War, U.S. citizens became increasingly restless and ambitious. Manifest Destiny had been realized, the frontier had reputedly (though not truly) disappeared, and the U.S. had become a major economic force. What was America to do with its newfound power?

When Cuba rebelled against Spanish rule in 1895, an answer presented itself. In 1898 President William McKinley led the U.S. into the "little war," in which fighting lasted only from April to August, with peace officially declared in December. Defeating the Spanish soundly and easily, the United States suddenly presented itself as a world military power.

In addition, the U.S. acquired new lands. According to the Treaty of Paris, which ended the Spanish-American War, Spain ceded Puerto Rico in the Caribbean and Guam in the Pacific to the U.S. America also bought the Spanish-held Pacific islands of the Philippines. Although Cuba had won its independence from Spain, it became a protectorate of the United States.

Along with the annexation of Hawaii the same year, these new acquisitions seemed to put the U.S. on the path to empire. But empire was a controversial concept among Americans, many of whom held to the old-fashioned belief that the U.S. should stand as an independent beacon of democracy and not force itself upon the rest of the world.

Yet, many of these new acquisitions remained U.S. imperial possessions. Hawaii received territorial status soon after its annexation, and its inhabitants were given the rights of U.S. citizens. Puerto Rico achieved the same status in 1900. Guam became a territory much later, in 1950. Cuba was at least nominally independent immediately after the Spanish-American War ended. As for the Philippines, U.S. control of the islands was plagued from the start by resistance and revolution. Filipino independence seemed inevitable long before it was fully granted in 1946.

Explosion sparks war fever On February 15, 1898, in the harbor of Havana, Cuba, an explosion ripped through the American battleship USS *Maine,* killing 266 of 354 officers and crewmen. President William McKinley had ordered the vessel to the Spanish colony, ostensibly on a "friendly" visit but in fact to protect American interests during the long-standing revolt of the Cubans against the Spanish government. Sensationalistic newspapers such as the *New York Journal* blamed the Spanish for the blast (although the real cause was an internal explosion) and whipped up war fever from east to west. The incident helped push McKinley toward war.

The German who imagined the West From 1875 to about 1900, German novelist Karl May—who did not set foot in the United States until 1908—crafted more than 60 vigorous, and often inaccurate, adventure novels set in the American West. Readers in Germany, Croatia, and elsewhere in Europe responded with wild enthusiasm to May's feel for action and colorful characters, particularly the Indian called Winnetou and Winnetou's German half brother, Old Shatterhand. To date, more than 100 million May novels have been sold in Germany alone. A Karl May museum opened there in 1985.

Sears catalog Along with Montgomery Ward & Co., Sears, Roebuck and Co. revolutionized American shopping, especially among farmers and rural folk who lacked access to the new department stores of the late 19th century. Packed with thousands of illustrations, the mail-order catalogs brought consumerism to the U.S. hinterlands. Bicycles, cars, tools, clothing, appliances, and even prefabricated houses were shipped throughout the U.S. High-quality items and easy credit terms made the catalogs such a success that neither Sears nor Ward built retail stores until the mid-1920s.

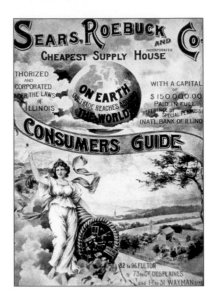

The roots of Berkeley In 1868 the College of California—founded by a former Congregational minister—merged with the state-run Agricultural, Mining, and Mechanical Arts College to form the University of California. In 1873 the university's 167 male and 222 female students moved to a new campus at Berkeley. Benjamin Ide Wheeler, who became university president in 1899, acquired research grants, library and scholarship funds, and a distinguished faculty. At the turn of the 20th century, Berkeley was not yet known for campus radicalism. In fact, military training was mandatory for all male students through 1962.

The copper capital Founded in 1882 by Marcus Daly and George Hearst, the Anaconda Mining Company was Montana's first copper mine and smelter operation—and the world's largest copper producer. John D. Rockefeller's Standard Oil Trust bought the company in 1899. Butte, the mine's "company town," was populated by tough Irish miners and their families. Strong unions and sensible management kept Butte's labor-management relations relatively peaceful up to World War I. Emerging electronics industries used Anaconda copper for wire, transformer windings, incandescent lightbulb elements, and electrical transmission lines. Copper also was required for manufacturing musical instruments and cartridge cases for cannons and firearms.

Labor Tensions

BY THE 1890s, the mining industry was plagued by tensions between labor and corporate managers and owners. Workers, who frequently suffered from low wages, excessive hours, and job insecurity, were fired or blacklisted when they tried to organize against their bosses.

In July 1892, violence erupted in Coeur d'Alene, Idaho, when workers retaliated against wage cuts, lockouts, and non-union hiring. Defiant miners dynamited a mill and engaged in gunfights with guards hired by mine owners. With the support of President Benjamin Harrison, federal troops imposed martial law in Coeur d'Alene. They rounded up about 600 workers in outdoor stockades called "bullpens," and broke the strike.

This ugly episode spurred the creation of the Western Federation of Miners (WFM) in 1893. The organization was strengthened by a successful 1894 confrontation in Cripple Creek, Colorado, during which miners again dynamited facilities. This time, cowed bosses granted strikers' demands for an eight-hour day and a daily wage of $3.

Simultaneous to the rise of the WFM, the nation was plunged into a financial depression by the Panic of 1893.

The resulting unemployment inspired Populist leader Jacob Coxey to organize workers from various locations to march to Washington, D.C. When "Coxey's Army" arrived on April 30, 1894, its leaders were promptly arrested for walking on the U.S. Capitol lawn, and the approximately 500 marchers were dispersed. However, other "armies" already had set out from western locations, including Los Angeles and San Francisco. Some 1,200 of these workers arrived in Washington during 1894.

Although such marches elicited public sympathy for American laborers, tensions continued in the West. Further confrontations between workers and owners occurred in Leadville, Colorado, in 1896, and again in Coeur d'Alene in 1899. In 1904 renewed labor violence broke out in Cripple Creek. This time, employers put down the uprising and banished the strikers from Colorado.

Under the leadership of William "Big Bill" Haywood, the defeated WFM sought allies in its struggle. In 1905 the WFM joined with other organizations to form the Industrial Workers of the World (IWW, or the "Wobblies") and Haywood stepped forward as the first chairman. The IWW remains an active organization today.

Bombing at Coeur d'Alene
After violence rocked the mining district of Coeur d'Alene, Idaho, in 1892, the area remained a powder keg of labor tension until trouble literally exploded there in 1899. The Western Federation of Miners, angered by low wages and the hiring of strikebreakers, organized about 1,000 miners to raid the town of Wardner on April 29. There they dynamited a huge mill owned by the Bunker Hill & Sullivan Mining and Concentrating Company, leaving the ruins shown here. Governor Frank Steunenberg quickly declared martial law. Some 600 miners were rounded up and forced to build stockades for their own incarceration.

December 10, 1898: Spain signs the Treaty of Paris, ending the Spanish-American War. Spain cedes Guam in the Pacific and Puerto Rico in the Caribbean to the United States. The United States also buys the Philippines in the Pacific, and Cuba (an island near Florida) becomes a protectorate of the U.S.

1899: In a treaty with Great Britain and Germany, the U.S. acquires the eastern islands of Samoa in the South Pacific.

1899: Robert Parker and Harry Longabaugh, aka Butch Cassidy and the Sundance Kid, embark on their crime spree across the West.

1899: The U.S. Army establishes Fort Rosecrans in San Diego, named for Civil War hero William Rosecrans.

1899: Novelist Frank Norris publishes *McTeague: A Story of San Francisco*, solidifying his reputation as a pioneer of literary naturalism. Norris shocks the sensibilities of Victorian readers with his tale about how one woman's character is destroyed by her all-consuming greed.

1899: A massive merger creates the mining conglomerate ASARCO, the American Smelting and Refining Company. Facilities will produce lead, silver, and copper (as well as pollution) throughout the Southwest and northern Mexico.

1900: Annual gold production peaks at $20 million at the productive gold camp in Cripple Creek, Colorado.

1900: The entire population of San Francisco's Chinatown is quarantined due to fears of a bubonic plague outbreak.

1900: Mining activity increases in Arizona and New Mexico, as lodes of zinc, copper, and silver are discovered.

A Socialist for president This 1900 presidential campaign button depicts American Socialist Eugene Debs. A staunch advocate of labor unionism, Debs headed the American Railway Union and helped found the Industrial Workers of the World. Following the failed Pullman Strike in Illinois in 1894, Debs served six months in jail. After alligning himself with the American Socialist Party in 1898, he ran as a Socialist presidential candidate five times. During Debs's final campaign in 1920, he was imprisoned for protesting the 1917 Espionage Act. Debs received approximately 920,000 votes, the most ever for a U.S. Socialist. President Warren Harding released Debs in 1921.

Cotton boom in Texas African Americans in Texas loading cotton bales onto freight trains. Texas's economy had long revolved around cattle, but after 1880 railroads made transport of commodities easier. Many Texans shifted to growing corn, and later cotton. The number of one-crop farms increased, and cotton production skyrocketed. Cotton remained generally profitable until the Great Depression began. Within a few years, indebted farm owners and sharecroppers "went bust" by the thousands.

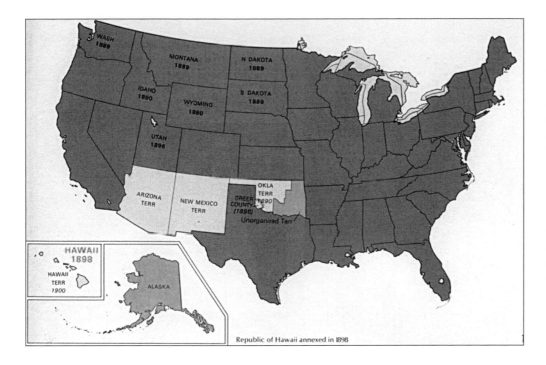

The remaining territories As this map of the western United States shows, all but three former territories had achieved statehood by 1900. The creation of the New Mexico (1850), Arizona (1863), and Oklahoma (1890) territories did not lead to immediate statehood for a variety of reasons, including the ethnic diversity of the three areas. The combination of Indians, Hispanics, and—especially in Oklahoma—African Americans caused considerable concern among many in a nation that was suspicious of such diversity.

Republic of Hawaii annexed in 1898

Roosevelt loves the great outdoors Theodore Roosevelt rides a moose in 1900, the year before he became president. A staunch advocate of the "strenuous life," Roosevelt was an avid outdoorsman. Taking advantage of what he called the presidential "bully pulpit," Roosevelt used executive orders to create national forests and wildlife refuges. He also pressured Congress to pass legislation to protect the environment from exploitation and to preserve Native American antiquities.

Bubonic plague strikes Chinatown Chinese residents of San Francisco check "Dead Walls" in Chinatown for information about an outbreak of bubonic plague there. When a suspected case appeared in 1900, city officials quarantined the area but soon lifted the cordon after complaints from businessmen that the local economy was suffering. Chinatown underwent a massive cleanup campaign in spite of some resistance from local residents and the governor's skepticism that the plague even existed. Deaths from the outbreak, which ended in 1904, totaled 122.

1900: Mexican American landowners in Texas are increasingly expelled from the territory, as the mining of salt becomes more widespread.

1900: The census reveals that nearly 76 million people now live in the United States.

1900: Katherine Tingley founds the Raja-Yoga School at Point Loma, California. It includes the first open-air Greek Theater in the United States.

1900: A "Tent City" is opened on the beach near San Diego's Hotel del Coronado to accommodate guests while the hotel is being renovated. The tents prove so popular with guests that they will remain for several decades.

1900: California novelist Jack London, whose work's central themes often center around the grandeur of nature, publishes his first work, *The Son of the Wolf*.

1900: Francis LaFlesche authors *The Middle Five*, the first Indian autobiography to be published in the U.S.

1900: Prohibition activist Carrie Nation begins her campaign of raiding saloons with her hatchet in hand.

January 3, 1900: Timber magnate Frederick Weyerhaeuser makes one of the largest land purchases in U.S. history, buying 900,000 acres in Washington State from the Northern Pacific Railroad.

March 14, 1900: The Gold Standard Act is ratified, establishing gold as the only means of exchange for paper currency.

May 1, 1900: An explosion at a coal mine in Scofield, Utah, kills some 200 miners.

Nation takes a hatchet to saloons Carrie Moore took up the temperance cause after a bad marriage to an alcoholic. When she married for the second time, her name became Carrie Nation (she had the version "Carry A. Nation" registered as a trademark in Kansas). In 1900–01, she became famous for marching into saloons, singing, praying, and smashing up the fixtures with a hatchet. Arrested about 30 times, Nation gave lectures that—along with the sale of souvenir hatchets—paid her jail fines. Seen here is a poster advertising a lecture tour. In her efforts to ban alcohol, Carrie Nation also published newsletters and appeared in vaudeville.

Utah's massive lake The Great Salt Lake is the largest surviving remnant of a prehistoric lake that covered half of present-day Utah. Sitting more than 4,200 feet above sea level, the Great Salt Lake stretches 75 miles from north to south and 35 miles from east to west. In 1847 Mormons founded Salt Lake City about 15 miles from the southeastern beach. In the southern part of the sea is big Antelope Island, where Mormon farmers grew alfalfa and raised cattle—alongside a wild buffalo herd. At Saltair Beach, 15 miles west of Salt Lake City, bathers could enjoy the buoyancy of the briny waters and the pleasures of Salt Lake Pavilion (*pictured*).

The Wild Bunch In 1900 these members of the Wild Bunch outlaw gang posed for this photo in Texas while celebrating a successful holdup. Standing are (*left to right*) William Carver and Harvey Logan ("Kid Curry"). Sitting are (*left to right*) Harry Longbaugh ("Sundance Kid"), Ben Kilpatrick ("Tall Texan"), and Robert Leroy Parker ("Butch Cassidy"). Soon afterward, a Pinkerton-led posse was in such close pursuit that Butch Cassidy, the Sundance Kid, and the Kid's girlfriend (Etta Place) fled to South America. Although Cassidy and Sundance were supposedly killed in a shootout in Bolivia, some evidence suggests that they actually survived and eventually returned to the U.S.

Wild Bunch bombs, robs trains Working in various combinations, members of the Wild Bunch rustled cattle and robbed banks and trains. In June 1899, they dynamited a Wyoming bridge to stop a Union Pacific train, then blew open both this express car and the safe inside, gaining about $30,000. On other occasions, the Wild Bunch mistakenly dynamited trains carrying no money. In one such unrewarding attempt in New Mexico, a gang member was killed and another arrested. In September 1900, Butch Cassidy, the Sundance Kid, and Bill Carver robbed a Nevada bank of $32,640. Butch and Sundance would use their shares to flee the country.

Settling in Oklahoma During the Cherokee Strip land run on September 16, 1893, towns such as this one sprang up overnight— or even in an afternoon. But while Oklahoma land run "Boomers" of 1889 and 1893 paid nothing for their claims except land-office fees, later settlers had to purchase land—a hard bargain in tough economic times. This burden finally was lifted in May 1900 when President William McKinley signed the Free Homes Bill, relieving settlers of all payments except filing fees. Oil discoveries brought more and more people to Oklahoma, spurring its achievement of statehood in 1907.

September 8, 1900: A devastating hurricane and accompanying 15-foot storm surge floods Galveston, Texas, claiming some 6,000 lives.

September 14, 1900: President William McKinley dies a week after being shot in Buffalo, New York. Vice President Theodore Roosevelt will succeed him.

1901: Butch Cassidy and the Sundance Kid, now notorious bank and train bandits, flee to South America.

1901: The U.S. Congress decrees that all Native Americans in Oklahoma Territory are to be given automatic U.S. citizenship.

1901: The Union Labor Party is formed to represent the political interests of San Francisco's working class.

1901: Frank Norris releases *The Octopus: A Story of California,* which details the struggles faced by wheat farmers in the San Joaquin Valley as they battle the powerful Southern Pacific Railroad.

January 10, 1901: A crew working on a small knoll called Spindletop near Beaumont, Texas, hits a massive gusher of oil, triggering an unprecedented oil boom in America.

April 26, 1901: Outlaw train robber "Black Jack" Ketchum hangs for his crimes in Clayton, New Mexico. He will be the only person in New Mexico ever executed for train robbery.

May 13, 1901: The U.S. Supreme Court rules that California's Cupa Indians are subject to the authority of Congress. Consequently, the Cupa will be moved to the Pala Reservation.

December 16, 1901: The Senate ratifies the Hay-Pauncefote Treaty, clearing the way for exclusive U.S. construction and administration of the Panama Canal.

Hollywood takes shape

In the 1870s, hay, grain, bananas, and pineapples grew on flourishing ranchos near Los Angeles. When the large Rancho La Brea was subdivided, H. H. Wilcox bought 160 acres. His farm was never very successful; he did better selling large building lots to wealthy Midwesterners. His wife, Daeida Wilcox, named the town they created. She had heard the name "Hollywood" from a woman she had met on a train, and liked the sound of it. By 1900 Hollywood, California, boasted about 500 residents as well as a post office, a newspaper, markets, and a hotel.

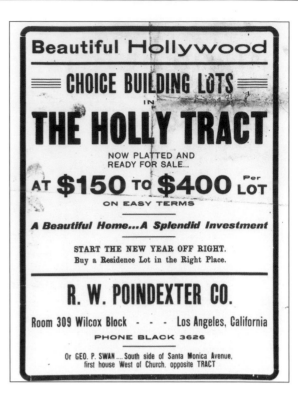

Hurricane destroys Galveston By 1900 Galveston, Texas, had weathered many storms, even though the city was on an island that was less than 10 feet above sea level. A seawall had been discussed, but none had been built. That September, reports of a tropical storm damaging the Louisiana and Mississippi coasts did not arouse much concern. Only a few Galveston residents evacuated. The great Galveston hurricane made landfall on September 8. It was a Category 4, with winds of 135 mph and a storm surge of more than 15 feet. Except for a few well-built mansions, Galveston was leveled, as shown in this tinted photo. Between 6,000 and 12,000 lives were lost, making it the deadliest natural disaster ever to strike the U.S.

The kings of preservation John Muir and John Burroughs were the two giants of the early 20th century wilderness preservation movement. Burroughs, a New Yorker from the Catskill region, was a prolific poet and essayist and a staunch defender of wilderness values. John Muir, a Scottish native who grew up in Wisconsin, went to San Francisco in 1868. Spending the next several years in the Yosemite Valley, California's natural wonderland, he spurred Congress to make it the second national park. In 1892 Muir founded the Sierra Club. Muir's eloquent opposition to the Hetch Hetchy Dam project made him unpopular with "pro-development" conservationists.

SAVE THE TREES

ANY FOOL CAN DESTROY trees. They cannot defend themselves or run away. And few destroyers of trees ever plant any; nor can planting avail much toward restoring our grand aboriginal giants. It took more than three thousand years to make some of the oldest of the Sequoias, trees that are still standing in perfect strength and beauty, waving and singing in the mighty forests of the Sierra. Through all the eventful centuries since Christ's time, and long before that, God has cared for these trees, saved them from drought, disease, avalanches, and a thousand storms; but he cannot save them from sawmills and fools; this is left to the American people.

—JOHN MUIR, IN THE *SIERRA CLUB BULLETIN*, 1920

Muir founds the Sierra Club In 1892 John Muir and others interested in preserving the natural features of the Sierra Nevada Mountains formed the Sierra Club. They wanted people to enjoy the wilderness in the right way—to look and learn without destroying it. The 182 charter members included many scientists, who mapped, photographed, and studied the mountain ranges. In 1901 the Sierra Club began annual outings so that members and visitors, such as the group seen here, could experience the wilderness. Muir was the first Sierra Club president; he held the office until his death in 1914.

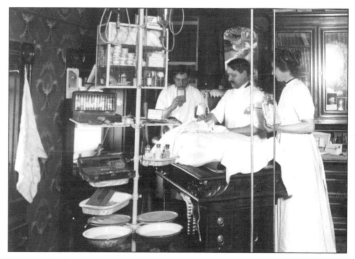

Turn-of-the-century medicine Midwestern settlers suffered from cholera, smallpox, typhoid, malaria, and pneumonia. These ailments were attributed to "miasmas"—bad air from stagnant water, marshes, mists, damp forests, and decaying matter. In those days, physicians were ill trained, widely scattered, and costly, meaning victims of disease or accident were often treated at home. In the late 1800s, medical practitioners learned why miasmas were indeed dangerous: because they bred germs and disease-carrying insects. By 1900 Midwestern medical schools were turning out well-trained doctors who provided better services. Seen here, a doctor, nurse, and anesthetist in 1901 Kansas operate in a well-equipped office. Even then, anesthetists were rare in the West.

Mellon forms Gulf Oil Pittsburgh banker William Mellon once compared the search for oil to an exciting treasure hunt. His family started in the oil business in Pennsylvania, sold their company to Standard Oil, then invested in Spindletop, Texas, oil explorations. They named their Texas company Gulf Oil, after the nearby Gulf of Mexico. When Spindletop production dropped, Mellon took over management, building a pipeline to bring Oklahoma crude to the Gulf refinery in Texas. Gulf Oil soon became one of the largest U.S. oil companies. In the 1920s, Gulf would begin investing in oil production in another gulf area—Bahrain and Kuwait in the Persian Gulf.

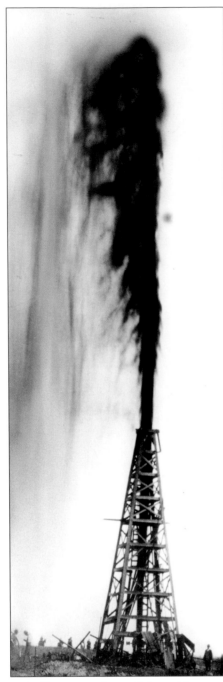

Spindletop gushes oil It had long been known that the gas bubbling from sulphur springs on Spindletop Hill south of Beaumont, Texas, would ignite if lit. In the late 19th century, oil prospectors began to dig there, but without success. Mining engineer Anthony Lucas persisted in the face of failure, and in January 1901 the Lucas gusher seen here struck oil at 1,139 feet, shooting it more than 100 feet into the air. The well's 100,000 barrels a day tripled U.S. oil production overnight.

Texas goes mad for oil By September 1901, there were six successful oil wells on Spindletop Hill near Beaumont, Texas. In 1903 there was the multitude of derricks seen here—an excess that soon caused production to decline to 10,000 barrels of oil per day (though later technologies would coax much more oil from Spindletop). By then, land prices in the Beaumont area had skyrocketed, and speculators were spending billions of dollars searching for oil in Texas. Companies were forming what would become huge corporations, such as ExxonMobil and Texaco. The nation's future dependence on oil and its byproducts was firmly established.

Roosevelt's "big stick" policy A political cartoonist takes aim at President Theodore Roosevelt's "big stick" foreign policy in the early 20th century. Actually, Roosevelt first used the African proverb "Speak softly and carry a big stick" in a 1900 letter about a local political matter while still governor of New York. He later adopted the phrase to describe his tough-minded approach to diplomacy. As president, he encouraged a revolution in Panama in 1903. He also browbeat European nations to stay out of Latin American affairs, while making the U.S. an active policeman of the area.

Chinese granted citizenship by birth In the late 19th century, Chinese laborers often were employed as strikebreakers by business owners in many different states. This led to resentment and anti-Chinese violence, but it also spread the Chinese into areas beyond California. In 1897 a U.S. Supreme Court decision in favor of Chinese American Wong Kim Ark reaffirmed the legal right of citizenship by birth for all Americans. With some protection from the law, Chinese Americans opened laundries, restaurants, and other businesses in major cities. Seen here is a Chinese general store in Virginia City, Nevada, circa 1900.

Wister creates noble western hero "What is become of the horseman, the cowpuncher, the last romantic figure upon our soil?" queried Owen Wister, addressing readers in the prologue of his 1902 novel, *The Virginian*. Wister was born to a wealthy Philadelphia family, studied in Europe and at Harvard, practiced law in Pennsylvania, and then decided to become a writer. Fascinated with the West, Wister helped create our enduring and much-loved western character—the naturally noble hero, strong and silent, always honest, who defeats the forces of evil. *The Virginian*, Wister's most famous work, is dedicated to his friend, Theodore Roosevelt.

U'ren and the "Oregon System" A former blacksmith, Oregonian political boss William U'ren was a believer in tools. So beginning in his youth, he wondered, "Why had we no tool makers for democracy?" To allow people direct participation in government, U'ren spearheaded the "Oregon System." The system's first major feature was the initiative, by which citizens voted on legislation proposed by other  citizens. Second was the referendum, by which citizens voted on measures proposed by the legislature. Third was recall, by which citizens could remove elected public officials. After its 1902 ratification in Oregon, most western and some midwestern states adopted the same system.

1902: Railroad magnate David Moffat begins construction of the Denver, Northwestern and Pacific Railroad.

1902: Owen Wister's signature novel, *The Virginian,* which romanticizes cowboy life and the American West, is published.

1902: The trans-Pacific telephone cable is laid from Canada to Australia.

1902: The Newlands Reclamation Act is passed, allowing for large-scale public works projects funded by land sales.

1902: The San Diego Public Library, the first of Andrew Carnegie's libraries west of the Mississippi, opens its doors.

January 1, 1902: The University of Michigan routs Stanford University 49–0 in the first Rose Bowl game, in Pasadena, California. The second Rose Bowl game will not be played until 1916.

1903: Montana's Amalgamated Copper Company effects the "Great Shutdown," putting 20,000 people out of work. The company's goal is to force the state legislature to permit a change of venue to avoid a judge whom the company feels is biased.

1903: Edward Adams, an editorial writer with the *San Francisco Chronicle,* establishes the Commonwealth Club of California. It will become the nation's largest and longest-running public affairs forum.

1903: President Roosevelt sponsors the Elkins Act, which prevents railroads from charging rates different from those they have published. The intent is to forbid rebates to preferred clients.

Wild times in Caldwell By the time this photograph of *The Caldwell Weekly Advance* presses was taken in the early 1900s, the Kansas town of Caldwell had tamed considerably. Founded in 1871 along the Chisholm Trail, Caldwell's wildest period was between 1880 and 1885, when it was a cattle town. Life there was worthy of a western movie, with boisterous cowboys, saloons, gambling, shootouts, hangings, and numerous murders—including those of lawmen. On September 16, 1893, Caldwell was the starting point of the Cherokee Strip land run—the largest land run in U.S. history.

Feisty Mother Jones
Mary Harris Jones lost her husband and four children to yellow fever, then lost her belongings and livelihood to the Chicago Fire. When she took up labor causes, the workers dubbed her "Mother Jones." The matronly, 5'0", profanity-spouting, Irish-born labor organizer helped to found the Industrial Workers of the World and to energize the United Mine Workers of America. In 1902 she led miners' wives in a "mop and broom brigade" against strikebreakers. In 1903 she organized the "Children's Crusade" march, protesting child labor. Arrested, sued, and deported from some states, Mother Jones fought for workers' rights until her death at 93 in 1930.

Newlands Reclamation Act

IN DISCUSSING IRRIGATION in the West, geologist John Wesley Powell proposed that communities be organized around existing water sources—instead of water being taken from one location and transferred to another. In 1902 the Newlands Reclamation Act authorized a much more ambitious approach to irrigation projects.

Proposed by U.S. Representative Francis Newlands of Nevada, and backed by President Theodore Roosevelt, this legislation provided for federal support and control of irrigation projects under a Bureau of Reclamation. It created a permanent revolving fund: Proceeds from the sale of public lands in western states would pay for the irrigation of arid lands; the irrigated lands would be sold to settlers; and

Francis Newlands

the profits would be reinvested in more irrigation projects. By putting science to work to transform the land, reclamation was expected to support agriculture, relieve urban congestion, and improve human lives.

By 1908 the Newlands Reclamation Act had created about 30 federal projects, and western politicians clamored for more in their home districts. Eventually, reclamation projects brought about the damming of nearly every major western river, the draining of some areas to provide water for others, and the redirection of governmental attention from small farms to mega-agriculture. These ambitious projects permanently altered both the western landscape and the western economy.

Combines produce greater yields Mechanized farming revolutionized the U.S. economy and transformed American farm life. Horse-drawn harvesting machinery was invented in the 1830s. In time, steam engines drove the machines, and then gas- or diesel-powered machinery appeared. The combined harvester was later patented. This device cut, threshed, and cleaned grain crops, then conveyed the product to wagons or other containers. Greatly accelerating the harvest, which took place within a critical time frame, the combines allowed for much larger areas to be planted, thus boosting profits for farmers. Such machinery, however, was expensive, and so it increased the amount of capital required for successful farming.

1903: *The Great Train Robbery*, considered the first true western film ever produced, is shot in New Jersey.

1903: President Roosevelt establishes the catchphrase that will define U.S. foreign policy for more than a century when he famously says that the United States should "speak softly and carry a big stick."

1903: The first juvenile court in the United States opens its doors in Denver, with Judge Ben Lindsey presiding.

1903: With the financial backing of the Scripps family, University of California zoologist William Ritter establishes the Marine Biological Association of San Diego. Its purpose is to found and endow the San Diego Marine Biological Institution, which will eventually be renamed the Scripps Institution of Oceanography.

April 20, 1903: Ojibwa Indian Charles Bender, nicknamed "Chief," becomes a major-league baseball player with the Philadelphia Athletics.

August 1903: A labor conflict ignites the Cripple Creek, Colorado, mining district. The violence and property damage will continue for nearly a year until the imposition of martial law restores the peace.

November 18, 1903: Frenchman Philippe Bunau-Varilla and U.S. Secretary of State John Hay sign the Hay–Bunau-Varilla Treaty, which establishes the terms of the sale of the Panama Canal Zone to the United States.

December 17, 1903: American aviation history begins in Kitty Hawk, North Carolina, with Orville Wright's first powered airplane flight.

1904: The first patrol along the U.S.-Mexican border is organized in response to the flow of Asian workers coming into the U.S. through Mexico.

The first western One of the earliest American films to tell a story, director Edwin Porter's 1903 *The Great Train Robbery* was the first true movie western (even though it was shot in New Jersey). In 12 swiftly paced minutes, it shows outlaws capturing a railroad telegraph office (*pictured*) and then hijacking and robbing a train, only to be gunned down by a posse in the end. *The Great Train Robbery* introduces story elements and images that would become staples (and clichés) in later westerns, ranging from murders, chases, and shoot-outs to dance-hall bullies forcing a "tenderfoot" to dance by shooting at his feet.

The first Mormon senator Did a U.S. senator take a "vengeance oath" against the nation? In 1903 Utah's Reed Smoot became the first Mormon U.S. senator. His opponents claimed that a vow to avenge the prophets' blood was required of all Mormon men, that Smoot was a polygamist (which he was not), and that members of his church still practiced outlawed plural marriages (apparently true). After years of hearings, the Senate in 1907 voted in Smoot's favor, and he remained a senator for another 26 years. He cosponsored the 1930 Hawley-Smoot Tariff Act, enacting high protective tariffs that some economists blame for deepening the Depression.

National Parks

"WHEN I FIRST VISITED California," wrote Theodore Roosevelt in his autobiography, "it was my good fortune to see the 'big trees,' the Sequoias, and then to travel down into the Yosemite, with John Muir. Of course of all people in the world he was the one with whom it was best worth while thus to see the Yosemite."

The year of Roosevelt's Yosemite visit was 1903, and he was then U.S. president. His three-day camping trip with celebrated naturalist and environmentalist John Muir proved lucky for America's environmental legacy.

Back in 1864, the spectacular Yosemite Valley and the nearby Mariposa Grove of giant sequoias had been the first wilderness locations cited for protection by the U.S. government, which ceded them to the state of California. Echoing the language of the Declaration of Independence, Congress's grant stipulated that Yosemite's treasures "shall be inalienable for all time." In 1872 Congress took a more sweeping action in declaring the newly explored region of Yellowstone to be the world's first national park.

The Yosemite Grant proved a disappointment. California mismanaged Yosemite, allowing commercial interests to take an environmental toll. Muir lobbied Washington until Congress created Yosemite National Park in 1890 (along with Sequoia and General Grant national parks). This victory was limited, because California still retained Mariposa Grove and Yosemite Valley. During his camping trip with Roosevelt, Muir persuaded the President that more needed to be done. And so, in 1906, Roosevelt signed a bill that brought Yosemite completely under federal control.

However, national parks remained under loose administration, with the departments of Interior, Agriculture, and War overseeing different sites. This system—or lack of a system—was clearly inadequate, causing activists and politicians to clamor for a central authority. In 1912 President William Taft asked Congress for a bill creating a Bureau of National Parks. At last, in 1916, President Woodrow Wilson signed a bill creating the National Park Service, which was organized the following year as a separate bureau of the Department of the Interior. The National Park Service has continued its valuable work ever since.

Mexican American miners
Mexican American laborers, such as the miners shown here, were crucial to the workforce of the U.S. Southwest. They also suffered from discrimination and prejudice. In 1903 Mexican Americans in the Clifton-Morenci, Arizona, mining district held a strike against poor working conditions and a dual-wage system that favored Anglo workers. In 1917 Mexican American copper miners were the primary victims of the Bisbee Deportation. The Industrial Workers of the World (IWW) and the United Mine Workers of America (UMWA) vigorously recruited Mexican American laborers.

Western shoot-outs The popular image of western gunfights—a revolver duel between two fast-draw artists—was a Hollywood concoction. In the real West, shoot-outs were spontaneous, angry events, often fueled by liquor. Westerners frequently did not use holsters, instead shoving their pistols into pockets or waistbands. Actually, most preferred a rifle or shotgun for accuracy. In this rare image from 1904, men from Quartzite, Arizona, have just quarreled in a saloon. The man wearing a vest has opened fire, while the man at the fence (*center*) will trigger one shot, then flee. The boy at right is a bystander.

Brave to the end Tom Horn was a compulsive adventure seeker who was drawn to the West as a teenager. He worked as a teamster, mastered cowboy skills, and competed in early rodeos. He wore a badge as a deputy sheriff and deputy U.S. marshal, and he engaged in frontier sleuthing as a Pinkerton agent and as a stock detective. Horn also served his country in the Apache Wars and the Spanish-American War. But as the frontier faded, Horn was hired by cattlemen to kill rustlers—$500 each. In 1903 he was hanged for murder. Reportedly, spectators admired his steely courage on the gallows.

Militant miners Members of the Western Federation of Miners (WFM) demonstrate in an uncharacteristically peaceful manner. The organization's founding was spurred by labor violence in the Coeur d'Alene, Idaho, mining district in 1892. The WFM's activities were marked by extreme militancy, including further violence at Coeur d'Alene in 1899 and in Telluride, Colorado, in 1901. By 1903 the WFM had locals throughout most of the western states and a membership of 27,000. But after unsuccessful alliances with other labor organizations, the WFM's influence waned. In 1916 it was renamed the International Union of Mine, Mill and Smelter Workers.

Deadly violence in Cripple Creek On August 11, 1903, more than 3,500 mine workers in Cripple Creek, Colorado, went on strike. In September, the Mine Owners Association (MOA) called upon Colorado Governor James Peabody to send militia troops into the district, alleging a "reign of terror" by the Western Federation of Miners (WFM). Peabody declared martial law on December 5, and the National Guard arrived in June 1904. Clashes among troops, strikebreakers, vigilantes, and striking miners caused more than 30 deaths, including the lynching of a union man (*pictured*). The strikers were defeated by the end of 1904, and the WFM was permanently weakened.

The appeal of Jack London
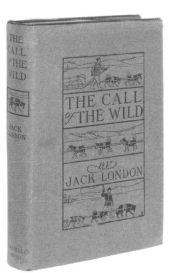
Writer Jack London published his most famous novel, *The Call of the Wild,* in 1903. The illegitimate son of a San Francisco woman, London spent his adolescence working a number of hard-labor jobs. His trip to the Yukon in 1897 provided rich material for *The Call of the Wild.* The novel focuses on the adventures of a large Alaskan dog that ultimately joins a pack of wolves when his loving owner is killed. London became a leading literary figure of his time. He earned fame for his strong masculinity, contradictory commitment to both rugged individualism and socialism, and his passion for adventure.

Hearst's media empire

William Randolph Hearst took over the *San Francisco Examiner* from his father and bought the *New York Journal*. He eventually owned more than two dozen newspapers, magazines, news services, radio stations, and film studios. Hearst's and Joseph Pulitzer's rival newspapers indulged in the sensationalism, hyperbole, and inventive newswriting that became known as "yellow journalism." Some claim that Hearst supported the 1895 Cuban Revolution—and actually ignited the Spanish-American War—to sell newspapers. He reportedly told artist Frederic Remington, "You furnish the pictures, I'll furnish the war." Beginning in the 1920s, Hearst built a lavishly decorated castle in San Simeon, California, for his longtime mistress, film actress Marion Davies. His wife and five sons lived in New York.

Homesteading more popular than ever While the early 20th century was marked by urbanization, rural population also increased steadily in the West. In fact, in the first two decades of the 20th century, homesteading flourished more than ever before, with 1913 being its peak year. This remote Colorado homestead was pictured during the 1910s. New homesteaders settled in the western Great Plains in large numbers, from the most northern states all the way down to Texas. Homesteading began to tail off around World War I.

May 4, 1904: The U.S. begins construction of the Panama Canal.

December 6, 1904: President Roosevelt makes a speech promoting his "Roosevelt Corollary to the Monroe Doctrine" to justify U.S. intervention in Latin America.

1904–07: Reuben Thwaites edits and publishes *Early Western Travels*, a 32-volume collection of narratives on travel and exploration in the American West.

1905: California's Salton Sea begins to form when water from the Colorado River breaches a levee and flows into a seabed that had been dry for hundreds of years.

1905: Political bickering and charges of voter fraud leave Colorado with three successive governors in one day: Alva Adams, James Peabody, and Jesse McDonald.

1905: An act of Congress establishes the U.S. Forest Service. President Roosevelt transfers management of all federal forests to the fledgling agency.

1905: Ground is broken on the Ocean Shore Electric Railway, planned to run between Santa Cruz and San Francisco.

1905: A series of articles is published in the *San Francisco Chronicle* asserting that Asian immigrants take sexual liberties with white women, undermine public schools, and exacerbate crime and poverty.

1905: The Japanese and Korean Exclusion League is founded. Membership soon will swell to 80,000.

1905: William "Big Bill" Haywood of the Western Federation of Miners (WFM) establishes the Industrial Workers of the World (IWW), which seeks to consolidate all industry unions under one massive umbrella union for the entire working class.

Rockefeller's "octopus" John D. Rockefeller's Standard Oil Company bought other oil companies, so that by the late 1870s Standard Oil controlled 90 percent of the nation's petroleum industry. According to a 1902–04 series of articles in *McClure's Magazine,* Standard Oil bribed politicians, controlled public opinion, and exacted tribute from other businesses—such as rebates from railroads. This 1904 cartoon depicts Standard Oil as a giant octopus grasping (*clockwise from top left*) the U.S. Capitol, shipping industries, a state house, the steel and copper industries, and the White House. In 1911 the U.S. Supreme Court decided that the monopoly should be dissolved.

Penney cashes in In 1902 young James Cash Penney opened a dry goods and clothing store in sparsely populated Kemmerer, Wyoming. Named the Golden Rule because of Penney's strong religious commitment, the store succeeded so well that he opened branches in other small western towns throughout the decade. Customers were attracted by the company's low prices and personal service. The various establishments became the JC Penney Company in 1913, and by 1917 175 stores dotted 22 states. Throughout the century, JC Penney grew into one of America's largest department store chains.

> "There was never a day when, looking back over the red and white men in my cavalcade, I did not know the thrill of the trail, and feel a little sorry that my Western adventures would thereafter have to be lived in spectacles."
>
> —BUFFALO BILL CODY

Buffalo Bill's Wild West

EVEN AS THE WEST was being settled, it was already becoming legendary. By the mid-1800s, eastern newspapers and magazines were publishing western adventure stories for eager readers. By the end of the century, a western spectacle was performed on tour in America and Europe.

William Cody rode with the Pony Express, served as an army scout, won the Congressional Medal of Honor for his bravery in battles with Indians, and earned the nickname "Buffalo Bill" for his hunting expertise. From the early 1860s to about 1910, dime-novel authors such as Ned Buntline wrote flamboyant fiction about Buffalo Bill Cody and other western heroes. When Cody took Russian Grand Duke Alexis on a buffalo hunt in 1872, a frenzied media covered every carefully staged moment.

In the 1870s, Buffalo Bill Cody, "Texas Jack" Omohundro, and occasionally "Wild Bill" Hickock played themselves on stage in New York City. Even though Cody often insisted that "I'm no actor," by 1883 his success led to his own re-creation of western legends. Buffalo Bill's Wild West—a four-hour outdoor event with hundreds of animals, cowboys, and Indians—staged battles, buffalo hunts, Indian war dances, an attack on a stagecoach, and a recreation of Custer's Last Stand.

Buffalo Bill's Wild West played in New York City's Madison Square Garden and was an outstanding attraction at the 1893 World's Columbian Exposition in Chicago. The show toured in the United States and Europe, and in 1887 performed in London before Queen Victoria. Among its sharpshooters, trick riders, skilled ropers, and other performers were Annie Oakley, Sitting Bull, and Geronimo.

In the 1890s and early 1900s, Cody recorded scenes from his Wild West show on film. His movie *The Life of Buffalo Bill* (1912) featured himself as the title performer. Then, with a cast of thousands shooting on actual locations, Cody re-created major battles from the Indian Wars for his 1914 *The Adventures of Buffalo Bill*. It was the first large-scale western movie, a genre that soon would rank among America's favorites.

Buffalo Bill's Wild West In this 1907 photograph, William Cody—probably the country's most recognizable celebrity at the time—leads a procession for his Buffalo Bill's Wild West show. The show, which opened in 1883 and toured for 30 years, was seldom as sedate as this publicity photo may seem to indicate. It was a dramatic, high-speed extravaganza with up to 1,200 performers. The cast included real Indians, some of whom had actually participated in the battles they reenacted. Buffalo Bill's Wild West also featured authentic working cowboys and colorfully costumed riders from around the world.

August 19, 1905: Roald Amundsen and his crew, traveling in a converted herring boat, make contact with a U.S. Coast Guard cutter, confirming their crossing of the Northwest Passage following a 26-month journey.

December 30, 1905: Former Idaho Governor Frank Steunenberg is assassinated, likely by a labor union sympathizer who felt that the governor had betrayed the unions.

1906: Japan claims that the United States is in violation of their bilateral treaties when the San Francisco school department segregates Asian children.

1906: Construction begins on the San Diego & Arizona Eastern Railroad, which will stretch from San Diego to Yuma, Arizona.

1906: The new United States Mint in Denver mints its first coins.

April 18, 1906: At least 3,000 people die and hundreds of millions of dollars in property damages result when a massive earthquake rocks San Francisco and sets off scores of fires.

May 8, 1906: Congress passes the Burke Act. Designed to delay the granting of U.S. citizenship to Indians, this act imposes a 25-year waiting period before granting Indians title to lands they were guaranteed under the Dawes Severalty Act of 1887.

June 8, 1906: The Preservation of American Antiquities Act becomes law. The act allows for the designation of important natural and historical sites as national monuments.

June 29, 1906: Congress creates Mesa Verde National Park, protecting both a beautiful natural area and important Anasazi Indian sites.

Chinese prostitution Because laws allowed the immigration of single Chinese men and severely restricted the immigration of women and families, Chinese men far outnumbered Chinese women in the United States. According to U.S. census figures, the American Chinese population was 90 percent male in 1900. This prostitute looks out from a "crib"—a street-level room with a barred window—in San Francisco's Chinatown, circa 1905. Higher-class prostitutes lived and worked in brothels.

Coast to coast auto race Two Oldsmobile runabouts—"Old Scout" (*left*) and "Old Steady"—leave New York City in the first transcontinental automobile race on May 8, 1905. After 44 days, Old Scout arrived first in Portland, Oregon, which helped open the Lewis and Clark Centennial Exposition. With only 150 miles of paved road in the entire country, the two cars endured rocks, mud, rain, cold, flooding, and herds of hogs and buffalo. Along the way, cowboys on horseback laughed at the drivers for their temerity. The two vehicles actually passed several wagon trains still heading west on the Oregon Trail, as America's past and future momentarily intersected.

Monument Valley A stagecoach travels along a dirt road through Monument Valley in northern Arizona, circa 1905. This iconic valley, which straddles the Utah-Arizona border and is home to the Navajo Nation Reservation, is most famous as the location for many movies, television shows, and commercials. Director John Ford was the first to recognize the cinematic value of the stark landscape, with its impressive formations rising from the flatlands. His western film classic, *Stagecoach,* was shot there in 1939.

Ex-Idaho governor assassinated During the 1899 labor violence in the Coeur d'Alene mining district, Idaho Governor Frank Steunenberg (*pictured*) declared martial law, and brought in federal troops to subdue the strikers. In 1905, four years after he left office, Steunenberg was assassinated outside his home by an explosive rigged to his gate. Harry Orchard, a member of the Western Federation of Miners (WFM), was arrested. He confessed to the killing and implicated WFM leaders Bill Haywood, Charles Moyer, and George Pettibone in the plot. Defended by attorney Clarence Darrow, the three leaders were acquitted. Orchard spent the rest of his life in prison.

"Big Bill" founds the IWW Charismatic and radical labor leader "Big Bill" Haywood joined the Western Federation of Miners (WFM) in 1896. In 1902 he became the organization's secretary-treasurer. Yearning for "One Big Union" to promote class struggle, Haywood helped spearhead the 1905 founding of the Industrial Workers of the World (IWW). In 1906 Haywood and two other WFM leaders were charged in the 1905 murder of former Idaho Governor Frank Steunenberg. Haywood was acquitted, but was later convicted for impeding U.S. efforts in World War I. Jumping bail in 1921, he fled to the Soviet Union, where he died in 1928.

June 30, 1906: The Food and Drug Administration is formed when Congress passes the Pure Food and Drug Act. The FDA will regulate the quality and labeling of medicines and foods.

August 13–14, 1906: African American soldiers of the 25th U.S. Infantry riot against racial discrimination in Brownsville, Texas.

1907: Economic disaster is averted when J. P. Morgan organizes a group of executives to prop up the U.S. economy during what has become known as the Panic of 1907.

1907: President Roosevelt convinces the San Francisco School Board to stop segregating Asian students. In exchange, Japan agrees to halt the immigration of Japanese and Korean laborers to the U.S.

1907: A streetcar strike paralyzes public transportation in San Francisco.

November 16, 1907: Oklahoma is admitted to the Union as the 46th state.

1908: In the case of *Winters v. United States,* the Supreme Court decides that western Indian tribes should retain first rights to limited water resources.

1908: President Roosevelt establishes the National Conservation Commission to develop a sustainable use policy for America's natural resources.

1908: Brothers Charles and Henry Greene design the Gamble House in Pasadena, California. The landmark will survive into the 21st century as one of the finest examples of the American Arts and Crafts style of architecture.

War with the Philippines Three American soldiers lie dead along a Philippine road during the Philippine-American War. When the U.S. occupied the Philippine Islands during the Spanish-American War and did not support independence in the Philippines, many Filipinos rebelled. Led by Emilio Aguinaldo, who had organized a rebellion against Spanish rule in 1896, Filipino soldiers fought a guerrilla war against U.S. soldiers beginning in 1899. Some 4,000 U.S. troops and an estimated 220,000 Filipinos, including civilians, died in the conflict. Although President Roosevelt officially declared an end to the hostilities when Aguinaldo was captured in 1901, isolated groups of rebels continued sporadic attacks for decades.

L.A. throws a parade Crowds line the streets to watch a parade during the *Fiesta de Los Angeles* in the early 1900s. The festival was the brainchild of businessman Max Meyberg, who wanted a celebration modeled after Mardi Gras but characteristic of Southern California. The five-day event, first put on in 1894, featured sporting contests, a queen and her court, and, of course, the parade. Its major colors—red, green, and yellow—symbolized the Golden State's major products: wine, olives, and oranges. Meyberg also hoped money spent at the fiesta would help local businesses recover from the depression of 1893.

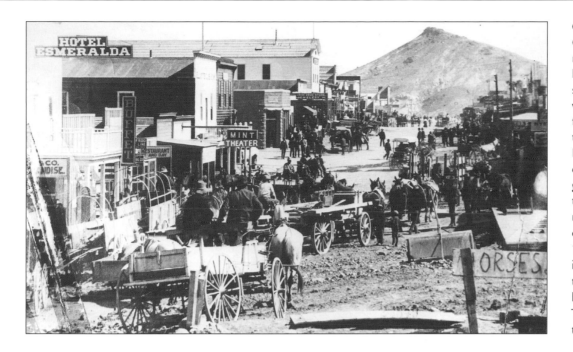

Goldfield's rise and fall Goldfield, Nevada, a few miles south of Tonopah, blossomed in 1902 when substantial gold deposits were discovered. The Goldfield Hotel was considered the finest hotel between Kansas City and San Francisco. At the height of the gold boom in 1906, the town boasted 30,000 residents, but the bust came only a few years later. In 1910 fewer than 5,000 inhabitants remained. By the early 1920s, Goldfield had become a ghost town. Today it remains an attractive tourist destination.

The San Francisco earthquake In the early morning of April 18, 1906, a violent earthquake devastated San Francisco. Shocks were felt in Oregon, Los Angeles, and central Nevada. The quake—estimated at 7.8 to 8.25 on the Richter scale—was followed by fires that destroyed more than 500 city blocks. Rather than watch people being burned to death, police officers sometimes resorted to mercy killings. Seen here, survivors view the rubble after the inferno. Deaths were estimated at more than 3,000. Between 225,000 and 300,000 people were left homeless. San Francisco parks and beaches were soon covered with makeshift tents. Police, under orders, shot some 500 looters.

Houses collapse; streets sink Onlookers examine several tilting houses on the verge of collapse after the 1906 San Francisco earthquake. Many buildings that did not fall were shifted off their foundations. One corner of the Call Building, a 12-story skyscraper, was moved two feet onto the sidewalk. In some places, streets sank several feet; in others, streets rose in five-foot humps. Afterward, the U.S. Army built 5,610 wooden houses, which they rented for $2 per month to displaced people. The houses, grouped in 11 camps, accommodated nearly 16,500 residents.

Final Four Contiguous States

IN 1853, WHEN ROGUISH LEADER Santa Anna became Mexico's president for the 11th and last time, it is said that he finally saw a map showing how much territory his country had lost to the United States during the Mexican-American War of 1846–48. The redoubtable dictator burst into tears.

By then, two parts of this vast land that had once belonged to Mexico—California and Texas—had already become U.S. states. All or parts of seven more states would be carved from that territory, including the last four of the 48 contiguous states of the U.S.

The first of these four states, Utah, found it hard to enter the Union. Settled by members of The Church of Jesus Christ of Latter-day Saints, or Mormons, Utah (then called Deseret) was an independent theocracy before becoming a state. Starting in 1849, the region's inhabitants made six unsuccessful applications for statehood. The most troublesome obstacles were the Mormon Church's involvement in politics and its acceptance of the practice of polygamy. The church had to renounce both before Utah became the 45th state, which occurred on January 4, 1896.

Only the western panhandle of the 46th state, Oklahoma, originally belonged to Mexico. For decades, this strip was so sparsely populated that it was called "No Man's Land." Oklahoma was once known as Indian Territory. The arrival of the railroad facilitated an influx of white settlers to the region, causing the western part of Indian Territory to become Oklahoma Territory in 1890. After these two areas combined and achieved statehood on November 16, 1907, Oklahoma's white and Indian inhabitants achieved a remarkable degree of integration.

New Mexico became the 47th state on January 6, 1912, quickly followed by Arizona on February 14 of the same year. The final two contiguous states share a desert border with Mexico, and are strongly influenced by Hispanic culture. In 2004, more than 43 percent of New Mexico's citizens (plus thousands of illegal aliens) were of Hispanic or Latino origin.

Tonopah's heyday Tonopah, Nevada, boomed in 1900 when prospector Jim Butler discovered silver, gold, copper, and lead deposits. In its heyday, Tonopah boasted a huge casino/dance hall/brothel complex that occupied an entire block. Fires destroyed parts of the town in 1908 and 1909, and mine fires—with some loss of life—occurred in 1911 and 1939. Tonopah's mines produced almost $121 million from 1900 to 1921, but the Great Depression heralded a permanent decline in productivity. Today, about 3,000 residents live in Tonopah.

One last drink for Oklahoma At the turn of the 20th century, Oklahoma's population had increased due to land runs and oil discoveries. The residents included immigrants from Europe, Native Americans from various tribes, and African Americans who had established a number of all-black towns. (When Oklahoma gained statehood, African Americans outnumbered both Indians and first- and second-generation Europeans.) On November 16, 1907, Oklahoma became the 46th U.S. state. Seen here, officers uncover hidden liquor in a kitchen. Oklahoma Territory entered the Union as a dry state, and revenue officers dumped some 28,000 barrels of beer into the streets.

Curtis photographs American Indians These portraits were taken by photographer Edward Curtis (*above left*). Curtis's career began in a Seattle photographic studio, but in 1898—thanks to a friendship with Indian expert George Bird Grinnell—he became the official photographer for the Harriman expedition to Alaska. Thereafter, he devoted his life to photographing Indians. Traveling over much of North America in search of subjects, Curtis created roughly 40,000 memorable, sometimes haunting, images. Though subjects were often "posed" for the best effect, Curtis's photographs document much about Native culture and life. From 1907 to 1930, he published an extraordinary 20-volume work entitled *The North American Indian*.

Dry farming in the Oregon desert Although much of Oregon is heavily forested, the southeastern part of the state is a desert. In the early 20th century, thousands of homesteaders—including many single women—secured low-cost federal land and developed small "dry farms" on this desert land. From 1905 to 1920, dry farming proved viable due to unusually wet years and long growing seasons. However, declining crop prices after World War I, compounded by drought and early killing frosts, wreaked havoc on small farmers. By 1920 most homesteaders' lands reverted to federal ownership or were bought by cattle ranchers, who thereafter dominated eastern Oregon's economy.

Yonkel the cowboy Yonkel the Mahzik, a Jewish cowboy, strikes a pose in this early 20th century photograph. A Civil War veteran who had migrated back to Russia, Mahzik was detained upon his return to America. Dressed in a long, dark coat and cowboy boots, he slugged and cursed—in a Russo-Texas drawl—at an immigration official who jostled him. He was readmitted when his identity was confirmed. Mahzik was one of thousands of Jews who went west looking for their fortunes, as well as an end to religious persecution, in the late 19th and early 20th centuries.

April 14, 1908: The Navy's Great White Fleet, with 27 ships and 16,000 sailors, makes San Diego its first port of call as it begins a worldwide tour.

May 9, 1908: Barney Oldfield shatters the automobile speed record, traveling one mile in 51.8 seconds at a racetrack in Lakeside, California.

July 7, 1908: The 12,500-seat Denver Municipal Auditorium is completed just in time to host the Democratic National Convention and perennial candidate William Jennings Bryan.

October 1, 1908: The first of Henry Ford's Model T automobiles, retailing for $825, is unveiled to the public.

November 3, 1908: William Howard Taft, a Republican from Ohio, is elected the 27th president of the United States.

1909: The Texas Folklore Society is established to safeguard, preserve, and publish Texas folklore.

1909: The Dawes Act opens some 700,000 acres of tribal land in Washington, Idaho, and Montana to settlement by white Americans.

1909: The Selig Polyscope Company, a major motion picture company in New York, relocates to Los Angeles, beginning the industry-wide exodus to the production-friendly natural climate of Southern California.

1909: The Chicago, Milwaukee, St. Paul and Pacific Railway, also known as the Milwaukee Road, is laid through the states of Montana, Idaho, and Washington.

1909: Naturalist John Muir leads the unsuccessful charge to protect the Hetch Hetchy Valley from being developed as the site of San Francisco's municipal water supply.

Water woes in the Southwest In the arid Southwest, farming used to be possible only near dependable streams or with irrigation. Native Americans had relied on canals for centuries, and early Spanish settlers also utilized irrigation ditches. After the U.S. took over the region, larger irrigation projects were created. From 1880 to 1930, hundreds of miles of canals were built, such as these in Mesa, Arizona, allowing vast increases in farm production. By the late 20th century, however, the huge aquifers—underground water sources—were being depleted. Deep well irrigation, as well as surface-water irrigation, continues to be used, though the future of water availability in the Southwest poses a serious challenge.

The Bradbury Building The stunning sky-lit interior atrium of the Bradbury Building in Los Angeles has been featured in many films, including *Blade Runner* in 1982. The Bradbury, finished in 1893, was commissioned by mining and real estate entrepreneur Louis Bradbury and designed by George Wyman. Inspired by Edward Bellamy's utopian novel, *Looking Backward*, the building was praised by architectural historians Kenneth Frampton and Yukio Futagawa for "its dramatically projecting stair and lift towers."

Church of the Nazarene Members of the Church of the Nazarene embark on a "Hallelujah March" around the tent that was the denomination's original home. The church was founded in 1908 in Pilot Point, Texas, by Phineas Bresee, a disillusioned Methodist minister who was doing missionary work in Texas at the time. Bresee found Methodism spiritually unsatisfying and was especially unhappy when church officials criticized his desire to minister to poverty-stricken non-Methodists. He broke from Methodism to form this new denomination, which preached religious inclusiveness.

"Killin' Jim" Miller "Deacon Jim" Miller, a black-clad, well-spoken churchgoer who neither smoked nor drank, worked as a lawman in Pecos, Texas. By 1891 Miller already had killed several men. When he took up murder-for-hire, he became "Killin' Jim." Miller is believed to have ambushed and murdered Pat Garrett (killer of Billy the Kid) for $10,000. Charges against Miller never stuck, as witnesses sometimes turned up dead. Western communities, tired of outlaws, formed vigilante groups—or lynch mobs—to clean up their towns. As seen here in 1909, Killin' Jim (*far left*) and other outlaws were caught and hanged by an Oklahoma vigilante group.

Oklahoma oil boom This Oklahoma refinery pumps out gasoline as part of the great gas and oil boom of the early 20th century. Oklahoma's first commercial well, colorfully called "Nellie Johnstone No. 1," was drilled in 1897, and by 1909 the boom was clearly on. The Oklahoma wells were part of the massive Mid-Continent Oil Region, which stretched from central Texas to eastern Kansas. From 1900 to 1935, some 8.8 billion barrels of crude oil were pumped from the region. The ensuing demand led to a frenzy of town building so furious that new workers often had to sleep in tents and even on rooftops.

1909: William "Big Bill" Haywood and his Industrial Workers of the World use violence and other extreme tactics in an effort to sabotage the Montana timber industry.

1909: William E. Smythe establishes the Little Landers colony, a utopian farm community, in what is now San Ysidro, California.

1909: Congress passes the Enlarged Homestead Act, doubling the size of a plot that a homesteader can "prove up" under 1862's Free Homestead Act from 160 acres to 320 acres. This measure is taken to assist homesteaders in arid western states, such as Montana, where effective farming practices require larger plots of land.

June 1, 1909: W.E.B. DuBois is among the founders of the National Association for the Advancement of Colored People (NAACP). The organization's objective is to obtain civil rights for African Americans via the legal system.

1910: Mexican American delegates at New Mexico's constitutional convention assert that the 1848 Treaty of Guadalupe-Hidalgo mandates that all state business be conducted in both English and Spanish.

1910: The Mexican Revolution begins, and Mexicans enter the U.S. in large numbers.

1910: Angel Island, the Ellis Island of the West, is opened. It was built in response to the Chinese Exclusion Act, and will serve as the U.S. point of entry for most Asian immigrants for the next 30 years.

1910: Forestry Division head Gifford Pinchot loses his job in a dispute with Secretary of the Interior Richard Ballinger, which underscores the ongoing battle between conservationists and mining, timber, and grazing interests.

Schreyvogel paints western riders
Charles Schreyvogel grew up in Hoboken, New Jersey, too poor to afford art lessons. He taught himself to draw, and by 1880 was teaching art classes. With support from patrons, Schreyvogel studied art in Munich. On his return, he took up western themes. He made a number of trips west, sometimes visiting Indian reservations, but painted his large canvases on the roof of his New Jersey studio. This Schreyvogel piece, entitled *In Safe Hands*, was painted in 1909.

California's progressive governor Hiram Johnson made his mark as a reformer in 1908, when he became the prosecuting attorney against political boss Abe Ruef. Johnson replaced Francis Heney, who had been shot in the courtroom. Johnson's success in the case helped spur his election as California's governor in 1910. A staunchly progressive Republican governor, he supported women's suffrage and the popular election of U.S. senators, while also weakening the Southern Pacific Railroad's hold on state politics. From 1917 until his death in 1945, he served as a U.S. senator from California, continuing to support such liberal causes as the New Deal.

Progressivism in the West

PROGRESSIVISM WAS NOT so much a movement as a belief that society could be transformed for the good of all. That belief produced several different progressive movements. As the 20th century approached, many Americans lobbied against unsafe and onerous working conditions, abuses of corporate power, wasteful uses of natural resources, increasing disparity between the wealthy and the poverty-stricken, and a government indifferent to the needs of everyday people.

Settlers had moved westward determined to make better lives for themselves. Western idealists were tough-minded, and they expected to see actual improvement in return for their efforts. Western states—the first to grant women full suffrage—were also concerned with the use of natural resources, children's rights, workers' causes, and a variety of struggles between corporations and individuals.

In Colorado, Judge Benjamin Lindsey pioneered the recognition of juvenile rights. In the early 1900s, Lindsey created and served on a Denver juvenile court that became world-famous for its applications of laws to children. Lindsey also worked to reform election laws, improve the rights of prison inmates and their families, and provide public baths and playgrounds.

Labor issues in the West included working conditions, hours, and workers' rights. When federal troops locked striking Idaho silver miners into an outdoor "bullpen," it led to the 1893 formation of the Western Federation of Miners (WFM) in Montana. The WFM played a role in the 1905 founding of the Industrial Workers of the World (IWW).

At the turn of the 20th century, laborers typically worked from 54 to 72 hours each week. Western states began to limit the hours that a worker needed to toil in order to keep a job. In 1898 Utah limited miners to an eight-hour workday, and in 1908 Oregon set a daily 10-hour maximum for female workers in laundries and factories. Both laws were disputed all the way to the U.S. Supreme Court, but in both cases the court upheld the limits. Most states eventually set minimum working ages and prohibited children from working more than 10 hours per day, although those laws were not always well enforced.

Child laborers on a beet farm in Colorado

In 1911 California Governor Hiram Johnson won the battle for an eight-hour workday for women and children. Johnson also tackled a corporation famously referred to as "The Octopus" in a popular novel by Frank Norris. The Southern Pacific Railroad had taken over the old Central Pacific along with several other railroads. The Southern Pacific demanded special privileges from towns that wanted to be served by the railroad. Moreover, reformers claimed that the company cheated farmers on land prices and raised shipping rates to cover bribes for public officials. As governor, Johnson broke up the Southern Pacific monopoly. He also initiated free textbooks in public schools, gave pensions to retired teachers, and improved election regulations and workers' compensation laws.

Reforms that began in states moved to the national level. Progressive reformers took up the Populist idea that a government should work for the economic well-being of the entire public. In 1903 President Theodore Roosevelt made social improvement a moral issue, insisting that every American deserved a "square deal."

1910: Western Montana is scorched by a series of wildfires.

1910: Washington State gives women the right to vote.

1910: The U.S. census indicates that more than 93 million people live in the country.

January 18, 1910: Aviator Eugene Ely completes his first successful takeoff and landing from a ship, near San Francisco.

May 8, 1910: Colorado's first long-distance phone call is placed, from Denver to New York City.

May 11, 1910: Montana's Glacier National Park is established by an act of Congress.

June 25, 1910: President Taft signs the Mann Act, which prohibits inter-state transportation of women "for the purpose of prostitution or debauchery, or for any other immoral purpose."

July 4, 1910: African American boxer Jack Johnson defeats Jim Jeffries in Reno, Nevada, retaining the heavy-weight title. The match triggers race riots that result in the deaths of more than 25 people.

October 1, 1910: Twenty-one die when the building housing the *Los Angeles Times* offices is bombed and burned in retaliation for the paper's anti-union stance. Union leaders and brothers James and John McNamara will plead guilty to the crime.

December 19, 1910: A Baltimore city ordinance segregating neighborhoods along racial lines is approved by the city council. This paves the way for similar ordinances in cities from St. Louis to Dallas to Oklahoma City.

1911: The Mexican Revolution is being fought so close to the United States border that Americans are able to watch the conflict from U.S. territory.

Indian "assimilation" A Crow family dines in "white man" style, complete with crockery, silverware, and a tea service, while the adult Indians retain traditional hair and clothing. Due to assimilation, Indians were faced with a spiritual crisis. Sioux medicine man Black Elk, a believer in the sacred power of circles, regretted that Indians were forced to live in square houses rather than tipis. "Our power is gone and we are dying, for the power is not in us any more," he said.

Otis pushes agenda in *L.A. Times* Centered in this group of newspaper VIPs and friends is Harrison Gray Otis, publisher of the *Los Angeles Times* from 1882 to 1917. Otis used newspaper stories to build the fear of drought in Los Angeles—making sure that citizens would vote to fund the aqueduct—and bought property that would soon be irrigated. Under Otis's guidance, the *Los Angeles Times* was a strident anti-union, conservative paper. Both the newspaper office and Otis's home were bombed in 1910. Although unions denounced the bombings, two union men confessed to the crime.

Bomb rocks the *Times* building
Only a shell of the *Los Angeles Times* building remains after an explosion on October 1, 1910, which killed 21 people. Brothers John and James McNamara, who were labor union activists angry at the anti-union stance of the publisher of the *Times,* were arrested for the crime. Famed lawyer Clarence Darrow defended them, but when he became convinced that the prosecution had sufficient evidence to convict and secure the death penalty, Darrow negotiated a plea bargain that garnered the brothers jail time but saved their lives. The incident was indicative of increased labor strife in a time of western growth.

California oil After the discovery of oil at La Brea in Los Angeles in 1892, rigs on the huge L.A. oil fields were constructed near neighborhoods and orchards. Oil discoveries in Santa Barbara County during the 1880s developed into major production in the early 1900s. California's San Joaquin Valley had the biggest gushers; the Lakeview well spouted uncontrollably at 18,000 barrels a day for 18 months in 1910–11. California produced four million barrels of oil in 1900 and 77 million barrels in 1910.

Indians in the workforce
In the late 1800s, most Native Americans lived on reservations as wards of the U.S. government. During the early 20th century, the closed reservation system ended and citizenship was granted to all Native Americans. Indians could thus seek employment off the reservation, such as these Apaches working on a road alongside Arizona's Salt River. Not surprisingly, Indians typically landed jobs that were strenuous, menial, and/or low paying.

1911: The last survivor of California's decimated Yahi tribe, an Indian named Ishi, is discovered when he walks to Oroville, California, in search of food.

1911: Mexicans are made exempt from immigrant "head taxes" when the Dillingham Commission reports that Mexican labor might be the answer to the labor shortage in the southwest United States.

1911: A group of Native Americans, including Sioux Charles Eastman and Yavapai Carlos Montezuma, establishes the Society of American Indians.

1911: The prolific American Film Manufacturing Company, also known as the Flying A Company, sets up shop in La Mesa, California, where it will eventually produce more than 100 films.

1911: Mrs. Arthur Dodge and other men and women form the National Association Opposed to Woman Suffrage.

1911: The Nestor Company is the first film studio to establish operations in the Hollywood section of Los Angeles. Others soon will follow.

January 29, 1911: Magonista rebels in Mexico, joined by members of the Industrial Workers of the World (an American-based union), capture Mexicali. They also will briefly occupy Tecate and Tijuana before being driven out by Mexican Federalists.

May 15, 1911: The U.S. Supreme Court finds Standard Oil guilty of violating the Sherman Antitrust Act. Standard Oil will be broken into several smaller companies.

May 24, 1911: Colorado National Monument, 32 square miles of cliffs and canyons on the Colorado Plateau, is established at the confluence of the Colorado and Gunnison rivers.

Aviation pioneer Glenn Martin of Iowa left an indelible mark on U.S. aircraft design and manufacturing. A few years after the Wright brothers' success at Kitty Hawk, Martin began producing experimental flying machines. In 1912 he created the company that he directed for almost 40 years. Among his employees were William Boeing, Donald Douglas, Lawrence Bell, and James McDonnell, all of whom later founded their own aircraft factories. "Martin Bombers" created the basis for modern airpower during WWI, and Martin supplied thousands of planes to the U.S. military.

The first transcontinental flight In 1911 Cal Rodgers made the first transcontinental flight in a Wright biplane. Rodgers followed railroad tracks and reportedly used a hanging shoe lace to judge vertical position. His support team on a train below repaired the plane and tended to the pilot after each of his 16 crashes. Rodgers is seen here with his plane, named *Vin Fizz* after the soft drink produced by his sponsor. The *Vin Fizz* left New York on September 17, arrived in Pasadena, California, on November 5, and continued to Long Beach on December 10. The 84-day flight required 70 landings.

Western Cities

WHEN RAILROADS CONNECTED western cities with the rest of the country, those cities grew rapidly. From 1870 to 1890, the population of Denver expanded from under 5,000 to over 100,000. Los Angeles had less than three percent of California's population in 1885; by 1900 it had seven percent. But during the economic depression of 1893, railroads, banks, and businesses failed. Some cities, including Denver, actually lost population.

As demonstrated in Chicago, 1893 was a time of conflicting signals about the future. Architects were designing the first spare, practical, truly modern buildings for downtown Chicago. Meanwhile, Chicago's Columbian Exposition presented an overblown, temporary "ideal city" of white plaster columns and domes. It was the Exposition's old-style opulence that stirred imaginations in western cities.

In 1895 Denver's leaders decided to cheer up everyone with three days of parades and festivities. Citizens who had gone broke dressed as though they were wealthy. This carnival continued annually until 1912, when Denver was financially secure and growing again. During that time, Denver, like most western cities, also took practical steps to diversify its economy—turning to tourism and service industries in addition to its traditional agricultural products and equipment.

Seattle, which had just finished rebuilding from an 1889 downtown fire, was crippled by the depression. That city recovered in 1898 when it became the gateway to Canada's Klondike Gold Rush. In Los Angeles, continuous growth was supported by the 1892 discovery of oil and the 1904 importation of water.

San Francisco had expanded wildly during the Gold Rush and grew at a slower rate afterward. The 1893 panic hit San Francisco hard, but the worst came in 1906. A devastating earthquake and fire destroyed 80 percent of the city. San Francisco rebuilt, and by 1910 it was growing again. In 1915 San Francisco held its own opulent Exposition to celebrate the opening of the Panama Canal. By 1918, after the United States had entered the First World War, San Francisco and other cities were strengthened by an influx of wartime workers.

The last Yahi Indian Ishi, which means *man* in his language, was allegedly the last living Yahi tribesman. Soon after he first appeared at Oroville, California, in 1911, Ishi was taken by Alfred Kroeber and Thomas Waterman to live at the University of California's anthropology museum in San Francisco. Until he died from tuberculosis (possibly contracted after he came to the city), Ishi taught his white associates much about his former lifeway. He also became a celebrity to thousands of admiring museum visitors who watched him make arrows and build fires. The Yahi Nation, like many other California "tribelets," had been pushed into extinction by whites' violence and by diseases.

Russell captures the Old West *Death of a Gambler,* a painting by Charles Russell, portrays a classic scene from the Old West, as rough justice prevails. Born in St. Louis, Russell fell in love with the West when he moved to Montana in 1880 as a boy of 16. He became a wrangler in 1882 and eventually perfected his self-taught artistic talents. Encouraged by his wife, Nancy, he continued to draw and paint scenes of a West that was rapidly disappearing. His authenticity combined with romanticism gained him fame, especially after his successful exhibit in New York in 1911.

October 10, 1911: California holds a special election to vote on an amendment to grant women's suffrage. The amendment passes by just over 3,500 votes.

December 10, 1911: After 84 days, Cal Rodgers lands his *Vin Fizz* in Long Beach, California, completing the first transcontinental flight.

1912: By this year, the epicenter of the American film industry has unmistakably moved from New York City to Los Angeles.

1912: Women are granted the right to vote in Arizona, Kansas, and Oregon.

1912: Zane Grey releases *Riders of the Purple Sage,* an American classic set in 1870s Mormon Utah.

1912: The U.S. military establishes itself on North Island near San Diego, building Rockwell Field and an aviation school.

1912: The Industrial Workers of the World stages a protest march in San Diego, one of several fights for free speech undertaken by the IWW in the early 20th century.

1912: Theodore Roosevelt's powerful Progressive Party, also known as the Bull Moose Party, is the first national political party to come out in support of women's suffrage.

1912: Pioneering aircraft engineer Glenn L. Martin establishes the Glenn L. Martin Aircraft Company in Santa Ana, California, to build planes for the Army Signal Corps. Martin will close his West Coast plant in 1917 and move operations to Ohio.

January 6, 1912: New Mexico becomes the 47th state to enter the Union.

February 14, 1912: Arizona joins the Union as the 48th state.

Indians stripped of land With the implementation of the Dawes Act, small parcels of tribal land were allocated to enrolled tribal members, but much reservation land was declared "waste" that could be auctioned off to non-Native bidders. By forcing Indians to "take up the plow,"

white policy-makers hoped to end tribalism and achieve assimilation. In actuality, much good Indian land was permanently lost to whites, and relatively few Indians benefited. By the time the Dawes Act was suspended in 1934, two-thirds of tribal land was gone, and Indians remained mired in poverty and despair.

The value of dams Built in 1911 on the Salt River, the Roosevelt Dam, like others in the West, was meant to prevent flooding, divert water to farms and towns, and turn hydroelectric turbines. After the 1902 Newlands Reclamation Act became federal law, numerous irrigation and dam projects transformed the arid West. As valuable irrigated public land was sold off, the government earmarked the proceeds to fund vast water and electric projects. Most of the major western rivers were dammed, sometimes destroying archeological sites and places of immense natural beauty.

Living with the Omaha Alice Cunningham Fletcher (*far left*) was an American anthropologist and ethnologist who spent years studying Native Americans. During a stay with them, the Nez Percé came to call her the "Measuring Woman." For a time, she lived among the Omaha of Nebraska. Her scholarly work included the transcription of hundreds of Plains Indians songs as well as her influential book, *The Omaha Tribe*. Fletcher's advocacy of Indian rights was sincere but ultimately ill-fated. Like most pro-Indian reformers of the time, she believed that Native Americans needed to become assimilated into white culture. Accordingly, she helped spearhead the Dawes Severalty Act of 1887, an ostensibly humane measure that led to the loss of much Indian land.

Mastermind of corruption Abe Ruef was the first Jewish leader of a major American political machine. Well educated and multilingual, Ruef was a mastermind of graft and corruption in San Francisco. He funneled bribes from businessmen to city officials before becoming the "little boss" of San Francisco with the 1901 election of his "puppet mayor," a bandleader named Eugene Schmitz. Ruef's ambitions for political power at the state and national levels were shattered by his 1908 conviction for corruption. Because no other officials were convicted, many regarded Ruef as unfairly singled out for imprisonment. He was paroled and pardoned in 1915.

Oklahoma's all-black towns In the late 19th century, African Americans discovered that they could own property, open businesses, and even form and govern their own communities in Oklahoma Territory. By 1890 more than 137,000 African American residents lived in all-black Oklahoma towns. Boley, incorporated in 1905, was one of the most prosperous. By 1911 Boley boasted more than 4,000 citizens, a newspaper, two banks, three cotton gins, and other businesses. The Boley Town Council is pictured here. After Oklahoma statehood in 1907, the legislature began passing segregation laws. By 1911 efforts were being made to completely block black immigration.

July 1912: Jim Thorpe, legendary Indian athlete, wins gold at the Stockholm Olympic Games in both the decathlon and pentathlon.

August 23, 1912: Spreckels Theatre, the first modern commercial playhouse in the West, opens on Broadway between 1st and 2nd streets in San Diego. *Bought and Paid For* is the opening-night production.

November 5, 1912: Woodrow Wilson, a Democrat from Virginia, is elected as the 28th president of the United States.

1913: The Territory of Alaska grants women the right to vote.

1913: *O Pioneers!,* novelist Willa Cather's masterpiece set on the Nebraska frontier, is published.

1913: Construction of the 200-mile Los Angeles Aqueduct is completed by engineer William Mulholland, bringing much-needed water to the rapidly growing city.

1913: The U.S. Mint begins producing the Indian head nickel, also known as the buffalo nickel.

1913: California's Alien Land Law forbids immigrants who are neither U.S. citizens nor eligible for citizenship from owning or signing a long-term lease on farmland in the state.

1913: The Raker Act is passed, allowing San Francisco to dam the Hetch Hetchy Valley and turn it into a reservoir.

February 3, 1913: The 16th Amendment is ratified, giving Congress the authority to levy and collect a federal income tax.

April 11, 1913: The federal government begins a program of official racial segregation in its offices, bathrooms, and cafeterias.

Athlete of the century Jim Thorpe, a descendent of several Native American tribes, was named "America's athlete of the century" by the U.S. Congress in 1999. Born in Prague, Oklahoma, Thorpe attended the Carlisle Indian School in Pennsylvania, where he excelled at football and track. At the 1912 Olympics, he won gold medals in the pentathlon and decathlon events. Thorpe played major-league baseball for six seasons, batting .252. He also toiled for six football teams and helped organize what became the NFL. Thorpe was active in Indian affairs, and sometimes worked as a movie extra.

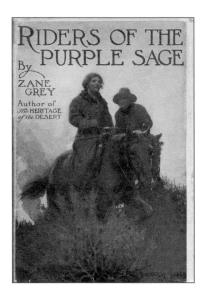

The prolific Zane Grey *Riders of the Purple Sage* was the first great hit of western novelist Zane Grey. Published in 1912, the book was a sweeping romance featuring Grey's most memorable character, the gunfighter known as Lassiter. *Riders of the Purple Sage* has been filmed five times, including a celebrated silent version in 1925 starring Tom Mix. In 1903 Grey was a 31-year-old dentist when he published the first of 78 novels. He traveled throughout the West on hunting and fishing expeditions, soaking up site and story material for his books. More than 100 motion pictures have been based on Zane Grey novels, a record unmatched by any other author.

A movie pioneer A poster tries to sell the virtues of the latest film from the Selig Polyscope Company. Founded in Chicago by William Selig in 1896, it was one of the first film companies in America. Selig constructed Los Angeles's first permanent motion picture studio (in 1908–09), and also produced the first "cliffhanger" serial, *The Adventures of Kathlyn* (1913). Because he specialized in short movies, Selig was unable to compete with new studios that focused on feature films, such as MGM. This major pioneer closed shop in 1918.

Environmental Thinking

"EVERYBODY NEEDS BEAUTY as well as bread," wrote preservationist John Muir in his 1912 book, *The Yosemite*. To Muir, this "beauty-hunger" could be seen "in the little window-sill gardens of the poor" as well as in the gardens of the wealthy, community parks, and national parks. To him, that was reason enough for leaving grand wilderness areas untouched. In 1892 Muir helped form the Sierra Club, an environmental organization, which he served as president until his death.

President Theodore Roosevelt generally agreed with Muir. However, Roosevelt was a conservationist who believed that protecting the nation's public resources did not exclude controlled commercial development. His primary concern was the public interest.

Conservationists and preservationists were divided on some issues. One example is the fight over water in Yosemite National Park's gorgeous Hetch Hetchy Valley. In 1903 and again in 1905, the city of San Francisco applied to the Department of Interior for the use of Hetch Hetchy water. Under President Roosevelt, both applications were denied as not being in the best interest of the public. However, after the destructive 1906 San Francisco earthquake damaged the city's water system (even though it did not reduce the water supply), the city reapplied.

Roosevelt's forest commissioner, progressive-minded conservationist Gifford Pinchot, argued that—although there were other water resources that could be put into use—damming and flooding the Hetch Hetchy Valley was the most cost-effective way to provide San Francisco with a long-term water supply. In 1908 Roosevelt's secretary of the Interior, James Garfield, granted the city a limited permit for the Hetch Hetchy project.

A battle began over Hetch Hetchy, pitching John Muir and the Sierra Club against conservationists who believed in managing resources and against those who—like San Francisco attorney Franklin Lane—wanted nature tamed. Lane, who later became Woodrow Wilson's first secretary of the Interior, explained, "The mountains are our enemies. We must pierce them and make them serve." In 1913 Congress passed the Raker Act, authorizing San Francisco to build a dam, turn the valley into a reservoir, and use the water. Muir died a year later, some say of a broken heart.

Miners strike in Colorado From 1884 to 1912, with death rates in Colorado mines twice the national average, the United Mine Workers of America (UMWA) succeeded in organizing Colorado miners, many of whom were immigrants from Southern and Eastern Europe. In 1913 the UMWA presented demands to companies such as the Colorado Fuel and Iron Company (*pictured*). They wanted union recognition, pay increases, an eight-hour workday, and enforcement of existing state mining laws. Miners also wanted the right to select their own stores, housing, and doctors, rather than being limited to those provided by the company. The demands were rejected, and 10,000 miners went on strike. Evicted from company housing, strikers and their families moved into UMWA-built "tent cities" nearby.

Micheaux's perspective

The Conquest by Oscar Micheaux was the first published novel written by an African American in the western United States. Born in Illinois in 1884 and raised in Great Bend, Kansas, Micheaux at age 20 moved to South Dakota, where he homesteaded for the next decade. In 1913 he "self-published" *The Conquest* and sold it door-to door to his rural white neighbors. Clearly autobiographical fiction, it told the story of a discontented black man who moved to the West to start anew. He revised the book in 1917 as *The Homesteader,* and two years later made it into a movie—the first of his 44 feature-length cinematic productions. In his fiction and movies, Micheaux challenged stereotypes of African Americans made popular in such films as *The Birth of a Nation.*

"Czar of the Greeks"

Leonidas Skliris, not so affectionately known as the "Czar of the Greeks," was an enormously successful labor agent in Utah in the early 20th century. A native of Sparta, he immigrated to the U.S. in 1897 and set up an office in Salt Lake City, with branches all over the nation. He was successful in bringing thousands of Greeks to labor in western mines. Skliris charged roughly $20 per person for finding a job, plus a dollar or two per month. He also received kickbacks from companies when he provided them with strikebreakers. Angered by his exploitation, Greek workers forced him out of his agency in 1912 with threats of labor violence.

Mulholland's shenanigans In 1902 William Mulholland became director of Los Angeles's new Department of Water and Power. Mulholland and former Los Angeles Mayor Fred Eaton realized that the city's future—and their personal fortunes—depended on bringing more water into the area. They found what they wanted in the Owens River Valley, where ranchers and farmers were expecting a federal Reclamation Bureau project to irrigate their valley. Pretending to support the reclamation project, Eaton bought up water rights in the valley. Mulholland widely proclaimed the aqueduct essential for Los Angeles. Meanwhile, he encouraged business cronies to buy land in the nearby San Fernando Valley, where he intended to divert much of the water.

Water pours into L.A. With the support of private investors whose newly purchased land would leap in value once it was supplied with water, a 1905 Los Angeles bond issue passed. Millions of dollars were made available to bring Owens Valley water to the city. In 1908 work began on the most ambitious engineering project so far undertaken in America, a construction that included 142 tunnels and stretched across more than 200 miles of desert and mountains. Using machinery, mules, and thousands of workers, Mulholland directed the building of tunnels, sluiceways, roads, railroad tracks, power lines, and the laying of giant pipes (*pictured*). Dedicating the Los Angeles Aqueduct on November 5, 1913, Mulholland turned on the water and announced, "There it is, gentlemen. Take it."

Cather's pioneer stories In 1883, when Willa Cather was nine, her family moved from Virginia to Red Cloud, Nebraska. Later, the experience of being a newcomer, the stories of everyday people, and the land itself would become dominant themes in her critically acclaimed novels. Her 1913 novel, *O Pioneers!*, is the story of Alexandra Bergson, a young Swedish immigrant who inherits the responsibilities and challenges of her family's prairie farm. The novel reflects Cather's admiration of courage, purpose, and spiritual values. Cather won the Pulitzer Prize in 1923 for her novel *One of Ours*.

Ufer favors realism, socialism "I paint the Indian as he is," said Walter Ufer. When Ufer moved to Taos, New Mexico, in 1914, he gave up the romanticized subject matter he had been taught to paint in American and European art schools in favor of simple scenes of Native American life. This painting is entitled *Callers*. As an ardent Socialist, Ufer took the side of striking workers and others he considered victims of social injustice. He was a founding member of the Taos Society of Artists.

Random shootings at Ludlow "The Ludlow camp is a mass of charred debris, and buried beneath it is a story of horror imparalleled [sic] in the history of industrial warfare," reported *The New York Times* on April 21, 1914. Seen here are the burnt ruins of the tent city at Ludlow, Colorado, after the Ludlow Massacre. During the 1913–14 strike, coal company detectives in an armored car sometimes fired randomly into the strikers' camps. The women and children who suffocated in the attack on Ludlow were hiding in a pit dug beneath their tent as protection from those gunshots.

The Film Industry

PHOTOGRAPHER Eadweard Muybridge's serial images of a horse in action, taken at a California racetrack in 1878, foreshadowed the motion picture era in America and the importance of the West Coast in film production. By 1903 experiment and innovation had resulted in silent movies, complete with narrative story lines, special effects, and creative editing. Three of the first such films—*The Great Train Robbery*, *Kit Carson*, and *The Pioneers*—all of which were westerns, were made in the East in 1903.

Although none of these one-reelers lasted more than 21 minutes, the new medium created a sensation, and the public demanded more. Companies that turned out "flickers" used equipment invented by Thomas Edison, who charged studios hefty fees for its use. Edison and a small group of companies attempted to control the filmmaking process through a trust known as the Motion Picture Patents Company. In response, small-scale, independent moviemakers fought back with lawsuits, imported film, pirated equipment, and clandestine shooting locales, some of them in California.

In 1908 the Selig Polyscope Company captured scenes in and around Los Angeles for the action-drama *The Count of Monte Cristo*. Impressed with Southern California's balmy weather, William Selig established a permanent studio in Los Angeles the following year. Soon, other moviemakers either relocated or established branch operations on the West Coast. By 1912 more than a dozen

Lillian Gish in *Birth of a Nation*

motion picture studios called the Los Angeles suburb of Hollywood home. Lower real estate and labor costs, less restrictive city governments, and an abundance of diverse and scenic shooting locations attracted film companies to other outlying communities as well. Universal Pictures established its own town, Universal City, in the San Fernando Valley north of Hollywood in 1915.

By the time the United States entered World War I, more than half of all the motion pictures produced in the United States were made in Southern California. During the 1910s, movies with western themes became a staple of the American cinema, with hundreds turned out annually. This era also produced the first major western movie stars: William S. Hart and Gilbert "Bronco Billy" Anderson.

Chaplin energizes Hollywood By 1910s standards, Charlie Chaplin (*center*) was the ultimate Hollywood success story. Raised in poverty in England, Chaplin later traveled in a vaudeville troupe in the United States, where he caught the eye of film director Mack Sennett. From 1914 to '17, Chaplin starred in 63 movies. In this 1914 film, *Kid Auto Races at Venice,* he made his first appearance as the "Little Tramp," his most famous persona. An ingenious comedic talent, with sentimental appeal as well, Chaplin was a boon for Hollywood, drawing millions to theaters. His subsequent works of art included *The Kid* (1921), *The Gold Rush* (1925), and *City Lights* (1931)—each of which he wrote, directed, and starred in.

Movie western icon This 1914 publicity poster shows Tom Mix doing his own stunt in one of the 308 confirmed films he made from 1909 to 1935—41 in 1914 alone. Mix became the epitome of the dashing cowboy hero, with his combination of physical agility, engaging personality, and showmanship (and a wonder horse named Tony). Before becoming an actor, he was a Texas Ranger, a champion rodeo rider, and a genuine cowboy. This popular icon died in a 1940 automobile accident in Arizona, the heart of his beloved West.

CALIFORNIA: FILM FRIENDLY

CECIL HAD PASSED UP Flagstaff as our shooting locale because the weather was bad when he stepped off the train in Arizona, and he suddenly realized there would be no facilities for processing film there. But he knew there must be film laboratories in California, because, while no one had yet made a feature picture in the West, a few companies making one-reelers had moved there from the East to take advantage of cheaper land, labor, and materials and to benefit from the milder climate and more dependable sunlight. The latter was a potent economic factor in as much as artificial lighting was still unknown to motion pictures.

—JESSE L. LASKY, DISCUSSING FILMMAKER CECIL B. DeMILLE

The Panama Canal After 19 years of French and American construction and the death of 30,000 workers and others, the Panama Canal officially opened on August 15, 1914. Because of the lock system, tugboats were needed to guide ships through the canal, as shown in this photograph. The canal provided a special economic boon to West Coast cities because it shortened the route from the East Coast by 8,000 miles. Previously, ships traveling from coast to coast had to sail some 14,000 miles around South America. By 2002, approximately 800,000 ships had passed through the Panama Canal.

Seminole Scouts In 1870 black Seminoles (descendants of escaped African American slaves who had assimilated with Seminoles in Florida, then migrated west) were recruited as U.S. scouts at Fort Duncan, Texas. The Seminole Scouts were transferred to Fort Clark in 1872. Never numbering more than 100, the scouts successfully fought raiding Indian parties. The scouts suffered resentment and violence from whites in the region, who wanted them and their families removed. In 1914 (the year this picture was taken) the Seminole Scouts were officially disbanded, and their brave services were largely forgotten.

1894-1918

August 1913: Four die when a riot begins at an Industrial Workers of the World protest at Wheatland, California's Durst hop ranch.

December 23, 1913: President Wilson signs the Federal Reserve Act, putting all federally chartered banks under the influence of the centralized Federal Reserve bank, which sets interest rates and monetary values.

1914: Memorial Hall in Topeka, Kansas, home of the State Historical Society, is dedicated before a crowd of 25,000 spectators.

1914: Socialist insurgents blow up the Western Federation of Miners' union hall in Butte, Montana. While the governor imposes martial law to restore order, mining interests withdraw recognition of the union.

1914: Osborne Russell publishes the autobiographical *Journal of a Trapper,* his account of the nearly 10 years he spent working as a beaver trapper in the Rocky Mountains as a young man.

1914: Hoping to overthrow Mexican President Victoriano Huerta, President Wilson sends U.S. troops into Veracruz. Huerta resigns soon afterward.

January 28, 1914: Beverly Hills, California, is incorporated.

April 20, 1914: Eighteen die, including 13 children, when the National Guard and mining company agents attack a tent city of striking miners and their families in Ludlow, Colorado. The bloodshed becomes known as the Ludlow Massacre.

June 28, 1914: The events that will trigger the First World War are set in motion with the assassination of Austrian Archduke Franz Ferdinand in Sarajevo.

The rebel girl Elizabeth Gurley Flynn, the subject of this song by fellow radical activist Joe Hill, was born to be a rebel. Her father was a socialist, while her mother was a feminist and Irish nationalist. After being expelled from high school in 1907 for making speeches favorable to the radical International Workers of the World, she became a full-time IWW organizer. She vigorously opposed U.S. entry into World War I and worked to help such immigrants as Sacco and Vanzetti, whom she believed were persecuted by the government for their political opinions. Flynn joined the American Communist Party in 1936 and remained a dedicated radical activist until her death in 1964.

Hawaiian vacations
This poster, advertising a winter festival in the Hawaiian Islands, tries to lure tourists with gorgeous scenery, a beautiful native woman in a grass skirt, and swimming in the ocean in late February. Tourism in Hawaii began with Captain William Matson, who started sailing merchant vessels between San Francisco and the islands in 1882. Enraptured by the beauty of Hawaii and the commercial prospects of hauling tourists as well as freight, he added passenger vessels to his line and built two resort hotels. More and more over the years, wealthy Americans—including Franklin Roosevelt—flocked to this tropical paradise.

Women's Suffrage in the West

WHEN JEANNETTE RANKIN of Montana became the first woman elected to the U.S. Congress in 1916, most women in the United States did not even have the right to vote. Rankin had been a teacher, social worker, and activist for women's suffrage in several western states. In 1914 Montana granted the right to vote to women, and Rankin went into politics.

As far back as the 1860s, while women's suffrage campaigns were getting organized in the East, voting-rights activists found quicker acceptance of their ideas in the West. The territorial legislature of Wyoming granted women suffrage in 1869. The following year, with Brigham Young's support, Utah Territory gave women the right to vote, though not to hold office. The Utah territorial law was over-ridden by an act of the U.S. Congress in 1887, in an effort to reduce Mormon political power.

By 1920, when the U.S. Congress passed the 19th Amendment giving women the right to vote, many western states already had done so. Wyoming entered the Union in 1890 as the first state with full women's suffrage. From 1893 to 1919, Colorado, Utah, Idaho, Washington, California, Oregon, Kansas, Arizona, Montana, Nevada, South Dakota, and Oklahoma granted women the right to vote. Texas and New Mexico refused women suffrage until the constitutional amendment was passed.

Members of the Woman Suffrage Party

Why was it easier for women to gain full voting rights in much of the West than in the East? Some historians suggest that western territories and states wanted to attract more settlers or to add voters who were likely to support a particular cause. Others believe that the types of women and men who settled in the West expected all individuals to maintain control over their own lives. It is clear that western women wanted the right to vote and worked for it. Activists argued that voting was a basic right for an American citizen, and that taxation without representation was nothing short of tyranny.

San Francisco World's Fair From February to December, 1915, San Francisco hosted the Panama Pacific International Exposition—or the San Francisco World's Fair. Officially celebrating the 1914 opening of the Panama Canal and the 400th anniversary of Balboa's sighting of the Pacific Ocean, the event rejuvenated San Francisco's economy. Among the thousands of exhibits in hundreds of temporary buildings were the Liberty Bell, a five acre reproduction of the Panama Canal, and a Ford assembly line that turned out cars every afternoon. Seen here is the main section of the 635-acre grounds. The tallest building was the 43-story Tower of Jewels, covered with 102,000 sparkling glass gems.

August 15, 1914: The Panama Canal opens, making the seaports of the American West readily accessible to shipping from the eastern seaboard and Europe.

December 31, 1914: President Wilson opens the Panama-California Exposition in San Diego's Balboa Park remotely from Washington, D.C. He does so by pressing a Western Union telegraph key wired to lights on the other side of the country.

1915: The U.S. Federal Trade Commission is created with a mandate to enforce fairness in business practices, including advertising, competition, and antitrust legislation.

1915: For the first time, tourists can drive automobiles through Yellowstone National Park.

1915: Utah becomes the first state to pass a law that makes the use of marijuana a criminal offense when the state legislature criminalizes all Mormon religious prohibitions.

1915: The U.S. Supreme Court rules in favor of the defendant in *Ozawa v. United States,* deciding that Japanese immigrants may not apply for U.S. citizenship or naturalization.

1915: An Act of Congress creates Rocky Mountain National Park in Colorado.

February 8, 1915: D. W. Griffith's *The Birth of a Nation,* the first significant epic film produced in the Los Angeles area, is released. The film portrays the Ku Klux Klan as heroic and African Americans as threats to the country.

May 7, 1915: The U.S. moves one step closer to war with Germany when the RMS *Lusitania* is sunk by a German submarine off the coast of Ireland, killing 128 U.S. citizens.

"Don't waste any time in mourning. Organize!"

—JOE HILL, A HIGH-PROFILE AGITATOR FOR THE IWW, ON THE EVE OF HIS EXECUTION FOR MURDER IN 1915

Leftist martyr A mural depicting Joe Hill's execution in 1915 clearly portrays him as a Christlike figure, unjustly convicted of murder and crucified by the state. In 1910 the Swedish-born Hill joined the International Workers of the World, a radical labor organization, and quickly became one of its most fiery spokespersons. He was most noted for his pro-union songs, including "The Preacher and the Slave" in which he coined the phrase "pie in the sky." Convicted of the murder of two Utah butchers, he stoutly maintained his innocence. Hill became an iconic hero for much of the Left.

The Non-Partisan League A. C. Townley, an American Socialist Party organizer, was best known for founding the Non-Partisan League (NPL) in 1915. Its platform advocated state ownership of industries that dealt with agriculture—such as mills, grain elevators, and rural banks—as a way of reining in corporate power. The NPL was most successful in North Dakota, where it controlled the state legislature and governorship under Lynn Frazier, who was elected in 1916. A goat, serving as the NPL's mascot, carried the politically charged name "The Goat That Can't Be Got." The League merged with the North Dakota Democratic Party in 1956.

Mexican bandit In 1910 a peasant bandit known as Francisco "Pancho" Villa (*pictured, center*) joined the Mexican Revolution and helped end the dictatorship of President Porfirio Díaz. In 1914 he turned against Mexico's new president, Venustiano Carranza. Carranza eventually forced Villa and his men to retreat to northern Mexico. In October 1915, U.S. President Woodrow Wilson infuriated Villa by recognizing Carranza's government. In January 1916, Villa's men killed 17 U.S. citizens in the state of Chihuahua, then staged a March raid on the town of Columbus, New Mexico. President Wilson decided to take military action against Villa.

Pershing pursues Pancho Villa
General John "Black Jack" Pershing was an open admirer of Pancho Villa when the Mexican rebel's power was at its height. Pershing even invited him for a 1914 visit to Fort Bliss, Texas, where they were photographed together. But in 1916, Pershing was put in command of a "punitive expedition" against Villa. The general is seen here leading his troops in Mexico. Through personal cunning and the loyalty of Mexican peasants, Villa escaped Pershing for 11 months, and the expedition ended in failure. Pershing went on to lead American troops in World War I, and Villa was assassinated in 1923.

Preparedness Day bombing Officials examine the bodies of two of 10 people who died from the bombing during the Preparedness Day parade in San Francisco on July 22, 1916. In a period of patriotism and anti-radicalism, police arrested two well-known labor union officials, Tom Mooney and Warren Billings, for the crime. In an almost lynch-mob atmosphere, the two were found guilty. Billings was sentenced to life in prison while Mooney was sentenced to death, although his punishment was later commuted to life in prison. When a later investigation revealed perjury and false testimony in the trial, California Governor Culbert Olson pardoned the two in 1939. The actual perpetrators were never found.

November 19, 1915: Songwriter and labor organizer Joe Hill is executed by a firing squad in Salt Lake City, following a controversial trial for a murder he allegedly committed (even though there were no witnesses and he seemingly did not have a motive). A national outcry fails to win him clemency, and he dies a martyr for the labor movement.

1916: Timber baron William Boeing establishes the Boeing Airplane Company in Seattle with a contract to build 50 biplanes for the U.S. Navy.

1916: The San Diego Zoo is formed unintentionally after its animals, which were brought to the city in 1915 for the Panama-California Exposition, were quarantined in Balboa Park.

1916: General John Pershing leads 10,000 U.S. troops on a chase through Mexico in search of Mexican General Francisco "Pancho" Villa, but comes up empty.

1916: With a total of 254,000 miles of track, America's railroads are as extensive as they will ever be. The advent of the automobile and the Great Depression will hasten the decline of railroading.

January 1916: Twenty people drown and many of San Diego's bridges are washed away when heavy rains flood parts of Southern California.

January 1, 1916: Colorado goes dry after the state legislature's adoption of prohibition.

June 5, 1916: Louis Brandeis, a Kentucky-born jurist known for his respect for individual rights and his tough stance against business monopolies, is sworn in as an associate justice of the U.S. Supreme Court.

Hart's authentic westerns William S. Hart was a respected New York stage actor when he saw his first movie western. Having grown up in the Dakotas, he was dismayed by the film's inaccuracies, and decided to tackle the genre himself. He starred in a number of silent westerns, including *Hell's Hinges* (1916), *The Toll Gate* (1920), and *Tumbleweeds* (1925). He frequently directed and wrote his own films, taking care to make them as authentic as possible. Hart created a screen persona that became a western archetype—the brave, taciturn antihero seeking redemption for past misdeeds.

Mexican refugees A U.S. cavalryman, acting as a border guard in El Paso, Texas, examines a Mexican immigrant. The year was 1913, and the Mexican Revolution of 1910–20 was raging. One government after another came to power in Mexico during those years, bringing waves of political refugees to the American Southwest. As those immigrants joined the Mexican American population, Latinos in the region grew more and more politicized. Mexican refugees and Mexican Americans unionized, fought discrimination, and increasingly asserted their language and culture. Women played a crucial role in this transformation of Southwestern Latino identity during the revolutionary era.

HOSTILE RECEPTION

THOSE WHO WITNESSED the actions of the Mexican mob at the end of the bridge will never forget it. Comprised largely of young girls, the mob seemed bent on destroying anything that came from the American side. As soon as an automobile would cross the line, the girls would absolutely cover it. The scene reminded one of bees swarming. The hordes of the feminine mob would claw and tear at the tops of the car. The glass rear windows of the autos were torn out, the tops torn to pieces, and parts of the fittings, such as lamps and horns, were torn away. All of this happened in view of the Mexican military, which had a sufficient force at hand to stop any kind of difficulty. But the commanders and soldiers seemed in sympathy with the mob. The impulse was to injure and insult Americans as much as possible without committing murder.

—*EL PASO TIMES*, JANUARY 29, 1917, ON MOB VIOLENCE OF THE PRECEDING DAY; THE MOB WAS PROTESTING THE CLOSED-BORDER POLICY OF THE UNITED STATES

World War I and the West

GERMAN LEADERS HOPED that the United States would steer clear of Europe during the First World War, but they laid plans to enlist Mexico on Germany's side if the U.S. did enter the conflict. In January 1917, German Foreign Minister Arthur Zimmermann sent a coded telegram to his ambassador in Mexico saying that Germany was about to begin "unrestricted submarine warfare." If the U.S. declared war, Zimmermann stated, Mexico should join sides with Germany and regain its "lost territory in Texas, New Mexico, and Arizona."

The British intercepted the telegram and decrypted it. Eager to draw the United States into the war on their side, the British gave the decoded message to President Woodrow Wilson in February 1917. When it was published in American newspapers, many readers thought it was a fake. But then Zimmermann himself announced that the message was authentic. Germany's submarines were already costing American lives, a fact that—coupled with the Zimmermann telegram—brought an end to neutrality. The U.S. entered the war on April 6, 1917.

Training camps sprang up in the West at such locations as Douglas, Arizona, and Fort Sill, Oklahoma. Balloonists trained at Fort Omaha, Nebraska, while pilots trained for overseas combat at Kelly Field and other Texas

Soldiers line up for induction in Camp Travis, Texas

airfields. Temporary stations for men about to be shipped abroad were named after distinguished soldiers: Camp Dodge, Iowa; Camp Travis and Camp Bowie, Texas; Camp Cody, New Mexico; and Camp Kearny, California.

Before World War I, Americans had experimented with airplanes and even aircraft carriers. The war accelerated the airplane industry. Western factories produced British-designed fighters and American-designed trainers. America had taken a key step to enduring military might.

San Diego's military camp
Built near San Diego in May 1917, Camp Kearny was one of 32 new camps designed to train U.S. troops for World War I. More than 65,000 men went through Kearny during the war, and it became a demobilization center in 1919. It ceased to function as an Army camp in 1920, suggesting America's desire for the rapid reduction of its large military. The site currently houses Marine Corps Air Station Miramar.

July 17, 1916: President Wilson signs the Federal Farm Loan Act into law, providing for loans to help small farmers compete with large agribusiness interests.

August 25, 1916: Congress creates the National Park Service to administer the growing number of national parks in the West and to keep natural and historical resources "unimpaired for the enjoyment of future generations."

November 5, 1916: Five die when violence breaks out at a protest rally during a six-month-long Industrial Workers of the World strike at an Everett, Washington, lumber camp.

November 7, 1916: Montana Republican Jeannette Rankin becomes the first woman elected to the U.S. Congress.

December 29, 1916: The Stock-Raising Homestead Act is passed, allowing homesteaders to stake claims on federal land previously designated for livestock grazing.

1917: North Dakota, Indiana, Rhode Island, New York, and Nebraska give women the right to vote in presidential elections.

1917: The U.S. Supreme Court declares a Louisville, Kentucky, city ordinance allowing for racial segregation by neighborhood to be unconstitutional.

January 10, 1917: William "Buffalo Bill" Cody dies at age 71. He will be buried in a rock tomb blasted from the Summit of Colorado's Lookout Mountain.

January 26, 1917: The Navy Radio Transmitter Facility at Chollas Heights, California, sends its first message. Its 600-foot antennas make it the most powerful radio transmitter in the hemisphere.

Lindsey reforms juvenile courts Judge Benjamin Barr Lindsey reformed the U.S. juvenile legal system. Lindsey served as the first judge of Denver's Juvenile Court system (1901–27), and his rehabilitation-oriented, humane treatment of youthful offenders became a model that many states adopted. When Lindsey denounced the infamous 1914 Ludlow Massacre, he became unpopular with Denver's anti-union politicians. Moving to California, he served on the Los Angeles Superior Court. While continuing his advocacy on behalf of children and youth, Lindsey endorsed the early feminist movement, birth control, and cohabitation prior to marriage.

The first congresswoman Jeannette Rankin took her seat as the first female member of Congress on April 4, 1917. Four days later, the representative from Montana cast her vote against entering World War I. Rankin explained in a 1972 interview, "I felt always that it was just a stupid, poor way of trying to settle a dispute." A noted suffragette, Rankin was again elected to the House in 1940. As a congresswoman and lobbyist, she promoted social programs such as maternal and child health care. She also protested every war that came along.

The Ludlow and Bisbee Incidents

"LITTLE CHILDREN roasted alive make a front page story," labor organizer Mother Jones bitterly observed concerning the Ludlow Massacre. "Dying by inches of starvation and exposure does not."

The massacre was the culmination of the 1913–14 Colorado coal strike. Dominated by the Colorado Fuel and Iron Company (CF&I), Colorado's Southern Coal Field was mined by men who lived in guarded company towns, where virtually all aspects of life were owned and controlled by their bosses. The mines, in which laborers worked long hours for poor wages, were extremely dangerous.

In September 1913, the United Mine Workers of America (UMWA) called a strike in the Southern Coal Field. Strikers were promptly evicted from the company towns. In cold weather, they and their families lived in nearby tent villages, the largest of which was at Ludlow. The following months brought increasing harassment and violence against the strikers.

On the morning of April 20, 1914, shooting broke out at the Ludlow camp between strikers and a militia consisting largely of former guards. After an entire day of fighting, militiamen set fire to the camp. At least 20 strikers and family members were killed, including two women and 11 children who suffocated while trapped in a pit beneath a burning tent. The strikers lost the 10-day war that ensued.

Three years later, another western labor confrontation shocked America. On July 12, 1917, more than a thou-

The Bisbee Deportation

sand striking copper miners in Bisbee, Arizona, were rounded up by armed vigilantes and loaded aboard boxcars. They were shipped across the state border into New Mexico, where they were unloaded and abandoned. Although food and water were brought to the strikers, they had no shelter until July 14, when U.S. troops escorted them to detention elsewhere.

Mother Jones, a prominent labor organizer, said that slain children demanded the public's attention. The Ludlow Massacre rallied public sympathy for American workers. It even prompted John D. Rockefeller, Jr., co-owner of the CF&I, to carry out labor reforms. Moreover, the Bisbee Deportation boosted membership in the Industrial Workers of the World (IWW) throughout the United States.

Haven for the wealthy Built in Pasadena, California, in 1893 for businessman W. C. Stuart, this mansion represented a haven for the wealthy who wished to escape the growing urban sprawl of Los Angeles. Incorporated in 1886, in part to provide the legal muscle to eliminate the area's only saloon, Pasadena went on to host the Valley Hunt Club's midwinter festival (the precursor of the Rose Bowl Parade), a Shakespeare Club, and a Grand Opera House. From 1900 to 1910, the population tripled to more than 30,000. Surrounding areas, such as Linda Vista, were annexed in 1914.

February 5, 1917: Congress overwhelmingly overrides President Wilson's veto of the xenophobic Asiatic Barred Zone Act, which effectively bans immigration of nonwhite Asians.

April 6, 1917: The U.S. Congress formally declares war against Germany.

July 12, 1917: Over 1,000 striking miners are herded into boxcars and deported from Bisbee, Arizona, when the copper mining interests in the town grow tired of the demands of the Industrial Workers of the World.

July 18, 1917: Camp Kearny is established in Southern California. Designed to house 40,000 troops, it is one of 32 new military camps built during the rush to bolster the U.S. military at the beginning of World War I.

August 23, 1917: Another race riot engulfs an American city when 13 people are killed in a Houston brawl between white citizens and African American soldiers. Eighteen more will die when some of the soldiers found guilty of participating are executed.

1918: The Sedition Act of 1918 makes speaking out against the government a federal crime punishable by fines and jail time.

1918: In Oklahoma, a group of Indians from several disparate tribes incorporates the Native American Church, famous for its ritual use of the hallucinogenic drug peyote.

1918: A women's suffrage amendment, publicly supported by President Wilson, passes the House of Representatives with two-thirds of the vote but dies in the Senate.

Spring 1918: Influenza breaks out at Camp Funston in Kansas and spreads like wildfire across the the nation. More than 600,000 Americans will die in the worldwide flu pandemic of 1918.

Socialist colony Curious visitors come to see the New Llano del Rio Cooperative Colony, which was developed in California in 1914 before being relocated to Louisiana in 1917. The community was founded by charismatic Socialist leader and lawyer Job Harriman. Attracting more than 600 adherents, the colony prospered until a water crisis prompted 200 members to move to Louisiana. The colonists thrived in their new home, putting Socialist principles into practice, with successful light industry as well as agriculture. Internal squabbling contributed to the colony's demise in 1939.

Court-martial of black soldiers In July 1917, a battalion of the black 24th U.S. Infantry was stationed in Houston. These "Buffalo Soldiers" endured legalized segregation and frequent racial slurs. On August 23, two soldiers interfered with the violent arrest of a black woman. Blows were struck and shots were fired. In the ensuing race riot, 16 white and four black citizens were killed. The Army court-martialed 118 black soldiers in trials such as this one. The Army convicted 110, hanged 19, and jailed 63 for life. Two white officers were charged but released, and no white citizens were charged. In 1938 President Franklin Roosevelt freed those still in prison.

> "In many of the cities, the bodies of the dead from Spanish influenza are piled up in morgues, and even garages are temporarily turned into places for the corpses...."
>
> —Sacramento native Anna Jamme

The Flu Epidemic

"Wear a Mask and Save Your Life! A Mask is 99% Proof Against Influenza," stated San Francisco's mayor in the fall of 1918. Most people wore masks; those who refused were jailed. Even so, influenza infected more than 23,000 people in San Francisco, killing 3,500.

In March 1918, an Army private at Camp Funston, Kansas, reported to sick call with a sore throat and achiness. The next day 40 men at the base were ill, and a week later the country was feeling the first wave of a flu epidemic. Officials everywhere, not wanting to alarm anyone, were slow to publicize the danger, but soon a worldwide pandemic was underway.

Like other cities, San Francisco closed schools, theaters, and other public gathering places, but too late. Medical professionals were overwhelmed. One doctor reported seeing 525 patients in a single day. Red Cross workers could respond to only half their calls for help. Immigrant communities and other areas of poverty were the hardest hit.

Scientists have suggested various origins for the deadly 1918–19 flu, including a genetic shift in a virus in

Seattle policemen during the epidemic

China; a virus exchanged between humans and pigs in America's heartland; a mutated virus from ducks, geese, and chickens; and a British training camp in France. Whatever the cause, the flu killed 20 to 40 million people worldwide in 1918–19, including an estimated 43,000 American servicemen—10 times those killed in the war.

Where the flu pandemic began In this 1918 photograph, hundreds of U.S. soldiers suffering from influenza are crammed into emergency facilities at Camp Funston, Kansas. This camp was home to more than 50,000 U.S. troops, many of whom would go overseas. In the United States, the pandemic may have originated with a new flu virus that appeared in Haskell County, Kansas, in January 1918. Recognized first by a local doctor, it was transmitted to three Haskell residents, including two soldiers, who then traveled to Funston. Ironically, a local paper said that one of them, Dean Nilson, looked like "soldier life agrees with him."

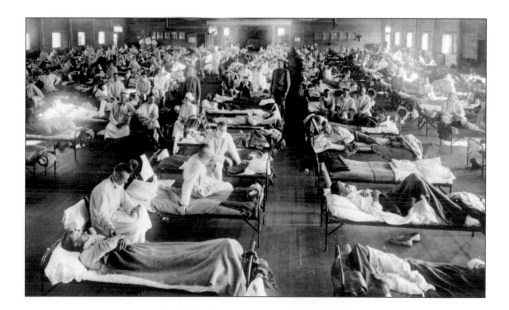

From Boom to Bust
∞ 1919–1939 ∞

THOUGH THE UNITED STATES joined the global conflict late, the First World War had a profound and lasting impact upon American society. Mobilization for the war effort touched every region of the nation. Military camps sprang up here and there overnight, as did war industries that provided everything from tanks and airplanes to boots and backpacks.

Entry was not without controversy, to say the least. Some Irish Americans and German Americans, for example, suggested that the United States had joined the war on the wrong side. Their opposition to the war effort created deep fissures in America, and they placed themselves at risk when they spoke out against it. Earlier, back in 1915, President Woodrow Wilson's secretary of state, William Jennings Bryan, resigned his office in protest when the President vehemently insisted that Germany's use of submarine warfare was against the rules of war.

World War I, at the time known as the Great War, led to fundamental changes in the lives of individual Americans and to the nation as a whole. Young men who had never lived far from where they had been born were sent to military bases throughout the nation, and then away to war in far-off Europe. They returned home as different people, and they returned to a different America than the one they had left behind.

After the stock market crashed in New York in 1929, this family felt the effects as far west as California. National unemployment rose from 3.2 percent in 1929 to 24.9 percent in 1933, and wages dropped precipitously.

"I am in the dust bowl. We didn't raise any crop this year. And we have to live off of the releif and theres no injoyment out of that.... My mother is sick and under the doctor's care most of the time and my Grandma that lives with me is very poorly. And that keeps my heart broken all the time."

—Letter by F. M., a 13-year-old boy from Kismet, Kansas, to First Lady Eleanor Roosevelt, November 3, 1937

With the end of the war in 1918, the United States attempted, in the words of Warren Harding, the 1920 Republican candidate for President, a "return to normalcy." Given Harding's landslide victory over his opponent, it is clear that such hopes resonated with the American people. The West was no different, and western voters cast their votes overwhelmingly in favor of Harding and his wishful optimism.

But a return to normal would be a difficult proposition—for the West and the entire nation. The world had changed too much, too fast, and things would never be the same again. Nor was it ever really clear what Harding's "normalcy" meant in the first place. Harding took office just as the 1920s began, and that decade would be anything but normal.

For one, much of the optimism that characterized progressivism in the first two decades of the 20th century—a faith that political and other reforms would improve American society—drifted away in the 1920s. The disillusionment caused by the war and its catastrophic impact on European nations, not to mention the new weapons of destruction it featured, was certainly partly to blame. The century had begun with great excitement over the promises and potential of America, but the war and its horrors cast a pall across the nation that made earlier hopes look ridiculously naive.

Federal policemen destroy a rumrunner's cargo in San Francisco in 1927. Western states led the way in the move toward Prohibition. Some states, such as Oklahoma, were already "dry" before the 18th Amendment was passed in 1919.

Albeit with less energy, the reform spirit did continue. Passage of two important amendments to the U.S. Constitution came as the 1920s beckoned. The arrival of both Prohibition and women's suffrage guaranteed that the nation would be very different indeed. Western voters and activists figured prominently in both movements. The West had provided an impetus for the 18th Amendment. With its ratification in 1919, the amendment and its enforcement legislation forbade the manufacture, distribution, or sale of alcoholic beverages across the land. Deeply rooted in western experience (the West had long had "dry" counties, even entirely dry states), Prohibition was far less experimental or revolutionary in the West than it was elsewhere in the country.

Prohibition failed on a grand scale. Enforcement of the laws governing alcohol sale and distribution proved to be impossible. In fact, antagonism to the new laws created a nation of lawbreakers. As a social worker in Reno pointed out, "the situation is much worse than before prohibition. It is now the smart thing to carry a flask. Nobody respects a law that cannot be enforced."

The insatiable demand for outlawed liquor created an even more threatening menace. Bootleggers and rumrunners operated within highly organized, and often brutally violent, criminal conspiracies and gangs. It would take more than a decade for Americans to fully grasp the scale of the Prohibition blunder. In the early 1930s, the 21st Amendment to the Constitution repealed Prohibition—an implicit acknowledgement that it had been a very bad idea in the first place.

On another front, the West's suffrage activists, men and women alike, pushed for equal voting rights for women—a reflection of the region's long-standing commitment to the issue. By 1920, when the 19th Amendment guaranteeing women the right to vote became the law of the land, the West was recognized as the region most closely identified with the issue and the significant changes it initiated.

With Prohibition proving a catastrophic failure, the 1920s rapidly became known as the "Roaring '20s." A spirit of carefree, if a tad overheated and perhaps even desperate, excitement characterized the era. In greater and greater numbers, Americans discovered the attractions of the city, where new strains of music, dancing, and other entertainments lured country folk. In the West, earlier patterns of migration accelerated. People left the countryside in greater numbers. Where did they go? They went to cities, and as a result places such as Minneapolis, Kansas City, Oklahoma City, Seattle, Denver, Salt Lake City, San Diego, and especially Los Angeles boomed. Once there, they found themselves in the midst of a social revolution. The 1920s inaugurated a new era in American history—a rush into modernity and all that it characterized.

A boy stands not in the middle of the desert but somewhere in the Midwest, in 1935. Overplowed land, a drought that lasted for much of the decade, and strong winds contributed to the infamous Dust Bowl.

The 1920s roared with the sounds of cars and airplanes, construction and jazz. And then the roaring stopped. Financial overconfidence, exuberance, and an unwillingness to read the signs of impending trouble created a storm of fiscal peril while people sang and danced their way through the decade. The handwriting was on the wall perhaps most glaringly in the West. Sales of western natural resources—among them oil, timber, coal, and farm produce—began to slide in the 1920s, and the national economy began to teeter. But few recognized the telltale signs or the brewing trouble. Not even Herbert Hoover, who in 1928 became the first president elected from the West, understood what was happening. By the end of the decade, it was too late. Speculation in the stock market, which had become rampant through the Roaring '20s, boomeranged when the stock market fell through the floor in the fall of 1929. The consequence was the Great Depression.

At the outset of the disaster, many assumed that the economy would rebound quickly. But as more and more Americans felt the sting of falling wages and rising unemployment, naive hopes about the ability of the economic ship to right itself faded away. And with them went support for President Hoover. Across the nation, angry, beleaguered, and frightened Americans—many of them newly homeless—built shanty communities they derisively called "Hoovervilles" and "Hoovertowns." Others sought refuge in caves and even sewer pipes. Breadlines and soup kitchens proliferated, and the average American income fell by 35 percent from 1929 to the early 1930s.

This couple, photographed by the renowned Dorothea Lange, settled in central California in the late 1930s. With their farms in ruins, thousands of "Okies" and "Arkies" headed to the Golden State, where they typically lived in migrant camps and made meager wages.

Political unrest roiled the country, and the West provided much of the energy for this turmoil. Western farmers banded together in fearful solidarity, in ways that they had not done since the heady days of Populism in the 1890s, and demanded that the federal government do something about falling crop prices. In the summer of 1932, veterans from World War I marched on Washington demanding that Congress authorize payment of their military bonuses, which had been promised them in the 1924 World War Adjustment Compensation Act.

In the 1932 election, Hoover had a strong base of Republican support in the West, especially in California, his adopted state. But with the Depression deepening, Hoover did not stand a chance against New Yorker Franklin Delano Roosevelt. Hoover had simply done too little to alleviate the suffering and fears of the American people in a time of national crisis. "FDR" won by a landslide; Hoover failed to carry even a single western state.

Roosevelt hit the ground running. Within a few short months of taking office, his administration responded to the Depression with a cascade of federal programs that he collectively called the "New Deal." These programs, varied and numerous almost beyond measure, attacked Depression problems large and small, and with solutions both trivial and inspired. Some were large-scale efforts at alleviating the worst of the suffering. Others had more to do with restoring confidence in such abstractions as the "American Dream" or American culture. New Deal legislation propped up banks, reset crop and commodity prices, initiated loans to companies and individuals, put people back to work in federal programs, and helped generate a renewed optimism about the economy and the nation.

Both the Depression and the New Deal remade the American West. As more and more Americans slid into poverty, many for the first time in their lives, the West beckoned as a place of proverbial, if not actual, new beginnings. Tens of thousands of farmers, ranchers, and small-town folk from Colorado, Kansas, Oklahoma, and Texas—many with nothing left to lose as Dust Bowl winds tore the topsoil off their land in swirling blizzards of dirt—simply picked up and moved further west with their families and meager belongings. Most went to California.

Immortalized through the lives of the fictional Joad family in John Steinbeck's novel *The Grapes of Wrath,* these hardscrabble Americans imagined a California that had somehow escaped the ravages of the Depression. That California did not exist in the early to mid-1930s, as the Depression was everywhere in America. The Roosevelt Administration succeeded only in blunting the very worst aspects of the crisis and its consequences. Despite the ambitions of Roosevelt's New Deal programs, it would take another world war to invigorate the American economy enough to put an end to the Great Depression.

Civilian Conservation Corps workers line an irrigation canal. Among the best of President Roosevelt's New Deal programs, the CCC employed three million young people. Among other jobs, the workers constructed buildings, installed power lines, and reportedly planted more than two billion trees.

In the meantime, the New Deal, especially the gigantic public works projects, turned the West into a different landscape than what it had been in the 1920s and before. Gargantuan dams arose in western places. They plugged up western rivers behind millions of tons of concrete in order to create water-preserving reservoirs and electricity-generating power plants. As FDR himself said at the dedication ceremonies for the Hoover Dam in 1935, "the transformation wrought here…is a 20th century marvel." And it was. Lake Mead, formed behind Hoover Dam from the waters of the Colorado River, was at that time the world's largest reservoir. It held enough water to cover the entire state of Connecticut to a depth of 10 feet!

In western mountains, armies of young men and women took part in the Civilian Conservation Corps and its affiliated organizations. They felled trees, made trails, built cabins, fought fires, and worked on flood-control projects large and small. To this day, evidence of the New Deal's impact on the western environment is plain to see. From irrigation projects and roadways to hiking trails and electrical grids, the New Deal's legacy is still very much a part of the American West.

1919: Labor leader Mary Harris "Mother" Jones continues to push for labor reform. She plays a prominent role in the steel strike of 1919.

1919: Colorado enacts one of the first gasoline taxes in the United States. The 1¢ per gallon levy will go toward road maintenance and improvement.

January 29, 1919: The 18th Amendment is ratified, establishing Prohibition.

February 1919: The city of Seattle is brought to a standstill by a massive general strike. Some 60,000 of the city's residents are idle.

February 26, 1919: The Grand Canyon, covering more than a million acres in northern Arizona, is designated a national park.

Spring 1919: The U.S. Navy establishes the home base of its Pacific Fleet in San Diego.

June 28, 1919: Germany and the European Allies sign the Treaty of Versailles, ending World War I.

September 1919: Governor William Stephens signs a bill establishing the University of California–Los Angeles (UCLA) as the southernmost branch of the University of California system.

October 1919: The Los Angeles Philharmonic holds its first rehearsal.

November 15, 1919: San Diego businessman John Spreckels drives the golden spike that completes the San Diego & Arizona Railroad.

November 19, 1919: Zion, 229 square miles of breathtaking canyons and monoliths in Utah, is designated a national park.

1920: The U.S. census finds that the national population has grown to nearly 106 million. For the first time, most Americans live in urban areas.

The Pearl Harbor base The American destroyer USS *Woolsey* lays down a smoke screen during 1919 war games near the Pearl Harbor naval base in Hawaii. Construction of the base began in 1908, and it officially opened three years later. It ultimately became the headquarters for the U.S. Pacific Fleet. After the Spanish-American War and the annexation of the Philippines, the American military needed such a base to protect U.S. interests in the Pacific. According to the National Park Service, the base is "significant historically as a strategic port that helped the United States become a formidable world power."

Pottery for tourists Native American artisans Maria and Julian Martinez decorate pottery intended for sale to white tourists. The Martinezes' famous black-on-black pottery designs attracted buyers from all over, transforming the Tewa farming village of San Ildefonso, New Mexico, into a center for the revival of Pueblo arts in the early 20th century. In the 1920s, the emergence of automobiles and the increased number of paved roads opened up tourism-based income possibilities for villages all across the Southwest.

Seattle General Strike On February 6, 1919, some 35,000 Seattle shipyard workers were already on strike when 25,000 union members joined them in a full-blown work stoppage. Obviously inspired by the recent Russian Revolution, the Seattle General Strike was all the more effective for being completely nonviolent, with organizers ensuring that necessary services continue throughout the city. Here, union men pick up their supplies of groceries. Although the strike lasted only until February 11 and ended without achieving any of its goals, it spurred an already-growing Red Scare throughout America.

Middle America Every 10 years, the U.S. Census Bureau gathers demographic data on the U.S. population. Among other things, censuses establish the "mean geographic center" of the U.S. population. In 1921 it was located on this farm eight miles west of Bloomington, Indiana. Mr. and Mrs. John Herrin proudly display a sign at their house in the town of Whitehall. In 1790 the geographical population center was on the Chesapeake Bay, but since then it has steadily moved westward. Today, it lies in south-central Missouri.

Cannery Row Laborers toil on Monterey, California's famed Cannery Row. The home of a small fishing industry since the 1850s, the city began to specialize in sardine canning as a result of mechanization during World War I. The canneries thrived in the 1920s and 1930s, but most of them eventually closed down. The Row has become a historic district frequented by tourists. Cannery Row is probably most famous today as the setting and title of a popular and critically acclaimed novel by John Steinbeck.

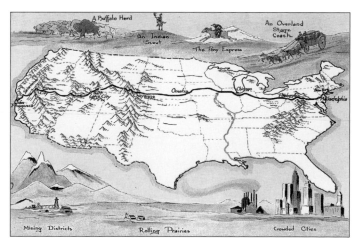

Coast-to-coast highway The Lincoln Highway, begun in 1913, was the nation's first interstate highway system. Spanning 14 states, it connected New York City with San Francisco. Initially, Henry Ford believed that the costs of building cross-country roads would be so great that the federal government would need to underwrite highway development. After Carl Fisher and some friends organized the Lincoln Highway Association in 1913, state and federal governments gradually supported the movement. President Franklin Roosevelt's Federal Aid Highway Act in 1938, and President Dwight Eisenhower's interstate highway system in 1956, elaborated upon the older Lincoln Highway ideas to create modern-day "superhighways."

1919-1939

1920: Tijuana becomes the place to be, as Americans fleeing Prohibition crowd the Mexican town's saloons.

February 14, 1920: The League of Women Voters is founded.

February 28, 1920: Congress passes the Esch-Cummins Act, which calls for returning the ownership and management of the railroads (nationalized during wartime) to private interests.

July 22, 1920: Pioneering aircraft manufacturer Donald Douglas establishes the Davis-Douglas Aircraft Company in Santa Monica, California.

August 26, 1920: The 19th Amendment becomes law following ratification by the states. The amendment grants women nationwide the right to vote.

1921: Farmers across the United States fall on hard times when postwar deflation forces bank closures and the decline of farm values.

March 4, 1921: Ohio Republican Warren Harding is inaugurated as the 29th U.S. president.

May 19, 1921: The Emergency Quota Act is passed, placing restrictions on the immigration of Southern and Eastern Europeans. Attempts to also restrict immigration of Mexicans fail, as agricultural interests have come to depend on cheap Mexican labor.

May 31–June 1, 1921: Dozens of people die when a violent race riot destroys a vibrant African American community in Tulsa, Oklahoma.

June 1921: Dozens drown when Pueblo, Colorado, is hit with a devastating flood.

June 23, 1921: Shell geologists strike oil on Signal Hill near Long Beach, California. Within several years, some 300 wells at Signal Hill will yield approximately 250,000 gallons of crude each day.

Birth of airmail The U.S. Postal Department's earliest experiments with airmail took place in 1911 between Garden City and Mineola, New York. Over the next several years, airmail service remained confined largely to the East and failed to attract widespread public use. However, 1920 brought cross-continental service that began in New York, included stops in Cleveland, Chicago, Iowa City, and Omaha, and terminated in San Francisco. That year, intrepid pilots flying biplanes—such as this De Havilland DH-4—were able to deliver mail across the nation 22 hours faster than by rail. The era of airmail had arrived.

Glacier among new national parks Fifteen thousand years ago, glaciers formed the valleys, two mountain ranges, hundreds of lakes, and flowing waters of what is now Glacier National Park (*pictured*) in Montana. The area became a national park in 1910— one of many such designations in the 1890s and early 1900s. In Washington, Mount Rainier became a national park in 1899, and the Olympic National Park was added in 1938. Utah's Zion Canyon and Bryce Canyon acquired park status in 1919 and 1928, respectively. Wyoming's Grand Teton became a national park in 1929.

Prohibition in the West

THE RISE OF SALOONS during the late 19th century—with a corresponding increase in gambling, prostitution, and public drunkenness—contributed to the appeal of Prohibition throughout the American West. In 1920 the 18th Amendment to the U.S. Constitution went into effect, prohibiting alcoholic beverages in the United States. At the time, only four states west of the Mississippi River (California, Louisiana, Missouri, and Minnesota) had not already

Prohibition raid in Wyoming

passed such laws of their own. No western states voted against ratifying the 18th Amendment.

Prohibition was related to western progressivism, which included such left-leaning causes as women's rights and the economic welfare of working people. Prohibition was consistent with progressives' belief in government solutions to social problems, and also with their

opposition to the "money power" of businesses—in this case, liquor distillers.

Of course, drinkers found ways of thwarting Prohibition in the West just as they did elsewhere. While urban centers had their furtive, illegal "speakeasies," rural and small-town America had local druggists. Physicians wrote prescriptions for alcoholic beverages without worrying much about medical necessity, and druggists filled those prescriptions. Thus, the local pharmacy became, in effect, the local liquor store.

However, Prohibition in the South and West was remarkably persistent. Oklahoma, Kansas, and Mississippi continued to enforce Prohibition even after the 21st Amendment of 1933 repealed the 18th Amendment. Although no states currently ban alcoholic beverages, some counties and communities remain "dry" even today.

The Tulsa riot On May 31, 1921, in Tulsa, Oklahoma, a white mob initiated a race riot that lasted 16 hours. They shot African Americans and burned 35 city blocks—an entire segregated neighborhood so prosperous that it had been known as "Black Wall Street." The ruins (*pictured*) left 10,000 people homeless. Thirty-nine deaths were officially reported, but estimates run into the hundreds. The riots began after a 19-year-old black shoeshiner—taking an elevator to reach a top-floor "colored" washroom—was accused by a shop clerk of attempting to rape a 17-year-old white female elevator operator. The young woman did not press charges and the case was dismissed.

The Pueblo flood The town of Pueblo, Colorado, was prospering as the "saddle-making capital of the world" and a rising western economic center until the flood of June 1921. The townspeople had believed they were well protected by levees, but three days of heavy rain swelled the Arkansas River, broke through the levees, and carried 11 feet of water into Pueblo's downtown area. One-third of the businesses were lost and as many as 600 houses wrecked, such as the one in this photograph. The death estimates range from 47 into the hundreds.

September 10, 1921: Film comedian Roscoe "Fatty" Arbuckle is indicted for murder following the death of Hollywood starlet Virginia Rappe. Though Arbuckle ultimately will be acquitted, the scandal furthers Hollywood's image as a colony of decadence.

1922: Initial planning begins on a 6.4-mile tunnel under the Continental Divide when the Colorado General Assembly creates the Moffat Tunnel Improvement District.

1922: Kid Ory's Creole Orchestra, based in Los Angeles, makes the first recordings by an African American jazz ensemble.

1922: Architect Lillian Rice begins designing Southern California's planned community of Rancho Santa Fe.

1922: Los Angeles's first three radio stations—KFI, KNX, and KHJ—all begin commercial broadcasts this year.

1922: Unidentified outlaws net $200,000 in a daylight holdup of a Federal Reserve truck in Denver.

February 1, 1922: In one of the most sensational crimes of the era, Hollywood director William Desmond Taylor is murdered in his Los Angeles home. His killer will never be caught.

April 7, 1922: The seeds of the "Teapot Dome Scandal" are sown when Secretary of the Interior Albert Fall leases part of the Naval Reserves at Teapot Dome, Wyoming, to private oil interests. *See* October 1923.

November 24, 1922: Seven states sign the Colorado River Compact, which is designed to ensure a fair distribution and use of the waters of the Colorado River.

1923: The U.S. Naval Training Center at Point Loma, California, is commissioned, with a staff of 10 officers.

Gas-powered tractors Internal-combustion engines revolutionized U.S. farming. This image shows a tractor on a North Dakota farm pulling 12 16-inch plows. Steam-powered tractors, used from about 1880 to 1920, proved dangerous; they sometimes exploded, and operators were often injured by the exposed moving parts. Diesel or gas engines, as seen in this image, were in wide use by 1920. Farmers utilized these expensive machines to produce more crops. Problems ensued as ever-greater wheat and corn harvests only further depressed commodity prices, causing economic distress. As more prairie was put under cultivation, the soil was exposed to high winds, thus contributing to the Dust Bowl disaster of the 1930s.

The conservative Coolidge President Calvin Coolidge (*left*) poses with Secretary of the Treasury Andrew Mellon (*center*) and Secretary of Commerce Herbert Hoover. After serving as vice president, Coolidge became president in 1923 because of the unexpected death of President Warren Harding. A staunch pro-business conservative, Coolidge won the 1924 election by a landslide, carrying even the once progressive West. Many voters in that region were disappointed, since one type of business Coolidge had no interest in supporting was agriculture.

Strict Immigration Laws

DURING THE MID-1800S, great numbers of Chinese immigrants arrived in California, first to prospect for gold, then to help build the western railroads. Whites in the region resented them from the start. California-based economist Henry George spoke for many in 1869 when he called the Chinese "utter heathens, treacherous, sensual, cowardly and cruel."

Anti-Chinese hostility led to the 1882 passage of the Chinese Exclusion Act, the first U.S. immigration law aimed at a particular group. Originally intended to prohibit Chinese immigration for 10 years, the law became permanent in 1902. This law did not apply to immigrants from Europe, who settled not only in major cities but in the western heartland.

Anti-immigrant xenophobia increased during the early years of the 20th century, partly because of the popularity of eugenics, a now-discredited philosophy that emphasized selective breeding for the improvement of the human species. Much eugenic thinking had a racist angle—especially the work of Madison Grant, whose 1916 book, *The Passing of the Great Race,* warned of the threat to "native Americans" (meaning the allegedly pure, "Teutonic" descendents of North American settlers) of rampant immigration of "inferior" breeds from Eastern and Southern Europe. Wrote Grant, "These immigrants adopt the language of the native American; they wear his clothes; they steal his name; and they are beginning to take his women, but they seldom adopt his religion or understand his ideals. . . ."

Grant's ideas influenced Congress's Emergency Quota Act of 1921. Grant himself supplied dubious statistics to support the more severe Immigration Act of 1924. The latter limited immigration of specific groups to two percent of their U.S. population as of the 1890 census. This calculation allowed immigrants from western and northern European countries to continue arriving in large numbers, but drastically curtailed immigration from southern and eastern European countries, such as Italy and Poland.

Immigrants from Latin America were exempted from this quota, because their cheap labor was considered essential to the United States economy. By contrast, immigrants from India and East Asia were prohibited altogether.

San Francisco's water supply These two photographs show the dramatic difference in the Hetch Hetchy Valley in Northern California after a major dam was completed there in 1923. In the aftermath of the 1906 earthquake that devastated San Francisco, the city petitioned the federal government for control of water rights in the valley, with a view toward creating a reservoir to provide water to the rebuilt city. Environmentalists, led by John Muir of the Sierra Club, bitterly opposed the project, believing that it would despoil the natural beauty of the valley. Muir lost, and the dam and reservoir went on to provide services to more than two million Californians.

1923: The Equal Rights Amendment is first promoted by the National Woman's Party. Although the amendment will surface in many forms during the 20th century, it will never be ratified.

1923: The Hollywoodland sign, complete with 4,000 lights and 50-foot letters, is erected in the hills above the new, upscale housing development of the same name in Los Angeles.

August 2, 1923: President Warren Harding dies of a heart attack while visiting San Francisco. Vice President Calvin Coolidge will be sworn in the next day.

October 1923: The Senate Committee on Public Lands and Surveys opens its hearings on the Teapot Dome oil lease. *See* January 31, 1924.

November 1923: The oil boom hits Colorado with a strike at Wellington Field near Fort Collins.

1924: The Ku Klux Klan infiltrates the Colorado Republican Party. A sympathetic governor and senator are elected.

1924: The popular jazz club Creole Palace, known as the "Harlem of the West," opens in San Diego's Hotel Douglas.

1924: The Immigration Act of 1924 curbs immigration for nationals of most countries, restricting most Asians and setting quotas for others. The act also will levy a tax against each person entering the United States.

1924: Congress passes the Snyder Indian Citizenship Act, granting citizenship to all American Indians.

1924: Ninety thousand Mexicans receive permanent visas, the most in any year in the 1920s.

Blumenschein enamored with Taos Ernest Blumenschein supported himself by playing first violin in the New York Symphony Orchestra while he studied art. In 1898 Blumenschein was traveling a mountain road near Taos, New Mexico, when his wagon broke a wheel. While waiting for repairs, he visited Taos. He returned nearly every summer until 1919, when he and his family moved there. Blumenschein helped establish the Taos Society of Artists. In his paintings, he typically mixed artifacts of different tribes. In his 1922 painting *The Gift* (*pictured*), the pipe bag, beaded leggings, and Pueblo pot do not belong with the Taos Indian.

Harvey Houses Five "Harvey Girls" pose in their trademark uniforms. Back in 1876, Kansas entrepreneur Fred Harvey had built a series of restaurants, lunchrooms, and hotels to serve the passengers of the Atchison, Topeka and Santa Fe Railway. He recruited hundreds of young women "of good character" and at least an eighth grade education to work in Harvey Houses, thus bringing a degree of respectability to waitressing. These establishments continued to be built into the 1940s and even inspired a musical film, *The Harvey Girls* (1946), starring Judy Garland.

Support for the KKK

JUST ABOUT EVERY WEEK OR SO, remembered American author Robert Coughlan, newspapers reported Ku Klux Klan atrocities in areas across the country, including lynchings, whippings, and tar-and-feather parties. According to Coughlan, "my father and my family were logical game in our locality." In 1923, when the Ku Klux Klan arrived in Coughlan's hometown of Kokomo, Indiana, his white family had reason to fear them. The Coughlans were Catholic.

The 1920s saw the rise of "nativism": the insistence of American-born white Protestants that "America must be kept American," as President Calvin Coolidge put it in 1924. Some U.S. citizens felt threatened by the millions of immigrants, including many Catholics and Jews, arriving from southeastern Europe and Russia. They also resented the population shift from rural to urban areas. Many people who lived in small towns and farming communities believed that modern ideas were destroying traditional values.

Mainstream America's resentment was especially high regarding people of other races. Even though the Chinese had been excellent workers, Chinese immigration was banned in 1882. In the early 20th century, Japanese workers made up half of California's agricultural workforce, but by 1908 Japanese immigration was restricted. Mexico became the next source of essential migratory workers. Meanwhile, a million African Americans moved from southern to northern states, and tens of thousands migrated westward. In the West, discrimination was a matter of whites against black, brown, red, and yellow—and also against Catholics, Jews, and city folk.

Soon after the 1915 premiere of D. W. Griffith's *Birth of a Nation*—a movie that extolled the history and virtues of the Ku Klux Klan—the KKK reorganized, gaining more than three million members. With their motto, "Native, white, Protestant supremacy," they found strong support in Indiana, Oklahoma, Oregon, and other western states. After 1925, the group declined following revelations of internal corruption and scandal.

The drive against immigration resulted in the National Origins Act of 1924, which continued the complete exclusion of Chinese and Japanese and severely limited immigration of people from all other nations. This restrictive immigration law remained in effect until the 1960s.

Boon years for the Klan Ku Klux Klan members march in Tulsa, Oklahoma, on September 21, 1923. Known mainly for their hatred of southern black Americans, Klansmen expanded into such farm states as Iowa, Oregon, and Indiana after 1915. Klan membership boomed, possibly reaching four million by 1920. Touting "100 percent Americanism"—and targeting "foreigners," Jews, Catholics, homosexuals, and progressives—the Klan disseminated hateful propaganda and helped elect a number of racist nativist politicians in the 1920s. Rapid decline came after Indiana's "grand dragon," D. C. Stephenson, was convicted of a brutal rape and murder in 1925.

Pickett's amazing stunt Born in Texas in 1871, Bill Pickett invented an exciting feat called "bull-dogging." Many African Americans were cowboys, but Pickett (of white, Indian, and black ancestry) was the most famous. He would leap from a galloping horse onto a cow, bite the cow's lip, and then fall backward, pulling the cow to the ground. First performed as a stunt, bull-dogging became one of professional rodeo's most popular events. Pickett toured with the 101 Ranch Wild West Show, and appeared in a few early films. He died at age 62 following a kick to the head by a horse.

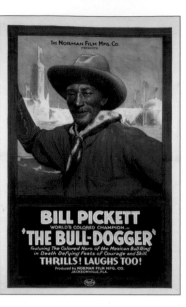

Montana's VP candidate In 1905 Massachusetts native and recent law school graduate Burton Wheeler headed for Seattle. In Butte, Montana, Wheeler got off the train and proceeded to lose his belongings in a poker game. He stayed in Montana, where he defended labor against the Anaconda Copper Mining Company. He also was elected to four terms as a Democratic U.S. senator. In 1924 Wheeler was the Progressive Party candidate for U.S. vice president. He supported the New Deal but opposed President Roosevelt's reorganization of the Supreme Court. Wheeler became an isolationist when World War II broke out in Europe.

Teapot Dome Scandal In this cartoon, a teapot-shaped steamroller rumbles toward the White House. The "Teapot Dome Scandal" centered around Albert Fall, President Warren Harding's secretary of the interior. In 1922 Fall secretly and noncompetitively leased federal oil reserves in Teapot Dome, Wyoming, and Elk Hills and Buena Vista Hills, California, to private oilmen. In return, Fall received cash gifts and interest-free loans. A Senate investigation revealed Fall's misconduct, and he was convicted of bribery in 1929. Although President Harding was not implicated, his administration is remembered as one of the most corrupt in U.S. history.

Artists flock to Santa Fe In 1892 the Santa Fe Railway began giving artists free rides from the New Mexico town to picturesque locations. The striking landscapes, rich cultural background, intense light, and healing dry air drew many artists and authors to Santa Fe. The artistic community worked to preserve the historic town and to renew Hispanic and Indian traditional crafts. Among them was John Sloan, a famous New York "Ashcan School" artist who painted scenes of everyday life. Sloan's 1924 *Traveling Carnival: Santa Fe* (*pictured*) depicts an eclectic mix of Santa Fe locals and visitors.

Ma Ferguson Miriam Amanda "Ma" Ferguson was the first woman to govern Texas. Her husband, James Ferguson, had served as governor from 1915 to 1917, but failed to get on the ballot in 1924. His wife ran, beating a pro-Ku Klux Klan, anti-liquor Democrat and her Republican opponent. Ma Ferguson won again in 1932. Regarding the use of Spanish in schools, she is alleged to have quipped,

"If English was good enough for Jesus Christ, then it's good enough for the children of Texas." Variants of the quote appeared much earlier, and evidence suggests that the attribution to Ferguson is a myth.

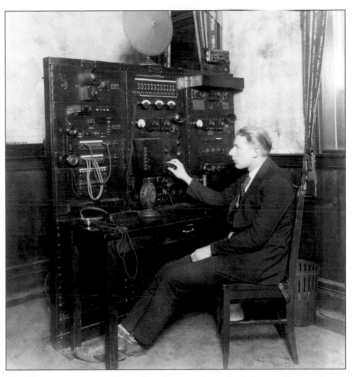

Radio creates national culture A technician adjusts the controls on a radio amplifier that allowed stations to connect to outside points for remote broadcasting. In the 1920s and '30s, radio technology improved markedly, and millions of Americans tuned in. From 1921 to 1940, the number of radio stations in the United States grew from five to 765. Radio's impact was especially powerful in small towns and rural areas, including those in the West. By bringing radio programs into people's homes, it helped create a national culture and broke down barriers imposed by isolation.

Lake of luxury In the early 1900s, more and more Westerners discovered the unspoiled natural beauty of Lake Tahoe. The lake rests in the Sierra Nevada, bordering California and Nevada. The area became a vacation haven for the well-to-do, leading to the building of several luxury hotels. When roads traversing the mountains around the lake were paved in the 1920s, tourism burgeoned, as thousands of middle-class Americans flocked to the area. This water-surfer "flipped" for Lake Tahoe in 1925.

A staunch progressive One of the most notable progressives in American history, Wisconsin Republican Robert Marion La Follette served as a U.S. representative (1885–91), the governor of Wisconsin (1901–06), and a U.S. senator (1906–25). Since he believed that politics was a conflict between "the people" and "selfish interests," his causes included progressive taxation, railroad regulation, women's suffrage, and direct democracy. His opposition to U.S. involvement in World War I prompted an unsuccessful effort to expel him from the Senate for treason. In postwar years, he helped investigate the "Teapot Dome Scandal" of President Warren Harding's administration. He made unsuccessful bids for the presidency in 1912 and 1924.

Los Angeles

ON NOVEMBER 5, 1913, Los Angeles water engineer William Mulholland opened a valve, releasing water that had traveled 200 miles. It had flowed to the city through tunnels across the Mojave Desert from a valley in the Sierra Nevada Mountains. The Los Angeles Aqueduct was open, and the city would never be the same.

After the 1892 discovery of oil in Los Angeles, it had seemed that the city could never accommodate the prospectors who flocked there. But with this new source of water, the city grew in area as well as in population, annexing dozens of neighboring communities that did not have their own water supplies.

Los Angeles in 1931

However, the success of the first aqueduct did not end the need for more water. By 1920 Los Angeles leaders began to look at the Colorado River. In 1928 Los Angeles and 12 suburbs incorporated the Metropolitan Water District of Southern California in order to finance, construct, and operate a Colorado River aqueduct. In 1931 work began on a 10-year project that would include the Hoover Dam—which began furnishing electric power to the city in 1935.

In 1920 the population of Los Angeles was 500,000, and real estate agents energetically promoted the city to Midwesterners. The Southern Pacific Railroad brought middle-class, conservative whites to L.A. By 1924 the population was in the high six figures, including 43,000 real estate agents. The newcomers spread out from the central city, creating a suburbia of mini-cities where frenzied construction of homes, apartment buildings, hotels, clubs, restaurants, stores, and industries made them comfortable. The movie studios moved to Hollywood, Beverly Hills, Brentwood, and Bel Air. In some of these suburban enclaves, the Ku Klux Klan maintained a strong influence, and racism against Asians and Mexicans thrived.

Near downtown was a Japanese settlement of more than 8,400 people, many of whom had migrated there after the 1906 earthquake in San Francisco. In 1913 Japanese flower growers and sellers started a Flower Market, which expanded into the Los Angeles Flower Market in 1924. The Chinese population had declined since the 1910s, and a new Los Angeles Chinatown would not emerge until the 1930s. Mexicans were the largest immigrant group in Los Angeles. Many had fled to L.A. during the revolution in their home country in the 1910s. In 1920 Mexican American neighborhoods in downtown were demolished for the creation and expansion of a new civic center and other public areas.

The word "sprawl" began to characterize Los Angeles. The large, red electric streetcars could barely make their way through automobile congestion on city streets. In 1920 a commission of city planning experts tried to ban automobile parking in downtown Los Angeles. *The Los Angeles Sunday Times* ran stories and cartoons about "The Perils of a Parkless Town." Two days later, tens of thousands of urbanites arrived—in their cars—to protest. The commissioners backed down, and the automobile ruled in L.A.

The Los Angeles Harbor, completed in 1914, profited from shipping traffic through the new Panama Canal. Air traffic also added to city growth when a daily air link with San Francisco opened in 1928. By 1930 the population of Los Angeles was more than 1.2 million—and growing.

Hollywoodland In 1923, at a cost of $21,000, this Hollywoodland sign was built on Mount Lee in Los Angeles. The 30-foot-wide, 50-foot-tall letters advertised a new housing subdivision. They were adorned by 4,000 lightbulbs that announced in sequence "Holly" . . . "wood" . . . "land" . . . "Hollywoodland." The sign deteriorated over the years until the Hollywood Chamber of Commerce repaired it in 1949— leaving off both the lightbulbs and the last four letters. The Hollywood sign is now a world-famous symbol for the Hollywood film industry.

Preacher and faith healer Rural Americans felt alienated by increasing urbanization and industrialization during the first half of the 20th century. Many took comfort in various forms of revivalist Christianity, including Pentecostalism. Charismatic preacher and faith healer Aimee Semple McPherson (*pictured*) was deeply influenced by such movements. With a remarkable flair for showmanship, she built the $1.5 million Angelus Temple in Los Angeles and founded the International Church of the Foursquare Gospel. She also preached to the entire nation via the new medium of radio. McPherson's flamboyant life was marred by scandal, including what is widely believed to have been a faked kidnapping in 1926.

Wine sales plummet Workers load grapes on railroad cars to ship to California wineries during Prohibition. The Volstead Act did allow the making of sacramental and medicinal wine, which helped some wineries survive in the 1920s. Others did well shipping grapes, the price of which shot up during a shortage of refrigerated train cars from 1920 to 1925. But by and large, Prohibition ruined the wine-making industry, with winery production dropping 94 percent from 1919 to 1925. Even after the repeal of Prohibition in 1933, some states remained dry while others exercised strict control over alcoholic beverage sales.

Cessna takes off In 1911 Kansas farmer and auto mechanic Clyde Cessna built his own wood and fabric airplane and taught himself to fly it—a trial-and-error method involving short flights between crashes. That winter, Cessna made a successful five-mile flight in Enid, Oklahoma. In 1924 he partnered with Lloyd Stearman and Walter Beech to manufacture biplanes in Wichita, and in 1927 Cessna formed his own company, producing monoplanes (advertised here as "foaled on the plains"). After the Depression, Cessna's nephew, Dwane Wallace, led the company to worldwide success in light-aircraft design and production. During World War II, the Cessna company built 5,000 military aircraft.

January 31, 1924: The Senate passes a resolution asserting that the Teapot Dome oil leases were "executed under circumstances indicating fraud and corruption."

February 1924: Secretary of the Navy Edwin Denby resigns in the fallout from the Teapot Dome Scandal. Interior Secretary Albert Fall resigned earlier. *See* October 17, 1927.

April 26, 1924: Colorado becomes the second state to ratify a constitutional amendment prohibiting child labor.

1925: The *History of the American Frontier* earns author Frederic Logan Paxson the Pulitzer Prize for History.

January 5, 1925: Nellie Tayloe Ross becomes the first female governor in the United States. She was elected to Wyoming's highest office after her husband's death just weeks prior to the 1924 election.

March 4, 1925: During prosperous economic times, President Calvin Coolidge is inaugurated for his second term.

November 11, 1926: Route 66 is commissioned as a major east-west U.S. artery, with nearly 2,500 miles of road.

November 15, 1926: The National Broadcasting Company (NBC) becomes the first radio network to broadcast across the continent, with the aid of some 24 affiliates.

1927: Upton Sinclair's *Oil* is published. It is the first significant American work of fiction about the oil industry.

1927: Okanagan Indian Mourning Dove becomes the first Native American woman to publish a book-length work of fiction, the novel *Co-ge-we-a*.

Indians become cowboys Many Native Americans, in the United States and Canada, became cowboys during the late 19th and early 20th centuries. Some tribes, such as the Idaho Shoshone-Bannocks, developed high-grade registered cattle herds by the 1930s. Other Indians worked for ranchers or as rodeo competitors and Wild West show performers. This Native American poses near Lodge Grass, Montana, circa 1927.

Huntington's treasures *The Blue Boy* by Thomas Gainsborough and *Pinkie* by Thomas Lawrence hang in The Huntington Library, Art Collections, and Botanical Gardens in San Marino, California. The complex was established in 1919 by Henry Huntington and his wife, Arabella. A real estate magnate in the Golden State, Huntington made a fortune, much of which he spent on art and rare books from the United States and Great Britain. In addition to such treasures, The Huntington's library holds original letters from presidents Washington, Jefferson, and Lincoln as well as one of the world's largest collections of Western Americana.

Higgins's landscapes As a nine-year-old on his parents' Indiana farm, Victor Higgins met an itinerant painter of advertisements on barns, and decided to become an artist. At 15, he took jobs in Chicago to pay for classes at the Art Institute of Chicago and the Academy of Fine Arts. Higgins also studied painting in Europe, but became determined to develop a purely American style. In Munich, he met artist Walter Ufer and heard of the art colony in Taos, New Mexico. Higgins later visited Taos, and settled there in 1914. His highly successful paintings—such as *Mountain Forms #2* (*pictured*)—reveal the landscape's basic shapes and rhythms.

A champion for farmers Quaker newspaper and magazine publisher Arthur Capper served as the Republican governor of Kansas from 1915 until 1919, then as a U.S. senator from 1919 to 1949. Deeply concerned about farming and young people, he created youth agricultural training organizations that merged into the 4-H movement. His efforts to help his farming constituency included the 1922 Capper-Volstead Act (often described as the "Magna Carta of farmer marketing cooperatives") and the Capper-Ketchum Act of 1928, which backed agricultural education with federal funds. A progressive Republican, he gave considerable support to President Roosevelt's New Deal programs.

Giannini's Bank of Italy In 1904 the director of a bank in San Francisco's Italian quarter, Amadeo Peter Giannini, and some friends decided to open their own banking institution. Giannini's Bank of Italy took a new approach, advertising for customers and encouraging loans to workers and small businesses. When the 1906 earthquake devastated San Francisco, the Bank of Italy was the first to reopen—even though Giannini had to do business from a plank set on two barrels in the street for a while. The Bank of Italy expanded, and in 1929 it became the Bank of America.

Quickie divorces in Reno According to a popular 1910 song, "I'm on my way to Reno" because "My wife and I don't get along." Throughout the early 1900s, Reno kept lowering the residential time required for a divorce, and the Nevada town soon became the divorce capital of the world. The six-week period advertised on this postcard attracted many short-term residents. From 1929 to '39, more than 30,000 divorces were granted in Reno. When Nevada legalized gambling in 1931, Reno developed the casino-style gambling houses popular in America today—creating new ways for divorce-seekers and other visitors to entertain themselves.

1927: Ansel Adams introduces his signature style of clearly focused, black and white photography with *Monolith, The Face of Half Dome,* taken in California's Yosemite National Park.

May 18, 1927: Sid Grauman opens his famous Hollywood Boulevard theater, built in the style of a Chinese pagoda. It will become one of Hollywood's most enduring landmarks, featuring the hand and footprints of generations of film stars on the sidewalk in front of the façade.

October 6, 1927: *The Jazz Singer,* Hollywood's first feature-length "talkie," is released. Al Jolson stars in blackface and sings "Mammy."

October 17, 1927: Harry Sinclair, lessee of Wyoming's Teapot Dome oil fields, appears at his trial for conspiracy and fraud. The case will end in a mistrial.

1928: The Dunbar Hotel is built on Central Street in Los Angeles, in the heart of a flourishing black business district. It will become a popular hangout for African American actors and entertainers.

1928: The Institute of Government Research releases the Meriam Report, which paints a bleak picture of American Indians' quality of life.

February 15, 1928: The Metropolitan Water District of Southern California is established in an effort to ensure distribution of scarce water resources throughout the arid region.

February 25, 1928: Utah's Bryce Canyon, a virtual forest of delicate stone spires that was described by its namesake, Ebenezer Bryce, as "a hell of a place to lose a cow," is established as a national park.

Oil Booms

I
N 1909, AT THE CORNER of Wilshire Boulevard and La Brea Avenue, an enterprising man set up a wagon bearing a gasoline tank to serve Los Angeles's growing automobile traffic. Though it was not, as has often been claimed, the world's first gas station (there was one in Seattle in 1907), it was certainly a far-sighted effort. For in the decades to follow, cars and gasoline came to dominate California life.

By 1930 approximately two million cars chugged along the streets of California. The state's oil production boomed accordingly, joining motion pictures as one of the region's two key industries. In the 1920s, during the peak of the Southern California oil boom, the Port of Los Angeles became a major hub of oil refinement and shipping. The California Petroleum Company constructed a terminal there in 1923.

But in a move that signaled a shift in power in the oil industry, the Texas Company (later Texaco) acquired California Petroleum, including its Los Angeles terminal. Texas was rapidly becoming the nation's center of petroleum exploration, production, and refinement. During the first three decades of the 20th century, many Texans left farms and ranches and moved to thriving oil boomtowns—appropriately packing their belongings aboard Model-T and Model-A Fords.

An oil field in Saratoga, Texas

While other states, including West Virginia and Pennsylvania, had their own oil booms, they were typically short-lived. Texas kept its own boom going by reinvesting profits into the industry. Such companies as Gulf Oil and the Texas Company built numerous refineries, and constructed pipelines that extended north into Oklahoma and east into Louisiana. From 1929 to 1940, Texas's oil-producing capacity increased fourfold.

The Great Depression was far from a devastating setback for Texas's oil industry. Oil exploration continued despite the financial catastrophe. Ironically, the business's greatest problem during that period was lowered prices caused by excess production. It was only in 1939, with decreased exports to Europe at the beginning of World War II, that Texas Oil production truly waned. When America joined the war in 1941, the industry further suffered from the diversion of steel and trained oil employees to military purposes.

Wildcatter
Harry Ford Sinclair began speculating in oil wells in south Kansas in the 1890s. By 1907 he was the richest man in the Sunflower State. He later became a successful wildcatter in Oklahoma and was a million-

aire before he was 30 years old. With a keen ability to select oil lands that would become profitable, he amassed enough money and savvy to establish the Sinclair Oil and Refining Company in 1916. By the end of World War I, his was the largest independent oil and refining company in the United States.

Lindberghs set speed record Charles Lindbergh and his wife, Anne Morrow Lindbergh—wearing electrically heated flight suits—stand outside their plane at Grand Central Airport near Los Angeles. On April 20, 1930, the couple flew from Los Angeles to New York in the record time of 14 hours, 45 minutes. Charles piloted the plane, and Anne (seven months pregnant) plotted their course with a sextant. Charles was already famous for making the first solo nonstop flight across the Atlantic Ocean in 1927. Anne, also a skilled pilot, became the first American woman to earn a first-class glider pilot's license.

Canned fruit Workers pack asparagus at a Del Monte plant in 1930. The Del Monte brand dates back to the late 19th century, when California became a major fruit and vegetable produce center. In 1898, 18 West Coast canning companies, including Del Monte, formed the California Fruit Canners Association (CFCA). In 1916 the CFCA became the California Packing Corporation (Calpak), using Del Monte as the principal name on its products. Calpak soon had operations throughout the far West as well as in Hawaii and the Philippines. Through shrewd marketing and advertising, the Del Monte label brought national prestige to canned produce.

"Fruit basket" of the world California's citrus industry dates to the early 1800s, when orange groves were established at several Spanish missions. By 1910 orange groves covered more than 100,000 acres of land, and sales surpassed $200 million. "Boosters" developed citrus fairs that continued well into the 20th century. Citrus led the way to other fruit and vegetable production, and California became known as the "fruit basket" of the world. This color lithograph, circa 1930, touts the beauty and productivity of California's citrus country, which was centered in the San Bernardino and San Gabriel valleys.

Folksy humorist
Born in 1879, Will Rogers became one of 20th century America's great humorists and entertainers. Part Cherokee, he grew up in Oklahoma, becoming an expert horseman and lariat artist. Rogers found work as a cowboy and Wild West show entertainer before becoming a star of stage, radio, and screen. His folksy,

humorous philosophy, and his philanthropy and fund-raising work, endeared him to fans around the world. Famous for saying "I never met a man I didn't like," he also claimed that "I belong to no organized party. I am a Democrat." Rogers died in a plane crash in 1935.

Hunt strikes it rich Soon-to-be Texas oil magnate H. L. Hunt (*second from right*) celebrates the discovery of a major new oil well, No. 3 Daisy Bradford, in East Texas in early 1930. Hunt, who had gone broke after making hundreds of thousands of dollars on oil in his home state of Arkansas, purchased the well and leases for much of the surrounding land in late 1930 with a $30,000 loan. He soon found himself sitting atop the largest oil field in the world at that time, with an estimated six billion barrels. By 1948 he was the richest man in the United States, according to *Fortune* magazine.

Wood's inspiration Although Grant Wood spent time painting in Europe and exhibited his work in Paris, he famously said that "all the really good ideas I'd ever had came to me while I was milking a cow. So I went back to Iowa." In 1932 he helped found the Stone City art colony to aid artists during the Depression. During the 1930s, Wood promoted Regionalism, which centered around the idea that American artists should focus on familiar American scenes. Wood's subjects include rural midwestern landscapes, such as the one seen here, entitled *Landscape*. His portraits (for example, the widely reproduced *American Gothic*) often reveal a touch of gentle irony.

"Alfalfa Bill" Murray Nicknamed "Alfalfa Bill" because of speeches he delivered in his alfalfa field, William Murray (seen here at left in 1931 with humorist Will Rogers) was a prominent figure in Oklahoma's political history. He participated in drafting the state's constitution, and was elected its governor in 1930. Alfalfa Bill's four-year governorship was marked by frequent and heavy-handed imposition of martial law and his bitter opposition to the New Deal—perhaps partly provoked by his loss of the 1932 Democratic presidential nomination to Franklin Roosevelt.

Car Trips

In THE EARLY DECADES of the 20th century, automobiles changed the way Americans spent their money and their time. From 1900 to 1930, the number of cars in the United States jumped from 8,000 to 23 million. To the middle class, owning an automobile signaled success and independence. A car was a way of escaping the ordinary for travel and adventure, and by 1919 nearly a third of Americans took their vacations by car.

Auto-tourists driving to see America often camped out in autocamps—and sometimes in farmers' fields. Cities, towns, historical places, and national parks gained income from fees, hotel accommodations, meals, and souvenirs. Tourist cabins, where travelers could park their cars right next to their cabins, eventually became more popular than camping out.

America's roads could barely accommodate all those Americans on wheels. By 1925 about 250 paved highways existed in the country, each with its own name and with locally supplied signs. That year, the Federal Aid Highway Act created a nationwide system of numbered standardized highways.

In 1926 U.S. Route 66 was established. It ran from Chicago through Missouri, Kansas, Oklahoma, Texas, New Mexico, Arizona, and all the way to the beach in

A road in Nevada, 1920

Santa Monica, California—a total distance of 2,347 miles. Route 66 brought new customers to small businesses in the towns it passed through, encouraging the building of service stations, restaurants, and motor courts. During the 1930s, the route was used heavily by farm families fleeing the Dust Bowl and heading west for agricultural jobs in California.

First drive-in restaurant
Employees show off the Pig Stand restaurant in Dallas in the early 1930s. The world's first drive-in restaurant was the brainchild of Dallas businessman Jesse Kirby, who operated on the wise assumption that "people with cars are so lazy, they don't want to get out of them to eat." The original Pig Stand was wildly successful, and by 1930 more than 120 of them dotted nine states, mainly west of the Mississippi. The signature dish was the Pig Sandwich, more genteelly known as barbecued pork.

November 18, 1928: Walt Disney's first animated film with sound, *Steamboat Willie*, is released. It includes the first appearance of Disney's Mickey Mouse.

1929: Authors Robert and Helen Lynd publish their groundbreaking sociological research with the release of *Middletown: A Study in Contemporary American Culture*. The town is based on Muncie, Indiana.

1929: Georgia O'Keeffe discovers new inspiration for her painting when she makes her first visit to New Mexico.

March 4, 1929: Herbert Hoover is inaugurated as the 31st president of the United States.

May 16, 1929: The first Academy Awards ceremony is held, at the Hollywood Roosevelt Hotel. *Wings* wins for best picture.

October 29, 1929: The value of the stock market plummets by 12 percent. This crash on what will become known as "Black Tuesday" will begin a run on the banks and trigger the Great Depression.

1930: After experiencing a tremendous boom since the turn of the century, the city of Los Angeles sees its population more than double from 1920 to 1930, from 500,000 to 1.2 million.

1930: California's Standard Pacific Gas Line begins construction on the world's largest natural gas pipeline, from Kettleman Hills, California, to San Francisco Bay.

1931: Nevada assures the future of Las Vegas with the statewide legalization of gambling.

1931: Black blizzards of dust develop in the Plains states. Throughout much of the decade, severe drought, over-plowing, and overgrazing will take their toll on the once-fertile land.

California water project The three men most responsible for the aqueduct that brought Colorado River water to Los Angeles stand on the construction site in 1931. F. E. Weymouth (*left*) built it, William Mulholland (*center*) conceived it, and W. P. Whitsett (*right*) was the first president of the Metropolitan Water District, which coordinated overall water policy for Southern California. Created in 1928, the district aided numerous communities in the area, but Los Angeles had a 50 percent share of the vote on the district's board of directors. The board, free from political control and influence, worked hard to secure sufficient water for the area.

Hoover's failures An Iowa blacksmith's son, Herbert Hoover was orphaned at age nine and spent the rest of his difficult childhood in Oregon. Consequently, he appreciated hard work and felt compassion for the needy. After making a fortune in mining, he became one of the greatest humanitarians of his time. This reputation suffered when the Great Depression broke out during his U.S. presidency (1929–32). Despite Hoover's aggressive government efforts to relieve the nation's misery, he failed to enact deficit-spending programs and handouts for the poor. His limited policies hurt the West, where later efforts—such as President Roosevelt's Civilian Conservation Corps—improved both morale and the quality of life.

Great Depression in the West

IN THE 1920S, CALIFORNIA'S booming population and rampant prosperity seemed like sure signs of a golden future. But as the '20s ended, people found themselves out of work, and jobs of any kind were hard to find. Every day, about 4,000 men competed for 1,500 jobs on the San Francisco waterfront, a situation that led to bribery, strikes, riots, and something approaching warfare. Even for those who still had work, incomes dropped drastically. Over a four-year period, pay for some agricultural field workers fell from 75 cents to 15 cents an hour. The Great Depression hammered the West as hard as it hit the rest of the country, and no social programs existed anywhere to feed the hungry or support the suddenly penniless.

California's population kept growing, but now the new arrivals were refugees from the Midwest, where farm prices had dropped by half. Farmers who could not sell their produce for enough to cover costs were dumping milk and vegetables—even while people in other parts of the country desperately needed food. Later in the 1930s, Dust Bowl refugees crowded into California.

Migrant worker in California

Migrants and many locals who had lost jobs were homeless. In 1931 unemployed workers in Seattle built a "Hooverville"—named after the president who kept insisting that prosperity was "just around the corner"—with shacks made out of cardboard, packing crates, scrap metal, or tar paper. Twice, the Seattle police burned down the shantytown, but each time the squatters rebuilt even sturdier shacks. Finally the city allowed them to stay. The 1934 census counted 632 men and seven women of varied nationalities and races living in 479 shanties.

Most other large cities also had their Hoovervilles. The one in Oklahoma City was 10 miles long and 10 miles wide. The largest was probably the one in St. Louis, populated by 1,000 people. Homeless people also lived under bridges, in public parks, and in unused sewer or drainage pipes. An empty pocket turned inside out was called a "Hoover flag," and old newspapers used for cover were a "Hoover blanket."

Banks go bust Anxious Californians hope to withdraw some of their funds from the United States National Bank in Los Angeles on August 24, 1931—a day after it closed. The Federal Reserve system proved incapable of quelling the national economic panic, which grew worse after 1931 and contributed to the Great Depression. By 1933, when Franklin Roosevelt was inaugurated, approximately 9,000 "busted" banks in the U.S. had left investors and depositors with no means of recouping their losses.

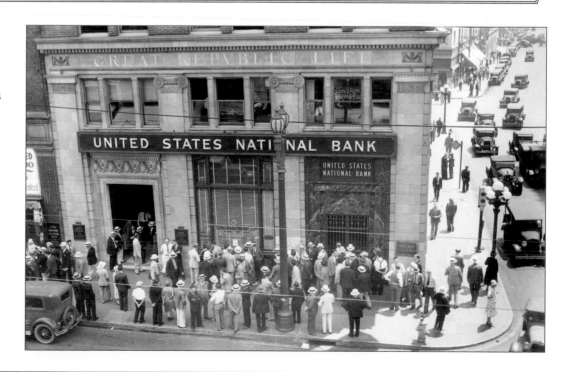

1931: In the midst of the Great Depression, Nelda and Clifford Clifton open their first Clifton's Cafeteria, in Los Angeles. Clifton's allows guests to pay as much or as little as they can, and never turns anyone away hungry.

1931: Colorado's population surpasses one million.

1931: Lynn Riggs, a Cherokee Indian, releases *Green Grow the Lilacs,* the inspiration for the Rodgers & Hammerstein musical *Oklahoma!*.

1931: *The Great Plains,* an acclaimed history of the territory by author Walter Prescott Webb, is released.

1931: An elementary school in Lemon Grove, California, turns away Mexican American children. Lemon Grove parents sue, leading to the first school desegregation case in U.S. history.

1932: California's aviation industry grows when Reuben Fleet moves Consolidated Vultee (which will be renamed Convair) to the West Coast.

1932: Fourteen major dust storms erupt on the Plains this year.

1932: Nearly one of four Americans is officially unemployed.

1932: The Bonus Army, a group of about 20,000 World War I veterans, marches to Washington. They demand that Congress authorize payment of their military bonuses, which were due to them according to the 1924 World War Adjustment Compensation Act. On orders from President Hoover, Army Chief of Staff General Douglas MacArthur leads armed troops against the protestors, dispersing them.

1932: Congress creates the Reconstruction Finance Corporation to stimulate the depressed economy by making loans to banks, corporations, and insurance companies.

"Hoovervilles" Youngsters in a "Hooverville" solicit donations from passersby in 1932. Hoovervilles appeared in many western states, with some of the largest in Washington, Oregon, and California. By January 1935, more than 26 percent of Seattle's workforce was unemployed, and 4,000 to 5,000 people dwelled in "shack towns" located along the city's waterfront and tidal flats. Similar Hoovervilles sprouted in Portland, San Francisco, Bakersfield, and Los Angeles.

Living in sewer pipes This Hooverville was located in Oakland, California's waterfront district. Named "Pipe City" because the "housing" consisted of surplus sewer pipes in a storage yard, it sheltered several hundred homeless men during the winter of 1932–33. Unsanitary and crowded, Hoovervilles became homes for many men, women, and children during the Great Depression. The name reflects how disappointed Americans were with President Herbert Hoover, who was unable to resuscitate the economy.

"Bonus Army" marches to Washington Members of the "Bonus Army" camp out on the U.S. Capitol lawn in 1932. In 1924 Congress had promised World War I veterans a bonus, deliverable in 1945. Walter Waters, a former sergeant from Oregon, began the march with some 300 men from Portland. By May 1932, about 15,000 destitute veterans, some with wives and children, assembled in Washington, D.C. Establishing Hoovervilles on nearby Anacostia Flats, they petitioned Congress for early payment. After Congress denied their petition, many departed. On July 28, police and soldiers tear-gassed and torched the camp. Several adults and children died, and many veterans were wounded. The incident practically guaranteed that President Hoover would not be reelected.

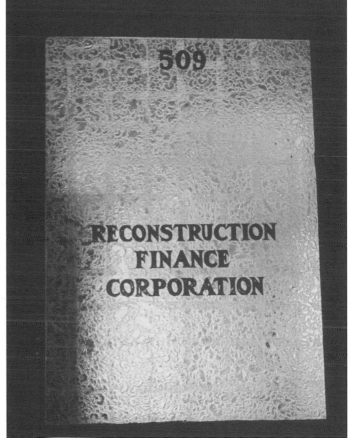

Bank relief Created in 1932 by the Hoover Administration, the Reconstruction Finance Corporation (RFC) was designed to help stem the tide of the Great Depression by providing low-interest federal loans primarily to banks experiencing financial difficulty. Although some small western banks received such loans, the amounts were simply too small to prevent hundreds of bank failures in 1932 and '33. Under President Franklin Roosevelt, the RFC increased loans to urban banks and also pumped more than $2 billion into banks that made agricultural loans, including many in the West. This helped alleviate some of the impact of the Depression on farmers.

The Los Angeles Olympics

In spite of economic depression and unsettled international conditions, the 1932 Summer Olympic Games were a resounding success, especially for American athletes and the city of Los Angeles. More than one million people attended, and 1,408 athletes from 37 countries participated. The city invested money to build the first Olympic Village and to expand Memorial Coliseum to seat 105,000. The athletes performed superbly, with 16 world and Olympic records falling in track and field alone. Of special note for Americans were Babe Didrickson's two gold medals and one silver in women's track and field, and

sprinter Eddie Tolan's two golds. The United States won the overall medal count with 103 to Italy's distant 36.

February 27, 1932: The Glass-Steagall Act is passed. It permits Federal Reserve banks to issue currency without being tied down to how much gold they happen to have.

March 23, 1932: President Hoover signs the Norris-LaGuardia Act, which outlaws contracts that force a worker to agree to not join a union as a condition of employment.

May 20–21, 1932: Kansas native Amelia Earhart flies solo across the Atlantic Ocean in record time (13 hours, 30 minutes).

July 22, 1932: The Federal Home Loan Bank Act is enacted to offset some of the effects of the Great Depression. The act makes more money available to lending institutions for loaning to individuals as home mortgages.

September 18, 1932: Depressed by her stalled career, actress Peg Entwistle takes her life by diving headfirst off the top of the Hollywoodland sign's "H." Ironically, her estate will receive a letter shortly thereafter inviting her to star in a production about a suicidal woman.

November 8, 1932: Democrat Franklin Delano Roosevelt defeats Republican President Herbert Hoover by a healthy margin. Republicans also lose control of Congress. Roosevelt promises "a new deal for the American people."

1933: By the end of this year, some 9,000 banks will have failed since the crash of the stock market.

1933: WXYZ in Detroit premieres its new radio show, *The Lone Ranger.*

1933: Dust storms are on the rise in the Midwest, with 38 this year—more than twice as many as were reported the previous year.

Hogue's harsh realism American artist Alexandre Hogue is most noted for his series of paintings depicting the Dust Bowl of the 1930s. This one, entitled *Dust Bowl,* combines a level of abstraction with harsh realism. The desolation and absence of human beings suggest the power of the dust storms that blanketed the Plains states during much of the Great Depression.

Animals die by the millions Domestic and wild animals suffered grievously during the drought years. Thousands of cattle, swine, sheep, and other creatures died from starvation, dehydration, or disease. In 1933 alone, 38 gigantic dust storms swept over the prairie states, darkening the skies and bringing misery to people and animals alike. One controversial New Deal program called for killing millions of domestic livestock in order to reduce the animals' demands on the land, and to improve prices for livestock ranchers. In September 1933, more than six million piglets—as well as many sheep and other animals—were slaughtered.

The Dust Bowl

FOR MUCH OF THE 1930s, the Oklahoma Panhandle, western Kansas, eastern Colorado, and land along the Texas-New Mexico border became a "Dust Bowl." Several factors contributed to this disaster, including a horrific drought that lasted most of the decade. In addition, Midwestern grasslands were no longer being naturally fertilized by buffalo herds. Farmlands had been overused for wartime food production and stripped of natural vegetation by poor agricultural techniques. When the drought hit, millions of acres of topsoil turned into dust and blew away.

In May 1934, one of the worst storms dumped dust and debris on far-away eastern cities. The equivalent of four pounds of dust per person fell on Chicago that month, and red dust colored the New England snow the following winter. On April 14, 1935, known as "Black Sunday," a Midwestern dust blizzard made it impossible to see farther than five feet away.

Photo journalist Margaret Bourke-White described where the dust came from: "Red, it is the topsoil from Oklahoma; brown, it is the fertile earth of western Kansas; the good grazing land of Texas and New Mexico sweeps by as a murky yellow haze." Bourke-White also commented that local people would say, "My uncle will be along pretty soon—I just saw his farm go by."

With their crops ruined and no possibility of growing more, farm families lost their homes because of debts

A dust storm approaching Springfield, Colorado

they could not pay. Many loaded whatever they could into cars and trucks, abandoned their land, and headed off to California on Route 66. It is estimated that 15 percent of the Oklahoma population left. Although the migrants came from many different states, they were all called "Okies."

During the 1930s, more than 300,000 people moved from the Dust Bowl states and nearby ones to California. Most went to either the Los Angeles area or the Central Valley, where they found agricultural jobs—low-paying, but better than what they had left behind.

Nationwide drought Sustained drought, unusually high temperatures, and poor farming practices devastated American farmland in the 1930s. The Dust Bowl years ravaged states from North Dakota to Texas. Thousands of "busted" farmers moved in desperation to other locales. The worst-hit areas were eastern New Mexico and Colorado, western Kansas, and the panhandles of Texas and Oklahoma. By May 1934, drought conditions afflicted more than 75 percent of the country, including portions of 27 states. This ruined cornfield lay somewhere in the Midwest.

1933: Ecologist Aldo Leopold releases *Game Management*. This groundbreaking, authoritative volume on wildlife management virtually introduces a new science.

March 4, 1933: Franklin Delano Roosevelt is inaugurated as president. He plans to introduce legislation that will stabilize the U.S. economy.

March 5, 1933: President Roosevelt declares a holiday to stop the run on financial institutions during yet another banking panic.

March 9, 1933: The Emergency Banking Bill is passed. It calls for mandatory shutdowns and inspections of U.S. banks in order to restore credibility and confidence in the system.

March 31, 1933: The Civilian Conservation Corps is established as another opportunity to get young American men back to work, in this case working on conservation-minded projects such as planting trees and maintaining parks.

May 1933: The Emergency Farm Mortgage Act allocates $200 million in federal aid to help destitute farmers avoid foreclosure.

May 12, 1933: The Agricultural Adjustment Administration is established with the goal of reducing crops in order to raise prices. • The Federal Emergency Relief Administration grants $500 million to individual states to provide unemployment assistance to residents.

May 18, 1933: President Roosevelt signs the Tennessee Valley Authority Act. The TVA will manage and maintain the means of production for billions of kilowatt-hours of electricity each year in the U.S.

May 27, 1933: Established by a presidential executive order, the Farm Credit Administration provides short- and long-term credit to farmers.

FDR's western projects President Franklin Delano Roosevelt was inaugurated in 1933 during the country's Great Depression and while the Midwest was suffering from drought. Roosevelt's New Deal programs that especially benefited the West included mortgage relief, payments to farmers for reducing production, and protection for grazing on federal range lands. New Deal projects also put young men to work improving national forests and building highways. The construction of large dams and irrigation systems—notably the Columbia River Basin Project—irrigated farmlands and provided hydroelectric power. Legislation under Roosevelt also ended the sale of American Indian lands and restored ownership of some areas to tribal groups. Roosevelt was elected to an unprecedented four terms in office, serving from 1933 until his death in 1945.

"Honest Harold" In 1933 progressive Republican Harold Ickes was appointed secretary of the interior by President Roosevelt. Ickes simultaneously served as head of the multibillion-dollar Public Works Administration (PWA). Ickes earned the nickname "Honest Harold" for his efforts to keep PWA free of political concerns and internal corruption. A civil rights supporter, Ickes urged the hiring of African Americans and openly criticized Japanese American internment during World War II.

Norris supports FDR, TVA

George Norris served Nebraska as a member of the House of Representatives from 1903 to 1913, then as a senator from 1913 to 1943. Though repeatedly elected as a Republican, he frequently defied his own party, saying that he "would rather be right than regular." He endorsed Democrat Franklin Roosevelt in all his presidential campaigns and was a staunch advocate of the New Deal. One of Norris's most significant achievements was introducing the 1933 bill creating the Tennessee Valley Authority (TVA), a government agency that brought flood control, electrical power, and better standards of living to people in seven states.

Building the dams

As dams were built throughout the United States during the 1930s, builders faced hardships and dangers. Hoover Dam workers, seen here excavating the foundation on the Colorado River, endured 120-degree heat in summer and subfreezing temperatures in winter. In their haste to complete the dam on schedule, contractors sacrificed safety for speed. The 96 deaths officially attributed to the construction did not include those that were caused by carbon monoxide poisoning from machinery. In times of high national unemployment, it took courage for Hoover Dam workers to strike in 1931. The strike ended quickly but brought some improvements in working conditions.

MGM rises to the top

The glass doors of a Metro-Goldwyn-Mayer cinema house—showing an MGM film, naturally—beckon to potential moviegoers in 1933. Founded in 1924, the studio went on to become a dominant force in Hollywood. In 1930 it released the first Technicolor all-talking film, as well as the first sound cartoon in color. MGM's stable of stars included Clark Gable, Jean Harlow, Robert Montgomery, and Nelson Eddy, and it released 50 movies a year in the 1930s. The MGM roaring lion became the most recognized film logo in the industry.

June 16, 1933: The Public Works Administration is established and given a multibillion-dollar budget. The money will be spent on massive public works projects that create large-scale employment opportunities. • The Federal Deposit Insurance Corporation is established to insure bank deposits up to $100,000 and instill consumer confidence in banks.

June 17, 1933: Five die in the "Union Station Massacre" when heavily armed men attempt to free just-recaptured prisoner Frank Nash. One of the dead is Nash, while the others are law enforcement officers.

June 20, 1933: The National Recovery Administration is formed with a mandate to establish fair employment practices, such as minimum wage and maximum hours.

September 1933: In an effort to stabilize pork prices, more than six million young pigs are slaughtered nationwide.

October 1933: In response to the public outcry over the waste of September's pork slaughter, the Federal Surplus Relief Corporation is established. The organization will distribute surplus comestibles to the poor. • Three die and hundreds are injured during the largest agricultural strike in U.S. history. Some 18,000 cotton pickers, members of the Cannery and Agricultural Workers Industrial Union, strike for 24 days in California's San Joaquin Valley.

December 5, 1933: The states ratify the 21st Amendment to the Constitution, bringing an end to Prohibition and putting a dent in organized crime.

1934: The economy begins to recover. Important economic indicators, such as the Gross National Product and the unemployment rate, improve across the board.

Bonnie and Clyde Bonnie parker, the petite (4'11") former honor roll student, poses with her lover, Clyde Barrow. From 1932 to 1934, the couple popularly known as "Bonnie and Clyde" robbed stores, gas stations, and banks in Texas and a cycle of mid-western states. All the while, a fascinated public eagerly followed newspaper stories about the outlaw couple. It is believed that Barrow and his gang members killed 13 people, but that Parker never fired a gun. In 1934 Bonnie's prediction that she and Clyde would die together came true in a Louisiana ambush laid by Texas and Louisiana lawmen.

Sinclair carries torch for Socialists After the publication of his 1906 exposé novel of the Chicago stockyards, *The Jungle,* author Upton Sinclair became an influential political figure. Like many Socialists, Sinclair believed that capitalism was ultimately doomed. He felt grimly vindicated by the arrival of the Great Depression, writing in 1934 that he had predicted such a crisis, which he dubbed the "permanent one," three decades earlier. In '34, Sinclair became the Democratic candidate for governor in California, campaigning on a platform he called EPIC—

End Poverty in California. EPIC specifically targeted California's unemployed, "so that they may work and support themselves and thus take themselves off the backs of the taxpayers." Sinclair was defeated in the election by Republican Frank Merriam.

Socialist Movements

IN 1934, AS THE AMERICAN Great Depression was about to enter its sixth year, California-based Socialist author Upton Sinclair described it as "the permanent crisis, the one which does not pass away." Sinclair and other leftists claimed that the Depression demanded drastic changes in human society. Indeed, Marxists and Socialists had long predicted such a worldwide economic catastrophe. With the arrival of the Great Depression, it seemed that their predictions had been realized and that their time of ascendancy had come.

Founded in 1901, the Socialist Party of America was one of the United States' most successful third parties. Even so, its reputation for atheism and in-fighting denied it a foothold in the American heartland. In 1915 former Socialist Party leader A. C. Townley created a new organization in North Dakota called the Non-Partisan League. The NPL adopted many Socialist positions, including state control of important industries. The league eventually dominated North Dakota politics, and its political influence spread throughout Middle America and much of the West. After a decline following World War I, the Non-Partisan League experienced a resurgence when the Great Depression began.

In 1934 Sinclair ran as the Democratic candidate for governor of California. His platform, called End Poverty in California (EPIC), boldly proposed that the state's abandoned factories and farmlands be turned over to the unemployed, who would run them as cooperatives. Sinclair lost the 1934 election to Republican Frank Merriam, 1,138,620 votes to 879, 537, and his EPIC program died with his campaign.

Moreover, during the end of the Great Depression, the Non-Partisan League's influence sharply declined. During the 1930s, many Americans on the political left supported President Franklin Roosevelt's New Deal program, with its assurance that the Great Depression was not a permanent crisis, and that government could relieve the economic sufferings of the American people.

Smear tactics The campaign against Upton Sinclair's California gubernatorial bid in 1934 is often cited as the earliest example of modern media smear tactics. This image is from an attack ad created by Hollywood producer Irving Thalberg, misleadingly edited into a movie newsreel that ran twice a week in theaters throughout the country. The segment showed respectable, articulate California citizens endorsing Sinclair's Republican opponent, Frank Merriam, while uncouth bums like these, arriving from out of state to take advantage of Sinclair's radical social schemes, declared their support for Sinclair. Many of these supposed vagrants were played by hired actors.

Branded a Communist Though an avowed Socialist, Upton Sinclair was not a Communist, and he outspokenly criticized the government of the Soviet Union. Nevertheless, the EPIC platform of his California gubernatorial campaign of 1934, with its emphasis on collective farming and manufacturing, made it easy for his enemies to attack him as a Communist. This phony currency, printed in red ink, signed by "Utopian Sinclair," and declared "good only in California or Russia," was widely circulated during the campaign. Other smear tactics included a fake poster in which Sinclair was supposedly endorsed by the Young People's Communist League.

1934: Disgusted by the lack of funds for Mexican American schools, San Antonio civil leader Eleuterio Escobar establishes the Pro Schools Defense League.

1934: The Motion Pictures Producers and Distributors Association begins to enforce the Production Code, also known as the Hays Code, in earnest. Initially adopted in 1930, the code includes fairly strict decency guidelines for American motion pictures.

1934: The new Wheeler-Howard Act, also known as the Indian Reorganization Act, allows for the return of local self-determination and government within autonomous Indian tribes.

1934: The Taylor Grazing Act provides for established, monitored livestock grazing districts to prevent the sort of land overuse that led to the Dust Bowl disaster. The new policy effectively ends homesteading.

1934: A massive maritime strike paralyzes shipping and ports along the Pacific seaboard from San Diego to Seattle.

January 1934: Retired Long Beach physician Francis Townsend develops a plan to provide a $200 monthly pension for everyone over age 60, the only obligation being that the money must be spent within the month in order to help stimulate the economy. The Townsend Plan is never passed.

January 1, 1934: The Army installation at Alcatraz Island on San Francisco Bay is reopened as a maximum-security federal prison for the most hardened convicts. *See* August 23, 1934.

March 24, 1934: The Tydings-McDuffie Act goes into effect. It provides a schedule for the gradual independence of the Philippines.

Collier fights for Indian rights John Collier poses with two Pueblo Indians in New Mexico. Collier, an eastern social worker, rose to prominence by defending Pueblo water and land rights from non-Native theft. A founder of the American Indian Defense Association in 1922, he headed the Bureau of Indian Affairs from 1933 to 1945. Fighting for legal and religious rights for Natives, Collier promoted "cultural pluralism" instead of "forced assimilation" programs. He was instrumental in persuading Congress to pass the 1934 Indian Reorganization Act, sometimes called the "Magna Carta of Indian Rights."

Early western talkies After gaining prestige in the silent period, the movie western briefly declined during the early sound era. Like 1934's *Wagon Wheels,* westerns were typically "B" movies, cheaply produced for the second half of a double feature. Such early western talkies continued to promote mythologized images derived from dime novels, stage melodramas, and spectacles such as Buffalo Bill's Wild West. Familiar elements included wagon trains, frontier towns, Indian attacks, and gunfights between outlaws and lawmen. The movie West was a romantic, moralistic world in which people lived by personal codes rather than the rule of law.

Maritime Strikes

DURING THE 1930S, Australian Alfred Renton Bridges was a longshoreman in San Francisco. Called Harry by his coworkers, Bridges was active in waterfront workers unions, and in May 1934 he planned a West Coast strike. Employers brought in strikebreakers under police protection, but Teamsters—in support of the longshoremen—refused to handle cargo unloaded by the strikebreakers. Although the Roosevelt Administration brokered agreements with various union leaders, union members refused to honor them.

Harry Bridges

On July 5, police shot tear gas canisters into a crowd of San Francisco strikers and supporters. A canister-tossing, rock-throwing melee followed. The day became known as "Bloody Thursday" after a policemen fired a shotgun into the crowd, killing two people. On Friday, thousands of strikers and sympathizers took part in a funeral procession. Finally, the National Guard was called in to control the waterfront situation.

Although some unions supported Bridges's call for a general strike, the maritime workers returned to their jobs. They later used smaller strikes to win improvements in workplace conditions. Bridges went on to become president of the International Longshoremen's and Warehousemen's Union (ILWU) from 1937 to 1977.

Many politicians, law officials, and employers attributed labor strife to the Communist Party, which had organized such groups as the Maritime Workers Industrial Union (MWIU). In 1938 and '41, the Roosevelt Administration attempted to deport Bridges on charges of Communist affiliation, but courts—including the U.S. Supreme Court in 1945—found the government's evidence insufficient.

Angel Island From 1910 to '40, an estimated 175,000 Chinese and 60,000 Japanese immigrants were processed at Angel Island in San Francisco Bay. With the severely restrictive Chinese Exclusion Act of 1882 still in force, the immigration center (*pictured*) detained Asians for weeks. Families were separated and crowded into communal barracks. Some were held for as long as two years, and thousands were denied entry and deported. The camp also processed German and Italian immigrants from Hawaii. During World War II, Angel Island held German and Japanese prisoners of war.

> "The dust storms have distinct personalities, rising in formation like rolling clouds, creeping up silently like formless fog, approaching violently like a tornado. Where has it come from?"
>
> —JOURNALIST MARGARET BOURKE-WHITE, *THE NATION*, MAY 22, 1935

Black Sunday April 14, 1935, started out as a pleasant, sunny day in Kansas. But once the winds kicked up, it became known as "Black Sunday." The enormous dust storm that resulted was so monstrous that some people believed the world was coming to an end. Kansans were caught off guard; those away from their homes ran manically for shelter. Not even airplanes could escape the massive Dust Bowl storms, which could affect visibility several miles high.

ALL COVERED IN DUST

AND THIS SAME DUST that coats the lungs and threatens death to cattle and men alike, that ruins the stock of the storekeeper lying unsold on his shelves, that creeps into the gear shifts of automobiles, that sifts through the refrigerator into the butter, that makes housekeeping, and gradually life itself, unbearable, this swirling drifting dust is changing the agricultural map of the United States. It piles ever higher on the floors and beds of a steadily increasing number of deserted farmhouses. A half-buried plowshare, a wheat binder ruffled over with sand, the skeleton of a horse near a dirt-filled water hole are stark evidence of the meager life, the wasted savings, the years of toil that the farmer is leaving behind him.

—JOURNALIST MARGARET BOURKE-WHITE,
THE NATION, MAY 22, 1935

Gone with the wind
Arthur Rothstein, a Farm Security Administration photographer, documented rural American Dust Bowl conditions. Rothstein took this photograph in Cimarron County, Oklahoma, in 1936. Many impoverished farm families lost what little they had during the terrible drought years of the 1930s. Here, a father and two little boys seek shelter in a shed during one of the "dusters" that blew away precious topsoil, making formerly productive farm land barren and useless. Among rural poor folk, the Dust Bowl years left many with a feeling of utter hopelessness.

Early-day environmentalist To plant a pine tree, wrote American ecologist Aldo Leopold, one need not be a god or a poet, but needed only to "own a good shovel." Leopold was often called the father of the United States' wilderness system. His many accomplishments included his role in officially declaring New Mexico's Gila National Forest the United States' first extensive wilderness area. As an outdoorsman, teacher,

philosopher, and writer, Leopold urged people to see the natural world "as a community to which we belong." His ideas contributed tremendously to the environmental movement in the late 20th century.

Novelty architecture A snappily attired vendor sells orange juice at an orange-shaped stand in El Monte, California, a state rife with novelty architecture. Unusual and eye-catching buildings advertised products and attracted customers. In recent decades, many such structures have been preserved or rehabilitated to help commemorate California's heady years of rapid development. From 1920 to 1940, the population jumped from 3,426,861 to 6,907,387.

Western hobos Not to be confused with beggars and idlers, such as bums and tramps, hobos were typically migratory, homeless working people. Their characteristic mode of transportation was the railroad boxcar, as in this photograph of a man traveling with his family (*off camera*) in the state of Washington. Hobo nicknames included "bindle stiffs," after the bedrolls they carried, and "harvest stiffs," who were hobos who followed ripening crops throughout the heartland. Other western hobos worked at jobs ranging from canning to logging. Although hobos originated in the 19th century, their numbers vastly increased during the Great Depression.

Eccles and the Federal Reserve Marriner Eccles, a millionaire Mormon from Utah, skillfully managed to steer his banks clear of trouble at the beginning of the Great Depression. Fittingly, he was tapped to help plan the U.S. government's strategies for coping with the economic catastrophe. In 1935 he became chairman of the Federal Reserve System, a network of "bankers' banks" throughout the United States that greatly influenced the nation's economy. As chairman during the Depression years, Eccles reshaped and strengthened the Federal Reserve into its present form. He also backed President Roosevelt's New Deal policies by promoting government deficit spending.

Oklahoma oil The oil wells of Oklahoma became commercially successful after 1897. The oil boom made many white men fabulously wealthy. Much oil was found on Indian land, but fraudulent contracts generally deprived Indians of oil revenues. Tulsa oil production flourished after 1905, and by the 1930s oil fields near Oklahoma City also produced enormous amounts. Oil money transformed the state's agrarian character. Oil barons lived lavishly, spent recklessly, built sprawling mansions, and helped modernize the region.

BRIGHT NIGHTS IN OK CITY

YOU TOP A LITTLE rise, and the fog of lights divides slowly into individualities. You see tall buildings all lighted up, still far away. You think what a big place Oklahoma City is, with lots of big office buildings—and lots of people working this late at night, too. Why, it looks like the New York skyline at night, only the buildings all seem about the same height. The tops make a ledge of light across the sky.

You think along like that, with the frogs croaking alongside the road and the motor purring through the night, and you getting closer and closer all the time. And then suddenly it hits you, right between the eyes. Those aren't buildings all lighted up. They're oil derricks! Oil derricks right in the city!

—SCRIPPS-HOWARD REPORTER ERNIE PYLE, 1936

The Townsend Plan In 1933 Dr. Francis Townsend wrote a letter to the editor of a Long Beach, California, newspaper. He proposed a simple plan for restoring the nation's purchasing power and ending the Depression: "Give all the aged a pension and the task of spending it every month." With the Townsend Plan, older citizens would receive $200 a month, with the money funded by a federal sales tax. The idea gained nationwide supporters, pushing President Roosevelt to include his own less generous pension plan in the Social Security Act of 1935. Townsend, shown speaking at the 1939 World's Fair in New York, continued to press for higher old-age pensions.

Relocating the destitute Rexford Tugwell, one of President Roosevelt's "Brain Trusters," served on FDR's drought commission in 1936. Here he examines drifting sand that covers a "busted" farm near Dalhart, Texas. Huge dust storms blew away topsoil and scattered sterile, loose sand over much of the West. Tugwell's New Deal agency, the Resettlement Administration, was designed to relocate urban poor people to suburbs and the rural poor to better farmlands. Renamed the Farm Security Administration in 1937, Tugwell's agency constructed three planned communities and improved conditions in some 200 towns.

"[When] they have finished harvesting my crops, I will kick them out on the country road. My obligation is ended."

—CALIFORNIA FARMER ON MIGRANT WORKERS, CIRCA 1935

Mexican Deportation

IN 1935 NINE-YEAR-OLD Emilia Castaneda was forced to leave Los Angeles to live in Mexico. What makes her deportation shocking was that she was not a Mexican immigrant to the United States. Though of Mexican descent, she was actually born a U.S. citizen. Her first language was English, not Spanish, and California had been her lifelong home. Her subsequent adjustment to life in Mexico was traumatic.

Forced removals of Latinos from Anglo society were not new in the 1930s; such episodes had begun shortly after Texas declared independence from Mexico in 1836. But in the 20th century, deportation took an especially ugly turn, beginning with the Immigration Act of 1924. This law targeted various immigrant groups for discrimination, including Mexicans.

Anti-Mexican xenophobia exploded after the Great Depression began in 1929. Mexicans throughout the West, especially in Texas, were scapegoated for the unemployment that afflicted staggering numbers of Americans. Moreover, white farmers fleeing the Dust Bowl during the 1930s suddenly introduced a new source of cheap agricultural labor, making Mexican immigrant labor unnecessary.

Such factors led President Herbert Hoover to support the Mexican repatriation movement, intended to make immigrants return to their home country. On the surface, methods of repatriation seemed benign. For example, immigrants were offered free train transportation back to Mexico, which appealed to adults who had never intended to make permanent homes in the U.S.

However, countless workers were forced to leave by many means, including firings and threats of violence. Estimates of the number of Latinos who left the U.S. during Mexican repatriation range between 500,000 and one million. Moreover, between 60 to 75 percent of deportees are believed to have been children born in the United States. Like Emilia Castaneda, they were U.S. citizens. Other Mexican Americans with longstanding family roots in the U.S. were misconstrued as immigrants and forced to leave. Such deportations were flatly illegal.

Although President Franklin Roosevelt withdrew federal support of Mexican repatriation, state and local governments continued to enforce it throughout the Great Depression. The deportation movement ended when America entered World War II and Mexican immigrant labor was again needed in the U.S.

Grasshoppers attack
As if economic depression, drought, and dust storms were not enough misery, Great Plains states saw a plague of grasshoppers unleashed on the land in the mid- to late 1930s. Pictured are corn plants chewed by grasshoppers in Montana. The infestation was caused by weather conditions. The hungry insects, according to a farmer in Nebraska, "had not only stripped their fields but had attacked their houses, eating the paint."

April 1934: The Legion of Decency is created from an effort that began when American Catholic bishops publicly asked Hollywood to stop producing films that romanticized gangsters.

May 1934: The Midwest continues to be consumed by dust storms resulting from the worst drought in U.S. history. As a result of the storms, 12 million tons of dust fall on Chicago this month.

May 23, 1934: Outlaws Bonnie Parker and Clyde Barrow, who committed murder and bank robbery in Oklahoma, Texas, and other states, are shot to death during a police ambush on a remote Louisiana road.

June 1934: The 900-seat Chicken Dinner Restaurant at Knott's Berry Farm in Buena Park, California, is begun with a 65¢ fried chicken dinner for eight served on Cordelia Knott's wedding china.

June 28, 1934: Congress enacts the Frazier Lemke Farm Bankruptcy Act, which prevents banks from foreclosing bankrupt farms. The act will be declared unconstitutional in 1935.

August 23, 1934: Al Capone is moved to Alcatraz Island along with 51 other new prisoners.

September 9, 1934: The Pico, the first drive-in theater in California, opens in Los Angeles.

November 1934: Author, Democrat, and onetime Socialist Upton Sinclair loses his bid for the governorship of California.

December 1934: According to the *Yearbook of Agriculture,* "35 million acres of formerly cultivated land have essentially been destroyed . . . 100 million acres now in crops have lost all or most of the topsoil."

Connecting San Francisco to Oakland In 1869 the first transcontinental railroad reached the east side of San Francisco Bay. This left San Francisco, on the west side of the bay, in danger of isolation. Many San Franciscans began calling for a bridge across the bay. Not until 1933 did construction on this $77-million, 8.25-mile-long structure get underway. The San Francisco-Oakland Bay Bridge, opened for traffic in 1936, consisted of two suspension bridges (*pictured*) that extended from San Francisco to Yerba Buena Island. They were followed by a tunnel through the island and then a cantilever bridge to Oakland.

FDR's adversary Oil industry millionaire Alfred Landon was a liberal Republican who supported many progressive policies. He was elected governor of Kansas in 1932, and was the only Republican governor reelected in 1934. Believing that progressivism must be practical, Alf Landon considered the New Deal wasteful and anti-business. He also thought that President Roosevelt was far too powerful for the nation's good. In 1936 Landon ran for president against Roosevelt, though he did very little campaigning. Landon carried only Maine and Vermont, receiving eight electoral votes to Roosevelt's 523—the most crushing electoral defeat in more than 110 years.

Civilian Conservation Corps

URING THE SUMMER of 1940, in California's White Mountains, a truckload of "grunts" serving in the Civilian Conservation Corps (CCC) was assigned a daunting task. They were to dig a huge "water retention pond" to satisfy the thirst of the area's herds of wild mustangs.

After a week's worth of hard work and a small rainfall, the workers—most of them teenagers—discovered to their dismay that a horse had died from drinking at the pond. Alkali deposits in the soil had poisoned the water. What was to be done with the pond? "Too much effort has been expended just to go off and leave it," the crew's foreman announced. "That would be admitting defeat." Instead, the workers used their feet to make mortar out of clay and water. They lined the pond with the mortar, sealing off the alkali and making the water safe. "I'll venture to say," mused team member Ed Braun many years later, "that that particular water hole has quaffed the thirst of several thousand mustangs and other wildlife since its creation."

This story of perseverance and ingenuity was typical of the efforts of the Civilian Conservation Corps, some-times affectionately called the "Tree Army." Possibly the most popular and successful of President Franklin Roosevelt's many New Deal programs, the CCC was created in 1933 for a two-fold purpose: to train and employ out-of-work youths, and to conserve and develop America's natural resources.

Throughout the nation, CCC members lived in camps under semimilitary discipline. They worked 40-hour weeks and earned $30 a month, $25 of which they were required to send back to their dependent families. Before the CCC was abolished in 1942 (against Roosevelt's wishes), it installed telephone and power lines, built numerous roads, fought forest fires and erosion, and planted some three billion trees.

For the program's duration, some three million young men served in the CCC. "Thank God for President Roosevelt," recalled CCC veteran Dawson H. Needham in 2001, "for his far-sighted wisdom in the creation of this marvelous work program that put many young men to work and gave them self-esteem."

CCC serves dual purpose
In his radio "fireside chat" of May 7, 1933, President Roosevelt described the federal government's new Civilian Conservation Corps as "killing two birds with one stone." It would give young men work to support their impoverished families, and it would deal with urgent environmental and infrastructure needs throughout the country especially the West. One branch of the CCC, called the Indian Emergency Conservation Work (IECW), targeted Native Americans for aid. This photograph shows IECW workers planting trees on the Nett Lake Reservation in Minnesota. During extraordinarily desperate times, the IECW employed and trained some 85,000 Native Americans.

1935: Consolidated Aircraft receives a big contract from the U.S. Army. The company will quadruple its workforce and open a plant along the Pacific Coast Highway.

1935: Author Paul Horgan publishes *No Quarter Given,* his first novel about the American West.

1935: *Tortilla Flat,* John Steinbeck's novel about Mexican Americans in the United States, is published.

1935: Laura Ingalls Wilder releases *Little House on the Prairie,* the first book in her enormously successful series about a young girl growing up on the American frontier.

January 15, 1935: The Drought Relief Service is organized to coordinate relief services for destitute Americans. The organization buys cattle from bankrupt farmers, and gives cattle fit for consumption to the Federal Surplus Relief Corporation.

April 8, 1935: The Emergency Relief Appropriation Act is signed by President Roosevelt. The act authorizes more than $500 million for drought relief and creates the Works Progress Administration, which will employ more than eight million people.

April 14, 1935: On this day, known as "Black Sunday," the Midwest is engulfed by the worst dust storm to date. Winds blow twice as much dirt as was dug to make the Panama Canal.

April 27, 1935: Congress establishes the USDA's Soil Conservation Service (SCS). By promoting farming techniques (such as crop rotation, terracing, and contour plowing) and offering financial incentives to farmers, the SCS will be able to stabilize and reverse damage to Midwest farmlands.

The Golden Gate Bridge Since the 1870s, forward thinkers had realized that San Francisco could easily become isolated and overcongested without a bridge to the north. However, the high winds and distance to span made that project seem impossible. In the 1920s, engineer Joseph Strauss became certain that he could span the Golden Gate Straight with a suspension bridge. He spent a decade drumming up support, and several more years wrangling over designs, before finally breaking ground in January 1933. Seen here is the Golden Gate Bridge under construction in July 1936. The 1.7-mile bridge was opened to traffic in May 1937—complete with suspension cables that held the roadway more than 200 feet above the water.

GOLDEN GATE ZANINESS

DONALD BRYANT, a San Francisco Junior College sprinter, was the first person across, wearing pants, sweater, and scarf against the early morning chill.... Carmen Perez and her sister Minnie were the first people to skate across.... Florentine Calegari, a houseman on strike from the Palace Hotel, was the first person to cross over on stilts; he then turned around and crossed back. Two Balboa High School girls were the first twins to cross the bridge; they were disappointed at not receiving an expected prize.... There were people who tapdanced across, a man blowing a tuba, people on unicycles and playing harmonicas. People walked backward, balanced on lines, and walked dogs and cats. Six sprinters from the *Chronicle* crossed both ways barefoot. Henry Boder, a seventy-four-year-old San Francisco man, who had crossed the Brooklyn Bridge on its opening day in 1883, now performed a comparable feat on the West Coast. A woman, apparently in physical distress, was stopped by police, who discovered that she wanted to be the first person across with her tongue out.

—AUTHOR JOHN VAN DER ZEE, DESCRIBING OPENING DAY FOR THE GOLDEN GATE BRIDGE

Faust's western pulps

"Max Brand" was one of five pseudonyms used by Frederick Schiller Faust. Faust wrote hundreds of pulp fiction tales and books, including *South of the Rio Grande* in 1936. During the '30s, he created the beloved Dr. Kildare character as well as western hero Harry Destry. Millions of readers enjoyed his formulaic novels that featured exciting tales and heroic cowboy

characters. Faust's popularity paved the way for later western novelists, such as Louis L'Amour. During World War II, Faust was killed in Italy while serving as a war correspondent.

Chinese pride Chinese Americans march in a parade in San Francisco's Chinatown, circa 1936. Boasting the world's largest Chinese population outside of China, San Francisco became the U.S. center of Chinese culture. Despite suffering broad discrimination in the 19th and early 20th centuries, California's Chinese American population thrived. Today, they continue to cherish and maintain 5,000-year-old cultural traditions, such as the Chinese New Year festival every February.

The desperate head to California The Dust Bowl drove thousands of "Okies," "Arkies," and other poor sharecroppers and tenant farmers off their land. Many headed to California in the 1930s, loading their belongings into jalopies and trucks and following U.S. Route 66 to the "Golden State." Hardship and disappointment greeted the influx of impoverished farm laborers when they reached California, including the Barnett family (*pictured*). Some towns prohibited migrants from stopping, unleashing discrimination and strife. As the new migrant workers competed for scarce jobs, wages dropped. Thousands lived in deplorable and unsanitary "ditch camps" established along irrigation canals.

Federal Art Project At its 1936 height, the WPA's Federal Art Project employed 5,000 visual artists. These artists produced 2,566 murals for state and county buildings in addition to thousands of easel paintings, photographs, sculptures, craft objects, prints, and posters, such as the one seen here. The artists also preserved antiquities and made paintings of important artifacts and architecture, such as the Spanish missions in California and New Mexico. At the Southwest Museum, Evelyn Hunt Nadeau painted watercolors recording American Indian pottery, baskets, and robes. Western artists John Steuart Curry, Thomas Hart Benton, Grant Wood, and Jackson Pollock also worked in Art Project programs.

May 11, 1935: An executive order creates the Rural Electrification Administration, which will bring electricity to millions of Americans, mostly the rural poor.

May 14, 1935: The Griffith Observatory opens its doors in Los Angeles. Opening exhibits include a Foucault pendulum, to demonstrate Earth's rotation, and planetarium shows about the solar system and the moon.

May 27, 1935: The U.S. Supreme Court rules that the National Recovery Administration is unconstitutional.

July 1935: Congress passes the Wagner Act, also known as the National Labor Relations Act, which guarantees the right for private sector employees to engage in collective bargaining and form labor unions.

August 14, 1935: The Social Security Act is signed into law. It establishes the Social Security Administration to administer a public, taxpayer-supported pension plan for older and disabled Americans.

September 30, 1935: Hoover Dam, the massive public works project on the Arizona-Nevada border, fires up its first generator. Sixteen more will be added over the next few decades.

1936: The Rural Electrification Administration begins to construct an electrical infrastructure in order to run electricity to rural Montana families.

1936: Dorothea Lange snaps her unforgettable photograph, *Migrant Mother,* at a pea-pickers camp in California.

1936: *The Plow That Broke the Plains,* a documentary film by Pare Lorentz, is released. It explains how the massive plowing of millions of acres of grassland led to the Dust Bowl.

Relief for the poor Men stand in line in 1937 to receive relief checks in Calipatria, California, located in the Imperial Valley a few miles from the Mexican border. The Social Security Act of 1935 helped millions of unemployed American workers. Widows, orphans, and out-of-work citizens began receiving small monthly relief checks. While insufficient to fully solve economic woes, the Social Security program significantly improved conditions for unemployed Americans, and helped restore hope during the dismal years of the Great Depression.

Flying with TWA A stewardess prepares to welcome passengers aboard a TWA airliner. TWA originated as Western Air Express, which introduced airline service between Los Angeles and Salt Lake City in 1926. In 1930 Western Air Express merged with Transcontinental Air Transport, which had already connected New York City and Los Angeles by combining air and train service across the continent. During the year of the merger, the newly named Transcontinental & Western Air linked the two coasts by air travel alone. In 1939 Howard Hughes purchased T&WA and began expanding its service throughout the world. In 1950 the company was appropriately renamed Trans World Airlines (TWA).

Curry's views of Kansas John Steuart Curry painted images of his native Kansas, as seen in *The Homestead and the Building of the Barbed Wire Fences* (*pictured*). Curry was a Regionalist painter who focused on rural midwestern subjects. In 1937 he was commissioned by the WPA to paint murals in the Kansas State House. He depicted Spanish explorer Coronado, abolitionist John Brown, a tornado, and a prairie fire, along with more pastoral scenes. Some felt that Curry was showing the worst side of Kansas. He was not allowed to finish his State House murals as he wanted, and refused to sign them.

The "Miracle Mile" In the early 1920s, developer A. W. Ross saw potential in Wilshire Boulevard, an unpaved Los Angeles road that ran through pastures and farmlands. Ross envisioned a new kind of commercial district, one designed for automobile traffic rather than for pedestrians. His plan included the first timed traffic lights in the nation, dedicated left-turn lanes, simple signs that could be read from moving cars, and large parking lots. This photograph shows the intersection of Western Avenue and Wilshire Boulevard in 1938, after Ross's vision became reality. The entire area was dubbed the "Miracle Mile" for its incredible commercial success.

Boeing's airliners In 1916 William Boeing and George Conrad Westervelt founded what became known as the Boeing Airplane Company (today's Boeing Company). Based in Seattle, the company pioneered the manufacture of airliners. In 1938 the Boeing Model 314 Clipper, a massive "flying boat," made transoceanic commercial travel possible. The same year, Boeing produced the Model 307 Stratoliner, the first airliner with a pressurized cabin. Shown here having its seams tested by Boeing workmen, the Stratoliner could cruise above most weather problems. In 1935 Boeing introduced the B-17 Flying Fortress, a bomber widely used during World War II.

Hollywood misfits Nathanael West, a transplanted New Yorker, wrote this scathing novel about the underside of Hollywood life in 1939. Populated with misfits in search of fame and fortune in not-so-sunny California, the novel ends with a mad, anarchic riot. *The Day of The Locust* illustrates the hollowness, amorality, lust, and despair that coexisted with the fabulously rich lifestyle of glamorous stars in Hollywood in the late Depression era. Oddly, West died in a car crash in 1940 while hurrying to novelist F. Scott Fitzgerald's funeral. Fitzgerald had touched on similar themes, albeit on the East Coast, in *The Great Gatsby*.

Dams and Bridges

By the time Los Angeles completed its 200-mile aqueduct in 1913 and the United States finished work on the Panama Canal in 1914, Americans were thinking big about other possibilities. The fast-growing western states were especially in need of infrastructure improvements. The idea of addressing public needs through huge public works programs took hold well before the Great Depression made job creation so urgent. By 1919 San Francisco was exploring the possibility of building a bridge across the Golden Gate Strait. By 1922 President Herbert Hoover was meeting with state governors of Arizona, California, Colorado, Nevada, New Mexico, Utah, and Wyoming to discuss building a dam on the Colorado River.

The Colorado River project aimed to control periodic floods, expand irrigated farming, generate electricity, and provide water for Los Angeles and other dry communities in Southern California. Construction on the dam, known as both the Boulder Dam and the Hoover Dam, began in 1930.

President Franklin Roosevelt's New Deal program would create scores of dams, locks, and reservoirs on other rivers. Montana's Fort Peck Dam on the Missouri River—authorized in 1933 for flood control, water quality management, and the generation of hydroelectric power—was completed in 1940. On the Mississippi River,

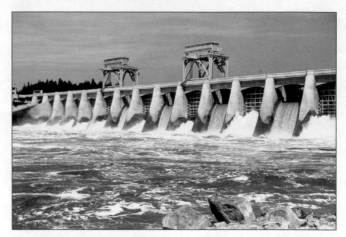

Bonneville Dam in Oregon

a series of locks and dams was designed to control flooding and keep an open channel for barge traffic.

With millions of cars on the roads, Americans demanded public works projects—such as bridges, tunnels, and freeways—to make private transportation more convenient. In 1933 construction began on a bridge to connect Oakland and San Francisco, and the Bay Bridge was opened to traffic in 1936. During the same period, voters in San Francisco and five surrounding counties put up their properties (homes, farms, and businesses) as collateral on a bond issue that financed the Golden Gate Bridge, which opened in 1937.

The Hoover/Boulder Dam From 1931 to '36, workers constructed the Hoover Dam on the Colorado River along the Arizona-Nevada border. More than 700 feet tall, 1,200 feet long, and 600 feet thick at the base, the dam at peak times generates more than 2,000 megawatts of electricity, and impounds 110-mile-long Lake Mead. In 1931 Congress named it Hoover Dam, honoring then-president Herbert Hoover. Franklin Roosevelt won the presidency in 1932, and his secretary of interior, Harold Ickes, unofficially—but effectively—changed the name to Boulder Dam. In 1947, two years after Roosevelt died, Congress passed a bill to restore Hoover's name, and President Harry Truman signed the bill into law.

Putting writers to work The Federal Writers' Project, established in 1935 under the WPA, provided financial support for 6,600 authors, editors, and researchers. The writers produced local histories, life stories, children's books, and nature studies, such as *Birds of the World*. Best known are the project's guides to U.S. states, territories, and significant places, such as California's Death Valley. Author Vardis Fisher developed several publications about Idaho, produced several novels, and served as director of the Idaho Writers' Project—all for an annual salary of $2,300. Other western writers included Utah historian Juanita Brooks, Los Angeles poet Arna Wendell Bontemps, and San Francisco poet and critic Kenneth Rexroth.

The controversial FSA The 1937 Farm Security Administration and its 1935 predecessor, the Resettlement Administration, were among the most controversial programs of President Roosevelt's New Deal. Designed to relieve farmers suffering from the Great Depression and the Dust Bowl, the RA and the FSA were sharply criticized for their "farmsteads"—cooperative homesteads in the West. New Deal opponents denounced farmsteads as imitations of Soviet-style collective farming. To counter such attacks, the FSA hired prestigious photographers to document the lives of farmers. The resulting vast collection includes this 1938 photograph by Dorothea Lange of a tenant couple applying for federal aid.

Teenage hobos Two teenage boys prepare to jump a freight train. During the height of the Depression, a quarter-million American teenagers lived a homeless existence. Train-hopping carried many youth to new jobs and new lives. Some became "professional hobos" who moved from one freight-yard "hobo jungle" to another. Young hobos jumped trains throughout the West, finding temporary work on farms and camping in remote freight yards, where they dodged railroad "bulls" (who policed the trains) and other law enforcement officials.

GNAWING HUNGER

I AM SENDING YOU a plea for the dirty bunch, we are getting tired of being so termed....

We do not dare to use even a little soap when it will pay for an extra egg a few more carrots for our children, pale and wobegone they look but dear to our hearts, dearer because of their helpless, needless, suffering.

Smoking their imported cig. that cost more for one day than growing children are allowed a month, how can these men and women that decree how much we eat, know the sacrifice of parents trying to get 21 meals out of 75¢.... Oh what can they know what it means for a mother to hear her hungry babe whimpering in the night and growing children tossing in their sleep because of knawing plain HUNGER.

—A LETTER SIGNED "UNWASHED, OREGON," TO FIRST LADY ELEANOR ROOSEVELT, FEBRUARY 28, 1935

February 1936: The American Civil Liberties Union sues Los Angeles after the city police chief admits to sending patrols to the state's borders to turn away "undesirables."

November 12, 1936: Traffic opens on the Bay Bridge, which links San Francisco and Oakland via Yerba Buena Island.

1937: President Roosevelt's proposed Shelterbelt Project gets underway. Workers plant vast numbers of native trees in a belt from Canada to northern Texas in a effort to protect farmland from erosion and stabilize the topsoil.

1937: *Of Mice and Men,* a classic California novel by John Steinbeck, is published.

1937: Editor Ray B. West begins publishing his *Intermountain Review,* which will subsequently be renamed *Rocky Mountain Review* and *Western Review.*

March 18, 1937: Due to a gas leak, a school blows up in New London, Texas, killing nearly 300 people.

May 28, 1937: The Golden Gate Bridge, spanning the mouth of San Francisco Bay, opens to vehicular traffic at noon.

June 24, 1937: Californian Richard Archbold makes the first transcontinental seaplane flight, traveling to New York City in a Convair-built craft.

1938: Ansel Adams publishes a volume of his best images in *Sierra Nevada: The John Muir Trail.*

January 1938: The first national unemployment census reveals that 7.8 million American workers are officially unemployed, although the actual number could be higher than 10 million. Total employment is estimated at 44 million.

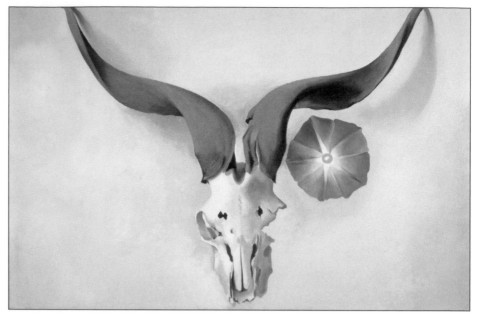

O'Keeffe's love of the desert In 1929 New York artist Georgia O'Keeffe vacationed in Taos, New Mexico. Although she was already famous for her close-up images of flowers, O'Keeffe found exciting new images in the desert. She collected and painted bleached white bones, sometimes along with flowers, as in *Ram's Head, Blue Morning Glory* (*pictured*). "I have used these things to say what is to me the wideness and wonder of the world as I live in it," she wrote. O'Keeffe returned to the desert every summer to paint, and in 1946 she became a full-time resident of New Mexico.

U.S. supports Japanese aggression At this rally on December 20, 1938, Chinese Americans in San Francisco protest the sale of scrap iron from the United States to Japan. As it expanded its Asian empire, Japan waged war against China throughout the 1930s. Lacking substantial iron deposits, Japan needed to buy iron to support industrial and military growth. Due to appeasement policies and fears that Communists would dominate China, the U.S. continued selling iron to Japan until shortly before the 1941 attack on Pearl Harbor. Chinese immigrants in California deplored Japan's ruthless Asian policies for several years before World War II began.

Experimental photographer In 1926 photographer Edward Weston moved to California and shot a series of natural forms and landscapes. Especially well received was a series of close-ups of natural objects that ranged from seashells to halved cabbages. In the 1930s, he shot experimental photographs of nudes and sand dunes near Point Lobos, which became his most famous works. This photo is of California's Oceano Dunes. After his death in 1958, Weston's ashes were scattered over the Pacific Ocean.

Mount Rushmore In 1923 South Dakota historian Doane Robinson began stumping for a state-sponsored stone memorial to American heroes. A year later, renowned sculptor Gutzon Borglum began work on the granite face of Mount Rushmore. Out-of-work miners blasted and drilled the cliff to rough out Borglum's massive visages of presidents Washington, Jefferson, Lincoln (*pictured*), and Theodore Roosevelt. Work continued intermittently from 1927 until Borglum's death in 1941. No workers died on the project, which cost $990,000. More than two million people visit the monument each year.

Shelterbelts protect the crops Shelterbelts, long rows of trees and shrubs planted in prairie states, helped control wind erosion, which had devastated farms during the Dust Bowl era. In 1935 a New Deal agency, the Soil Conservation Service, began persuading farmers to implement prairie-grass restoration projects, and to plant rows of hardy native trees as windbreaks. By 1938 the Great Plains states boasted almost 80 million trees in shelterbelts, some of which remain in place today.

Paving the Los Angeles River Construction laborers work on a bridge that spans a section of the Los Angeles River, which had been artificially "channelized" with cement in the late 1930s. A devastating flood on the river in 1938 had caused millions of dollars in damage and roughly 100 deaths. Engineers discovered that the few portions of the river that had previously been channelized suffered the least damage, so much of the rest of the waterway underwent a similar process. The "paving of the Los Angeles River" infuriated many environmentalists, not to mention some landowners who had hoped to develop the riverbank areas.

California's atheist governor Culbert Olson, governor of California from 1939 to '43, was one of the few atheists ever elected to high political office in the United States. Although he did not publicly profess atheism—he called his philosophy "secularism"—he had rejected his Mormon faith at a young age. When he took the oath of office in 1939, he refused to say "so help me God," noting to the Supreme Court justice who swore him in that "God couldn't help me at all [since] there isn't any such person." Olson lost his bid for reelection in 1942.

The Grapes of Wrath John Steinbeck often wrote about the hardships of working-class people during the Great Depression. His Pulitzer Prize-winning 1939 novel, *The Grapes of Wrath,* weaves a tale of the Joad family. The Joads are driven from their Oklahoma home by financial crisis and dust storms. They lose two elderly family members while crossing the desert in their beat-up car, then face mistreatment in a job-poor California. A somewhat less bleak 1940 movie version of *The Grapes of Wrath* starred Henry Fonda and was directed by John Ford. In 1962 Steinbeck won the Nobel Prize for Literature.

The struggle to adjust A South Dakota family on the road to California seeks work in 1939. Impoverished and often ill-educated, such families faced many adversities on the road and after they arrived in California. Of course, finding work, shelter, and food were the primary concerns. In addition, Midwesterners from conservative, religious families struggled to adjust to their new, more progressive communities. Many migrants remained in the Golden State, and in time they contributed to California's evolving social, cultural, and political life.

Dryland farming Midwestern and southwestern farmers developed dryland agricultural techniques to make the best use of whatever moisture was available. Deep planting allowed roots to reach subsoil moisture. Turning the soil quickly after rainfalls held moisture beneath a mulch. Leaving strips of lands fallow allowed those areas to store moisture for planting the following year. Crops were chosen for quick growth and drought resistance. By the 1920s, dryland farming methods were in wide use on the Great Plains. If a water source was available, farmers in dryer areas relied on row-crop irrigation, as seen on this farm in Yuma, Arizona.

Filipino immigration Filipino farmworkers cut and load lettuce in Imperial Valley, California. Filipino immigration did not begin on a large scale until after the Spanish-American War, and even then most of the early arrivals were students. But in the 1920s, large waves of working-class immigrants arrived from the Philippines. The Filipino population in the U.S. grew from 5,603 in 1920 to 45,208 in 1930. Almost all settled in the West, and most were agricultural workers. Although legally able to immigrate, unlike the Chinese and Japanese, Filipinos faced significant hostility. They were forced to use segregated facilities, such as restrooms, and were the subjects of anti-miscegenation laws in California and other states.

Immigration and deportation During labor shortages caused by World War I, some 125,000 Mexicans entered the U.S. legally, most of them to work on western farms. After the war, there was a xenophobic backlash against the growing number of Mexican immigrants. During the Great Depression, staggering numbers of Mexicans and American citizens of Mexican descent were deported from the U.S. Those who remained, like the migrants shown here working in a Texas cotton field in 1939, endured discrimination, poor wages, and appalling working conditions. Their efforts to organize, while largely futile during the Depression, paved the way for a powerful migrant rights movement.

Stagecoach The 1939 release of *Stagecoach* finally established the western as a significant genre of the sound era. Directed with great visual style by John Ford (including spectacular outdoor scenes at Utah's Monument Valley), the film featured a stellar ensemble cast in vivid roles. *Stagecoach* boosted the career of a young, little-known "B" movie actor named John Wayne, who would go on to define the western hero. The movie told the story of a troubled group of stagecoach passengers wending their way through hostile Indian territory. It was nominated for seven Academy Awards.

Hard times for Natives Few Americans were worse off than Native Americans during the Great Depression. By the late 1930s, as national conditions began to improve, the majority of Indians still lived in poverty on isolated reservations. Subjected to legal discrimination and racially based mistreatment, Natives faced many challenges. However, thanks to the "Indian New Deal," Native life gradually improved after 1934. Despite discriminatory signs such as this one in a tavern near the Sisseton Reservation in South Dakota, Native Americans began establishing tribal governments and developing economic programs on reservations.

1939: The military buildup associated with the threat of war in Europe, combined with the end of the drought, begins to pull the United States out of the Great Depression.

1939: John Steinbeck is awarded the Pulitzer Prize for *The Grapes of Wrath,* his novel about a family struggling in the Oklahoma Dust Bowl. John Ford's film version of the book will be released in 1940 and will garner an Academy Award for best picture.

1939: *Apache Gold and Yaqui Silver* by J. Frank Dobie wins the first-ever Texas Institute of Letters Award for best book by a Texan.

1939: Radio evangelism reaches the mainstream with the broadcast of Charles Fuller's *Old-Fashioned Gospel Hour* on some 150 stations nationwide.

1939: Stanford graduates Bill Hewlett and Dave Packard found the Hewlett-Packard Company in a garage in Palo Alto, California.

February 15, 1939: The classic western *Stagecoach,* directed by John Ford and starring John Wayne, is released.

July 6, 1939: Richard Archbold, Steve Barinka, and Russell Rogers return to California after becoming the first people to complete an around-the-world equatorial seaplane flight.

September 1, 1939: World War II begins in Europe with the German invasion of Poland.

October 27, 1939: A motion to amend the U.S. Neutrality Act to allow the sale of arms to besieged allies passes the Senate, and will clear the House on November 4. As a result, millions of Americans—including large numbers in the West—will begin jobs in war materiel factories.

REA brings power to farms These electric meters were installed on U.S. farms. The Rural Electrification Administration was one of the most successful New Deal reforms, as the agency lent millions of dollars to rural cooperatives that were run by groups of farmers. The money could be used to construct and operate generating plants, transmission lines, and distribution lines that would bring electric power to many American farms. In 1944 Congress contributed further to rural electrification by passing an act that stabilized low interest rates and extended the loan repayment period.

Tons of timber This Alfred Eisenstaedt photograph depicts the enormous output of the Seattle Cedar Lumber Manufacturing Company in 1939. Pacific Northwest timber first became important during California's Gold Rush, and remained significant throughout the 20th century. Oregon, Washington, and Northern California produced immense timber harvests, with substantial portions of the product sold to Japan. In May 1958, a fire consumed millions of board feet of cedar and destroyed several of the company's facilities in the Seattle suburb of Ballard.

Electricity on the Farms

BEFORE THEY HAD electricity, farmers spent as many as 63 days of work time each year simply hauling water to their farms. Water for washing and cooking was carried into the house and heated on a wood-burning stove that had to be constantly tended to and replenished with fuel. To iron clothes, women kept heavy metal flatirons heating on those stoves. In the summer, women labored over their wood-burning stoves to prepare fruits and vegetables for canning. Because kerosene lamps produced weak light, few adults read much. Without radios, people knew little about the outside world.

In 1935 only 10 percent of America's farms had electricity. Although cities were electrified, running lines to every individual farm seemed impossible—and the companies that held monopolies on the marketing of electricity were not interested in the idea. President Franklin Roosevelt, a believer in public utilities, decided to change all that.

In 1936 the Rural Electrification Act provided loans to rural cooperatives, making it possible for farmers to get electric power at relatively low rates. In 1929 the Bureau of Reclamation undertook major electricity-producing engineering projects, such as the Hoover Dam in Nevada and Arizona and the Grand Coulee Dam in the state of Washington. About one-third of farms were electrified by 1940, and about 90 percent received electricity by 1950. Some farms in Nebraska and thinly populated areas in other states had to wait several more years for electric service.

With electricity, farm families could run radios, and they could use artificial lighting for reading or to extend their work hours. They could utilize the same electric irons, clothes washers, and other household appliances that city people used. For the first time, a farmer could milk more than one cow at a time with a milking machine. He or she could take care of other jobs while the milk was being processed in an electric cream separator. All the while, an electric pump sent water flowing into the farmer's own home.

A western "quack" John Brinkley was one of America's most famous medical "quacks." Dr. Brinkley claimed he could remedy male impotence by implanting portions of a male goat's testicle in a patient. In 1923 Brinkley created the first radio station in Kansas and pitched his "therapy" over the airwaves. After opposition from radio competitors and local politicians, Brinkley relocated to Del Rio, Texas, and in 1931 built a powerful radio facility in Mexico. He continued broadcasting "medical" advertisements, along with cowboy music and political chat, until 1939, when the U.S. and Mexican governments nabbed him for tax evasion and other violations.

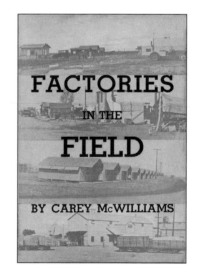

Factory farm exposé In *Factories in the Field* (1939), California writer Carey McWilliams documented the deplorable working and living conditions of low-paid farm laborers. Published just two months after John Steinbeck's blockbuster fictionalized work, *The Grapes of Wrath,* McWilliams's book included journalistic documentary prose to portray the plight of workers employed on vast corporate farms. Comparing corporate farm workers to factory workers, McWilliams argued that only unionization and collective bargaining could improve their conditions and prevent ruthless exploitation.

FACTORIES
IN THE
FIELD
BY CAREY McWILLIAMS

The West Goes to War
∽ 1940-1949 ∽

THE SECOND WORLD WAR utterly transformed the American West. In fact, it would be virtually impossible to find a corner of the West not affected by wartime mobilization. Military personnel trained in the West in huge numbers. Western factories—some brand new, others retrofitted by the war's demands—pumped out planes, tanks, and ships by the hundreds of thousands. Americans from other parts of the nation streamed westward in search of good wartime jobs. The West was a different place after the war than before, and Westerners themselves were different, too.

In his groundbreaking 1985 book, *The American West Transformed: The Impact of the Second World War,* historian Gerald Nash daringly proposed that the closing of the frontier during the 1890s had less impact upon the West than events in the 20th century. According to what has become known as the "Nash thesis," the greatest expansion and transformation of the American West took place not during westward expansion or the "cowboy and Indian" era, but rather in the 20th century and especially during World War II. "In four short years," wrote Nash, "the war brought a maturation to the West that in peacetime might have taken generations to accomplish."

After the 1941 Japanese attack on Pearl Harbor, the West became essential to the war effort because of its wide-open spaces (most of them already

Workers at the Lockheed plant in Burbank, California, construct a B-17 Flying Fortress. The planes, tanks, and ships that Westerners built helped the Allies crush Germany and subdue Japan.

"[I]t could be said that the entire American West
became a giant boom town in the World War II era."

—Historian Gerald Nash

owned by the federal government), abundant natural resources, and already-thriving industries. Important, too, was the West Coast's proximity to the Pacific Theater of the war. Western states quickly became dotted with military bases, supply depots, and training camps, while mining and manufacturing soared throughout the region. Products ranged from raw materials—including synthetic rubber, aluminum, steel, and magnesium—to state-of-the-art technologies and weaponry.

Shipbuilding thrived in Northern California, while the aircraft industry dominated Southern California. During the four years of war, the federal government spent an estimated $40 billion in the West as a major part of the national war effort. What the New Deal era had initiated—giant federal projects enacted in western settings—the Second World War greatly expanded upon.

Such developments brought a huge migration to western states. As populations grew, so did service industries, including banks, restaurants, health care services, and schools. Western cities and their partners in the federal government and the defense industries struggled to provide enough housing and services for the newly-arrived. Moreover, the expansion of western urban areas led to an increase in racial and ethnic diversity, marked by an especially rapid growth in the numbers of Native Americans and people of Mexican and African descent. Such groups experienced new opportunities in western cities, as well as the age-old effects of bigotry and discrimination.

J. Robert Oppenheimer headed the team of scientists that worked in Los Alamos, New Mexico, to develop the atomic bomb. Their goal was realized on July 16, 1945, when the first A-bomb was detonated in Alamogordo, New Mexico.

Perhaps most strikingly, the wartime West suddenly became a center of scientific research, much of it federally funded and military in nature. In Southern California, engineers and scientists at such institutions as the California Institute of Technology and the Jet Propulsion Laboratory studied and manufactured rocketry. The Scripps Institute of Oceanography in La Jolla, California, examined ocean currents, while a laboratory in San Diego specialized in submarine detection and underwater operations. The Lawrence Berkeley National Laboratory became one of several western centers for nuclear research, along with such places as the Hanford Engineer Works in the state of Washington. Other western institutions studied radar, electronics, aerodynamics, and torpedoes. Also during these years, the most extraordinary gathering of scientists in human history secretly assembled at the "science city" of Los Alamos, New Mexico, to produce the atomic bomb.

Even psychiatry experienced a boom, as many European intellectuals fled Nazi persecution and settled in the American West, forming the basis of the Topeka Institute and the San Francisco Psychoanalytic Institute. The influx of Old World intellectuals and artists also affected cultural affairs, especially in Los Angeles. L.A. welcomed prestigious authors, composers, directors, designers, and actors into the entertainment industry. For its part, Hollywood embraced wartime opportunities to aid the efforts of the United States and its allies. The government recognized that the motion picture industry had the potential to shape public opinion across the nation and the world. The federal Office of War Information aggressively lobbied filmmakers and the film community to include wartime propaganda in Hollywood movies, and Hollywood responded accordingly.

An American battleship goes down in Pearl Harbor, Hawaii, on December 7, 1941. The Japanese aerial assault killed more than 2,300 military personnel and prompted the U.S. to declare war on Japan the following day.

The wartime transformation of the American West ran much deeper than shifts in population and industry. Westerners experienced nothing less than an altered sense of identity. They no longer felt like colonial outsiders in American culture, but saw themselves as playing an essential role in the present and future of a burgeoning superpower.

It cannot be said, however, that the war's effects on the West and Westerners were without a dark side. In the far West, a federal order signed in the wake of the attack on Pearl Harbor forced the evacuation of people of Japanese descent from the Pacific Coast because they ostensibly represented a threat to national security. Torn from their homes, jobs, and friends, about 120,000 people, most of them U.S. citizens, were sent to internment camps (mostly in the interior and desert West), where they languished for several years before being allowed to leave. Dillon Myer, director of the "relocation" of Japanese and Japanese Americans, called internment "the greatest involuntary migration in the history of the United States." Nearly 50 years later, the United States issued an apology to the internees and authorized the payment of reparations to internees or their families.

1940: *Melody Ranch,* featuring America's favorite singing cowboy, Gene Autry, premieres on the radio.

March 4, 1940: California's Kings Canyon is designated a national park.

Spring 1940: The U.S. Navy's Pacific Fleet transfers its home base to Pearl Harbor, on the Hawaiian Island of Oahu.

June 29, 1940: The Smith Act is passed, making an attempted overthrow or plotting to overthrow the U.S. government a federal offense.

September 6, 1940: The Selective Training and Service Act is passed, requiring all young men ages 21 to 36 to register for the military draft. The draft age will be lowered to 18 in November 1942.

1941: Potato processing giant and agribusiness pioneer J. R. Simplot opens a potato-dehydration plant in Caldwell, Idaho.

1941: The Southern Pacific Railroad draws protests by the League of United Latin American Citizens for failing to offer skilled apprenticeships to Mexican Americans.

1941: The San Diego Naval Air Station welcomes the first of 31,000 U.S. Army Air Corps pilots it will train during the course of World War II.

1941: Robert Oscar Peterson, future founder of Jack in the Box, establishes Oscar's, his first drive-in restaurant, in San Diego.

1941: Nellis Air Force Base, near Las Vegas, is established as a U.S. Army Air Corps gunnery school.

1941: The development of the Las Vegas Strip as we know it today begins with the opening of the El Rancho Vegas resort hotel and casino.

Boom time for Colorado A Colorado farmer hauls peaches to market in 1940. The decade turned out to be a fruitful one for the Centennial State. World War II ignited a surge in agriculture, while new military installations also spurred the state's economy. In addition, a scientific-research industrial-military community emerged in Colorado after the war. A uranium rush in the late 1940s and an increase in higher education enrollments generated by the GI Bill also added to Colorado's boom. Finally, postwar prosperity nationwide led to a rise in tourism in the state's glorious mountain areas.

Laborers flock to Oakland Oakland, California, on the eastern shore of San Francisco Bay, became a major rail terminus in the late 19th century. After the 1906 San Francisco earthquake and fire, refugees doubled Oakland's population, and by 1920 the city was an industrial center. During World War II, naval shipbuilding jobs attracted laborers from other parts of the country. Many were African Americans from Texas, Louisiana, Oklahoma, and Arkansas. In this photograph, an integrated crowd appears for a free Thanksgiving dinner at Oakland's Ringside Bar. After the war, shipbuilding and other industrial jobs declined, and Oakland's prosperity waned.

Black Migration to the West

IN THE EARLY 1940s, poverty, racial discrimination, and the lack of opportunities drove large numbers of African Americans to move out of the South. As in earlier black migrations, many moved to northern cities. This time, however, others headed westward, swelling the black populations of cities such as Los Angeles, San Francisco, and Oakland. From 1940 to 1945, the African American population in the West grew from 171,000 to 620,000.

Even before World War II erupted, African American leaders had been pushing for the integration of work forces. In California's aircraft industry, for example, very few workers were black and most of them were janitors. In 1941, faced with the probability of a public African American protest, President Roosevelt issued an executive order banning discrimination in defense industries and government based on "race, creed, color, or national origin." Even though the immediate effect of Roosevelt's order was limited, it did open up some new possibilities for minorities.

As the war progressed, West Coast shipyards, aircraft plants, and other defense industries were in serious need of more workers. In the West, African Americans still faced discrimination and segregation, but they also found opportunities for job training and for employment as skilled workers. As that news spread, more black workers moved westward. From 1942 through '45, some 340,000 African Americans settled in California.

The Ox-Bow Incident In classic stories of the Old West, a hero often must take the law into his own hands against bad men—normally with commendable results. In *The Ox-Bow Incident* (1940), author Walter Van Tilburg Clark turns this morally simple, audience-pleasing formula inside out. Set in 1885, the story tells of a deputized posse's pursuit of cattle rustlers. The posse catches and brutally lynches three men, who are later proved innocent of the crime. The novel was turned into a low-budget but highly respected 1943 film, which was directed by William Wellman and starred Henry Fonda.

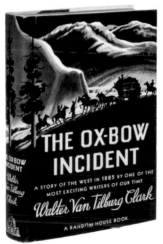

Cowboys test skills in rodeos After the big cattle drives ended, cowboys used their skills and supplemented their incomes in "cowboy competitions." These became known as *rodeos*, Spanish for roundups. In such towns as Cheyenne, Wyoming, and Prescott, Arizona, the annual rodeo soon became the highlight of the year. Professional cowboys competed in bareback riding, steer wrestling, team roping, saddle bronc riding, calf roping, barrel racing, and bull riding. In 1945 the Cowboy Turtles organization changed its name to the Rodeo Cowboys Association and set the standards for modern rodeos.

March 1941: Congress passes the Lend Lease Act, authorizing President Franklin Roosevelt to offer material support to U.S. allies in Europe without violating America's official position of neutrality.

Mid-March 1941: A ferocious blizzard in the Red River Valley claims 90 lives. The death toll is 39 in North Dakota alone.

March 28, 1941: U.S. government researchers ascertain that plutonium is fissionable and can be used in the manufacture of massively destructive bombs.

June 9, 1941: President Franklin Roosevelt signs an executive order that authorizes and directs the secretary of war to take possession of and operate the Inglewood (California) plant of North American Aviation, Inc. The intent of the order is to prevent a strike by union employees from crippling aircraft production.

June 25, 1941: President Roosevelt puts some muscle behind the Fair Employment Practices Committee by signing Executive Order 8802, which prohibits racial discrimination in federal hiring procedures.

August 14, 1941: President Roosevelt and British Prime Minister Winston Churchill issue the Atlantic Charter, a joint declaration of their mutual goals for the postwar world.

December 7, 1941: Japanese warplanes attack the U.S. Navy's Pacific Fleet at Pearl Harbor, Hawaii, triggering America's entrance into World War II.

December 8, 1941: The United States declares war against Japan. The American West will become the staging ground for the World War II Pacific Theater.

Mealtime A family sits down for a meal in Pie Town, New Mexico, in 1940. Rural Westerners ate essentially simple fare in the 1940s, with some regional variations: Green chilies were almost a staple in New Mexico, while a salsa craze hit San Antonio in 1947. As the jars on the table indicate, most rural families in the West still relied heavily on home canning, which was far cheaper than buying commercial products.

Agricultural revolution Because of their lower yields, farms in the drier regions of the Midwest and West had to be larger than in other areas. This made farms in the Heartland hard to plow and harvest with traditional animals. The increasing sophistication of farm machinery, including the truck and combine harvester shown in this 1941 photograph of Washington's Walla Walla County, characterized what has been described as a "second American agricultural revolution." By 1954 the number of tractors on American farms finally exceeded the number of horses and mules.

Attack on Pearl Harbor On December 7, 1941, 360 Japanese aircraft launched a devastating attack on Pearl Harbor, a U.S. naval base in Hawaii. The assault sank or damaged eight battleships, including the one pictured here in flames (*above*) and the USS *Arizona*, shown here as a tangled hulk (*top right*). Many smaller vessels were also hit, as were 160 U.S. airplanes on the ground. More than 2,300 Americans died, and more than 1,000 were wounded. Ironically, a message that warned of the likely outbreak of war arrived too late to put the base on red alert. The attack galvanized American opinion and led President Roosevelt on December 8 to ask Congress for a declaration of war.

Big changes in small towns Cascade, Idaho, seen here in 1941, was typical of many small towns in the Midwest and West. In the early 20th century, electricity reached these towns in an irregular pattern, depending at first on private utility companies and later on federal New Deal programs. At the same time, local governments built better streets and installed sewer systems. These amenities improved the quality of small-town life, but people had to earn more money to pay for them. By midcentury, better cars and roads meant that consumers had a wider range of places to shop, which began to hurt some small-town economies.

Chinese Americans embraced as allies In Oakland's Chinatown, the Japanese American Masuda family placed this banner across its grocery store the day after the Pearl Harbor attack. Proclaiming themselves Americans did not save the Masudas from internment. Their Chinese American neighbors, however, experienced a different change of fortune. After a century of vilification and segregation, they suddenly found themselves embraced as allies in the war against Japan. The Chinese Exclusion Act of 1882, which had barred Chinese immigration, was repealed in 1943, and jobs and opportunities that had long been closed suddenly opened for Chinese Americans. Many served in the military during the war, while others raised money for the Red Cross, sold war bonds, and participated in scrap metal drives.

1940-1949

December 11, 1941: Germany and Italy, the other two Axis powers, declare war on the United States, drawing the U.S. into the European Theater of World War II.

1942: A bumper wheat crop finally restores prosperity to the Northern Plains, following more than a decade of economic depression and drought.

1942: The Japanese conquer the Commonwealth of the Philippines, a territory under the control of the U.S.

1942: The U.S. Navy acquires the land to establish the Camp Pendleton Marine base, on the 126,000-acre Rancho Santa Margarita in Southern California.

1942: The Columbia River's 24-turbine Grand Coulee Dam is completed. Eventually, it will irrigate 500,000 acres in Washington State and bring electricity to 11 states.

1942: Japanese forces bomb Alaska's Dutch Harbor and invade the Aleutian Islands.

February 19, 1942: President Roosevelt signs Executive Order 9066, officially authorizing the internment of, ultimately, some 100,000 Japanese Americans during World War II, as well as some 20,000 Japanese nationals.

April 11, 1942: Construction begins on the Alaska–Canada Military Highway, from Dawson Creek, British Columbia, to Delta Junction, Alaska.

August 4, 1942: The Bracero Program, which will permit the issuance of temporary agricultural work permits to Mexican nationals, is instituted by the U.S. and Mexican governments.

August 7, 1942: U.S. Marines land on the Pacific island of Guadalcanal for what will be one of the pivotal battles of the World War II Pacific Theater.

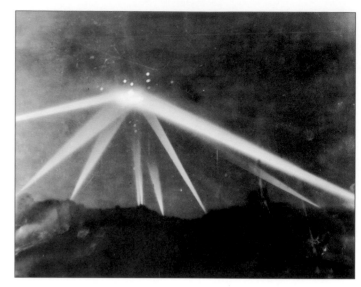

"Battle of Los Angeles" Spotlights and antiaircraft fire appear over Los Angeles in February 1942. In the early morning hours of the 25th, a mysterious object was picked up by radar 120 miles west of the city. Gun batteries again went on alert and a blackout was instituted. Dozens of people called authorities to report enemy planes. When a balloon carrying a red flare was sighted over Santa Monica, American antiaircraft weapons opened fire, whereupon, according to one observer, "the air over Los Angeles erupted like a volcano." Experts disagree over whether the object was an American weather balloon or a Japanese fire balloon. Such was the "Battle of Los Angeles."

Massive steel mill In November 1941, while concerned that a West Coast invasion or an attack on the Panama Canal might cause steel shortages in the West, the U.S. government financed a $200 million steel mill. The government located Geneva Steel in Utah near raw materials, railroads, highways, and air service, and far enough inland to be safe from invasion. After the Japanese attack on Pearl Harbor, excavations (seen in this 1942 photograph) and building continued day and night with the manpower of 10,000 construction workers. The Geneva plant opened in December 1944. This and other defense spending in Utah rejuvenated the state's economy.

Japan attacks the West Coast Although Japanese attacks on the continental U.S. were rare during World War II, they put Westerners on edge. Attacks sometimes came by submarine, as in the incidents pictured here. Above, U.S. soldiers examine damage to a pier from such an attack on the Ellwood oil field and refinery near Santa Barbara, California, in February 1942. A similar attack occurred near Astoria, Oregon (*above right*), in June of that year, as a shell fell harmlessly in a field at Fort Stevens. The Japanese also launched more than 9,000 bomb-carrying balloons, some 300 of which landed on the U.S. and Canada. The only casualties from those attacks occurred when a woman and five children died in Oregon when they attempted to move a bomb.

Italian and German exclusion During World War II, immigrants and Americans of certain foreign backgrounds were treated as "alien enemies." As seen on this sign from Terminal Island near Los Angeles, Italians and Germans were sometimes excluded along with the more heavily targeted Japanese. Those considered alien enemies were forbidden to enter or stay in certain areas, even if they had been living or working there. These exclusion zones eventually made up more than a third of the United States. Approximately 11,000 German Americans were interned in camps.

Indians help on the homefront Navajo Indians repair tracks on the Southern Pacific Railroad near Yuma, Arizona, in 1942. Although more famous for their role in cryptology, Navajos—like other Native Americans—worked in numerous civilian positions as well during the war, from farm laborers to factory workers to clerks. In spite of Nazi propaganda, American Indians at home remained loyal. Most fully intended to return to their reservations after the war, where they expected improved conditions that would reflect the triumph of American democracy.

Japanese Internment

IN 1942 THE PACIFIC COAST was designated "Military Area No. 1." In California, western Oregon, western Washington, and southern Arizona, as many as 120,000 people were declared "excluded" from the military area. They were rounded up and moved to camps that were fenced with barbed wire and patrolled by armed guards. The 10 internment camps were located in hot, remote areas where detainees lived in tar paper-covered barracks and used communal bathroom and dining facilities.

Children about to be relocated

A majority of those interned were American citizens by birth. Most of the rest had been U.S. residents for many years, usually decades, but had not been allowed to apply for citizenship. Peter Ota, 15 at the time, said that his father, like most, went without protest. Mused Peter: "After all those years, having worked his whole life to build a dream—an American dream, mind you—having it all taken away, and not one vindictive word." Peter was later inducted into the Army, but his father and sister were held in the camp until the end of World War II.

This nightmarish scenario was the largest forced relocation in U.S. history. America was fighting a war against Germany, Italy, and Japan, but almost entirely those of Japanese ancestry were interned. They were given just a few days notice, and could keep only what they could carry with them. Speculators bought their homes and businesses at a fraction of the actual value. Most families never recovered what they had lost.

The relocation and internment of Japanese Americans was carried out under an executive order signed by President Franklin Roosevelt in February 1942. The U.S. Supreme Court upheld the legality of the action. Japanese Americans were given seasonal furloughs to work in California agriculture, and about 4,300 young people were allowed to return to college if they transferred to schools outside the military zone. They were also allowed to enlist in the armed services.

In 1945, before the war ended, the exclusion order was rescinded. In 1980 under President Jimmy Carter, a bipartisan commission condemned the internment as unjust. In 1988 President Ronald Reagan signed the Civil Liberties Act, which provided $20,000 for each surviving internee.

Japanese forced to relocate In February 1942, Lieutenant General J. L. DeWitt told the War Department that Pacific Coast security required the evacuation of all people of Japanese ancestry. Originally, the government encouraged these citizens to relocate voluntarily; about 8,000 did so. Those with limited resources or who were concerned about hostility in new areas did not move. In March, DeWitt—acting on Executive Order 9066—put a halt to voluntary relocation and made evacuation to internment camps mandatory. Approximately 120,000 Japanese people, most of whom were American citizens, were forcibly removed from their homes, held under guard, and bussed to 10 camps located between the Sierra Nevada Mountains and the Mississippi River.

Evacuating Little Tokyo The empty streets of Los Angeles's Little Tokyo present an eerie sight. Little Tokyo was home to about 30,000 Japanese Americans at its height before World War II. But when this photograph was taken on July 12, 1942, all of its residents had been forcibly moved to internment camps. During the war, African Americans moved into the district, but some of them left when Japanese Americans returned from the camps after the war. Although Little Tokyo never regained its former ethnic population, it remains Los Angeles's center of Japanese business and culture.

THE LIFE OF A DOG

"THE DESERT WAS bad enough. The mushroom barracks made it worse. The constant cyclonic storms loaded with sand and dust made it worse. After living in well furnished homes with every modern convenience and suddenly forced to live the life of a dog is something which one cannot so readily forget. Down in our hearts we cried and cursed this government every time when we were showered with sand. It was not the question of protection. It was because we were Japs! Yes, Japs!"

—JOSEPH Y. KURIHARA, AN AMERICAN SOLDIER DURING WORLD WAR I WHO WAS INTERNED AT MANZANAR DURING WORLD WAR II

Life in the camps People of Japanese descent were interned in remote camps that were fenced with barbed wire and overseen by armed guards in watchtowers. The Manzanar War Relocation Center, ironically located just outside of Independence, California, housed more than 10,000 people and was the most famous of the camps. Because the internees had to leave their homes hurriedly, and did not know where they were going, most did not bring suitable clothing for the extremes of heat and cold at the camps.

The bare essentials Japanese Americans arrive at the Heart Mountain Relocation Center in Wyoming, where they would live for more than three years. Internees were allowed to bring only the baggage that they could carry with them. Each family's room was furnished with a stove, one light fixture hanging from the ceiling, and an army cot with two blankets for each occupant. The relocation centers had to be self-sufficient, and internees provided services at very low pay. For example, an internee doctor in charge of pediatrics at the Heart Mountain Hospital made $228 per year while white nurses there made annual salaries of $1,800.

> "There was a teen-ager at Manzanar who walked out into the desert one day.... He was mentally deranged. And he got shot. They shot him in the back. So we all knew exactly where we stood."
>
> —Dr. Yoshiye Togasaki

Overcrowding at Manzanar "At the very beginning . . . there weren't enough barracks built yet," recalled Paul Kusuda in a 2004 interview about his internment at the Manzanar War Relocation Center. Kusada's family of five shared a room with a widowed mother and her teenage son, while the detainees pitched in to help finish their own detention quarters. As seen here, each family made the space as comfortable as possible. Kusada commented that Japanese American women were especially uncomfortable with the unpartitioned toilets in communal bathhouses, and sometimes stood in line outside to use the facilities one at a time.

Resistance at Tule Lake Overseers of all the Japanese detention camps operated farms, paying workers about $12 a month. Internees who passed character and loyalty investigations could receive seasonal work furloughs to relieve field labor shortages on outside farms. Seen here are workers at California's Tule Lake Relocation Center. After a farmworker died in a 1943 truck accident, Tule Lake laborers went on strike to protest the tiny compensation offered the victim's widow. The administration brought in 234 Japanese Americans from other centers as strikebreakers. Tule Lake was the largest detention center, and its 18,000 residents were the most resistant to relocation. The center was ruled under martial law and was the last to close, in March 1946.

Hirabayashi takes U.S. to court When Japanese Americans were removed from Seattle for internment in 1942, college student Gordon Hirabayashi refused to leave the city. He turned himself in to the FBI, was tried and convicted of defying the U.S. government's curfew and expulsion orders against Japanese Americans, and spent 90 days in prison. In 1943 Hirabayashi appealed his conviction to the U.S. Supreme Court, which ruled unanimously against him. After many years as a sociology professor, Hirabayashi again legally challenged his conviction. In 1986 a U.S. District Court judge reversed the conviction; an appeals court upheld the reversal in 1987.

Battle of the Philippines The Philippines came under United States control in 1898, after the Spanish-American War. In 1935 the Pacific nation was placed on a 10-year path toward independence. However, this process was interrupted by the Battle of the Philippines in 1941–42. The city of Manila fell to the Japanese on January 2, 1942. Here, Japanese soldiers lower the American flag on the strategic Philippine island of Corregidor in May 1942. Although the U.S. lost the first Battle of the Philippines, it drove the Japanese out in 1945. In 1946 the Philippines at last achieved independence.

Battle of Midway American dive bombers patrol coral reefs at the beginning of the Battle of Midway, which raged from June 4 to 7, 1942. The Japanese had planned an attack against Midway Island, which is located about halfway between Japan and California. The Japanese hoped to use their naval superiority to destroy the U.S. aircraft carrier force that was based at Midway. However, American intelligence decoded Japanese messages and allowed Admiral Chester Nimitz to set an ambush. American planes destroyed four irreplaceable Japanese carriers, while the U.S. lost only one and retained its island base. According to historian Mary Beth Norton, the American victory at Midway "was a turning point in the Pacific war, breaking the Japanese momentum."

Guarding the West Coast Given the fears of Japanese aerial attacks on the West Coast during World War II, a number of antiaircraft batteries were activated or built to counter such a move. This one was entrenched along the California coast. Although a few Japanese balloon-carried bombs did land on the coast, there was only one verified attack by an airplane: A seaplane tried to start a forest fire in Oregon by dropping an incendiary bomb.

1940-1949

September 1942: The Navajo code talkers program is established on the recommendation of a former Navajo missionary's son who recognized that the rich but unwritten Navajo language could be useful in secret military communications. The code will never be broken.

1943: Per capita, the state of North Dakota leads the nation in the sale of war bonds.

1943: The U.S. government creates the Venetie Reservation for the Neets'aii Gwich'in Indians on approximately 1.8 million acres surrounding the Alaskan town of Venetie.

February 27, 1943: The worst coal mining disaster in Montana's history claims 74 lives when an explosion rocks Smith Mine #3 in the town of Washoe.

March 1943: The Convair aeronautics firm is founded in San Diego when Consolidated Aircraft merges with Vultee Aircraft to form the Consolidated Vultee Aircraft Corporation, headquartered in San Diego.

March 15, 1943: J. Robert Oppenheimer's top-secret Manhattan Project laboratory is relocated to a site in Los Alamos, New Mexico.

June 1943: The Zoot Suit Riots flare in Los Angeles when U.S. servicemen attack Mexican American and African American youths for wearing distinctive "zoot suits."

Mid-June 1943: Authorities declare martial law in Beaumont, Texas, after the outbreak of a race riot.

July 1943: The federal government builds a German prisoner-of-war camp in Concordia, Kansas, the first and largest of several such camps built in Kansas during World War II.

FSA labor camps Children pass the time at the Farm Security Administration's Robstown, Texas, labor camp. In 1942 the FSA set up a Migratory Camp Program, which offered basic shelters, showers, day care centers, and health clinics to farmworkers and their families—mostly Mexican Americans in the West. Camps such as this one were permanent, while mobile FSA camps provided floored tents. The labor camps were generally an improvement on living conditions previously available to migrant workers. Also, since they were independent of company facilities, workers in FSA camps could bargain with employers regarding salaries and working conditions.

On behalf of Japanese Americans The Japanese American Citizens League (JACL) was established in 1929. Fearing the consequences of impending war, Nisei (second-generation Japanese Americans) attempted to promote understanding between Japanese Americans and the dominant white population. Some members aided the government's incarceration efforts in order to soften the social and economic hardships that ensued.

These JACL members stand in line to receive registration cards that will certify them as United States citizens.

Rosie the Riveter

THE IMAGE OF a sturdy female laborer appeared on a 1942 poster that proclaimed "We Can Do It!" A 1943 song gave her a name, "Rosie the Riveter." Then artist Norman Rockwell made her really famous by depicting her on the May 29, 1943, cover of *The Saturday Evening Post.*

Across the nation, many "Rosies" were making history. With so many American men overseas in the armed forces, the nation faced a critical labor shortage. The government mounted a propaganda campaign proclaiming that it was a woman's patriotic duty to take a job. In the San Francisco Bay area, women quickly outnumbered men seeking defense work. Overall, western states had the highest percentage of female industrial workers.

Except for some noncombat flying, the 350,000 American women who joined the military generally worked in clerical, communications, and health care fields traditionally assigned to women. Civilian women often worked as riveters, welders, blast furnace cleaners, drill press operators, mechanics, and other traditionally male occupations.

Women who already held low-paying jobs took the opportunity to move up the salary scale. (In 1942, hundreds of laundries closed when their female workers left for better pay.) About six million women who had never before worked outside the home took jobs. African American women were a substantial part of the new labor

A riveter at an aircraft company in 1943

force, although they usually worked for low pay at canneries, railroads, military supply facilities, and shipyards. Native American women also worked in defense industries. By 1945 women comprised 36 percent of the labor force. They still earned less than men, and they still had to manage child-care and housework duties.

Rosie the Riveter had always been considered a temporary worker. At the end of the war, women's jobs went back to returning servicemen. Many women became full-time homemakers, though some continued to hold on to their jobs.

Westerners build military aircraft Military aircraft construction boomed during World War II, and much of the manufacturing took place in the American West. Boeing constructed B-29 bombers in the states of Washington and Kansas, while Consolidated built B-24 bombers in San Diego and Fort Worth, Texas. Douglas manufactured fighters, transport planes, and bombers in Tulsa, Oklahoma, and in Santa Monica, El Segundo, and Long Beach, California. Hughes, Lockheed, Martin, Northrop, and North American also operated military aircraft factories throughout the West. Women proved valuable in aircraft construction, partly because their dexterity and typically smaller size were useful in assembling delicate parts.

The Bracero Program

AFTER THE UNITED STATES' entry into World War II, much of its labor force moved into military industries. The nation suddenly faced huge shortages of workers, especially in western agriculture. Meanwhile, skilled farmworkers in Mexico suffered from declining crop yields. In 1942 the governments of the U.S. and Mexico signed an agreement that seemed a humane and sensible solution to both nations' problems.

That year, the Mexican Farm Labor Program Agreement—better known as the Bracero Program—allowed Mexican workers to enter the United States legally as temporary agricultural workers. Although the program began modestly with a few hundred beet workers in California, some 4.5 million Mexicans went to work in the U.S. during the next 22 years. Called braceros (a term indicating strength, taken from the Spanish word *brazo,* or arm), Mexican farmworkers performed an enormous role in transforming U.S. agriculture into a mechanized industry.

At least on paper, the Bracero Program assured fair treatment of migrant workers, including decent housing and health care, wages equal to those of U.S. farmworkers, the right to organize and participate in unions, and con-

Bracero worker, 1942

tracts written in Spanish. However, U.S. agriculture businesses resisted these standards from the beginning. Texas farmers refused to even participate in the program for its first five years, preferring instead to hire illegal workers directly from Mexico.

Despite repeated attempts at reform, Mexican bracero workers frequently lived in deplorable conditions, made poor wages, signed English-language contracts that they could not understand, and were fired and deported for participating in unions. They also often found themselves hired as strikebreakers, putting them at odds with U.S. laborers.

By the time it ended in 1964, the Bracero Program was universally regarded as a huge human rights failure. U.S. Department of Labor administrator Lee G. Williams described it as "nothing short of legalized slavery." Indeed, scandals surrounding the program have persisted into the 21st century. Ten percent of braceros' weekly checks were withheld and put into savings accounts in Mexico, with the promise that the funds would be returned after workers went back home. This seldom happened. Today, surviving braceros are still trying to recover their lost wages.

Progressive Indian policies Two Havasupai children pose outside their home on the smallest Indian reservation in the United States, in Havasu Canyon, Arizona. At the time that this photograph was snapped in 1942, the U.S. government was reforming its policies toward reservations. The Indian Reorganization Act of 1934 (also called the Wheeler-Howard Act, or the Indian New Deal) gave Indians greater rights of self-government. In the years following the act, more than two million acres of land were returned to Indians, and federal funds poured into health care and education. By 1950 more than half of all Indian children attended public schools.

Douglas Aircraft The aircraft company founded by Donald Douglas in 1920 became famous during the 1930s and '40s for its "DC" commercial planes. During World War II, Douglas Aircraft Company produced military versions of the DCs in addition to torpedo bombers for the Navy, observer aircraft, and other military planes—as well as ejection seats, missiles, bombs, and bomb racks. At this Long Beach plant, women work on transparent noses for attack bombers. During the war, 160,000 employees in seven Douglas factories (located in California, Oklahoma, and Illinois) built nearly 30,000 planes.

The war effort throughout the West During World War II, war-related production and training facilities proliferated not just in California but throughout the West. Shipbuilding became a leading industry in Seattle, where Henry J. Kaiser's innovative manufacturing techniques produced seagoing vessels in record time. Excellent year-round flying conditions led to the creation of training facilities in southwestern states. Albuquerque, New Mexico, developed a bombardier training school, and Corpus Christi, Texas, supported a huge naval air station (pictured), where thousands of pilots, bombardiers, navigators, and gunners received training.

44,000 Indians enlist At Little Eagle, South Dakota, Standing Rock Sioux Chief White Bull displays a bow and arrow while young Sioux soldiers show off an armored vehicle with a machine gun. Some 44,000 Indians served in World War II, making their contribution to the war effort greater per capita than that of any other American group. Indeed, the U.S. War Department calculated that if all Americans had enlisted in the same proportion as Indians, the draft would not have been necessary. Indian soldiers received numerous awards for their service, including three Congressional Medals of Honor.

Kaiser's clout During World War II, industrialist Henry J. Kaiser (*second from left*) built shipyards in California and Oregon. He developed mass-production techniques for ships, and pioneered tract housing and health care organizations for his employees. Beginning well before the war, when he built dams and roads, Kaiser was a regular visitor to the nation's capital. He was one of the first American entrepreneurs who worked closely with executive branch officials to accomplish what he needed. Here, President Roosevelt (*right*) visits the Kaiser shipyard in Portland. FDR and Kaiser are accompanied by Oregon Governor Charles Sprague (*far left*) and Kaiser's son, Edgar.

1940-1949

August 15, 1943: A 34,000-man Allied invasion force lands on Kiska, the last Japanese-occupied island in Alaska's Aleutians, only to discover it had been abandoned by the Japanese weeks earlier.

October 3, 1943: The Hauser Creek fire in Southern California's Cleveland National Forest claims nine lives and some 10,000 acres.

December 17, 1943: The Magnuson Act is signed into law. The act allows Chinese nationals living in the U.S. to become American citizens, and allows a small number of Chinese citizens to immigrate to the U.S.

1944: Congress approves the Pick-Sloan Plan, a joint Bureau of Reclamation and Army Corps of Engineers plan to regulate the waters of the Missouri River.

1944: After some 60 years and $80 million worth of gold production, the Alaska-Juneau Gold Mine is shut down.

1944: The U.S. Navy begins construction of an aqueduct to bring water from the Colorado River all the way to San Diego. *See* 1947.

1944: The Western Defense Command issues orders releasing Japanese Americans from the internment camps, except those who are considered potentially dangerous to national security.

1944: The National Congress of American Indians is founded in Denver. It eventually will become the largest Indian tribal government organization in the U.S.

June 6, 1944: The Allies land on the beaches of Normandy, France, to take Western Europe back from Hitler's Nazi forces.

Stars support the war effort
Hollywood celebrities threw tremendous support behind America's involvement in World War II. Some big-name actors, including Jimmy Stewart and Clark Gable, enlisted for active duty, while countless others entertained troops abroad in USO shows. Here, actress Rita Hayworth (who also supported the sale of war bonds) displays her bumper-less car to promote wartime salvage drives. Americans on the home front were encouraged to donate a huge range of materials, including paper, rags, tin, iron, steel, and rubber. Spare cooking fat was useful in making munitions, and silk from stockings went into the manufacture of parachutes.

Ansel Adams The Grand Tetons loom over Wyoming's Snake River in this 1942 photograph by Ansel Adams. The legendary photographer received his first camera, a Kodak Brownie, at age 14 while his family vacationed at Yosemite National Park. He was hooked, and for the next 60 years he took thousands of photographs, primarily of his beloved West. Adams was best known for his ability to manipulate light and shade to create especially striking contrasts. Shortly after his death in 1984, a mountain in the Sierra Nevada range was named in his honor.

Different schools for different kids Children pose in a rural school in Saint Augustine, Texas, in 1943. K-12 education varied dramatically in the West during the 1930s and 1940s. In some rural areas, the one-room schoolhouse remained the norm. In larger towns and cities, consolidation led to larger schools. All the while, minority students faced an uncertain education. In California, many black students wound up in schools segregated because of residential patterns, while Mexican American children were legally segregated in California until 1947. Most Japanese American children were sent to relocation camps during World War II.

Hopalong Cassidy Middle-aged actor William Boyd (*pictured*) played quite a different Hopalong Cassidy than the character in early 20th century novels. As created by author Clarence E. Mulford, Hopalong was a foul-mouthed cowboy who limped from an old wound. The name was all that remained in the 66 movies made from 1935 to 1948. Boyd's Hopalong never cursed, drank, smoked, or chewed tobacco, and he let the villain draw first. Always dressed in black, he rode a white horse. In the 1950s, Boyd made a well-loved TV series, put Hopalong's image on a lunchbox, and endorsed other merchandise.

Western pulps Pulp magazines (named for the cheap wood pulp paper they were printed on) thrived between the world wars. Crime, science fiction, horror, and the Old West were popular pulp genres. *Texas Rangers* (the December 1943 issue is seen here) won readers with a recurring character, Ranger Jim Hatfield, who inhabited a simplistic, largely mythical West, aided by his wonder horse, Goldy. Although the fast-paced short stories weren't exactly literature, they delivered the thrills and adventure needed to draw readers back, month after month.

The Big Inch Pipeline Before the Japanese attack on Pearl Harbor, most of America's oil was shipped by tankers from Texas to the East Coast. By 1942 German submarines were sinking many of these tankers. To protect America's wartime oil supply, U.S. Secretary of the Interior Harold Ickes made plans for the largest oil pipelines ever constructed. The Big Inch Pipeline (*pictured*) stretched from Longview, Texas, to Norris City, Illinois. The Little Big Inch, a second pipeline built with 20-inch pipes, ran from Beaumont, Texas, to Linden, New Jersey.

The Zoot Suit Riots

ON AUGUST 2, 1942, the body of a young man named José Diaz was found in the Sleepy Lagoon reservoir in southeast Los Angeles. Racial tensions were already running high in the city, and in the ensuing hysteria, some 300 Mexican American youths were rounded up and arrested for the alleged murder. In a highly flawed trial, three defendants were convicted of first-degree murder, nine of second-degree murder, and five of assault. (These convictions would be overturned in 1944.)

The Sleepy Lagoon affair was a prologue to the Zoot Suit Riots of 1943. Members of the Mexican American subculture known as *pachucos* wore fancy outfits called zoot suits, which featured broad-brimmed hats, suit jackets with wide shoulders, and gold chains. On June 3, these suits made *pachucos* easy targets for about 200 American sailors on leave, some of whom claimed to have been assaulted by groups of the youths. The sailors went on nightly rampages, raiding bars and movie theaters to attack and beat *pachucos*. By June 7, ranks of sailors, soldiers, and civilians attacking *pachucos* had swelled into the thousands. The police arrested hundreds of *pachucos,* many of them badly injured, but only nine sailors.

Victims (*on ground*) of the Zoot Suit Riots

During the riots, city newspapers egged on the sailors. "Zoot Suiters Learn Lesson in Fights with Servicemen," announced a *Los Angeles Times* headline. When U.S. First Lady Eleanor Roosevelt responded to the riots with concern about racism against Mexican Americans, the *Times* accused her of Communist leanings and provoking racial discord.

War in the Aleutians
American landing craft stream toward the shore of Kiska Island in the Aleutians (west of Alaska) in August 1943. Japanese forces occupied the island chain in June 1942 and soon endured U.S. aerial attacks. U.S. forces invaded Attu Island in May 1943 and fought one of the bloodiest battles of the entire war, suffering almost 4,000 casualties at the hands of entrenched Japanese troops. At Kiska Island, American forces discovered that Japanese soldiers had already been evacuated. Nonetheless, more than 300 Allied troops died from friendly fire, land mines, and booby traps while taking control of Kiska.

African Americans prefer L.A. Members of the Los Angeles National Association for the Advancement of Colored People (NAACP) meet in 1944. The African American population of Los Angeles skyrocketed in the 1940s, from 75,000 in 1940 to 250,000 in 1950. Most new black residents, such as Mary Trimble, migrated both to escape blatant racism and for economic opportunity. "I was through 'Missing' and 'Mistering,'" she said. "I could get a job in a war plant [in Los Angeles]." Many African Americans did find decent jobs in L.A., especially in manufacturing industries.

Navajo code talkers Two Navajo Marines operate a portable radio on the island of Bougainville off present-day Papua New Guinea. These "code talkers" used a deliberately jumbled version of their native language to transmit vital military information to U.S. forces in the Pacific Theater. The Navajo code talkers served a crucial role in Marine combat missions against the Japanese from 1942 to 1945, baffling the enemy at every turn. Remarked signal officer Major Howard Connor, "Were it not for the Navajos, the Marines would never have taken Iwo Jima."

From governor to chief justice Earl Warren became the district attorney of Alameda County, California, in 1925. During his years as California's attorney general (1939–43), he supported the internment of Japanese citizens—a position he would deeply regret later in life. After Warren's three terms as California's governor (1943–53) and an unsuccessful Republican candidacy for vice president of the United States (1948), President Dwight Eisenhower appointed him chief justice of the U.S. Supreme Court in 1953. Long regarded as a staunch conservative, Warren surprised his contemporaries—including Eisenhower himself—with his liberal Supreme Court decisions, most famously *Brown v. Board of Education*.

June 22, 1944: President Roosevelt signs the Servicemen's Readjustment Act, better known as the GI Bill of Rights. It provides for federal funding, home loans, and scholarships to help World War II veterans reenter American society.

July 17, 1944: An explosion at Port Chicago Naval Magazine in California kills 320 sailors and civilians. More than 200 of the dead are African American. In August, 258 black sailors will refuse to load ammunition at Port Chicago due to safety concerns. Fifty of them will be court-martialed and sentenced to eight to 15 years of hard labor, and 208 will receive bad-conduct discharges.

August 25, 1944: The Allies liberate Paris from the Nazi occupation.

September 1944: The Hanford Site in Richland, Washington, built to produce plutonium for the Manhattan Project, fires up its first reactor.

1945: John Steinbeck releases his classic novel *Cannery Row,* which is set in early 20th century Monterey, California.

1945: After years of consolidation, San Francisco's Bank of America emerges as the world's largest bank.

1945: Las Vegas, Nevada, planners begin to promote the city as a tourist destination. They hire advertising guru J. Walter Thompson to run their campaign.

1945: The U.S. Senate ratifies a treaty that would divert some of the waters of the Colorado River across the border to Mexico.

1945: Josephina Niggli's anthology *Mexican Village,* which explores issues affecting Mexican Americans, is published.

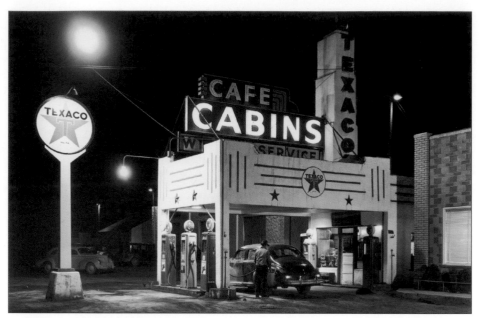

A place to sleep for travelers Tourist cabins provided a bed and bath for automobile travelers. They were built in local architectural styles and named after colorful attractions and characters, such as Buffalo Bill Cody. By 1939 half of the better motor hotels, or motels, also included cafés. Usually located outside of town, with individual room doors opening onto a parking area, motels offered considerable privacy for occupants. However, they also gained a reputation as hideouts for sexual trysts and for criminals. In his 1940 magazine article "Camps of Crime," FBI Director J. Edgar Hoover warned Americans to stay away from motels, though with little effect on their popularity.

West Coast shipbuilders When the U.S. entered World War II, shipbuilding suddenly became a major industry all along the West Coast. By 1943 San Francisco and Los Angeles shipyards alone employed 280,000 workers, many of whom had moved from other parts of the country for the jobs. Here, workers pray for victory in June 1944 at the California Shipbuilding Corporation (Calship) in Los Angeles. At Calship, 40,000 men and women completed more than 450 cargo ships, which were used to move weapons, supplies, and personnel.

The Atomic West

ON JULY 16, 1945, a hundred or so people watched in anxiety and then in awe from a shelter in Alamogordo, New Mexico, as the world's first atomic bomb was detonated. The explosion released heat four times the internal temperature of the sun and broke windows 120 miles away. This successful project—code-named "Trinity"—meant that the United States possessed the world's most destructive weapon. Even while the Trinity test was being set up, a second atomic bomb was being readied for use against Hiroshima, Japan. A third bomb would fall on Nagasaki, Japan.

Those first nuclear weapons were developed by the top-secret Manhattan Project under the direction of physicist Dr. J. Robert Oppenheimer, and coordinated at Los Alamos Laboratory in New Mexico. Plutonium, the element used as fuel for the explosions, was produced at the Hanford, Washington, Nuclear Site.

During the 1950s, the Atomic Energy Commission and other U.S. governmental agencies developed the remotely located Nevada Proving Ground for testing bombs. The mushroom-shaped clouds created by those blasts could be seen from 100 miles away. Tourists enjoyed watching the explosions from their hotel windows in Las Vegas.

Within two years of a particularly large 1953 atomic blast at the Nevada Proving Ground, cancer began to

A component of the first atomic bomb

show up in farmers and livestock living downwind of the tests. Decades later, the government financially compensated those victims as well as some stricken nuclear plant workers and other fallout casualties. Radiation was also released into the atmosphere from byproducts of plutonium processing at the Hanford site.

The long-term effects of low-level doses of radiation are still being investigated by federal agencies, and further compensation is under discussion. Large-scale nuclear cleanup efforts have been made at the New Mexico, Nevada, and Washington sites. Meanwhile, the Proving Ground has become a popular tourist destination.

Hanford's "tank farm" The Hanford Engineer Works in Washington State was built in 1943 to manufacture plutonium for making atomic weapons. During World War II, Hanford supplied plutonium for the Trinity test bomb in New Mexico in July 1945 as well as for "Fat Man," the bomb dropped on Nagasaki, Japan, on August 9, 1945. This 1944 photograph shows the construction of a "tank farm" to store nuclear waste at the site. By the time of its permanent closing in 1989, Hanford had built 177 such underground tanks, plus other above-ground storage facilities. Waste storage eventually presented serious environmental problems in the area.

A scientist at the Berkeley Radiation Laboratory in California examines a cyclotron. First built by American nuclear physicist Ernest Lawrence in 1930, the cyclotron vastly speeded up the process of the acceleration of particles such as electrons and protons. This advance was crucial for the development of the atomic bomb during World War II. The lab was renamed after Lawrence in 1958 and was combined with another nuclear research laboratory, the Livermore, in 1979. Under any name, it has been a major center of U.S. nuclear research for more than 70 years.

The brains behind the bomb General Leslie Groves (*left*) was the head of the project that developed the world's first nuclear device. Dr. J. Robert Oppenheimer (*right*) was the physicist who directed the scientific team headquartered in Los Alamos, New Mexico. For three years, these two men worked within the secret Manhattan Project, planning and developing the atomic bomb. Oppenheimer, later known as the "father of the atomic bomb," recruited top physicists to tackle the problems of splitting the atom. When the first bomb exploded successfully, Oppenheimer muttered a line from a Hindu text: "I am become death, the shatterer of worlds."

FIRE IN THE SKY

SUDDENLY, without any sound, the whole world lit up. When I came to my senses, I was lying on the ground with my back to where the light was coming from. I put my hands over my eyes to protect them and I could see the bones in my fingers. It was as if I was looking at an X-ray.

I whisked around and looked towards the light. I could hear a rumble and the Earth shook. I saw a big fireball rising in the sky—it looked like it was pouring gasoline out there, all the way around. The fireball was getting bigger and bigger and we just stood and watched.

This was followed by a long rumbling—I'd say it went on for 10 minutes. In and out and round the mountains. The fire began going down and then I saw a swirl of black smoke rising in the sky.

I was scared at the time. I didn't know what was going on. I remember the man running the camera beside us hollering that it was the most beautiful picture he had ever taken in his life—he said it maybe 25 times. All he was interested in was the picture and all I was wondering was if we were going to get out of there or not.

No one was allowed to talk about what we saw. Anyone who did was shipped out pretty quickly.

—PRIVATE DANIEL YEAROUT, AFTER WITNESSING THE FIRST-EVER ATOMIC EXPLOSION, THE TRINITY TEST, ON JULY 16, 1945

The Trinity test "We were reaching into the unknown and we did not know what might come of it," wrote General Thomas Farrell, who witnessed "Trinity"—the first nuclear test—from an observation hut. Many had concerns about the upcoming blast. Might it launch some sort of cataclysmic reaction that would lead to world destruction? Or might it fail completely? In the early morning of July 16, 1945, the Trinity explosion created a ball of flame, then a mushroom cloud that soared more than seven miles high. The bomb released energy equal to about 19 kilotons of TNT, creating a shock wave that was felt 100 miles away.

A monstrous blast A protective force officer watches the New Mexico sky for violations of the no-fly zone over atomic experimentation. The Trinity test at Alamogordo created 100 million-degree heat that vaporized the metal tower holding the bomb. Beneath the blast, sand was fused into a green glass, named "Trinitite," that uninformed local residents collected to sell to tourists. Effects reached far beyond the zone, exposing nearby ranch families to radioactivity and creating pockets of intense radiation. Thirty miles north, cattle lost their hair (which grew back in a different color) and fallout particles were found in packing material products 1,000 miles away.

Nothing to come home to
Given a week to 10 days to report for relocation in 1942, many Japanese Americans quickly sold what they could not take with them—farmland, houses, cars, appliances, furniture, and personal belongings—generally for far less than their worth. Evacuees also left behind about $200 million worth of commercial and personal property. Many, like this Seattle family, returned to their homes in 1945 to find them vandalized or even destroyed. In 1948 the U.S. government made some compensation payments to Japanese Americans, but most did not recover their losses.

1940–1949

1945: New York's Museum of Modern Art hangs a retrospective of Georgia O'Keeffe's work. It is the first time the museum has staged a show of this scope for a female artist.

February 1945: As World War II winds down, Allied leaders Roosevelt, Churchill, and Stalin meet to discuss international relations in the emerging world order. • Allied troops storm the border of Germany with the German troops in retreat.

April 12, 1945: President Franklin Roosevelt dies of a cerebral hemorrhage at Warm Springs, Georgia. Vice President Harry Truman is sworn in as the 33rd president of the United States.

May 8, 1945: The Allies accept the unconditional surrender of Germany.

June 26, 1945: Fifty nations sign the United Nations Charter.

July 16, 1945: The U.S. executes the Trinity test at Alamogordo, New Mexico, the world's first detonation of an atomic bomb.

August 6, 1945: The U.S. destroys Hiroshima, Japan, with an atomic bomb, killing (by year's end) 140,000 people.

August 9, 1945: The U.S. drops a plutonium explosion weapon over Nagasaki, Japan. The death toll will be half that of Hiroshima.

August 15, 1945: Japan surrenders unconditionally.

September 2, 1945: World War II officially ends in the Pacific Theater with the surrender ceremony on the deck of the battleship USS *Missouri*.

1946: The U.S. Congress establishes the Indian Claims Commission. It will serve as a forum for American Indians to formally air grievances against the federal government.

Texas war hero Audie Murphy, the son of poor Texas sharecroppers, was initially rejected by Army recruiters because he was too young. He went on to become the most decorated American soldier in World War II. He fought in nine major battles, including one in which he leaped on top of a burning, munitions-laden tank and held off attacking German soldiers with the tank's machine gun. After the war, Murphy embarked on a successful movie career, appearing in 44 films, including *The Red Badge of Courage* (1951). He was also a successful rancher, businessman, and songwriter, penning hits for such performers as Dean Martin. In spite of his youthful appearance, he once said, "I can't ever remember being young in my life."

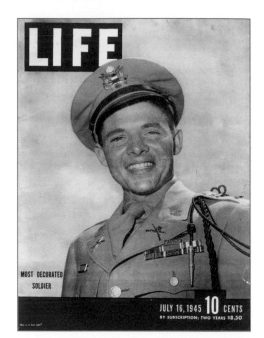

LIFE

JULY 16, 1945 **10** CENTS
BY SUBSCRIPTION; TWO YEARS $8.50

MOST DECORATED SOLDIER

Neutra's California designs Born and trained in Vienna, Modernist architect Richard Neutra settled in Los Angeles in 1925, opening a practice with his wife, Dione. Believing that architecture could work for human betterment, Neutra carefully created designs around the needs of each client. He made inventive use of glass, steel, mirrors, water, and unusual lighting effects to open up space and enhance the building's relationship with its natural setting. In his light and airy "California Modern" buildings, he frequently used a stucco finish over a metal framework. Seen here is the living room of Neutra's own California home.

Gambling in the Pacific During the 19th century, the ocean boundary of the United States was set at three miles beyond the coastline. This meant that gambling was legal beyond the three-mile limit, no matter what laws were in force on shore. Enterprising 20th century mobsters, such as Tony "Admiral" Cornero, took advantage of this loophole by anchoring gambling ships, or "floating casinos," more than three miles out in the Pacific. Clientele could reach these ships in minutes by water taxis from the shore. Pictured here in 1946 is Cornero's gambling ship, *Lux,* a converted mine layer that was anchored off Long Beach, California.

Government settles claims President Harry Truman signs the Indian Claims Commission Act on August 13, 1946. Intending to permanently settle outstanding Native claims against the U.S. government, Congress mandated the commission to adjudicate cases involving Indians' land, mismanagement of tribal funds by the Bureau of Indian Affairs, and questionable resource-extraction agreements. By the late 1970s, the commission had settled almost 300 cases, dispersing more than $800 million to Indians. Moreover, the commission helped restore significant tribal sovereignty.

The Black Dahlia murder In a tragic irony, aspiring actress Elizabeth Short might have remained unknown forever if it were not for her gruesome murder at the age of 22. On January 15, 1947, her body was found in a vacant lot in Hollywood, mutilated and cut in half at the waist. Newspapers quickly nicknamed Short the "Black Dahlia" because she often had

worn a dahlia in her jet-black hair. Short's killing both horrified and fascinated the public. In a weird frenzy of publicity-seeking, about 60 people confessed to her murder. The case remains officially unsolved today.

Western fashions By the mid-20th century, cowboy fashions—including a hat, blue jeans, colorful or fringed shirt, and fancy boots—seemed to express American ideals of heroism and virtue. Manufacturers began producing blue jeans for adult leisure wear, and in children's sizes as well. Even little girls could buy a "cowboy outfit" complete with hat, gun and holster, chaps, scarves, and fancy boots. Here, actor Dennis Morgan poses with two young winners of a 1947 western fashion show in Cheyenne, Wyoming—a type of event that continues today.

1940-1949

1946: For the first time, Nevada exacts a tax from gamblers.

1946: In Las Vegas, the Golden Nugget and Bugsy Siegel's Flamingo Hotel open for gambling.

1946: *Citizen 13660,* the first major literary work on the Japanese American experience in the World War II detention camps, is released by Japanese artist Mine Okubo.

1946: Construction begins on the Kortes Dam on the North Platte River, about 60 miles outside of Casper, Wyoming.

March 5, 1946: Winston Churchill introduces the concept of a Soviet Bloc "Iron Curtain" in a speech delivered at Missouri's Westminster College. Referring to Europe, he proclaims that "an iron curtain has descended across the continent."

July 25, 1946: The U.S. performs the world's first subsurface nuclear test detonation at Bikini Atoll in the Marshall Islands.

August 1, 1946: The Atomic Energy Act is signed by President Truman. It includes a mandate to regulate and control the development and proliferation of nuclear weapons.

1947: The House Un-American Activities Committee holds hearings regarding the infiltration of Communists in the Southern California film industry.

1947: Colorado River water begins to flow into San Diego with the opening of the San Diego Aqueduct.

1947: A federal district court in California rules that it is unconstitutional to segregate Hispanic students.

1947: The U.S. Department of Defense establishes the Alaskan Command. It will be the first unified command of the Army, Air Force, and Navy.

The GI Bill The Servicemen's Readjustment Act of 1944, better known as the GI Bill of Rights, eased the return of U.S. military personnel into civilian life after World War II. The GI Bill provided veterans with unemployment compensation, loans to buy homes and start businesses, and opportunities for college or vocational education. Keith Peterson, seen here with his wife and son in 1947, attended college in Iowa on the GI Bill. By offering home loans, the bill continued the wartime western population boom. It also encouraged midwestern farmers to study new agricultural technologies.

The California ranch A California couple enjoys the amenities of a ranch house in 1947. This single-story architectural style typically featured large windows and few interior walls. The first such house, designed by Cliff May, was built in San Diego in 1932. By the late 1940s, the style had spread far beyond the Golden State. Ranch houses, as well as stucco and adobe homes, were seen as California architectural innovations.

Burgeoning Suburbs

IN THE MID-1900s, suburbs multiplied around major cities. These housing clusters shared some common characteristics: the housing was less dense than city housing; the homes were similar, sometimes identical; and those who lived there were from comparable income levels and cultural backgrounds. However, suburbs developed in several different ways.

In some cases, older communities became attractive to city workers. Bothell, Washington, for example, was a logging and agricultural community before post-WWII road improvements made it easily accessible for Seattle commuters. New housing developments soon sprang up among the older residences.

In some areas, industrial suburbs developed around factories. In 1934 the Federal Housing Administration (FHA) was created to provide mortgage insurance and loans to individuals and contractors. Over the following decades, FHA financing helped spur the development of such industrial suburbs as the 5,000-house project near a Schlitz brewery and a General Motors plant outside of Los Angeles. Like many others, that project, called Panorama City, originally barred nonwhites from buying houses. Other industrial suburbs began as African American or Latino communities, and many changed in cultural identity over time. (Panorama City is now mostly Latino.)

By the 1940s, huge commuter suburbs encircled most major cities. Trains and improved highways made it possible to work in a city and live outside it. Because of new

New homes in metro Los Angeles, 1947

mass-production building techniques, government financing, and low interest rates, families could afford to buy these homes. When the war ended in 1945, servicemen on the GI Bill created an even greater demand for suburban development.

Architectural styles such as split-level and ranch were promoted as "dream homes" in indistinguishable suburban communities. For young families with children—a demographic enlarged by the postwar baby boom—these were relatively safe and pleasant places to live. In this new suburban lifestyle, a typical family consisted of two parents and their children. Fathers left for work and mothers took responsibility for the household.

By 1943 Portland, Oregon, and San Diego, California—followed by other western cities—engaged in city planning. These communities strove for a balance between suburban and inner-city development.

L.A.'s postwar boom War-related industrial development, seaport facilities expansion, petroleum development, and the growing film industry fueled a rapid population growth in Los Angeles, which boomed after World War II. Inexpensive house construction in subdivisions generated a vast suburban sprawl that radiated outward from the old city center. L.A.'s population grew from 1.5 million in 1940 to almost two million in 1950. But while the white population increased by 25 percent, the nonwhite population increased by 115 percent. "White flight," the massive freeway complex, and changing social-economic and immigration patterns produced the ethnic enclaves that mark modern-day Los Angeles.

1947: The Tlingit and Haida people of Alaska file the Alaska Native Brotherhood land-claims suit in the U.S. Court of Claims.

March 1947: President Truman becomes the first U.S. president to visit Mexico City.

March 22, 1947: President Truman issues Executive Order 9835, authorizing the Federal Employee Loyalty Program. The program allows for the investigation and termination of federal employees deemed disloyal to the United States.

April 16, 1947: Ammonium nitrate explosions aboard vessels in the harbor of Texas City, Texas, kill some 600 people and injure thousands. The force of the explosions triggers a 15-foot tidal wave.

April 25, 1947: Congress passes a bill establishing the Theodore Roosevelt National Memorial Park in the North Dakota Badlands.

July 1947: A New Mexico rancher located about 75 miles outside of Roswell reports that a large flying disk has scattered debris on his property. The UFO report triggers a media frenzy.

1948: The 1,390-mile-long Alaska Highway, open since 1942 to military vehicles, opens to civilian traffic for the first time.

1948: The American GI Forum is founded in Texas with a mandate to promote the welfare of Mexican American veterans.

1948: The state supreme court in Arizona and a U.S. district court in New Mexico rule that American Indians have the right to vote.

1948: Bernard DeVoto wins the Pulitzer Prize for history with his volume *Across the Wide Missouri.*

The Texas City explosion Flames engulf Monsanto storage tanks and refinery facilities after a massive chemical explosion at Texas City on Galveston Bay in Texas on April 16, 1947. When a fire started in the hold of a French-registered ship, the *Grandcamp*—which was loaded with 17 million pounds of highly explosive ammonium nitrate—crewmen directed pressurized steam into the hold to extinguish the flames. The vessel blew up. Another vessel, *High Flyer,* carrying millions of pounds of ammonium nitrate and sulphur, exploded shortly thereafter. The blasts killed 600 people, injured 5,000, and caused fires and tidal waves that ravaged Texas City. Shock waves shattered windows in Houston, 30 miles away.

Gangster Bugsy Siegel Born in 1906 to a poor Jewish family in Brooklyn, Benjamin "Bugsy" Siegel began his crime career as a boy by extorting "protection" money from pushcart peddlers. He teamed with another young gangster named Meyer Lansky to engage in bootlegging, car theft, and murder. The pair quickly rose to prominence in the National Crime Syndicate. Siegel envisioned a gambling paradise in Las Vegas, and in 1945 he began building the Flamingo Hotel and Casino with Syndicate money. The construction ran hugely over budget, sparking mob suspicions that Siegel was skimming funds. This police photograph shows Siegel's body after his contract murder in his Beverly Hills home on June 20, 1947. The Flamingo had opened its doors just six months earlier.

UFO over Roswell? Major Jesse Marcel examines debris of an aircraft near Roswell, New Mexico in June 1947. That month, as the Cold War began, reports surfaced that an unidentified flying object (UFO) had been recovered at the Roswell Army Air Field. Military personnel and scientists said the "UFO" was the wreckage of a high-altitude experimental balloon, but others argued that it was a "flying saucer." The following decades produced numerous books, articles, and television programs about the alleged UFO. Despite the lack of credible proof, many people believe that government officials conspired to cover up the incident.

Hughes pushes the limits Howard Hughes inherited his father's Houston-based Hughes Tool Company after being orphaned as a teenager. He then divided his energies between the movie industry and aviation. As a Hollywood mogul, he produced such movies as *Hell's Angels* (1930), *Scarface* (1932), and *The Outlaw* (1941). As an aircraft tycoon, engineer, and aviator, he designed and flew innovative aircraft, personally breaking a speed record in 1935 and an around-the-world record in 1938. In 1939, upon becoming the principal stockholder of Transcontinental and Western Air (later TWA), he brought his innovative talents to commercial airline travel. An obsessive-compulsive, Hughes became increasingly reclusive after 1950.

The "Spruce Goose" During World War II, the U.S. government helped fund Howard Hughes's efforts to design and construct the Hughes H-4 Hercules, a massive military transport plane. Built almost entirely of wood because of wartime metal restrictions, the H-4 was mockingly nicknamed the "Spruce Goose." About five stories tall with a 320-foot wingspan, it remains the world's largest aircraft. Only one H-4 was built, and it was completed after the war was over. Seen here in 1947 making its only flight, it reached an altitude of 70 feet and flew a little less than a mile. Hughes was at the controls.

"Highway 66 is the main migrant road. 66—the long concrete path across the country, waving gently up and down on the map, from the Mississippi to Bakersfield—over the red lands and the gray lands, twisting up into the mountains, crossing the Divide and down into the bright and terrible desert, and across the desert to the mountains again, and into the rich California valleys."

—AUTHOR JOHN STEINBECK, *THE GRAPES OF WRATH*

The "Mother Road" The popular song "Get Your Kicks (On Route 66)" by Bobby Troup expressed America's fascination with the highway that connected the Midwest with the West. The first stores, gas stations, cafés, and motels that appeared along Route 66 reflected local styles and building materials. Soon, oil companies standardized their gas stations, using consistent colors and big, easily recognizable signs—as on this Texaco station on Route 66 in Arizona. During World War II, workers attracted by jobs in war-related industries streamed westward on Route 66. After the war, the "Mother Road" (as it was called) carried tourists east and west.

Founder of Regionalism Thomas Hart Benton rejected his family's political aspirations and decided to become an artist. After studying in Chicago and Paris, he founded the midwestern representational movement known as Regionalism in the 1920s. A heavy drinker, Benton said he would rather have his paintings hang in bars than in museums. When he painted murals of Indiana life for the 1933 Chicago World's Fair, he included Ku Klux Klan members among his unflattering images of everyday people. Many of Benton's paintings depict tranquil midwestern scenes, including 1948's *The Boy* (*pictured*).

A strong black voice During World War II, many African Americans in the military shipped out through San Francisco. After the war, many returned to make their homes there. Some black workers in wartime industries also opted to stay in western cities. African Americans in the West faced postwar unemployment, segregated and inadequate housing, and sometimes police brutality, but their numbers generated a powerful voice. In 1947 black citizens in Oakland, California, protested the showing of the Walt Disney movie *Song of the South*. They objected to the passive black characters who seemed thoroughly content with their subservient positions in the South.

Dole's pineapples Women process pineapples in the Honolulu cannery of the Hawaiian Pineapple Company (now the Dole Food Company, Inc.) in 1948. James Drummond Dole, nicknamed the "Pineapple King," bought his first pineapple plantation on Oahu in 1899. In 1901 he began canning his pineapples and founded the Hawaiian Pineapple Company. The assembly-line activity seen here became possible after the 1911 invention of the Ginaca pineapple processing machine, which automatically cut pineapples into can-sized cylinders and cored them. The Ginaca machine was eventually able to process 100 pineapples per minute.

Gruening pushes for Alaska statehood Ernest Gruening, governor of Alaska Territory since 1939, lives it up at a governors conference in 1948. Alaska did not fully engage America's attention until 1942, when Japan occupied some of the territory's neighboring Aleutian Islands, stirring fears of another Pearl Harbor. Billions of military dollars suddenly poured into Alaska. From 1940 to 1943, its population increased from 75,000 to 233,000. When Alaska became a state in 1959, Gruening served as one of its first U.S. senators.

Eccentric billionaire
J. Paul Getty was a colorful and flamboyant western oilman. After attending the University of Southern California and Berkeley, he graduated from Magdalen College, Oxford in Great Britain. Getty worked in his father's oil fields, then formed his own company in Tulsa. After making his first million by 1916, he decided to retire at 25 to become a Los Angeles-based playboy, much to his father's chagrin. He

returned to work and became an eccentric billionaire who installed pay phones in his mansion, saved bits of string, and washed his own underwear. He also married five times, and when he died, he left his eldest son a mere $500.

Nixon goes after Reds Future president Richard Nixon (*left*) used Red-baiting to propel his political career. Nixon was elected as a U.S. representative (R–CA) in 1946 after strongly suggesting that his opponent had Communist sympathies. In Congress, he rose to prominence in the House Un-American Activities Committee (HUAC). Here he examines testimony concerning the Communist threat with New Jersey Representative J. Parnell Thomas (*right*) and HUAC's lead investigator, Robert Stripling. Nixon's aggressive interrogation of Alger Hiss, a former State Department official accused of spying for the Soviet Union, established his reputation as tough on communism. So did his successful 1950 campaign for the U.S. Senate, in which he again smeared his opponent with accusations of extreme left-wing views.

1940-1949

1948: The U.S. government makes token reparations to Japanese who were forced into internment camps during World War II. The government returns 10 cents for every dollar a prisoner could prove he or she lost as a result of the internment.

April 1948: The U.S. military begins a series of nuclear tests on Eniwetok Atoll, in the South Pacific Marshall Islands chain.

June 1948: The Palomar Observatory in San Diego County, California, officially opens.

July 26, 1948: President Truman issues an executive order to end segregation in the U.S. Armed Forces.

October 1, 1948: In *Perez v. Sharp,* the California Supreme Court rules that a state law banning interracial marriages is unconstitutional.

November 2–3, 1948: In an electoral result that catches many by surprise, incumbent President Harry Truman beats challenger Thomas Dewey • Texas Democrat Lyndon Johnson wins a seat in the U.S. Senate by a razor-thin 87-vote margin.

Winter 1948–49: A blizzard sweeps through Nebraska, Wyoming, and the Dakotas, bringing transportation and commerce to a standstill.

1949: Idaho's National Reactor Testing Station opens near Arco. In a 90-minute experiment in 1955, it will become the world's first nuclear reactor to provide power to an entire town.

April 4, 1949: The U.S., Great Britain, Portugal, Italy, Norway, Denmark, Iceland, the Netherlands, Luxembourg, Canada, Belgium, and France charter NATO, the North Atlantic Treaty Organization.

August 24, 1949: The medical school at the University of Texas in Galveston admits its first African American student.

A kindly cowboy Roy Rogers (born Leonard Franklin Slye) and his second wife, Dale Evans, stood for clean living and decent fun to their many fans. As a young man, Slye sang with a western cowboy music group and took small parts in films. In 1938 he got his break when Gene Autry walked out on a movie contract. Slye changed his name to Roy Rogers and became the hero of a string of musical westerns. Rogers would shoot the gun out of a villain's hand rather than kill the man. Rogers's palomino horse (Trigger) and his grouchy sidekick (Gabby Hayes) added to his myth.

San Diego's population explosion A housing boom occurred in San Diego County, California, after World War II. The county's population grew from 289,348 in 1940 to 556,808 10 years later. The growth was fuelled by marvelous weather, job opportunities, and a city and county government committed to expansion. Voters were more than willing to support bond issues for building, including one in 1945 to begin development of Mission Bay and another in 1946 to fund the construction of an aqueduct.

The "Singing Cowboy" Gene Autry (*left*) was a 17-year-old telegrapher in Oklahoma when his vocal talent was first noticed and encouraged by Will Rogers. After a stint in radio, Autry—the "Singing Cowboy"—moved into film in 1934, becoming a top western star by 1937. In nearly 100 "B" movies and a television show that ran from 1950 to 1956, Autry played an amiable, singing western lawman—a character whose name was his own. Pat Buttram (*right*) was Autry's frequent comic sidekick. A shrewd businessman, Autry retired from show business in 1964 and endowed the Autry Museum in Los Angeles in 1998.

Bowron takes control in L.A.
Fletcher Bowron, mayor of Los Angeles from 1938 to 1953, cleaned up the city in what he called the "Los Angeles Urban Reform Revival." He replaced officials who had been tainted by corruption, including the police chief. In 1942 he created an uproar and rebellion among women when he expressed his disapproval of female employees wearing slacks to work. Bowron met with African American leaders, proclaimed the first official celebration of Negro History Week in Los Angeles, and attended festivities in the Mexican American and Japanese American communities. Nevertheless, he was in complete agreement with the World War II internment of Japanese Americans.

Comic book cowpokes
Cowboy comics were for kids, and their advent coincided with the rise of the Hollywood "B" western in the 1930s. Like the B movies, western comics gloried in criminal activity and shootouts, with little regard for historical fact. In "Gun-Mad Lil," the liveliest story in this 1949 issue of *Saddle Justice,* the beautiful but crazed protagonist guns down nine "ornery rats" in just four pages.

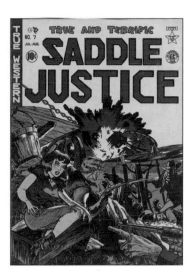

L.A. highways When this six-mile Arroyo Seco Parkway opened in Los Angeles in 1940, it was the first freeway in the West. The sprawling city's streets were clogged with vehicles, and transportation engineers believed that freeways would solve all their traffic problems. Leaders of surrounding cities—such as Whittier, South Gate, Long Beach, and Pasadena—urged a system that would connect the entire area, and residents agreeably supported higher taxes and bonds to build it. Two more freeways opened during the 1940s, and by 1949 plans had been drawn for a wide-ranging Los Angeles freeway system.

Rise to Prominence
⤜1950–Today⤛

S INCE 1950, LIFE IN THE UNITED STATES has changed dramatically—
especially in the American West. The West of 2005 was bigger—in
numbers of people and, more importantly, in the life of the nation—
than it was in 1950. While the entire United States roughly doubled
in those 55 years, the West more than tripled, rising from 13 percent of the
national population to nearly 23 percent. As was true in other regions, nearly
all of the West's increase took place in large cities and suburbs rather than
in rural areas.

The Great Plains—where so much homesteading, town-building, and railroading took place between 1870 and 1920—stabilized, aged, and in many
counties actually lost population beginning in the 1920s. That depletion continued steadily after 1950. Small towns shriveled and literally blew away.
Farmsteads were abandoned, railroads and post offices were shut down, and
young people fled. The American frontier of farm settlement passed its peak
by 1920. It suffered a grievous blow in the 1930s when the Great Depression
was compounded by drought and the Dust Bowl, and it never recovered after
World War II. Agriculture expanded but in mechanized, large-scale units.
Small farmers moved to towns and cities, retired, or simply died off, while
their children found other challenges in the West's expanding cities.

Populated by just 11,000 people in 1880, Los Angeles
boasted a population of 3.8 million in 2005. L.A.'s
metropolitan area is home to 12.9 million people,
making it one of the largest metro areas in the world.

"By 1965 the West had ceased to be a frontier in any traditional sense. Yet it seemed to be forever pioneering, originating, creating. In the next two decades it became the cockpit of several great national events, none of them momentary, all reflecting long-term, basic demographic change: the end of the baby boom, a wholly new immigration, environmental concerns, and inexorable metropolitanism."

—AUTHOR WALTER NUGENT, *INTO THE WEST*

1950–TODAY

1950: A rich lode of uranium is discovered near Grants, New Mexico, triggering a uranium mining rush.

1950: Western novelist Louis L'Amour releases *Westward the Tide,* the first of his 90 novels.

1950: Historian Henry Nash Smith publishes *Virgin Land: The American West as Symbol and Myth,* his seminal work on the West.

1950: More than 30,000 productive oil wells are operating in Kansas.

June 5, 1950: The U.S. Supreme Court orders the University of Texas Law School to desegregate.

June 25, 1950: The Korean War begins with the surprise invasion of South Korea by Communist North Korea.

1951: Restauranteur Robert Peterson opens his first Jack in the Box drive-through in San Diego.

1951: The Bracero Program, which brings agricultural workers from Mexico into the U.S., is revived.

1952: John Steinbeck publishes *East of Eden,* his largely autobiographical novel set in Salinas, California.

November 1, 1952: The U.S. detonates its first hydrogen bomb, nicknamed "Mike," at the South Pacific proving grounds at Eniwetok Atoll.

1953: In an action dubbed "Operation Wetback," the U.S. Immigration and Naturalization Service deports 1.5 million Mexicans.

1953: The General Dynamics aerospace giant grows larger with the acquisition of Convair.

August 1, 1953: Congress approves House Concurrent Resolution 108, which seeks to abdicate all federal responsibility for American Indian affairs.

A housing boom in the San Francisco suburb of Richmond reflected the phenomenal growth in California in the early 1990s, as the small city's population grew by almost 20 percent.

Those cities, however, were a huge success story. The only significant western city that actually lost population between 1950 and 2005 was San Francisco—which slipped from 775,000 to 739,000. That, however, was something of a rebound from its 679,000 of 1980, and the metropolitan Bay Area as a whole grew to more than four million, 12th largest in the nation. Meanwhile, Los Angeles sped past Chicago in the 1980s to become the nation's second most populated city (behind New York).

Of the largest 50 cities in 2005, 18 were in the 13-state West and nine more were in Texas and Oklahoma—over half of the national total. A few that had not been among the top 100 or 200 in 1950 rocketed to prominence. Several that had fewer than 100,000 people in 1950 boasted a half-million or more by 2005. The most spectacular examples were Mesa, Arizona, which went from 17,000 to 443,000; Colorado Springs, from 45,000 to 370,000; Tucson, from 45,000 to 516,000; Las Vegas, from 25,000 to 545,000; and Phoenix, with a 14-fold increase from 107,000 to 1,462,000, making it the sixth largest city in the country.

As long-established eastern and midwestern cities shrank and dropped in the national rankings of populations, western cities replaced them. In 1950 San Jose (95,000) was dwarfed by Detroit (1,850,000), but in 2005 San Jose was the larger, with 912,000 versus Detroit's 887,000. San Jose, in fact, is larger than Indianapolis, Baltimore, and Milwaukee. Phoenix, which had about 5 percent of Philadelphia's population in 1950, was poised to pass it before 2010. Places unheard of in 1950 except locally—such as Glendale and Scottsdale, Arizona; Modesto, Fresno, Stockton, and Bakersfield in California's Central Valley; and Henderson, Nevada, near Las Vegas—each were home to hundreds of thousands.

The mental picture of the West that many Americans traditionally had—wide-open spaces, men on horseback racing across the emptiness of Monument Valley, the unpeopled peaks of the Rockies and Sierras—was simply out of date by the end of the century. Some people tried to deal with this disjuncture between reality and mythology by defining the West Coast's metropolises, especially Los Angeles, as not really part of the region. But if Los Angeles, the Bay Area, Portland, and Seattle were not in the West, where were they? The truth is that the West was urban and metropolitan, more so in percentage terms than any other region—and had been for a long time.

The peculiarity of the West, which has made its demography difficult for Easterners to grasp, is that it is both metropolitan and expansive, a region of cities but also of those wide-open spaces. To reconcile these seeming opposites, it helps to think of the West's cities as oases—large and growing population centers at considerable distances from each other, with "empty" land in between. People in Boise, Idaho, for example, like to think of themselves as central, which, in a sense, they are: centrally located in a subregion whose other cities (Seattle, Portland, Salt Lake City, and Denver) are several hundred miles distant. Phoenix is a two-hour drive from Tucson and almost five hours from Las Vegas. Las Vegas is six hours from Los Angeles and a lot more to anywhere else. Albuquerque and El Paso are similarly isolated in ways that cities on the East Coast and around the Great Lakes are not.

A historic cathedral contrasts with modern skyscrapers in Phoenix, America's largest state capital. Between 1990 and 2000, the city's metro population grew by 34 percent.

Portland, Oregon, ranks among America's most "livable" cities, due to such factors as clean air and water, natural beauty, numerous parks, and smart city planning.

January 20, 1954: Republican Dwight D. Eisenhower is inaugurated as the 34th U.S. president.

March 14, 1954: The film *Salt of the Earth* is released. It offers a window into the lives of Mexican Americans as they struggle to make their way in the United States.

May 17, 1954: In the landmark case *Brown v. Board of Education of Topeka,* the U.S. Supreme Court rules that racially segregated schools are unconstitutional.

July 17, 1955: Walt Disney's longtime dream becomes reality when Disneyland opens its gates in Anaheim, California.

1956: *Old Yeller,* Fred Gipson's classic novel about a boy and his dog in mid-19th century Texas, is released.

1956: Edward Abbey publishes his western classic, *The Brave Cowboy.*

June 29, 1956: The Federal-Aid Highway Act, which commits $25 billion in federal funding toward construction and maintenance of the federal highway system, is signed into law by President Eisenhower.

October 15, 1956: Construction begins on Arizona's massive Glen Canyon Dam. The 3,700-foot dam, built with more than five million cubic yards of concrete, will take 10 years to complete.

1957: Writer Theodore Geisel of La Jolla, California, writes *The Cat in the Hat* under the pen name Dr. Seuss, revolutionizing children's literature in America.

October 1957: The Vallecitos nuclear power plant near Pleasanton, California, goes online, making it the first privately funded nuclear plant in the nation.

In three or four cases, the image of an oasis as a solitary peak should be expanded into something more like a range, or strip—stretched along a natural boundary and including several more or less contiguous cities. Two examples, 500 miles apart, are the metropolitan strips on either side of the Rocky Mountains. On the east side, along the Front Range, lies a line of cities and towns of which the largest is Denver. But it also includes Colorado Springs, Boulder, and (stretching it not too much) Pueblo on the south end and Cheyenne on the north end. The west side of the Rockies, the Wasatch Front, similarly has a north-south strip with Salt Lake City at the center, Provo on the south, and Ogden at the northern tip.

In the Pacific Northwest, an increasingly contiguous strip runs from the Willamette Valley cities of Eugene, Corvallis, and Salem north through Portland and up to Tacoma and the Seattle metro area. Largest of all of these strip oases is southern California. From Santa Barbara south for more than 200 miles to the Mexican border, through Los Angeles, Orange County, and San Diego, "the Southland" strings together tens of millions of people. This strip runs almost continuously along land bordered by the Pacific on the west and mountain ranges and deserts on the east.

Smaller population clusters have appeared that were virtually nonexistent before 1950. Las Vegas is the only million-plus metro area in the United States that did not exist at all before 1900. Phoenix is one of the only major cities between New Orleans and California that had no Spanish or Mexican colonial origins. The appeals of Las Vegas are initially to the libido and the pocketbook—what happens in Las Vegas stays there—but hundreds of thousands of people have chosen to stay and live there. Phoenix has never been a gambling town, but like Vegas—and many other large and small cities from California all the way east to Florida—it has grown because of its resorts (Camelback, Biltmore, and others since the 1920s) and more recently because of its climate, tax leniency, and welcome to senior citizens (and other not-so-senior early retirees).

Senior citizens learn tai chi at the Sun City Retirement Home in Arizona. Opened in the 1960s, the home has inspired many similar establishments as the U.S. population has aged.

The Las Vegas Strip shines alluringly. The gambling mecca, which attracts roughly 35 million visitors a year, also has a permanent metropolitan population of more than 1.7 million.

As part of the Sunbelt, the Southwest expanded rapidly in the late 20th century, as retirement in new places became realistic possibilities because of Social Security and other pensions. Del Webb's Sun City near Phoenix; Leisure World in Orange County, California; Lake Havasu City along the Colorado River; and other retirement communities less famous drew the elderly from the Midwest and beyond as places to live out "the golden years." In certain cities, retirement opportunities combined with a strong military or naval presence to attract ex-officers and their families to a permanent place in the sun. Examples include San Diego and its suburb, Coronado, for the Navy; Colorado Springs for the Air Force; and several western cities for the Army.

In the early 20th century, many people went to Denver, Los Angeles, and points in between to cure their tuberculosis. In the late 20th century, people went west for happier reasons, one of them to take part in all sorts of leisure and recreation that scarcely existed in 1950. Hardly anyone had heard then of Aspen, Vail, Jackson Hole, or even Palm Springs. By 2000 they were common verbal currency, symbolizing attractive lifestyles. Skiing in the winter, surfing in the summer, visits to state and national parks and beaches during all seasons . . . these were more and more accepted parts of people's lives, at least part of the time.

Some of the new centers of population emerged after 1950 because the public's level of educational achievement kept rising. This happened through-

December 17, 1957: San Diego's Convair company completes the first successful test-firing of an Atlas A missile. It is the forerunner of the Atlas D, which will launch the spacecraft of the Mercury astronauts.

February 1958: Traffic opens on California's Interstate 8, which was built over well-worn American Indian trails through Mission Valley.

April 18, 1958: The Los Angeles (formerly Brooklyn) Dodgers play their first game, facing off against the San Francisco (formerly New York) Giants.

October 1, 1958: The National Aeronautics and Space Administration (NASA) begins operations.

1959: Stars Marilyn Monroe, Tony Curtis, and Jack Lemmon shine at the Hotel Del Coronado near San Diego during the production of Billy Wilder's *Some Like It Hot*.

1959: Seven of the year's 10 most popular prime-time television programs in the U.S. are westerns.

January 3, 1959: Alaska becomes the 49th state to join the Union.

August 21, 1959: Hawaii becomes the 50th state admitted to the Union.

1960: Developer Del Webb sells the first homes in his new planned community, Sun City, Arizona. Sun City is unique in that it is marketed exclusively to retirees. Webb's idea will catch on in several other American communities.

1960: The state of California approves a plan to transport water from the northern half of the state to supply the arid south.

1961: Seeking greater control of their destinies, delegates attending the American Indian Chicago Conference adopt a "Declaration of Indian Purpose."

out the country, but most notably in the West. The most prominent example is Silicon Valley, the cluster of once separate towns and villages around the south end of San Francisco Bay that merged to become one of the world epicenters of computing. Smaller but powerful mini-Silicon Valleys developed south of Salt Lake City and in the Seattle suburbs, where Microsoft and other computer companies flourished.

Universities, very few of them large in the West before 1950, became engorged with students when the Baby Boomers reached college age in the 1960s. After 1950, formerly small institutions gained enrollments, faculties, facilities, and laboratories as well as clerical staff, bookstores, and coffee shops—indeed, whole new economies and populations. UCLA, La Jolla, and other campuses of the University of California system topped a pyramid of educational institutions that included dozens of four-year and community colleges around the state. The universities of Washington, Colorado, Oregon, Arizona, and the other western states served similarly as flagships leading

fleets of state-supported educational institutions. The United States expanded its knowledge industries after 1950 as it had not done before, and the West—particularly California, but other coastal and border states as well—led the way.

Even the Baby Boom of 1946–64, a national phenomenon and hugely important demographic event, took place with more vigor and speed in the West than in other regions. In 1961, for example, 12 of the 16 states

Anticipating an explosion of aspiring college students (due to the baby boom and increasing affluence), California adopted a Master Plan for Higher Education in 1960. UCLA (*pictured*) was part of the nine-campus University of California system.

with the highest birthrates were in the West. All seven Mountain states were among the 12, with Utah's birthrate leading the country. The West also led the way down, becoming the first region to experience a "baby bust."

Waves of Immigrants

Populations can increase in only two ways: by births outnumbering deaths ("natural increase"), or by more people coming to a place than leaving it (i.e., high net immigration). The West produced more than its share of natural increase. It also continued, after 1950, as a preeminent region of immigration.

A large number of students arrives at California's newly constructed Lakewood Elementary School in 1953, a sure sign of early Baby Boomers reaching school age. This trend would continue into the 1970s.

To pick up and move, a person needs not only the will but the way. In the years following 1950, the ways to go west became significantly easier. Railroads still carried millions of passengers in 1950, taking them from Chicago and St. Louis and New Orleans to the Rockies and the West Coast on the *California Zephyr*, the *Super Chief*, and the Southern Pacific's streamliners. The Union Pacific railroad station in Ogden, Utah, saw more than a hundred passenger trains a day go through in 1950. By the 1980s, daily train traffic through Ogden dwindled to two. Passenger trains still existed in 2005, but there were very few—and they were not the usual way people chose when they went west.

The preferred methods that developed after 1950 were cars and planes. Auto trips from the Midwest to the West Coast, and points in between, had been happening since the early 1900s, but as late as 1941 they were still fairly rare and exotic. The Depression and Dust Bowl of the 1930s sent several hundred thousand dispossessed farm people rattling along Route 66 from Oklahoma to Santa Monica, paralleled by less famous migrations from the upper Midwest to the Pacific Northwest. But those numbers were nothing like the traffic after 1960. The enabling element was the interstate highway system.

The federal government had underwritten much of the transcontinental and other railroad building in the 19th century, and it stepped in and paid about 90 percent of the cost of the interstates in the late 20th. Gradually shrinking the vast distances of the West, they made it possible to drive 500 or 600 miles in a day—in other words, from one of the region's oasis cities to another. As the network developed, it spawned secondary businesses. Innu-

1961: Santa Fe, New Mexico's, Institute of American Indian Arts opens its doors.

January 20, 1961: Massachusetts Democrat John F. Kennedy takes the oath of office as the 35th U.S. president.

September 1961: NASA opens its Manned Spacecraft Center near Houston. The facility will eventually be renamed Johnson Space Center.

1962: Labor leader César Chávez establishes a union for agricultural workers: the National Farm Workers Association.

1962: For the first time, the population of California exceeds that of New York State.

1963: The Jonas Salk Institute for Biological Studies is established in La Jolla, California, by Salk, who developed the first polio vaccine in 1953.

November 22, 1963: President Kennedy is assassinated by Lee Harvey Oswald while riding in a motorcade through the streets of Dallas. Vice President Lyndon Johnson of Texas is given the oath of office, becoming the 36th president.

1964: Author Ken Kesey and his Merry Pranksters leave California on a cross-country bus trip. Their voyage, which will become emblematic of the '60s counterculture that is just getting underway, will be immortalized in Tom Wolfe's book *The Electric Kool-Aid Acid Test*.

1964: The Bracero Program is repealed once again, for the final time.

March 1964: San Diego's flagship SeaWorld amusement park opens its gates in Mission Bay Park.

merable gas stations, motels, restaurants, car dealerships, tourist spots, and other enterprises sprouted due to the highways.

Another post-1960 accelerator of travel and migration was the commercial jet. The pre-1960 four-engine, propeller-driven airliner took many hours to go from Chicago to Los Angeles, and it could carry only a few dozen people. The jet-driven 707 or DC-8 that came into use at the end of the 1950s, followed by jumbo jets in the late 1960s, transported many more people at much faster speeds. Some stayed, some only visited; but in either case the West became accessible and familiar to Americans from other regions as it never had been before.

Through easier transportation as well as natural increase, the post-1950 West grew in population faster than any of the other regions of the country. Growth in the 1950s was largely a continuation of patterns that had developed in the wartime 1940s: More African Americans migrated from Texas and nearby southern states. War veterans who had first seen the West, compliments of Uncle Sam, now returned with their young families. Ex-farmers and their children saw greater opportunities in western cities. War brides, both European and Asian, and many others all moved to the West, particularly to California, most especially Southern California. By 1960 California led the states in both foreign-born residents and new arrivals, passing New York. California also replaced New York (in 1962) as the state with the largest population.

Massive improvements in aircraft technology after 1950, exemplified by this Boeing 707, made travel to the West much easier and led to increased tourism and migration throughout the region.

Westward migration took a different turn in the 1960s, and again the federal government played a huge role. The Immigration Act of 1965 repealed the race-based national-origins quotas that had been legislated in the 1920s to virtually stop immigration from Eastern Europe and Asia. In doing so, the new law opened the door to Latin Americans and Asians, who began entering through it in 1968–69. It gave preference to persons with education and skills, or who already had family members in this country. The unexpected result of the 1965 act was to change the sources of immigration from Europe and Canada to Asia and Latin America, which together contributed about 85 percent of new arrivals in the 1970s and 1980s.

Although some of the newcomers settled in other parts of the country, the West naturally took the large majority because it was the region closest to the Mexican border and the Pacific. Each year from 1968 on, when the law fully kicked in, the net inflow of people from other countries seldom fell below a half-million, and in several years topped a million (as in 1990, when 1.5 million arrived, and 2005, with 1.1 million). These figures do not include refugees, more than 200,000 of whom arrived in 1980 (mostly from Vietnam), nor does it include undocumented or illegal immigrants. California consistently took in at least one out of five newcomers, more than twice as many as New York and many more than any other state. Fewer than 10 million foreign-born people were living in the United States in 1960, but by the early 1990s there were more than twice as many. In 2004 the United States boasted more than 34 million foreign-borns, of whom 13 million were naturalized citizens.

Immigration from Mexico and elsewhere in Latin America was nothing new in 1950. Before and after that date, numbers rose and fell according to the demand for workers, particularly in the border states of Texas and California. Sought after in the 1920s, Mexicans were expelled *en masse* when the Depression struck in the early 1930s. They were welcomed and hotly recruited as contract laborers from 1942 to 1964, under the Bracero Program, when native-born potential farmhands entered the armed services during World War II and chose other occupations afterward. After the 1965 law started operating, Mexicans (and smaller numbers of Guatemalans, Salvadorans, Hondurans, and others from Central America) entered entirely legally, often to reunite with family members and much more often than not to take up service positions in cities, not as farmworkers.

By the early 21st century, the Latino population of the West included many different kinds of people, from the descendants of the first entrants of

Most of the millions of Mexicans who have migrated to the U.S. after 1950—both legally and illegally—have lived in the Southwest, with many engaged in agricultural labor.

March 27, 1964: A massive earthquake strikes Alaska, literally liquefying acres of land and triggering huge tsunamis. Remarkably, only 131 people die in this disaster, the third largest quake in recorded history.

July 13, 1964: The Republican National Convention opens at the Cow Palace in San Francisco. The Republican nominee, Arizona Senator Barry Goldwater, will assert in his acceptance speech: "Extremism in the defense of liberty is no vice."

October 1, 1964: Berkeley's Free Speech Movement erupts when former student Jack Weinberg is arrested for promoting the Congress for Racial Equality on campus, in violation of school rules. Thousands will protest over the next several weeks.

1965: The Immigration and Naturalization Act of 1965 abolishes immigration quotas based on nation of origin. It will spur a massive influx of immigrants from Latin American and Asian nations, a trend that continues today.

1965: Archaeologists begin digging at Presidio Park, the site of the earliest Spanish settlement in San Diego.

1965: The Mexican government permits the establishment of *maquiladora* factories, which will allow American manufacturing concerns to take advantage of cheap Mexican labor by opening plants entirely or partially owned and managed by non-Mexicans.

August 1965: Members of the Seventh Marine Division out of California's Camp Pendleton conduct "Operation Starlite," considered the first significant U.S. ground engagement in Vietnam.

Mexicans living in Los Angeles demand their rights in a 2006 demonstration. Roughly 80 percent of Mexicans coming to America from 1990 to 2005 were illegal immigrants.

1598 and of Spanish colonists over the next 200 years as well as the newest arrivals crossing at El Paso, Nogales, Tijuana, or other border points. They also ranged in class, education, and occupation, from unskilled farmworkers to the most highly qualified professionals and business executives. Although the heaviest concentrations of Spanish-speaking and Spanish-descended persons lived in California and the other three border states, Latinos were spreading well beyond the West.

Massive Asian immigration also resulted from the 1965 law. The three Chinas—mainland, Taiwan, and Hong Kong—were all major contributors. Many of them were professionals or students, with some bringing substantial wealth (in sharp contrast to the bachelor railroad and laundry workers of the 19th century). India sent tens of thousands of people to America. They, too, became prominent in certain professions, notably health care. After the end of the Vietnam War, several waves of immigrants arrived from that country and Cambodia, with California taking in the largest number.

Koreans arrived, too. Among the traditional sources of Asian immigration—small and restricted as it was—only Japan declined to send many people after 1950. The Philippines, the former American colony in the western Pacific, provided the largest number of any Asian group, aided as they were by knowing the English language before they arrived. The immigration law of 1965 deci-

By 2000, 2.7 million Americans identified themselves as Chinese, with a large number living in the West. In 1996 Gary Locke (*pictured*) of Washington State became the first Chinese American elected governor.

sively changed the faces and raised the number of people in the West. Further legislation in 1986, 1990, and later attempted to control the flow, especially of illegals, but did so only moderately at best.

Migration to the West from other parts of the country was as old as the Gold Rush. In 1950 and beyond, the stagnating Great Plains sent many of its young people to California, Washington, and other urbanized states in the West. New York contributed substantial numbers, and so did such midwestern states as Illinois. African Americans from Texas, Louisiana, Arkansas, and nearby had begun to trickle into California in the late 1930s. When the aircraft and shipbuilding industries on the West Coast finally dropped their discriminatory hiring policies in 1943, black people surged to the Los Angeles and San Francisco Bay areas, never to return to the South. Other western cities experienced an influx of black people, some for the first time in a serious way. After 1970, increases in the West's black population came from natural increase—very little from new migration—which was also true in the Midwest.

Within the West, native-born people migrated in the 1950s to 1970s from the Mountain states to the coast. After 1990, due to the resultant problems of overcrowding, Californians relocated to Oregon, Washington, and interior states, such as Idaho. During the first five years of the 2000s, some western states received more migrants from other states than from other countries, specifically Arizona, Idaho, Nevada, and Oregon. Other states lost considerable numbers of native born people while continuing to attract foreigners. So it went in Utah (which lost 34,000 native-borns but took in 50,000 foreign-borns), Alaska, Hawaii, and spectacularly California (which lost 664,000 native-borns chiefly to other states but attracted more than 1.4 million foreign-borns, mostly Mexican, Central American, and Asian).

The result of all the natural increase, internal migration, and immigration from other countries between 1950 and 2005 was the emergence of a region not only much more populated, but much more diverse. Some states ceased to have a native-white majority. In 2004 California was 44.5 percent white, 34.7 Hispanic or Latino, 12.1 Asian, and 6.8 African American. Demographers and economists uniformly predicted that immigration would continue, that the West would maintain birth rates at a strong level, and that the region would consequently keep growing faster than the national average.

The large Korean and African American communities of Los Angeles were often at odds, culminating in violence during the 1992 L.A. riot. Here, market owner Jae Yul Kim, who rebuilt after the riot, and longtime customer McKinley Gipson greet each other in 1997.

August 11–16, 1965: Thirty-four people die when race rioting erupts for six days in the Watts neighborhood of Los Angeles.

August 1, 1966: Charles Whitman kills 14 and injures dozens from the University of Texas tower in Austin as he opens fire on the campus below.

January 14, 1967: San Francisco's Golden Gate Park hosts the Human Be-In, an event that will give rise to the influx of young hippies to the Haight-Ashbury neighborhood several months later, during the "Summer of Love."

1968: Diné College, formerly Navajo Community College, opens in Tsaile, Arizona, as the first tribally chartered higher-education institution.

1968: Naturalist Edward Abbey pens *Desert Solitaire,* his seminal work about the American desert landscape.

June 6, 1968: Presidential candidate Robert Kennedy is shot and killed by Sirhan Sirhan at the Ambassador Hotel in Los Angeles moments after announcing his win in the California Democratic primary.

Summer 1968: American Indian activists found AIM, the American Indian Movement, in Minneapolis.

August 10, 1968: Police in Oakland fire shots at the headquarters of the militant Black Panthers. Throughout the late 1960s, law enforcement works nationwide to disrupt the activities of the Panthers, considered dangerously subversive by the federal government.

November 1968: In an effort to force the creation of a college of ethnic studies, students at San Francisco State University will embark on what will become the longest student strike of the 1960s. University officials will accede to the students' demands in March 1969.

Explosive Economies

With all the population growth and migration into the West after 1950, it is not surprising that the region's economic development also outpaced the national average. It did so, however, in ways that diverged from tradition. No longer was the West the place to find gold miners, homesteaders, and cowboys (though some of each were still there). More likely, one would find a tourist, a bureaucrat (public or private), a software writer, or a restaurant worker. Along with the rest of the American economy, the West modernized into new forms.

The World War II years were boom times in the West, as the war and its immediate aftermath yanked the region out of the Great Depression. During the war, soothsayers from *Fortune* magazine and other prognosticators warned that when the war ended, the economy of the West, and probably the nation, would relapse into depression again. But nothing of the sort happened. The West continued to take off, fed by migration (as previously described); by opportunities—many of them different from any before; by the Sunbelt climate; by the relative lack of racial discrimination, compared to the South and other places; and by the sheer lure—and here, tradition continued—of the western idea.

Since the Gold Rush, the West had always been thought of and dreamt of as the region of freedom and opportunity. For many, the wartime and post-

So-called "big oil," represented by such companies as Exxon, Shell, and Phillips, has dominated oil drilling in the Southwest for much of the period since 1950, eliminating most wildcatters. Pictured is an oil refinery in Texas.

war years were like a new Gold Rush. As workers went west looking for jobs, and usually finding them, people with money to invest or with ideas to try out also decided that the West was the most fertile and promising place to be. By 1950 the West already had enough people, money, and ideas of its own to generate its rapid development. Outsiders simply accelerated the pace.

Looking at the economies of the West after 1950, certain long-term trends and themes stand out. In the first place, size and speed: Economic development expanded more rapidly in the West than elsewhere in the country, taking an ever larger share of national product. Second, while extractive industries continued to be significant—mining, fishing, lumbering, farming, ranching, oil-drilling—they took a back seat to newer, less traditional western activities. Extraction occupied a shrinking share of the regional economy.

Third, manufacturing became prominent to a degree unknown before World War II. Some manufacturing involved consumer durables, such as cars and aircraft, while some of it included building military equipment or ships. Additional manufacturing industries included steelmaking, metal-processing, and oil-refining. All of these were traditional forms of manufacturing, although the West had seen little of such activity before the war. Other manufacturing, however, was unknown anywhere before the 1950s, and here the West took the lead—most notably in computer technology.

Fourth, more and more of the region's economic activity lay in the service sector, which included a vast range of activities: from personal services such as hair-styling or fashion design to finance, insurance, banking, government, and many other ways in which people worked not to produce some tangible good but something intangible but essential, at least to modern life.

Fifth, construction became a huge industry. Every new suburb pushing out of Los Angeles or Phoenix or the other metropolises required houses, post offices, fire trucks, gas stations, streets, sewers, phone and electric lines, city halls and police stations, lawn care, schools, and churches. And much more. Every city center demanded new, tall buildings, and up they soared. Enterprises needed factories or, as the new computer companies preferred to call their headquarters, "campuses," such as the Microsoft campus in Redmond, Washington. Highways, aqueducts, airports, and other forms of "infrastructure" emerged everywhere.

An iron worker toils on the Lincoln Tower office building in Denver in 1964. Like many western cities, Denver has experienced major construction booms since 1950, especially in the 1980s, as symbolized by voter approval of a new multibillion-dollar airport.

1969: Country singer Merle Haggard records his cowboy classic, *Okie from Muskogee.*

1969: N. Scott Momaday, a Kiowa Indian, is awarded a Pulitzer Prize for his novel *House Made of Dawn.*

January 20, 1969: California Republican Richard Nixon is inaugurated as the 37th U.S. president.

July 20, 1969: Under the watchful eye of the NASA Mission Control technicians at Houston's Manned Spacecraft Center, Neil Armstrong takes mankind's first steps on the moon.

August 1969: Followers of sociopath hippie guru Charles Manson go on a Los Angeles killing spree that claims eight lives, including that of Sharon Tate, a film starlet who is more than eight months pregnant. Captured by the end of the year, most of the members of Manson's "family" will be imprisoned.

August 3, 1969: The San Diego–Coronado Bay Bridge opens to traffic.

November 20, 1969: A group of American Indian activists occupies Alcatraz Island in the San Francisco Bay, demanding the use of the facility for an Indian cultural center. The occupation will continue until June 1971.

December 6, 1969: Four die when violence erupts at a free Rolling Stones concert at California's Altamont Speedway.

1970: After a five-year strike, Filipino and Hispanic agricultural workers win concessions from California grape growers.

1971: Wallace Stegner releases *Angle of Repose,* based on the life of reluctant western pioneer Mary Hallock Foote. The book will win a Pulitzer Prize for fiction.

Sixth, the federal government had vast economic impacts, directly and indirectly. The surging economy of World War II slackened only momentarily after V-J day. For more than 40 years after that, the Cold War seemed to require constant new infusions of aircraft and missiles, maintenance of dozens of military and naval bases, and support systems, all of which the West happily provided. The Korean War (1950–53) and U.S. involvement in the war in Vietnam (1962–73) only intensified Cold War preparedness. Nor did the end of the Cold War in 1991 put an end to war-related economic activity. Other than a quite temporary cutback in aircraft and aerospace spending in the early 1990s, no serious "peace dividend" reversed the federal government's inputs. Nor was all federal activity military connected, as we shall see.

These six features give only a bare-bones idea of the western regional economy in the second half of the 20th century. Some of them deserve more detailed comment. As to the first, more rapid growth than elsewhere: California contained roughly half of the West's people through the period, the equal of the other 12 states, and it generated at least half of the region's economic product. By the 1980s, one heard often that if California were an independent country (and economy), it would be the world's seventh largest. Moreover, the state's economy was well balanced, leading most other states in

The headquarters of Intel stands aglow in California's Silicon Valley. The leading U.S. producer of microprocessors for computers, Intel helped make Northern California a major center for technology companies.

agricultural output as well as manufacturing, technology and "the knowledge industry," and services both public and private. Of course, California wasn't the only economic engine in the region. The Seattle area, Silicon Valley just south of San Francisco, the Utah and Colorado oases, and the Texas metropolises were all substantial economic centers.

Conversely, the parts of the West dependent on traditional extractive activities—such as agriculture, mining, lumbering, fishing, and even (by 2000) oil production—stabilized and, consequently, took reduced shares of the regional output. As historians Michael P. Malone and Richard W. Etulain remarked, "The West's older extractive industries, based on the harvesting of its natural resources, crested during the prosperous 1950s and 1960s; then, generally speaking, they began to decline, some of them seemingly never to rise again."

Periodic energy crunches, most notably from the mid-1970s to just after 1980 when the oil-producing OPEC nations embargoed or choked off oil exports, sent energy companies into headlong searches to find new oil reserves, to extract oil from shale, or to mine more coal from Wyoming's near-inexhaustible beds. In 1970 the largest coal mine in the United States was not in Pennsylvania or West Virginia, but outside Farmington, New Mexico, in the Four Corners area. But these scrambles subsided when oil prices came down. (In the early 21st century, another price rise threatened to become more permanent.)

Precious-metals mining, another mainstay of the pre-1950 western economy, never actually ceased. However, it faded for several reasons: exhaustion of gold and silver ores that could economically be refined; similar problems with copper, causing the shutdown of Anaconda and the other great copper companies of Montana and Arizona; and the search to replace those metals with more exotic ones such as uranium (sought in Utah and New Mexico), but with no equivalent success.

Lumbering, so much a part of the Northwest's traditional economy, also flourished for a while because of immense new demand for materials for houses and other buildings. But clear-cutting of forests—faster than new growth could possibly catch up—forced many companies out of business or, at best, encouraged them to press the Forest Service (and Congress) to permit cutting in national forests. Of course, there was plenty of opposition to that from recreation interests, environmentalists, and the general public. Around Coos Bay in southwestern Oregon, for example, where the smell of logs and

"The men and women who populated Silicon Valley in the 1960s were optimists. . . . They would be famous and rich, have beautiful children and live in a Winterless Paradise and own a modernistic house and collect fine wines—all at the same time."

—AUTHOR MICHAEL S. MALONE, INFINITE LOOP

lumber yards meant the smell of money, the forests were depleted by 1990 and the industry collapsed. By 2000 lumbering around Coos Bay was replaced, in part, by the Bandon Dunes Golf Resort. That shift from lumbering to leisure typified much of the West's economic change.

The other traditional western extractive enterprise, besides mining and lumbering, was agriculture. What happened in this sector was not shutdowns but changes in business organization and technology. As long as water was available, crops would grow and livestock would feed. In California and Texas, ranchers and farmers made sure that water would stay available, making farming nearly drought-proof through irrigation. Billions were spent to create California's aqueduct system, both in the Central Valley—the world's greatest agricultural factory—and in the Imperial Valley, inland along the Mexican border.

On the other side of the West, on the Great Plains, irrigation also made crops flourish, but this irrigation was different. Center-pivot wells sucked up water from the Ogallala Aquifer, the great underground lake (the size of Lake Huron) that had accumulated since Pleistocene times. Unfortunately, the Aquifer was not renewable, and agribusiness drew it down so fast that in the 30 years

The California Aqueduct, begun in 1960, includes more than 400 miles of canals, tunnels, and pipelines, and provides up to three million acre feet of water to Southern California each year.

after center-pivots first appeared in the 1950s, its southern extremities were already going dry. For a few decades, however, Texas cotton and Kansas wheat sprouted on Ogallala water.

As for the organization of agricultural production, the trend was toward larger and larger units—and the force-out of small producers. In California, large units had been typical since Spanish and Mexican times, and corporate farms—agribusinesses—dominated in the Central Valley. There, no tidy farmhouses marked the landscape, but rather mile after mile of irrigated fields and orchards. On the Great Plains, such large units had been rare prior to 1950, with the exception of the great cattle ranches of south and west Texas and of Wyoming and Colorado, the independent homestead had been the ideal, and often the reality.

From the 1950s on, however, the small farmer struggled to compete with larger neighbors, even in growing corn or wheat. Tractors became too expensive; harvesters and combines (and people to operate them) had to be rented or hired; fertilizers and pesticides became essential, or one's yield-per-acre simply could not match the big outfit's chemistry; center-pivot irrigation required major investment; and the farmer practically needed an MBA to keep up with the taxes and accounting. On top of all that, small farms did not pay very well, and the sons and daughters of the farmers who had survived the 1920s and 1930s saw opportunities beckoning in towns or, better, in cities—especially the young people who had seen part of the world in the military, or who had gone to college.

A third of the farms of Texas were swallowed up by larger ones in the 1950s and 1960s. Similar scenarios occurred in Oklahoma, Kansas, Nebraska, and the Dakotas. The homesteaders of the early 20th century— or more precisely, their children and grandchildren—could not stay on the land even

when they wanted to. When they left, agribusinesses using up-to-date (and very expensive) machinery superseded them. They kept labor costs low by hiring large numbers of migrant workers, including many from Mexico.

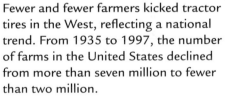

Fewer and fewer farmers kicked tractor tires in the West, reflecting a national trend. From 1935 to 1997, the number of farms in the United States declined from more than seven million to fewer than two million.

As the small farmers grew old and folded, and their children moved elsewhere, the remaining population of the small towns of the Great Plains aged and faded away. The Plains never became wholly depopulated, but between 1950 and 2005 the farm population of the West, particularly the western Great Plains, fell by about three-fourths. It was an exaggerated, concentrated example of a trend that had been manifest in American farming since the 19th century: As a sector of the economy, *agriculture* flourished and produced food and fiber at ever higher levels, but *farmers* as a population grew older, thinned in numbers, and did not prosper.

Western manufacturing, on the other hand, spread in size and shape after 1950. The war had brought large steel mills to the region, notably Henry J. Kaiser's mill in Fontana, California, east of Los Angeles, and another at Provo,

1975: Phelps Dodge, the lifeblood of the copper mining town of Bisbee, Arizona, shuts down operations.

1975: Gillette, Wyoming, and other prolific Rocky Mountain coal-producing towns boom on the strength of the fossil fuel market.

January 4, 1975: The Indian Self-Determination and Education Assistance Act is signed into law. This act will establish a framework for funneling social services to American Indians through the Bureau of Indian Affairs.

April 30, 1975: Saigon falls, and the first of nearly three million refugees flee Communist Vietnam. Nearly half of the Vietnamese refugees will reach North America, with the vast majority of them settling in California.

June 26, 1975: A shootout at South Dakota's Lakota Pine Ridge reservation leaves one Indian and two FBI agents dead.

April 1976: Steve Wozniak and Steve Jobs launch Apple Computer, Inc., in Palo Alto, California, with the introduction of the Apple I computer, the first computer with a single circuit board.

July 31, 1976: A cloudburst over the Big Thompson River results in a devastating flood that claims more than 140 lives.

January 20, 1977: Georgia Democrat Jimmy Carter is sworn in as the 39th U.S. president.

June 20, 1977: The Trans-Alaska Pipeline is completed, linking interior oil fields to the coastal port of Valdez.

August 11, 1978: The American Indian Religious Freedom Act is signed into law. It underscores the existing constitutional right to freedom of religion that so often was denied Indians in the past.

Utah. It also brought or greatly expanded aircraft factories—Boeing in Seattle; Lockheed and Douglas in Los Angeles; Cessna, Beech, Learjet, and again Boeing (B-52s and other warplanes) in Wichita, and others. Shipbuilding and fitting continued in Long Beach, Richmond, Portland, and Puget Sound. Cars came out of new factories in Torrance, California, and elsewhere.

But all these were familiar elsewhere in the country, if new in the West. The West's virtually indigenous contribution to manufactur-

Cold War tensions led to an increase in military aircraft purchased by the Air Force—including the Boeing B-52 bomber (*pictured*). The USAF received 47 percent of the defense budget in 1960.

ing was in wholly new fields, particularly aerospace and computing. The number of large firms that were located in the West tripled between 1950 and 2000, and some of the very largest of them, incredibly, had started in tinkers' garages in and around San Jose. Hewlett Packard was such a start-up. So was Apple Computer, Inc., founded by Steve Jobs and Stephen Wozniak. Intel, the chip-maker, had its home there. In Seattle, Bill Gates and Paul Allen created the largest of all, Microsoft, from a tiny beginning.

Microsoft Corporation's Windows has become the world's dominant computer operating system. Founded in 1975 by Bill Gates (*pictured*), the Seattle-based company helped make Gates the wealthiest person in the world.

The inventor entrepreneur of past decades, such as Thomas Edison or Henry Ford, still appeared—but on the West Coast rather than in the Midwest. Success came not only from invention but also from organization. The dean of Stanford's engineering school, Frederick Terman, meshed the resources of his university with government agencies and such companies as Hewlett Packard and Fairchild Semiconductor, and in 1951 started Silicon Valley. This was one of the first, and no doubt the most famous, university-corporate-government industrial parks.

Business historians point out that even more than manufacturing, the service sector became the outstanding part of the economy of the West after 1950. Perhaps it should because "service" is defined to include so much, including banking. In 1950 Amadeo P. Giannini's Bank of America—from humble beginnings before the 1906 San Francisco earthquake and fire—reigned as the largest bank in the world. In 1958 Giannini introduced BankAmericard (later, Visa), the first general-purpose credit card, which revolutionized consumer practice everywhere. Other western banks, including Wells Fargo and Security Pacific, ranked high as well.

Insurance and financial services of all sorts arose to aid both businesses and private individuals. Governments at all levels expanded to serve communities. Like corporations, they provided jobs (the "public sector") for millions. Governments also created public works: the interstates, other roads and bridges, streets, and buildings. Denver became a center for federal agencies, and by 1975 had more federal employees than any place except Washington, D.C.

Fun-seekers pour into Disneyland in Anaheim, California. Walt Disney's dream theme park opened to huge crowds in 1955 (*pictured*) and over the years has hosted more than 500 million visitors.

Recreation and tourism was, like computing, an industry almost unknown in 1950 but which grew to be a very major part of the regional economy. To be sure, railroad and auto tourism took place before the war, as did visits to the national parks and resort hotels. But the scale and the variety simply exploded, especially after 1960. Disneyland opened in Anaheim, California, in 1955. Motel chains such as Holiday Inn and Best Western did not start in the West but found fertile ground there, as did McDonald's and other fast-food chains. The interstates, as mentioned earlier, brought visitors as well as permanent migrants to the West.

September 25, 1978: One hundred forty-four people die and some 20 houses are destroyed when a Cessna collides with a Pacific Southwest Airlines jet on approach to San Diego International Airport.

November 8, 1978: The President signs the Indian Child Welfare Act, which puts jurisdiction over Indian adoptions in the hands of the tribes.

November 27, 1978: San Francisco Mayor George Moscone and Supervisor Harvey Milk are assassinated by former Supervisor Dan White for their support of gay rights in San Francisco, home of a large homosexual population.

1980: Coal mining production peaks at mines throughout the western slope of the Colorado Rocky Mountains.

May 18, 1980: Fifty-seven people lose their lives when Mount St. Helens, an active volcano in the state of Washington, erupts.

September 14, 1980: Televangelist Dr. Robert Schuller dedicates his Crystal Cathedral in Garden Grove, California. It has seating for nearly 3,000 parishioners and a massive outdoor screen for "drive-in" worship.

January 20, 1981: Former California Governor Ronald Reagan is inaugurated as the 40th U.S. president.

1982: The Mexican peso suffers a dramatic devaluation, triggering a corresponding increase in the non-Mexican owned *maquiladoras* (factories).

1982: Thousands lose their jobs when Exxon closes its oil shale development fields in the Colorado counties of Rio Blanco, Mesa, and Garfield.

Telluride, Colorado, home to a ski resort and an annual film festival, has contributed to the growth of western tourism since 1950. In 2002 alone, 22 million "leisure" visitors flocked to Colorado.

Upscale and full-service resorts attracted the expanding American middle class. Tourists flocked to Vail, Colorado; Jackson Hole, Wyoming; Scottsdale, Arizona; and, of course, Las Vegas. Tourism replaced mining as the major income-producer in many states, and as early as 1949 it outran everything except aircraft manufacturing as a moneymaker in Southern California. In smaller places along the interstates, communities stayed alive by touting the historic significance (and fun for the family) of any fort or other artifact that could be called historic. Car dealerships and service stations proliferated, as did auto ownership.

Construction was another mark of the late 20th-century West. All those suburbs meant millions of new homes, and they required wood products, cement, plaster, bricks, wall board, fixtures, electrical equipment, streets, schools, municipal government, retail shops (often in the form of shopping centers and malls), and freeways and other roads. The ranch-style house, pioneered in Southern California as a postwar adaptation of the early 20th-century California bungalow, swept back eastward. Ranch homes appeared in towns and suburbs throughout the Midwest, the South, and, eventually, even the Northeast.

The federal government played an enormous role in the western economy, even though many Westerners, especially in the interior, were federal-phobic. The Defense Department had bases old (Fort Sill, for example) and new (air bases from the Plains to the Pacific), as well as facilities such as the Jet Propulsion Laboratory connected with the California Institute of Technology in Pasadena, and the Rocky Mountain Arsenal outside of Denver. The Atomic Energy Commission, later the Department of Energy, operated nuclear laboratories and factories from Hanford, Washington, (later closed down) to Los Alamos, New Mexico, to the Lawrence Livermore Laboratory in Berkeley, California. In Utah, 11 percent of the state's workforce in the 1960s were federal employees, led by Hill Air Force Base with 14,000 civilian workers. In Colorado, the Air Force Academy opened in 1958, and the North American Air Defense Command started about that time.

Denver also housed its branch of the U.S. Mint as well as a customs house, the Rocky Flats plutonium site, the National Park Service headquarters, and a large veterans hospital. By 1980 the Denver area totaled 33,000 federal workers. As early as 1962, the

Two military personnel enter the Cheyenne Mountain Complex headquarters for the North American Air Defense Command. Founded in 1958, NORAD provides aerospace warning and aerospace control for North America.

West Coast enjoyed nearly half of the nation's defense contracts for research and development. Defense Department contracts in dollars and in payrolls quadrupled in the West from 1963 to 1983 and kept rising. On the Plains, from Kansas north to North Dakota and Montana, air bases and missile silos seemed to be everywhere. North Dakota, people joked, would have been the world's third largest nuclear power if it were an independent country.

The military aside, the federal government functioned as custodian of the West's public land. Through the Bureau of Reclamation and the Army Corps of Engineers, irrigated acreage doubled from the end of the war to 1975, which meant dams, straightened riverbeds, aqueduct systems, and more—notably in California, Arizona, Utah, and Washington. In that way, the federal government subsidized agriculture, along with making direct payments to farmers and farm companies.

The West was the region of choice for many federal contractors because labor was available and unions were weak. Many western states, practically all in the interior, passed "right to work" laws that outlawed compulsory union membership. Continuing the tradition of the "Rosie the Riveters" of World War II, women were no novelty in the outside-the-home workforce. The least attractive jobs, such as the "stoop labor" of picking field crops, or

March 31, 1982: Seven die when a massive avalanche slams into the base of the Alpine Meadows ski resort near Lake Tahoe, California. It buries the parking lot and main lodge and destroys several buildings.

1983: Washington-based technology firm Microsoft releases "Multi-Tool Word" word processing software. Known simply as Microsoft Word, it will soon become the global standard.

1983: Spinsters Ink publishes *The Woman Who Owned the Shadows*, considered the first feminist American Indian novel.

1984: The Soviet Union and several of its Communist satellites boycott the Summer Olympic Games in Los Angeles.

July 18, 1984: Twenty-one people die when an assailant opens fire in a McDonald's restaurant in San Ysidro, California.

October 13, 1984: Interstate 40 bypasses Route 66 at Williams, Arizona, making the iconic American highway officially obsolete.

June 30, 1985: A wildfire destroys nearly 70 homes in the San Diego neighborhood of Normal Heights.

December 1985: The California oil industry's annual production peaks at 424 million barrels.

1986: Congress approves the Immigration Reform and Control Act, which seeks to tighten regulations designed to keep illegal aliens out of the U.S.

November 1986: Ben Nighthorse Campbell, a Northern Cheyenne Indian, is elected to the U.S. House of Representatives by his Colorado constituency.

busboys and dishwashers in restaurants, could always be filled by migrants from Mexico or farther south—some legal, some not. Migrants kept on coming, and the regional economy depended on them, as was true elsewhere in the country.

Red State, Blue State

As the West's economy changed after 1950, so did its politics. Many Westerners supported the "New Deal consensus" that began with Franklin Roosevelt in the 1930s and continued through the Truman Administration and the Kennedy-Johnson years in the 1960s. However, the West shifted gradually to the right from around 1970 through the rest of the century. Mainstays of the Democratic West, such as small farmers and the industrial miners of the Mountain states, disappeared as their economies faltered. The rising service economy often meant suburban living and lifestyles, and with them more conservative politics. The interior West, in particular, joined the Great Plains and Texas in moving rightward along with the South, and together the two sections pulled the nation in that direction.

Texas was represented through the 1950s by such Democratic officials as House Speaker Sam Rayburn, Representative Maury Maverick, and Senators Ralph Yarborough and Lyndon Johnson. But in the 1960s, Texans moved toward the right by electing Governor John Connally and, later, the two George Bushes. Oklahomans voted in the 1950s for such liberals as Senator Mike Monroney and Speaker Carl Albert, but by the 1970s they backed conservative Republican governors Henry Bellmon and Dewey Bartlett. Texas and Oklahoma followed a pattern as much southern as western when they shifted from solidly Democratic into the 1960s to true two-party states through the 1970s to firmly Republican from the Ronald Reagan years onward.

New Mexico moved away from the liberal Clinton Anderson and Dennis Chavez to the conservative Ed Mechem and (a little later) Pete Domenici. Arizona swung from liberal Carl Hayden to conservative Barry Goldwater for U.S. senator. Wyoming elected liberals Gale McGee and Joseph O'Mahoney but later chose conservatives Milward Simpson, Alan Simpson, and Dick Cheney. Idaho elected the liberal Frank Church to the Senate four times beginning in 1957, but has not chosen a Democratic senator since 1980. Similarly in Utah, Frank Moss became a senator in 1959, but he was the last Democrat to do so.

Western Conservatism

URING THE 20TH CENTURY, the progressivism that had once marked western politics gave way to increasing conservatism. This shift was dramatized at the 1964 Republican National Convention, when Arizona Senator Barry Goldwater (who had been born in Arizona when it was still a territory) gave a firebrand speech accepting his party's nomination for president. "Extremism in the defense of liberty is no vice," Goldwater thundered.

Goldwater's strident anti-New Dealism and hawkish anticommunism proved too unsettling for voters in 1964. He lost all states except his native Arizona and five in the South. Incumbent Democratic President Lyndon Johnson defeated him in a landslide. However, within a couple of years of his defeat, Goldwater's distinctly western style of conservatism began to take hold in American politics.

A former Hollywood actor named Ronald Reagan made his political debut campaigning for Goldwater in 1964, then was elected governor of California in 1966. As governor, he appealed to conservative sentiments nationwide by calling in the National Guard to put down student protests at the University of California at Berkeley. After a failed attempt to win the Republican presidential nomination in 1976, Reagan was nominated and elected in 1980.

Reagan's ascent to the presidency is widely regarded as the culmination of the conservative revolution that Goldwater had set in motion in 1964. As president, Reagan declared the Soviet Union an "evil empire," instituted

Ronald Reagan

a massive military buildup, defied labor unions, and cut back on New Deal programs. He also presided over the decline of the Soviet Union, which collapsed shortly after he left office.

Known as the "Great Communicator," Reagan was a master of political imagery. Frequently photographed on horseback, he promoted his conservative agenda by cultivating the laconic, self-effacing image of a movie cowboy (which he had actually played in westerns).

Ironically, the "extremist" Goldwater seemed moderate during Reagan's presidency. Serving as senator until 1987, he supported legalized abortion and gay and lesbian rights. He also objected strenuously to the increasing influence of religious fundamentalists in the Republican Party.

Republican presidential candidate Barry Goldwater (*far left*), perceived as representing the ultraconservative wing of his party, lost every western state in 1964 except his home state, Arizona. Nevertheless, his campaign is credited with invigorating the "New Right." "Goldwater Girls" (*left*) supported his campaign.

February 25, 1987: The U.S. Supreme Court upholds the right of a California tribe to conduct bingo games, opening the door for Indian gaming nationwide.

June 1987: The NAMES project, which will create the vast AIDS memorial quilt, begins as an informal gathering in a San Francisco storefront.

1988: The Indian Gaming Regulatory Act passes Congress, with a mandate to regulate casino gambling on Indian reservations.

1989: The Mirage, the first of the modern Las Vegas mega-resort casinos, opens for business.

January 20, 1989: George H. W. Bush is inaugurated as the 41st U.S. president.

March 24, 1989: The oil tanker Exxon Valdez runs aground in Prince William Sound, Alaska, covering hundreds of square miles of pristine waters and coastline with a thick coating of crude oil.

October 17, 1989: The Loma Prieta earthquake rocks San Francisco, causing serious infrastructure damage and collapsing part of the Bay Bridge. Sixty-three people are killed.

June 1990: The battle between Pacific Northwest logging interests and environmentalists reaches a fever pitch as the northern spotted owl is officially listed as a threatened species.

November 16, 1990: President Bush signs the Native American Graves Protection and Repatriation Act.

1991: Montana's Custer Battlefield is rechristened the Little Bighorn Battlefield National Monument.

In 1955 the western states' U.S. senators were split evenly (11 Democrats and 11 Republicans), but in 2005 Republicans outnumbered Democrats 15 to 11. By the 1970s, the Rocky Mountain and Great Basin states consistently voted Republican in presidential elections, although they frequently elected Democrats to congressional and statewide offices. Only on the West Coast was the pattern different, and there not until the 1990s, when for various reasons California, Oregon, and Washington generally opted for Democrats. The Great Plains had trended Republican for some time, but after the 1950s were almost undeviatingly so.

There were, however, exceptions to almost all of these generalizations. While more true than false, they can be a little misleading. Conservatism was already abundantly evident in the West by 1950. For example, Richard Nixon's campaign for the Senate in 1950 was based on anticommunism and Red-baiting, preceding the more famous McCarthyism of the early 1950s. Conservative Republicans such as Nixon, Zales Ecton of Montana, Karl Mundt of North Dakota, Herman Welker of Idaho, and Democrat Pat McCarran of Nevada were on Senator Joe McCarthy's side.

Nonetheless, voters elected liberal Democrats to the Senate with some frequency. Mike Mansfield of Montana, Richard Neuberger of Oregon, Henry "Scoop" Jackson of Washington, Gale McGee of Wyoming, and Frank Moss of Utah were all first elected during the 1950s even though that decade is often remembered as "the age of Eisenhower"; i.e., a conservative time. When

The son of a Texas sharecropper, Tom Bradley became the first African American mayor of Los Angeles in 1973. He served for 20 years, overseeing the tremendous growth of his city.

Alaska and Hawaii were admitted to the Union in 1959 as the 49th and 50th states, three of their first four senators were Democrats. Hawaii generally stayed that way, while Alaska went Republican.

Even within states, political divisions were common—for example, the more liberal coasts of Washington and Oregon versus their conservative interiors, or the coexistence in Colorado of conservative Colorado Springs and liberal Boulder. Ethnic and racial minorities, often newly immigrated, affected an area's political coloration. African Americans formed a strong part of the Democratic base. Supported by black and progressive white voters, African American Tom Bradley served as mayor of Los Angeles from 1973 to 1993. The fast-growing Latino population leaned Democratic, and swung strongly that way when the Republican governor of California, Pete Wilson, backed the anti-immigrant Proposition 187 in 1994. Asians were divided politically. In general, most of the West's metropolises, led by Los Angeles, San Francisco, Seattle, and Denver, but joined by others, voted with a liberal or centrist cast. Conversely, the states, counties, and cities that remained largely white-Anglo voted Republican.

The Nevada delegation howls its support for President Ronald Reagan at the 1984 Republican convention. Immensely popular in the West, the charismatic, individualistic Reagan won a landslide reelection.

In presidential elections, the rightward trend was fairly clear. Candidates with western roots or identification helped pull western votes, and most of those candidates were Republicans: Eisenhower, Nixon, Goldwater, Reagan, and the Bushes. Of all the Democratic presidential nominees since 1950, only two could call themselves Westerners: Lyndon Johnson in 1964 and George McGovern in 1972.

The West that once had strongly backed Democrat Franklin Roosevelt and his followers moved into the Republican "sure thing" column, especially after the 1960s. Eisenhower carried every western state in both his campaigns. Nixon carried 10 in 1960. Johnson swept all but Barry Goldwater's Arizona in 1964, but that was far and away the Democratic presidential candidates' apogee. Nixon carried all but Washington and Hawaii in 1968 and swept completely in 1972. Democrat Jimmy Carter took only Hawaii in 1976 and 1980. Reagan took the rest in 1980 and carried every western state in 1984. In 1988, Democrat Michael Dukakis managed Hawaii, Oregon, and Washington; George H. W. Bush took the other 10. Bill Clinton made serious inroads,

January 1991: Five months after Iraq invades Kuwait, initiating the Gulf War, the United States attacks Iraqi forces. One of the workhorses of this primarily air war is the F-15E Strike Eagle, a California-built jet designed to strike long-range targets deep behind enemy lines.

October 20, 1991: A deadly firestorm sweeps through Oakland Hills, California, killing 25 and destroying some 3,500 homes.

1992: Clint Eastwood earns critical acclaim for *Unforgiven,* his grim take on the classic Hollywood western.

1992: The observance of the 500th anniversary of Columbus's voyage to America is denounced by many Native American groups.

February 1, 1992: The U.S. signs a friendship treaty with the Russian Federation, symbolically ending the Cold War.

April 29, 1992: South Central Los Angeles erupts in violence following the acquittal of the white police officers videotaped beating black motorist Rodney King.

June 18, 1992: In the case of *Nordlinger v. Hahn,* the U.S. Supreme Court upholds the constitutionality of Proposition 13, the California voter initiative enacted in 1978 that caps property taxes statewide.

August 1992: A 10-day standoff between Alcohol, Tobacco, and Firearms agents and the Weaver family of Idaho results in the deaths of Weaver's son, wife, and dog, as well as one of the federal agents. The incident underscores national concern over abuse of power by the federal government.

taking eight of the 13 in 1992 and seven in 1996, but George W. Bush captured eight to Al Gore's five in 2000 and nine to John Kerry's four in 2004.

For the Democrats, the one bright spot—a very bright one—was that the Gore and Kerry states included four of the five on the West Coast: Hawaii, Washington, Oregon, and the great prize of California with its 54 electoral votes. By 2000 the

The two Bushes, father and son, continued the West's political tilt toward the national Republican Party, as both won a great majority of interior western states when they were elected to the presidency.

evidence from presidential and senatorial elections was that the West had moved to the right politically since the 1950s, but also that it had divided into a rather solidly Republican-voting interior and a solidly Democratic-voting coast.

Why did these shifts happen? No one has conclusively and persuasively explained them. Personalities were important at the national level, especially with the charismatic Reagan. But the Democrats boasted state and local leaders with ability and charisma, such as the senators already mentioned, governors Pat Brown and Jerry Brown of California, congressmen Ron Dellums of Berkeley, Ed Roybal and Augustus Hawkins of Los Angeles, Stuart and Mo Udall of Arizona, and Patricia Schroeder of Colorado.

There were tectonic shifts as well. The New Deal base of small farmers and labor-union members had withered as agriculture consolidated and mine yields dwindled. The New Deal had provided support for such people through laws that upheld collective bargaining, price supports for crops, Social Security, and progressive taxes. These were eroded from the late 1940s onward by more pro-business, Republican majorities in Congress and state legislatures. A rhetoric of individual self-sufficiency and, in Reagan's words, the notion that government was the problem rather than the solution, gained traction. By the 1980s, religious groups—many of which had supported the New Deal and perforce the Democrats—all seemed to be headed right, becoming part of the Republican base instead.

Furthermore, certain events outraged moderate as well as right-wing opinion, and those events seemed consistently to be connected to liberal (or

In 1969 Governor Ronald Reagan called up the National Guard to prevent demonstrators from blocking construction of a new dormitory in People's Park at the University of California-Berkeley.

radical) groups. Ronald Reagan, when governor of California in the late 1960s, confronted the later stages of student unrest at the University of California at Berkeley, perhaps the most notorious of student uprisings at major American universities. By doing so, he added centrist voters to the conservative platform he inherited (and modified) from Goldwater's campaign of 1964.

Voters in California were also mindful of, and put off by, the 1965 Watts riots in Los Angeles, a serious episode of racial unrest. The assassinations of John F. Kennedy in 1963, and of Martin Luther King and Robert Kennedy in

Los Angeles's primarily African American neighborhood of Watts erupted in five days of violence in August 1965, directed primarily at white-owned businesses. Thirty-four people were killed.

November 3, 1992: Bill Clinton is elected president over incumbent George Bush and businessman Ross Perot. • Native American Ben Nighthorse Campbell is elected to the U.S. Senate from Colorado.

April 19, 1993: In Waco, Texas, a 51-day standoff between the Branch Davidians and the FBI ends in the deaths of cult leader David Koresh and 80 of his followers, including 25 children, when the Davidians burn their compound to the ground.

July 1993: The U.S. Navy announces that San Diego's Naval Training Center will be closed due to budget cuts and consolidation.

January 1, 1994: NAFTA, the North American Free Trade Agreement, goes into effect. It will stimulate trade with Mexico and dramatically increase the population along both sides of the international border, as people rush to the area to take advantage of commerce opportunities.

January 17, 1994: Fifty-seven people are killed when the Northridge earthquake rocks Los Angeles.

April 29, 1994: President Clinton invites the leadership from all federally recognized American Indian tribes to a White House meeting.

April 19, 1995: One hundred sixty-eight people are killed when the Alfred P. Murrah Federal Building in Oklahoma City is bombed in what is arguably the worst act of domestic terrorism in U.S. history.

October 3, 1995: Perhaps the most sensational American criminal trial to date comes to a close, as athlete-celebrity O. J. Simpson is found not guilty of killing his ex-wife and her male friend in the Brentwood neighborhood of Los Angeles.

1968, were upsetting enough, and the urban riots sparked by the King killing further disoriented many whites and convinced them that a swing to the right was called for. As historian Richard White writes:

> Reagan made urban demonstrators, striking farmworkers, black rioters, radical students, criminals, and wasteful bureaucrats from Johnson's War on Poverty his targets. He lined them up like ducks in a shooting gallery.... Until 1960 westerners in opinion polls had favored government intervention to provide jobs, health care, and other basic necessities. After 1960 they began to opt for individualist solutions. Before 1960 federal intervention had largely benefited whites; by 1966 [after Watts] it appeared to many whites to favor minorities and to threaten the existing pattern of race relations.

No doubt they did feel threatened. All of this helped elect Reagan as president in 1980, and his incumbency solidified the right-wing coalition. By the time he left office in 1989, that coalition was adding ideology from neoconservative think tanks (some in the West, more in Washington) and conviction from the "Religious Right," whose roots in California, Texas, and other western states dated back to the 1920s.

Supporting issues played a role as well in the interior West's shift to the right. Initially, the environmentally conscious had produced Earth Day in 1970, the creation of the Environmental Protection Agency in 1970, and other laws such as the Federal Land Policy and Management Act of 1976. Nixon, while president, found it prudent to adopt a pro- rather than anti-environmental stance. But counterpressures arose. By the late 1970s, a "Sagebrush Rebellion" had taken shape in the West, as people adopted the old idea of turning over the federal government's extensive landholdings to the states (and from there, certainly to private ownership by companies and persons with the money to buy them).

California environmentalists celebrate the first Earth Day (April 22, 1970), which prefigured new laws in the 1970s to protect the environment. Many of those laws were gutted in later decades.

Environmentalism

ENVIRONMENTALIST GROUPS frequently disagree on issues and solutions, but they all address concerns about the present and future condition of our planet. Some focus on specific problem areas. The Surfrider Foundation, founded in 1984 by Malibu, California, surfers, is dedicated to the protection and enjoyment of the world's oceans, waves, and beaches. In 1985 Earth First! members began "tree-sitting" to defend Oregon forests and started using other kinds of direct personal intervention to prevent the destruction of wildlife habitats.

The Sierra Club (founded by John Muir in 1892) still combats the destruction of wilderness areas, such as Yosemite National Park, Grand Canyon National Park, and Sequoia National Monument. The Sierra Club has also moved on to concerns for humans—such as clean air and water—as have many conservationist groups.

In addition to their ambitious preservation efforts in the Sierra Nevadas, The Trust for Public Land supports such projects as the EcoVillage Farm Learning Center for children in Richmond, California. It also supports Parks for People in Los Angeles and other cities.

Greenpeace, started in Vancouver, British Columbia, in 1971, practices activism on a wide range of environmental issues. The Natural Resources Defense Council, which maintains offices in San Francisco and Los Angeles (as well as at its New York City base), works for the passage and enforcement of legal safeguards, such as the Clean Air Act and the Clean Water Act.

Sierra Club Executive Director David Brower in 1966

The concerns of environmental groups include man-made pollution, animal rights, pesticides, human nutrition, environmental equality for different racial and income groups, energy sources and uses, global biodiversity, greenhouse gases, ozone depletion, global warming, and many other issues. In recent years, even some environmental activists have criticized other environmentalists for their fragmentation of interests and opinions, reliance on short-term solutions, and lack of evaluation of their programs. Announcing "the death of environmentalism," these activists have stirred new discussion and debate among the organizations concerned with the preservation of Earth and its inhabitants.

With Reagan's election and his appointment of anti-environmentalist lawyer James Watt as secretary of the interior, the Sagebrush Rebellion had achieved success. The Reaganites loosened or overturned environmental regulations and protections. (The George W. Bush Administration continued to gut what was left, beginning in 2001.)

The Right's lavish support of military bases and defense contracts throughout the West also helped solidify the region's rightward trend. Minimum-wage laws were frozen, anti-union laws strengthened. Tax reduction laws, most notably California's Proposition 13 referendum of 1978, capped property taxes and thereby shut down many state programs and services, such as education, welfare, libraries, and much else.

August 12–15, 1996: The Republican National Convention is held in San Diego, marking the first time the city has ever hosted a national political convention.

Fall 1996: President Clinton promises a crackdown on illegal immigration while campaigning in border states.

March 27, 1997: The 39 participants of the largest mass suicide on U.S. soil are discovered in a home in Rancho Santa Fe, California. Believing they were preparing for the arrival of an alien spaceship hiding behind the Halle-Bopp comet, they decided to "shed their earthly containers."

May 6–7, 1997: President Clinton becomes the first U.S. president to visit Mexico since Jimmy Carter's 1979 trip. Clinton promises Mexican President Ernesto Zedillo that U.S. immigration enforcement will steer clear of mass deportations.

December 16, 1997: The Richard Meier-designed Getty Center, home of the world-class J. Paul Getty Museum, opens in Los Angeles to critical acclaim.

1998: President Clinton and Mexican President Zedillo commit to joint enforcement of international drug trafficking regulations.

1998: The Sundance Film Festival's Audience Award for Dramatic Films is given to the American Indian production *Smoke Signals.*

March 20, 1999: The Legoland amusement park welcomes its first guests in Carlsbad, California.

June 22, 2000: NASA's Mars Global Surveyor, created by the Jet Propulsion Lab in Pasadena, California, discovers evidence of water, a key requirement for life, on Mars.

The West changed politically between 1950 and 2005—not always to the right, but more often than not, especially in the interior states. The "Left Coast," however, continued to live up to its nickname.

Cultural Mecca

Thus, the people of the West multiplied and migrated, the western economy expanded, especially into technology and services, and the political West moved rightward, though ambivalently. In the second half of the 20th century, the West more closely resembled the rest of the nation than it had before. Such was true of the cultural products of the West, varied and unexpected as they were. In a host of fields, the West equaled or set the pace for the nation in the arts, the media, architecture, lifestyles, sports, and even religion and social tensions.

Until 1958, Major League Baseball consisted of 16 teams located within a parallelogram, with St. Louis and Boston at its far corners. Commercial jet air service changed all that, and in 1958 the Brooklyn Dodgers started playing in Los Angeles and the New York Giants in San Francisco. Other major-league teams followed—to Houston, Oakland, Dallas, Denver, and Seattle. So did teams (expansion or migrant) in the National Football League and the National Basketball Association. The National Hockey League even brought a team to the desert (the Phoenix Coyotes). The West was no longer Triple-A country, and in 1974 the first all-western World Series took place, with the Oakland A's defeating the Dodgers. UCLA's 10 NCAA championships in 12 years in men's basketball was perhaps the most remarkable of many athletic achievements in the region.

The postwar population boom in Los Angeles led to huge crowds at Dodgers games beginning in 1958. Since then, the team has drawn more fans than any other major-league franchise.

Los Angeles had been the home of motion pictures since early in the 20th century, and remained so. Television, like the movies, originally centered around New York, but after the TV industry matured in the 1960s, more production and more shows began coming out of Hollywood. When Johnny Carson moved the immensely popular *Tonight Show* from New York to the NBC studios in "beautiful downtown Burbank" in 1972, a symbolic corner was turned. Again, California (by then the most populous state) led the way. It never quite succeeded in doing so in the newspaper, magazine, book publishing, and fashion fields, but the state nonetheless attracted significant market share in those sectors too.

In another sense, the West remained a powerful force in both films and television: Westerns were more popular than ever. Seven of the top-rated TV shows of the late 1950s had western heroes and themes. Western films starring John Wayne, Gary Cooper, and other stars perpetuated traditional western mythology and its traditional box-office success. The dominance of westerns on TV slipped from its 1960 high, but late-night reruns kept playing. Western films could still win audiences and Oscars; *Dances with Wolves* (1990) and *Unforgiven* (1992) won for best picture. Neither of those propagated traditional western myths, however. *Dances with Wolves* took a strongly pro-Indian, anti-military position, and Clint Eastwood in *Unforgiven* portrayed the amorality and futility of gunfighters and outlaws.

Already in 1974, Mel Brooks's *Blazing Saddles* ridiculed the serious, traditional westerns of Wayne and others with its many iconoclastic characters and scenes. Nonetheless, the romantic and hero-worshipping novels of Louis L'Amour flew off bookshelves into the hands of a loyal public—and a huge one. His estimated sales are 200 million copies in many languages (and still counting). Like the West itself, the audience for westerns split into traditionalists and sophisticates.

L'Amour was not the only novelist from the West (he lived outside of Telluride, Colorado). From Texas, Larry McMurtry wrote of the days of the range cattle industry, the rancher, and the cowboy. His *Lonesome Dove* (which won a Pulitzer Prize for fiction in 1986) was the most popular of his many novels. Ivan Doig (on Scots sheep raisers in Montana), Tom King (on Blackfeet Indians), Louise Erdrich (on Chippewas), Joan Didion (on her native California), James Michener (*Centennial*, 1974, a fictional history of Colorado from the dinosaurs to the present), and many others wrote fine, serious—and entertaining—literature probing western locales and themes.

Producers of *Dances with Wolves* (1990), which won an Oscar for best picture, tried to explode myths about the Old West. Kevin Costner (*pictured*) plays a former Army officer who goes west and is accepted into the Sioux tribe.

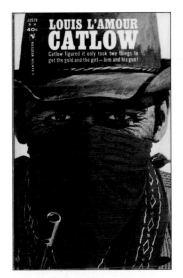

North Dakota-born Louis L'Amour, America's most prolific western writer, wrote 90 novels. He focused on the grand theme of the encroachment of civilization on Native American culture.

In the 1960s, such California bands as the Jefferson Airplane (*pictured*) and the Grateful Dead popularized psychedelic, revolutionary rock 'n' roll.

Music flourished, from the West Coast Jazz of the 1950s and 1960s to the contributions of Westerners to rock 'n' roll and other genres. The classics were presented with excellence by the symphony orchestras of Los Angeles, San Francisco, Seattle, Salt Lake City, and other places. Grand opera ornamented the cultural scenes of Los Angeles, San Francisco, and Seattle. Santa Fe began its innovative summer operas in 1957. Splendid performing arts centers arose, some of the largest and most notable being Denver's Center for the Performing Arts (1978), Abravanel Hall in Salt Lake City (1979), the San Francisco War Memorial and Performing Arts Center (1980), Anchorage's Alaska Center for the Performing Arts (1989), Seattle's Benaroya Hall (1998), and the Walt Disney Concert Hall in downtown Los Angeles, designed by architect Frank Gehry (2003). The West boasted magnificent venues for good music and performances of all kinds.

Architecture also flourished through the second half of the 20th century. Some buildings became symbols of their cities, such as the Transamerica Building in San Francisco, the Space Needle in Seattle, and (less proudly) the Enron Building in Houston. The Seattle Public Library, designed by Dutch architect Rem Koolhaas, opened in 2004 to deserved acclaim. Every city, even in earthquake zones, had its tall office boxes, convention centers, sports arenas, and monuments.

Western cities also pioneered domestic and vernacular architecture. Planners and critics deplored the sprawl of Los Angeles, but cities farther east, from Phoenix to Fort Worth to Atlanta, accepted the decentralized, indeed multicentered, Los Angeles format, with freeways, malls, and a middle-class lifestyle. By the 1980s, the planned (and, in more affluent cases, gated) community was the Sunbelt norm, from California east to Florida. California styles blew back across the country in more than housing; fast-food chains, clothing, and kitchen and bathroom technology often were adopted first in the West.

When the huge Baby Boom population began reaching its late teens in the early 1960s, higher education experienced an unprecedented expansion. It was not unpredicted. In 1960 California, expecting an enrollment explosion, produced a three-tier plan for higher education: two-year community colleges, four-year state colleges, and at the top, the nine-campus University

The Space Needle, the centerpiece of the Seattle World's Fair in 1962, presaged good fortune. Thanks to great natural beauty and Microsoft's nearby presence, Seattle has become a symbol of mellow prosperity.

> **"I was sitting in a room with four or five friends, and someone else came into the room. . . . He said hello to everybody in the room, and they said hello back. I said hello to him, and he said hello to me. And then I looked at him and he was me."**
> —STAN KAPLAN, RECALLING AN LSD EXPERIENCE IN SAN FRANCISCO DURING THE 1960S

Western Counterculture

DURING THE EARLY 1960S, a new and startling kind of frontier spirit wended its way through the American West, where alternative lifestyle communities began to spring up. The Himalayan Academy took root in Virginia City, Nevada, and Gorda Mountain began near Big Sur, California. These were followed in 1963 by Tolstoy Farm outside of Davenport, Washington, and in 1965 by Drop City near Trinidad, Colorado.

Such centers, which often promoted communal living, free love, and psychedelic drug use, dramatically shaped the U.S. counterculture during the 1960s—especially hippies. The hippie lifestyle, which largely rejected mainstream mores, revolved around an eclectic range of ideas that included Eastern religion and philosophy, anarchism, anti-materialism, hedonism, radical individualism, communism, sexual freedom, feminism, astrology, organic farming, natural medicine, vegetarianism, and consciousness expansion (although few, if any, hippies embraced all of these values). When drug guru Timothy Leary introduced the hippies to the mind-altering properties of LSD, he also gave them one of their most succinct and potent slogans: "Turn on, tune in, and drop out."

A commune in Sunny Valley, Oregon

Hippies cultivated "nonconformist" modes of appearance, marked especially by long hair. Both sexes donned beads, ankhs, peace symbols, and colorful tie-died clothes. Some hippie apparel paid homage to frontier ways—for example, denim jeans, handmade clothes of natural fabrics, and "granny" glasses. Hippies' use of drugs to achieve shamanic states also owed something to western Native American cultures.

The western phase of hippie culture reached its height in 1967 with San Francisco's "Summer of Love," for which some 75,000 people rallied in a "Human Be-In." By then, San Francisco's Haight-Ashbury District was the nation's dominant hippie center. By 1971 the hippie movement was generally considered to be over.

However, its influence had already been incalculable. Many faces of American counterculture during the 1960s, including the Berkeley Free Speech Movement and the Youth International Party (Yippies), owed a great deal to the hippies. Their legacy continues today in peace movements, environmentalism, and alternative spirituality—to say nothing of a society that is markedly more morally permissive than in pre-hippie days.

of California system. Entrance requirements tightened at each level, but high achievement at, say, a community college would permit entry into a state college or a UC campus. From the 1960s until the 1990s, the California system was widely acknowledged as the country's best. After that, the belt-tightening forced by the 1978 Proposition 13 tax reform had a baleful impact. Despite that, UC-Berkeley and UCLA remained near the summit of lists of the best universities in the world.

September 8, 2000: Kevin Gover, the assistant secretary of the Interior and a Pawnee Indian, publicly apologizes on behalf of the Bureau of Indian Affairs. He admits that the agency has "profoundly harmed the communities it was meant to serve."

November 2000: Former Texas Governor George W. Bush is elected 43rd president of the U.S. by the slimmest of margins.

September 11, 2001: Radical Islamic terrorists hijack four jets en route to the West Coast and slam them into the Pentagon and the Twin Towers of the World Trade Center. The fourth plane is brought down in Pennsylvania (with no survivors) by the heroic actions of the passengers and crew.

December 2, 2001: The Houston-based Enron Corporation files for Chapter 11 bankruptcy protection. The subsequent collapse of the company's blue-chip stock, followed by the indictments and convictions of several of its top officials, will make the Enron name synonymous with corporate greed and corruption.

February 8–24, 2002: Salt Lake City hosts the Winter Olympics.

May 13, 2002: President Bush signs the Farm Security and Rural Investment Act, which contains provisions to help support America's independent farmers in the face of competition from large-scale agribusiness.

October 9, 2002: The "Dot-Com" crash is complete as the NASDAQ composite index bottoms out at 1,114, representing a near 80-percent loss since its March 2000 high of 5,046.

February 1, 2003: The Space Shuttle Columbia breaks apart upon reentry into Earth's atmosphere, above Texas. The seven astronauts on board perish.

Other western states (though unfortunately not all) boasted excellent universities. Private higher education had never been as strong in the West as in the Northeast and South, yet Stanford, Cal Tech, the Claremont complex, Brigham Young, Loyola Marymount, and liberal-arts colleges such as Reed and Occidental continued in a tradition of excellence. Elementary and secondary education was not often so excellent, though that was true across the United States. Pockets of poverty, and the problems associated with the dozens of languages spoken by pupils in certain places such as Los Angeles, were not peculiar to the West but were certainly perennial.

As to religious affiliation and practice, the West presented a number of contradictions. The region had always been known for religious innovation, from the arrival of the Latter-day Saints in Utah in the late 1840s to the evangelists of the 1920s and 1930s. That phenomenon continued, most popularly in the megachurches that flourished in the new suburbs of Los Angeles (notably, Robert Schuller's Crystal Cathedral, which opened in 1980), Phoenix, and other cities. Cults, some derived from East Asian religions, sometimes combined with the region's history

Designed by renowned architect Philip Johnson, the Crystal Cathedral in Garden Grove, California, became the home of television minister Dr. Robert Schuller's Reformed Church of America congregation in 1980.

of utopian communities and communes. A famous example was the Rajneeshpuram in north-central Oregon during the 1980s.

The mainline denominations were not absent, either. The Catholic archdiocese of Los Angeles opened its new Cathedral of Our Lady of the Angels in downtown Los Angeles (two blocks from the Disney Concert Hall) in 2002. The church was modeled in a modern way after the Spanish missions of 200 years earlier. Large, but not alone, it was among thousands of new churches built around the region after 1950—Mormon, Southern Baptist, Pentecostal, and others.

Yet the West stood out among the regions of the country for its *lack* of formal religion. The Pacific Northwest was known among scholars of Amer-

Alternative Religions

DURING THE 1960S AND '70S, millions of Americans joined traditional churches and alternative religious groups—of which there were many. In the 1960s, Hindu swamis and Japanese Zen masters brought Eastern methods of acquiring spiritual insight to the United States. The first widely noticed Hindu devotees were likely the saffron-clad Hare Krishnas, who danced and chanted in western cities. In the 1970s, the Transcendental Meditation movement—started in the 1950s by Maharishi Mahesh Yogi—launched a plan to create 3,600 TM meditation centers worldwide, one for each million people.

Korean Christian minister Sun Myung Moon moved to the U.S. in 1971. His Unification Church missionaries found success in San Francisco and spread to other cities. Saying he was designated by God as a successor to Jesus to create the Kingdom of Heaven on Earth, Moon was outspoken about religion, politics, and other issues.

Elizabeth Clare Prophet, widely seen in television interviews, and her husband, Mark Prophet, combined Eastern and Western religious teachings. They claimed to be messengers for spiritual beings called Ascended Masters. Their organization, The Summit Lighthouse, moved from Colorado Springs to Santa Barbara and Pasadena, California, and finally to a ranch in Montana near Yellowstone Park.

Emphasizing the importance of personal responsibility, Werner Erhard founded his mind-training est seminars in San Francisco in 1971. Erhard adopted concepts

Followers of Bhagwan Shree Rajneesh

from Zen Buddhism and from the Church of Scientology, founded by science fiction author L. Ron Hubbard in 1953.

Alternative movements often aroused suspicion, and in some cases criminal investigation. In 1981 followers of Indian teacher Bhagwan Shree Rajneesh bought an Oregon ranch and elected a majority of members for a nearby town council. By 1985 the ostentatiously wealthy Rajneesh, under investigation for multiple felonies and vote fraud, was arrested and deported.

A Christian religious movement, the Children of God, was started in Huntington Beach, California, in 1968. This group advocated sexual activity to attract converts and adult-child sexual contact. Children of God leaders, who later admitted that some children had been abused, changed their policies and excommunicated some members.

ican religion as "The None Zone," because more people there than anywhere else answered "none" when asked what their religious affiliation was. Things were not much different elsewhere in the West, with the one great exception of Utah and neighboring parts of Idaho, Arizona, Wyoming, and Colorado— the "Mormon culture area." Wrote Patricia O'Connell Killen, a historian of religion, "Fewer people in Oregon, Washington, and Alaska affiliate with a religious institution than in any other region of the United States. . . . What's more . . . the Pacific Northwest has pretty much always been this way, to the longstanding frustration and bewilderment of its religious leaders."

Around the year 2000, 63 percent of Pacific Northwest people claimed no church affiliation, compared to 41 percent nationally. California and the

October 7, 2003: In a rare recall election, California Governor Gray Davis is replaced by Austrian-born actor and former Mr. Universe Arnold Schwarzenegger.

2004: The North American Aerospace Defense Command completes a $14 million upgrade of its Cheyenne Mountain underground command facility near Colorado Springs, Colorado.

2005: The booming city of Phoenix has seen its population grow by nearly 50 percent in the past 15 years, making it the sixth largest city in the United States.

March 16, 2005: The U.S. Senate votes 51–49 to permit oil exploration on the calving grounds of the Porcupine caribou herd in Alaska's Arctic National Wildlife Refuge.

April 2005: The "Minuteman Project" launches efforts to patrol the Arizona-Mexico border to prevent the influx of illegal immigrants.

September 28, 2005: A brushfire near Los Angeles triggers the Topanga fire, which will burn large swaths of land in the Santa Monica Mountains before firefighters are able to completely contain it on October 13.

April 10, 2006: Hundreds of thousands of Latino immigrants and their supporters march in the streets of cities across America. They demand immigration reform in response to federal government efforts to increase oversight of the U.S. border.

September 2006: Spinach contaminated with E. coli is traced to California's Salinas Valley after a massive outbreak sickens more than 150 people nationwide.

November 7, 2006: Democrats regain control of the U.S. Senate thanks in part to wins in California, Washington, Hawaii, New Mexico, North Dakota, and Nebraska.

rest of the Mountain and Pacific West—but for the Mormon exception—were almost as unchurched. The three coastal states plus Hawaii, Alaska, and Nevada occupied the lowest six places in percent of church members listed by state. In Utah, however, 84 percent of the people were churchgoers, most of them Mormon. Elsewhere in the West, Catholics (Hispanic and non-Hispanic) have invariably been the largest group, but percentage-wise they were not as numerous as in most other parts of the country.

A Matured West

As this chapter has shown, the American West since 1950 has grown in population, both through natural increase and immigration, more rapidly than the rest of the nation. Its economy developed faster, too, especially in the high-technology and service sectors. It became more important as a factor in the nation's politics, although neither Right nor Left exclusively benefited. It influenced lifestyles and nearly every conceivable aspect of culture to other Americans. But we should not leave the West with a sense that all has been well, that it has been a happy near-utopia. It also has had its crises, problems, and unwelcome events.

Nature itself could be cruel. In March 1964, an earthquake measuring 9.2 on the Richter scale devastated Anchorage; almost miraculously, only 131 people were killed. In May 1980, the topmost 1,300 feet of Mount St. Helens in southwest Washington blew off when that volcano erupted, send-

The Loma Prieta earthquake that struck San Francisco during evening rush hour on October 17, 1989, caused 63 deaths, injured more than 3,500, damaged 100,000 buildings, and postponed the World Series.

ing a tremendous amount of ash and dust eastward across the Northwest and Great Plains. Its larger neighbors, Mt. Hood east of Portland and Mt. Rainier south of Seattle, while quiescent, are regarded as "dormant" rather than "extinct"; future eruptions would be horrific. An earthquake in October 1989 jolted the San Francisco Bay area just as a World Series game was beginning there, collapsing bridges and freeways. The "Northridge quake" of January 1994 damaged the Los Angeles area. All were warnings of a possible "big one" to come. In California, in Yellowstone Park, and on the Great Plains, drought and forest fires ravished forests and grasslands in 1988 and other years.

Dry conditions have made the West, with its vast forests and brushlands, especially prone to wildfires. This one, in California in July 2006, destroyed more than 70,000 acres.

Man-made problems, some chronic and others sporadic, also beset the West. Indian reservations from the Dakotas to California consistently touched lows of poverty and deficient education. The thousands of Indians who moved to Los Angeles and other western cities improved their lot only partially. Migrant farmworkers lived in conditions that mocked the traditional idea of the West as a land of opportunity. Racial tensions twice erupted into lethal riots in Los Angeles, first in the Watts area in 1965, and again in the South Central district in 1992 after police who were videotaped beating an African American named Rodney King were acquitted by a suburban jury. Like everyplace else, life in the West was far from perfect.

By 2005, more than in 1950 and far more than in 1900, the West had become integrated into the broad patterns of American life. It remained different in many ways, with its own regional identity—or rather, identities, since differences within the West were great—still clear. Moreover, it was no longer the land of cowboys and Indians, Gold Rushers and stagecoaches, if indeed it ever really was. It had matured. People's notions about the West have matured less rapidly. At times they fail to catch up with the West's realities and remain caught in myths that, though often enjoyable and comforting, should be understood to be the fictions they are. For reality checks, the best thing is to examine the West as it truly exists, and to learn, as this book helps us to do, how the West is the product of its history.

Despite the inevitable modernities, the West—especially the interior western states—has retained much of its heritage. Without question, the spirit of the Old West still permeates the region.

Index

438

Acknowledgments

Page 119: Cover of *The Life and Adventures of Joaquin Murieta: The Celebrated California Bandit,* by (Yellow Bird) John Rollin Ridge. Reprinted with permission of University of Oklahoma Press. Available through www. oupress.com, 800-627-7377.

Page 141: Passage from *Sod and Stubble,* by John Ise. © 1996 The University Press of Kansas. All rights reserved.

Pages 327, 334: Passages from the May 22, 1935, article "Dust Changes America" by Margaret Bourke-White, in *The Nation.* Reprinted with permission of *The Nation.*

Pages 330, 331: Passages from the October 13, 1934, article "End Poverty in California: The EPIC Movement" by Upton Sinclair. © 1934, Time, Inc. Reprinted with permission.

Page 336: Passage from the Depression-era writings of Ernie Pyle. Reprinted with permission of Scripps Howard Foundation.

Page 340: Passage from *The Gate: The True Story of the Design and Construction of the Golden Gate Bridge* by John Van Der Zee. © 1986 John Van Der Zee. Reprinted with permission of Simon & Schuster Adult Publishing Group.

Page 346: "Ram's Head, Blue Morning Glory," by Georgia O'Keeffe, 1938. © 2007 Georgia O'Keeffe Museum/Artists Rights Society (ARS) New York. Reprinted with permission.

Page 347: "Dunes, Oceano," by Edward Henry Weston, 1936. © 1981 Arizona Board of Regents. Reprinted with permission from the Collection Center for Creative Photography.

Page 376: Passage, as recalled by Private Daniel Yearout, in "The Day the World Lit Up" by Kathryn Westcott from the July 15, 2005, issue of *BBC News* on bbc.co.uk/news. Text reprinted with permission of *BBC News.*

Page 384: "The Boy," by Thomas Hart Benton. © T. H. Benton and R. P. Benton Testamentary Trusts/UMB Bank Trustee, licensed by VAGA, New York, NY. Reprinted with permission.

Photo Credits

Front cover:
Wyoming State Archives, Department of State Parks and Cultural Resources Cowboy bronco rider Billy Cramer, ca.1899 (inset). "The Wild, Spectacular Race for Dinner," 1904-1905 (oil on canvas), Wyeth, Newell Convers (1882-1945), **Buffalo Bill Center of the West, Cody, Wyoming, U.S.A.**, Gift of John M. Schiff; 44.83 (inset). **Getty Images** (inset). **Shutterstock.com** (background).

Back cover:
Shutterstock.com (background);
Getty Images (inset).

The Academy of Natural Sciences, Ewell Sale Stewart Library: 38 (center); **Alamy Images:** Chad Ehlers, 391 (bottom); Popperfoto, 325 (bottom left); **Aldo Leopold Foundation Archives:** 335 (top left); **American Automotive Manufacturers Association:** 321 (top); **American Heritage Center, University of Wyoming:** 158 (bottom), 216 (bottom), 232 (bottom); **American National Insurance Company, Fine Art Collection, Galveston, Texas:** 34 (top); **AP Wide World Photos:** 76, 163, 236-237, 244 (top), 248 (top right), 252 (top), 257 (top right), 273 (bottom), 286 (top), 297 (bottom), 302, 311, 315 (bottom left), 317 (top right), 319 (top right), 320 (bottom right), 323 (bottom), 327 (top), 328 (top), 330 (bottom), 334 (top), 336 (bottom right), 340, 341 (bottom left), 343 (bottom left), 349 (top right), 359 (top left & top right), 363 (top left), 368 (bottom), 369 (top left, bottom left & bottom right), 370 (top), 371 (top right), 372 (top), 373 (bottom left & bottom right), 374 (bottom), 375 (bottom), 377 (bottom), 382, 385 (bottom right), 396, 399, 405, 412, 415 (top), 420 (top); **Archive Photos:** 253 (top left); **Arizona Historical Foundation:** Roscoe G. Wilson Collection (1904), Quartzite, Arizona, 262 (top left); **Arizona Historical Society Library:** 195 (bottom right), 201 (left), 203 (top right), 208 (bottom); **Arizona State University Libraries:** Henry S. McCluskey Photographs, Arizona Collection, 262 (bottom); Western History Collection, 281 (top left); **Art Resource:** National Portrait Gallery, Smithsonian Institution, 55, 99 (bottom left), 322 (bottom); The New York Public Library, 37 (top left), 50 (bottom); The Newark Museum, 122 (top); Georgia O'Keeffe Museum, Santa Fe, 346 (top); Réunion des Musées Nationaus, 57 (bottom right); Scala, 59 (right); Schomburg Center, 52 (top); Smithsonian American Art Museum, Washington, D.C., 134 (bottom), 161 (bottom right), 169 (left center), 177 (left center), 285 (top right), 310 (top), 312 (bottom right), 317 (top left), 320 (bottom left), 326 (top), 343 (top left); Snark, 250 (top), 323 (top); **Between the Covers Rare Books:** 263 (bottom left), 282 (center), 285 (top center), 341 (top left), 348 (top center), 357 (right),

419 (bottom); *Bismarck Tribune,* **Bismarck, North Dakota:** 181 (top right); **Boot Hill Museum:** 167 (bottom right); **Bridgeman Art Library, London/New York:** Sacagawea with Lewis and Clark during their expedition of 1804–06 (color litho), Wyeth, Newell Convers (1882-1945), Peter Newark American Pictures, Private Collection, 28–29; "The Oregon Trail," 1869 (oil on canvas), Bierstadt, Albert (1830–1902), Gift of Joseph G. Butler III 1946, © Butler Institute of American Art, Youngstown, Ohio, USA, 93 (left); Track-layers gang-building the Union Pacific Railroad through American wilderness, 1860s (b/w photo), American Photographer, 19th century/Peter Newark American Pictures, Private Collection, 144 (bottom); Loading Texas cattle onto a train at Abilene railhead, Kansas, c.1870 (color litho), American School, 19th century, Peter Newark American Pictures, Private Collection, 177 (top); Postcard depicting the stockyards and abattoirs in Chicago, c.1910 (colored photo), American School, 20th century, Archives Charmet, Private Collection, 229 (bottom left); "Dead Sure," a U.S. Cavalry trooper in the 1870s (color litho), Schreyvogel, Charles (1861–1912), Peter Newark Western Americana, Private Collection, 274 (top); "Dunes, Oceano," 1936 (gelatin silver photograph), Weston, Edward Henry (1886–1958), Art Gallery of New South Wales, Sydney, Australia, 347 (top left); Pinkerton's National Detective Agency, "We Never Sleep" (litho), American School, 19th century, Peter Newark American Pictures, Private Collection, 167 (bottom left); Black Cowboys at Bonham, Texas, c.1890 (b/w photo), American Photographer, 19th century, Peter Newark American Pictures, Private Collection, 182 (top); Colonel John M. Chivington (1821–92) (b/w photo), American Photographer, 19th century, Peter Newark Western Americana, Private Collection, 145 (top); **Brigham Young University, Museum of Art:** "Joseph Mustering the Nauvoo Legion," by CCA Christiansen, all rights reserved, 89 (top); **Bringham Young University, Provo, Utah:** L. Tom Perry Special Collections, Harold B. Lee Library, 246 (top); **Brown Brothers:** 41 (bottom left), 45 (top left), 49, 60 (bottom), 72 (top), 78 (bottom), 126 (top), 147 (top), 166 (bottom), 183 (top right), 200 (top), 228 (top), 235 (top), 256 (center), 257 (bottom right), 264 (bottom), 271 (top left), 288 (top); **Buffalo Bill Historical Center, Cody, Wyoming:** Gift of the artist's heirs, WHD Koerner, III and Ruth Koerner Oliver; P.78.4311., 316 (top); **California Historical Society:** #FN-08767, 175 (right), #FN-13836, 242 (top); **California History Room, California State Library, Sacramento, California:** 111 (center), 112 (bottom), 113 (bottom); **California State Archives:** 114 (bottom); **California State Railroad Museum:** 173 (top), 230 (bottom); **Carey Sublette, nuclearweaponarchive.org:** 375 (top); **Chicago History Museum:**

Chicago Daily News, DN-0068779, 267 (bottom left); **City of Los Angeles Department of Water and Power:** 284 (bottom right); **Clymer Museum of Art:** "Salt Makers" by John F. Clymer, Courtesy of Mrs. John F. Clymer and the Clymer Museum of Art, 39 (top); **Coffrin's Old West Gallery, Bozeman, Montana:** L. A. Huffman, 206 (bottom); **Community of Christ Library-Archives, Independence, Missouri:** 84 (bottom); **Colorado Historical Society:** 40 (top), 71 (top left), 86 (bottom), 135 (top left), 161 (top right), 200 (bottom), 204 (top left & top right), 263 (top left); **© Corbis:** 229 (top left), 233 (bottom right), 252 (bottom), 337, 349 (top left), 386 (bottom); Bettmann, 366 (bottom), 376 (left); Lake County Museum, 223 (right center); Medford Historical Society Collection, 146 (bottom left); PEMCO-Webster & Stevens Collection; Museum of History and Industry, Seattle, 305 (top left); Peter Turnley, 6; **Donald Corner & Jenny Young, GreatBuildings.com:** 272 (bottom); **Culver Pictures:** 68 (bottom), 120 (top), 121 (right center); **Cumberland County Historical Society, Carlisle, Pennsylvania:** 206 (top left & top right), 211 (top left & top right); **Denver Public Library, Western History Collection:** 61 (top left & right), 73 (top left & left center), 88 (bottom), 91 (top left), 92 (top), 106 (top), 124 (center), 134 (top), 137 (top), 140 (bottom), 149 (top right), 150 (bottom), 151 (bottom), 153 (bottom), 154 (top), 155 (top right), 157 (bottom left), 166 (top), 172 (bottom left), 176 (bottom), 178 (top), 192 (bottom), 193 (top left), 197 (bottom), 201 (right), 211 (bottom), 212 (bottom left), 220 (top), 223 (left), 224 (top right), 225 (top), 226 (bottom), 227 (top left), 233 (top), 235, 246 (bottom), 263 (bottom right), 275 (bottom), 304 (bottom), 307 (top); **Collection of Brent C. Dickerson:** 268 (bottom); **Digital Vision Collection:** endsheets; **Collection of Ellwood House Museum, DeKalb, Illinois:** 217 (top); **Federal Reserve Bank of San Francisco:** 243 (top); **Folio, Inc.:** 33, 149 (left); **Fort Smith National Historic Site:** 193 (bottom right); **Gary R. Lucy Gallery, Inc., Washington, Missouri, www.garylucy.com:** "Lewis and Clark: The Departure from the Wood River Encampment, May 14, 1804," by Gary R. Lucy, 36 (top); **George Eastman House:** 172 (bottom right); **Getty Images:** contents, 14, 15, 17, 21 (bottom), 22, 24, 25, 43 (bottom right), 45 (top right), 56 (top), 57 (top right), 58 (top), 69, 81 (top left & top right), 83 (left center & right center), 84 (top), 85 (top), 87, 88 (top), 92 (center), 93 (right), 95 (bottom right), 96 (bottom), 99 (top), 104, 105, 116 (top), 118 (top), 119 (top), 121 (top & left center), 123 (bottom), 124 (top), 125 (bottom), 127 (bottom right), 131, 132, 133, 139 (center & bottom), 144 (top), 145 (bottom left), 150 (top), 158 (bottom), 160, 161 (top left), 164 (bottom), 165 (top), 168 (top), 174 (top), 178 (right